BIOLOGICA
BEHAVIORAL DET
OF LANGUAGE DE

BIOLOGICAL AND BEHAVIORAL DETERMINANTS OF LANGUAGE DEVELOPMENT

Edited by

Norman A. Krasnegor
National Institute of Child Health and Human Development

Duane M. Rumbaugh
Language Research Center, Georgia State University
Yerkes Regional Primate Research Center, Emory University

Richard L. Schiefelbusch
University of Kansas

Michael Studdert-Kennedy
Haskins Laboratories

 LAWRENCE ERLBAUM ASSOCIATES, PUBLISHERS
1991   Hillsdale, New Jersey   Hove and London

Lawrence Erlbaum Associates, Inc., Publishers
365 Broadway
Hillsdale, New Jersey 07642

Library of Congress Cataloging-in-Publication Data

Biological and behavioral determinants of language development /
edited by Norman A. Krasnegor . . . [et al.].
    p.   cm.
Includes bibliographical references and index.
ISBN 0-8058-0635-0. — ISBN 0-8058-0993-7 (pbk.)
1. Language acquisition.   2. Biolinguistics.   I. Krasnegor,
Norman A.
[DNLM: 1. Language Development.   WS 105.5.C8 B6144]
P118.B54   1991
401'.93 — dc20
DNLM/DLC
for Library of Congress   91–16139
                                                        CIP

Printed in the United States of America
10   9   8   7   6   5   4   3   2   1

Table of Contents

Preface   ix

PART 1:
CRITICAL THEORETICAL ISSUES

1
Language Development from an Evolutionary Perspective
Michael Studdert-Kennedy   5

2
Symbols and Syntax: A Darwinian Approach
to Language Development
Elizabeth Bates, Donna Thal, and Virginia Marchman   29

3
How the Acquisition of Nouns May Be Different
from That of Verbs
Michael P. Maratsos   67

4
Concepts and Meaning in Language Development
Katherine Nelson   89

5
Representation and Expression
Lois Bloom   117

PART 2:
PRECURSORS OF LANGUAGE IN PRIMATES

6
Comparative Perspectives of Brain, Cognition,
and Language
**Duane M. Rumbaugh, William D. Hopkins,
David A. Washburn, and E. Sue Savage-Rumbaugh**   145

7
The "Postural Origins" Theory of Primate
Neurobiological Asymmetries
Peter F. MacNeilage   165

8
Developmental Changes in Nonhuman Primate Patterns
of Brain Lateralization for the Perception of Speech Cues:
Neuroelectrical Correlates
Dennis L. Molfese and Philip A. Morse   189

9
Language Learning in the Bonobo: How and Why
They Learn
E. Sue Savage-Rumbaugh   209

10
Imitation, Grammatical Development, and the Invention
of Protogrammar by an Ape
Patricia M. Greenfield and E. Sue Savage-Rumbaugh   235

PART 3:
LANGUAGE ACQUISITION IN CHILDREN

11
The Phylogeny and Ontogeny of Language Function
A. Charles Catania   263

12
The Role of Social Interaction in Early Language
Development
Andrew Lock   287

13
Language Comprehension: A New Look
at Some Old Themes
Kathryn Hirsh-Pasek and Roberta Michnick Golinkoff   301

14
Recharting the Course of Language Acquisition:
Studies in Elicited Production
Stephen Crain and Rosalind Thornton   321

15
Motor Aspects of Emergent Speech:
A Dynamic Approach
Esther Thelen   339

16
Linguistic and Spatial Development: Dissociations
Between Cognitive Domains
Ursula Bellugi, Amy Bihrle, and David Corina   363

PART 4:
ACQUISITION BY INSTRUCTION IN THE
LANGUAGE DELAYED

17
On Differentiated Language-Learning Models and
Differentiated Interventions
Keith E. Nelson   399

18
Patterns of Language Learning by Instruction: Evidence
from Nonspeaking Persons with Mental Retardation
Mary Ann Romski and Rose A. Sevcik   429

19
Children with Specific Language Impairment:
Toward a Model of Teachability
Mabel L. Rice   **447**

20
Communicative Intent and Its Realizations
Among Persons with Severe Intellectual Deficits
James E. McLean and Lee Snyder-McLean   **481**

Author Index   **509**

Subject Index   **523**

Preface

Many animals, besides humans, reliably communicate with each other to convey the information necessary to help conspecifics locate sources of nourishment, avoid danger, and reproduce. With respect to the social insects, for example, Karl von Frisch, who, along with Konrad Lorenz and Niko Tinbergen, was awarded a Nobel prize in physiology, elucidated how the dance of worker bees imparts data to other drones concerning the location of nectar. Although this aspect of the foraging honeybee's (*Apis mellifera*) behavior is truly remarkable, it, along with communication systems of all other animals, is differentiated from the one used by our own species. In fact language, as our communication system is called, is so unique that it was made an inclusion criterion for the definition of what it means to be human. Did this distinctive neurobehavioral system evolve? How do our children reliably develop their capacities to become active participants in the language community?

The 20 chapters that comprise this book are devoted to an examination of the biobehavioral bases of language acquisition. What sets this book apart from others is its emphasis upon the development of language within the dual contexts of evolution and ontogeny. Major themes herein addressed revolve around the questions of how language came to be the dominant form of hominid communication and how language emerges in humans during the sequence that spans infancy through childhood. Additional foci are upon the centrality of grammatical structure as a defining characteristic of language development and precursors of language in closely related species (chimpanzees). This latter work on *Pan paniscus* presents a significant challenge to the notion that language is an exclusively human trait.

Both biological and behavioral factors involved in the mapping of meaning onto utterances during the acquisition process are explicated for both normal children and those who are language delayed.

The book should be of interest to developmental psychologists, psycholinguists, neuropsychologists, and those investigators interested in cognitive development. Researchers and clinicians who work with retarded children and the learning disabled should also find the volume of interest because the theoretical discussions and empirical findings bear directly on diagnosis and treatment of children with impaired language capacity. Finally, the volume may find immediate use in medical and graduate level courses that focus upon pediatric psychology, behavioral medicine, child development, and pediatrics.

The ideas, overviews, and data contained in this book are at the cutting edge of research on language acquisition. The presentations provide important examples of the scope of both the critical theoretical issues that help frame empirical questions and the innovative methodologies being employed to ask such questions. The volume is divided into five parts: Introduction, Critical Theoretical Issues, Precursors of Language in Primates, Language Acquisition in Children, and Acquisition by Instruction in the Language Delayed.

The book was inspired by a conference sponsored by the Human Learning and Behavior Branch of the National Institute of Child Health and Human Development, held at the Xerox Center, Leesburg, Virginia in June of 1988. However, the contents were written and submitted independently of the meeting. The contributions are original manuscripts presented in the form of peer-reviewed scholarly chapters. As such, the book may be viewed as a useful addition to the growing literature on language development.

I

Critical Theoretical Issues

This section is composed of five chapters that provide perspectives upon evolution, cognition, and mental mechanisms as these factors relate to the development of language. The topics addressed represent some of the most basic issues of current interest to the community of scholars who are studying the ontogeny of productive and receptive language during the first 3 years of life.

In the first chapter, Michael Studdert-Kennedy evaluates language development from the viewpoint of Darwinian and modern evolutionary theory. He conceptualizes language development as "a sort of postnatal embryology." The author argues that the neural substrate for language was shaped during phylogeny and language performance continues that shaping as the child uses language. His main thesis for elucidating the way language develops is that: "Language function thus determines language form, and form is viewed as an a posteriori description of rather than an a priori prescription for development." Studdert-Kennedy employs the general principles that emerge from the evolutionary biology model as a framework within which to explicate the emergence of phonetic segments. He discusses the role of perception and analyzes the mechanisms involved in production (integration and differentiation) as these contribute to the acquisition of language. Finally, he details how gestures become integrated in a manner that leads to the expression of phonemes.

Next, Elizabeth Bates, Donna Thal, and Virginia Marchman employ a Darwinian model to gain insights into the origins and ontogeny of language. They argue that a dilemma exists regarding the presumed (e.g., Chomsky) discontinuity between a uniquely human generative grammar and the rest of

1

both human and nonhuman cognition. To account for the existence of language, they say, one would have to either invoke a nonevolutionary mechanism (e.g., creationism) or postulate the occurrence of unique mutation in hominids that would be ". . . a cognitive equivalent of the Big Bang." The authors outline a way out of this dilemma by asserting that language ". . . must be viewed as a new machine built out of old parts." They outline and summarize the data concerning three continuities (mechanisms, motives, and representations) that they assert could form the framework for language development.

In chapter 3, Michael Maratsos provides his overview of the differentiation between the semantic and structural factors that govern how nouns and verbs become part of a developing child's lexicon. His general argument concerning the contrast in acquisition is that ". . . the conceptual-object core of nouns is more important in acquisition than the respective actional core of verbs." Maratsos suggests that cross-linguistic evidence supports the idea that nouns are organized on the basis of concrete object reference. Verbs, on the other hand, are parts of the syntactic order that are grouped together due to their small-scale structural properties (e.g., Maratsos & Chalkley). The author also critiques the notion that children are unbiased analyzers of language input during development. To the contrary, he asserts that ". . . strong biases in weighting input data are evidenced by what is known about nouns and their likely course of development."

Katherine Nelson describes, in chapter 4, the factors that she feels must be thoroughly elucidated to gain a deep understanding of the acquisition of both lexical terms and meaning during a child's development. In order to find out how these aspects of language become known to the child, she indicates that those studying this problem must comprehend ". . . the language system, the way it is presented to the child, and the internal workings of the child's mind at different points in development." Nelson outlines three distinctive phases during lexical development. These are: Phase 1 (9 to 14 months of age), a period during which the child must find a way into the system and become sensitized to the forms of language; Phase 2, a point in development when the child has acquired some 30 words or more and begins to ask "What's that?"; and Phase 3 (3 to 4 years of age), during which ". . . revision, reorganization, and consolidation of lexical items within domains of related words" occurs. She provides an insightful analysis of different theories of the acquisition of meaning and highlights the importance of the social and cognitive contexts in which language is acquired.

The final chapter in Part 1, by Lois Bloom, presents the thesis that to understand language acquisition one must explore how the individual's mind is constructed. More specifically, she states that by gaining access to representations that exist in the mind's "mental spaces" and determining what developmental factors contribute to the establishment of these entities, one can better explain how language is acquired. She states that ". . . what is represented in language is less concerned with objects and events in the external world than with the relations between them that we set up in consciousness." She also expresses the view that children acquire language to express ". . . what the contents of intentional states are about." Bloom indicates that mental spaces exist prior to language and relate initially to perception. These elements unite to form primitive mental schemas which can be recalled in the context of cues that eventually become more temporally removed from the ones to which they were originally linked. Subsequently, infants generate their own cues to access memory. Bloom asserts that speech heard by the infant ". . . will be the preeminent source of cues for constructing the representations that underlie acts of interpretation and intentions." Bloom believes that to gain a full understanding of language acquisition researchers need to consider the capacity of mental spaces, the notation systems that encode representations, and the paths in and out of the knowledge base. The author describes both her own and others' empirical studies that lend support for the existence and organization of the mental spaces she postulates.

1 Language Development from an Evolutionary Perspective

Michael Studdert-Kennedy
University of Connecticut,
Yale University,
and Haskins Laboratories

In his famous course of lectures at the University of Geneva (1906–1911), de Saussure distinguished *langue,* language as a system, a cultural institution, from *parole,* language as spoken and heard by individuals: ". . . language is not complete in any speaker; it exists only within a collectivity . . . only by virtue of a sort of contract signed by members of a community" (de Saussure, 1966, p. 14). Language thus was seen as an abstract property of a group, related to its variable individual speakers somewhat as a species is to its variable individual members.

Nineteenth-century attempts to apply evolutionary principles to language did indeed view each language as a species. For example, Darwin (1871) wrote: "The formation of different languages and of distinct species . . . [is] curiously parallel . . . We find in distinct languages striking homologies due to community of descent, and analogies due to a similar process of formation" (pp. 465–466). Here, Darwin was following in the steps of August Schleicher (1821–1868), who drew on the earlier work of Darwin himself, and on the vast scholarship of 19th-century European philology, to construct a taxonomy of Indo-European languages. Later work has continued to draw on Darwinian principles to construct evolutionary trees of language families (Lehmann, 1973).

However, a strict analogy between languages and species is untenable for both linguistic and biological reasons. For the historical linguist, the most obvious difficulty is that a biological species is a reproductively isolated population: Properties of one species cannot pass to another. Yet languages in contact clearly do influence one another, even after they have become discrete sociopolitical entities. Often, we cannot then know how far shared properties have arisen from contact, how far from common descent.

A more serious difficulty follows from two central tenets of neo-Darwinian theory (the modern synthesis of Mendelian genetics with Darwinian natural selection). First, in the evolution of a species, the principal unit of variation and selection is not the species, but the individual organism. Individuals within a species differ in the number of offspring they produce; genes whose expression increases the relative number of an individual's offspring will increase their own relative number in the species' gene pool. The characteristics of a species therefore are determined by competition among individuals of that species. And, by analogy, the characteristics of a language are formed by competition among speakers of that language. So far, so good.

The difficulty arises when we combine the principle of individual selection with the so-called central dogma of modern biology, the "Weismann barrier," insulating germ cells from body cells: Genes alter body cells, but body cells cannot alter genes. In other words, biological evolution does not proceed by the transmission of acquired characters across generations, and this is precisely what an evolutionary model of language change requires. We therefore must distinguish the cultural, or Lamarckian, evolution of language, a concern of historical linguistics, from its biological, or neo-Darwinian, evolution, a concern of developmental biology.

This distinction was first clearly formulated by Chomsky (1965, 1986), who recognized that de Saussure's (1966) definition of language as a property or product of a social group did not lend itself to treatment in biological evolutionary terms. Chomsky made the necessary move by reformulating the *langue-parole* distinction as competence (what a speaker-listener knows) and performance (what a speaker-listener does in implementing knowledge). He thus set the locus of human language capacity in the individual's mind/brain. He also set the stage for the modern study of language acquisition.

Form and Function

Nonetheless, the competence-performance distinction as usually formulated also does not lend itself to evolutionary treatment. Competence is knowledge of a particular language, formed by interaction between an innate schema, the "universal grammar," and the grammar of the language being learned. Universal grammar is ". . . a theory of the 'initial state' of the language faculty, prior to any linguistic experience" (Chomsky, 1986, pp. 3-4). Performance thus is said to be a product of a partially innate competence. In what follows, I argue that this precisely reverses the true course of development. Universal grammar is not a prescription, or program, for development, but a partial and a posteriori description of the phenotypic product of the developmental system (cf. Oyama, 1985). Universal grammar is a consequence, not a condition of development.

What is at stake here is the relation between form (competence) and function (performance). Zoologists traditionally have stressed the harmonious match between form and function, as expressed in an animal's mode of life, but they have disagreed on how the match comes about. From classical times down into the 19th century, the standard belief was that species and genera had fixed, unchanging forms or essences: Departures from the species prototype were "unreal," and structure took precedence over function. For example, according to Mayr (1982), Georges Cuvier (1769–1832), the great French zoologist, held that ". . . structure has primacy over function and habit, and . . . only a change in structure might necessitate a change in function" (p. 367). Certain non-Darwinian French zoologists still hold such views: ". . . evolution originates in parent forms; if these are absent, new types of organization never appear" (Grassé, 1977, p. 75). Thus, Chomsky and his structuralist forebears in linguistics align themselves with the essentialist tradition in biology by asserting the primacy of form over function.

For Darwin and modern evolutionary biologists working within the British empricist tradition, the form-function relation is reversed. Species are not eternally fixed. A species is a genetically variable population of individuals, adapted to a particular ecological niche and thereby reproductively isolated. No aspect of an animal's structure determines a unique function. Rather, a structure determines an unbounded range of functions, to some of which it is more nicely tailored than others. (We can use a screwdriver to drive screws, or as a dagger, a lever, a drumstick, a fork, etc.) If certain members of a species are forced by competition with their fellows, or by an environmental change, into a new mode of life, a new habitat, they may call on some hitherto unused potential function of their structure. The new mode of life then confers a reproductive advantage on those individuals whose structure is marginally better suited (due to small differences in their genetic makeup) to the new mode. Little by little, as with the beaks of Darwin's famous finches (Lack, 1961), the new selection pressures reshape the old structure to its new function. Behavior is thus the great "pacemaker of evolutionary change" (Mayr, 1982, p. 612), the cause not the consequence of speciation and of species form.

In short, a commitment to gradual evolution by natural selection entails a commitment to the primacy of function over form. My central assumption, then, is that language competence (the neural substrate of language form) was shaped in phylogeny, and is still shaped in ontogeny, by language performance (function, behavior).

Behavior as the Pacemaker of Development

If we extend Mayr's (1982) dictum on evolution to development, we see development in a new light. We are freed from preoccupation with the "initial state" as an index of genetic endowment, and from the nativist–empiricist controversy that has dominated studies of language development almost since their inception.

At birth, an organism suffers an abrupt change in the quality and quantity of environmental conditions that may affect its growth. But the discontinuity does not change the developmental system. Gene action does not cease at birth, nor does regulation of gene action by the cellular environment. Rather, the developmental circle widens. The new external environment affords a broader range of stimulation, eliciting a broader range of response. Changes in the organism's environment and behavior now mediate, to a steadily increasing degree, changes in the cellular environment that controls genetic action.

The developmental course is not one of simple maturation (cf. Borer & Wexler, 1987). Language development will not go forward merely because the environment meets general conditions of survival—air, food, other people, and so on. Specifically, linguistic input and, probably, output are called for so that if either is set to zero, development stops. Specific extralinguistic processes of perceptuomotor and cognitive development—a growing grasp on the physical and social modes of being and acting that language represents—also must feed into the language system. Thus, the proper study of language growth is the sequence of behavioral and cognitive conditions, linguistic and extralinguistic, that precipitate language change. The task of this "postnatal embryology," as we might call it, is to chart the course by which perceptual and motoric functions induce structure, from undifferentiated infant performance to differentiated adult competence.

In short, I am proposing that principles of growth, generally accepted in the development of the peripheral anatomy, also apply to the central nervous system. For example, writing of the plasticity of growing bones, D'Arcy Thompson (1917/1961) remarked:

> . . . the very important physiological truth that a condition of *strain,* the result of a *stress,* is a direct stimulus to growth itself. This indeed is no less than one of the cardinal facts of theoretical biology. The soles of our boots wear thin, but the soles of our feet grow thick the more we walk upon them: for it would seem that the living cells are "stimulated" by pressure, or by what we call "exercise" to increase and multiply. (p. 238, italics in the original)

Bosma (1975) invoked this principle of exercise in describing the development of the vocal apparatus: Perhaps the development of the neural representations of speech and language is also an instance of ". . . one of the cardinal facts of theoretical biology."

Ontogeny (Sometimes) Parallels Phylogeny

Complex functions, and the physical structures that support them, arise in evolution by gradual differentiation from simpler forms. Every evolutionary change is a change in development that is preserved in later generations. Accordingly, when a complex function is an evolutionarily coherent, hierarchically developed system, ontogeny may parallel, or recapitulate, phylogeny. I should emphasize that I am not proposing to reinstate the discredited "biogenetic law" of Ernst Haeckel (1834–1919). I am merely drawing attention to developmental facts well known since the embryological studies of Karl Ernst von Baer (1792–1876) in the early 19th century (Gould, 1977).

Of course, if we lack, as we largely do for language, precursor forms that confirm the sequence, we cannot be sure that the order of development we now observe was the actual order of evolution. Such precursors as we may establish—for example, lateralized systems for neural control of body posture and manual function (MacNeilage, chapter 7), or certain capacities for symbolic representation (Savage-Rumbaugh, chapter 8)—do not help us in the present context. Some "stages" may have been inserted into the evolutionary sequence later than others that now follow them in development. This may be true, for example, of left-hemisphere sensitivity to speech at, or soon after, birth because it is unlikely that a specialized neural substrate for speech evolved before speech itself.

Yet other processes may have evolved independently, parallel to processes with which they were later integrated. For example, some form of segmental phonology, affording at least a modest lexicon, would seem necessarily to have evolved before syntax began to take shape, and we still observe this sequence in development. But later stages of phonology and syntax may have evolved, as they still seem to develop, more or less independently. Similarly, prosodic variations in pitch, amplitude, and duration, characteristic of both human and nonhuman systems of communication, perhaps first followed an independent course of evolution, to be modified and integrated into the linguistic system only as longer utterances and more finely differentiated syntactic functions emerged. The double dissociation of right and left hemispheres for emotional and linguistic uses of prosody may reflect such a course of evolution.

Yet further limits on a phylogenetic interpretation of language ontogeny may seem to arise because the child is born into a community of companions who already speak a language. Moreover, the child is born with a vocal tract and a pair of hands that soon mature into forms adaptable for spoken or signed language, and with a rich, plastic neural substrate fit for shaping by cognitive and linguistic function. The exogenous and endogenous conditions of development therefore differ radically from those that must have prevailed in a hominid community where language was not yet fully formed.

Nonetheless, language acquisition is not instantaneous. The child does not have immediate access to the full adult language that surrounds it. The effective linguistic environment changes, step by step, as the child comes into possession of new cognitive and linguistic capacities. The problem of how linguistic input is ordered so as to ensure coherent development is solved by the child's own increasingly differentiated linguistic attention. With each new step the child finds the next step waiting, as it were, in the adult language because the adult language is adapted to the child no less than the child to the language. The reason for this is simply that language, like every evolved form, is the product of successive ontogenies, its structure a record of its own evolution (cf. Locke, 1983). Looked at in this way, language is not an object, or even a skill, that lies outside the child and has somehow to be acquired or internalized. Rather, it is a mode of action into which the child grows because the mode is implicit in the human developmental system.

We conclude that language, as a complex, hierarchical, behavioral structure with a lengthy course of development, is a good candidate for (circumspect) study in a recapitulatory framework because its development is rich in sequential dependencies: syllables and formulaic phrases before phonemes and features (as I argue later), holophrases before words, words before simple sentences, simple sentences before lexical categories, lexical categories before complex sentences, and so on. Thus, if we assume that each of the subsystems, phonology and syntax, evolved hierarchically by repeated cycles of differentiation and integration, we may recover their course of evolution by tracing the course of their growth. The general heuristic value of the assumption is that it not only throws light on evolution, but also promises an understanding of development in functional terms.

Development Is Not Teleological

If we combine the principles of gradual evolution and of a limited, functional recapitulation, we are freed from the temptation to assign purpose to development. At each point in its development an organism is already complete, adapted and adapting, as best it can, to present conditions, internal and external. Just as earlier evolutionary forms existed for themselves, not for any later forms to which they might give rise, so the present form of a developing organism has its own present function. A child does not learn its first words so that it may later combine them into sentences. First words have their own economy. More generally, a child's grammar, at each stage of development, is a possible adult grammar.

This last statement is limited exactly to the extent that the principle of recapitulation is limited. Some stages may have been inserted into the developmental sequence relatively late in evolution. Others now may serve a new function, having lost the function for which they originally arose. Such stages, perhaps particularly during the early months of rapid growth before linguistic functions have begun to differentiate, would have survived through successive generations because they facilitated later adaptive changes, while not infringing on present functions. In this sense, an early form may "preadapt" for a later. However, it would be an error to see such preadaptations as literal preformations. Development, like evolution, is a tinker, putting to present use whatever chance has laid to hand (cf. Jacob, 1977).

Individuals Reach the Same Developmental Ends by Different Routes and at Different Rates

Many linguists believe that universal aspects of language are innate. Universals are said to be purely genetically determined, and either to be present at birth (Chomsky, 1986) or to mature without contribution from the environment (Borer & Wexler, 1987). Aspects that vary across languages, though perhaps constrained to a few values by principles of universal grammar, are said to be learned from, or "fixed" by, the surrounding language. This is the model of "parameter setting" in syntactic theory (Chomsky, 1981; Roeper & Williams, 1987) and, in effect, of Jakobson's (1968) account of phonological development (cf. Goad & Ingram, 1987).

I do not challenge the descriptive adequacy of such theories. What I question is the proposed developmental mechanism, the attribution of species invariance to the genes, within-species variability to the environment—for, in fact, both invariance and variability arise from both genes and environment. The point is important because individual similarities in language development often are taken as support for a "biological" account of the process, whereas individual differences are seen as a threat (Goad & Ingram, 1987).

Consider, first, that identical phenotypes may be induced either by a genetic change in an unchanged environment or by a changed environment acting on an unchanged genome. For example, a yellow (as opposed to gray) body in the fruit fly (*Drosophila melanogaster*) can be produced either by mutation or by feeding the fly larva on fruit jelly impregnated with yellow dye (Dobzhansky, 1957). Similarly, the lack of a posterior cross-vein in fruit fly wings can result either from mutation or from subjecting the fly pupa to a brief high-temperature shock early in development (Waddington, 1975). Another example, not due to experimental intervention, comes from Piaget (1978) who studied freshwater snails in Swiss lakes during the late 1920s. He described three species. One species (*Limnaea stagnalis*), found in deep, calm waters, has an elongated shell; two other species (*L. lacustris* and *L. bodamica*), found in shallow, rough waters, have almost indistinguishable stubby, contracted shells. If the two stubby species are bred in the calm water of a laboratory aquarium, *L. bodamica* retains its stubby shell over many generations, whereas *L. lacustris* gradually takes on the elongated form characteristic of *L. stagnalis*. Had Piaget simply described the two stubby species, he might have attributed their similarity to shared genes. But we cannot reliably infer genotype from phenotype, as discussions of language development often assume. Without controlled breeding studies, we cannot determine whether an invariant, species-typical form reflects genetic constancy or environmental constancy.

Notice, moreover, that even when we have isolated genetic or environmental factors that contribute to some aspect of phenotypic variation, we have not demonstrated that the variable held constant has no effect. The snail species that takes an elongated form after generations in calm water, a contracted form after generations in rough water, can adapt to the environmental change because it is genetically equipped to do so. The snail species that retains its contracted form, whether bred in rough waters or in calm, lacks this genetic potential. But we cannot conclude from this that the environment has no effect on the form of its shell. We can conclude only that the two environments to which the snail was exposed did not suffice to select for a change in form although other environments might have done so.

In short, phenotypic form is both genetically and environmentally determined, a fact of some importance to language development. If we cannot assign phenotypic invariance, even in these "simple" examples, either to genes alone or to environment alone, we surely are not justified in doing so for language universals, or for the within-language constancies in linguistic development that often are cited as evidence for an innate language competence.

By the same token, variability in development among children learning the same language cannot be assigned solely to the environment. Certainly, different children, even within the same social class, must be exposed to widely varying patterns and frequencies of linguistic input, and such differences are likely to affect the course and rate of development. At the same time, children differ genetically, and these differences too affect development (Locke & Mather, in press). The problem is not to assign variability to a genetic or environmental source, but to understand how children resist the effects of genetic and environmental variation so as to arrive at a common language.

Development Is Buffered Against Extreme Variation

The problem of uniformity within and across languages is, in some respects, the obverse of the problem of language diversity. Languages, like species, differ because individuals differ. If all members of a species were genetically identical, followed an identical course of development, and arrived at an identical developmental term, new species could never arise. Genetic variation within a species, affording subtle individual differences in adaptive response to new environments, is the basis for the origin of species by natural selection. Similarly, if all speakers of a language followed an identical course of development to an identical linguistic term, new languages could never arise.

Of course, differences among speakers that lead to language change are unlikely to rest on genetic differences, because speakers of different languages do not differ systematically in their language-related genetic endowment: Children learn any first language to which they are exposed. In fact, from a genetic point of view, language differences rest on commonalities rather than differences: the shared capacity to adapt to any linguistic environment and to learn the surrounding language. In other words, it is precisely because language is supported by (we must presume) many thousands of genes, which depend on the environment to trigger their expression, that languages can be learned—and that languages differ. Subtle, environmentally induced individual differences in language development, selected and transmitted to other individuals by sociocultural forces of which we understand at present, very little, are one source of language diversity.

What then are the forces that resist change, guiding speakers into a common language? The problem is a special case, analogous to the general problem in developmental biology of how species maintain their identities across generations. We can gain conceptual leverage on the question by invoking the principle of "canalization" (Waddington, 1957, 1975). The term is purely descriptive, intended to capture ". . . a large number of well-known facts in genetics and embryology, all of which are summarized in the statement that the development of any particular phenotypic character is to some extent modifiable, and to some extent resistant to modification, by changes either in the genotype or in the environment" (Waddington, 1975, p. 72). In other words, both genetic and environmental variations are buffered against extreme divergence, canalized toward equifinality by constraints from the developing system. Genes and environment act in reciprocal, mutually constraining concert to assure a stable trajectory of growth.

To characterize the constraints on language growth in any detail is well beyond the scope of present knowledge. There would seem, however, to be two main sources of constraint: one in the child itself; one in the physical, social, and linguistic environment. Within the child, each step in cognitive and linguistic development opens new paths and closes others, an automatic consequence of the selection, and increasing differentiation, of the neural structures that support language and cognition, continuing the processes of tissue differentiation in the embryo. Once launched, the learning of a particular language becomes increasingly constrained by structural changes in the child's brain. These changes open paths into the language being learned, and perhaps into other languages of the same general type. Presumably, development along these paths will cease if the child is transferred abruptly to a markedly different linguistic environment. (Studies of "savings," that is, of the head start or lack of it, displayed by children who have switched languages or been exposed to a second language, might then throw light on cognitive and linguistic commonalties between the languages and on their inferred neural substrates.)

The external constraints on the child arise, first, from a general social context that invites the child to engage with its companions and to match its behavior to theirs. The second source of constraint is the language that the child's companions speak. Every language is a solution, one of an uncountable, but presumably limited, set of solutions to the problem of developing a communicative system within the perceptuomotor, memorial, and cognitive limits of humans (cf. Lindblom, 1983). The child then is guided easily into its language because, as we have already remarked, every language has evolved under constraints very like those that limit the child.

Given the increasing strength of endogenous and exogenous constraints as the child grows, we would expect phenotypic variation in phonology and syntax, if not in lexicon, to diminish as children come into possession of their language. Nonetheless, individual variability, far from being evidence against a biological account of language development, is a hallmark of developing biological systems.

In the following section, I attempt to illustrate some of the principles sketched earlier as they might apply to the development of phonological form over the first 2 years of life.

THE EMERGENCE OF PHONETIC SEGMENTS

Perception

The first systematic studies of infant capacity to perceive speech derived from the well-known studies of adult categorical perception. In a seminal set of experiments, the model for many others, Eimas and his colleagues (Eimas, Siqueland, Jusczyk, & Vigorito, 1971) demonstrated that 1- and 4-month-old infants displayed the same pattern of discrimination between syllables on a synthetic voice onset time (VOT) continuum as adults: They discriminated significantly better between syllables belonging to different English phoneme categories than between syllables belonging to the same phoneme category. Much the same result came from later infant studies of stop consonant place of articulation, consonant manner, the [r]-[l] distinction, and almost every other synthetic continuum on which infants were tested (see Aslin, Pisoni, & Jusczyk, 1983, for a comprehensive review).

From this accumulated wealth of evidence, Eimas (1975) concluded that categorical perception reflects the operation of innate mechanisms, specialized for processing speech, and that ". . . these early categories serve as the basis for future phonetic categories" (p. 342). This conclusion often is cited by students of language acquisition whose primary interest is in syntax. For example, Gleitman and Wanner (1982) summarily dismissed the problem of the origin of discrete phonetic segments (a problem no less severe than the problem of the origin of morphemic units to which they devote much attention) by citing the work of Eimas and others to support the claim that: ". . . no learning apparatus is required for an initial segmentation of the acoustic wave into discrete phones. The segmentation has been provided in the nervous system" (p. 16). Exactly how this capacity for segmentation came to be evolutionarily, or comes to be ontogenetically, "provided in the nervous system," they did not consider.

In any event, many reasons to doubt Eimas's interpretation of the infant data have been given by Jusczyk (1981), Kuhl (1987), Studdert-Kennedy (1986), and Walley, Pisoni, and Aslin (1981). I do not rehearse the reasons in detail, but here briefly note three. First, we now know that categorical perception is peculiar to neither speech nor audition (see Harnad, 1987, for several relevant papers). Second, Kuhl and her colleagues have demonstrated categorical effects on labial, alveolar, and velar VOT continua in chinchillas (Kuhl & Miller, 1975), and on a place continuum in macaques (Kuhl & Padden, 1982, 1983). Thus, whatever the bearing of categorical studies on the development of speech perception, they clearly do not reflect a perceptual specialization. Third, the claim that categorical perception reveals the basis for future phonetic categories confuses two types of category. The categories mimicked by a synthetic series vary along a single acoustic dimension in a fixed context; they comprise, at most, the random variations that we might observe in a single syllable, spoken repeatedly with identical stress and at an identical rate by the same speaker. However, the phonological categories that a child must form are equivalence classes of intrinsic and extrinsic allophonic variants, formed by execution of a particular phoneme in a range of phonetic contexts, spoken with varying degrees of stress, at different rates, and by different speakers.

For study of the infant's potential grasp on these equivalence classes, we must turn to another body of research. In a systematic series of studies Kuhl and her colleagues have demonstrated that 3- to 6-month-old infants can learn to recognize the equivalence of: (a) isolated vowels spoken by a man, a woman, or a child; (b) syllables with the same consonantal onset before different vowels; (c) syllables with a particular consonantal acoustic pattern in initial, medial, or final position; and (d) syllables that share an initial "feature" (stop, nasal). (For a comprehensive review, see Kuhl, 1987.) Yet we should be cautious in interpreting even these studies as evidence that infants can recognize phonetic (as opposed to acoustic) invariants, if only because Kluender, Diehl, and Killeen (1987) have successfully trained Japanese quail to form equivalence classes across syllables spoken with different pitch contours, by different speakers, or with the same consonant before different vowels. In short, we have no grounds for claiming that perceptual analysis of the acoustic structure of a spoken syllable, and the formation of categories from the resulting components, engage distinctively human capacities, whether infant or adult.

In fact, these infant studies seem to have no more than a general bearing on the specialized development of language. They are psychophysical studies, demonstrating that infants at, or soon after, birth have the capacity to discriminate and categorize certain acoustic patterns that occur in speech. They provide detailed support for a general observation, suggested by the fact that speech sounds are concentrated in the few octaves of the acoustic spectrum to which humans (and many other animals) are most sensitive: Spoken language has evolved and develops within the constraints of prelinguistic auditory capacity. Surely, it would be surprising if this were not so. We do not expect an animal to have a communication system that is not matched to its sensory capacities!

However, the most serious objection to the standard interpretation of these studies is that by assuming the child to be innately endowed with sensitivity to the smallest phonetic units of which spoken utterances are composed, they implicitly adopt a view of development as proceeding from the specific to the general rather than the reverse. Yet, as we already have seen, it is a general rule of both phylogeny and ontogeny that complex structures evolve by differentiation of smaller structures from larger. Accordingly, we should not expect children to build words from phonemes as adults do; rather, we should expect phonemes to emerge from words. We may note, in passing, that a similar principles must apply to the development of word classes and syntactic structures, a fact not generally recognized in developmental psycholinguistics.

From this vantage we can take a different view of infant speech perception than has hitherto prevailed, one that emphasizes development of function rather than psychophysical capacity. One aspect of this work will entail charting the process of "attunement" to the surrounding language, the course by which the infant learns to perceive speech, bringing to bear capacities evidenced in the laboratory on the speech it hears at home. Work along these lines, in fact, has already begun, with studies of infants' loss of sensitivity to phonetic contrasts not deployed in their native language (see, e.g., Best, McRoberts, & Sithole, 1988; Werker & Tees, 1984). Other studies by Hirsh-Pasek and her colleagues (see, e.g., Hirsh-Pasek et al., 1987; see also chapter 13 of this volume) are tracing the development of sensitivity to prosodic patterns that specify clausal units, perhaps the thin end of an infant wedge into syntactic structure.

Here, however, I wish to pursue another aspect of perceptual function: its role in guiding the development of production. I assume that the development of speech depends not only on the maturation and use of the vocal motor system, but also on the infant's gradual discovery of structure in the speech it hears: By learning how to listen, the infant learns how to speak. The speech signal therefore comes to specify for the infant the actions — or, more exactly, the motoric components of articulatory action — by which speech is produced. Yet neither phonemes nor features, the perceptual units typically posited in infant studies, can be defined either acoustically or motorically. They are abstract units beyond the reach of an infant who does not yet know a language. If we are to understand speech development, we must couch our descriptions and frame our experiments in terms of auditory and motoric units to which an infant might reasonably be expected to have access. In what follows I briefly sketch a speculative account of the process by which infants gradually harness prelinguistic motoric elements to communicative use.

Production

We may discern at least four broad stages in the early development of speech, successive cycles of differentiation and integration that carry the infant from prelinguistic cries and mouthings to the emergence of phonetic segments and the beginnings of phonology in early words. The stages form a necessary hierarchical sequence from the general to the specific, from the nonlinguistic to the linguistic. However, they are not sharply delimited: Processes that begin in one stage may continue more or less unchanged into several later stages — for example, a child may continue to babble long after it has begun to produce words. Also, we must be cautious in characterizing a stage as differentiative or integrative for two reasons. First, differentiation at one level (for example, breaking a syllable into its component gestures) entails integration at another (coordinating movements to form gestures), and vice versa. Second, even within a level both differentiation and integration go on during a single stage: For example, integrating gestural patterns into consonants and vowels entails simultaneously differentiating a syllable into its segmental components.

Nonetheless, because even a coarse and tentative taxonomy of development may lend insight into its process, let us consider the following four stages: (a) early vocalizing: differentiation of respiratory and vocal tract activities into patterns of sound making associated with different nonspeech actions (0 to 7 months of age); (b) canonical babbling: integration of nonspeech movement patterns into rhythmic syllabic structures (7 to 10 months of age); (c) variegated babbling and early words: differentiation of the syllable into its component gestures (10 to 15 months of age); and (d) integration of recurrent gestural patterns into canonical phonetic segments (15 to 24 months of age). The suggested time periods are, of course, approximate, because children differ widely in the time courses of their development.

Differentiation: Early Vocalizing.   Over the first half-year of life, infant sounds progress systematically from clearly nonspeech vocalizations to canonical babbling that invites phonetic transcription. The changing forms presumably are determined, at least in part, by general maturation and by exercise of the vocal apparatus and of its neural control structures (for review, see Kent, 1981). Stark (1986) divided the development of sound making over the first 7 to 8 months of life into three stages: reflexive crying and vegetative sounds (0 to 8 weeks of age), cooing and laughter (8 to 20 weeks of age), and vocal play (16 to 30 weeks of age). These stages are of interest in the present context because they reflect changes in the topography of vocal tract activities and in the forms of the resulting sounds by which prelinguistic elements are differentiated and marshalled for protolinguistic use (cf. Oller, 1986).

Reflexive crying, like the distress calls of other animals, has, of course, a communicative (though nonlinguistic) function. Cries, executed with a relatively unconstricted vocal tract, are predominantly voiced, often with the formant structure of low to mid front vowels. Vegetative sounds—the grunts, sighs, clicks, stops, and pops associated with breathing and feeding—may be either voiced or voiceless, formed with either an open, vowellike or a constricted, consonantlike configuration of the vocal tract. The cooing, or comfort, sounds of Stark's (1986) second stage tend to occur in a series of 3 to 10 segments, each of about 500 ms, separated by voiceless intakes of breath and glottal stops. Their energy is concentrated in frequencies below about 1,500 Hz, a pattern that Oller (1980) has termed a "quasi-resonant" nucleus, having the form of a nasal consonant or nasalized vowel.

Thus, by the end of the 5th month, the infant's sound repertoire already contains a variety of protoconsonantal and protovocalic elements. The important changes in the next stage are not so much in the size and quality of the repertoire as in its function and organization. First, sounds begin to lose their original functional moorings: They become ". . . divorced from their previous cry, vegetative or comfort sound contexts, and are used in a variety of communicative situations" (Stark, 1986, p. 159). Second, sounds become longer (700 to 1,500 ms), and form longer, more complex sequences. The infant emits repetitious strings of consonantlike clicks, trills, friction noises, syllabic nasals with a constriction at the front of the mouth, and lip smackings. Vowellike sounds, now with a "fully resonant" nucleus (Oller, 1980) often carrying extreme pitch glides, are executed with increased variation in tongue height and front-back placement.

However, the key change during this stage is combinatorial: The infant begins to superimpose movements of tongue, jaw, and lips on the laryngeal actions associated with cry (Koopmans-van Beinum & Van der Stelt, 1986), so that the proportion of supraglottal to glottal articulations gradually increases (Holmgren, Lindblom, Aurelius, Jalling, & Zetterstrom, 1986). Even at this early stage, children may differ quite sharply in their preferred types of vocalization (Stark, 1986). Toward the end of the stage increasingly long and complex combinations of tract constrictions and openings appear, forming sequences that Oller (1980) termed marginal babble.

The functional value of the differentiation of early sound making into these diverse patterns is not obvious. Teleologically, of course, exercise of the vocal apparatus must contribute to its neural and anatomical development, laying the basis for later integration of sounds into syllables. However, the immediate function may lie simply in the increased range of emotional expression that it affords, with a consequent tightening of dyadic social bonds (cf. Stern, 1985; Trevarthen & Marwick, 1986). Interestingly, P. F. MacNeilage (personal communication, October, 1985) has noted a possible precursor of such differentiation in the repetitive girneys (lip smacks, accompanied by a low murmur) exhibited by Japanese macaques in intimate, affiliative situations (Green, 1975).

In any event, I have dwelt on this early stage because it is here that we can see most clearly the tinkering together of disparate nonlinguistic patterns of vocal tract activity into the beginnings of phonological structure (cf. Bates, Thal, & Marchman in chapter 2 of this volume).

Integration: Canonical Babble. With the onset of canonical babble, often a sudden event over a few days in the 7th or 8th month of age, the infant begins to integrate patterns of vocal tract constriction and opening into unitary, cohesive syllables. Rhythmic, reduplicated sound sequences are common: [bababa], [nenene], [dIdIdI]. However, the convenient use of phonetic transcription should not mislead us into supposing that the infant has independent control over segments within a syllable. In fact, rhythmic lowering and raising of the jaw in canonical babble seems to occur with little or no independent movement of the tongue (Davis & MacNeilage, 1990). This rhythmic jaw oscillation often begins about the same time as rhythmic movements of the legs and arms (Thelen, 1981; see also chapter 15 of this volume), and perhaps facilitates the integration of vocal tract activities into cohesive syllabic patterns.

We owe the clear distinction between early vocalization and canonical babble to Oller (1980, 1986). He described some half-dozen acoustic properties of structures that listeners recognize as canonical, adult consonant-vowel (CV) (constricted-to-open), or consonant-vowel-consonant (CVC) syllables. Of these properties, the most important in the present context (because they are the only ones that appear rarely, if ever, in early vocalizations) are temporal. The canonical syllable has a duration of no less than 100 msec, no more than 500 msec; onset (and, when present, offset) formant transitions display smooth changes in frequency and amplitude with durations between 25 and 120 ms. These acoustic patterns reflect the infant's increasing skill in integrating the closing and opening phases of jaw movements.

Patterns of movement in babble are not random. During the constriction phase of the syllable, complete closure, as in stops, is favored over partial closure, as in fricatives. Points of closure are biased toward the front of the mouth, engaging lip and tongue tip muscles active in sucking. During the open phase, the favored tongue positions are those associated with low front vowels, indicating that the tongue tends to ride up and down on the jaw with little or no active movement of its own (Davis & MacNeilage, 1990). The glottis typically is approximated throughout the syllable, giving the impression of voiced consonants at syllable onset.

These "phonetic" biases have been reported for infants growing in a number of language environments (Locke, 1983). The biases also are present in many adult languages, perhaps reflecting the infant proclivities from which languages have evolved (Locke, 1983; cf. Lindblom, 1989). Here we have a tangle that cross-linguistic data on babble are still too sparse to resolve. How far do the perhaps universal biases of infant babble reflect the maturational state of the infant vocal apparatus, and how far do they reflect the surrounding language? We may ask much the same question concerning individual differences in babbling repertoire within a language: Do they reflect differences in the development of the vocal apparatus or differences in the language patterns that the infants happen to have heard? Whatever the answers to these questions, recent work with deaf infants has shown that the emergence of canonical babble is not purely an effect of maturation.

Deaf infants once were said to exhibit the same babbling patterns as hearing infants, at least over the first year of life (cf. Locke, 1983).

However, recent comparisons have demonstrated that canonical babble does not appear on schedule in deaf infants (Oller & Eilers, 1988; Oller, Eilers, Bull, & Carney, 1985; Stoel-Gammon & Otomo, 1986). Whether this is due to the lack of auditory input from the infant's own vocalizations, from those of its adult companions, or both, we do not know. If self-stimulation were the only essential, a purely maturational account could still hold. To the extent that communicative interchange, or the impulse to imitate the actions of conspecifics, plays a role the onset of canonical babble would be determined, at least in part, by experience of a surrounding language. Persuasive evidence for the role of the surrounding language comes from reports that deaf children exposed to sign language begin to "babble" with their fingers at about the same age as hearing infants begin to babble with their mouths (Newport & Meier, 1985; Laura Petitto, personal communication, April, 1989).

Finally, what is the function of canonical babble? "None" has been the answer of some (e.g., Jakobson, 1968; Lenneberg, 1967) who viewed babble as random mouthing, sharply discontinuous from truly linguistic utterance. However, Locke and Pearson (1988) recently reported a severe (though not irremediable) delay in the development of speech in a tracheostomized child, deprived of the opportunity to babble from 5 to 20 months of age. This suggests that babble is a necessary step in normal linguistic development. Moreover, several studies now have shown that babble merges smoothly into early words and that the phonetic structure of a child's first words tends to reflect its babbling preferences (Locke, 1983; Oller, Wieman, Doyle, & Ross, 1975; Vihman & Miller, 1988; Vihman, Macken, Miller, Simmons, & Miller, 1985). The immediate function would seem then to be to continue the "imitative" process of aligning the infant's communicative skills more closely with those of its adult companions.

Differentiation: Variegated Babble and Early Words.   Toward the end of the first year of age full syllable reduplication fades. The infant begins to differentiate the closing and opening gestures of successive syllables so that "variegated" sequences (Oller, 1980) appear, giving the impression of variations in consonant and/or vowel (e.g., /nenI/, /mɛnə/, /dædi/). Also, at about this time the child produces its first recognizable attempts at adult words or phrases ("All gone," "What's that?"), usually (in English children) single syllables or disyllables. The two modes of output then proceed concurrently, often for many months, with words gradually coming to predominate. Over this period the child gradually is forging links between its perceptual and productive capacities.

The perceptual ground for this development seems to be laid by the child's growing attention to words in the surrounding language. Data on early comprehension are scarce, but children evidently accumulate sizeable receptive lexicons before attempting their first words. Benedict (1979) has reported a longitudinal study of comprehension and production in eight children from the age of 9 or 10 months to a point where they had achieved a productive lexicon of 50 words (between 15 and 22 months of age). In every child, comprehension comfortably outstripped production. On the average, the children understood more than 60 words by the time they could produce 10, with a range from 30 to 182 words; and on the average, their receptive lexicon over the period of the study was three times their productive lexicon (Benedict, 1979).

The gap between perception and production demonstrates that a perceptuomotor link is not innate, as some have proposed (Liberman & Mattingly, 1985), but must develop. Many studies have shown that the phonetic forms of early words are similar to those of concurrent babble (see Vihman, 1990, for review). A child selects for imitation words that match "vocal motor schemes" (McCune & Vihman, 1987) already present in its babble and avoids words that do not match (Menn, 1983). Thus, the child initially grows into a lexicon, as it were, by discovering correspondences between adult words and auditory feedback from its own babbled output. Because the structure of auditory feedback must correspond, in some fashion, to the structure of motor controls that produced it, the child's recognition of babble-to-word correspondences presumably facilitates growth of perceptuomotor links, and their gradual extension to new words.

Each word (or formulaic phrase) seems to be a prosodic unit (Macken, 1979), its production planned as a whole (Menn, 1983). Evidence for this comes from gestural interactions. A child often fails to execute two different places or manners of articulation within the same word, thus maintaining some of the reduplicative tendencies of canonical babble: *dog* [gag], *lady* [jeiji], *duck* [tʌt]. Closing and opening gestures also interact. For example, Davis and MacNeilage (1990) reported an extensive study of a child's concurrent babbling and speech over the period from 14 to 20 months of age. Their data are replete with instances not only of consonant, but of vowel and even consonant-vowel assimilation. The latter is revealed by the child's preference for high front vowels following alveolar closures and for low, front-central vowels following labial closures. At the same time, these authors also reported an inverse relation between consonant and vowel reduplication: Where the child succeeds in combating assimilation in the open phases of a disyllable, she often fails to do so in the closing phases, and vice versa. This demonstrates an incipient segregation of consonants and vowels into phonetic classes.

The study by Davis and MacNeilage (1990) is particularly important because the child deployed an unusually large lexicon, growing from about 25 words at age 14 months to over 750 words at age 20 months. Evidently, a child may have a substantial lexicon long before it has fully mastered segmental structure. The principal phonological achievement of this period, then, is internal modification of the integrated syllable by differentiation of its gestural components.

Integration: From Gestures to Phonemes. The final step in the path from mouth sounds to segments is the integration of gestural patterns of syllabic constriction and opening into the coherent perceptuomotor structures we know as consonants and vowels (Studdert-Kennedy, 1987). As is well known, the status of the segment is problematic, for, on the one hand, we can neither specify the invariant articulatory-acoustic properties shared by all instances of a particular consonant or vowel, nor isolate any given segment as a discrete articulatory-acoustic entity within a syllable. On the other hand, across-word metathetic errors in adult speaking ("spooner-isms") attest to the functional role of segments in the planning and execution of an utterance (Shattuck-Hufnagel, 1983). Moreover, such errors typically entail exchanges between consonants and vowels that occupy corresponding slots in their respective syllables. Because the exchanging elements may be physically quite disparate, it is evident that their exchange is premised on shared function (onset, nucleus, coda) in the formation of a syllable.

There are therefore two aspects to the emergence of segments as elements of word formation in a child's lexicon. First is the grouping of all instances of a particular gesture-sound pattern into a single class presumably on the basis of their perceptuomotor, or phonetic, similarity (e.g., grouping the initial or final patterns of *dad, dog, bed,* etc. into the class /d/). Second is the distributional analysis and grouping of these gesture-sound patterns into higher order classes (consonants, vowels) on the basis of their syllabic functions. These processes of phonetic category formation are perhaps analogous to those proposed by Maratsos and Chalkley (1980) for the formation of syntactic categories.

Evidence from across-word metathetic errors for the formation of these classes in young children is sparse. The only systematic data known to me come from Jeri Jaeger (personal communication, April, 1986). She reported her daughter's first across-word metathesis as occurring in her 27th month of age: *ummy takes* for *tummy aches.* This was followed in her 30th month of age by *fritty pace* for *pretty face, sea tet* for *tea set,* and *Bernie and Ert* for *Ernie and Bert.* Jaeger did not report data on the size of her daughter's lexicon at this time, nor on the complexity of her multiword utterances. But the collection of errors suggests that both were well advanced.

Two possible selection pressures may precipitate formation of consonant and vowel classes. One pressure is toward economy of storage as the lexicon increases in size. We have seen that a child may accumulate an appreciable lexicon of some 750 words without showing signs of independent segmental control (Davis & MacNeilage, 1990). But this lexicon is roughly one hundredth of the size that it will eventually become; and it seems reasonable to suppose that, as the lexicon increases, words should organize themselves on the basis of their shared gestural and sound properties. Recurrent patterns of laryngeal and supralaryngeal gesture thus would form themselves into unitary classes of potential utility for recognition and activation of lexical items (cf. Lindblom, 1989; Lindblom, MacNeilage, & Studdert-Kennedy, 1983).

A second possible selection pressure is toward rapid lexical access in the formation of multiword utterances. Several authors (e.g., Branigan, 1979; Donahue, 1986) have argued that the form of early multiword combinations may be constrained by the child's limited ability to organize and execute the required articulatory sequences. One such constraint might be a child's inability to produce two successive words with different initial places of articulation. Donahue, for example, described two strategies adopted by her son in his first two-word utterances. One strategy was to attempt only those words that conformed to his preexisting rule of labial harmony: *Big book, big bird, big ball* were all attempted, but *big dog* and *big cooky* were "adamantly refused" (p. 215). The second strategy was to circumvent the consonant harmony rule by adopting vocalic words lacking consonants (e.g., *where* [ejə], *want* [wa]) as pivots that could be combined comfortably with many of the words already in his vocabulary. Such findings imply that the integration of gestures into independent phonemic control structures, or articulatory routines (Menn, 1983), may serve to insulate them from articulatory competition with incompatible gestures and so facilitate their rapid, successive activation in multiword utterances.

CONCLUSION

I have proposed that the study of language development might be cast fruitfully in an evolutionary and recapitulatory framework, as a sort of postnatal embryology. Language universals (like other species characters) are the endpoint of development (and evolution), a consequence, not a condition, of learning a natural language. Language function thus determines language form, and form is viewed as an a posteriori description of, rather than an a priori prescription for, development. We thus are freed from the habit of viewing universals as innate, language-specific properties as learned. Both sets of characters are the product of a species-specific developmental system, in which genetic and environmental conditions cannot be separated.

I have attempted to illustrate the approach with a sketch of the process by which the universal phonological categories of consonants and vowels might emerge. They are viewed as deriving by successive cycles of differentiation and integration from prior nonlinguistic perceptual and motor capacities.

REFERENCES

Aslin, R. N., Pisoni, D. B., & Jusczyk, P. W. (1983). Auditory development and speech perception in infancy. In M. Haith & J. Campos (Eds.), *Infancy and the biology of development: Vol. 2. Carmichael's manual of child psychology* (4th ed., pp. 220–284). New York: Wiley.

Benedict, H. (1979). Early lexical development: Comprehension and production. *Journal of Child Language, 6,* 183–200.

Best, C. T., McRoberts, G. W., & Sithole, N. W. (1988). Examination of perceptual reorganization for nonnative speech contrasts: Zulu click discrimination by English-speaking adults and infants. *Journal of Experimental Psychology: Human Perception and Performance, 14,* 345–360.

Borer, H., & Wexler, K. (1987). The maturation of syntax. In T. Roeper & E. Williams (eds.), *Parameter setting* (pp. 123–172). Dordrecht, Holland: Reidel.

Bosma, J. F. (1975). Anatomic and physiologic development of the speech apparatus. In D. B. Tower (Ed.), *The nervous system: Vol. 3. Human communication and its disorders* (pp. 469–481). New York: Raven.

Branigan, G. (1979). Some reasons why successive single word utterances are not. *Journal of Child Language, 6,* 411–421.

Chomsky, N. (1965). *Aspects of the theory of syntax.* Cambridge, MA: MIT Press.

Chomsky, N. (1981). *Lectures on government and binding: The Pisa lectures.* Dordrecht, Holland: Foris.

Chomsky, N. (1986). *Knowledge of language.* New York: Praeger Special Studies.

Darwin, C. (1871). *The descent of man.* New York: Modern Library.

Davis, B. L., & MacNeilage, P. F. (1990). Acquisition of correct vowel production: A quantitative case study. *Journal of Speech and Hearing Research, 33,* 16–27.

de Saussure, F. (1966). *Course in general linguistics* (W. Baskin, Trans.). New York: McGraw-Hill.

Dobzhansky, T. G. (1957). *Human genetics.* New York: Columbia University Press.

Donahue, M. (1986). Phonological constraints on the emergence of two-word utterances. *Journal of Child Language, 13,* 209–218.

Eimas, P. D. (1975). Auditory and phonetic coding of the cues for speech: Discrimination of the /r-l/ distinction by young infants. *Perception and Psychophysics, 18,* 341–347.

Eimas, P. D., Siqueland, E. R., Jusczyk, P., & Vigorito, J. (1971). Speech perception in infants. *Science, 171,* 303–306.

Gleitman, L. R., & Wanner, E. (1982). The state of the state of the art. In E. Wanner & L. R. Gleitman (Eds.), *Language acquisition* (pp. 3–48). New York: Cambridge University Press.

Goad, H., & Ingram, D. (1987). Individual variation and its relevance to a theory of phonological acquisition. *Journal of Child Language, 14,* 419–432.

Gould, S. J. (1977). *Ontogeny and phylogeny.* Cambridge, MA: Belknap Press.

Grassé, P. P. (1977). *Evolution of living organisms.* New York: Academic.

Green, S. (1975). Variation of vocal pattern with social situation in the Japanese monkey (*Macaca fuscata*): A field study. In L. A. Rosenblum (Ed.), *Primate behavior* (Vol. 4, pp. 1–102). New York: Academic.

Harnad, S. (Ed.). (1987). *Categorical perception*. New York: Cambridge University Press.

Hirsh-Pasek, K., Kemler Nelson, D. G., Jusczyk, P. W., Cassidy, K. W., Druss, B., & Kennedy, L. (1987). Clauses are perceptual units for young infants. *Cognition, 26,* 269-286.

Holmgren, K., Lindblom, B., Aurelius, G., Jalling, B., & Zetterstrom, R. (1986). On the phonetics of infant vocalization. In B. Lindblom & R. Zetterstrom (Eds.), *Precursors of early speech* (pp. 51-63). New York: Stockton Press.

Jacob, F. (1977). Evolution as tinkering. *Science, 196,* 1161-1166.

Jakobson, R. (1968). *Child language, aphasia and phonological universals*. (A. R. Keiler, Trans.). The Hague, Netherlands: Mouton.

Jusczyk, P. W. (1981). Infant speech perception: A critical appraisal. In P. D. Eimas & J. L. Miller (Eds.), *Perspectives on the study of speech* (pp. 113-164). Hillsdale, NJ: Lawrence Erlbaum Associates.

Kent, R. D. (1981). Sensorimotor aspects of speech development. In R. N. Aslin, J. R. Alberts, & M. R. Petersen (Eds.), *Development of perception* (Vol. 1, pp. 161-189). New York: Academic.

Kluender, K. R., Diehl, R. L., & Killeen, P. R. (1987). Japanese quail can learn phonetic categories. *Science, 237,* 1195-1197.

Koopmans-van Beinum, F. J., & Van der Stelt, J. M. (1986). Early stages in the development of speech movements. In B. Lindblom & R. Zetterstrom (Eds.), *Precursors of early speech* (pp. 37-50). New York: Stockton Press.

Kuhl, P. K. (1987). Perception of speech and sound in early infancy. In P. Salapatek & L. Cohen (Eds.), *Handbook of infant perception,* (Vol. 2, pp. 275-382). New York: Academic.

Kuhl, P. K., & Miller, J. D. (1975). Speech perception by the chinchilla: Voiced-voiceless distinction in alveolar plosive consonants. *Science, 190,* 69-72.

Kuhl, P. K., & Padden, D. M. (1982). Enhanced discrimination at the phonetic boundaries for the voicing feature in macaques. *Perception and Psychophysics, 32,* 542-550.

Kuhl, P. K., & Padden, D. M. (1983). Enhanced discriminability at the phonetic boundaries for the place feature in macaques. *Journal of the Acoustical Society of America, 73,* 1003-1010.

Lack, D. (1961). *Darwin's finches: An essay on the general biology of evolution*. New York: Harper & Row.

Lehmann, W. P. (1973). *Historical linguistics*. New York: Holt, Rinehart & Winston.

Lenneberg, E. H. (1967). *The biological foundations of language*. New York: Wiley.

Liberman, A. M., & Mattingly, I. G. (1985). The motor theory of speech perception revised. *Cognition, 21,* 1-36.

Lindblom, B. (1983). Can the models of evolutionary biology be applied to phonetic problems? In A. Cohen & M. P. R. v. d. Broecke (Eds.), *Proceedings of the Tenth International Congress of Phonetic Sciences* (pp. 67-81). Dordrecht, Holland: Foris.

Lindblom, B. (1989). Some remarks on the origin of the "phonetic code." In C. von Euler, I. Lundberg, & G. Lennerstrand (Eds.), *Brain and reading* (pp. 27-44). Basingstoke, England: Macmillan.

Lindblom, B., MacNeilage, P., & Studdert-Kennedy, M. (1983). Self-organizing processes and the explanation of language universals. In B. Butterworth, B. Comrie, & O. Dahl (Eds.), *Explanations for language universals* (pp. 181-203). The Hague, Netherlands: Mouton.

Locke, J. (1983). *Phonological acquisition and change*. New York: Academic.

Locke, J. L., & Mather, P. L. (in press). Genetic factors in the ontogeny of spoken language: Evidence from monozygotic and dizygotic twins. *Journal of Child Language*.

Locke, J., & Pearson, D. M. (1988). Linguistic significance of babbling: Evidence from a tracheostomized infant. *Report from the Neurolinguistics Laboratory at Massachusetts General Hospital*.

Macken, M. A. (1979). Developmental reorganization of phonology: A hierarchy of basic units of organization. *Lingua, 49,* 11–49.

Maratsos, M. P., & Chalkley, M. A. (1980). The internal language of children's syntax: The ontogenesis and representation of syntactic categories. In K. Nelson (Ed.) *Children's language* (Vol. II, pp. 121–143). New York: Gardner.

Mayr, E. (1982). *The growth of biological thought.* Cambridge, MA: Belknap Press.

McCune, L., & Vihman, M. (1987). Vocal motor schemes. *Papers and Reports on Child Language Development, 26,* 72–79.

Menn, L. (1983). Development of articulatory, phonetic and phonological capabilities. In B. Butterworth (Ed.), *Language production* (Vol. 2, pp. 3–50). London: Academic.

Newport, E. L., & Meier, R. P. (1985). The acquisition of American Sign Language. In D. I. Slobin (Ed.), *The cross-linguistic study of language acquisition: Vol. 1. The data* (pp. 881–938). Hillsdale, NJ: Lawrence Erlbaum Associates.

Oller, D. K. (1980). The emergence of the sounds of speech in infancy. In G. Yeni-Komshian, J. F. Kavanagh, & C. A. Ferguson (Eds.), *Child phonology: Vol. 1. Production* (pp. 93–112). New York: Academic.

Oller, D. K. (1986). Metaphonology and infant vocalizations. In B. Lindblom & R. Zetterstrom (Eds.), *Precursors of early speech* (pp. 21–35). New York: Stockton Press.

Oller, D. K., & Eilers, R. E. (1988). The role of audition in infant babbling. *Child Development, 59,* 441–449.

Oller, D. K., Eilers, R. E., Bull, D. H., & Carney, A. E. (1985). Prespeech vocalizations of a deaf infant: A comparison with normal metaphonological development. *Journal of Speech and Hearing Research, 28,* 47–63.

Oller, D. K., Wieman, L. A., Doyle, W., & Ross, C. (1975). Infant babbling and speech. *Journal of Child Language, 3,* 1–11.

Oyama, S. (1985). *The ontogeny of information.* New York: Cambridge University Press.

Piaget, J. (1978). *Behavior and evolution.* Chicago: Chicago University Press.

Roeper, T., & Williams, E. (Eds.). (1987). *Parameter setting.* Dordrecht, Holland: Reidel.

Shattuck-Hufnagel, S. (1983). Sublexical units and suprasegmental structure in speech production planning. In P. F. MacNeilage (Ed.), *The production of speech* (pp. 109–136). New York: Springer-Verlag.

Stark, R. E. (1986). Prespeech segmental feature development. In P. Fletcher & M. Garman (Eds.), *Language acquisition* (2nd ed., pp. 149–173). New York: Cambridge University Press.

Stern, D. N. (1985). *The interpersonal world of the infant.* New York: Basic.

Stoel-Gammon, C., & Otomo, K. (1986). Babbling development of hearing-impaired and normally hearing subjects. *Journal of Speech and Hearing Disorders, 51,* 33–41.

Studdert-Kennedy, M. (1986). Sources of variability in early speech development. In J. S. Perkell & D. H. Klatt (Eds.), *Invariance and variability of speech processes* (pp. 58–76). Hillsdale, NJ: Lawrence Erlbaum Associates.

Studdert-Kennedy, M. (1987). The phoneme as a perceptuomotor structure. In A. Allport, D. MacKay, W. Prinz, & E. Scheerer (Eds.), *Language perception and production* (pp. 67–84). London: Academic.

Thelen, E. (1981). Rhythmical behavior in infancy: An ethological perspective. *Developmental Psychology, 17,* 237–257.

Thompson, D. W. (1917/1961). *On growth and form* (abridged ed.). New York: Cambridge University Press.

Trevarthen, C., & Marwick, H. (1986). Signs of motivation for speech in infants, and the nature of a mother's support for development of language. In B. Lindblom & R. Zetterstrom (Eds.), *Precursors of early speech* (pp. 279–308). New York: Stockton Press.

Vihman, M. M. (1990). Ontogeny of phonetic gestures: Speech production. In I. G. Mattingly

& M. Studdert-Kennedy (Eds.), *Modularity and the motor theory of speech perception* (pp. 69–84). Hillsdale, NJ: Lawrence Erlbaum Associates.

Vihman, M. M., Macken, M. A., Miller, R., Simmons, H., & Miller, J. (1985). From babbling to speech: A re-assessment of the continuity issue. *Language, 61,* 397–445.

Vihman, M. M., & Miller, R. (1988). Words and babble at the threshold of lexical acquisition. In M. D. Smith & J. L. Locke (Eds.), *The emergent lexicon: The child's development of a linguistic vocabulary* (pp. 151–183). New York: Academic.

Waddington, C. H. (1957). *The strategy of the genes.* New York: Macmillan.

Waddington, C. H. (1975). *The evolution of an evolutionist.* Ithaca, NY: Cornell University Press.

Walley, A. C., Pisoni, D. B., & Aslin, R. N. (1981). The role of early experience in the development of speech perception. In R. N. Aslin, J. Alberts, & M. R. Petersen (Eds.), *Development of perception* (Vol. 1, pp. 219–255). New York: Academic.

Werker, J. F., & Tees, R. C. (1984). Cross-language speech perception: Evidence for perceptual reorganization during the first year of life. *Infant Behavior and Development, 7,* 49–63.

2 Symbols and Syntax: A Darwinian Approach to Language Development

Elizabeth Bates, Donna Thal, and Virginia Marchman
Center for Research in Language
University of California, San Diego

The species on this planet have had millions of years to develop mechanisms for coping with light, heat, gravity, space, time, cause and effect, and the boundaries of common objects and events. By contrast, human language is a relative newcomer, a coping mechanism that has been around for a mere 300,000 years or less (Harnad, Steklis, & Lancaster, 1976; Lieberman, 1982). How did such a complex and exquisite system evolve in such a short time? In this chapter, we sketch out a neo-Darwinian approach to the development of symbols and syntax, an approach that may help to resolve this evolutionary dilemma.

THE LINGUISTIC DILEMMA

Most linguists and psycholinguists working within the generative grammar tradition subscribe to the view that natural language is part of our biological endowment, a defining and perhaps unique characteristic of our species (Bickerton, 1981; Borer & Wexler, 1987; Chomsky, 1965, 1976, 1980). This claim is, of course, quite compatible with Darwinian theory. However, Chomsky and his colleagues go on to argue that our faculty for language is discontinuous from the rest of human and nonhuman cognition. As currently formulated, this discontinuity argument is difficult to reconcile with Darwin's theory that innate structures evolved gradually by natural selection from prior forms. This is the linguistic dilemma: Arguments for the biology of language rest on biologically implausible claims.

Specifically, the human capacity for language is attributed to universal grammar, a set of innate linguistic elements, operations, and constraints on operations that determine the form(s) that a natural language can take (Berwick & Weinberg, 1984; Lightfoot, in press; Pinker, 1984; Roeper & Williams, 1987; Wexler & Culicover, 1980). The argument that universal grammar is innate comes in three parts:

1. Universality: Universal grammar is, by definition, a description of the structural features shared by all natural languages. These include elements and operations that are found in every language (e.g., noun phrases, and rules that move noun phrases from place to place in a bracketed string), together with principles that take a disjunctive or "parameterized" form (e.g., languages either may or may not permit omission of an overt subject in a free-standing declarative sentence). The very existence of such universal structure (intensive or disjunctive) is offered as prima facie evidence for the biological basis of language (Chomsky, 1976).

2. Poverty of the stimulus: When they are described in this form, the symbols, rules, and constraints of universal grammar appear to be so abstract that it is difficult to see how they could be induced from the limited data to which human children are exposed, within the brief span of time that apparently is sufficient for language acquisition in our species. If this conclusion is correct, then universal grammar is not "learnable" (Borer & Wexler, 1987; Pinker, 1979, 1984).

3. Domain specificity: Even if universal grammar is not learnable, we might want to argue that it is constructed out of preexisting cognitive and perceptual elements that are innate but not specific to language. In other words, there may be a top-down solution to language learning where bottom-up solutions fail. However, the objects and operations of universal grammar appear to be radically different from anything that has ever been described for other cognitive domains (i.e., general principles of sensation, perception, memory, and/or motor planning; e.g., Chomsky, 1980). Because of these structural dissimilarities, it is difficult to see how children could build their language out of nonlinguistic components. If this conclusion is correct, then universal grammar is not "derivable."

Unfortunately, these arguments for innateness at the ontogenetic level present equally serious problems at the phylogenetic level. How did language evolve in our species in the first place? If the basic structural principles of language cannot be learned (bottom-up) or derived (top-down), there are only two possible explanations for their existence: Either universal grammar was endowed to us directly by the Creator, or else our species has undergone a mutation of unprecedented magnitude, a cognitive equivalent of the Big Bang. Is there any way out of this dilemma? Can we find an evolutionary scenario for language that is more compatible with Darwinian theory?

TOWARD A DARWINIAN SOLUTION

The major obstacle to a Darwinian solution comes from the generativist belief that linguistic and nonlinguistic systems are discontinuous. This argument precludes any attempt to identify "protoforms," prelinguistic structures and mechanisms that serve as the phylogenetic and (perhaps) ontogenetic building blocks of language. What protoform can we possibly envision that could have given birth to constraints on the extraction of noun phrases from an embedded clause? What could it conceivably mean for an organism to possess half a symbol, or three quarters of a rule? We can provide at least a partial answer to this puzzle, presenting a view of the biological basis of language that invokes five concepts from evolutionary theory: preadaptation, dual function, limited recapitulation, heterochrony, and functional branch points.

Preadaptation.   The discontinuity problem is not unique to language (Gould, 1977, 1980). Because the principle of natural selection presupposes the existence of intermediate forms, the greatest challenge to Darwinian theory has always come not from the half-baked products of nature (where the incompleteness of natural selection is clearly displayed), but from nature's most intricate and apparently perfect structures. For example, wings are beautifully designed for flight, and the selective advantages of flight are obvious to any observer. But it is not at all obvious what advantage half a wing might confer on an ancestor who could not fly at all.

Observations of this kind led Darwin's contemporaries to postulate teleological explanations for evolution, mysterious vital forces that move species onward and upward toward a higher (human) plane. Darwin's genius lay not in the discovery of evolution (a popular idea in his time), but in his elucidation of the blind and mechanical force of natural selection as a replacement for such vitalist accounts. How, then, could he explain exquisite adaptations like wings or universal grammar, adaptations that could not have conferred any advantage on their owners until the work of natural selection was nearly complete? Darwin's answer lay in the principle of preadaptation. According to this doctrine, new functions evolve out of structures that originally served a different, preexisting function; this old function maintains the evolving form during the phase in which natural selection for the new adaptation is underway. In other words, intermediate forms are maintained not for the work they will eventually do, but for the work that they are doing right now (like a law student working his way through college as a waiter). A typical example is the preadaptationist scenario for flight (Gould, 1977). Evidence now suggests wings evolved from flaps of skin between the trunk and limbs, flaps that initially served a thermoregulatory function. From this point of view, flight can be viewed as a serendipitous discovery, a secondary function that emerged (perhaps gradually) from body parts that initially served an entirely different purpose. This scenario also makes it easier to see how the behavior patterns of flight might have evolved, from the flapping movements that initially helped to distribute and maintain body heat.

Dual Function. The principle of dual function is a corollary of preadaptation: Old and new functions may continue to exist side by side, particularly when the adaptation in question is relatively new. Lieberman (1982) offered a variant of the dual function argument in language evolution. He proposed that our capacity for grammar is grafted directly onto neural wiring that originally evolved in the service of rapid and efficient speech-motor planning. Furthermore, he offered several lines of evidence to suggest that these brain structures continue to carry out both functions today. Whether or not we accept Lieberman's argument in detail,[1] the basic concept of dual function has considerable heuristic value in any theory of language evolution.

Limited Recapitulation. The combined notions of preadaptation and dual function lead to a fascinating prospect: Traces of the causal route by which a new function evolved still may be evident in the ontogenetic record (Bates, 1979; Gould, 1977; Lamandella, 1976). By examining those functions that reliably precede or co-occur with the development of language, we may find some clues to the construction route that nature used to build this system in the first place.

This is a highly inferential enterprise, and it must be approached with caution. Natural selection operates not only on the finished product, but also on the ontogenetic way stations that make the final product possible. An organism must be viable at every stage in its development, surviving in the relevant (albeit temporary) environment long enough to make it to the next stage. For this reason, ontogeny cannot and does not recapitulate phylogeny in all its glory and detail. For example, tadpoles use an undulating tail to swim, a tail that disappears at a later point. We would not want to conclude from this fact that tail-driven swimming is a logically

---

[1]In our view, Lieberman's (1982) arguments for the origins of grammar in speech are greatly weakened by recent research on American Sign Language and other visual-manual code (Klima & Bellugi, 1979; Newport & Meier, 1985; Poizner, Klima, & Bellugi, 1988). Sign languages apparently can evolve complete grammatical systems, obeying all the principles that are believed to govern grammar in a spoken language. Children acquire these grammars with alacrity, on a schedule that is not markedly different from the acquisition of spoken language. Finally, several different forms of sign aphasia can result from damage to the classical language areas in the left hemisphere. However, if we broaden the claim that grammar is built on motor cortex to include hand coordination as well as speech, these disparities could be resolved.

necessary stage in the ontogenetic or phylogenetic construction of an adult frog. Rather, tail-driven swimming is the cheapest and best solution to locomotion through water in the period before the strong legs of the adult frog are developed and in place. It is an adaptation that exists for the good of tadpoles, and it is good for the adult frog only insofar as it helps to keep the tadpole alive. Consider also the human umbilical cord, a structure that is essential for the existence and growth of the fetus. We would not want to conclude from the fact that umbilical cords precede language development (in every known case) that umbilical cords play any interesting role in the evolution of universal grammar. At best, ontogeny can give us only an indirect view of the construction process that our species followed. However, if we want to understand the origins of complex behavioral systems that leave no fossil record, an indirect view may be better than no view at all. The good that we can make of this indirect view will depend upon our capacity to construct a coherent theory that puts all the relevant pieces together.

Heterochrony.   The term "heterochrony" refers to adaptation resulting from a change in the timing and growth function of a preexisting structure. As outlined by Gould and Eldredge (Eldredge & Gould, 1972; Gould, 1977), current evidence suggests that evolution has taken place not in a smooth and continuous line, but with a series of spurts and plateaus called "punctuated equilibrium." In other words, phenotypic changes (when they occur) tend to be rather large. This observation is difficult to reconcile with the slow rates of genetic change associated with mechanisms like sexual reproduction (a major source of variation) and mutation (a source of variation that rarely leads to anything good). In a nutshell, the theory of punctuated equilibrium requires a mechanism that can produce large and discontinuous phenotypic changes at a relatively small genetic cost. The need for such a mechanism is particularly urgent in hominid evolution, given the finding that human beings share 98% of their genes with their nearest phylogenetic neighbor, the chimpanzee (King & Wilson, 1975). To meet this need, geneticists have found it useful to distinguish between *structural genes* (the xerox originals that are used to create larger structures) and *regulator genes* (genes that operate across large sets of structural genes to control their onset and offset). In principle, one small change in a regulator gene can bring about relatively large changes in the rate and patterning of growth – producing something for (almost) nothing. Hence the theory of punctuated equilibrium can be reconciled with natural selection through known genetic mechanisms, if we assume that regulator genes play a major role in evolution.

There are undoubtedly upper limits on the point in ontogeny at which these changes can apply. Each increase in complexity places serious limits on the range of variation that is possible from that point on. Once we get close to the adult endpoint, it is difficult to conceive of any way to bring about a serious change. Gould (1980) put the matter as follows: "Few systems are more resistant to basic change than the strongly differentiated, highly specified, complex adults of 'higher' animal groups. How could we ever convert an adult rhinoceros or a mosquito into something fundamentally different?" (p. 189). However, large changes are possible if the adjustment is made early in development. Thus, as D'Arcy Thompson (1942) observed in his classic text on biology and mathematics, the difference between a starfish and a mouse is very small at the embryonic stage; a small shift in the growth function of all or part of the embryo could result in a qualitatively different adult form.

Functional Branch Points.   A continuous (quantitative) change in one or more organ systems can lead to a discontinuous (qualitative) result, if it permits or forces the organism to solve a problem it would never have encountered without that quantitative change. To illustrate, consider the phylogenetic consequences of the increase in size that took place during the evolution from bacteria to higher organisms (from Thompson, 1942). Elephants, water beetles, and bacteria all live in the same (objective) world, a world that simultaneously contains the effects of gravity, fluid dynamics, and electromagnetism. However, these three aspects of the physical world have very different consequences depending on one's position along the (continuous) dimension of size. Bacteria are buffeted about by Brownian movement and electromagnetic fields, but they have nothing to fear from gravity or the surface tension atop a drop of water. For a water beetle, surface tension is a life or death matter; gravity has few consequences, and Brownian movement matters not at all. For the elephant, surface tension poses no threat, but gravity is a serious constraint on life and movement. Scaling matters. Variation along a continuous dimension can place the organism in a new "problem space," requiring qualitatively different solutions to ensure survival and reproductive success. Lieberman (1982) referred to these moments in evolution as "functional branch points."

The discontinuities that we observe from one species to another result from a combination of genetic factors (varying continuously) and the shape of the problem space that the animal has entered (sometimes quite suddenly) because of this continuous change.[2] Language acquisition can be viewed as a formal problem space that lies outside the reach of other primates: specif-

---

[2]We are stressing changes in the problem space that result entirely from changes that occur within the animal (e.g., "bootstrapping" into a new level of cognitive or social competence). We certainly do not want to rule out those situations in which the animal is forced to confront problems that result from a change in environmental conditions (e.g., a prolonged drought, or the introduction of literacy). Our point is that environmental changes are not necessary for the creation of a new problem space.

ically, the problem of mapping complex, nonlinear ideas onto a highly constrained linear channel. This does not mean, however, that the mechanisms we use to solve that problem are discontinuous with the mechanisms displayed by other primates. Even if the products of language acquisition are discontinuous, we can seek continuity in the processes (and processors) that make language acquisition possible. That is, the same set of (preexisting) processors may be able to handle a new and qualitatively different set of problems as a result of a relatively small quantitative change.

If generative grammarians are correct, is not this effort doomed from the start? Chomsky (1976, 1980) consistently claimed that the principles of universal grammar are so eccentric, so opaque, so peculiarly linguistic, that they cannot be derived directly or indirectly from other systems. However, Chomsky's argument does not distinguish between the domain specificity of outcomes, and the domain specificity of the processes and mechanisms used to achieve those outcomes. Every complex problem has its own unique properties, including artificial problems like the ones encountered in chess or tennis. When we apply general cognitive and perceptual mechanisms to solve a chess problem, we may come up with a solution that is utterly peculiar to chess. Furthermore, when we look across the solutions to many different chess problems, we will find some interesting commonalities (universals?). But these commonalities still are going to be uniquely "chesslike"; indeed, the universal properties shared by chess solutions may be just those properties that make chess different from any other game. We are not trying to argue here that language is "just another cultural artifact"; the robust and pervasive nature of language in our species argues strongly to the contrary. But we are trying to make a logical point that becomes more obvious when we move away from systems that have a strong biological base: Structural eccentricity does not constitute, ipso facto, evidence for the existence of peculiar and domain-specific cognitive mechanisms. A general mechanism can produce a unique and domain-specific result, if it is applied to a problem space with unique properties of its own.

To summarize, we assume that recent adaptations in the primate line have come about primarily through quantitative changes in the size, power, and interactive potential of preexisting components. Language (like other complex cognitive systems) must be viewed as a new machine built out of old parts (Bates, Benigni, Bretherton, Camaioni, & Volterra, 1979). Through careful investigation of intermediate stages in the "embryology" of language, we may be able to discern some of this componential structure. But to do so, we have to abandon any strong version of the discontinuity claim that has characterized generative grammar for 30 years. We have to find some way to ground symbols and syntax in the mental material that we share with other species. In the remaining pages we summarize results of our search for continuity, in three parts:

1. Continuous mechanisms: Following a line of research that began in the 1970s (e.g., Bates et al., 1979), we continue to search for cognitive developments that reliably co-occur with specific milestones in the development of language. This is a developmental version of a common research strategy in neuropsychology: the search for reliable patterns of association and dissociation that provide clues to the componential structure of brain and mind. In this chapter, we provide a brief update of results from this established research program, suggesting that language development is fueled not by "general intelligence," but by a variety of distinct and partially dissociable cognitive and perceptual mechanisms.

2. Continuous motives: The use of these learning mechanisms is ensured by certain evolutionary changes in the hominid social-motivational system. Specifically, our species has evolved a peculiar passion for certain key activities like imitation and object-oriented communication. These passions ensure our entry into the problem space of language, and greatly increase the probability that normal language acquisition will occur.

3. Continuous representations: Finally, we consider a new approach to symbols and rules, based on computational models of cognition and learning that are called alternatively *parallel distributed processing* (Hinton & Anderson, 1981; McClelland, Rumelhart, & PDP Research Group, 1986; Rumelhart, McClelland, & PDP Research Group, 1986), *connectionism* (Elman, 1988; Smolensky, 1987, 1988), and/or *neural modeling* (Churchland & Sejnowski, 1988, 1989). These models offer a way of characterizing the microstructure of mental representations, a subsymbolic level of analysis that may have the ragged and continuous properties that we need to explain piecemeal evolution. Although we cannot provide an adequate treatment of this complex and controversial topic in one short article, we provide a few interesting facts about language development that illustrate the descriptive and explanatory advantages of distributed symbols and probabilistic rules.

Continuous Mechanisms

If we believe that the formal problem of language acquisition could (at least in principle) be solved by a coalition of more general mechanisms, then it behooves us to demonstrate what set of mechanisms young children actually use in the course of language development. In this regard, O'Grady (1987) has offered a useful distinction between *specific nativism* and *general nativism*. In specific nativism (the view embraced by most generative grammarians), language acquisition is explained by innate principles that are unique to language. In general nativism, the same events are explained by innate principles that operate across cognitive domains.[3]

General and specific nativism are both compatible with the conclusion that children play an active and creative role in the acquisition process, developing "guesses" about the structure of their native language that bear only a very indirect relationship to the structures they hear from adults. Indeed, this conclusion seems inescapable after 25 years of developmental psycholinguistics, and may be the only claim about child language endorsed by the majority of researchers in this field. Aside from this, there are some important a priori differences between these two approaches to the biology of language. First, because general nativism does not require a belief in discontinuity of mechanisms, it is more plausible on evolutionary grounds. Specifically, it is more compatible with the principle of natural selection, and easier to explain within the short time constraints in which language has evolved. Second, because a general nativist account uses fewer mechanisms to explain the same range of cognitive phenomena, it is preferable to specific nativism on grounds of elegance and theoretical austerity (Langacker, 1987).

There are several different linguistic and psycholinguistic programs to choose from within the general nativist framework, many of which predate O'Grady's (1987) felicitous distinction. O'Grady offered his own version of general nativism, a detailed account of linguistic universals in terms of *dependency* and *adjacency,* two basic structural principles that language shares with other complex cognitive systems (i.e., pattern perception and motor planning). Other approaches within linguistics and psycholinguistics include *functional grammar* (Bates & MacWhinney, 1982, 1987, 1990; Foley & Van Valin, 1984) and *cognitive grammar* (e.g., Langacker, 1987). Although they differ in detail, these models all try to explain syntax and morphology in cognitive, perceptual, and/or communicative terms.

Within the field of language acquisition, a version of general nativism can be traced back to the 1970s, when a number of theoretical papers appeared independently arguing in favor of a Piagetian approach to language development (Bates, Camaioni, & Volterra, 1975; Beilin, 1975; Bloom, 1973; Bruner, 1975a, 1975b; Edwards, 1973; Greenfield & Smith, 1976; MacNamara, 1972; Ryan, 1975; Schlesinger, 1974; Sinclair, 1971; Slobin, 1973). These proposals differ in detail, but the basic insight that they share can be summarized briefly: Children actively assimilate lexical and gram-

---

[3]Fodor (1983) made a related distinction between *horizontal modules* (general-purpose processing modules that cut across content domains) and *vertical modules* (processors that evolved to deal only with a particular kind of content). However, he went on to argue that horizontal modules are so vague and unbounded that they cannot be studied scientifically; progress will be made only if we concentrate on the study of vertical modules. For a rejoinder, see Bates et al. (1988).

matical forms to more general cognitive and communicative content (e.g., basic event structures like agent-action-object, basic communicative functions like topic-comment), with the assistance of more general cognitive mechanisms (e.g., a general capacity for symbolic representation that permits the discovery of naming; changes in working memory that permit the child to "chunk" two or more symbols together). This approach retains the 1960s conclusion that children play an active and creative role in language acquisition, while rejecting the Chomskian claim that grammatical development is cognitively autonomous.

Shortly after the aforementioned theoretical papers appeared, investigators in many different laboratories set out in search of cognitive prerequisites to language (for reviews, see Bates & Snyder, 1987; Harris, 1983; Johnston, 1985). Most researchers followed a correlational strategy: Find out which linguistic and cognitive milestones reliably "hang together" in populations of normally developing children, and relate those milestones to a common set of underlying meanings and mechanisms. A more interesting variant of this research strategy involves children who are developing at an abnormal rate (e.g., mentally retarded, language-delayed, and/or autistic children; "early talkers" and "late talkers" within the normal range). The logic of this research is identical to accepted practice in adult neuropsychology, where patterns of association and dissociation in brain-damaged patients are used as clues to the componential structure of the mind and brain (for a detailed discussion, see Bates, Bretherton, & Snyder, 1988, chapters 2 & 3).

Piaget's theory of cognitive development was the point of departure for most of these studies. The majority focused on Piaget's (1962) claim that early linguistic symbols (i.e., naming) are just one manifestation of a general capacity for mental representation that emerges at roughly the same time across all relevant cognitive domains (e.g., object permanence, deferred imitation, representation of space, and causality). Summarizing briefly, it now appears that this hypothesis was incorrect, at least in its original form (for reviews, see Bates & Snyder, 1987; Harris, 1983; Johnston, 1985). Some aspects of nonverbal cognition indeed are correlated significantly with the emergence of language (e.g., symbolic play, imitation, aspects of tool use); but other domains of sensorimotor development appear to be quite independent of early language (e.g., spatial cognition, traditional measures of object permanence). Furthermore, significant positive correlations tend to hold only at specific points in development. For example, performance on the Uzgiris–Hunt means-ends scale at age 9 months is a good predictor of language comprehension and production from 9 months through (at least) 17 months of age; but performance on the same test at 12 months of age is not related to language at any point.

Results like these have led most investigators to abandon the orthodox

Piagetian view, in favor of what has been called alternatively the local homology model (Bates et al., 1979), skill theory (Corrigan, 1978; Fischer, 1980), and/or the specificity hypothesis (Gopnik & Meltzoff, 1986). These models share the belief that language comprises of many separate, underlying skills or mechanisms. Some of these components may be specific to language; other components are shared by several cognitive domains, resulting in significant cross-domain correlations primarily at those points in development when a shared component is "coming on line" (Bates, Thal, Whitesell, Fenson, & Oakes, 1989).

Our research group has been working within the local homology model for the past 10 to 12 years, seeking reliable patterns of association and dissociation, synchrony and asynchrony, in the early stages of language and cognitive development (Bates, Bretherton, Snyder, Shore, & Volterra, 1980; Bates et al., 1988; Bretherton & Bates, 1984; Bretherton, Bates, McNew, Shore, Williamson & Beehgly-Smith, 1981; Snyder, Bates, & Bretherton, 1981; Thal & Bates, 1988a, 1988b; Thal, Bates, & Bellugi, 1989). In this research, we make an important distinction between domain-specific mechanisms and domain-specific content (see also, Johnston, 1985). Because grammars represent a solution to the formal problems posed by language (i.e., mapping nonlinear meanings onto a linear channel), those solutions will have many properties that are unique to the language problem (in line with our earlier comments about chess). We therefore do not expect to find direct analogues to grammatical structure in any nonlinguistic domain. There is nothing outside of language proper that "looks like" the universal or language-specific content of grammar, that is no nonlinguistic analogue to constraints on pronoun interpretation, case inflection in Turkish, or the peculiarities of gender assignment in German. However, the mechanisms that are used to acquire and process language may be shared with other cognitive domains. The patterns of association and dissociation that we observe in our developmental research provide clues about the nature of these mechanisms.

Because of this emphasis on the basic mechanisms that make language possible, we have focused on four early developmental milestones: word comprehension, word production, first-word combinations, and the "burst" of grammatical development that takes place between 20 months and 30 months of age. In our first round of studies, we examined aspects of nonlinguistic cognition that co-occur with each of these milestones, in relatively large samples of normally developing children. More recently, we have concentrated on smaller samples of children at the extreme ends of the normal range: late talkers (with or without concomitant delays in comprehension) and early talkers (with or without corresponding degrees of precocity in comprehension). This research strategy pushes general nativism to its limits, uncovering those aspects of nonverbal cognition that necessarily co-occur with specific aspects of production and/or comprehension.

As a result, we have begun to identify at least two or three of the basic mechanisms that children use to acquire language.

Table 2.1 summarizes results from comparative studies of language and cognitive development across the normal range, from 9 months through 30 months of age. Although this is a complex literature (far more than we could hope to summarize adequately here), there is a simple take-home message: Every major milestone in early language development co-occurs reliably with reorganizations in at least one area of nonlinguistic cognition. The pace of early language development appears to be set by factors that transcend the boundaries of language proper, underlying mechanisms that have repercussions in more than one domain. Are these putative mechanisms necessary and/or sufficient for normal language development to take place? The normative data in Table 2.1 cannot be used to support strong causal inferences. To identify the "smoking gun" behind each language milestone, we need a stronger test.

Our studies of children at the extremes of normal variation take us one step closer to a precise fractionation of the human language faculty. First, children at the extremes have shown us that language itself is not "all of a piece." Some aspects of language apparently can develop out of synchrony with others, at least up to a point. Furthermore, these asynchronies cut across the traditional componential boundaries of language. That is, they appear to reflect dissociations among information processing modalities (e.g., comprehension versus production, analytic versus holistic processing), as opposed to content-specific modules (e.g., phonology, semantics, grammar). Finally, each of these dissociated language processing components seems to map onto a different aspect of nonverbal processing, leading to the conclusion that we have identified mechanisms that have some phylogenetic continuity. Let us take a closer look at each of these within-language dissociations, to arrive at a better characterization of the mechanisms that are responsible.

Comprehension Versus Production.   In all of our studies to date, we have found three groups of children: those who are above the median on both comprehension and production, those who are below the median on both, and a final group in which comprehension massively outstrips current levels of language production (Bates et al., 1988; Bates, O'Connell, & Shore, 1987). Children who follow the third pattern are the most interesting, because they clearly demonstrate that comprehension is a necessary but not sufficient condition for the development of expressive speech. The same disparities also are observed in the early stages of grammatical development; furthermore, our longitudinal findings suggest that comprehension/ production profiles are stable across the first 2 years of language develop-

TABLE 2.1
Studies of Language and Cognitive Development in Normal Children

Average Age	Language Milestones	Cognitive Milestones	References
9–10 mos.	Word Comprehension	*Deictic Gestures (giving, pointing, showing)	Bates, Benigni, Bretherton, Camaioni, & Volterra, 1979; Snyder, 1975.
		*Gestural Routines (e.g., Pattycake)	Bates, Camaioni, & Volterra, 1975; Bates et al., 1979;
		*Tool Use	Bates et al., 1979; Curcio, 1977; Snyder, 1975; Sugarman-Bell, 1978.
		*Causal Understanding	Harding & Golinkoff, 1979.
		*Shifts in Categorization (Habituation Paradigm)	Cohen & Younger, 1983.
12–13 mos.	Word Production	*Recognitory Gestures in Symbolic Play	Acredolo & Goodwin, 1985a, 1985b; Bates et al., 1975, 1979; Bates, Bretherton, Snyder, Shore, & Volterra, 1980; Bretherton, Bates, NcNew, Shore, Williamson, & Beeghley-Smith, 1981; Escalona, 1973; Werner & Kaplan, 1963; McCune-Nicholich & Bruskin, 1981; Snyder et al., 1981; Volterra & Gaselli, 1983.
		*Deferred Imitation	Meltzoff, 1985, 1988
18–20 mos.	"Vocabulary Burst"	*Gestural Combination in Symbolic Play	Brownell, 1988; Fenson & Ramsay, 1980; Nicolich, 1977; Shore, 1986.
		*Shifts in Categorization (Sorting and Touching)	Brownell, 1988; Gopnik & Meltzoff, 1986; Shore, 1986; Sugarman, 1979.
		*Changes in Patterns of Block Building	Brownell, 1988; Shore, 1986.
		*Gestural Combinations in Motor & Social Play	Brownell, 1988.
24–36 mos.	"Grammar Burst"	*Active sequencing in Symbolic Play	Genson & Ramsay, 1980; Nicolich, 1977; O'Connell & Gerard, 1985; Shore, O'Connell, & Bates, 1984.

ment (e.g., children with a high comprehension/low production pattern at 12 to 13 months of age tend to have the same pattern in early grammar).

These comprehension/production disparities are particularly clear in our studies of late and early talkers (Thal & Bates, 1988a, 1988b). Late talkers are defined as children in the bottom 10th percentile of expressive vocabulary development across the second year, according to a series of parental report instruments developed and validated in our laboratories (Bates, Snyder, Bretherton, & Volterra, 1979; Dale, Bates, Reznick, & Morriset, 1989; Reznick & Goldsmith, 1989); early talkers correspondingly are defined as children in the top 10th percentile on the same measure. In each group, there are children who are equally late (or equally precocious) in both comprehension and production; however, the remaining children in each sample are indistinguishable from age-matched controls on measures of receptive vocabulary (including parental report and structured testing in the laboratory). This fact has permitted us to conduct a new and more interesting test of the relationship between language and nonverbal cognition: How will the nonverbal correlates summarized in Table 2.1 align with comprehension versus production in children who show a marked dissociation between the two?

So far, the answer seems to be that most nonverbal measures follow the child's current level of language comprehension. Put somewhat differently, we might say that language and cognition are most closely related at the level of language understanding, that is, what the child knows rather than what she does. However, for children with expressive vocabularies under 50 words (before the oft-cited vocabulary burst), specific measures of symbolic gesture do align quite closely with the child's current level of language production.[4] For reasons that we discuss in more detail later, we have speculated that this second pattern may reflect constraints on fine motor control that are shared by language and gesture.

Analytic/Holistic Learning Strategies. A second type of dissociation within language can be found in the literature on "learning styles" (Bloom, Lightbown, & Hood, 1975; Dore, 1974; Horgan, 1979, 1981; Nelson, 1973;

---

[4]In several different studies, we have found a class of gestures that are reliably associated with production, but not comprehension: so-called recognitory gestures that are associated with common objects (e.g., drinking, combing, telephoning), elicited one at a time out of context, with little or no perceptual support from the object itself (e.g., "drinking" from a wooden block, "combing" with a substitute object like a spoon). As we have noted elsewhere (Bates, Bretherton, Shore, & McNew, 1983), this specific correlation between gesture and language bears an interesting resemblance to a relationship often reported in the literature on brain-damaged adults, between anomia (difficulty with object naming) and ideomotor apraxia (difficulty with gestural pantomime). We have proposed that this gestural deficit may be viewed as a kind of anomia (see also, Kempler, 1988).

Peters, 1977, 1983). This is (again) a complex literature, but it can be summarized briefly as follows: So-called "analytic children" enter into language development by breaking the input down into small units, and working out the meaning of those before attempting a synthesis. This pattern shows up at every level of language development: in babbling (where short consonant-vowel [CV] segments predominate), in first words (where the child concentrates on object naming), and in first-word combinations (telegraphic speech with function words and inflections eliminated). In contrast, so-called "holistic children" seem to enter into language development from the opposite extreme: They start by using relatively large, global chunks of speech in familiar contexts, giving their speech a more adultlike sound while they gradually break speech units down into their component parts. This style also can be found at every level of language development: in babbling (where sporadic consonants are nested within long streams of sentencelike intonation), in first words (with heterogeneous vocabularies that often include formulaic expressions like "Want dat"), and in first-word combinations (where inflections, pronouns, and other function words may be present from the beginning, in frozen expressions, and/or in formulas with limited productivity).

It is important to point out that this is a characterization of children at the far ends of a normal distribution. Most children use a mix of both strategies, with output that cannot be characterized at either extreme. However, the pure cases clearly illustrate the need to invoke at least two learning mechanisms: an analytic mechanism that segments the input and extracts regularities of meaning and form, and a second mechanism that permits the storage and reproduction of larger units whose internal structure is not yet clear to the child. Both mechanisms are necessary for normal language development to take place; however, children may vary in the extent to which they rely on one or the other. As we have pointed out elsewhere (Bates et al., 1988), there are many reasons why such dissociative patterns emerge, for example, differential rates of maturation, differences in temperament, and/or a tendency for parents to encourage one style more than another. These explanations are not mutually exclusive, and they are all compatible with the view that (at least) two partially dissociable mechanisms are at work in early language development.

The analytic-holistic distinction is obliquely related to the aforementioned comprehension-production contrast. Specifically, children at the analytic extreme tend to be high comprehenders, and more precocious overall. However, our recent work with early talkers suggests that this association is not logically necessary. This point can be illustrated most clearly by considering a case study of two children who are extraordinarily precocious in expressive language (from Thal & Bates, 1988b). M is a 21-month-old with an expressive vocabulary of 627; S is a 17-month-old with an expressive vocabulary of 596. The two children also are quite advanced in comprehension—although they are less exceptional in this regard (i.e., fewer standard deviations from the mean). Both children produce a wide array of verbs and adjectives as well as nouns—a development that typically signals the onset of grammar. And they have both begun to master English grammatical morphology, producing contrasting endings on at least a few nouns and verbs (e.g., "talk" vs. "talking"). The one clear difference between these two exceptional children revolves around sentence length: S has a mean length of utterance (MLU) in morphemes of 2.39, equivalent to a 30-month-old child; M has just begun to combine words, with an MLU of 1.19, exactly what we would expect for a child her age. Because these two children are not measurably different in their mastery of noun and verb endings, we would not want to conclude that they represent a dissociation between vocabulary and grammar. Nor would we want to conclude that S is advanced in syntax, because her long sentences contain very little evidence for transformation, extraction, inversion, or any of the operations that define and characterize the syntactic component of the grammar. We suggest instead that M and S vary markedly in the size of the unit they are able to store and reproduce at any given time. This interpretation is supported by the fact that S has a repertoire of idioms like "No way Jose!" and "You little monkey!" Her ability to manipulate and even blend these units is illustrated by the expression "No way you little monkey," which she produced for the first time for our cameras. In short, we suggest that M and S represent an analytic-holistic dissociation with levels of comprehension and expressive vocabulary held constant.

Is the analytic-holistic distinction peculiar to language, or can we trace these mechanisms outside the boundaries of language? There is still no clear answer to this question. Some evidence is available suggesting a link between language style and the approach children take to symbolic play and other symbol manipulation tasks (Bauer & Shore, 1986; Thal & Bates, 1988b; Wolf & Gardner, 1979). On the other hand, we have found no clear difference between our subjects M and S in their symbolic play abilities (which matched their levels of language comprehension), or in tests of spatial cognition. We are still open to the possibility that variations in the size of the unit reflect factors that are peculiar to speech perception (e.g., auditory short-term memory) and/or speech production (e.g., speech-motor planning). This is a topic that we plan to pursue actively in our studies of late and early talkers, and in studies across the normal range. It comes up again later when we turn to the issue of imitation in our species.

Putting these lines of evidence together, we can propose at least three partially dissociable mechanisms that are responsible for variations in early language learning:

1. The first is an analytic mechanism that segments the input, extracting invariant features and establishing patterns of correlation between sound and meaning. This mechanism yields high comprehension, and is strongly associated with many other aspects of nonverbal cognition.

2. Second is a fine-motor control factor that is partially responsible for turning patterns of analyzed and comprehended speech into expressive language. Because this factor is correlated with aspects of gestural production in the early stages of development, we suggest that it is not modality specific.

3. A memory device that permits storage and retrieval of large input patterns (which may or may not be specific to the speech channel) is the third mechanism. Individual differences in "language style" reflect the degree to which this mechanism develops ahead of or behind the analytic and motor devices described in items 1 and 2.

This picture is still quite speculative, and it is certainly incomplete. It is quite likely that other mechanisms also are involved in early language learning — perhaps even some of the domain-specific mechanisms proposed within the generative grammar camp (Borer & Wexler, 1987; Crain & Fodor, 1988). However, the three factors that we have tried to characterize here are the ones most clearly illustrated by asynchronies and dissociations in the ontogenetic record, and in that sense they could be viewed as the most robust and "natural" boundaries in the language acquisition device. Because all three of these proposed mechanisms have antecedents in the hominid line, these patterns are compatible with a general nativist approach. However, it also is clear that these three mechanisms are developed to a much greater extent in our species — which brings us to the next point.

Continuous Motives

Use of the aforementioned information-processing mechanisms is further ensured in our species by certain crucial adaptations in our social-motivational system, adaptations that maximize the likelihood that infants will enter into the problem space of language and seek the appropriate solutions.

Object-Oriented Communication. The role of motive systems that predispose humans for language is well illustrated by what might be called a preverbal "passion for small talk," a tendency to establish reference and communicate about the existence of external objects through showing, giving, and pointing (Bates et al., 1975; Bates, Benigni, Bretherton, Camaioni, & Volterra, 1979; Bates, O'Connell, & Shore, 1987; Werner &

Kaplan, 1963). These behaviors are universal in our species, appearing spontaneously (i.e., without explicit training or reinforcement) some time between 8 months and 12 months of age (although a nonfunctional variant of the pointing gesture has been observed as early as 4 to 5 months of age; Hannan, 1982). Giving and showing tend to precede pointing to objects at a distance by 1 to 2 months of age, on the average, but all three forms of reference are highly correlated within samples of normal children. These gestures are used not only in requests (which have an obvious payoff), but in "pure" acts of reference that are satisfied if the adult simply acknowledges the object or event of interest.

The emergence of these three referential gestures is strongly correlated with the subsequent emergence of naming, and with other aspects of language learning in the second year: Early pointers tend to be early talkers, late pointers tend to be late talkers (Marchman, Miller, & Bates, 1991; Snyder, 1975), and autistic children (who manifest serious problems in language development) typically do not show, give, or point to objects at all (Curcio, 1977). We are not trying to argue that showing, giving, and pointing actually "cause" language in any direct way. However, the appearance of these gestures seems to signal a new level of understanding, establishing the quintessential triangle of symbolic communication, the I/Thou/It relationship. Furthermore, the gusto with which human infants engage in this behavior suggests that the system draws on its own intrinsic motivational base: It is fun to do, for its own sake. (Indeed, one 9-month-old of our acquaintance entertained a visitor across the course of an afternoon by dragging most of the movable objects in the house to his feet, demanding acknowledgment of each one, and responding with a satisfied smile when each act of reference was complete.)

The establishment of such a tendency prior to speech all but guarantees that the child will attend to and acquire names for common objects; indeed, adults typically respond to referential gestures by providing the relevant object name ("Yes, that's a doggie, isn't it?"). The establishment of nominal reference will (in turn) facilitate the acquisition of verbs, adjectives, and other relational terms that depend on nouns for their meaning and function (O'Grady, 1987). Thus, by this indirect chain of events, the appearance of preverbal "small talk" helps to ensure timely and enthusiastic acquisition of language.

Imitation.   Arguments about the arbitrary nature of language may have been overstated; many linguists now are convinced that the more opaque and (apparently) mysterious aspects of grammar do have some functional motivation (e.g., Bates & MacWhinney, 1990; Foley & Van Valin, 1984; Langacker, 1987). For example, gender and number agreement phenomena may help the listener to keep track of reference across long passages of discourse. Complex constraints on pronominal coreference across clauses also may have their explanation in discourse terms (Kuno, 1986). But these facts are of little help to a 2-year-old child who is trying to break into grammar well before he or she knows about the mysteries of discourse. Whether or not grammars are motivated from an adult point of view, children must have a means of acquiring linguistic phenomena that they do not understand at all—at least not yet. They must be able to store and reproduce speech patterns that are poorly understood, just as they must store and reproduce vast amounts of cultural activity that is quite arbitrary from their point of view. The human capacity for imitation may provide a shortcut into the acquisition of language and culture: It permits quick storage of behaviors in context, allowing us to "get by" in social interaction while we analyze at our leisure the cause-and-effect relations that make these behaviors functional.

In our discussion of continuous mechanisms, we provided evidence for a partially dissociable memory device that permits storage and reproduction of large units of speech. This system is clearly implicated in the process of imitation, that is, the process by which a perceptual image is transformed into its motor analogue. We do not know yet whether this is a speech-specific mechanism, or whether it is merely one manifestation of a more general system that works in other modalities as well. In other words, there may be more than one mechanism for mapping perception onto action. At this point, however, we want to underscore the fact that mere possession of an imitative capacity may not be sufficient to ensure its regular use. Imitation has been observed in other primates; indeed, some version of the verb "to ape" is used in many languages to describe imitative behavior (Visalberghi & Fragaszy, 1990). Analogous to the passion for small talk described previously, our species also seems to have evolved a passion for imitation. Infants and children engage in imitative behavior (immediate and/or deferred) for hours at a time, with no obvious reinforcement other than the sheer joy of repeating what other people do. Indeed, it even has been argued that humans have a propensity for imitation that is detectable in the first hours of life (Meltzoff & Moore, 1977).

Of course, this capacity for imitation does have antecedents in the hominid line, and other primates do engage in some form of imitation without extrinsic reinforcement of any kind. For example, there are observations of infant chimpanzees in the wild trying to imitate their mother's "termite fishing" (i.e., using a stick to extract termites from their nest); these infants will persist in their imitation for weeks or months before they have any success at all in capturing a termite "reward" on their own. An even more striking example of unreinforced imitation comes from Savage-Rumbaugh's studies of the pygmy chimpanzee (see chapter 9 of this volume); in contrast with their cousins the common chimpanzee, these animals appear to have acquired skill in the comprehension and use of an artificial symbol system through pure observation, with no explicit reward of any kind. Nevertheless, there are sharp differences between humans and other primates in the level and amount of imitation that is likely to occur under natural conditions. A direct comparison can be found in Kellogg and Kellogg (1933), who raised their infant son Donald together with an infant chimpanzee called Gua. As social-learning theorists, they were aware of the existence and importance of imitation and observational learning, and they hoped that exposure to naturalistic modeling would demonstrate previously unseen capacities in the chimpanzee. Alas, the experiment was placed in jeopardy several times because of its unintended effects on Donald: Whereas the chimpanzee made relatively little progress in imitation of Donald, the human child imitated and made productive use of many chimpanzee behaviors!

In the modern cognitive era, the mysterious process of imitation has not been a fashionable topic of study (no doubt because it smacks too much of behaviorism). We suggest, however, that imitation is one of the crowning achievements of our species. It is indeed continuous with mechanisms and motives that appear in other primates, but the qualitative implications of our quantitative passion for imitation should not be underestimated.[5]

Continuous Representations

Let us suppose for a moment that everything we have said about continuous mechanisms and continuous motives is true. For most linguists working within the generative tradition, the Maginot line that separates language from the rest of human and nonhuman cognition would still be intact. For these theorists, claims about the uniqueness of language are based on the discontinuous (unlearnable and underivable) nature of linguistic representations.

To see why this is so, we must remember that generative grammar is inspired by an influential computational metaphor: the serial digital

---

[5]This list of social-motivational factors is by no means exhaustive. For example, Markman and Hutchinson (1984) have proposed a number of constraints on categorization and word learning that could greatly simplify the task of language learning if they are part of the child's innate repertoire. These include a tendency for 10- to 14-month-old children to attend more closely to an object if the parent labels or describes that object while pointing. The domain specificity of such constraints is questionable. For example, Roberts and Jacob (1988) have shown that children also will attend more closely to a display and learn more quickly and efficiently if it is accompanied by a nonlinguistic sound (i.e., a passage of music). However, we agree with Markman and Hutchinson that the establishment of reference involves a range of social and attentional components beyond the few we have listed here. See Savage-Rumbaugh, Rumbaugh, and Boysen (1978) and chapter 6 of this volume for a detailed discussion.

computer. This device is essentially a symbol cruncher; it manipulates symbols by applying a series of mapping operations or rules that take one symbol (or string of symbols) as input, and yield another symbol (or string of symbols) as output.

Two forms of discontinuity follow from this architecture. First, the symbols manipulated by a serial digital computer are discrete and monadic. That is, a symbol is either present in the input, or it is not. Partial symbols (e.g., 75% of the letter *A*) can have no computational effect.[6] Second, rules are discrete operations that fire obligatorily whenever their relevant input conditions are met. This assumption complements the notion of monadic symbols: If a symbol is present in the input, then its associated operations are always triggered; if the symbol is absent, or if it falls below some threshold of detectability, the rule will not fire. It is therefore meaningless to speak in terms of partial rules, weak rules, or 25% of a mapping operation.[7]

Arguments for the nonlearnability of grammar turn crucially on these classical assumptions about the discrete nature of symbols and rules (Pinker, 1979; Wexler & Culicover, 1980). Learnability theorists invoke a proof by Gold (1967), demonstrating that context-sensitive grammars (the class to which natural languages are said to belong) cannot be learned in a finite amount of time if the learner is exposed only to positive data — that is, if the learner is given examples of sentences that are in the language, but no information about range of sentences that are forbidden (i.e., negative evidence). However, Gold's theorem holds only if we accept a very strong assumption: The learner invents and tests whole grammars, one at a time, against each incoming symbol string; grammars are accepted or rejected in their entirety depending on the outcome of a single test. Under these

---

[6]Traditional symbolic architectures can mimic the internal structure of subsymbolic systems by feeding a macrosymbol into an array of smaller symbols that we might call *features* (Pinker & Prince, 1988). For example, a lexical symbol can be decomposed into a list of phonetic features plus a list of semantic features. However, to achieve this kind of mapping it is always necessary to access the macrosymbol that controls this feature set. One cannot build a representation up in pieces. As a result, even though a similar list of microfeatures may be involved in both cases, there are serious differences in the learnability of symbolic and nonsymbolic representations.

[7]In traditional architectures, it is possible to have a situation in which two rules are in competition; that is, both their symbols are present, but their firing conditions are otherwise incompatible. To resolve such competitions, rules can be assigned a relative weight or rank order. However, such weightings must be assigned post hoc, after each participating rule has been acquired as a whole. Furthermore, because rule ordering does not fall out of the learning process in any natural way, we need some kind of exogenous mechanism to assign the proper weights after learning has occurred. By contrast, probabilistic differences between individual rules or mappings come "for free" in subsymbolic networks, as a natural by-product of learning.

conditions, a learning device could wander aimlessly about in the world of possible grammars, "guessing" new ones one at a time, without ever converging definitively on the right one. If we accept these assumptions as a characterization of human language learning, and if we accept (as many researchers do) the claim that little negative evidence is available to young language learners, then we must conclude that a great deal of innate structure is necessary to ensure acquisition of grammar.[8]

However, if the assumptions that underlie Gold's (1967) theorem are correct, then they also lead to a phylogenetic learnability problem. How could there be an intermediate stage, in phylogeny or ontogeny, when organisms operate "quasi-symbolically"? What intermediate state could have supported the system or rules and representations that are used in modern language? How could we conceivably derive linguistic representations from nonlinguistic mental stuff, and how could an extant processor manipulate both linguistic and nonlinguistic representations when the two forms of representation look so different? One way out of this dilemma is to deny the monadic status of linguistic representations, in favor of distributed, "fuzzy" representations with a coarsely coded internal structure. Such representations could exist in bits and pieces, and they could activate their associated operations by degree. In short, distributed representations would have the requisite properties to permit a preadaptationist scenario for the evolution of language, one that still may be evident in the ontogenetic record.

The distributed approach to mental representation has received considerable attention recently within a new movement in cognitive science that is inspired by a very different computational metaphor: the connection machine, a massive, "brainlike" system of densely interconnected local units that converge in parallel on one or more dynamic solutions to an input problem (Churchland & Sejnowski, 1988, 1989; Rumelhart & McClelland, 1987). In these systems, knowledge is contained not in individual symbolic units or "engrams," but in patterns of weighted connections among many different units. Smolensky (1988a) distinguished between the classical symbolic architecture and distributed systems as follows:

The name "subsymbolic paradigm" is intended to suggest cognitive descriptions built up of entities that correspond to constituents of the symbols used

---

[8]Gold's (1967) theorem usually is invoked in discussions of Universal Grammar, principles and parameters that are presumed to be innate on other grounds as well. However, M. Maratsos (personal communication, March, 1988) has pointed out that the learnability problem is often just as serious for language-specific lexical and grammatical phenomena that could not possibly be innate. Bowerman (1987) has made a related argument in her study of the semantic factors that underlie our use of prefixes like *un,* for example, the fact that we can say *undo* but not *undrop* or *unhug.* The point is that these regularities must be inferred from very indirect and incomplete information, just like the principles of universal grammar.

in the symbolic paradigm; these fine-grained constituents could be called subsymbols, and they are the activities of individual processing units in connectionist networks. Entities that are typically represented in the symbolic paradigm by symbols are typically represented in the subsymbolic paradigm by a large number of subsymbols. Operations in the symbolic paradigm that consist of a single discrete operation (e.g., a memory fetch) are often achieved in the subsymbolic paradigm as the result of a large number of much finer grained (numerical) operations. (p. 3)

Several important consequences for general nativism follow from this distributed or subsymbolic approach to representation:

1. The same unit may participate in many different patterns.
2. The mappings that hold between distributed patterns are not necessarily modular; instead, one subsymbolic pattern can "penetrate" another, mapping onto some select portion of its internal structure.
3. Stable patterns may emerge or "fill out" across the network on the basis of degraded or partial input.
4. The relationships that hold between representations are probabilistic.

These four properties can be used (at least in principle) to solve the discontinuity problem, in phylogeny and ontogeny. In a system with the first two properties, we can see how linguistic representations might be derived from a more general cognitive base. Units that participate in a nonverbal concept may be recruited for use within a linguistic representation, and representations that mix verbal and nonverbal information can be maintained indefinitely. In a system with the last two properties, it is reasonable to speak in terms of half a symbol or three quarters of a rule. The set of representations that contain linguistic knowledge can pass through a variety of intermediate states, and they can continue to operate probabilistically even in their mature adult form.

If we can show that language processing and language acquisition are based upon such distributed "mental stuff," then it becomes easier to construct a plausible model of language evolution. Although the study of parallel distributed processing is still in its infancy, there is some reason to believe that certain classic problems in language acquisition can be handled with an architecture of this kind. Consider a paradigmatic example in the study of language acquisition, the phenomenon of morphological overgeneralization: An English child who has spent months or years correctly producing past-tense forms like *went* and *came* suddenly begins to produce unexpected errors like *goed* or *comed*. These phenomena have been used to support the view that children switch from one form of representation to another, that is, from rote memory to use of productive rules (Berko, 1958; MacWhinney, 1978; Pinker & Prince, 1988). However, Rumelhart and McClelland (1987) have been able to simulate all these phenomena within a single homogeneous architecture. Childlike overgeneralizations and novel forms apparently can emerge without explicit, discrete symbols or rules; insofar as rules and symbols can be said to exist in these systems at all, they exist in a probabilistic and highly distributed form.[9]

On the other hand, many developmental phenomena that are difficult to handle in the classic architecture can be expressed naturally and gracefully with distributed representations. Here are just a few examples.

Undergeneralization/Overspecification.   We often learn how to use a word in context without real insight into the meaning of that word in isolation. For example, consider the sentence "John left the room in high dudgeon." We know that John left feeling angry and insulted. But few of us (including Webster's dictionary) know what the word *dudgeon* actually means, that is, where it came from or how to use it in any other context. This kind of context boundedness frequently characterizes the first words that children use in comprehension and/or production (Nelson & Nelson, 1978; cf. Huttenlocher & Smiley, 1987; Volterra, Bates, Benigni, Bretherton, & Camaioni, 1979). For example, a child might first produce the sound "woo-woo" only to refer to the family pet, or only in a book-reading situation in which "woo-woo" is the correct response to the question "How does a doggie go?"; weeks later, the same sound is used to name new doggies in a wide range of situations. It is not at all obvious how the classic architecture can be used to represent word meanings that are deeply embedded in context, nor is it obvious how to use traditional notation to describe the gradual process of decontextualization.

The problem of context boundedness can be rephrased as a problem of *undergeneralization* (i.e., the term is not or cannot be generalized beyond a restricted set of external contexts), or alternatively, as a problem of *overspecification* (i.e., the internal representations that define a term contain too much irrelevant information). Undergeneralization is the

---

[9]Critics have pointed out some serious problems in the original Rumelhart/McClelland (1987) model. Among other things, they have argued that rules are "sneaked in" by the simulator (Lachter & Bever, 1988), and that artifacts of data entry are responsible for the sudden appearance of overgeneralization errors during the simulated learning process (Pinker & Prince, 1988). However, most of these problems have been addressed in more recent connectionist simulations of morphological learning, in English (Mozer, 1989; Plunkett & Marchman, 1991), German (MacWhinney, Leinbach, Taraban, & McDonald, 1989), Hungarian, (Hare, 1990), and Turkish (Hare, Corina, & Cottrell, 1989). It now seems clear that subsymbolic architectures can acquire and produce many of the same regularities that were used previously to argue for a classical architecture based on discrete symbols and rules.

appropriate description from an external observer's point of view (i.e., extension); overspecification is a more appropriate description if we are talking about those representations inside the speaker (i.e., intension) that generate the undergeneralized behavior. In traditional symbolic architectures, efforts to describe and explain these phenomena usually have involved use of a feature notation (i.e., a set of smaller symbols that represent internal structure). Within this framework, an overspecified representation can be said to contain too many features, compared with the "correct" representation for the concept in question. For example, the representation underlying the context-bound use of a word like *dog* contains a number of "incorrect" features (e.g., brown, large, responds to "Fido") as well as the correct features (e.g., animate, fuzzy, four-legged, barks). From this perspective, children recover from undergeneralization by canceling out some features while reconfirming others.

Feature-based semantics appear to have some prima facie validity for words like *dog,* but it is not at all obvious how the contextual frames that surround terms like *high dudgeon* can be reduced to a feature notation, without making cumbersome and ad hoc decisions about segmentation of the context. Furthermore, even for straightforward cases like *dog,* it is difficult to see how a 1- to 2-year-old child might arrive at the features that are necessary to represent word meanings before the words themselves have been acquired. If we insist on symbolic-featural representations as an account of word meaning, then there are only two possible solutions to the problem of word learning: (a) In order to derive the featural primitives that they will need to set up word meanings, 1-year-old children have to carry out a detailed segmentation of reality (presumably before word learning can get under way); alternatively, (b) the set of semantic features that will be needed to represent word meanings are innate. On the second account, word learning is a process by which children learn how to "package" innate features into language-specific configurations. On the surface, this is not an unreasonable proposal; on closer inspection, it is difficult to envision how nature could have provided us with the features we will need to represent meanings like *responds to "Fido,"* and even more difficult to understand how the murky contextual frames that surround terms like *high dudgeon* could be built from innate semantic atoms.

This problem becomes more tractable if we assume instead that word knowledge and contextual information are represented together in the same distributed format, with relatively little segmentation. Word meanings thus emerge gradually through a process of *superposition*. That is, we first store a word together with salient facts about its context of use, and superimpose successive uses of the word across contextual frames. Eventually, within this large distributed array, we may arrive at a central tendency that is sufficiently stable and bounded to permit a dictionary definition. But this final status is not crucial to the representation of meaning. With a word like *dudgeon,* no such central tendency has been reached. With a word like *dog,* a central tendency may emerge quite early. And with many words, once we are good at the naming game, it may be possible to carve out the word's center with just a few trials (e.g., "fast mapping"; Carey, 1978). Our point is that shades and gradations of meaning in context can be handled with distributed representations, without invoking any discontinuous boundary between denotation and connotation, sense and reference, and without performing an ad hoc and unnecessary segmentation of the contexts in which words are used.

Overgeneralization/Underspecification. In the aforementioned example of a context-bound representation, a distributed pattern of sound is associated with a distributed pattern of meaning that is larger than it should be. During development the irrelevant variations in context must be "shaved off" — a process that is easy to realize with representations of this kind. There are other developmental phenomena that move in the opposite direction: The term in question is used in an overly general way (i.e., extension), presumably because the meaning of that term is underspecified (i.e., intension). For example, take the 20-month-old who calls all mammals "doggie." In traditional symbolic architectures, this phenomenon can (again) be described by use of a featural notation, attributing to the child a representation with too few of the correct features (e.g., animate, fuzzy, and four-legged, but not barks). From this point of view, the child can be said to recover from overgeneralization by adding new features. Once again, however, we must assume that the child has carried out a detailed segmentation, extracting old and (perhaps) new features on every trial. This process is much less cumbersome if we assume that learning proceeds through the superposition of word-context pairs, with no initial segmentation beyond the rather primitive segmentations offered by the visual and auditory systems. The boundaries around a distributed representation of this sort can expand or contract with experience (see Bates & MacWhinney, 1989, for an application of this approach to grammatical categories).

Submappings. If representations take a distributed form (at every stage of learning), then we also can explain cases in which one representation appears to be "penetrated" by another. To illustrate, consider an observation by Camarata (1988), who described an apparent case of rule invention by a single child. This child achieved pluralization in English not by adding an *s,* but by lengthening the vowel inside a pluralized noun. For example, the word *key* would become *ke-e-y* when describing two or three members of that class. Camarata argued that this rule invention is based on an iconic relationship between sound and meaning: The idea of increased quantity (within the semantic representation that underlies pluralization) is expressed with an increase in duration at the level of sound. But where did the idea of increased vowel length come from? In fact, any time we add an *s* to pluralize a noun, the overall duration of the word is increased. In a sense, the phonetic feature of increased duration is contained inside the set of sound features associated with pluralization in English (see Fig. 2.1). This English child apparently has mapped a subregion of meaning (quantity) directly onto a subregion of sound (duration). As Camarata pointed out, the iconicity between quantity-in-sound and quantity-in-meaning may be partly responsible for this error, attracting these two subregions together in a premature mapping. In an architecture based on discrete symbols, this kind of phenomenon could not occur; features nested within one representation cannot penetrate or invade the internal structure of another. However, the same morphological mapping operation can be understood and represented fairly easily in distributed terms.

Competition, Substitution, and Blends.   In connectionist models, the probabilistic nature of knowledge can be represented in two ways: by the

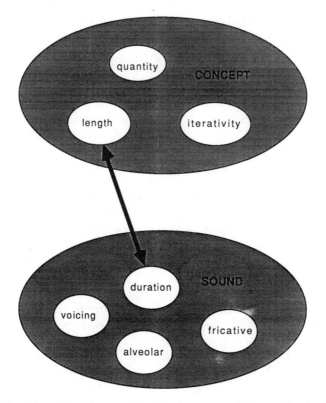

FIG. 2.1.   Phonetic and conceptual features association with plurality in English.

degree of activation associated with a given unit (by default, or at a given moment in time), and by the strength of the connection that links one unit to another. This property permits network models to capture the "in-between" nature of language behavior under different conditions of change: in language learning by children, in second-language acquisition by adults, in historical language changes, and in language loss due to different forms of brain damage. For example, when a child vacillates between *came* and *comed,* we are able to represent the current state of his system in statistical terms. In the same fashion, we can capture facts about interlanguage transfer and interference during second-language acquisition (Kilborn & Ito, 1989; Klein & Perdue, 1989). We have a graceful way of describing and predicting the degree of loss displayed by an aphasic patient (Bates & Wulfeck, 1989). And we have a convenient notation for describing the nature of linguistic knowledge in a single, in-between generation as a language changes from one type to another (e.g., as English gradually lost its case inflections and took on its current, rigidly ordered form).

This kind of statistical competition can be modeled within a more traditional architecture, by adding weights to individual symbols and rules (Pinker & Prince, 1988, Footnotes 5 & 6). However, because rules and symbols have no internal structure in these models, there is no way to represent a competition that involves only one "piece" of a complex representation. Many examples of morphological substitution and blending can be handled gracefully if we assume that competitions take place at a subsymbolic level, between different subregions of sound or meaning. Linguistic forms can share a partial overlap in internal structure, a fact that may result in competition when the two forms are both active at a given point in comprehension or production. Similarity leads to competition, competition can lead to confusion, and substitution and blend errors occasionally result. This kind of explanation has been offered in several recent studies of speech errors in normal and brain-damaged adults (Dell, 1976; Stemberger, 1985), and connectionist simulations based on this principle apparently can generate speech errors that are quite similar to the ones observed in normal and aphasic speech (Dell 1988; Shallice, 1988).

The same principle also may account for many of the errors produced by children. An excellent example of a substitution based on semantic overlap comes from Clark and Carpenter's (1989) description of prepositional errors during acquisition of the passive. Children occasionally produce utterances like *The ball was hit from John* or *of John* instead of the correct form *by John;* but they never produce *to* as a substitute for *by.* According to Clark, the prepositions *from, of* and *by* share the semantic notion of "source," whereas the preposition *to* conveys the opposite meaning (i.e., goal). Hence, substitution errors seem to be affected by the internal semantic structure of the target, with substitutions occuring along a gradient of similarity. Substitutions based on a combination of phonetic and semantic similarity can be seen in the more amusing errors produced by small children, for example, a child of our acquaintance who was terrified to take a bath because of a long-standing confusion between the words *drown* and *drain.*

At the morphological level, a similar mechanism has been invoked to account for errors based on an analogy between forms. For example, children sometimes produce *brang* as the past tense for *bring,* due perhaps to interference from legal pairs in the language like *sang* and *sing.* This process of analogy is difficult to explain in a system based on discrete symbols and rules; it is much easier to understand if we assume that mappings operations are sensitive to the internal, distributed structure of two competing forms. The same is true for errors that blend regular and irregular forms (e.g., *camed* or *branged*), errors that appear to cross the strict separation between rote and rule-governed mechanisms that are maintained in traditional symbol systems (see Pinker & Prince, 1988, for a detailed discussion of this problem).

Modularization.   Probabilistic systems can take a continuous array of values—including the absolute values zero and one. Hence, it is possible for a probabilistic system to mimic the results of a system based on deterministic rules. In a distributed representation based on many probabilistic links, it is also possible for an outcome to be massively overdetermined, that is, 300% or 1,000% compared with the 100% ceiling that is encountered in traditional symbol systems. This means that modularity can be constructed or derived in a distributed system, when it proves necessary or useful to do so. The system can be "tuned" by experience (or by nature) to behave as though it were made up of impenetrable elements and operations. In ontogeny, a child may pass through an intermediate phase of probabilistic mappings, arriving eventually at an adult endpoint where the same mapping behaves exactly like an absolute and irrevocable rule. In phylogeny, a species may pass through a ragged intermediate state when a protoform looks very unlike the grammatical determinism of our species; and yet, we can at least discern a route whereby our more deterministic behaviors might have been derived.

The converse does not hold: There is no graceful way to derive probabilistic behavior from a system that is modular to its core. We can always add weights and probabilities by hand, from the outside; but this behavior does not derive in any natural way from the internal structure of the system itself. This is of course the learnability dilemma that we described at the outset: Monadic symbols, absolute rules, and modular systems must be acquired as a whole, on a yes-or-no basis—a process that cries out for a creationist explanation. With distributed symbols and probabilistic syntax, we can resolve the problem of origins and yet, at the same time, foresee a way to arrive at all the advantages of a deterministic architecture.

To summarize, many different phenomena in language acquisition can be described and explained economically, if we assume that representations of meaning and sound take a distributed form. Distributed representations can expand, shrink, and blend as needed. Because they have permeable boundaries, they can be penetrated: One small region within a word meaning can be mapped directly onto one small region within a phonetic string. Above all, development can take place without discrete shifts in the nature of representation: Instead, knowledge can reorganize by a shift in the strength of individual units or a change in the strength of mapping from one unit to another. These are the properties we need to construct a plausible model of language acquisition, one that is also plausible on evolutionary grounds.

Connectionist models are currently a matter of heated debate, and their power and limitations are still not fully understood (Fodor & Pylyshyn, 1988; Lachter & Bever, 1988; Pinker & Prince, 1988). Some opponents have argued that connectionism is nothing but old wine in new bottles, discredited old associationism presented in a modern package. Supporters respond by pointing out that the nonlinear, multilayered associative nets used in current models are far more powerful than the simple nets of old, capable of the complex and often counterintuitive behavior that we have long used as evidence for discrete symbols and rules. Eventually, we may have to invoke some combination of symbolic and subsymbolic architectures to account for human cognition.[10] For present purposes, we simply want to

---

[10]For those who are repelled by the associationistic flavor of connectionism, there are at least two other approaches to cognition that exploit the advantages of distributed representation and parallel processing without invoking notions of linkage or association among the small local units that are responsible for computation. In Rosch's prototype theory (Rosch, 1973; Rosch & Mervis, 1975) and variants thereof (Bates & MacWhinney, 1982), categories are described as fuzzy, probabilistic, and heterogeneous representations organized around a real or idealized "best member"; new instances of the category are recognized by their degree of fit to this prototypic member. In Selfridge's classic pandemonium model (Selfridge, 1959), complex patterns are recognized by a large assembly of small, local "demons," feature detectors that respond when they see themselves in the input; pattern recognition occurs across the system as a whole, as an emergent property of all this local behavior. A more detailed version of the Selfridge approach can be found in the classifier system recently proposed by Holland, Holyoak, Nisbett, & Thagard (1986). In these theories, the various subcomponents of a representation are not linked directly; information is "broadcast" simultaneously to all the various bits, and all computations are carried out locally. Unfortunately, these theories do not offer an explicit learning algorithm, and features have to be put into the system "by hand"; this contrasts markedly with the powerful algorithms that are now available to describe learning in neural nets. For example, back propagation is an algorithm that permits multilayered networks to "discover" the features they need for further learning, given relatively gross and unsegmented input (e.g., raw speech; Elman & Zipser, 1988).

point out that the enigma of language learning may have a solution that is compatible with Darwinian theory, if we assume that distributed representations are involved at some point in the evolution and development of language.

CONCLUSION

In this chapter, we have argued in favor of continuity in the mechanisms, motives, and representations that underlie the evolution and development of language. None of these arguments should be taken as a denial of the undeniable fact that language is special. It is our prized possession, something that no other species really shares. Our children burst into language learning with talent and enthusiasm, and they seem to be ideally suited for it. But the beauty of language will not be compromised if we rob it of some mystery; continuity can give birth to discontinuity, and exquisite products can be constructed with humble tools. In this regard, we turn one more time to S. J. Gould (1980): "The effect of our large brain has far outstripped the relative ease of its construction. Perhaps the most amazing thing of all is a general property of complex systems, our brain prominent among them—their capacity to translate merely quantitative changes in structure into wondrously different qualities of function" (p. 133).

REFERENCES

Acredolo, L., & Goodwyn, S. (1985a, April). *Spontaneous signing in normal infants.* Paper presented at the biennial meeting of the Society for Research in Child Development, Toronto.

Acredolo, L., & Goodwyn, S. (1985b). Symbolic gesturing in language development. *Human Development, 28,* 40–49.

Bates, E. (1979). On the evolution and development of symbols. In E. Bates, L. Benigni, I. Bretherton, L. Camaioni, & V. Volterra (Eds.), *The emergence of symbols: Cognition and communication in infancy* (pp. 1–32). New York: Academic.

Bates, E., Benigni, L., Bretherton, I., Camaioni, L., & Volterra, V. (1979). *The emergence of symbols: Cognition and communication in infancy.* New York: Academic.

Bates, E., Bretherton, I., Shore, C., & McNew, S. (1983). Names, gestures, and objects: Symbolization in infancy and aphasia. In K. Nelson (Ed.), *Children's language* (*Vol.* 4, pp. 59–123). Hillsdale, NJ: Lawrence Erlbaum Associates.

Bates, E., Bretherton, I., & Snyder, L. (1988). *From first words to grammar: Individual differences and dissociable mechanisms.* New York: Cambridge University Press.

Bates, E., Bretherton, I., Snyder, L., Shore, L., & Volterra, V. (1980). Vocal and gestural symbols at 13 months. *Merrill–Palmer Quarterly, 26,* 407–423.

Bates, E., Camaioni, L., & Volterra, V. (1975). The acquisition of performatives prior to speech. *Merrill–Palmer Quarterly, 21,* 205–226.

Bates, E., & MacWhinney, B. (1982). Functionalist approaches to grammar. In E. Wanner &

L. Gleitman (Eds.), *Language acquisition: The state of the art* (pp. 173–218). New York: Cambridge University Press.

Bates, E., & MacWhinney, B. (1987). Competition, variation and language learning. In B. MacWhinney (Ed.), *Mechanisms of language acquisition* (pp. 157–193). Hillsdale, NJ: Lawrence Erlbaum Associates.

Bates, E., & MacWhinney, B. (1989). Functionalism and the competition model. In B. MacWhinney & E. Bates (Eds.), *The crosslinguistic study of sentence processing* (pp. 3–73). New York: Cambridge University Press.

Bates, E., O'Connell, B., & Shore, C. (1987). Language and communication in infancy. In J. Osofsky (Ed.), *Handbook of infant competence* (2nd ed., pp. 149–203). New York: Wiley.

Bates, E., & Snyder, L. (1987). The cognitive hypothesis in language development. In I. Uzgiris & J. M. Hunt (Eds.), *Infant performance and experience: New findings with the ordinal scales* (pp. 168–204). Champaign-Urbana: University of Illinois Press.

Bates, E., Snyder, L., Bretherton, I., & Volterra, V. (1979). The emergence of symbols in language and action: Similarities and differences. *Papers and Reports on Child Language Development, 17,* 106–118.

Bates, E., Thal, D., Whitesell, K., Fenson, L., & Oakes, L. (1989). Integrating language and gesture in infancy. *Developmental Psychology, 25,* 1004–1019.

Bates, E., & Wulfeck, B. (1989). Crosslinguistic studies of aphasia. In B. MacWhinney & E. Bates (Eds.), *The crosslinguistic study of sentence processing* (pp. 328–371). New York: Cambridge University Press.

Bauer, P., & Shore, C. (1986). *Nonlinguistic concomitants of stylistic differences in early multiword speech.* Unpublished manuscript.

Beilin, H. (1975). *Studies in the cognitive bases of language development.* New York: Academic.

Berko, J. (1958). The child's learning of English morphology. *Word, 14,* 150–177.

Berwick, A., & Weinberg, A. (1984). *The grammatical basis of linguistic performance.* Cambridge, MA: MIT Press.

Bickerton, D. (1981). *The roots of language.* Ann Arbor, MI: Karoma.

Bloom, L. (1973). *One word at a time: The use of single word utterances before syntax.* The Hague, Netherlands: Mouton.

Bloom, L., Lightbown, L., & Hood, L. (1975). Structure and variation in child language. *Monographs for the Society for Research in Child Development, 40* (Serial No. 160).

Borer, H., & Wexler, K. (1987). The maturation of syntax. In T. Roeper & E. Williams (Eds.), *Parameter·setting* (pp. 123–172). Dordrecht, Holland: Reidel.

Bowerman, M. (1987). Commentary: Mechanisms of language acquisition. In B. MacWhinney (Ed.), *Mechanisms of language acquisition* (pp. 443–466). Hillsdale, NJ: Lawrence Erlbaum Associates.

Bretherton, I., & Bates, E. (1984). The development of representation from 10 to 28 months: Differential stability of language and symbolic play. In R. Emde & R. Harmon (Eds.), *Continuities and discontinuities in development* (pp. 229–261). New York: Plenum.

Bretherton, I., Bates, E., McNew, S., Shore, C., Williamson, C., & Beeghly-Smith, M. (1981). Comprehension and production of symbols in infancy. *Developmental Psychology, 17,* 728–736.

Brownell, C. (1988). Combinatorial skills: Converging developments over the second year. *Child Development, 59,* 675–685.

Bruner, J. S. (1975a). From communication to language: A psychological perspective. *Cognition, 3,* 255–287.

Bruner, J. S. (1975b). The ontogenesis of speech acts. *Journal of Child Language, 2,* 1–19.

Camarata, S. (1988). Iconicity in semantics: A case of suprasegmental marking in the acquisition of English plural. *Papers and Reports on Child Language Development, 27,* 123–130.

Carey, S. (1978). The child as word learner. In M. Halle, J. Bresnan, & G. A. Miller (Eds.), *Linguistic theory and psychological reality* (pp. 264-293). Cambridge, MA: MIT Press.

Chomsky, N. (1965). *Aspects of a theory of syntax.* Cambridge, MA: MIT Press.

Chomsky, N. (1976). *Reflections on language.* New York: Pantheon.

Chomsky, N. (1980). Rules and representations. *Behavioral and Brain Sciences, 3,* 1-61.

Churchland, P. S., & Sejnowski, T. J. (1988). Perspectives on cognitive neuroscience. *Science, 242,* 741-745.

Churchland, P. S., & Sejnowski, T. J. (1989). Neural representation and neural computation. In L. Nadel (Ed.), *Neural connections, mental computation.* Cambridge, MA: MIT Press.

Clark, E., & Carpenter, K. L. (1989). On children's uses of from, by and with in oblique noun phrases. *Language, 65,* 1-30.

Cohen, L., & Younger, B. (1983). Perceptual categorization in the infant. In E. Scholnick (Ed.), *New trends in conceptual representation: Challenges to Piaget's theory?* (pp. 197-220). Hillsdale: NJ: Lawrence Erlbaum Associates.

Corrigan, R. (1978). Language development as related to stage 6 object permanence development. *Journal of Child Language, 5,* 173-189.

Crain, S., & Fodor, J. D. (1988). *Competence and performance in child language.* Unpublished manuscript, University of Connecticut, Storrs.

Curcio, F. (1977, October). *A study of sensorimotor functioning and communication in mute autistic children.* Paper presented at the Boston University Conference on Language Development, Boston.

Dale, P., Bates, E., Reznick, S., & Morisset, C. (1989). The validity of a parent report instrument of child language at 20 months. *Journal of Child Language, 16,* 239-250.

Dell, G. (1976). A spreading activation theory of retrieval in sentence production. *Psychological Review, 93,* 283-321.

Dell, G. (1988, December). *Frame constraints on phonological speech errors.* Paper presented at the First Annual Conference on Language and Connectionism, Rome, Italy.

Dore, J. (1974). A pragmatic description of early language development. *Journal of Psycholinguistic Research, 4,* 423-430.

Edwards, D. (1973). Sensorimotor intelligence and semantic relations in early child grammar. *Cognition, 2,* 395-434.

Eldredge, N., & Gould, S. J. (1972). Punctuated equilibria: An alternative to phyletic gradualism. In T. J. M. Schopf (Ed.), *Models in paleobiology* (pp. 82-115). San Francisco: Freeman.

Elman, J. L. (1990). *Finding structure in time Cognitive Science, 14,* 179-211.

Elman, J. L., & Zipser, D. (1988). Learning the hidden structure of speech. *Journal of the Acoustical Society of America, 83,* 1615-1626.

Escalona, S. (1973, October). On precursors of language. Paper presented at Teacher's College, Columbia University, New York.

Fenson, L., & Ramsay, D. (1980). Decentration and integration of the child's play in the second year. *Child Development, 51,* 171-178.

Fischer, K. (1980). A theory of cognitive development: The control and construction of hierarchies of skill. *Psychological Review, 87,* 477-526.

Fodor, J. (1983). *The modularity of mind.* Cambridge, MA: MIT Press.

Fodor, J., & Pylyshyn, Z. (1988). Connectionism and cognitive architecture: A critical analysis. *Cognition, 28,* 3-71.

Foley, W., & Van Valin, R. (1984). *Functional syntax and universal grammar.* Cambridge, England: Cambridge University Press.

Gold, E. (1967). Language identification in the limit. *Information and Control, 16,* 447-474.

Gopnik, A., & Meltzoff, A. (1986). Relations between semantic and cognitive development in the one word stage: The specificity hypothesis. *Child Development, 57,* 1040-1053.

Gould, S. J. (1977). *Ever since Darwin: Reflections in natural history.* New York: Norton.

Gould, S. J. (1980). *The panda's thumb: More reflections in natural history.* New York: Norton.

Greenfield, P., & Smith, J. (1976). *The structure of communication in early development.* New York: Academic.

Hannan, T. E. (1982). Young infant's hand and finger expressions: An analysis of category reliability. In T. M. Field & A. Fogel (Eds.), *Emotion and early interaction.* Hillsdale, NJ: Lawrence Erlbaum Associates.

Harding, C., & Golinkoff, R. (1979). The origins of intentional vocalizations in prelinguistic infants. *Child Development, 50,* 33–40.

Hare, M. (1990). The role of similarity in Hungarian vowel harmony: A connectionist account. *Connection Science, 2,* 123–150.

Hare, M., Corina, D., & Cottrell, G. (1989). A connectionist perspective on prosodic structure. *Proceedings of the 15th Annual Meeting of the Berkeley Linguistics Society, 15,* 114–125.

Harnad, S. R., Steklis, H. D., & Lancaster, J. (Eds.). (1976). Origins and evolution of language and speech. *Annals of the New York Academy of Sciences* (Vol. 280).

Harris, P. (1983). Infant cognition. In J. Campos & M. Haith (Eds.), *Handbook of clinical psychology* (Vol. 2, pp. 689–782). New York: Wiley.

Hinton, G. E., & Anderson, J. A. (Eds.). (1981). *Parallel models of associative memory.* Hillsdale, NJ: Lawrence Erlbaum Associates.

Holland, J. H., Holyoak, K. J., Nisbett, R. E., & Thagard, P. R. (1986). *Induction: Processes of inference, learning, and discovery.* Cambridge, MA: MIT Press.

Horgan, D. (1979, May). *Nouns: Love 'em or leave 'em.* Address to the New York Academy of Sciences, New York.

Horgan, D. (1981). Rate of language acquisition and noun emphasis. *Journal of Psycholinguistic Research, 10,* 629–640.

Huttenlocher, J., & Smiley, P. (1987). Early word meanings: The case of object names. *Cognitive Psychology, 19,* 63–89.

Johnston, J. (1985). Cognitive prerequisites: The evidence from children learning English. In D. I. Slobin (Ed.), *The crosslinguistic study of language acquisition* (pp. 961–1004). Hillsdale, NJ: Lawrence Erlbaum Associates.

Kellogg, W., & Kellogg, L. (1933). *The ape and the child: A study of environmental influence upon early behavior.* New York: Whittlesey House.

Kempler, D. (1988). Lexical and pantomime abilities in Alzheimer's disease. *Aphasiology, 2,* 147–159.

Kilborn, K., & Ito, T. (1989). Sentence processing strategies in adult bilinguals: Mechanisms of second-language acquisition. In B. MacWhinney & E. Bates (Eds.), *The crosslinguistic study of sentence processing* (pp. 257–291). New York: Cambridge University Press.

King, M., & Wilson, A. (1975). Evolution at two levels in humans and chimpanzees. *Science, 188,* 107–116.

Klein, W., & Perdue, C. (1989). The learner's problem of arranging words. In B. MacWhinney & E. Bates (Eds.), *The crosslinguistic study of sentence processing* (pp. 292–327). New York: Cambridge University Press.

Klima, E., & Bellugi, U. (1979). *The signs of language.* Cambridge, MA: Harvard University Press.

Kuno, S. (1986). *Functional syntax: Anaphora, discourse and empathy.* Chicago: University of Chicago Press.

Lachter, J., & Bever, T. G. (1988). The relations between linguistic structure and associative theories of language learning—A constructive critique of some connectionist learning models. *Cognition, 28,* 195–247.

Lamandella, J. T. (1976). Relations between the ontogeny and phylogeny of language: A neorecapitulist view. In S. R. Harnad, H. D. Steklis, & J. Lancaster (Eds.), *Origins and evolution of language and speech.* Annals of the New York Academy of Sciences (Vol. 280).

Langacker, R. (1987). *Foundations of cognitive grammar.* Stanford, CA: Stanford University Press.

Lieberman, P. (1982). *The biology and evolution of language.* Cambridge, MA: Harvard University Press.

Lightfoot, D. (in press). The child's trigger experience: Degree-0 learnability. *Behavioral and Brain Sciences.*

MacNamara, J. (1972). The cognitive basis of language learning in infants. *Psychology Review, 79,* 1–13.

MacWhinney, B. (1978). The acquisition of morphophonology. *Monographs of the Society for Research in Child Development, 43* (Serial No. 174).

MacWhinney, B., Leinbach, J., Taraban, R., & McDonald, J. (1989). Language learning: Cues or rules? *Journal of Memory and Language, 28,* 255–277.

Marchman, V. A., Miller, R., & Bates, E. (1991). Babble and first words in infants with focal brain injury. *Applied Psycholinguistics, 12(1),* 1–22.

Markman, E., & Hutchinson, J. (1984). Children's sensitivity to constraints on word meaning: Taxonomic vs. thematic relations. *Cognitive Psychology, 16,* 1–27.

McClelland, J. L., Rumelhart, D. E., & the PDP Research Group. (1986). *Parallel distributed processing: Explorations in the microstructure of cognition* (Vol. 2). Cambridge, MA: Bradford Books.

McCune-Nicolich, L., & Bruskin, C. (1981). Combinatorial competency in symbolic play in language. In D. Pepler & K. Rubin (Eds.), *The play of children: Current theory and research* (pp. 30–45). Basel, Switzerland: Karger.

Meltzoff, A. (1985). Immediate and deferred imitation in fourteen- and twenty-four-month-old infants. *Child Development, 56,* 62–72.

Meltzoff, A. (1988). Infant imitation and memory: Nine-month-olds in immediate and deferred tests. *Child Development, 59,* 217–225.

Meltzoff, A., & Moore, K. (1977). Imitation of facial and manual gestures by human neonates. *Science, 198,* 75–78.

Mozer, M. (1989). *A focused back-propagation algorithm for temporal pattern recognition.* (Tech. Rep. No. CRC-TR-88-3). Toronto: University of Toronto.

Nelson, K. (1973). Structure and strategy in learning to talk. *Monograph of the Society for Research in Child Development, 38*(1 & 2, Serial No. 49).

Nelson, K. E., & Nelson, K. (1978). Cognitive pendulums and their linguistic realization. In K. E. Nelson (Ed.), *Children's Language* (Vol. 1, pp. 223–285). New York: Gardner Press.

Newport, E., & Meier, R. (1985). Acquisition of American Sign Language. In D. I. Slobin (Ed.), *The crosslinguistic study of language acquisition: The data* (Vol. 1, pp. 881–938). Hillsdale, NJ: Lawrence Erlbaum Associates.

Nicolich, L. (1977). Beyond sensorimotor intelligence: Assessment of symbolic maturity through analysis of symbolic play. *Merrill–Palmer Quarterly, 23,* 89–99.

O'Connell, B., & Gerard, A. (1985). Scripts and scraps: The development of sequential understanding. *Child Development, 56,* 671–681.

O'Grady, W. (1987). *Principles of grammar learning.* Chicago: University of Chicago Press.

Peters, A. (1977). Language learning strategies: Does the whole equal the sum of the parts? *Language, 53,* 560–573.

Peters, A. (1983). *The units of language acquisition.* Cambridge, England: Cambridge University Press.

Piaget, J. (1962). *Play, dreams and imitation in childhood.* New York: Norton.

Pinker, S. (1979). Formal models of language learning. *Cognition, 1,* 217–283.

Pinker, S. (1984). *Language learnability and language development.* Cambridge, MA: Harvard University Press.

Pinker, S., & Prince, A. (1988). On language and connectionism: Analysis of a parallel distributed processing model of language acquisition. *Cognition, 28,* 73–193.

Plunkett, K., & Marchman, V. (1991). U-shaped learning and frequency effects in a back-propagation network: Implications for language acquisition. *Cognition, 38,* 43–102.

Poizner, H., Klima, E., & Bellugi, U. (1988). *What the hands reveal about the brain.* Cambridge, MA: MIT Press/Bradford Books.

Reznick, S., & Goldsmith, S. (1989). Assessing early language: A multiple form word production checklist. *Journal of Child Language, 16,* 90–100.

Roberts, K., & Jacob, M. (1988, November). *Linguistic vs. attentional influences on nonlinguistic categorization in 15-month-old infants.* Paper presented at the Annual Meeting of the American Speech-Language-Hearing Association, Boston.

Roeper, T., & Williams, E. (Eds.). (1987). *Parameter setting.* Dordrecht, Holland: Reidel.

Rosch, E. (1973). On the internal structure of perceptual and semantic categories. In T. E. Moore (Ed.), *Cognitive development and the acquisition of language* (pp. 111–144). New York: Academic.

Rosch, E., & Mervis, C. (1975). Family resemblances: Studies in the internal structure of categories. *Cognitive Psychology, 7,* 573–605.

Rumelhart, D. E., & McClelland, J. L. (1987). Learning the past tenses of English verbs: Implicit rules or parallel distributed processing. In B. MacWhinney (Ed.), *Mechanisms of language acquisition* (pp. 195–248). Hillsdale, NJ: Lawrence Erlbaum Associates.

Rumelhart, D. E., McClelland, J. L., & the PDP Research Group. (1986). *Parallel distributed processing: Explorations in the microstructure of cognition* (Vol. 1). Cambridge, MA: Bradford Books.

Ryan, J. (1975). Mental subnormality and language development. In E. Lenneberg & E. H. Lenneberg (Eds.), *Foundations of language development* (Vol. 2, pp. 269–277). New York: Academic.

Savage-Rumbaugh, E. S., Rumbaugh, D. M., & Boysen, S. (1978). Linguistically mediated tool use and exchange by chimpanzee (pan troglodytes). *Behavioral and Brain Sciences, 1,* 539–554.

Schlesinger, I. M. (1974). Relational concept underlying language. In R. Schiefelbusch & L. Lloyd (Eds.), *Language perspectives: Acquisition, retardation and intervention* (pp. 129–151). Baltimore: University Park Press.

Selfridge, O. G. (1959). Pandemonium: A paradigm for learning. In *Symposium on the mechanization of thought processes.* London: HM Stationery Office.

Shallice, T. (1988, December). *Connectionist modeling of aspects of acquired dyslexia.* Paper presented at the First Annual Conference on Language and Connectionism. Rome, Italy.

Shore, C. (1986). Combinatorial play: Conceptual development and early multiword speech. *Developmental Psychology, 22,* 184–190.

Shore, C., O'Connell, B., & Bates, E. (1984). First sentences in language and symbolic play. *Developmental Psychology, 20,* 872–880.

Sinclair, H. (1971). Sensorimotor action patterns as a condition for the acquisition of syntax. In R. Huxley & E. Ingram (Eds.), *Language acquisition: Models and methods* (pp. 121–135). New York: Academic.

Slobin, D. I. (1973). Cognitive prerequisites for the development of grammar. In C. Ferguson & D. I. Slobin (Eds.), *Studies in child language development* (pp. 175–226). New York: Holt, Rinehart & Winston.

Smolensky, P. (1988). On the proper treatment of connectionism. *Behavioral and Brain Sciences, 11,* 1–74.

Smolensky, P. (1987). *The constituent structure of connectionist mental states: A reply to Fodor & Pylyshyn. Southern Journal of Philosophy, XXVI,* 137–161.

Snyder, L. (1975). *Pragmatics in language-deficient children: Prelinguistic and early verbal performatives and presuppositions.* Unpublished doctoral dissertation, University of Colorado, Boulder.

Snyder, L., Bates, E., & Bretherton, I. (1981). Content and context in early lexical development. *Journal of Child Language, 8,* 565–582.

Stemberger, J. (1985). Bound morpheme loss errors in normal and agrammatic speech: One mechanism or two? *Brain & Language, 25,* 246–256.

Sugarman, S. (1983). Children's early thought: Developments in early classification. Cambridge University Press.

Thal, D., & Bates, E. (1988a). Language and gesture in late talkers. *Journal of Speech and Hearing Research, 31,* 115–123.

Thal, D., & Bates, E. (1988b, November). *Relationships between language and cognition: Evidence from linguistically precocious children.* Paper presented at the Annual Convention of the American Speech-Language-Hearing Association, Boston.

Thal, D., Bates, E., & Bellugi, U. (1989). Language and symbolic gesture in two children with Williams syndrome. *Journal of Speech and Hearing Research, 32,* 489–500.

Thompson, D. W. (1942). *On growth and form.* New York: Macmillan.

Visalberghi, E., & Fragaszy, D. (1990). Do monkeys ape? In S. Parker & K. R. Gibson (Eds.), *"Language" and intelligence in monkeys and apes: Comparative developmental perspectives.* Cambridge, England: Cambridge University Press.

Volterra, V., Bates, E., Benigni, L., Bretherton, I., & Camaioni, L. (1979). First words in language and action: A qualitative look. In E. Bates, L. Benigni, I. Bretherton, L. Camaioni, & V. Volterra (Eds.), *The emergence of symbols: Cognition and communication in infancy* (pp. 141–222). New York: Academic.

Volterra, V., & Caselli, C. (1985). From gestures and vocalizations to signs and words. In W. Stokoe & V. Volterra (Eds.), Sign language research '83 (pp. 1–9). Rome: Linstock Press, Inc. & Instituto di Psicologia, CNR.

Werner, H., & Kaplan, B. (1963). *Symbol formation: An organismic-developmental approach to the psychology of language.* New York: Wiley.

Wexler, K., & Culicover, P. (1980). *Formal principles of language acquisition.* Cambridge, MA: MIT Press.

Wolf, D., & Gardner, H. (1979). Style and sequence in symbolic play. In M. Franklin & N. Smith (Eds.), *Early symbolization* (pp. 117–138). Hillsdale, NJ: Lawrence Erlbaum Associates.

3

How the Acquisition of Nouns May Be Different from That of Verbs

Michael P. Maratsos
University of Minnesota

ARE NOUNS DIFFERENT FROM VERBS?

Practiced speakers of a language (who may include 3- and 4-year olds) know something about both the semantic cores and the structural properties of major formal categories like noun and verb, or subject and object. Brown (1957) showed that preschool children know that concrete object reference is characteristic of nouns, and actional reference characteristic of verbs. Simultaneously, preschool children's patterns of overregularizations and lack of form-class errors show that they are skillful in categorizing words on structural bases even when the words do not share the semantic core properties of their category (Maratsos & Chalkley, 1980).

Because both types of knowledge are available to speakers, it is clearly a key problem of acquisitional theory to discover the relationship of semantic core properties to more purely structural properties, both in the adult state of knowledge and in the course of acquisition itself. Indeed, analyzing this relationship is a key aspect of most extant theories of syntactic category acquisition (e.g., Braine, 1987; Grimshaw, 1981; MacNamara, 1982; Maratsos & Chalkley, 1980; Pinker, 1984, 1987; Schlesinger, 1982).

Most such theories, whatever position they take on the particular course of interaction for such factors, propose that the correct answer to the problem is essentially the same for all the categories in the domain of the theory. Gentner (1982) was perhaps the first to propose an important cleavage within the form-class categories. She theorized that nouns are acquired differently from verbs and adjectives; that for nouns, the central property of referring to concrete objects was more central in acquisition, whereas for verbs and adjectives, analysis of structural properties played a more central role.

The core of Gentner's (1982) proposal was the conceptual difference between nouns and other categories: Objects, she argued, are more coherent packets of conceptual information. Aside from the intuitive appeal of this statement, Gentner noted various kinds of evidence. In memory experiments with adults, she found that adults remember object concepts more exactly than actional ones. Across languages, actional verbs are more likely to vary in the semantic shape of analogous concepts than are nouns. Children appear to acquire nouns more quickly in early development as part of their vocabulary; this fact is also accounted for, she argued, by the greater coherence and stability of concrete objects. Within languages, the relationship of object words to nouns is more exact than the relationship of action words to verbs; not all nouns refer to objects, but all clear object words do seem to be nouns; as for action words and verbs, not all verbs are action words, and furthermore, not all action words are verbs (e.g., *game, trip, busy, coronation, action*) (Maratsos & Chalkley, 1980).

In this chapter, arguments are given on other grounds to support Gentner's (1982) general conclusion, that the conceptual-object core of nouns is more important in acquisition than the respective actional core of verbs; indeed, it is argued that this remains true even for the adult structure. These conclusions were derived by a somewhat different analytic path than Gentner's; they arose in the author's own continuing consideration of the adequacy of the theory of form-class ontogenesis in Maratsos and Chalkley (1980). Yet the general conclusion is much the same as for Gentner's original proposal: For nouns, relatively speaking, the conceptual-object core is relatively more important than is the corresponding actional core of verbs; for verbs, the analysis by structural properties per se appears to receive greater weight, both in acquisition and in the final forms of adult categories.

Organization of the Chapter

The basic points to be presented in the chapter are organized as follows:

1. Cross-linguistic evidence about the form-class repertoires of natural languages indicates that the only candidate for a universal form-class category is nouns, and the only universal distinction, that of noun-other. This is taken to support the notion that concrete object reference is a strong categorical organizer, because it is the core of the noun category.

2. The claim is outlined that in adult categories, verbs and nouns differ in the way in which semantic and structural factors serve to organize them. In particular, verbs are found to be describable as terms that share a

common group of small-scale structural properties, like those discussed in Maratsos and Chalkley (1980). Such analysis, it is argued, fails for nouns. Although small-scale structural properties partly organize aspects of noun structure, concrete object reference acts as an internal brace to hold the category together as well. Furthermore, semantic factors may override structural factors in determination of noun subclasses as well.

Supplementary to the aforementioned arguments about adult structure, developmental evidence about the acquisition of Tagalog adjective auxiliaries, and the semantic nature of early verbs and nouns are considered, as partial empirical supports. A brief hypothetical account of the developmental course of the noun category is given.

3. Finally, some general consequences for acquisitional theory are elaborated. Among these, a critique is given of the presuppositional foundations of the theory in Maratsos and Chalkley (1980) for which the present arguments have special relevance; this essential problem is that their theory presupposes children are unbiased analyzers of the input data, when in fact strong biases in weighting input data are evidenced by what is known about nouns and their likely course of development.

With this picture of the prospective expository path in mind, we turn to the first consideration outlined earlier, a (brief) description of relevant cross-linguistic patterns, which shows the marked stability of the general noun category among the form-class categories.

CROSS-LINGUISTIC PATTERNS

English and many other languages have a four-way split in major form-class categories: nouns, verbs, adjectives, and prepositions. These have as their respective semantic cores, concrete objects, actions, stable properties, and locative relations. Such a repertory, although common, is by no means universal. Many languages, for example, do without either prepositions or postpositions to mark locative relations, and simply use stem-bound morphology. In a few languages (e.g., Mixtec; Brugman, 1983), even morphological markers to mark locative relations are lacking.

More central to this article, languages are quite common in which there is no split between adjectives and verbs. In many languages, linguists describe the language as having only verbs. This is because in the structure of the language, words that typically would be conveyed by verbs versus adjectives in a language like English, act alike in the structures of sentences. For example, words like *push* and *sad* and *big* may all be inflected alike for tense, subject person, or aspect in such languages; or as in Chinese, they all alike may be unmarked on the stem, and at the same time share many critical positive structural properties.

Thus, across the world's languages, the verb-adjective distinction may be lost, or the distinction among prepositions and other classes may be lost. Nouns, in contrast, reliably remain a separate category, organized around the core of concrete object reference. The general opinion is succinctly stated by Dixon (1979): "It is an empirical fact there is *always* a major class that is aptly called Noun: there is *never* any doubt as to the applicability of this traditional label, and *never* any doubt as to which class should be called *Noun*" (p. 1).

This pattern thus accompanies the other kind of fact previously noted: Nouns typically contain all the clear concrete object reference terms; action terms may be concentrated primarily on one category, such as the verb category, but they may appear in other categories as well. These broad facts point to a similar conclusion: Concrete object terms tend to stick together as a grammatical category, and serve to preserve the separateness of the category in which they reside from other grammatical categories.

WITHIN-LANGUAGE PATTERNS: VERBS VERSUS NOUNS

Small-Scale Structural Properties and Verbs

It is widely held that the adult form-class categories are best defined by the shared structural properties of their members, rather than a shared semantic property or set of semantic properties (e.g., Braine, 1987; Grimshaw, 1981; Lyons, 1968; MacNamara, 1982; Maratsos & Chalkley, 1980; Pinker, 1984). The thesis of this chapter is that this is true for verbs, but not for nouns, which comprise a family resemblance category composed partly of semantic and partly of structural properties.

Because the structural property definitional basis is held to work for verbs, it is reasonable to begin with a discussion of them. Then the contrastive status of nouns may emerge more clearly.

The reason actionality fails as a definitional basis for the verb category is well known: Many verbs do not denote actions, that is, verbs such as *feel* (*good*), *like, resemble, consist, belong, believe, think* (*so*), *have,* and many others. Indeed, many of the nonactional verbs appear to be less actional than members of other form-class categories, such as *busy, active, noisy, loud,* and *obnoxious* among adjectives, or *game, trip, coronation,* and *party* among nouns. Some verbs and adjectives are almost identical in meaning, for example, the verb *like* and the adjective *fond* (of), or the verb *know* and the adjective *aware* (*of*).

What verbs do share in common in a mostly reliable way is a set of combinations with small-scale grammatical markers. In English in particular, these include various ways in which the verb stem can be marked for tense (present tense *s*, past tense *ed*), ways of marking negation (use of forms of *do*, e.g., *does, doesn't, did, didn't, do, don't* in front of the verb), use of *to* to mark the verb as an infinitive complement head, and the ability to appear unmarked for tense in any way after an initial noun-phrase subject. For example, consider the semantically close words *like* and *fond*. One can encode a present tense occurrence of liking, with a third-person subject, by adding *s* to the word *like*, that is, *John like* + *s dogs*. With the word *fond*, this would give **John fond* + *s of dogs*, which contains a form-class error (*marks an ungrammatical utterance, as in usual linguistic use). Similarly, present nonoccurrence of liking is marked with *doesn't* or *don't*, for example, *John doesn't like dogs;* parallel marking of *fond* gives **John doesn't fond of dogs*. With first- and second-person noun-phrase subjects, or third-person plural, a main verb can appear unmarked, that is, *I like dogs,* something that is impossible for adjectives, for example, **I fond of dogs.*

Indeed, it is difficult to find anything but such small-scale grammatical differences between the overall grammatical potentialities of verbs and adjectives. For example, both adjective and verb forms can appear as prenominal modifiers, as can be seen from the forms *the sleeping dog* and *the big dog;* the difference (among other things) is that a verb form has to be marked as either a progressive participle or a perfective participle to be used as an adjectival modifier, whereas adjectives can do so in unmarked form.

Thus overall, adjectives and verbs can be most reliably and clearly distinguished from each other, at least in adult structures, by their different patterns of combination with various small-scale grammatical markers.

Developmental Data

Data from the Acquisition of English.   As far as is known, children during acquisition are very skillful at making the appropriate analyses of small-scale marker patterns for verbs versus adjectives. Form-class errors in which verb markings are applied, for example, to adjectives, are extremely rare (Cazden, 1968), even as children appropriately extend verb markings to actional and nonactional verbs alike. That is, even as children say things like *he feeled good* or *I knowed it,* which show active extension of verb markings to nonactional terms, they do not say things like **he sadded* or **he happies.*

Data from the Acquisition of Tagalog.   More interesting evidence about the importance of small-scale markers for delineating the main verb category comes from the acquisition of the Filipino language Tagalog (for the most complete linguistic description of Tagalog, see Schachter, 1976; Schachter & Otanes, 1972). The structural distinction between verbs and adjectives in Tagalog can be grounded very clearly on morphological grounds: Verbs are marked luxuriantly for aspect on the stem by a system of prefixes, infixes, suffixes, and combinations of these that interact richly with other aspects of sentence grammar; adjectives are unmarked for aspect, though they are marked for comparative degree on the stem.

In addition to these two major classes, Tagalog also has a class of auxiliarylike terms that are translateable by English "want," "know," "love," "like," "must," "can," "not like" (= "don't like"), and others. Like auxiliary verbs, they take infinitival complements to produce sentences equivalent to "he must come" or "he can sing" or "he likes (to) sing." What is interesting about them is that in some ways, they act structurally like main verbs, whereas in other ways they do not. First, we see how they—or at least some of them—are like main verbs. This similarity lies in what kinds of noun phrase arguments they take. Tagalog, like many languages, makes a distinction between oblique objects and direct relations. In English, for example, noun phrases that are the objects of prepositions are oblique objects; noun phrases unmarked by a preposition are direct relations (either subject or direct object). This distinction is marked in Tagalog by the form of article for common and proper nouns, or by pronominal form for pronouns. As in English, only main verbs can take direct objects in Tagalog. Adjectives may take only oblique objects. (Thus in English, there is no sentence like *he is angry the girl or *he is positive the proposal; the girl or the proposal would have to have a prepositional marker, e.g., he is angry at the girl or he is positive about the proposal, and thus be oblique objects.) Tagalog observes the same general stricture; adjectives can take only oblique objects; only main verbs can take direct objects.

The way in which some of these auxiliarylike terms, such as want, know, and like, are like main verbs, and unlike adjectives, is that they take noun-phrase arguments marked like direct objects or subjects; they do not take oblique objects, in sentences that are the translation equivalents of "I like dogs" or "he knows Mary." Thus, they share an important characteristic of many main verbs. On the other hand, this set of auxiliarylike terms is always unmarked for aspect, which is unlike main verbs.

Thus on grounds of noun-phrase constituent structure, these terms are main verblike; indeed their meanings are rather main verblike as well, including "want," "know," "like," and "love." Hypothetically, children might occasionally overregularize them as main verbs on this basis of similarity by marking them at least once in a while for aspect. There is evidence of various kinds that they do not do this. The present author and Dr. Nelly Cubar have records from six children at various developmental points in the age range of 2 to 5 years (about 6 hours in all, for six children), and no such errors show up, though the children have productive aspect marking systems by the age of 3 or 4 years. More conclusively, the Filipino linguist Gonzales (1984) kept weekly diaries on his nephew and niece from the ages of roughly $1\frac{1}{2}$ through $3\frac{1}{2}$ years. During this time, they clearly entered into productive marking of aspect, including making errors of overregularizing irregular uses. Gonzales in general paid attention to errors, but noted none in which nonmain verbs were marked for aspect.

So it appears that despite their main verblike major constituent structure, and rather verblike meaning, these terms never were categorized, or were categorized tentatively, as main verbs by the children. A strong interpretation of this result is that the children took stem marking for aspect as a critical feature for main verb constituency (much as Schachter and Otanes [1972] also did, in fact). A complete absence of it thus led them to classify these predicates as not being main verbs of Tagalog.

In summary, it appears that the verb category cannot be defined satisfactorily by its core semantic properties; small-scale grammatical combinations do serve to provide a unique and commonly shared set of defining properties for the category; developmental evidence is consistent with a claim that children use such analysis to formulate the category; at least at some point early enough to lead to appropriate patterns of error and nonerror; the Tagalog data further may indicate a greater relative importance of such small-scale analysis compared to analysis, for example, of aspects of combination with noun phrase constituents.

SMALL-SCALE STRUCTURAL PROPERTIES AND NOUNS; PROBLEMS WITH PRONOUNS AND PROPER NAMES

Successes of Small-Scale Analysis

At first glance, it appears that nouns, like verbs, are properly defined largely by small-scale combinatorial properties. Like verbs, nouns appear to have a semantic core, this core being one of concrete object reference. But also as for verbs, this semantic definition appears inadequate, because nouns also include terms like *idea, energy, trip, party,* or *game (verb* and *action* are nouns, for that matter), which are not easy to analyze as some kind of concrete object. Again, such terms seem to be incorporated into a general category because they share various kinds of small-scale combinatorial properties. For example, *idea* and *dog* both can appear after the articles *a* and *the* to denote indefinite and definite reference to members of the class respectively; they can appear after demonstratives like *this* and *that;* plural marking with *s* is possible for both. Common nouns share a number of such properties. Mass nouns like *mud* or *attention* do not share all of them, but share a great many of them. All common nouns readily can appear after possessive determiners, that is, *my idea, my dog, my attention, his idea, his dog, his attention,* and so on.

Failures of Small-Scale Analysis

The problem, however, is that nouns traditionally are taken to include pronouns and proper names, like *I, you, Mary,* and *John.* But these nouns do not share the small-scale structural patterns characteristic of other nouns. They do not appear with articles like *a* or *the* (**a Mary,* *the you) or demonstratives (**this you,* *this Robert), or take pluralization with *s.* They do not appear with possessive determiners, that is, **John's you.* They also do not take other characteristic noun patterns like appearing after adjectives (e.g., one can say *a big dog,* but not *a big Mary or *big you). Thus, small-scale grammatical patterns do not seem to provide a clear set of unifying defining properties for nouns as they do for verbs.

Indeed, it commonly is assumed that small-scale structural properties account for the differences among the noun subclasses such as pronouns, proper names, and common nouns; but it is not clear they even do this very well. The class of proper names in particular can be divided into first names like *Mary,* and last names like *Smith.* Last names, in fact, often resemble common nouns in their structural behavior. One can apply noun plurals to them, and use articles (e.g., *the Smiths*), or use prenominal quantifiers (*some of the Smiths*). In contrast, first names like *Mary* essentially resemble pronouns in much of their structural behavior, in not taking articles, plurals, quantifiers, adjectival modifiers, and the like. On small-scale structural grounds, one might propose that first names belong with the pronouns, whereas last names are a type of common noun. The general intuitive rejection of this analysis indicates that the essential bases for proper noun subclassification are in large degree semantic-denotational in nature; small-scale properties again have only limited application.

PREDICATE-ARGUMENT ANALYSIS: ANOTHER BASIS FOR NOUNS?

Predicate-Argument Analysis Briefly Outlined

Is it possible, though, that there is another structural-combinatorial basis for nouns? At least one other does exist, though it is one that is not in the domain of small-scale grammatical patterns. This is *predicate-argument* analysis (Braine, 1976, 1987; Maratsos, 1988). What it is will require some initial exposition; then its applicability to the problem of noun definition can be analyzed.

Predicate-argument analysis frequently is used in symbolic logical analysis of propositions (Reichenbach, 1947). It has been explored extensively in abstract forms by linguists as well (e.g., Lakoff, 1970). For the purposes here, the basic idea is that propositions can be analyzed as composed of two major kinds of morphemes or phrases: (a) predicates, terms that serve to denote a property or relation of, or between, entities, and (b) arguments, terms or phrases that denote the entities of which properties and relations are predicated. Thus, in the sentence *the boy kissed the girl,* the word *kiss(ed)* is the major predicate term. Its two arguments are *the boy* and *the girl,* corresponding to the kisser and kissed argument roles of *kiss.* Adjectives also may be analyzed as major predicates. Thus, the sentence *John is angry at Joan* may be analyzed as having *angry (at)* as its major predicate; its arguments are *John* and *Joan* corresponding to the experiencer and object of anger respectively.

As can be seen in the aforementioned examples, nouns typically either comprise an argument (as in *John likes Joan*), or they are the conceptual cores of argument phrases, as in *the boy* and *the girl,* in which *boy* and *girl* are the core terms. That is, they are typically argument heads, where this may mean comprising an argument by themselves, or comprising the clear core of an argument. Thus, one could say that the basic semantic-structural function of nouns is to be argument heads, whereas the basic corresponding function of verbs and adjectives is to be predicates.

This larger scale structural analysis does seem to show more potential for unifying nouns as a single structural category. Despite their semantic and small-scale structural differences, words like *Mary, dog,* and *attention* all share the property of typically functioning as major argument heads; they function alike in sequences like *John liked you, John likes Mary, John likes the dog, John likes (the) attention.*

Furthermore, as noted in the cross-linguistic section, the minimal form class split appears to be between nouns and nonnouns; this translates very well into a statement that the minimal form-class split is that between argument head terms and predicate terms. Indeed, at the broadest level of semantic-structural analysis, predicate-argument structure is one of the major universal structural properties all languages share in common.

Some Problems for Predicate-Argument Analysis

There are two major problems, however, with using predicate-argument analysis as a defining basis for nouns, at least as a sole basis. First, the difference in function between nouns and other categories in this respect is not always reliable. In the totality of language use, nouns can have predicate uses, and verbs can have argument head uses. As an example of the first case, consider predications like *John* (*is*) *a dog.* Here *a dog* clearly predicates a property of *John,* and so is predicatelike. This use of nouns is even clearer in languages that lack or rarely use the verb *to be,* so that the sentence form is *John dog.*

As an example of verbs used as argument heads, one can consider a sentence like *I like to sing.* In this sentence, *like* predicates a relation between the liker *I* and what is liked, which is *to sing.* In the latter, *sing* is a verb, but is the head of the argument.

The second major problem is that the cross-linguistic data still do not quite make sense. If the predicate-argument is the central split, what would be consistent is for there to be two major form classes universally, which might be called noun and predicate. Furthermore, we are still left with the problem of why the noun category should be unified by one type of structural-semantic property (that of usually denoting an argument head), whereas the verb category should be sharply unified by another type of property, that of shared small-scale structural patterns.

CONCRETE OBJECT REFERENCE AS A SOLUTION TO THESE VARIOUS PROBLEMS

There are, then, two sets of problems presented by the aforementioned considerations. First, what holds together the noun category when small-scale structural properties fail to do so? Second, why should predicate-argument analysis succeed as an explanation for part, but not all, of the problems of defining nouns and accounting for the cross-linguistic patterns? The solution to these problems apparently lies in the key role, again, of concrete objects as a definitional core of nouns.

Vis-à-vis the small-scale structural properties and nouns, the proposed solution here is that nouns are, in fact, a family resemblance category, partly defined by core semantic properties, and partly defined by structural properties. The core semantic property, of course, is that of denoting a concrete individual or class of such individuals. This property unifies terms like *you, Mary, Smith,* and *dog,* despite their semantic and structural differences.

Some of these terms also have characteristic small-scale structural patterns in a given language. In English these include manner of marking for definiteness, plurality, quantity, and other such patterns. Terms such as *idea, game, trip,* or *explosion* do not denote concrete objects. But they are used in small-scale patterns identical to those used for concrete terms, such as *dog* or *table;* they also are used in similar argument head positions. These structural similarities are apparently important enough to cause their inclusion in the same category as *dog* and *table*. Thus, some nouns are nouns because they make concrete object reference; some nouns are nouns because of their structural identity with subclasses of concrete nouns. The noun category is thus a family resemblance category, in which neither concrete object reference nor structural use by itself can explain membership patterns.

The concrete object reference core of nouns in all probability also explains why argument head terms (that is, terms that typically are used as argument heads) correspond to a universal form-class category, whereas predicate terms do not. In all likelihood, a large part of cognition consists of seeing the world as made up of objects, properties of objects, and relations among objects. Arguments, as noted previously, are those terms or phrases of which predicates denote relations or properties. Thus, concrete object terms are natural argument head terms. Argument head terms are in turn a universal form class because they contain the concrete object terms which give the class much of its resultant unity and distinctiveness.

A DEVELOPMENTAL ACCOUNT FOR NOUNS; SOME DEVELOPMENTAL DATA

The preceding description of the structure of the noun category suggests in a natural way an overall sketch of how nouns develop. In the initial stages, children group together object-referring words into a single category. Thus, words like *I, mommy, Mary,* and *dog* are given a common category description. Important other semantic properties of such terms, such as whether they are animate, human, or inanimate, refer to a category or an individual, and so on, are also encoded.

Over time, the child then can analyze what structural properties are distinctive either to the category as a whole, or to semantic subclasses of the category, for the child's particular native language. Much is entailed in this analysis that cannot be speculated on here; for example, one would want to answer the question "distinctive of this category compared to what?" It also seems, as Pinker (1984) pointed out, that there must be some limitation on what will count as a possible structural property to be tabulated at all.

Nevertheless, with these problems duly noted, the general idea is fairly clear. Over time, the concrete object terms and their subclasses accumulate various clusters of distinctive structural properties. At some point, these properties become well enough established that a new term like *idea* or *game,* used in an environment that matches enough of the relevant structural uses, is incorporated into the relevant subclass. The category thus acquires its mixed semantic and structural definition.

On the whole, of course, this account very much resembles well-known accounts of formal category ontogenesis from a semantic core like those in MacNamara (1982), Pinker (1984), or Schlesinger (1982). Indeed, the present author believes that nouns are perhaps the one structural category for which accounts of this type actually have a good chance of working in some reasonably straightforward fashion. The major addition in the present article is that, as noted earlier, most accounts of formal category formation assume that the noun category ends up being defined solely by shared structural properties of its members. In the present account, it perhaps is assumed that this is so for common nouns; but for the noun category as a whole, shared concrete object reference remains an internal partial definitional brace that holds the category together as a unity, even as structural properties develop in partly disparate ways within the category.

It would be a good thing if developmental data clearly supported these formulations. By and large, the available data on these problems are not very extensive. To this author, there seem to be two small sets of empirical analyses, both from relatively early grammar, that do bear (both positively) upon the discussions of nouns in this chapter. These are presented in the following sections.

MACNAMARA'S DATA REINTERPRETED: EARLY NOUNS AND VERBS

The first of these data analyses is a set of data adduced by MacNamara (1982) to support the hypothesis that children's formal categories indeed do grow out of initial analyses centered around their semantic cores: concrete objects for nouns, actions for verbs, and attributes for adjectives, for example.

MacNamara's (1982) claim was that children's early speech shows this process in an active fashion: They initially actively avoid using nonconcrete nouns or nonactional verbs in the combinations appropriate for those categories. To support this claim, he analyzed the spontaneous productions of one of Roger Brown's (1973) three subjects, Sarah in Samples 1 to 10 (these are samples of ½ hour of speech, 1 week apart). He also analyzed the usage of Sarah's mother. His general claim was that the percentage of nonobject nouns and nonaction verbs is much higher in Sarah's mother's speech than in Sarah's own speech; thus, Sarah's speech is claimed to show active avoidance of semantically noncharacteristic nouns and verbs.

Let us look at the data, as MacNamara (1982) presented them. Sarah's mother, he found, used nonconcrete nouns 15% of the time, and nonactional verbs 23% of the time. He could not give figures of this precision for Sarah, for a number of reasons. Sometimes one cannot really tell for certain what meaning a term has for a child, for example. Or one cannot tell for certain whether or not an adult noun or verb really is receiving a distinctively nounlike or verblike use in children's early speech. For this reason, he gave ranges of estimation for Sarah's uses.

For nouns, MacNamara (1982) found that just 2.5% to 3.6% of Sarah's noun uses were nonconcrete in meaning. This is indeed much lower than her mother's percentage of 15%, both absolutely and proportionally, and indeed is not much above absolute zero. For nouns, the thesis appears well supported by the data. For nonaction verbs, he reported a range of 9.3% to 19% nonactional verbs in Sarah's speech, compared to her mother's 23%.

To the present author, these data do not seem to support a thesis of active avoidance of nonactional verb uses at all. The top of the range, 19%, is not much below the adult percentage of 23%. If one takes the middle of the range as an estimate, it is 14%. This figure is still about two thirds the proportion of the adult percentage, and is well above absolute zero. There seems to be a noun-verb asymmetry. The early noun uses appear to stick much more closely to their concrete object core than do early verblike uses; such an asymmetry, although not required by the general thesis of this article, is certainly very consistent with it.

The present author has done a much briefer analysis of data in the Stage 1 sample of Adam, another of Brown's (1973) subjects. For these analyses, the first 20 types (not tokens) of nouns and verbs respectively were analyzed. The results are consistent with the aforementioned. Of the first 20 nouns, 19 were clear concrete object references. Only one, *checkers* in *play checkers* might have been nonconcrete, if it referred to the game rather than the pieces; and obviously, this is at best a dubious case. Of the first 20 verbs, when context was used to make an interpretation, 3 appeared to be very clearly nonactional in meaning. These included contextually stative uses of *like, see,* and *got* (*got* often is used colloquially to mean "have," and this is how Adam appeared to use it in the utterance). So the proportion of nonobject noun types was 0 to 5%, and the proportion of nonactional verbs, 15%. Thus, again a noun-verb asymmetry is found.

We must note that these results have many qualifications. They are not from the earliest part of grammatical development, but come from a time when the children's mean length of utterance (MLU) is at least 1.75, well after the earliest two-word combinations (see Brown, 1973, for discussion). Also, certainly there are other interpretations. Perhaps children who use nonactional verbs early on do not consider them as part of the same category as adult action verbs at all; they may analyze them as part of another category, or analyze them as individual word patterns. Perhaps the nonconcrete nouns children hear early on happen to be relatively abstract as vocabulary meanings, so they are unassimilated because of word-meaning difficulties, not as part of a process of active grammatical avoidance.

Nonetheless, the asymmetry between early nouns and verbs in these analyses is an interesting one, and at least consistent with the general asymmetries for them claimed in this article; it would be interesting if further investigation showed the effect to be a general one.

PREDICATE-ARGUMENT ANALYSIS AND EARLY COMBINATIONS

From Stage 1 speech, we turn now to an earlier period, the period of initial two-word combinations, when MLU is often 1.1 to 1.4. These data bear upon the question of whether predicate-argument analysis indeed will form a clear sole basis for developmental beginnings for the child; or whether some of the difficulties discussed for adult language also might obtain for analyses of early child language.

As noted in the discussion of difficulties for predicate-argument analysis as a form-class basis, the major problem was that nouns are not always argument heads, and verbs are not always predicates. Early combinations that children make show that this is likely a problem in the input that they analyze; for their own combinations show these kinds of cases as well.

For example, early corpora (see, Braine, 1976) show productive combination patterns with the word *want* like the following: *want jump, want open, want come in.* In these, the predicate terms *want* has a clear structure *want + wanted,* in which the things that are wanted constitute an argument of *want.* Thus, in the aforementioned combinations, *jump, open,* and *come in,* denote what is wanted, and so they are arguments of *want,* though they are not adult nouns. Some other relevant sentence types in early grammar include sentences of the *more + X* type, that is, *more cook, more change, more sing, more read* (examples from Briane, 1976; Maratsos, 1988), in which *cook, change, sing,* and *read* are argument heads for *more,* denoting what recurs or what is desired to have recur.

One also finds cases in which nouns appear to take on predicatelike roles. Brown (1973) noted a pattern found in many early combinations that he called Demonstrative + Entity. Examples include *it ball, it Dennis, that hat,* and the like; the child seems to be saying something about a property of an object. (there are even a few early examples such as *mommy lady =* "mommy is a lady.") These are instances in which nouns serve a predicate-like function, that of denoting a property. Early combinations also include many possessives, in which a proper noun serves to modify a noun (Bloom, 1970; Braine, 1976; Brown, 1973; Schlesinger, 1971). Examples include *pie Tafale, house Sina, balloon mama* (Samoan possessives), *Adam checker,* and many others.

Thus these data, which are selected from a wider set of examples, point out that the relations between predicate, argument, nonnoun, and noun are not transparent even in children's early combinations. This nontransparency in turn indicates that children cannot classify the use of terms or phrases as simply being predicate and argument, and from there form an appropriate basis for the noun and nonnoun categories, for this procedure would give an initial classification in which many adult nouns and nonnouns go together in the same grammatical category.

Indeed, what one intuitively selects as the "appropriate" grammatical arguments for forming the noun category are, in these data, essentially those grammatical arguments that refer to concrete objects. Thus, an account (e.g., Braine, 1987) that attempts to incorporate predicate-argument analysis into the analysis of grammatical categories and relations would do well to posit that the child uses the object–nonobject distinction to select the appropriate groups of argument phrases and argument heads to group together initially. The results of doing this are much the same as the analysis offered in prior discussions, in which object-terms (and now also phrases) serve as a primary basis for the child's initial analysis of nouns and noun phrases. The analysis "denotes an argument of a predicate" can now be added, however, to the list of semantic-structural properties that we can propose that children use in their developing analysis of the noun category.

SUMMARY AND SOME GENERAL CONCLUSIONS

Summary

It would be repetitive to go through the various strands of evidence considered in any detail. Basically, they are as follows:

1. Cross-linguistically, only the noun category is universal (or very nearly so); predicate terms are subdivided or not into different major formal categories, depending on the language.

2. Within languages like English, small-scale combinatorial marking systems, such as stem marking or closed-class combinations, often give a complete basis for the internal organization of verbs. Nouns, on the other hand, show more of a family resemblance nature, being unified in part by the internal brace of concrete object denotation, and in part by small-scale combinatorial marking operations.

3. Concrete objects have special perceptual and ontological status within the conceptual system (Gentner, 1982, in press).

4. Developmentally, some asymmetries also show up in children's early vocabularies between nouns and verbs, which may show a more active grammatical category organizing influence for concrete object terms; some

data from Tagalog indicate the relative superiority of small-scale markers over large-scale constituent analysis for determining verb class boundaries.

5. Predicate-argument analysis, although an interesting and important part of grammatical analysis, does not prove a probable sole source for the noun–nonnoun distinction; again, a probable role for the object–nonobject distinction is indicated.

Some General Theoretical Entailments

What are the implications of these conclusions, and their general thrust, for a theory of formal category development? The major general implication is that we should not expect children's evolution of formal categories to be uniform. Perhaps this should follow from the cross-linguistic patterns per se. If sometimes there is an adjective versus verb category, sometimes not, and if the category of adjectives can range down to 10 members in all (Dixon, 1979), whereas nouns are more constant across languages, one would expect there to be something different about the internal structure, and the acquisitional course, for nouns, verbs, and adjectives. This seems to be the case.

ENTAILMENTS FOR PARTICULAR THEORIES OF FORM-CLASS DEVELOPMENT

These considerations also have more particular consequences for various theories of form-class acquisition. Their clearest implication, perhaps appropriately, is for the framework that implicitly governs the discussion in Maratsos and Chalkley (1980). The underlying framework of that analysis is that children are highly accurate, broad, and unbiased inductive analyzers who have the goal of producing the most accurate predictive system possible. They favor characterizing the internal system of verb-defining properties by small-scale tensing, negation, and aspect markings, for example, over basing verb category description on actional properties, because actional properties are a less accurate predictor of the relevant combinatorial operations, than are the combinatorial operations themselves. (For example, whether or not a term takes *s* to mark third-person present tense is better predicted by whether it can take *don't, doesn't,* or *didn't* to mark negation, than by whether it denotes an action.) Similarly, how productive a grammatical operation is should be predicted according to their theory by the internal predictive coherence of the system of analyzed properties.

In fact, according to the analyses discussed here, children do not operate in this unbiased fashion. Some properties, such as concrete object reference, simply are given very high weight as categorical organizers compared to others, high enough to overcome internal problems in the small-scale combinatorial patterns. For predicate categories, in contrast, some small-scale operations, especially stem marking on predicates, have very high organizing force. Of course, stem marking in general for certain sets of semantic-structural functions is no doubt generally important in grammatical category ontogenesis of all formal categories; but the point remains that for nouns in particular, the type of reference (concrete object reference in general reference to individuals rather than classes within the class) seems to bear an unevenly high category-defining weight. The system is not an unbiased predictive analyzer.

ENTAILMENTS FOR SEMANTIC-BASED MODELS

The considerations in this chapter also have implications for other theories. For example, a number of theories (Grimshaw, 1981; MacNamara, 1982; Pinker, 1984; though see Pinker, 1987, for important revisions) hold that children innately use certain semantic meanings of terms either to organize formal categories initially (MacNamara, 1982) or to recognize their membership in an innately given category (Grimshaw, 1981; Pinker, 1984). Thus, concrete object organizers or cues nouns, action organizers or cues verbs, attribute organizers or cues adjectives, and so on. From there, distributional properties of the core terms are analyzed to give the formal adult category.

As discussed earlier, this kind of account, if properly adjusted, could work for the noun category, given the universality of a clearly object-based, form-class category in the world's languages. But it would have to be adjusted seriously, in a way that undermines its basic spirit, to deal with the nonuniversality, and very different nature of determination for the major predicate categories. At the most general level, there is the problem that most such theories presuppose a standard list of formal categories in the world's languages. This assumption is incorrect for the form-class categories (and probably incorrect for the grammatical relations as well [Maratsos, 1988]). At a more detailed (and tangled) level, one might consider those languages whose adjective repertoires are smaller than more familiar adjective-verb languages (as few as 10 adjectives). Surely some of the terms that are verbs in these languages are very highly stative, and in use early on; a strict application of the Semantic Bootstrapping hypothesis (Grimshaw, 1981; Pinker, 1984; though see Pinker, 1987, for some revisions) could have great difficulties in such languages, as would a related theory like that of MacNamara (1982). Although semantic-based theories can no doubt be adjusted to deal with these and other problems, to this author's knowledge no present account exists that deals appropriately with the known variations of word-class repertoires.

Language-Specific Versus More General Mechanisms

What about the more general problem of language-specific determining mechanisms for acquisition versus more general mechanisms? Here the present results are not highly determinative. For example, take the fact that concrete object reference serves as an important noun-category organizer. This could be expected in a view of acquisition as largely driven by general analytic mechanisms, for it would follow from the centrally coherent status of concrete objects in the cognitive system that such reference would serve to be a stronger organizer in the linguistic system as well. Similarly, the importance of tense and aspectual markers on the predicate stem could be taken to follow from the natural relevance of tense and aspect to the specification of event types, in combination with some intuitive notion of structural closeness that would give high weight to stem marking or local marking for these highly relevant notions.

On the other hand, it is very natural that as an innate linguistic analytic system evolves, it would build on those cracks and divisions already implicit in the cognitive system. Thus, in evolution, an innate linguistic program naturally might incorporate a salient cognitive category as a basis for linguistic analysis, and give more weighting to more highly weighted conceptual categories. Similarly, the natural relevance of tense and aspect marking to events could be specialized or slightly modified to give the analytic weightings useful in building event-related formal categories. Such systems furthermore could operate either with or without innate specification of the possible category sets. Given the general evidence for some degree of innate specialization of language faculties (e.g., Poizner, Klima, & Bellugi, 1987; see discussion in Maratsos, 1988, 1989 or see Chomsky, 1986), such hypotheses are highly plausible. Making these analyses take advantage of cognitively natural or available analyses is an evolutionarily natural proposal (Bickerton, 1981; Pinker, 1984). Unfortunately, the complexity of the sets of possibilities, once a mixture of innate and noninnate mechanisms is admitted, is very great. A system that naturally captures these, and the cross-linguistic variations, is perhaps the greatest present task of theories of formal category formation.

SOME METHODOLOGICAL CONSEQUENCES

Finally, if the thrust of this article is correct, there are some important methodological and interpretive consequences, both for the analysis of linguistic method and for the analysis of acquisition. It seems reasonable to assert that the chief presupposition of much linguistic and acquisitional study is that the child's analysis of the incoming data will be, in some sense, the best analysis from some possible third-person point of view. For example, arguments over whether two categories are separate concern whether the structural properties differentiating them are sufficient from an objective point of view to justify their differentiation. Nouns should share uniformly a number of structural properties distinct from those of other categories, as should verbs, adjectives, prepositions, and the like.

The argument here has been that the structural properties shared overall by nouns are quite tenuous, compared with those of verbs. Essentially, it is argued, children see the noun subclasses so strongly bound together by concrete object reference that they form a single category even though the objective structural evidence is not good, even though, in fact, adjectives and verbs could be put together as a single category at the same level of analysis. Within nouns, it is argued, some proper names act more like common nouns (e.g., family names), whereas others act a great deal like pronouns. Yet no one could seriously consider splitting the proper names in this way. The basis for the split we have, of course, is referential. Similarly, pronouns could be badly split between first or second versus third person. Yet intuitions have not considered this split seriously.

Actually, much the same kind of argument could be made about the predicate categories, though it has not been. Perhaps a more significant general structural property could be considered to be transitive versus intransitive, in which case some adjectives would be grouped with many verbs, and intransitive verbs and adjectives would form a separate category. But it is instead chiefly the distribution of small-scale properties that actually correlates, and excellently, with the understood formal category divisions within the predicate category.

What this comes to is that, assuming the reasonableness of these arguments, the problem of judging category membership is the problem of judging similarity of items. As is well known, everything is both similar to everything else in some way, and different in some way. So what counts is what similarities are seen as important in what degree. That is, there is probably no third-person objective viewpoint from which categorizations can be made according to some objective "best" fit of the data. This is not necessarily a serious problem for learning a conventional system, of course. It is not necessary that in some objective sense, an individual achieves the best analysis. All that is necessary is that his or her analysis, however biased, agrees reasonably well with the analysis of everyone else who learns the language.

In judging children's acquisition of formal categories, again, the usual idea is that at some point, members of a putative category will show enough similarity of structural uses by the child to be profitably judged by the analyst as grouped together in a category. But, if the previously discussed arguments about nouns and their subclasses are correct, children never do have "sufficient" objective grounds for the groupings they arrive at; nor does the adult analyst. Children might make the proper name-common noun subdivision immediately and intuitively, for example, before these show any division in the uses in their speech, because the grounds are apparently not particularly structural in the first place. Then again, children's speech sometimes shows various divisions of use, such as those between people's names and inanimate objects (see Bloom, 1970; Bowerman, 1973), especially early on. But they might well still analyze all these as being members of a larger category, even though the particular semantic relations they are interested in expressing give different structural patterns for them.

All this does not, of course, mean that no analyses of children's speech can give evidence as to the acquisition of categories. What is chiefly possible is, often, a reasonably well-based conservative estimate. For example, when English-speaking children overregularize verb past tenses in a way that observes the formal adjective-verb boundary, but goes across both actional and nonactional verbs, it is reasonable to take this as strong evidence for a predicate categorization much like that of the adult. Again, when children consistently place articles before common nouns, but not proper nouns, this is good evidence for a division (actually, between first-name proper nouns and common nouns, because family proper names can take articles, as discussed earlier). What these are, are good conservative estimates. It is much more difficult, perhaps impossible, to make good estimates that are not conservative.

Are linguists' classifications the same as those of native speakers? Of course, it is possible that linguists are simply wrong in their classifications, or that they are mostly right, with a few difficulties here and there. For example, perhaps pronouns, proper names, and common nouns are not all members of the same lexical category noun. More broadly, as has been shown here, linguists typically judge a language to have an adjective-verb distinction when tense and aspect marking on the stem are different for two (or more) classes of predicates, but no such distinction when they are not, as in Chinese, or other languages. Perhaps, though, native speakers actually always divide predicate categories into adjective versus verb based on properties such as likelihood of being used as a modifier, or some combination of this with stative qualities. Sometimes the language fails to observe this distinction in the kinds of structural differentiations linguists habitually use. Alternatively, perhaps the predicate categories really are members of one category, with slight formal differentiations at a lower level, as generative semanticists of the 1960s came to argue (Lakoff, 1970).

In short, we tend to suppose that the bases for classification used by linguists actually approximate those tacitly used by native speakers. If they do, or if linguists' intuitive decisions, which they justify by appeal to appropriate structural properties, are similar to the tacit categorizations of speakers, things are fine. If they are not, and if linguists' categories differ seriously from speakers' tacit categories, what can be done? The answer is, nothing on a major level—if the arguments of this chapter are roughly correct. That is, given that there are both reasons to put pronouns, proper names, and common nouns together as a single lexical category, and reasons not to, direct intuitions are probably as good as we can get. Conscious analysts simply will append various arguments to justify these decisions, partly educated by the fates of their structural analyses. Structural properties that support the analysis then will be emphasized. Structural properties that do not (for example, both English adjectives and prepositions must take tensing and negation with forms of the verb *to be*, but are not commonly considered members of the same category) will be taken less seriously. We may as well then accept intuitive judgments, presumably informed to some degree by structural concerns, as being as reasonable as any we are likely to get.

ACKNOWLEDGEMENTS

This article has benefited from discussions with a number of persons, including Melissa Bowerman, Martin Braine, Brian MacWhinney, Clifton Pye, Joe Stemberger, and others in audiences. Special acknowledgment goes to James Morgan, who pointed out to me the common nounlike behavior of family names.

REFERENCES

Bickerton, D. (1981). *The roots of language,* Ann Arbor, MI: Karoma.

Bloom, L. (1970). Language development: Form and function in emerging grammars. Cambridge, MA: MIT Press.

Bowerman, M. (1973). *Early syntactic development: A cross-linguistic study with special reference to Finnish.* Cambridge, England: Cambridge University Press.

Braine, M. D. S. (1976). Children's first word combinations. *Monographs of the Society for Research in Child Development, 41.*

Braine, M. D. S. (1987). What is learned in acquiring word classes—A step toward an acquisition theory. In B. MacWhinney (Ed.), *Mechanisms of language acquisition* (pp. 103-137). Hillsdale, NJ: Lawrence Erlbaum Associates.

Brown, R. N. D. (1957). Linguistic determinism and the part of speech. *Journal of Abnormal and Social Psychology, 55,* 1-5.

Brown, R. N. D. (1973). *A first language: The early stages.* Cambridge, MA: Harvard University Press.

Brugman, C. (1983). The use of body-part terms as locative in Chalcatongo Mixtex. In *Survey of California and Other Indian Languages* (Report No. 4, pp. 235–290). Berkeley, CA: University of California.

Cazden, C. B. (1968). The acquisition of noun and verb inflections. *Child Development, 39,* 433–448.

Chomsky, N. (1986). *Knowledge of language.* New York: Praeger.

Dixon, R. M. W. (1979). Where have all the adjectives gone? In R. M. W. Dixon (Ed.), *Where have all the adjectives gone?* (pp. 1–78). Berlin: Walterac Gruyter.

Gentner, D. (1982). Why nouns are learned before verbs: Linguistic relatively vs. natural partitioning. In S. Kuczaj (Ed.), *Language development: Language, cognition, and culture* (pp. 38–62). Frankfurt, Germany: Springer-Verlag.

Gentner, D. (in press). More on why nouns are learned before verbs. *Linguistics.*

Gonzales, A. (1984). *Acquiring Philippino as a first language: Two case studies.* Manila: Linguistic Society of the Philippines.

Grimshaw, J. (1981). Form, function, and the language acquisition device. In C. L. Baker & J. J. McCarthy (Eds.), *The logical problem of language acquisition* Cambridge, MA: MIT Press.

Lakoff, G. (1970). *Linguistics and natural logic* (Studies in generative semantics, No. 2). Ann Arbor: University of Michigan, Linguistics Department.

Lyons, J. (1968). *Introduction to theoretical linguistics.* Hillsdale, NJ: Lawrence Erlbaum Associates.

MacNamara, J. (1982). *Names for things: A study of child language.* Cambridge, MA: Bradford Books/MIT Press.

Maratsos, M. P. (1988). Crosslinguistic analysis, universals, and language acquisition. In F. Kessel (Ed.), *The development of language and language researchers: Essays in honor of Roger Brown.* Hillsdale, NJ: Lawrence Erlbaum Associates.

Maratsos, M. P. (1989). Innateness and plasticity in language acquisition. In M. L. Rice & R. L. Schiefelbusch (Eds.), *The teachability of language* (pp. 105–125). Baltimore: Brookes.

Maratsos, M. P., & Chalkley, M. (1980). The internal language of children's syntax: The ontogenesis and representation of syntactic categories. In K. Nelson (Ed.), *Children's language* (Vol. 2, pp. 185–257). New York: Gardner Press.

Pinker, S. (1984). *Language learnability and language development.* Cambridge, MA: Harvard University Press.

Pinker, S. (1987). The bootstrapping problem in language acquisition. In B. MacWhinney (Ed.), *Mechanisms of language acquisition.* Hillsdale, NJ: Lawrence Erlbaum Associates.

Poizner, H., Klima, E. S., & Bellugi, U. (1987). *What the hands reveal about the brain.* Cambridge, MA: MIT Press.

Reichenbach, H. (1947). *Symbolic logic.* Los Angeles: University of California Press.

Schachter, P. (1976). The subject Philippine languages: Topic, actor, actor-topic, or none of the above. In C. N. Li (Ed.), *Subject and topic* (Vol. 15, pp. 491–518). New York: Academic.

Schachter, P., & Otanes, S. (1972). *A reference grammar of Tagalog.* Los Angeles: University of California Press.

Schlesinger, I. M. (1971). Production of utterances and language acquisition. In D. I. Slobin (Ed.), *The ontogenesis of grammar* (pp. 73–117). New York: Academic.

Schlesinger, I. M. (1982). *Steps to language.* Hillsdale, NJ: Lawrence Erlbaum Associates.

4 Concepts and Meaning in Language Development

Katherine Nelson
City University of New York Graduate Center

The central problems of the acquisition of lexical terms and meanings are not greatly different from those of other aspects of language acquisition: They have to do with the questions of how the language system gets into the mind of the child. The problem of the child's acquisition of a system of conventional lexical meanings is a subset of the question of how language in general is acquired and at the same time it is a much larger question — involving all of learning and knowledge acquisition. Although the lexical system seems to be much more closely connected to the child's general knowledge system (language seems much less "special" in this domain), the answers that are proposed for this component of the system are similar to those proposed for grammar. And many of the problems are similar. For example, as with the syntactic component, each language organizes its lexicon in a different way: Different concepts are lexicalized, semantic domains are structured differently (Lyons, 1977), and classifiers and covert categories relate lexical items differently in different languages (Bowerman, 1982; Lakoff, 1987). Yet the child is not tutored directly in these systems any more than in grammar; the systems must be induced from the language in use.

In this chapter, I focus on the problems of the acquisition of a lexical system. An adequate approach to these problems involves understanding the language system, the way it is presented to the child, and the internal workings of the child's mind at different points in development. Taken each alone these are not simple domains, and finding how they work together in development can be daunting. No approach has yet managed this difficult task. I emphasize "in development" here and throughout, in contrast to models and theories that make the simplifying assumption that processes of acquisition do not change and that the same mechanisms are employed throughout the acquisition process.[1] In my view, first language acquisition is a developmental problem and must be understood as such; that is, it takes place over time, exhibiting different organizations at different points despite apparent similarity of linguistic input.

There are at least three standard views as to the proper answer to the question of how language structure in general and semantic structure in particular gets into the child's mind: language as innately given, language as a cognitive construction, and language as a social-cultural construction. Before considering different versions of these views and their potential as theories of semantic development, I first review what relevant research in the area of lexical acquisition has revealed about the processes involved. This sets the stage for a critical evaluation of some current theories and the description of a framework that I think is promising for further work in this area.

THE COURSE OF LEXICAL DEVELOPMENT

Lexical development consists, in brief, of acquiring word forms and the conventional meanings associated with them as agreed upon by adult users in a language community. It further involves establishing relations among words and meanings of specific kinds, for example, synonyms, antonyms, and superordinate terms within a system of lexical relations. The words and their meanings that the child must learn are displayed in uses by the language community of which she is a part. The conventional meanings must be inferred by the child from the way the words are used in context. In this section I consider what we know from empirical research about how lexical meaning develops from first words to the large and complex vocabulary of the school child, which incorporates relations of contrast, similarity, and hyponomy. A central question is whether these relations are

---

[1]For example, after specifying that mechanisms are stationary over time, Pinker (1984) turned to defending the assumption of task specificity, asserting: "Unless a model is capable of acquiring the complex and elegant linguistic systems of the sort characterized by linguists . . . it is irrelevant to the debate over task-specificity" (p. 33) But the point is that the young child is not initially capable of these things. Given the stationary assumption (learning mechanisms do not change over time) and the assumption that variation in input is not significant and does not change over time, there appears to be no way to account for order of acquisition and development of organization. In the end these assumptions reduce to the instantaneous acquisition assumption made by Chomsky whereby, given knowledge of word meanings, syntactic structures are inferred all at once as a grammar is selected to fit the entirety of the input.

relied upon in the acquisition of a first lexicon, or whether they are derived later. The description here reflects a view of conceptual and semantic development that my colleagues and I have developed over a number of years that seems to fit the accumulated data. This view is elaborated in a later section.

To understand lexical development one must make some assumptions about what it is to know the meaning of a word. There is no simple and straightforward account of what a meaning is; indeed, philosophers and linguists have written volumes in recent years without resolving the issue (see, e.g., Putnam, 1975; 1988; Schwartz, 1977; and the references in the next section). I believe the best operative assumption is to consider word meaning as a tripartite system of reference, denotation, and sense (Lyons, 1977). This assumption provides a framework within which lexical development may be viewed, which becomes clearer as the description unfolds.

Empirical research has uncovered three distinct periods of lexical development that are suggestive of the three parts of the lexical system (Barrett, 1986; Kuczaj & Barrett, 1986; Nelson, 1985; Nelson & Lucariello, 1985). Each of the three periods has distinct problems and tasks that are reflected in the word-learning procedures used during the period, and in the eventual establishment of lexical relations. Thus, as emphasized earlier, acquiring a lexicon is an essentially developmental process, in which the nature of meanings and their relations changes as the subjective lexical system develops.

Phase 1

The first period of development is one in which the child faces the problem of finding a way into the language system. This period lasts for 6 to 12 months for most children, from the time that the child first becomes sensitive to language forms and begins to respond to some of them consistently (sometimes as early as 9 months of age but often as late as 14 or 15 months) until the production of 30 or more words and the first two-word combinations (which may be as late as 24 months). The problems the child faces during this period are of the following sort: What is a word? What do words do? How are words used to refer? Can a single word refer to more than one category of things or events? That these are real problems is evident in the data from many observational studies, for example in the data on "errors" in word use.

From the 19th century until the present, most observers have reported that during this initial period children engage in overextended or complexive uses of words, as well as using them in overly restricted and idiosyncratic ways. For example, a child may restrict the use of the term *car* to the situation of watching cars move on the street outside the window (Bloom,

1973; Nelson, 1973). Barrett (1986; Barrett, Harris, Jones, & Brookes, 1986), who has closely analyzed a number of context-restricted uses in the early months of word learning, claims that such restriction is typical of this first period, a position shared by many if not most observers of early child language (e.g., Bates, Benigni, Bretherton, Camaioni, & Volterra, 1979; Braunwald, 1978; Dore, Franklin, Miller, & Ramer, 1976; Dromi, 1987; Gopnick & Meltzoff, 1986; McShane, 1979; Nelson & Lucariello, 1985; Nelson, Rescorla, Gruendel, & Benedict, 1978; Rescorla, 1980). In this early period children also use words to refer to complexes of objects or features. A familiar example is that of a child who applied the term *clock* to real clocks and watches, to meters, dials, and timers of various sorts, to bracelets, a buzzing radio, and telephone, and to a chevron-shaped medallion on his dishwasher, suggesting that *clock* referred to an associative complex of features, rather than to a particular type or category of object (Rescorla, 1980). Different researchers have had different interpretations of these early complexive overextensions, suggesting on the one hand that they might be comments on similarity between objects rather than real category errors (Nelson et al., 1978); or that children have formed complexive rule systems (Rescorla, 1980); or that early word meanings are formed around prototypes, thus accounting for extension on the basis of one or a few features (Barrett, 1986; Bowerman, 1976; Lucariello, 1987); or that the word's semantic role (i.e., its function in combination with other elements) rather than its referential meaning dictated shifting references (Greenfield & Smith, 1976). Although the problem of inferring the child's word meaning from the child's word use is a sticky one, children's apparently anomalous uses cannot be simply dismissed. Rather than looking for a single definitive interpretation, I suggest that these observations indicate uncertainty on the child's part as to the nature and function of words. The child during this period seems to be engaged in learning what word meanings are, what words can refer to, and what words do (Dromi, 1987; Nelson, 1988a; Nelson & Lucariello, 1985; see also discussion that follows).

Children typically learn and use many object labels during this period; on the average, for middle-class American children learning English, about 40% of the first 50-word vocabulary consists of generic names of object categories (Nelson, 1973). But they also acquire many proper names, relational terms, nouns that are not object labels, action words, and social and expressive phrases. This picture contrasts with the claims of some constraints theorists (discussed in the following section) who believe that children initially are constrained to take words to refer to object classes and thus assert that the overwhelming majority of first words are count nouns. Moreover, individual differences in the type of words learned and used are the rule, with some children focusing on object labels and others focusing on other types of words that are useful in social interactions, indicating emphasis on referential or expressive functions, respectively. In addition, some words are used to refer to both objects and actions or properties so that their target categories are indeterminate, for example the use of the word *hot* as a name for heaters and ovens as well as for the property of either hot or cold. Dromi (1987) reported that most of the words acquired during the first 2 months and 16% of all the words in her daughter's vocabulary in the single-word period were indeterminate in reference in this way. Also during these early months children understand many more words than they use, acquiring a receptive vocabulary of 50 words 6 months prior to the equivalent productive vocabulary (Benedict, 1979). Moreover, known words typically are produced infrequently, and many that are initially productive drop out of use after a brief period.

Taken together, the characteristics of this long period of beginning language use—comprehension much superior to production, restricted, complexive and indeterminate uses, and emphasis on one or a few functions—strongly suggest that during this time children are learning what words do. That is, contrary to the suggestion that children enter the language-learning period with clear constraints on lexical reference, children must acquire these ideas in the course of early experience with the language itself.

I believe that developments during this period are important to understanding the foundation of lexical acquisition. Primary language acquisition (i.e., acquisition of basic grammar and vocabulary, not including the complexities and subtleties within the capacity of mature language users) takes place over roughly 4 years (between 1 and 5 years of age). The first year of that time (between 1 and 2 years) is crucial to understanding the process of acquisition in that it lays the foundation for the more visible developments in productive language that follow. The 1-year-old child is an intelligent, problem-solving creature who is rapidly acquiring knowledge about the physical, social, and linguistic world. The slow and quirky developments during this period are clearly at odds with the "simplifying assumption" of an instantaneous language acquisition device (e.g., Chomsky, 1965; Wexler & Culicover, 1980). I believe that serious theorists should ask: What is being learned during this long period of exposure and sensitivity to linguistic input? Study of the child's first uses of linguistic forms can provide clues, but we need to go beyond these clues to construct and test theories with implications for how language is constructed by the child.[2]

---

[2]The proposal that language is constructed by the child is not the same as the claim that the "mind" is so constructed, a view attributed to Piaget (see, e.g., Pinker, 1984). That is, the same cognitive mechanisms may be attributed to the child as to the adult (although they may be less efficient). But in constructing knowledge of the language, the organization of that knowledge

Phase 2

The second period of lexical development begins when the child has acquired about 30 productive words or more and seems to have achieved the realization that words name categories of objects and events. This realization often is manifested in a naming explosion when the child asks for and names everything in sight (McShane, 1979; Nelson, 1973). At this point the child, who has heretofore learned a handful of object names, and has used them infrequently, often inflexibly, and unpredictably, suddenly seems to want to know the name for everything in her world, and doubles or triples her vocabulary in the space of a few weeks. This phenomenon often is accompanied by the child's first and subsequently incessant use of the question "What's that?"[3] Although not all children evidence this insight so dramatically, its onset is important: It signifies the entry into the acquisition of a productive language. The formation of word combinations follows a few months after, and is in turn succeeded by the acquisition of morphological and ordering principles of grammatical structures. The fact that vocabulary building is so sudden and so fast at this point in the child's development clearly implies that the child has formed concepts that are in some sense available for naming, once she realizes that that is "what words do."

We need to pause at this point, however, to reflect that naming concepts is not simply "what words do," although the child might believe this to be the case. The words of the adult language simply cannot be mapped directly onto the child's experientially derived concepts. Words do have conventional meanings, meanings established through use by a language community, although they are not static or deterministic. The child's experientially based concepts might be quite different from that of the language community in some seemingly bizarre ways. For example, the child might begin with a concept of "small four-legged house animals" rather than individual concepts of "dog" and "cat." Then the term *dog* will be extended to cats as well. Such overextensions of words to close category members are frequent during this period, replacing the earlier complexive overextensions (Dromi,

---

changes over time in the direction of greater complexity. Thus, different mechanisms may be called upon at different points in the acquisition process. These are points that are overlooked by learnability theorists and that are well illustrated in the work of Bowerman (1982) and Karmiloff-Smith (1979).

[3]It also has been called the "Helen Keller phenomenon" because of the dramatic episode described in the autobiography of the deaf-blind child, when, as her teacher was pumping water over her hand and at the same time tapping the sign of water into the other, Helen had the sudden insight that "everything has a name" and that the tapping signified the thing's name. Subsequently, she raced about demanding to know the name of everything, just as many children of about 18 to 21 months of age do.

1987; Nelson et al., 1978; Rescorla, 1980). But the child's concept of "dog" also might include specifications relating to the child's own pet, such as "friendly, excitable, chews socks." These are legitimate characterizations of a particular dog, and are also generalizable to some subset of the category of dogs. However, they are not legitimately part of the conventionally accepted "meaning" of the term *dog* in the parent language. The term *dog* in the conventional language denotes a particular species of animals (with many differentiable subspecies or breeds). Characteristics of or experiences with particular animals are irrelevant to the abstract denotation of the term, although they may enter into an individual's concept, and thereby be part of the connotation of the term for that individual. There is no evidence, however, that when the child first begins to use words she distinguishes between her own experientially based concepts and the meaning of the term in the larger language community. We can say that she uses words denotatively (that is, that there is a conceptual basis for what the word can be used to refer to), but that what the words denote are her own subjective, possibly idiosyncratic, concepts. This developmental view is clearly at odds with the universal innate concept view considered in the next section.

As previously stated, the sudden onset of names at the outset of this period can best be explained by the assumption that the child has already formed conceptual categories for things and events in the world, and now realizes that words can be used to denote them. During this period the child tends to assume that words and concepts are in one-to-one correspondence; that is, there is a word for every concept and a concept for every word. The child's problem at this time is one of identifying the words for all of the conceptual categories that represent the child's world of things, people, actions, and events. The process may work both ways—the child looks for words for established concepts and also tries to form concepts for new words.

This second period may last several years, as basic knowledge of words and related conceptual distinctions is built up. A number of recent experimental studies of the extension of a novel word to new instances during this period have been reported (e.g., Gelman & Markman, 1986; Markman & Hutchinson, 1984; Merriman, 1986, 1987; Taylor & Gelman, 1988; Waxman & Gelman, 1986). These studies have shown that young preschool children are excellent strategists: They employ a number of cues—syntactic, categorical, contrastive—to determine to which instances a novel word might legitimately apply, whether it might be a noun or an adjective, a higher order category term, or something else. A notable characteristic of this period, studied initially by Carey and Bartlett (1978), is the "fast mapping" of words onto meanings, in their study the acquisition of a new word for a novel color after a single exposure to its use. Fast mapping as a strategy has been invoked to explain the evident fact that children acquire words at a very rapid rate—on the order of 5 to 10 new words a day during the preschool period. As discussed later, I believe it can best be understood in terms of the growth and differentiation of the child's conceptual structures.

This is a period (from 2 to 5 years of age) when linguistic knowledge of all kinds is accumulating at a rapid rate: knowledge of grammar, of how linguistic forms are used in the community (pragmatics), as well as lexical knowledge of how things and events may be referenced and how relations between them may be expressed. Two simultaneous developments are taking place within and across these domains: The child is learning to use language communicatively; at the same time, the child's language is itself gaining increasingly complex internal structure.

Phase 3

The third period of lexical development is one of revision, reorganization, and consolidation of lexical items within domains of related words. This is a period of growth, beginning in the preschool years (about 3 to 4 years of age) that leads into the less turbulent period of the established lexical system by the early school years. The characteristics of this period (which overlaps the second—no hard and fast boundaries or discontinuities are projected here) are less well studied than the earlier periods, and less accessible to observation. However, available research strongly suggests some important characteristics that point to reorganization processes. For example, during the second period there appear to be contextual limitations on the child's use of some words, such as relational terms and superordinates denoting hierarchical relations among terms (French & Nelson, 1985; MacNamara, 1982; Markman, 1983; Nelson, 1985) that begin to be overcome during the third period as the lexical system is reorganized and new relations are established. Bowerman (1982) has documented evidence for the process of reorganization of terms and the establishment of new semantic relations within a number of different domains during this period. Karmiloff-Smith (1979) has described the movement from the child's use of a term in an undifferentiated way to the restriction of its use to one function, and finally its use in a multifunctional adult way, reflecting a similar process of reorganization of meaning within the lexical system during this time. Ehrlich (1979) characterized the change that took place in terms of a move from restricted situational uses to "free elements" that could combine with other terms without restriction. In addition, the beginning understanding of the relation between superordinate and subordinate terms within a general semantic domain, such as *food* or *furniture,* indicates that the semantic system is becoming organized along conventional lines.

All of these otherwise disparate findings suggest a system that is at first characterized by independent lexemes, that are related to experientially based concepts but are not related directly to other lexemes, subsequently becoming reorganized in terms of relations between the lexical items themselves, a process that in turn leads to new insights into both the linguistic and the conceptual systems.

Summary

To conclude, lexical development involves all of the characteristics and problems described here, and a theory of word learning must encompass all. No theory that does not account for differences in the processes of acquisition of words and their meanings at different developmental points will be adequate. The view put forward here under the assumption of the successive development of a tripartite system can be summarized as follows. The child can be seen as beginning the acquisition of lexical meanings by mastering notions about the reference of words, that is, what words can refer to in the real world. Thus the first period of development may be considered the *referential* period. After a point the child comes to the realization that beyond the word-world relation of reference there is a word-concept relation of denotation, wherein concepts denote what words may potentially refer to. At this point words become mapped onto concepts in the child's conceptual system; words are learned rapidly for concepts that already exist, and new concepts are formed or differentiated to match newly learned words for which no previously formed concept is available in the child's mind. This second period then may be called the *denotational* period. Still later, a period of lexical relations emerges, when words are related to one another (word-word) in terms of their semantic properties of similarity, contrast, and inclusion. At this point (late in the preschool years), the semantic system becomes differentiated from the conceptual system, and the two may operate semi-independently. This period of reorganization then may be termed the *sense* period. Of course, each relation is operative in the mature semantic system (see, e.g., Lyons, 1977).

THE ACQUISITION OF MEANING:
ALTERNATIVE THEORIES

The developmental account just summarized reflects a cognitive constructive view of lexical development that is further elaborated in the last section. As noted previously, a number of alternative accounts have been put forward that attempt to explain lexical acquisition in terms of specific innate linguistic knowledge. In this section these accounts are critically examined (see also, Nelson, 1988a), and the possible contribution of social determinism views is briefly considered.

Innate Knowledge Theories

The nativist proposals considered here assume that there is an innate species-specific universal linguistic constraint that determines the domain and structure of word meanings: what can be the meaning of a word and how the meaning is specified.[4] The nativist view is held in its most stringent form by Fodor (1975, 1981), but it is evident as well in several other recent proposals about constraints on word learning (see Nelson 1987, 1988a). Fodor claimed that all *lexical concepts,* that is, all concepts that are expressed by single words, are innate, composing a limited and universal language of thought that serves as the conceptual base for the natural language to be acquired. Lexical concepts are not learned; they are part of the conceptual structure specified by the genetic code and are simply "triggered" by appropriate environmental conditions. Complex concepts may be composed of the biologically given set by combinatory principles that operate much like chemical compounds (Fodor, 1981).

It is difficult to see how this proposal can deal with the fact that different concepts are lexicalized in different languages, or especially that different lexical cuts are made across the same conceptual fields. (See Lakoff, 1987; Lyons, 1977; Sampson, 1980, for discussion and examples; see also, Putnam, 1988 for arguments against this and all other functional/ computational theories of meaning; and Shannon, 1988, for arguments against semantic representations in general.) This account is also at odds with the slow, uncertain, and idiosyncratic process of acquisition documented in the previous section.

Fodor's (1975, 1981) proposal is only the most extreme form of the nativist views, in that it does not propose components out of which word meanings may be constructed, but claims rather (for logical reasons) that lexical concepts do not have internal structure. A more common and seemingly more acceptable proposal is the notion of universal lexical *components* (e.g., Bierwisch, 1970; Katz, 1972; Katz & Fodor, 1963) out of which all word meanings are constructed. The assumption here is that "semantic features cannot be different from language to language, but are rather part of the general human capacity for language, forming a universal inventory used in particular ways by individual languages" (Bierwisch, 1970, pp. 181–182). In commenting on this general class of theories, Sampson (1980) pointed out:

---

[4]Innate cognitive constraints on the structure of knowledge in general are not in question here.

that the features are by no means restricted to Lockian "simple ideas," i.e., immediate sensory qualities such as "cold," "yellow"; properties like YOUNG or MALE are only distantly related to the qualities which our physical organs of sense are designed to detect, so linguists are solving the problem posed by the fact that we have ideas not directly derived from experience by holding that such ideas are built-in from birth. (p. 22)

The universal semantic component proposal received considerable attention in the developmental literature, specifically in terms of the semantic feature hypothesis (Clark, 1973). But today this particular proposal is no longer influential among developmentalists, having fallen before an onslaught of empirical and theoretical objections well summarized by Carey (1982). Keil's (1979) claim that a universal ontological hierarchy constrains children's acquisition of word meanings also has fallen on rough empirical and theoretical ground (Carey, 1983; Gerard & Mandler, 1983).

Lexical nativism has not vanished from the developmental scene, however. A variety of proposals characterized as "constraints" theory populate the area. The alleged need for constraints on word learning derives in many discussions from claims made by Quine (1960) about the indeterminacy of radical translation, and from Goodman's (1955) puzzle of what constrains natural concepts (for example, why we do not have a concept of "grue" that refers to the color green before the year 2000 and the color blue after that year). The child, it is claimed, must be constrained from forming wild hypotheses about the meaning of a word such as *rabbit* uttered in the presence of rabbits. The child must somehow be prevented from taking this word to refer to rabbit running, the color brown, rabbit ears, or other irrelevant concepts; the child must be constrained to assume that the word refers only to the object rabbit if word learning is to proceed properly. For example, Markman and Hutchinson (1984) echoed Quine's dilemma:

Young children beginning to acquire their native language continually face this problem of narrowing down the meaning of a term from an indefinite number of possibilities. Someone points in some direction and then utters a word. On what grounds is the child to conclude that a new unfamiliar word, e.g., "dog" refers to dogs? What is to prevent a child from concluding that "dog" is a proper name for that particular dog? What prevents the child from concluding that "dog" means "four-legged object" or "black object" or any number of other characteristics that dogs share? And finally, what prevents the child from concluding that "dog" . . . also refers to the bone the dog is chewing on or the tree the dog is lying under?[5] (p. 2)

---

[5]Note that Fodor's (1981) notion of words "triggering" innate concepts fails to deal with this problem of narrowing down possibilities.

The answer favored by Markman and Hutchinson is in terms of "an abstract constraint children place on possible word meanings" (p. 22).

A number of researchers have been taken with this notion that there must be built-in, species-specific linguistic constraints on word learning (Huttenlocher & Smiley, 1987; Markman & Hutchinson, 1984; Seidenberg & Pettito, 1987). These constraints typically are conceived to operate in such a way as to prevent the child from assuming that a word may denote two different ontological categories, such as action and object. In several proposals, children are held to believe that words refer to whole objects; thus, when presented with a novel word they take it as an object name, and not say as an object part or property or relation.[6] The evidence from naturalistic studies of early word learning reviewed in the previous section (e.g., Barrett, 1986; Bowerman, 1976; Dromi, 1987; Rescorla, 1980) runs counter to these proposals, indicating that at the outset children do not confine word reference to one ontological category or to whole objects. Most of the evidence supporting these claims comes from experiments with preschool children who are highly experienced in lexical acquisition, with several years of word learning behind them. Thus, it appears that ontological constraints on word learning (or more appropriately, biases to assume words refer to single ontological categories, and preferably to object categories) seems to derive from experience with the language, rather than being a built-in guide to lexical acquisition.

Sampson (1980) raised a point that is relevant to the ontological constraints proposal as well as to the semantic feature proposal: "One might ask how a child can know a banana when he sees one . . . The answer is that he cannot, and nor can anyone else; we *guess* that what we see is a banana, and sometimes our guess is refuted by subsequent experience" (p. 40). The point that Sampson emphasized and that is crucial to the developmental story outlined here is that semantics is not and cannot be deterministic in the way proposed by what he terms the "limited mind" view (that is, that our knowledge, including our linguistic knowledge, is innately determined). As Sampson pointed out, children as well as adults guess at the meanings of novel words, using whatever inferential grounds may be available at the moment based on prior knowledge of both the language and the world.

Moreover, despite its hoary history (Augustine, 397/1950), the picture of child word learning painted by Quine (1960) and by Markman and Hutchinson (1984), with the adult pointing to an object and uttering its name, presenting the child with the task of discovering the word's reference, is the reverse of the usual actual situation. As outlined in the previous section, after an initial period of unstable and indeterminate word learning

---

[6]See Putnam (1988) on the problem of delimiting the notion of "object" for discussion of the basic difficulty with this claim.

during the first half of the second year of age, children tend to take over the game and themselves point and ask "What's that?" Thus the child is not in the situation of guessing the referent; the child knows the referent but not its name. In this situation there is no need for constraints on the child's hypotheses about the meaning of a word.

Clark (1983, 1987) has proposed a theory of lexical contrast, positing the constraint notions that all lexical items contrast (that is, there are no true synonyms), and that there are conventional ways of expressing concepts. The notion of contrast has received substantial support in the literature, although, as with ontological constraints, most studies have found that children's tendency to follow a contrastive principle emerges with development rather than being the basis on which a lexicon is founded at the outset. (See Gathercole, 1987 for critical review, and Clark, 1988 for a defense of the claims; see also, Merriman & Bowman, 1989.) The consensus view seems to be that, however important the principles of convention and contrast may be in the structure of an ideal lexicon, they are too weak in themselves to support a general theory of the development of word meaning. Moreover, having abandoned the theory of semantic features, Clark has not been clear as to how word meanings are constituted, that is, what it is that contrasts in meaning if it is not features.[7]

There are stronger arguments to be raised against the notion of a contrast constraint as well. The general argument that Sampson (1980) presented, that there can be no "rigorous, scientific account of the semantics of a human language" (p. 46), is based on the view that word meanings are not determinate, and that they change as social and cultural understandings change. For example, Labov's (1973) research indicated that adults will shift their acceptance of a term such as *cup* in reference to a particular instance, depending on a variety of properties, including width, height, the presence of handles, and the function of the object (holding coffee or flowers). These findings suggest that the attempt to specify the lexical entry for CUP in terms of a set of invariant features is misguided. Rather, they indicate that acceptance of a word reflects "the state of mind of an individual English-speaker at a particular point in his biography . . . and . . . could not count as a scientific prediction—this is just the kind of issue on which a thinker is liable to change his mind at any time . . ." (Sampson, 1980, pp. 46–47). The point in relation to the notion of contrasts is that the term *cup* may be held to contrast with *bowl* in specifying an object with one handle, rather than two or none, as well as along the dimensions of height and width, and in its

---

[7]The contrast constraint seems to be a constraint on the process of constructing a lexicon, rather than on its structure. Clark (1983) has argued strongly that meanings cannot be identified with concepts. Thus, it remains unclear as to how word meanings are constituted in her view.

use, but not in its general shape or material; but a particular object may confound these contrasts: It may be handleless, the general size, shape and material of a prototypical cup, and filled with hot liquid (tea or soup). Is the ambiguous object a cup or a bowl? English speakers may differ among themselves and within themselves over time, indicating that the terms *cup* and *bowl* do not contrast decisively as the theory claims.

Moreover, as Sampson (1980) argued:

> . . . even in the case of technical words such as *atom,* though society arranges things in such a way that they receive standard definitions to which a considerable measure of authority is ascribed . . . nevertheless there is a limit to the influence of that authority. Were there not, it would have been impossible for scientists ever to have discovered that atoms are composed of particles, since at one time . . . the stipulative definition of *atom* implied that atoms have no parts. Had the meaning of the word *atom* been determined by the stipulative definition, the discovery that things previously called "atoms" were composite would have led people to cease applying the word *atom* to them; what happened instead was that the word remained attached to the same things, and the new knowledge about those things changed the meaning of the word. (p. 47; Putnam, 1988, made a similar argument.)

Here the point in relation to contrasts is that, whereas once the essential contrast of the term *atom* was with all terms denoting entities that are composed of parts, it now does not contrast along that dimension at all.

Specific innate constraints on word learning then are difficult to defend for the reasons just summarized. Three additional considerations I believe to be particularly important to the development of word meanings follow:

1. Constraints are in the eye of the observer, not in the mind of the child. The discussion of formal constraints by Fischer and Bullock (1981) is highly relevant to the issues raised here. They define formal constraints as special patterns of data: "Of the many formally possible developmental outcomes, only a small set are ever actualized" (p. 6) They go on to note:

> . . . one might be tempted to treat them [formal constraints] as restrictions on the operation of the human cognitive system. We believe that in this regard, the word *constraint* may be misleading. It suggests restricting the natural inclination of something, as when ill-designed clothing constrains movement. In many instances when the data are formally constrained, however, there is no sense in which *some part of the cognitive system acts to restrict the natural inclination of another part.* The constraint in such instances exists primarily in the eyes of beholders *who have learned the skill of symbolically generating all formally possible combinations.* For these cases, the theorist's task is not to

explain how the system eliminates possibilities but how it *actualizes* (only some) possibilities. There is a difference. (pp. 6–7, emphases added)

2. A second point may be raised against the claim that children must be constrained from entertaining wild hypotheses. What counts as a wild hypothesis? As the discussion in the previous section indicated, children first learning language take words to mean actions, objects, objects and actions, parts of objects, whole situations, and a number of other allegedly "unacceptable" meanings (Dromi, 1987; Nelson, 1988a). If constraints were to be useful, they should operate during the initial period of word learning when there are no other linguistic clues to word classes (e.g., syntactic markers), but as we have seen, they do not. The notion of innate constraints may be contrasted with the notion of innate preparedness. Children appear to be prepared to learn words in reference to the world that they experience, but they do not appear to be constrained to apply them exclusively to any particular aspect or combination of aspects of that experience. They do, however, appear to be prepared to learn which aspects of experience words typically denote, as I argued earlier.

3. There are reasons on aesthetic and metaphysical grounds for preferring the notion of preparation to the notion of constraint, as discussed by Sampson (1980) in terms of the limited mind versus the creative mind views. In the limited mind view (which Sampson attributed to Chomsky and Fodor among others), the basic substance for all human knowledge is given innately in the mind. Generally this view is put forward in contrast to a radical empiricist view. For example, Chomsky claimed (as quoted in Sampson, 1980): "If we were plastic organisms without extensive pre-programming, the state that our mind achieves would . . . be a reflection of the environment, which means that it would be extraordinarily impoverished" (p. 18). But one does not need to accept as an alternative that all human knowledge is derived from the environment. Rather, one may hold that the human mind is designed to creatively construct knowledge: new previously unknown concepts, for example, the idea of a jet engine, or of a "talking cure" for neurosis. If one believes that the invention or creation of truly novel ideas is humanly possible (and it is hard for me to see how one could reject that belief), it seems reasonable further to believe that *all* human minds are equipped to be creatively constructive. Thus they may be prepared to encounter and make sense of the world, inventing the language as they go along, so to speak. This will seem to many at the present time to be a radical claim, and indeed it is beyond the pale of current linguistic theorizing. But I believe it is an important and fruitful avenue to pursue.[8]

---

[8]See Lock (1980) for detailed discussion of such an alternative.

I do not expect that this brief summary of arguments against innate constraints will be persuasive to readers inclined toward these views. For further discussion of these points, see Nelson (1988a) on developmental issues, Sampson (1980) on linguistic issues, Shannon (1988) on cognitive issues, and Putnam (1988) on philosophical issues.

Social Determinism

A standard alternative answer to the question of how language gets into the child's mind is through learning or enculturation. The extreme form of this view was of course (and still is) the stance of behaviorists, with B. F. Skinner as a foremost exponent. A more moderate transactionist view, that language and other cultural knowledge are acquired through transactions with the social environment, can be found in theories of semiotic mediation. This position bears little resemblance to the simplified instrumental conditioning position of behaviorism. Rather, it suggests a kind of taking over of the child's mind by the language of the community. How children come to understand and to own — that is, to internalize — the meanings of the groups of which they are a part were critical questions for developmentalists such as G. H. Mead, Heinz Werner, and the Russian psychologist Lev Vygotsky in the first half of the 20th century. During the same time period, the work of Pierce, Boas, Sapir, and Benjamin Lee Whorf implied that the system of meanings embedded in a language would in time absorb thought. Where Piaget saw the growth of universal logical structures as the central thrust of development, these semiotically inclined theorists viewed human development in terms of induction into different modes of thinking, modes that varied across languages, cultures, and historical epochs. This general view currently is being revived along lines suggested by Vygotsky (1962; see Bruner, 1983; Wertsch, 1985), but it has had relatively little impact as yet as a serious theory of semantic development. Although social influences are critical to a full theory of meaning acquisition (Nelson, 1985), at the present time these views are not worked out in detail, and therefore I do not discuss them further here.[9] Rather, I suggest how these ideas may be combined with a cognitive constructive perspective.

LEXICAL DEVELOPMENT IN A SOCIAL-COGNITIVE PERSPECTIVE

The perspective that I have adopted is based on the proposal that in ontogenetic development representation of knowledge of the world is in the

---

[9]See Adams and Bullock (1986) for suggestive research and discussion of the potential contribution of the Vygotskian position.

first instance primarily in terms of important events and that more static and abstract knowledge is derived from the resulting dynamic and interactive event knowledge base (Nelson, 1983, 1985, 1986; Nelson & Gruendel, 1981; Nelson & Lucariello, 1985). For the prelinguistic infant, experience is represented in terms of event schemas, conceptual wholes that incorporate the actors, actions, and objects that can be expected on any given occasion of that event. This proposal has important consequences. It explains the child's entry into the word-learning situation disposed to learn words that are embedded in significant events (e.g., games, bathing, feeding). But, because events are conceptual wholes, their constituent parts — objects — are not at first salient referents for the words being learned. Rather, the words may be used in association with the event as a whole or any of its parts, whether object, action, or person (see Barrett, 1986, and Dromi, 1987 for relevant data, discussed earlier).[10]

Some important characteristics of event representations in contrast with object concepts may be noted. Events are situated in a social context, as well as within a temporally and spatially particular situation. When the focus is upon objects qua objects, it is possible to conceive of the object world in static, even abstract, terms. But when the emphasis is upon events, this is not possible. Moreover, when the focus is upon objects they can be conceived of as physical entities independent of all social and cultural meanings. Events, however, are always socially and culturally meaningful.

In this view, objects take on meaning for the child because of their place in significant events. Object concepts then may be considered derivative of or secondary to event schemas. But this is true only in the sense that objects are represented in terms of the events in which they play a part. Thus, balls are those things that can be rolled and bounced; bottles are those things that hold milk or juice and come after a meal or before sleep. The event defines the function of the object for the child. Thus, the concept of the object is formed around its functions in an event or events. To the extent that this is true, object concepts will be at first embedded in event representations. Thus, when the child first begins to use words to refer to particular objects she will use them in familiar events or to refer to the object in a particular event (Barrett, 1986; Dromi, 1987). Whereas children in our society tend to learn many names of objects when they first begin to talk, the object words that they learn tend to be for those things that have importance to the child because they function in particular ways in the child's life.

In brief, the claim I am making here is that when the child begins to

---

[10]It is important that the hypothesis of the primacy of event representations was formulated on the basis of observations of older children's and adults' event knowledge, not on the basis of the data from first-word learning. Thus, the fact that the data support the hypothesis is independent of its genesis.

acquire words, these are first mapped directly onto preexisting experientially derived representations of the child's world, and that in those representations events are primary. Thus, words learned to refer to objects take on meanings derived from those events. Concepts of object categories are formed on the basis of the roles that the objects play in the event. Beyond this point, learning words to refer to objects gives the objects themselves an importance independent of their place in familiar events, and this is reflected in the phenomenon of the naming explosion discussed earlier. Lexical knowledge is at first mapped directly onto the experientially derived (event-based) representational system. This must change over the course of time if the child is to achieve a mature understanding of the semantics of the conventional language.

Some of the developments during the preschool years that provide evidence for the changing relation between the child's conceptual representations and the emerging conventional semantic system were noted previously. Among these is the problem of constructing semantic hierarchies, which I consider here in more detail in conjunction with its relation to the type of event-based conceptual structure that I have just sketched.

Children's growing understanding of taxonomic relations has been intensively studied over the years. The conventional wisdom (based largely on Piaget's work) has been that young children are deficient in regard to taxonomic knowledge, because they lack the logical basis for comprehending class relations, that is, knowledge of class inclusion. But it is important to note that semantic hierarchies are linguistically and culturally specific, defined in the language and not in universals of the physical world nor in universals of the human mind. Although there may be innate predispositions to respect ontological distinctions such as animate and inanimate, the variety of possible higher order categories (i.e., category terms that dominate other terms) is far too diverse and culturally specific to be based on universal kinds (see Lakoff, 1987; see also Barsalou, 1983, on ad hoc categories). Taxonomic hierarchies are only one type of conceptual/semantic relations. Thus mastering taxonomic relations must be understood as a semantic problem. The perspective of event knowledge provides a link between the conceptual and the semantic representation of taxonomic relations.

As already indicated, young children have well-organized knowledge of familiar well-structured events, such as the "having lunch" event. Thus they can be said to have an *event category* of eating lunch, a category whose *extension* includes all the successive occasions of lunch, and whose *intension* includes the specification of necessary components—actions, objects, and persons within a particular spatial and temporal goal-oriented configuration. Some common object categories can be seen to be related to event categories in an interesting way, as *slot-filler categories,* that is, categories of items that can fill a particular object slot in a particular type of event, for example, foods that can be eaten at lunch. The lunch schema includes the action of eating, and that action takes specified foods as its complements. Not just any foods will fill the lunch food slot, however, but only certain types of foods that generally are offered for lunch; in common child cases, for example, peanut butter or cheese sandwiches. Foods that can fill a particular slot in a particular event type form a category based on the fact that they are functional alternatives to one another, a relation of substitutability. Prior to understanding that different foods can be alternatives within the particular event type of lunch one must have constructed the event type itself. Thus the category of foods eaten at lunch is dependent on the category of lunch events.

This conception of slot-filler categories contrasts with the notion of food as an abstract superordinate concept whose intension is roughly "anything that can be eaten" and whose extension is all possible foods. This is an abstract notion of a functionally based and context-free, higher order category. It generally has been assumed that when the young child gives evidence of knowing terms such as *food* and using them in relation to terms such as *apple, meat, cereal,* and so on, that the child has a concept of food that is the equivalent of the adult's, namely that it is functionally based, context-free, and reflects class-inclusion relations such as asymmetry and transitivity. However, evidence indicates that young children do not work with such abstract context-free concepts, even when they have the terms. Our research has shown that their first understanding of superordinates such as *food* and *clothes* is in relation to experientially based slot-filler categories (Kyratzis, Lucariello, & Nelson, 1989; Lucariello & Nelson, 1985; see Nelson, 1988b for an overview). Such categories are functionally based, in that they are formed as alternative possible complements of an action in an event, but they are not context-free, in that the items that can occur in one event type are not the same as those that can occur in another.

The claim here is that categories like *food, clothes,* and *animals* are semantic, defined in the language, in terms of the lexical items that they dominate. They do not exist in the world waiting to be discovered, but rather are constituted by the language community. The child, however, is exposed to the use of these terms in situations where they are applicable to the child's own experientially based slot-filler conceptual categories. These categories provide a hook, a way into the more abstract, context-free semantic relation represented in the conventional adult language. They provide a way of bootstrapping to a higher level of abstraction, a level where relations are represented semantically, and not in terms of direct experience. And the most advantageous way for the child to reach this level is to experience the language being used by others in situations where his or her own proto-categories are the topic of discussion, for example, in situations where an adult says "Let's put on your *clothes*" or "eat your *food*."[11]

Parallels Between Syntactic and Semantic Development.   This analysis has been confined to issues of lexical meaning and their relation to the child's conceptualizations. However, there are evident parallels between the formation of lexical categories (for the denotation of single words, and for categories of words that enter into semantic hierarchies) and the formation of grammatical categories such as noun and verb, or grammatical roles such as subject and object, or argument roles such as agent and patient. In particular, the principles of similarity of function and of substitutability within a frame may be applicable to the construction of grammatical categories.

The parallel between the type of conceptual representation and development proposed here and the structure of linguistic categories can be made explicit in the analysis of paradigmatic and syntagmatic relations (Nelson, 1982). De Saussure (1915/1959) identified these interdependent relations as basic to linguistic structures at all levels. Syntagmatic relations hold between unlike elements in a linear configuration, for example, between /b/, /a/, and /t/ in the word *bat,* or between *girl,* and *sings* in the sentence "The girl sings." Paradigmatic relations hold between elements that share similar positions in syntagmatic frames, for example, /b/ and /p/ in the words *bat* and *pat,* or *girl* and *boy* in the sentences "The girl sings" and "The boy dances." As de Saussure pointed out originally, syntagmatic relations are apparent in presentations in the real world, in what is now referred to as the surface structure of sentences. But paradigmatic relations, he noted, are not apparent in the world, but are products of the human mind, abstractions from experienced structures.

The syntagmatic-paradigmatic relation plays an analogous role in the analysis of event structures. Event representations are linear, based on syntagmatic relations between unlike elements (e.g., particular actors, actions, and objects). Paradigmatic relations are formed between those elements of events that share similar positions in a syntagmatic frame, for example, the slot-filler categories. Analogously, general categories of agents, actions, objects of action, beneficiaries, and so on also might be formed on this principle. Consistent with de Saussure's claim, such paradigmatic categories are mental abstractions based on the analysis of previously represented, experientially based event structures. But as with slot-filler categories, the general categories formed might be more contex-

---

[11]This is not to deny that there may be more direct teaching of superordinate category labels and category membership, as studies by Watson (1985, 1987) and Adams and Bullock (1986) have shown.

tually restricted than such terms as *agent* suggest. (See Braine, 1976, for evidence of children's initially restricted categories.) Smaller categories then might be combined on the grounds that they may both be substituted for by the same terms, for example *that* and *it*.[12]

The claim that categories are derived from cognitive analysis of event representations requires the assumptions that: (a) Children form general representations of recurrent events that include specifications of items that can fill slots, and (b) there exist cognitive operations of analysis and integration that provide the mechanisms for abstracting elements from such representations to form categories based on substitutability within a frame. Evidence to support these assumptions is presented in Kyratzis et al. (1989), Lucariello and Nelson (1985), and Nelson (1986, 1988b).

Given that the mechanisms for forming abstract paradigmatic categories from syntagmatic representations exist, it seems not unreasonable that abstract paradigmatic grammatical categories might be formed in the same way. In fact, Maratsos (1982) and Braine (1987) presented models of grammatical category formation that rely on similar principles. Based on Maratsos's (1988) survey of linguistic categories in natural human languages, from which he concluded that only a predicate-argument structure is universal, it does not seem unreasonable to suggest that, although the child is prepared biologically to construct grammatical categories from the evidence available in the language to be acquired, such categories are not built-in universals. Rather, such categories are likely to be formed by utilizing basic human conceptual capacities.

Developmental parallels between lexical and grammatical development also may be noted. As pointed out earlier, the first two-word grammatical constructions tend to appear soon after the naming explosion in the latter half of the second year of age. The naming explosion was attributed to the child's insight that words denote concepts, and thus words can be learned for all concepts already available. Also, because concepts are embedded in and derived from the event structures that form the conceptual representations, combinations of concepts are already available in that base, that is, as constituents of event representations. Thus, word combinations can be constructed from the event representation model. This conceptual basis for early grammatical constructions is easily reconciled with the kind of conceptual category foundation already postulated.

Beyond this, of course, the particular grammatical structures of the language to be learned must be acquired. In principle, this grammatical phase also parallels the formation of semantic structures subsequent to the

---

[12]Evidence related to this suggestion is found in an analysis by Levy (1989) showing that acquisition of the phrases "do it (that)" was generalized over time from coreference to specific verbs to generalized coreference to an extended activity.

acquisition of lexical-concept bonds as described earlier. That is, both the grammar and the lexicon can be seen as moving from a phase closely connected to the underlying conceptual base to a phase in which complex specifically linguistic structures reorganize the system.

CONCLUSION

The picture I have been presenting is very much a creative mind view, to use Sampson's (1980) phrase, or a cognitive constructivist view, to use a more familiar formula. But such a view by no means denies the importance of a biological basis for language development. Rather, it requires that this basis be formulated in terms that are consistent with what we know about phylogenetic as well as ontogenetic development. No one denies that our close primate relatives do not speak or use a humanlike language: We can find no close evolutionary models for our linguistic abilities. But it seems important to recognize that apes do solve problems and can be taught to use symbols communicatively. The chimps' cognitive wherewithal for symbol usage (see, e.g., chapter 9 of this volume) must have existed prior to the human effort to bring them into the symbol-using community, and it seems likely that that wherewithal includes an ability to represent events and categorize objects, just as it does for human children. It seems probable, however, that the more complex human brain is equipped to form more abstract (e.g., paradigmatic) categories and to construct more abstract rules for the use of those categories. The difference between apes and humans might be the kind of quantitative difference that results in a qualitative leap. But this difference need not be specifically linguistic. Certainly language makes it possible to engage in abstract thought, but at the same time acquiring language itself rests on the ability to engage in abstractions. Greater cognitive capacity, specific perceptual and productive mechanisms, brain centers designed to process speech: These all can be taken as biological preparations for language. More specifically, the ability to represent events, to categorize objects, to reflectively analyze the representations and integrate the information, and to organize those integrations into systems seem necessary cognitive preparations not only for the language-learning task, but also for the acquisition of knowledge of complex cultural systems of all kinds. Jackendoff (1983) proposed a set of innate conceptual/semantic categories that seems consistent with the present proposal.

There also may be specific linguistic preparations for language learning, although to my thinking these are likely to be less complex and extensive than those posited by linguistic nativists. For example, it seems most probable that there is a predisposition to acquire words, or speech chunks, within a social context where others are communicating to each other and to the child with such sounds. Such a predisposition would not, however, dictate that any particular ontological category be given preference over any other as the referent of a speech sound pattern. Indeed, present evidence suggests that reference is not an innate but a constructed relation, the result of experience with word use during the early period of word learning. Reference is, after all, only one function of words, others including instrumental, expressive, conative, phatic, and poetic (see Bruner, 1975; Jakobson, 1960). There also may well be predispositions for forming grammatical rules for combining category elements (e.g., Slobin, 1973, 1985). What I and other cognitive constructivists are inclined to deny is that there are specific built-in symbols or rules, much less whole grammars, that dictate how a language should be constructed.

In summary, I conclude by claiming that there is no evidence for, and no evident need for, any innate specifically linguistic capacity in the formation of a semantic component of the language, but rather that this component emerges from general cognitive processes. I suggest further that the same may be true of grammar in general; that grammatical capacities may be constructed out of general conceptual capacities for representing and analyzing categories and conceptual relations. To return to an earlier theme: The species may not need to be constrained by an innate grammar any more than by an innate lexicon. Rather, the species may be prepared in a variety of ways — neurologically and cognitively — to construct a grammar and a lexicon on the basis of the representations of experiences with language in use. We gain a new perspective when we turn the nativists familiar dictum — "Human minds must be such that language can be learned by them" — to the inverse: "Languages must be such that human minds can learn them." In this formula the constraints are on languages, not minds, which seems to be a defensible interpretation that deserves further investigation.

REFERENCES

Adams, A. K., & Bullock, D. (1986). Apprenticeship in word uses: Social convergence processes in learning categorically related nouns. In S. A. Kuczaj II & M. D. Barrett (Eds.), *The development of word meaning: Progress in cognitive development research* (pp. 155–197). New York: Springer-Verlag.

Augustine, St. (1950). *The confessions of St. Augustine,* (E. B. Pusey, Trans.). New York: Dutton. (Original work published 397).

Barrett, M. D. (1986). Early semantic representations and early word-usage. In S. A. Kuczaj II & M. D. Barret (Eds.), *The development of word meaning: Progress in cognitive development research* (pp. 39–68). New York: Springer-Verlag.

Barrett, M. D., Harris, M., Jones, D., & Brookes, S. (1986, September). *The first words of the infant: Their characteristics and their relationship to maternal speech.* Paper presented at the British Psychological Society Developmental Section Annual Conference, Exeter, England.

Barsalou, L. W. (1983). Ad hoc categories. *Memory and Cognition, 12,* 211–227.

Bates, E., Benigni, L., Bretherton, I., Camaioni, L., & Volterra, V. (1979). *The emergence of symbols: Cognition and communication in infancy.* New York: Academic.

Benedict, H. (1979). Early lexical development: Comprehension and production. *Journal of Child Language, 6,* 183–200.

Bierwisch, N. (1970). Semantics. In J. Lyons (Ed.), *New horizons in linguistics* (pp. 166–184). Baltimore: Penguin.

Bloom, L. (1973). *One word at a time: The use of single word utterances before syntax.* The Hague, Netherlands: Mouton.

Bowerman, M. (1976). Semantic factors in the acquisition of rules for word use and sentence construction. In D. M. Morehead & A. E. Morehead (Eds.), *Normal and deficient child language* (pp. 99–180). Baltimore: University Park Press.

Bowerman, M. (1982). Reorganization processes in lexical and syntactic development. In E. Wanner & L. R. Gleitman (Eds.), *Language acquisition: The state of the art* (pp. 319–346). New York: Cambridge University Press.

Braine, M. D. S. (1976). Children's first word combinations. *Monographs of the Society for Research in Child Development, 41* (Serial No. 164).

Braine, M. D. S. (1987). What is learned in acquiring word classes—A step toward an acquisition theory. In B. MacWhinney (Ed.), *Mechanisms of language acquisition* (pp. 65–88). Hillsdale, NJ: Lawrence Erlbaum Associates.

Braunwald, S. R. (1978). Context, word and meaning: Towards a communicational analysis of lexical acquisition. In A. Lock (Ed.), *Action, gesture and symbol: The emergence of language* (pp. 485–528). London: Academic.

Bruner, J. S. (1975). The ontogenesis of speech acts. *Journal of Child Language, 2,* 1–19.

Bruner, J. S. (1983). *Child's talk.* New York: Norton.

Carey, S. (1982). Semantic development: The state of the art. In E. Wanner & L. R. Gleitman (Eds.), *Language acquisition: The state of the art.* (pp. 347–389). New York: Cambridge University Press.

Carey, S. (1983). Constraints on the meanings of natural kind terms. In Th. B. Seiler & W. Wannenmacher (Eds.), *Concept development and the development of word meaning* (pp. 126–143). New York: Springer-Verlag.

Carey, S., & Bartlett, E. (1978). Acquiring a single new word. *Papers and reports on child language development* (No. 15, pp. 17–29). Stanford, CA: Stanford University, Department of Linguistics.

Chomsky, N. (1965). *Aspects of a theory of syntax.* Cambridge, MA: MIT Press.

Clark, E. V. (1973). What's in a word? On the child's acquisition of semantics in his first language. In T. E. Moore (Ed.), *Cognitive development and the acquisition of language* (pp. 65–110). New York: Academic.

Clark, E. V. (1983). Meanings and concepts. In J. H. Flavell & E. Markman (Eds.), *Cognitive development.* In P. Mussen (Ed.), *Manual of child psychology* (4th ed., Vol. 3, pp. 787–840). New York: Wiley.

Clark, E. V. (1987). The principle of contrast: A constraint on language acquisition. In B. MacWhinney (Ed.), *Mechanisms of language acquisition* (pp. 1–34). Hillsdale, NJ: Lawrence Erlbaum Associates.

Clark, E. V. (1988). On the logic of contrast. *Journal of Child Language, 15,* 317–336.

de Saussure, F. (1959). *Course in general linguistics.* New York: Philosophical Library. (Original work published 1915)

Dore, J., Franklin, M. B., Miller, R. T., & Ramer, A. L. H. (1976). Transitional phenomena in early language acquisition. *Journal of Child Language, 3,* 13–28.

Dromi, E. (1987). *Early lexical development*. Cambridge, England: Cambridge University Press.

Ehrlich, S. (1979). Semantic memory: A free-elements system. In C. R. Puff (Ed.), *Memory organization and structure* (pp. 195–218). New York: Academic.

Fischer, K. W., & Bullock, D. (1981). Patterns of data: Sequence, synchrony, and constraint in cognitive development. In K. W. Fischer (Ed.), *Cognitive development* (pp. 1–19). San Francisco: Jossey-Bass.

Fodor, J. A. (1975). *The language of thought*. New York: Crowell.

Fodor, J. A. (1981). *Re-presentations*. Cambridge, MA: MIT Press.

French, L., & Nelson, K. (1985). *Young children's knowledge of relational terms: Some ifs, ors and buts*. New York: Springer-Verlag.

Gathercole, V. C. (1987). The contrastive hypothesis for the acquisition of word meaning: A reconsideration of the theory. *Journal of Child Language, 14,* 493–532.

Gelman, S. A., & Markman, E. M. (1986). Categories and induction in young children. *Cognition, 23,* 183–209.

Gerard, A. B., & Mandler, J. M. (1983). Ontological knowledge and sentence anomaly. *Journal of Verbal Learning and Verbal Behavior, 21,* 507–523.

Goodman, N. (1955). *Fact, fiction, and forecast*. Cambridge, MA: Harvard University Press.

Gopnick, A., & Meltzoff, A. N. (1986). Words, plans, things, and locations: Interactions between semantic and cognitive development in the one-word stage. In S. A. Kuczaj II & M. D. Barrett (Eds.), *The development of word meaning: Progress in cognitive development research* (pp. 199–224). New York: Springer-Verlag.

Greenfield, P. M., & Smith, J. H. (1976). *The structure of communication in early language development*. New York: Academic.

Huttenlocher, J., & Smiley, P. (1987). Early word meanings: The case of object names. *Cognitive Psychology, 19,* 63–89.

Jackendoff, R. (1983). *Semantics and cognition*. Cambridge, MA: MIT Press.

Jakobson, R. (1960). Linguistics and poetics. In T. A. Sebeok (Ed.), *Style in language* (pp. 350–357). Cambridge, MA: MIT Press.

Karmiloff-Smith, A. (1979). *A functional approach to child language*. Cambridge, England: Cambridge University Press.

Katz, J. J. (1972). *Semantic theory*. New York: Harper & Row.

Katz, J. J., & Fodor, J. (1963). The structure of a semantic theory. *Language, 39,* 170–210.

Keil, F. C. (1979). *Semantic and conceptual development: An ontological perspective*. Cambridge, MA: Harvard University Press.

Kuczaj, S. A. II, & Barrett, M. D. (Eds.). (1986). *The development of word meaning: Progress in cognitive development research*. New York: Springer-Verlag.

Kyratzis, A., Lucariello, J., & Nelson, K. (1989). Schemas and categories as knowledge organizers for young children. Manuscript submitted for publication, City University of New York.

Labov, W. (1973). The boundaries of words and their meanings. In C.-J. N. Bailey & R. W. Shuy (Eds.), *New ways of analyzing variation in English* (pp. 340–373). Washington, DC: Georgetown University Press.

Lakoff, G. (1987). *Women, fire and dangerous things*. Chicago: University of Chicago Press.

Levy, E. (1989). Monologue as development of the text-forming function of language. In K. Nelson (Ed.), *Narratives from the crib*. Cambridge, MA: Harvard University Press.

Lock, A. (1980). *The guided re-invention of language*. London: Academic.

Lucariello, J. (1987). Concept formation and its relation to word learning in the second year. *Journal of Child Language, 14,* 309–332.

Lucariello, J., & Nelson, K. (1985). Slot-filler categories as memory organizers for young children. *Developmental Psychology, 21,* 272–282.

Lyons, J. (1977). *Semantics* (Vol. 1). Cambridge, England: Cambridge University Press.

MacNamara, J. (1972). The cognitive basis of language learning in children. *Psychological Review, 79*, 1-13.

Maratsos, M. (1982). The child's construction of grammatical categories. In L. R. Gleitman & H. E. Wanner (Eds.), *Language acquisition: The state of the art* (pp. 240-266). Cambridge, MA: Harvard University Press.

Maratsos, M. (1988). Crosslinguistic analysis, universals, and language acquisition. In F. S. Kessel (Ed.), *The development of language and language researchers: Essays in honor of Roger Brown* (pp. 121-152). Hillsdale, NJ: Lawrence Erlbaum Associates.

Markman, E. M. (1983). Two different kinds of hierarchical organization. In E. Scholnick (Ed.), *New trends in conceptual representation: Challenges to Piaget's theory?* (pp. 165-184). Hillsdale, NJ: Lawrence Erlbaum Associates.

Markman, E. M., & Hutchinson, J. (1984). Children's sensitivity to constraints on word meaning: Taxonomic vs. thematic relations. *Cognitive Psychology, 16*, 1-27.

McShane, J. (1979). The development of naming. *Linguistics, 17*, 879-905.

Merriman, W. E. (1986). Some reasons for the occurrence and eventual correction of children's naming errors. *Child Development, 57*, 942-952.

Merriman, W. E. (1987, April). *Lexical contrast in toddlers: A reanalysis of the diary evidence.* Paper presented at the Biennial Meeting of the Society for Research in Child Development, Baltimore.

Merriman, W. E., & Bowman, L. L. (1989). The mutual exclusivity bias in children's word learning. *Monographs of the Society for Research in Child Development, (54*, 3-4, Serial No. 22).

Nelson, K. (1973). Structure and strategy in learning to talk. *Society for Research in Child Development Monographs, 38*, (1-2, Serial No. 149).

Nelson, K. (1982). The syntagmatics and paradigmatics of conceptual representation. In S. A. Kuczaj II (Ed.), *Language development: Vol. 2. Language, thought and culture* (pp. 335-364). Hillsdale, NJ: Lawrence Erlbaum Associates.

Nelson, K. (1983). The derivation of concepts and categories from event representations. In E. Scholnick (Ed.), *New trends in conceptual representation* (pp. 129-149). Hillsdale, NJ: Lawrence Erlbaum Associates.

Nelson, K. (1985). *Making sense: The acquisition of shared meaning.* New York: Academic.

Nelson, K. (1986). *Event knowledge: Structure and function in development.* Hillsdale, NJ: Lawrence Erlbaum Associates.

Nelson, K. (1988a). Constraints on word learning? *Cognitive Development, 3*, 221-246.

Nelson, K. (1988b). Where do taxonomic categories come from? *Human Development 31*, 3-10.

Nelson, K., & Gruendel, J. (1981). Generalized event representations: Basic building blocks of cognitive development. In M. Lamb & A. Brown (Eds.), *Advances in developmental psychology* (Vol. 1, pp. 131-149). Hillsdale, NJ: Lawrence Erlbaum Associates.

Nelson, K., & Lucariello, J. (1985). The development of meaning in first words. In M. Barrett (Ed.), *Children's single word speech* (pp. 59-86). Chichester, England: Wiley.

Nelson, K., Rescorla, L., Gruendel, J., & Benedict, H. (1978). Early lexicons: What do they mean? *Child Development, 49*, 960-968.

Pinker, S. (1984). *Language learnability and language development.* Cambridge, MA: Harvard University Press.

Putnam, H. (1975). The meaning of meaning. In *H. Putnam, Philosophical Papers: Vol. 2. Mind, language and reality* (pp. 215-271). Cambridge England: Cambridge University Press.

Putnam, H. (1988). *Representation and reality.* Cambridge, MA: MIT Press.

Quine, W. V. O. (1960). *Word and object.* Cambridge, MA: MIT Press.

Rescorla, L. A. (1980). Overextension in early language development. *Journal of Child Language, 7*, 321-335.

Sampson, G. (1980). *Making sense*. Oxford, England. Oxford University Press.

Schwartz, S. P. (1977). *Naming, necessity and natural kinds*. Ithaca, NY: Cornell University Press.

Seidenberg, M. S., & Pettito, L. A. (1987). Communication, symbolic communication, and language: Comment on Savage-Rumbaugh, McDonald, Sevcik, Hopkins, and Rupert (1986). *Journal of Experimental Psychology: General, 116*, 279–287.

Shannon, B. (1988). Semantic representation of meaning: A critique. *Psychological Bulletin, 104*, 70–83.

Slobin, D. I. (1973). Cognitive prerequisites for the development of grammar. In C. A. Ferguson & D. I. Slobin (Eds.), *Studies of child language development* (pp. 175–208). New York: Holt, Rinehart & Winston.

Slobin, D. I. (1985). Cross-linguistic evidence for the language-making capacity. In D. I. Slobin (Ed.), *The cross-linguistic study of language acquisition* (Vol. 2, pp. 1157–1249). Hillsdale, NJ: Lawrence Erlbaum Associates.

Taylor, M., & Gelman, S. A. (1988). Adjectives and nouns: Children's strategies for learning new words. *Child Development, 59*, 411–419.

Vygotsky, L. S. (1962). *Thought and language*. Cambridge, MA: MIT Press.

Watson, R. (1985). Towards a theory of definition. *Journal of Child Language, 12*, 181–197.

Watson, R. (1987, April). *Features of discourse and the development of categorical organization*. Paper presented at the Biennial Meeting of the Society for Research in Child Development, Baltimore.

Waxman, S. R., & Gelman, R. (1986). Pre-schoolers' use of superordinate relations in classification and language. *Cognitive Development, 1*, 139–156.

Wertsch, J. V. (1985). *Culture, communication, and cognition: Vygotskian perspectives*. Cambridge, England: Cambridge University Press.

Wexler, K., & Culicover, P. (1980). *Formal principles of language acquisition*. Cambridge, MA: MIT Press.

5 Representation and Expression

Lois Bloom
Teachers College, Columbia University

The present-day cognitivist perspective in psychology was born with Miller, Galanter, and Pribram's (1960) now classic response to behaviorism: *Plans and the Structure of Human Behavior.* The problem addressed in that book was the task of describing "how actions are controlled by an organism's internal representation of its universe" such that "cognitive representation" is mapped into "the appropriate *pattern* of activity" (pp. 12–13, italics in original). Two aspects of cognitive representation were invoked by Miller et al. One was a mental plan for acting. The other was the individual's knowledge base. In short, what determines how we act is what we know and how we make use of what we know in a plan for acting.

Acts of expression and interpretation require underlying plans just as other acts that we do. The plans we use for expressing and interpreting include procedures for language and the representations "that we set up as we talk or listen and that we structure with elements, roles, strategies, and relations" (Fauconnier, 1985, p. 1). These representations are "mental spaces" (to use Fauconnier's term) set up in the part of the mind that traditionally has been called *working memory* or *consciousness*. They are the mental contents that individuals express when they talk and that they construct when they interpret the speech of others. The purpose of this chapter is to show how attending to the representations in these mental spaces, and the developments that contribute to them, can help to explain how language is acquired.

COGNITIVE DEVELOPMENT AND CHILD LANGUAGE

The cognitivist perspective in child language research has, by and large, had two thrusts. One is the focus on the child's knowledge base and one or another version of the traditional child language "mapping problem": How children attach the forms of language to what they know about objects, events, and relations in the world (e.g., Bloom, 1970, 1973; R. Brown, 1956, 1958; Gopnik & Meltzoff, 1986; Mervis, 1984; Nelson, 1974, 1985; and many others). The importance for language of object concepts and knowledge of events is, by now, self-evident. Most simply, children learn to talk about what they know something about. The second cognitive focus in child language research concerns how children acquire the processes of thought that make possible the acquisition of concepts and event knowledge (e.g., Bates, 1976; Bloom, 1973; Bloom, Lifter, & Broughton, 1985; Brown, 1973; Gopnik & Meltzoff, 1984; McCune-Nicholich, 1981; Tomasello & Farrar, 1984; and others). These processes of thought include development of such Piagetian constructs as object permanence, means-end relations, and, perhaps most ubiquitously, the symbolic capacity.

Each of these cognitive perspectives in child language research—one with a focus on the acquisition of knowledge, and the other with a focus on development of the thought processes for acquiring knowledge—has contributed to understanding changes in the child's ways of knowing about the world. The result is that we now have some idea of how these cognitive developments contribute to the acquisition of words and the structures of language. The notion of representation has been central in these views of the mind of the child. In fact, *representation,* is one of our most overused words because we have meant many different things in using the term. For example, we talk of the experience of objects and events in the world represented in memory as schemas, concepts, and event knowledge. Language is represented in the mind symbolically, and language represents aspects of objects and events in the world in messages.

The object of representation that I emphasize in this chapter is none of the above. It is, nevertheless, implicit in virtually all models of language acquisition although it is rarely made explicit or taken as the object of inquiry.[1] Language is a vehicle for representation. But what is represented in language is less concerned with objects and events in the external world than with the elements and relations between them that we set up in consciousness. Consciousness is that aspect of mind that intervenes between events in the world and the knowledge we have stored in memory.[2]

---

[1]For exceptions, see Campbell (1986); Gopnik (1982); Hamburger and Crain (1987).

[2]I do not mean consciousness in the metacognitive sense of "to be conscious of" or "knowing that we know."

Representations in consciousness are the products of attention and ordinary thinking (Miller, 1962) or the experiences produced by the "computational mind" (Jackendoff, 1987). Percepts and aspects of knowledge come together in consciousness to connect with words, sentences, and discourse. The mental elements, with their roles and relations that we set up, are directed at objects in the world but they are internal to the individual. They require language to make them external and known to other persons. Thus, the sense of representation emphasized here has to do with the momentary contents of mind that underlie our acts of expression and interpretation. The "thinking" required for language consists of these representations that a child is able to set up for interpretation and expression, and is the critical aspect of thinking required for the process of language acquisition (Bloom, 1974).

The theory of language development presupposed here draws on psychological theory concerned with attention and the contents of awareness and philosophical theories of intentionality. In psychology, the importance of representation in infant attention has been stressed in numerous accounts of infant cognition (e.g., Mandler, 1983; Moscovitch, 1984). For example, the "quiet alert states" of the neonate and young infant are generally considered to be those moments during which the infant focuses on and attends to objects and events in the environment (e.g., J. Brown, 1964). The objects of infant attention are constructed out of data from perception and determine what the infant learns about objects and events. Measures of infant attention provide an index of such learning: For example, when an infant compares a new stimulus with a familiar stimulus and evaluates the discrepancy between them (e.g., McCall & McGhee, 1977). Similarly, what a child is able to hold in awareness guides such problem-solving tasks as the search for absent objects (e.g., Wellman & Somerville, 1982). The literature is full of descriptions of the attentional capacities of the infant and young child and their importance for cognitive development in general. The representations that are the objects of the child's attention are no less important for language development.

In philosophy, the representations underlying acts of expression and interpretation are intentional states in the sense of Brentano (1966), Danto (1973), Fodor (1979), and Searle (1983), among others. Intentional states are constructed out of what we perceive in the immediate context and what we recall from knowledge stored in memory. They are about contents recalled from the past, perceived in the present, and/or anticipated in the future. These representations are directed at some object in the world with a psychological attitude that the individual has toward them. These psychological attitudes are the beliefs, desires, and feelings directed toward what these representations are about.

In theory and research in child language, the emphasis is ordinarily on desires that are intentions to achieve a goal or to communicate. But the intention to act or intentions to communicate are what Searle (1984) has called only the "ordinary" sense of the term *intention:* "Intending to do something is just one kind of Intentionality along with believing, desiring, hoping, fearing, and so on" (p. 60). More fundamental is the fact that children acquire words and construct the grammar of a language in their efforts to express what the contents of intentional states are about. These contents of beliefs, desires, and feelings have rarely been addressed in child language theory and research. However, they are determinative for language development. They determine what children express through language, what they interpret of the language they hear, and most important, how language is learned for acts of expression and interpretation. The developments contributing to the representations in these mental spaces are the developments we need to consider in our efforts to explain language acquisition.

CONTENTS OF MIND AND LANGUAGE

First, let us consider what is required for learning linguistic units (words and syntactic structures) in the first place. At the minimum, the infant has to attend to some aspect of the context along with an acoustic signal (or visual signal, in the case of sign language). The product of this attention is, at first, a representation consisting largely if not exclusively of the data from these combined perceptions. However, elements in this perceptually based representation cue recall from memory of some aspect of related prior experience to construct another representation. The elements in these mental spaces are about objects in the world perceived in the context and recalled from memory.

Early in development, objects recalled from memory are no doubt prior experiences that are not discrepant, or are only minimally discrepant, from the original objects of perception. They are episodic. For example, a child might first hear the word *ticktock* while looking at the clock on the kitchen wall. When hearing the word *ticktock* again and seeing the clock in a playroom, the child remembers the clock on the kitchen wall. With development, the child will recall such events from memory and compare them with objects in perception that are related, but increasingly discrepant: for example, a wrist watch or a compass. The point is that the elements in any of these representations can include a word (such as *ticktock*) that is also stored in memory for future recall.

Second, let us consider what is required for understanding and saying words and sentences. When we understand what someone else says, the word or words we hear cue recall of prior knowledge to set up objects, roles, and relations between them. The resulting representation is our interpretation of what was said. To say words and sentences, some element or elements, with their roles and the relations between them, are set up in consciousness. These representations come from objects retrieved from memory using data from perception as cues. Linguistic forms are recalled from memory for expressing some aspect of this representation.

Very young children on the threshold of language depend on hearing speech about objects and events in the immediate perceptible context, just as they use speech to talk about the objects they see and act on. This is so because perceived objects and events set up representations and cue recall of prior knowledge in the absence of language. Cues from the immediate context become less and less important as children learn more of the units and structures of language. Once enough of the language is learned, words, sentences, and discourse become the cues for recalling objects and representing them in a mental space. (See Bloom, 1974, for a more explicit account of the part played by different kinds of contexts, especially the linguistic context, for expression and interpretation.)

The essence of the central claim, then, is as follows. The cognitive work that underlies acts of learning, using, and interpreting linguistic units consists of forming representations. These representations are "interconnected *mental spaces* . . . [they] are not part of the language itself, or of its grammars; they are not hidden levels of linguistic representation, but language does not come without them . . . Language, then, is not merely interpreted with respect to worlds, models, contexts, situations, and so forth. Rather, it is involved in constructions of its own. It builds up mental spaces, relations between them, and relations between elements within them" (Fauconnier, 1985, pp. 1–2). Hearing speech or seeing signs provides cues for setting up the elements in a mental space with relations between them, and for setting up relations between mental spaces, and the result is an act of interpretation. And language provides the procedures for articulating such representations for acts of expression. However, these plans or mental spaces are not themselves a part of language. In short, the plans constructed for acts of expression and interpretation are cognitive, not linguistic, representations of the content that the expression or interpretation is about.

Consider, as an example, what is happening as you read this paragraph. What the paragraph is about has nothing whatever to do with the room that you sit in, what you might be able to see out of the window, the music that might be coming from the next room, and so forth. Nevertheless, these things, especially now that the words you have just read called your attention to them, are part of what you have in mind right now, at this immediate moment in time as you read these words. Data from perception are one source of the representations that we form in awareness, and perceptual data can be more or less important for constructing representations for expression and interpretation.

However, the words and sentences on the page are your only cues for attempting to understand what this paragraph is about. Within the narrow confines of the context afforded by this printed page you are engaged in an act of construction whereby new information is assimilated to what you already know (Miller, 1979). The words and their arrangements are familiar to you, familiar enough so that they can cue recall of things stored in memory to construct what you have in mind at this precise, immediate moment. This representation of what the words are about is not a picture; that is, it is not a literal image. It is also not just the words themselves. In fact, the words and their syntactic arrangement underdetermine the representation you construct as you read. The words are only cues for accessing aspects of what you already know from prior experience for constructing a new experience in consciousness: a configuration of elements linked by the relations between them. As you continue to read, other elements and the relations between them will be added to the configuration. This act of construction is taking place as you read the words. It is taking place here, in the immediate context of your reading the words. The representation you are constructing is what you are attending to, what you have in mind now. These "here and now" contents of mind are what you understand about what is printed on this page.

Everything else you know, the record of many other experiences you have had or imagined or dreamed before this time and place is "somewhere else" in your head. Everything else you know is irrelevant to what you have in the mental space you are constructing, here and now, until you read a word, like *ducklings,* or hear the strains of a Mozart sonata, or someone suggests a drink before dinner. These new events would cue recall of other things from your knowledge base and your mental work would shift to constructing new mental spaces. But at the precise time and place you were reading the words on this page, the mental configuration you were constructing was your interpretation of the paragraphs on the page. That interpretation is what the contents of your intentionality were about and we might expect that others who read this page will construct mental spaces with similar contents.

DEVELOPMENTS FOR CONSTRUCTING MENTAL SPACES

Mental spaces are ontogenetically prior to language. Early in infancy, long before the infant has had much experience with objects and events in the world let alone experience with language, the contents of these representations are pretty much constrained to perception. What the child sees, hears, and feels in the immediate present determines what the child holds in mind. Nonetheless, memory begins in earliest infancy with the formation of the first mental schemas. These begin with what Baldwin, and Piaget (1947/1960) after him, called "circular reactions" as the infant acts to reproduce a result that had, at first, happened only fortuitously with a chance movement (p. 101). Short-term retention of objects and events in the immediate context has been demonstrated in habituation studies with young infants (e.g., Cohen, 1976; Fantz, 1964; Ruff, 1976). And infants as young as 8 weeks old already demonstrate memory for prior events (Vander Linde, Morrongiello, & Rovee-Collier, 1985). But this early retrieval from infant memories depends on cues from the immediate context that are literally "reencounters" with the same episodic experiences (Rovee-Collier, Sullivan, Enright, Lucas, & Fagen, 1980).

What develops is the ability to recall aspects of prior events using cues that are farther and farther removed from the original presenting events. Children eventually come to be able to think about, and talk about, objects outside the episodes in which they were originally experienced (e.g., Bloom, 1973; Bloom, Lifter, & Broughton, 1985; Corrigan, 1983; Mandler, 1984; Nelson, 1982, 1985; Piaget, 1937/1954). However, although the representations in mental spaces are no longer constrained to perceptible objects and events in the immediate context, recall from memory for objects in these representations nevertheless depends on visual, auditory, and other cues afforded by the context. The early gestures and words of infants depend on such cued recall: waving "byebye" when someone leaves the room; looking up at a clock on the wall of the playroom and saying "ticktock"; walking toward the stove and saying "hot"; and so on. In each of these instances, the child has to have recalled something that was not there in the context, such as, for instance, Mommy leaving home in the morning and waving "byebye"; the clock on the kitchen wall and the word *ticktock*. In sum, the child's gesture or word is an expression of mental contents constructed with the benefit of cues from the context. Development occurs in the sorts of cues the child uses for recall to construct these representations: beginning with the same cues (the clock on the kitchen wall cues recall of the same clock at a previous time), and then similar cues (the clock in the playroom cues recall of the clock on the kitchen wall), and then linguistic cues ("ticktock" or "What time is it?").

Eventually, infants become able to generate their own cues for accessing memory. This means that the elements of a mental space cue recall to set up a related mental space. For example, the child might see a pile of blocks on the floor and then go to the toybox for a doll to ride a train. The pile of blocks (a perceptual cue) cued a plan to build a train, and the representation of a train cued recall of a likely passenger. Infants come to be able to anticipate events that are not present in the context, to discover new means to an end, or to construct a mental space with novel contents never actually experienced before, as in dreams or pretend play. Ultimately, the speech the child hears (or signs the child sees), in the absence of more literal cues from the context, will be the preeminent source of cues for constructing the representations that underlie acts of interpretation and expression.

What developments contribute to the ability to set up mental spaces and make these representations possible? At the least, we have to consider developmental changes in (a) capacity, (b) notation systems, and (c) pathways into and out of the knowledge base. These aspects of mental activity have received a good amount of attention in psychological theory and research. However, their importance for language development has barely been touched on.

We can expect the capacity for representation in mental spaces will change dramatically in the period during which the basics of language are acquired, in the first several years of life. The use of language can be diagnostic of these changes in capacity. For example, in the single-word period, 1-year-olds progress from representations with focus on a single element (saying a single word) to representing more than one element with a relation between them (saying successive single words) (e.g., Bloom, 1973). Setting up a mental space with a relation between two elements is required for syntactic word combinations (Ewing, 1984). And the beginning of complex sentences between 2 and 3 years of age depends on the ability to represent two propositions and the relation between them (Bloom, Lahey, Hood, Lifter, & Fiess, 1980). We can use children's language to infer that such developments have taken place, but we need to understand the processes by which these developments in capacity occur independent of language. The young child does not begin with language and early ontogenetic categories are not linguistic. Language makes the underlying representations manifest and so reveals that developments contributing to them have occurred, but the developments themselves take place independently of language, at least in the early years.

The notation system adults use for representations in consciousness is the subject of some debate and speculation (e.g., Pylshyn & Demopoulos, 1986). In fact, the study of development during the period in which language is acquired might shed light on such questions as, for example, whether the required notation systems are componential (a system of symbols and procedures for assembling them) or holistic (propositional or imagistic). At the least, we might expect that the ways mental content is encoded would differ before and after language is acquired. However, language will not be acquired unless the child possesses the capacity for notation systems that will: (a) capture the phonetic features of speech, or the formational features of signs, and (b) represent the elements and the relations between elements that can point to objects and events in the world. We have paid some attention to the first kind of notation system, in studies of infant speech perception, for example. But aside from invoking development of the symbolic capacity, we know very little about the second.

In addition to inquiring into the developments in capacity and notational systems that make acquiring a language possible, we also need to consider the path to and from the knowledge base. If acquiring language depends on the construction of mental spaces, then setting up the elements and relations of mental spaces requires integrating data from perception and memory. In this regard, we need to consider the cues that infants and young children can use for recall and recognition and how these change in the first few years of life. Early in life, such cues are reencounters with the same or similar episodes evoked from memory and are necessarily quite literal. With development, episodes recalled from memory become increasingly discrepant from the perceptual cues that evoked them. Ultimately, with language, speech and signs provide the cues for recall and representing elements and relations in consciousness. In order for this to happen, children must have recorded, in the knowledge base, the auditory-vocal or visual-manual gestures they have heard or seen other persons make along with something of the circumstances of these encounters as, for example, R. Brown (1956) described in the "original word game."

When a child hears a word (and perhaps a larger speech unit like a phrase or sentence), the word is entered in memory along with other perceptual and personal data about its circumstances of use. The fundamental importance of this kind of associative learning has long been recognized in language studies: "[f]or both the 1-year-old and the adult, the relationship between the word "shoe" and the object it refers to is learned by association" (Bates, Benigni, Bretherton, Camaioni, and Volterra, 1979). The data for these associations consist of the perceptual and functional contingencies experienced with the word. These can include an action, by the child or someone else, as well as an object in the context. The speech unit, then, is one element of an episode with other elements that include persons, objects, and actions. Virtually all developmental accounts of children's first words have noted the strong association between word and object, word and action, or word and event.

Infants begin to have pairings of words (nouns and verbs) with events (objects and actions) in memory at least as young as 12 to 14 months of age, according to data reported by Oviatt (1980, 1982) and by Golinkoff and Hirsh-Pasek (1987). When the word is heard again, or the event is seen again, either the word or the event (or both, if the word game is repeated) cues recall of the original word-event pair to set up a representation in consciousness. This representation, then, is the joint product of the contextual cue and the word-event pair that the cue accessed from memory. The important point here is that if the child then says the word, that word is an expression of this representation.

REPRESENTATION AND EXPRESSION IN DEVELOPMENT

We can say that an action is an expression when it is an embodiment (medium) of some represented content (meaning). An expression is "a set of material properties . . . [which] embody a given representation" (Danto, 1983, pp. 251–252). The same representation may find different embodiments, "the same meanings . . . appearing in different media": For example, speech, sign language, and printed text are different embodiments of meaning in language (Danto, 1983, pp. 251–252). Language makes the contents of our internal representations manifest and puts them in a public space (Taylor, 1985). Language is a vehicle of expression because it provides the materials and procedures for making something manifest. The study of language acquisition, then, is the study of expression. It follows that a theory of language development needs to address what the representations that underlie children's acts of expression and interpretation are about. This requires that we understand how mental spaces are constructed, and the developments that contribute to their construction and their expression.

To this end, we are in need of what Miller et al. (1960) called a "re-enactment," a model simulating the process of language development, in addition to our descriptions of what is acquired:

> Description is of course important. Even more, it is *essential* to science that we have accurate descriptions available. But there is another ingredient required, one that we seem to forget and rediscover in every generation of psychologists, at least since Brentano's Act first competed with Wundt's Content. Life is more than a thing, an object, a substance that exists. It is also a process that is enacted. We have a choice in our approach to it. We can choose to describe it, or we can choose to re-enact it. Description . . . is the traditional approach of the scientist. Re-enactment has been the traditional approach of the artist. And just as description depends upon an Image, re-enactment depends upon a Plan. (pp. 213–214, italics in the original)

We have many descriptions of children's language and how their language changes from one point in time to another. But language acquisition is a process that is enacted each time a child learns the system of expression available in a culture or society. If we are to reenact or model the process our plan must closely resemble the child's. This entails understanding the representations underlying the acts of expression and interpretation for which language is learned, and how these change as language is being learned. We have to understand, at least, the mental spaces that the child is capable of setting up, the cues the child uses for setting up mental spaces, and how these representations are made manifest through the linguistic forms and structures afforded by the language.

Descriptions of language acquisition have typically been concerned with reference, designation, and the instrumental function of language. Each of these has to do with observable events and bypasses the unobservable, internal dimension of language. Thus, when we explain the development of language in terms of instrumental "tool use" we are describing one of the things that can happen through language. Using language can influence the actions of other persons and get things done in the world. However, we influence the actions of other persons only because our words have the power to influence their beliefs. A word or words can be successful as a tool only to the extent that the speaker is successful in setting up a representation in the listener's mind that matches the representation in the speaker's mind (Bloom, 1974; Fauconnier, 1985; Fodor, 1979).

The perspective taken here also argues against the notion that by saying a word the child (or, for that matter, anyone) "makes reference" to an object that is "out there." Ordinarily, characterizing a child's use of words as reference simply describes the facts that the child said a word, and that the word named something in the context. But this description omits the important facts that to use a word, a child has to recall the word along with something of its prior experience from memory, and then has to construct a mental space representing these objects from memory in relation to the objects in context. It is the elements in the mental space that are directed at objects in the world and that refer to those objects. The words, or the forms of language, name these elements. We can speak of "elements being *set up mentally, pointed to,* and *identified* by language forms; [but] the language forms do not *refer* to such elements. If there is to be reference, it will go from the elements in mental spaces to the objects referred to . . . Theories of truth and reference for natural language cannot bypass the space construction process" (Fauconnier, 1985, p. 2).

When we speak of language in terms of designation we come closer to taking account of internal processes. However, the familiar mapping problem in child language research often takes designation to mean that words are learned to "stand for" the concepts and other sorts of knowledge that we have stored in memory: mapping between words and elements of knowledge. These accounts also bypass the mental activity whereby elements in mental spaces are the objects set up and designated by words. The crucial developments for language are those that contribute to (1) constructing connections between perceptions and items in memory for representations in consciousness, and (2) accessing words to express what these representations are about.

REPRESENTATION AND LANGUAGE DEVELOPMENT

If we are correct in the assumption that what the infant can construct in mind is determinative for learning language, then we ought to be able to see the effects of how the infant constructs mental spaces on resulting behavior. We have explored this question in our studies of infant expression in the period of early word learning, from the last quarter of the first year and continuing through the second year. In one study, for example, we have made attributions of the contents of beliefs and desires underlying infants' expressions, and compared these for expression through speech and through affect in the single-word period (Bloom, Beckwith, Capatides, & Hafitz, 1988).

For young children, beginning to respond to words they hear others say and beginning to say words are tentative beginnings at best. The early behaviors that we see are fragile, unpredictable, and inconsistent. Nevertheless, prelinguistic infants and infants making the transition to language are not in a state of limbo with respect to communication. Virtually from birth, infants begin to display affect signals that their caregivers interpret as meaningful. Toward the end of the first year, by the time they begin to learn language, the development of affect expression is well underway. At a time when early words are tentative and inconsistent, the infant's affect signals — the whole gamut of smiles, giggles, laughs, frowns, whines, and cries — are in place. We have looked, in this period of early word learning, at the relation between these two systems of expression: infants' emerging words and their relatively well-developed affect signals. Here I present the results of only one of these studies of the developmental relation between affect expression and the emergence of words in the single-word period. (A summary of other studies can be found in Bloom, 1990.)

We would expect that children would be most likely to begin to say words that express things they also have feelings about. That is to say, the infant who is experiencing pleasure or displeasure, is already able to express that feeling through affect. But the affect expression cannot articulate what the pleasure or displeasure is about. Only words can do that. In saying a word, the infant must have constructed a mental space and recalled the word for its expression. This mental activity requires attention and reflection.

The expression of emotion also requires cognitive activity. The experience of emotion entails representation of the causes and consequences of the emotion. These are often centered on an evaluation of the goals that the individual has in mind in relation to circumstances and situations in the context (e.g., Oatley & Johnson-Laird, 1987; Rothbart, 1973; Stein & Jewett, 1986). When the goal is obtained, the experience is a positive emotion; when the goal is blocked, the emotional experience is one of anger or sadness. Such mental activity for the experience and expression of emotion competes with the mental activity required in saying a word for the limited cognitive resources of the young language-learning child. We have, in fact, tested such a competition model for early word and affect expression in our research.

We devised a system of transcription for reducing the overwhelming amount of data that comes from a video recording of infant behavior (described in Beckwith, Bloom, Albury, Raqib and Booth, 1975; Bloom, in press). We have not attempted a rich transcription of all the recorded behaviors and accompanying contexts, as is commonly done with audio and video data. Instead, we have pulled the video record apart, exploded it, so to speak, and separated out the variables of interest to one or another research question. Relevant variables in our research so far have included, for example, child speech, mother speech, child affect expression, mother response to child affect expression, child object play, child object search, and so forth. Independent coders, naive to the research questions or hypotheses in our studies, were assigned to transcribe or code only one variable at a time. For instance, one group of coders only transcribed child speech; another only coded child affect expression.

However, because these variables in the stream of behavior covary, we must have a way of putting them back together again. We recorded a computer readable time code (SMPTE FOR-A) on the second sound track of the video tape at the time of the original observation. The video deck (Sony stereo Betamax) was interfaced at the time of playback and coding with a microprocessor (Apple II plus) which could read the time code. Every coding decision is associated with a time of onset and, for most variables, a time of offset. Because the computer can read the time code, the separate coding passes made by the independent coders could be merged subsequently. The merging produces an integrated transcription with the relevant behaviors lined up according to the original temporal relations between them. This allows us to look very carefully at the timing of one behavior relative to another, such as the timing of infant emotional expression and speech.

Richard Beckwith and I have reported an analysis that exploited these capabilities of the system (Bloom & Beckwith, 1989). The procedure is a form of lag sequential analysis (Bakeman, 1978; Sackett, 1974, 1979), where the word that a child says is the target event and the occurrence of an expression of emotional affect before and after the word is lagged against it. At the time of this analysis, the infants whom we studied ($N = 12$) had been saying words at home, according to their mothers' diaries, but had just begun to use words in our laboratory playroom (mean age = 13.6 months). These First Words playroom sessions provided the data for analysis. The mean duration of speech (primarily single words but occasional phrases) was .89 sec for the 12 children. With the occurrence of a word considered as the anchor lag, 15 1-sec lags before and 15 1-sec lags after each word were scanned for the occurrence of emotionally toned affect expression. A baseline rate of emotional expression was determined by dividing the amount of time each child spent in emotional expression overall (Bloom, Beckwith, & Capatides, 1988) by the total amount of coded time. This was then considered the expected frequency of expression per 1-sec lag.

To determine whether emotion was expressed during a lag, the onset and offset of every emotional expression was examined and its occurrence in a lag was noted. A running count was kept for each instance of emotional expression that occurred in each of the 15 1-sec lags before and after a child's words. A proportion of emotional expression was obtained for each lag and compared to the baseline rate of emotional expression. The baseline was then subtracted from the proportion of affect in each lag to obtain a difference score from baseline. This yielded an emotion expression profile for each child which consisted of the percentages of the difference from baseline in the 30 lags. The differences from baseline were then divided by the standard deviation of the differences for each child (Z scores) and the means for the Z scores were used to generate a composite profile for the group of children. This profile was then plotted as the mean difference in standard deviation units from the baseline expression of emotion.

If the two sorts of expression, affect and words, were unrelated to one another, then we would expect an essentially random interaction between expressing emotion and saying words. The result would be a lagged function similar to baseline. However, if the content of the child's words and the feelings underlying the child's affect expression were about the same thing, as we might expect, then we should find words and emotionally toned affect expression tending to cluster together, which is what we found. However, the competition for constructing the representations required for the experience and expression of an emotion, and for expressing a word that articulates what the emotion is about, should be reflected in the temporal relation between word and emotional expression. And this is what we also found.

The result of the lag sequential analysis is presented in Fig. 5.1. The horizontal line represents the baseline rate or expected frequency of emotional expression per 1-sec lag, based upon the amount of time the children spent in emotional expression overall. The observed frequency of emotional expression is presented as the difference in mean standard deviation units from the baseline expression of emotion in each of the 15

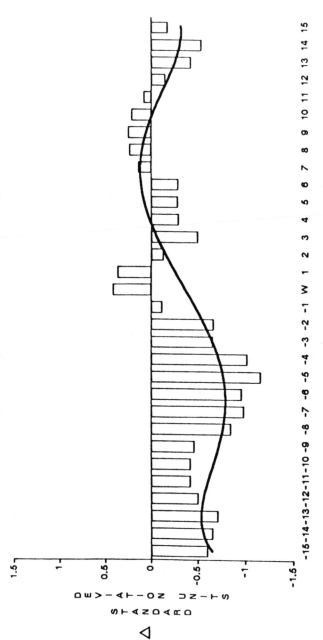

FIG. 5.1 FW: Profile of emotional expression in moments before and after a word. (From "Talking with Feeling: Integrating Affective and Linguistic Expression" by L. Bloom and R. Beckwith, 1989, *Cognition and Emotion, 3*, p. 313–342. Copyright Lawrence Erlbaum Associates. Reprinted by permission.

pre- and 15 postword 1-sec lags, plotted in relation to the word. The graph represents the collapsed data from the 12 children, with the resulting curve smoothed by a least squares best fit of the data.

The expression of emotionally toned affect clustered around the words, but the resulting function had the shape of a sine wave. The critical features of the function were a dip in the frequency of affect expression at about 5 sec before the word lag, with a steep rise through the word lag and a peak just after the word.

We are interpreting the dip before the word as the time during which the mental activity associated with the experience and expression of emotion is, essentially, suspended. This is the time the child uses for the cognitive work that saying a word involves: constructing a mental space and recalling a word for expressing an element in this representation. The peak in affect expression comes after having said the word, when the child's cognitive resources are now free once again for constructing the representations associated with feeling states. Because most of the affect expression we observed was positive affect, the peak after saying the word can be likened to the smile of recognition observed by McCall and McGhee (1977) in their studies of infants' visual perception.

The effect shown in Fig. 5.1—a dip in emotional expression just before the word and a peak immediately after—was, in fact, diminished at the end of the single-word period, when words were more well known, easier to recall, and more automatic (see Bloom & Beckwith, 1989, for the same analysis at the end of the single-word period). We would expect a similar effect, however, throughout life, because constructing the representations underlying expression are more or less effortful according to content and circumstances. We, as adults, might not smile or frown, for instance, when we are talking about or hearing others talk about something that is particularly abstract or complex.

OTHER RESEARCH

Other examples from the child language literature can be cited to demonstrate the value in considering the representations underlying children's acts of expression and interpretation. Studies of infants and mothers have revealed again and again that communication between them occurs in a context of "joint attention" (e.g., Bruner, 1983; Lock, 1978; Sugarman, 1978). Infants' early gestures in these contexts (pointing in particular) have been interpreted as "orienting" responses by the infant, indicating attention to something in the context, rather than as communicative acts (Bates et al., 1979; Lempert & Kinsbourne, 1985). Mothers in such interactions as these have been shown to differ in the timing of their response to their infants' vocalizations, and also in their tendency to name the object that their infants are attending to. Both factors influence subsequent vocabulary size and differences among mothers are reflected in differences among their children (Masur, 1982; Roth, 1987; Tomasello & Farrar, 1986). Children evidently learn more words when their mothers respond promptly to their vocalizations and also say something about the objects of the infant's attention. Similarly, an optimum occasion for learning language forms is provided when caregivers fail to understand an infant's expression and "negotiate" the form of the message in subsequent exchanges (Golinkoff, 1983). When this happens, infants hear (or see) the forms that can more successfully articulate what they have in mind.

The meanings of children's relational words (for example, *there* and *more*) in the single-word period are directed at the plans they have in mind (Gopnik, 1982). In particular, they use such words to express something about their goals in relation to their actions and aspects of the context. For example, *there* expresses the success of a plan; *no* and *gone* express failure to attain a goal; *more* expresses repetition of a plan, and so forth. In a series of experiments with older children who were 4 years old, Hamburger and Crain (1987) took explicit account of the computational demands attributable to underlying plans in sentence processing. They found that certain phrases varied in difficulty for children as a function of their relative cognitive demands rather than their syntactic complexity.

Finally, a key component in learnability-theoretic research is the child's hearing and making use of sentences in the input. In any learnability theory, input sentences are required for the acquisition of latent principles of grammar assumed to be a part of the child's endowment. The structures of syntax cannot be realized, that is, acquired in a grammar, unless the child ascertains their relevance to something in the input. This process of matching an input sentence to a grammatical principle would have to include setting up a mental space based on hearing the sentence. Most learnability-theoretic research assumes that this mental space is limited to the sentence the child hears. However, in addition to representing the input sentence, the child also sets up a mental space with elements from the situation that the sentence is about, indexing correspondences between participants in the situation and items in the sentence. The child uses such representations of sentence-situation pairings to learn sentence types from the input (Beckwith, 1988).

OVEREXTENSIONS IN WORD LEARNING

Children's underextensions and overextensions of early words have typically been interpreted as evidence for the limits of a word's meaning for the child (e.g., Clark, 1973; Greenfield, 1973; Rescorla, 1980). In one classic example, Werner (1948), citing an example from Darwin, reported that a child said *qua-qua* to refer to both a duck and water, after having first heard the word spoken when a duck was swimming in water. Werner suggested that the child had not differentiated between the duck and the water on hearing the word originally, and so both were stored together with the word. Other examples in the literature involve "chains" of associations (as described by Vygotsky, 1962) in which each succeeding experience of a word adds another aspect to the word's putative meaning for the child. An example is the word *water* when the child is splashing in a pool, then when the child is holding a glass of water, and then when the child sees a window pane. In cases like these, and hundreds of like examples in the literature, the tendency has been to take the child very seriously and to assume that the circumstances of the word's use is an indication of what the child believes the word means.

But perhaps we should not take the child's so-called "reference" quite so seriously. I suggest that such overextension often consists only of cued recall. In the aforementioned examples, seeing the water cued recall of the duck (Werner [1948] did say that the two were stored together in memory); seeing a window pane cued recall of the water glass. To cite one of the most familiar instances in the literature, the child who says "Daddy" on seeing a man who is not Daddy, could have recalled the real Daddy to mind. Saying "Daddy" would then be an expression of the element represented in a mental space that is directed at the child's real Daddy. The child was not calling the stranger *Daddy*. Neither did the child really believe that *Daddy* is a name to use for all large, male persons in jeans or a business suit. Similarly, when hearing the telephone ring cues recall of Daddy's voice on the phone, the child saying "Daddy" is not naming the telephone "a daddy." Seeing another man or hearing the telephone ring cued recall of the real Daddy which the child then expressed.

Nonetheless, such events are important, although for a different reason than the one ordinarily offered: that they indicate the meaning the word has for the child. In most of these situations, a "good enough" (to borrow from Winnicott) language tutor (mother, father, big brother, caregiver) will provide an alternative for the child, for example, "that's a *window*" or "that's a *man*" or "Daddy's on the *telephone*." In this way, the child has another word-object pair to store away, waiting to be called up in future encounters with the same or slightly discrepant objects.

CONCLUSIONS

In order to reenact or model the process of language acquisition we have to study infants and young children in what Chomsky (1964) once called "devious and clever ways" (p. 36). Several such examples have been touched on here. For one, in studies of the beginning of infant memories, Rovee-Collier et al (1980) tied a baby's foot to a mobile suspended above a crib. They were able to demonstrate that infants as young as 8 weeks old, given the right cues, could recall prior experiences (like kicking the foot and moving the mobile). Closer to home, Golinkoff and Hirsh-Pasek (1987) gave infants not one but two Sesame Street vignettes on separate TV screens. Their infants chose to watch the one that was most interesting because it matched the word or phrase they heard at the same time. In a series of these experiments, they have shown that young children have experiences of words paired with objects and actions in memory, and even knowledge of aspects of English word order. Thus, in highly focused contexts, with cues for recall carefully constrained, and the contrivance of response variables devious and clever enough, infants show us that they can access this knowledge and set up mental spaces. What remains to be done is to determine the developments needed for the infant to get from there to here — to get from knowing and recalling certain linguistic units only under optimal conditions, to using those linguistic units in acts of interpretation and expression.

I began this chapter by pointing out that the perspective taken here is rarely the object of inquiry nor ordinarily even made explicit in studies of child language. It is nonetheless implicit in much theoretical and empirical work in the field. I mentioned a few such instances from research reported by others, and described an example of research from my own laboratory. Some, however, will object to an appeal to contents of consciousness. In response, I can only point to other research domains in which enormous strides have been made precisely because the contents of awareness have been taken into explicit account. This is certainly the case in the study of infant perception, for example. We would not have the insights that we now have concerning infants' perceptions of objects, speech sounds, and the like, if researchers had not devised the means to tap into the contents of the infant's attention. Similarly, theory and research in cognitive science have made heavy use of representation in on-line processing models for understanding the exchange of information that takes place between the brain and the context.

One criticism of the position taken here will no doubt be the strong emphasis on the mind of the individual and its development. In an era in which the place of society has come to be revered by many who study language and its acquisition, a decidedly mentalist view such as this one may be distasteful. However, a social perspective on language acquisition cannot ignore the cognitive activity of constructing the mental spaces that underlie acts of expression and interpretation. In essence, the social context cannot determine language and language development because social interaction depends on the contents of the child's mind. The child is not a sponge. What children take from and contribute to an interaction has to do with the elements (including representations of other persons), roles, and relations represented in the mind. This hidden mental life of the individual child, the child's intentionality, must be taken into account in even the most interactionist of social views on language and its acquisition.

Individuals exist only by virtue of their relation to one another. But this is possible because of the power of individuals to take what is hidden in themselves and make it public. A micro–macro debate is not really relevant in this context because languages are social products and to acquire a language is to become a member of society. A large part of why languages began in the first place is no doubt because of the need in a society for individuals to have expressive power—to make external and public to other persons what is otherwise internal and private to themselves.

ACKNOWLEDGEMENTS

Support for the preparation of this article was provided by research grants from the National Science Foundation and the Spencer Foundation, and a James McKeen Cattell Sabbatical Award in Psychology. I thank Richard Beckwith for his comments on an earlier draft of the manuscript and for collaborations that resulted in many of the ideas presented here, and Michael Studdert-Kennedy for his careful and thoughtful editorial comments. The material in this chapter also appears in the book, *The Transition from Infancy to Language: Acquiring the Power of Expression* (Bloom, forthcoming).

REFERENCES

Bakeman, R. (1978). Untangling streams of behavior: Sequential analyses of observational data. In G. Sackett (Ed.), *Observing behavior: Vol. 2. Data collection and analysis methods* (pp. 63–78). Baltimore: University Park Press.

Bates, E. (1976). *Language in context.* New York: Academic.

Bates, E., Benigni, L., Bretherton, I., Camaioni, L., & Volterra, V. (1979). *The emergence of symbols: Communication and cognition in infancy.* New York: Academic.

Beckwith, R. (1988). *Learnability and psychological categories.* Unpublished doctoral dissertation, Teachers College, Columbia University, New York.

Beckwith, R., Bloom, L., Albury,, D., Raqib, A., & Booth, R. (1985). Technology and methodology. *Transcript Analysis, 2,* 72–75.

Bloom, L. (1970). *Language development: Form and function in emerging grammars.* Cambridge, MA: MIT Press.

Bloom, L. (1973). *One word at a time: The use of single-word utterances before syntax.* The Hague, Netherlands: Mouton.

Bloom, L. (1974). Talking, understanding and thinking: Developmental relationship between receptive and expressive language. In R. Schiefelbusch & L. Lloyd (Eds.), *Language perspectives: Acquisition, retardation, and intervention* (pp. 285–312). Baltimore: University Park Press.

Bloom, L. (1990). Developments in expression: Affect and speech. In N. Stein, B. Leventhal,

& T. Trabasso (Eds.), *Psychological and biological approaches to emotion* (pp. 215-295). Hillsdale, NJ: Lawrence Erlbaum Associates.

Bloom, L. (*in press*). Transcription and coding for child language research. In J. Edwards & M. Lampert (Eds.), *Transcription and coding methods for language research*. Hillsdale, NJ: Erlbaum.

Bloom, L. (forthcoming). *The transition from infancy to language: Acquiring the power of expression*.

Bloom, L., & Beckwith, R. (1989). Talking with feeling: Integrating affective and linguistic expression. *Cognition and Emotion, 3,* 313-342.

Bloom, L., Beckwith, R., & Capatides, J. (1988). Developments in the expression of affect. *Infant Behavior and Development, 11,* 169-186.

Bloom, L., Beckwith, R., Capatides, J., & Hafitz, J. (1988). Expression through affect and words in the transition from infancy to language. In P. Baltes, D. Featherman, & R. Lerner (Eds.), *Life-span development and behavior* (Vol. 8, pp. 99-127). Hillsdale, NJ: Lawrence Erlbaum Associates.

Bloom, L., Lahey, M., Hood, L., Lifter, K., & Fiess, K. (1980). Complex sentences: Acquisition of syntactic connectives and the semantic relations they encode. *Journal of Child Language, 7,* 235-261.

Bloom, L., Lifter, K., & Broughton, J. (1985). The convergence of early cognition and language in the second year of life: Problems in conceptualization and measurement. In M. Barrett (Ed.), *Single word speech*. London: Wiley.

Brentano, F. (1966). *The true and the evident*. (R. Chrisholm, (Ed); Trans. by R. Chrisholm, I. Politzer, & K. Fischer). New York: Humanities Press. (Original work published 1930).

Brown, J. (1964). States in newborn infants. *Merrill-Palmer Quarterly, 10,* 313-327.

Brown, R. (1956). Language and categories. In J. Bruner, J. Goodnow, & G. Austin, *A study of thinking* (Appendix). New York: Wiley.

Brown, R. (1958). How shall a thing be called? *Psychological Review, 65,* 14-21.

Brown, R. (1973). *A first language, the early stages*. Cambridge, MA: Harvard University Press.

Bruner, J. (1983). *Child's talk, Learning to use language*. New York: Norton.

Campbell, R. (1986). Language acquisition and cognition. In P. Fletcher & M. Garman (Eds.), *Language acquisition: Studies in first language development* (2nd ed, pp. 30-48). Cambridge, England: Cambridge University Press.

Chomsky, N. (1964). Formal discussion. In U. Bellugi & R. Brown (Eds.), The acquisition of language. *Monographs of the Society for Research in Child Development, 29* (Serial No. 92), 35-39.

Clark, E. (1973). What's in a word? On the child's acquisition of semantics in his first language. In T. Moore (Ed.), *Cognitive development and the acquisition of language* (pp. 65-110). New York: Academic.

Cohen, L. (1976). Habituation of infant attention. In T. Tighe & R. Leaton (Eds.), *Habituation: Perspectives from child development, animal behavior, and neurophysiology* (pp. 207-238). Hillsdale, NJ: Lawrence Erlbaum Associates.

Corrigan, R. (1983). The development of representational skills. In K. Fischer (Ed.), *Levels and transitions in children's development. New Directions for Child Development, 21,* (pp. 51-64). San Francisco: Jossey-Bass.

Danto, A. (1973). *Analytical philosophy of action*. Cambridge, England: Cambridge University Press.

Danto, A. (1983). Toward a retentive materialism. In L. Cauman, I. Levi, C. Parsons, & R. Schwartz (Eds.), *How many questions? Essays in honor of Sidney Morgenbesser* (pp. 243-255). Indianapolis: Hackett.

Ewing, G. (1984). *Presyntax: The development of word order in early child speech*. Unpublished doctoral dissertation, University of Toronto.

Fantz, R. (1964). Visual experience in infants: Decreased attention to familiar patterns relative to novel ones. *Science, 146,* 668-670.

Fauconnier, G. (1985). *Mental spaces: Aspects of meaning construction in natural language.* Cambridge, MA: MIT Press.

Fodor, J. (1979). *The language of thought.* Cambridge, MA: Harvard University Press.

Golinkoff, R. (1983). The preverbal negotiation of failed messages: Insights into the transition period. In R. Golinkoff (Ed.), *The transition from prelinguistic to linguistic communication* (pp. 57-78). Hillsdale, NJ: Lawrence Erlbaum Associates.

Golinkoff, R., & Hirsh-Pasek, K. (1987, October). *A new picture of language development: Evidence from comprehension.* Paper presented at the Boston University Child Language Conference, Boston.

Gopnik, A. (1982). Words and plans: Early language and the development of intelligent action. *Journal of Child Language, 9,* 303-318.

Gopnik, A., & Meltzoff, A. (1984). Semantic and cognitive development in 15- to 21-month-old children. *Journal of Child Language, 11,* 495-513.

Gopnik, A., & Meltzoff, A. (1986). Words, plans, and things: Interactions between semantic and cognitive development in the one-word stage. In S. Kuczaj & M. Barrett (Eds.), *The development of word meaning* (pp. 199-223). New York: Springer-Verlag.

Greenfield, P. (1973). Who is "Dada"? Some aspects of the semantic and phonological development of a child's first words. *Language and Speech, 16,* 34-43.

Hamburger, H., & Crain, S. (1987). Plans and semantics in human processing of language. *Cognitive Science, 11,* 101-136.

Jackendoff, R. (1987). *Consciousness and the computational mind.* Cambridge, MA: MIT Press.

Lempert, H., & Kinsbourne, M. (1985). Possible origin of speech in selective orienting. *Psychological Bulletin, 97,* 62-73.

Lock, A. (Ed.). (1978). *Action, gesture and symbol: The emergence of language.* New York: Academic.

Mandler, J. (1983). Representation. In J. Flavell & E. Markman (Eds.), P. H. Mussen (Series Ed.), *Handbook of child psychology: Vol. 3. Cognitive development* (pp. 420-494). New York: Wiley.

Mandler, J. (1984). Representation and recall in infancy. In M. Moscovitch (Ed.), *Infant memory: Its relation to normal and pathological memory in humans and other animals* (pp. 75-101). New York: Plenum.

Masur, E. (1982). Mothers' responses to infants' object-related gestures: Influences on lexical development. *Journal of Child Language, 9,* 23-30.

McCall, R., & McGhee, P. (1977). The discrepancy hypothesis of attention and affect in infants. In I. Uzgiris & F. Weizmann (Eds.), *The structure of experience* (pp. 179-210). New York: Plenum.

McCune-Nicolich, L. (1981). The cognitive basis of relational words in the single word period. *Journal of Child Language, 8,* 15-34.

Mervis, C. (1984). Early lexical development: The contributions of mother and child. In C. Sophian (Ed.), *Origins of cognitive skills* (pp. 339-370). Hillsdale, NJ: Lawrence Erlbaum Associates.

Miller, G. (1962). *Psychology, the science of mental life.* New York: Harper & Row.

Miller, G. (1979). Images and models, similes and metaphors. In A. Ortony (Ed.), *Metaphor and thought* (pp. 202-250). Cambridge, England: Cambridge University Press.

Miller, G., Galanter, E., & Pribram, K. (1960). *Plans and the structure of behavior.* New York: Holt-Dryden.

Moscovitch, M. (Ed.). (1984). *Infant memory: Its relation to normal and pathological memory in humans and other animals.* New York: Plenum.

Nelson, K. (1974). Concept, word and sentence: Interrelations in acquisition and development. *Psychological Review, 81,* 267-285.

Nelson, K. (1982). The syntagmatics and paradigmatics of conceptual development. In S. Kuczaj (Ed.), *Language Development (Vol. 2): Language, thought, and culture* (pp. 335-364). Hillsdale, NJ: Earlbaum.

Nelson, K. (1985). *Making sense: The acquisition of shared meaning.* New York: Academic.

Oatley, K., & Johnson-Laird, P. (1987). Towards a cognitive theory of emotions. *Cognition and Emotion, 1,* 29-50.

Oviatt, S. (1980). The emerging ability to comprehend language: An experimental approach. *Child Development, 51,* 97-106.

Oviatt, S. (1982). Inferring what words mean: Early development in infants' comprehension of common object names. *Child Development, 53,* 274-277.

Piaget, J. (1954). *The construction of reality in the child.* New York: Basic. (Original work published 1937).

Piaget, J. (1960). *The psychology of intelligence.* Paterson, NJ: Littlefield, Adams. (Original work published 1947)

Pylshyn, Z., & Demopoulos, W. (Eds.). (1986). *Meaning and cognitive structure: Issues in the computational theory of mind.* Norwood, NJ: Ablex.

Rescorla, L. (1980). Overextension in early language development. *Journal of Child Language, 7,* 321-335.

Roth, P. (1987, April). Longitudinal study of maternal verbal interaction styles. Poster presented at the Biennial Meeting of the Society for Research in Child Development, Baltimore.

Rothbart, M. (1973). Laughter in young children. *Psychological Bulletin, 80,* 247-256.

Ruff, H. (1976). Infant recognition of the invariant form of objects. *Child Development, 49,* 293-306.

Rovee-Collier, C., Sullivan, M., Enright, M., Lucas, D., & Fagen, J. (1980). Reactivation of infant memory. *Science, 208,* 1159-1161.

Sackett, G. (1974). A nonparametric lag sequential analysis for studying dependency among responses in behavioral observation scoring systems. Paper presented at the meeting of the Western Psychological Association, San Francisco.

Sackett, G. (1979). The lag sequential analysis of contingency and cyclicity in behavioral interaction research. In J. Osofsky (Ed.), *Handbook of infant development* (pp. 623-649). New York: Wiley.

Searle, J. (1983). *Intentionality: An essay in the philosophy of mind.* Cambridge, England: Cambridge University Press.

Searle, J. (1984). *Minds, brains and science.* Cambridge, MA: Harvard University Press.

Stein, N., & Jewett, J. (1986). A conceptual analysis of the meaning of basic negative emotions: Implications for a theory of development. In C. Izard & P. Read (Eds.), *Measurement of emotion in infants and children* (Vol. 2, pp. 238-267). New York: Cambridge University Press.

Sugarman, S. (1978). Some organizational aspects of preverbal communication. In I. Markova (Ed.), *The social context of language,* London: Wiley.

Taylor, C. (1985). *Philosophy and the human sciences: Philosophical papers* (Vol. 1). Cambridge, England: Cambridge University Press.

Tomasello, M., & Farrar, M. (1984). Cognitive bases of lexical development: Object permanence and relational words. *Journal of Child Language, 11,* 477-493.

Tomasello, M., & Farrar, J. (1986). Joint attention and early language. *Child Development, 57,* 1454-1463.

Vander Linde, E., Morrongiello, B., & Rovee-Collier, C. (1985). Determinants of retention in 8-week-old infants. *Developmental Psychology, 21,* 601-613.

Vygotsky, L. (1962). *Thought and language.* Cambridge, MA: MIT Press.

Wellman, H., & Somerville, S. (1982). The development of human search ability. In M. Lamb, & A. Brown (Eds.), *Advances in developmental psychology* (Vol. 2, pp. 41–84). Hillsdale, NJ: Lawrence Erlbaum Associates.

Werner, H. (1948). *Comparative psychology of mental development.* New York: Science Editions.

II

Precursors of Language in Primates

This part of the volume is composed of five chapters that provide overviews of research bearing directly on language precursors in nonhuman primates. An important feature of this section is the empirical work presented on chimpanzees (*Pan paniscus* and *Pan troglodytes*). These unique investigations probe the capacity of *Homo sapien*'s closest living relatives to acquire aspects of language.

In chapter 6, Duane Rumbaugh, William D. Hopkins, David A. Washburn, and E. Sue Savage-Rumbaugh provide a selective review of the pertinent literature that relates primate brain complexity with learning, environmental factors, and competence as these relationships inform language development. More specifically, Rumbaugh et al. discuss findings concerning primate brain size and asymmetry and relate these measures to learning capacity and other behaviors that appear necessary for acquisition of language. The authors also address the importance of brain maturity at birth in a comparative context and relate how this variable could influence basic learning in developing primates. Rumbaugh et al. detail studies that demonstrate the role played by environmental enrichment on brain development. They then review some of the similarities and differences in capacity of the common chimpanzee (*Pan troglodytes*) and the bonobo (pygmy chimpanzee, *Pan paniscus*) for language acquisition. Their review of the data leads the authors to conclude that

> . . . the major dimensions of human competence for language, numbers, calculations, extrapolations, and so on, are reflections of (a) genetically possible modes and levels of development, as (b) modulated by degree of

environmental complexity, and as (c) topically declared and limited by recurring themes and ever-increasing difficulty of "object lessons" encountered by the organism across the days and years of its maturation to adulthood.

Due to their relatedness, these same factors, they assert, can influence the development of both man and his closest living relative, chimpanzees.

Next, Peter McNeilage discusses a theory of how cerebral hemispheric specialization evolved in primates. McNeilage argues that asymmetries in cerebral function emerged due to an adaptation of posture in the aboreal habitat of early primates. The author postulates that both handedness and communicative capacity became dependent on ". . . whole-body postural organization." Further, McNeilage asserts that the validity of the theoretical position hinges in part upon the observation that "human footedness, a necessarily postural specialization, has a stronger contralateral relation to language specialization in humans than does handedness." Evidence for the theory is reviewed in the context of studies that indicate a preference for left-hand-right-hemisphere specialization of visually guided reaching and a corresponding right-side-left-hemisphere postural control specialization in primates. The author reviews the implications of his theory for the ontogenesis of language.

In the following chapter, Dennis L. Molfese and Philip A. Morse review research findings on the comparison of evoked potential investigations of humans and nonhuman primates regarding voice onset time (VOT). The authors point out that ". . . this cue has long been recognized as important for the perception of human speech information." Molfese and Morse's overview of the data on VOT provides an analysis of both the capacity for speech discrimination in humans and a comparison of brain responses across species to identify similarities and differences relating to this measure. An examination of evoked potential data from the human brain reveals that the right hemisphere is involved in VOT discrimination. Data from rhesus monkeys display a different pattern. Thus, at 1 month and 1 year of age, evoked response to VOT is lateralized to the right hemisphere. At 3 years of age lateralization is to the left hemisphere in the same species. The authors review the implications of these and other findings for the evolution of primate brains relating to categorical, linguistically relevant, perception mechanisms involved in lateralization of function.

E. Sue Savage-Rumbaugh next describes her language studies of the Bonobo (*Pan paniscus*). The author suggests that because ". . . no clearly documented anatomical structures present in man's brain are completely absent in the chimpanzee . . . that more of the behavioral differences between *Pan* and *Homo* may be attributable to learning than previously acknowledged." Further, Savage-Rumbaugh asserts that based upon this premise ". . . language may have been an 'invented' behavior rather than a biological endowment." The author outlines the logical prerequisites for identifying behavior that implies knowledge of meaning and relates these criteria to studies carried out, by her and her colleagues, on language learning in chimpanzees. Savage-Rumbaugh characterizes the procedures used to rear Bonobo chimpanzees, from birth, in a language environment that parallels the one in which human babies are raised. She focuses upon the concept of "routine" to illustrate how the chimpanzees map meaning onto specialized symbols (lexigrams) and ultimately come to comprehend the spoken utterances of their human caretakers. Savage-Rumbaugh argues that her observations of chimpanzees are not incompatible with the idea that homologous processes are at work in both apes and children as language is acquired.

In the final chapter, P. M. Greenfield and E. S. Savage-Rumbaugh discuss their observations of language learning in the pygmy chimpanzee (*Pan paniscus*). The authors assert that their data support the conclusion that during the course of development, in the language project, pygmy chimpanzees developed both a simple grammatical rule and symbol-ordering rules that govern language production. Greenfield and Savage-Rumbaugh also indicate that pygmy chimpanzees exposed to language employ imitation in a manner akin to humans ". . . to fulfill a variety of conversational functions such as agreement and request." The data analyzed represent samples over a 5-month period of sequential language-related interactions between one of the chimpanzees and his human caregivers. What is important about the data set is its completeness and similarity to the corpus collected by Brown in his pioneering work on language acquisition in children. The corpus allows independent investigators to apply rigorous methodological approaches to test hypotheses about the existence and/or development of grammar and syntax in the production of the pygmy chimpanzee. Greenfield and Savage-Rumbaugh conclude that ". . . these results suggest the potential to invent (as well as learn) a rudimentary grammar (or protosyntax) and to use language conversationally was present approximately 5 million years ago when hominids, chimpanzees, and gorillas split in the phylogenetic tree."

6 Comparative Perspectives of Brain, Cognition, and Language

Duane M. Rumbaugh, William D. Hopkins,
David A. Washburn, and E. Sue Savage-Rumbaugh
Language Research Center, Georgia State University, and
Yerkes Regional Primate Research Center, Emory University

The origins of language remain controversial. It is held by many that language is unique to the genotype of our species. By implication, even our nearest living relatives—the great apes (*Pongidae*)—should have no capacity for it. In contrast, the view advanced in this chapter is that language is neither monolithic nor totally beyond the competence of the chimpanzee (*Pan*).

Language is viewed as consisting of a large number of component parts and interacting functions. Although speech is the most salient aspect of language and the most highly evolved and efficient means for using language, it is not held from a comparative psychological perspective as the sine qua non of language. Rather, language is basically an achievement of cognitive operations made possible to the degree that a species has a highly encephalized brain that has been uniquely organized by early experiences in an environment steeped with symbolic communication.

The emergence of language and its communicative value rest upon a number of interacting nonspeech building blocks, the cornerstone of these being the ability to learn to use an arbitrary symbol to represent something that is not necessarily present in space or time. Such symbols are used in exchanges with other social partners to refer to things and events and thereby to alter, to plan, and to coordinate behavior. Both the use of and response to these symbols are profoundly different from highly predictable, species-specific patterns of behavior (e.g., fixed action patterns, etc.; see Alcock, 1984, for a discussion of ethology) brought forth in response to stimuli and signals (e.g., sign-stimuli and releasers). Species-characteristic behaviors, such as the newborn gull's readiness to peck at the red dot on its parent's beak to obtain food, are predominantly under genetic control. By contrast, the evolution of an essentially arbitrary stimulus into a communicative symbol is primarily the product of complex learning and cognition.

It is the comprehension of symbols — be they spoken words, geometric symbols, or of American Sign Language — that is the foundation of language. That the symbols of a language system might not be spoken, as is the case with lexigram symbol use (see chapters 9 & 18 of this volume), does not deny their basic semantic value and function.

It is the appropriate use and interpretation of symbols — not speech per se — that are critical to language. Speech produces sounds, and only those sounds, not meanings, are propagated to the listener. The final event of a linguistic communication is the determination of meaning, and that is contingent upon competent comprehension of symbols by the listener. Short of that, literally nothing but sounds have been generated by a speaker. It is surely safe to proffer that even if speech had never evolved in *Homo sapiens,* our species would have devised a symbol-based language system — though it would not be called "language."

Without symbols being used representationally and communicatively there can be no syntax or grammar; there can be no sentences, paragraphs, or lectures. Unless the participants of conversation are symbol competent (e.g., able to use symbols representationally), their verbal exchanges can be no more informative than those one might have with an automatic-bank machine. It is the comprehension of symbols with acquired meanings that is held in this chapter to be the essential component of language.

Most language research with nonhuman subject populations has been done with the chimpanzee (*Pan*). Research at our laboratory (see Rumbaugh, 1977; Savage-Rumbaugh, 1986, for reviews) indicates that they have a profound ability to learn meanings of hundreds of arbitrary visual symbols (called *lexigrams*) and through their use to accomplish social discourse that would otherwise be impossible. The bonobo (*Pan paniscus*) has advanced capacities to understand an essentially unlimited number of spoken sentences (Savage-Rumbaugh, 1988). Because of these kinds of abilities, it is said that these chimpanzees have language.

However, no claim is advanced that they have fully mastered, or even have the capacity to master all aspects of human language. They may never speak as humans (Hayes & Nissen, 1971). Perhaps because of this constraint, they will remain relatively limited with respect to both linguistic flexibility and syntactic structure (but see chapter 10 of this volume). There are many functions served by human language that are not evinced in nonhuman primate communications. Notwithstanding, chimpanzees have given clear scientific evidence of representational and referential use and comprehension of symbols with acquired meaning. To state it differently, chimpanzees have learned to comprehend and use words and sequences of words.

This chapter relates brain complexity, learning processes, early environmental influences, and the patterning of competence through development to the end of producing a better understanding of these language processes.

SELECTED PERSPECTIVES OF THE BRAIN, LEARNING, AND TRANSFER

The expansion of the neocortex and the emergence of asymmetrical functioning within the brain have been heralded as the hallmarks of anthropoid ape, early hominoid, and modern *Homo* evolution. Important cognitive advances, such as tool use (Frost, 1980) and speech (Lieberman, 1975), have been associated with evolution of cerebral lateralization (see Passingham, 1982). Demands of the environment have served to shape and organize an increasingly complex nervous system in the order *Primates* and their attendant capacity to meet those demands through problem solving and learning.

Just as the course of evolution of organisms has been generally toward complexity, in response to environmental demands, so has been that of ontogeny. Because mammals' neurological system, and specifically the brain, is not fully mature at birth, the environment can have a profound impact upon neurological development. Examples of this abound in the perceptual literature in which organisms reared with selective environmental stimulation or sensory deprivation develop abnormal neurological systems which result in altered psycho-perceptual performances (see Riesen, 1982, for a review). Similarly, evidence for cerebral plasticity is suggested by the influence that early experience may have on neurological development. For instance, human children but not adults with acquired brain damage, particularly within the left cerebral hemisphere, can partially recover language functioning (Lenneberg, 1967; Witelson, 1987).

Relative Proportion of Brain Size and Development in Primates

Several efforts have been made to relate the quantitative differences between the brains of various species of primates to understand their behavior, learning, and cognition. Jerison's (1985) encephalization quotient (EQ), for instance, permits the comparison of brains between species by factoring out the overall body size of the organisms. Theoretically, the EQ measures that proportion of brain tissue in excess of the amount of tissue necessary for motor and sensory functions, which should be proportional to body size. Jerison noted that, within the order *Primates,* there are disproportionately large increments in EQs as one compares the relatively small-bodied, small-brained prosimians and simians with the great apes (*Pongidae*) and humans. Humans have the largest EQ of all primates.

Among primates, there has been radical expansion of the neocortex of the great apes and humans that cannot be accounted for by their relatively large body sizes. It would be tempting to conclude that this relative abundance of neocortex provides the capacity for advanced cognition. Cortical expansion alone, however, cannot account for all advanced competencies such as speech. For example, microcephalics have approximately one third the brain size of normal human adults and, in fact, have brain sizes approximating chimpanzees'. Notwithstanding, these individuals quite commonly are able to speak and to communicate without deficits being readily detected (Passingham & Ettlinger, 1974).

A specific component of these analyses that has been of particular interest is the proportion of different association cortex between species. For humans, the auditory association cortex area is 2.3 times larger than would be predicted for a species of our size, whereas in Old World monkeys this area is 1.2 times smaller than would be predicted (Passingham, 1982). By contrast, the visual association cortex is about the normal size as predicted by human body weight, whereas in Old World monkeys the size is about 2.4 times larger than would be predicted. Thus, in humans there is an expansion in the auditory cortex whereas in monkeys there is an expansion in the visual cortex. The evidence for differential cortical expansion between related primate species suggests that auditory-processing capacity became an important modality as the role of vocalizations in the processes of communication increased.

Passingham (1975, 1982) has studied the sizes of various brain structures relative to the size of the medulla and cerebellum, two structures through which all motor and sensory functions must pass, in the evaluation of species-specific ecological adaptations. Thus, with respect to body size, the relative proportion of the cerebellum and medulla to brain volume differs across primate families, but the differences follow a linear function that sets primates generally apart from other mammals. The same interpretation applies to the relationship of neocortex to brain volume, with humans having disproportionately more neocortex than apes, apes disproportionately more than Old World monkeys, and Old World monkeys disproportionately more than prosimians.

Data supporting the expansion of neocortex also have been documented by a number of paleontological studies (Holloway & de la Costa-Lareymondie, 1982; LeMay, 1985). In particular, Holloway and colleagues examined brain endocast in a variety of ape and hominoid species, including *Gorilla,*

Pan, and *Pongo,* for the overall petalia patterns of the skulls. They found that all ape species and early hominoids demonstrate expansion of the occipital lobe of the left hemisphere. For *Pan paniscus* and early hominoids, there is also a significant expansion of the frontal lobe of the right hemisphere. Although other ape species did not show this pattern identically, LeMay's findings support the left occipital-right frontal petalia patterns in *Pongo, Pan troglodytes,* and *Gorilla.*

ASYMMETRIES

There are differences between the right and left cerebral hemispheres that might assist attempts to explain the behavioral and cognitive differences between human and nonhuman primates (Passingham, 1982; Warren, 1980). It is well known that there are anatomical asymmetries in adult and neonate human brains (Geschwind & Levitsky, 1968; Wada, Clarke, & Hamm, 1975; Witelson, 1977). For example, the planum temporale of the left hemisphere is an average of 1.4 cm longer and is more posterior than it is in the right hemisphere in approximately 65% to 70% of specimens examined.

Furthermore, a growing corpus of research indicates that the left and right hemispheres of the human brain have, in part, different functions or specializations (e.g., Beaton, 1986; Bryden, 1982). How the observed anatomical asymmetries interact with functional asymmetries has yet to be fully disambiguated. Some have suggested that such asymmetry may be related to an innate disposition for language in infants (Entus, 1977; Molfese & Betz, 1988; also see chapter 8 of this volume). Others have suggested that these anatomical asymmetries are related to basic asymmetries of attention, measured by head turning or posture (Turkewitz, 1977), and to a disposition for right-handedness in most humans and infants (Young, Segalowitz, Corter, & Trehub, 1983).

Interpretation of these findings will have to allow for the fact that many of these same anatomical asymmetries are found in nonhuman primate species, particularly in the great apes. For example, Yeni-Komshian and Benson (1976) found that the Sylvian Fissure of the left hemisphere was longer than the right in humans and chimpanzees but not in rhesus monkeys (*Macaca mulatta;* but see Falk, Cheverud, Vannier, & Conroy, 1985). It is reasonable to expect, however, that given the overlap between apes and humans in many anatomic asymmetries (also see LeMay & Geschwind, 1975) together with the robust evidence for functional asymmetries in humans, similarities between the species in asymmetrical function should exist.

Some researchers found no solid bases for concluding that there were population-level functional asymmetries in organisms other than humans (e.g., Warren, 1980). In contrast, several recent studies do strongly suggest functional asymmetries in nonhuman primates, including asymmetrical processing of form stimuli (Hopkins, Washburn, & Rumbaugh, 1990), visual-spatial discrimination (Hamilton & Vermeire, 1988a, 1988b; Hopkins & Morris, 1989), dot localization (Jason, Cowey, & Weiskrantz, 1984), processing of species-specific vocalizations (Petersen, Beecher, Moody, Zoloth, & Stebbins, 1978), and processing of tones (Dewson, 1977; Pohl, 1983).

Early studies gave no reason to anticipate cerebral lateralization and handedness in our apes. Notwithstanding, recent laterality research with our language-competent subjects indicate that they are predominantly right-handed (Bolser, Runfeldt, & Morris, 1988), and that they exhibit functional cerebral asymmetries similar to many of those found in human subjects (cf. Hopkins & Morris, 1989; Levy, 1982).

It appears that the asymmetries may differ functionally in degree and direction between species. Handedness in prosimians might well be opposite to that for humans (see MacNeilage, Studdert-Kennedy, & Lindblom, 1987; see also chapter 7 of this volume). The mean reaction times for the processing of form stimuli presented unilaterally to humans, chimpanzees, and rhesus monkeys (Hopkins, Washburn, & Rumbaugh, 1990) are quite different in that both humans and chimpanzees evidence a right-hemisphere advantage whereas monkeys show a left-hemisphere advantage.

Furthermore, two language-trained chimpanzees, Sherman and Austin, have evidenced faster reaction times to meaningful lexigrams when presented to the right visual field than to the left visual field (Hopkins, Morris, & Savage-Rumbaugh, 1991). This indicates that for these two chimpanzees meaningful symbols are processed more rapidly by the left hemisphere, a finding consistent with the human literature (Beaton, 1986; Bryden, 1982). Whether and how their rearing and language training produced these important results merits further study.

Brain Development and Learning Skills

Learning in relation to brain size and specific structures has been studied from a comparative perspective by several investigators (e.g., Masterson & Berkley, 1974; Masterson & Skeen, 1972; Rumbaugh & Pate, 1984). The main hypothesis derived is that learning abilities will differ in relation to relative size of the brain and its specific structures.

Masterson and Berkley (1974) determined that delayed matching-to-sample skills in a variety of mammals was very dependent on the premotor cortex. They also compared intact hedgehogs, tree shrews, and bush babies (a prosimian primate) on a delayed position-alternation task (1 to 256 sec). The varying degrees of prefrontal lobe elaboration for these species correlated positively with task performance. All subjects could delay without alternation and, also, alternate without delay; but neither hedgehogs nor tree shrews could delay and alternate at levels comparable to the bush baby, with its relatively enhanced prefrontal lobes.

Rumbaugh and Pate (1984) examined the complex-learning and transfer skills for 11 species of primates with various levels of brain complexity and size, including three species of prosimian, four species of monkey, and four species of ape. The transfer index (TI; Rumbaugh, 1969) learning levels of 67% and 84% correct criterion were established, in turn, on blocks of problems prior to cue reversal. There was a strong, positive relationship between learning criterion and transfer-of-training for all the great ape species. That is, reversal performance for chimpanzees, orangutans, and gorillas improved as prereversal criterion was increased from 67% to 84%. Conversely, the relationship was either null or strongly negative for all monkeys and prosimians for which data were available.

Fobes and King (1982) found that performance at the 84% criterion TI correlated .72 with the neocortex and telencephalon values reported by Stephan, Bauchot, and Andy (1970). (Data at the 67% level were not then available for the rhesus monkey; however, recent work in our laboratory [Washburn, Hopkins, & Rumbaugh, 1989] revealed that the 67% transfer values for the rhesus monkey are comparable to the great ape data. Unlike the data from other monkey species, but similar to great ape TI data, transfer-of-training for rhesus was significantly positive.)

In a related study, these same 11 species again were tested for learning capacities, with particular attention given to the emergence of mediational or relational learning vis-à-vis basic associative learning. Associative learning is viewed as the acquisition of specific responses or habits to specific stimuli based on cumulative reward strength. By contrast, mediational learning entails sensitivity to relationships among stimuli and responses and the emergence of rules that can facilitate problem solving and learning. As with TI values, only the three species of great apes demonstrated significant mediational patterns of responding, whereas the remaining species appeared to be primarily associative learners. Rumbaugh and Pate (1984) concluded that the great apes demonstrate learning processes that are qualitatively different from most monkeys, with apes utilizing mediational learning strategies. Except for rhesus (Washburn & Rumbaugh, in press), monkeys for which data are currently available are best characterized by associative learners.

In sum, evolution of the brain has been toward complexity. With complexity have come specialization and advancements in the ability to transfer learning to an advantage and to learn of relationships. In all probability, these developments are requisites to the emergence of language.

MATURATIONAL FACTORS

Bruner (1972) argued that protracted years of infancy allow organisms frequent and varied opportunities to learn social and communicative skills. The role that learning plays in the acquisition and refinement of such skills becomes increasingly significant as the brain becomes more complex. What is to be learned and what can be learned by the great ape infant is relatively less restricted than it is for the monkey infant, and behavior is not as limited to species-specific patterns.

A related factor is the maturity of the brain of an organism at birth. The relative maturation levels of the monkey, ape, and human brain differ significantly at birth (Passingham, 1982), with the human brain being the least mature. The more immature the brain at birth, the greater flexibility there is in what can be learned by an developing organism. Learning, in turn, affects neural organization.

Thus, although differences in learning abilities are evident across a broad range of species with differing brain size, maturational factors also affect the types of information that can be learned at various ages. Harlow, Harlow, Rueping, and Mason (1960) reported that 60-, 120-, and 360-day-old rhesus monkeys differed on learning-set proficiency, with the older animals being the more accomplished.

There are still other cognitive tasks that reflect maturational factors of the brain. Goodall (1986) described the development of tool-use skills in the wild chimpanzees of Gombe. Piagetian tasks have been useful in elucidating the sensorimotor stages of development in a variety of species (Chevalier-Skolnikoff, 1982; Dore & Dumar, 1987). It is noteworthy that only the great apes, of all nonhuman primates, develop all six sensorimotor stages as described by Piaget (see Scarr-Salapatek, 1976).

These studies indicate that species differences as well as individual and maturational factors affect performance of basic learning tasks in normally developing primates.

What Is Sensitive in a "Sensitive" Phase

The importance of a "sensitive" phase has been viewed as important for a variety of song birds (Kroodsma, 1982; Marler, 1970). Only if birds are exposed to the song repertoire of their species early in life will they be optimal in singing as adults.

For primates, sensitive phases in the development of vocalization are less compelling. On the other hand, Hopkins and Savage-Rumbaugh (in press) report that the vocalizations of a young bonobo (*Pan paniscus*) were structurally altered by exposure to human speech during infancy.

Seyfarth, Cheney, and Marler (1980) and Struhsaker (1967) have described three distinct vocalizations used by vervet monkeys that are reliably associated with the appearance of different predators. When emitted, other members within the troop respond as though they, too, have had direct perception of the predator for which the alarm call was emitted. The sounds are, however, natural to the vervet's development. What is learned is the appropriate context in which to produce them (Seyfarth & Cheney, 1986; Cheney & Seyfarth, 1990).

Environmental Factors and Development

Environmental enrichment and impoverishment during the years of infancy can have pronounced effects upon maturation (see Alcock, 1984) and the social and cognitive functioning of humans and many other animals (Hinde & Stevensen-Hinde, 1973). Fortunately, instances of complete isolation of human infants have been rare (see Curtiss, 1977).

Research with nonhuman primates has contributed substantively to our understanding of the social requisites for normal social and cognitive functioning (Harlow, Gluck, & Suomi 1972; Suomi, 1982). Gluck, Harlow, and Schiltz (1973) discerned that it was only in very complex tasks (i.e., oddity concept) that rhesus monkeys reared in isolation learned significantly poorer learning than those reared with their parents.

Studies of apes reared in partial or complete isolation have confirmed the findings with monkeys with the important addendum that the cost to cognitive development is probably more severe and enduring in apes. Davenport, Rogers, and Rumbaugh (1973) reported that six adult chimpanzees with early restricted laboratory environments throughout their first 2 years of life performed significantly worse on the transfer index than did eight wild-born chimpanzees of similar age. Furthermore, even though all animals shared common social and environmental experiences after the first 2 years and on to adulthood, the deficits remained for the chimpanzees reared initially in impoverished environments. In fact, two of those with impoverished rearing could not even be tested because of aberrant behaviors! These findings indicate that for the chimpanzee, with its relatively complex brain, the cognitive deficits incurred by early impoverished rearing are more resistant to remediation or correction through social stimulation than is the case for the rhesus monkey.

Rumbaugh (1970) reported an apparent interaction between species, age, and rearing condition for the learning-set competencies of six species of apes and monkeys ranging in age from infants to adults. Specifically, the orangutans, not previously used in psychological studies and with life histories primarily of standard maintenance in zoo caging, displayed great variation in learning. Two-year-old orangutans achieved the highest Trial-2 learning-set performance of all; however, adult orangutans were the lowest and near chance. By contrast, the chimpanzees, gorillas, and macaques with similar histories demonstrated increasing performance levels or stable performance levels across the 8-year age span. It was suggested that optimal cognitive development and functioning of the orangutan might be particularly dependent on appropriate and sustained environmental stimulation.

Menzel, Davenport, and Rogers (1970) contrasted tool-using abilities of adult wild chimpanzees and chimpanzees who, early in life, had been reared in a restricted environment. Notwithstanding the "equal opportunity" given them to become familiar with sticks, wild-born subjects were nearly twice as effective in raking banana slices into their cages as were the laboratory-born subjects. Also noteworthy is the lack of "self-awareness" in apes that have been reared in restricted environments (e.g., they did not recognize themselves in mirrors; see Gallup, 1987).

Early restricted social and environmental experiences can have profound adverse effects on long-term cognitive performance. The more complex the brain (i.e., the chimpanzee brain vs. that of the rhesus monkey), the greater seems to be the importance of appropriate and enriched environmental stimulation to the full development of cognitive competence.

Environmental Enrichment

Enrichment can have relatively specific effects on brain development. Stimulation through handling can affect later manifestations of lateralized functions in rats (Denenberg, 1981). Furthermore, rats reared in larger spaces and with a variety of play items demonstrated improved problem-solving skills compared to rats raised under restricted conditions and also showed differences in brain weight and chemistry (Bennett, Rosenzweig, Morimoto, & Herbert, 1979; Krech, Rosenzweig, & Bennett, 1962).

Similar interactions between neurological development and type of environmental stimulation are indicated with primates. Stell and Riesen (1987) reared macaques under various environmental conditions and found that the number of branchings of basilar dendrites of motor I cortex increased significantly in the condition associated with the greatest skills and activities that entailed climbing, swinging, and grasping of objects. The development of visual cortex had been shown previously to be sensitive to amount and kind of light that prevailed in the rearing environment of infant primates (see Riesen, 1982, for a review). Stell and Riesen concluded that genetic factors determine the basic formats for the development of neurological patterns, but environmental parameters serve to increase or decrease the dendritic branchings, hence the fine tuning and functional effectiveness of the neural organization in specific parts of the brain.

LEARNING, LANGUAGE AND APES

Laboratory studies, particularly those of recent years, have served to substantiate the claim that the chimpanzee has considerable language skills (Gardner & Gardner, 1969; Rumbaugh, 1977; Savage-Rumbaugh, 1986; Savage-Rumbaugh, MacDonald, Sevcik, Hopkins, & Rubert, 1986; Savage-Rumbaugh, Murphy, Sevcik, Gilmore, & Rumbaugh, in press; also refer to the introduction of this chapter). These studies suggest either that the ape shares a capacity for language with humans that takes other forms in the wild or that the ape-human interaction and environment early in the chimpanzee's life uniquely cultivates a capacity for some language.

Matata, an adult female bonobo (i.e., "pygmy" chimpanzee, *Pan paniscus*) who had a history of feral living until the age of about 5 years, provides a good case in point. As an adult, after several years of social maintenance, she entered the language studies at our laboratory. Matata appeared very bright, particularly when in the 55-acre forest that surrounds our laboratory. She has been sociable and has adapted readily to humans interacting with her during cleaning, feeding, playing, and even as she gave birth. Nevertheless, she has done poorly at learning the meanings of lexigrams and learning tasks readily mastered by other apes in our programs. In 2 years of language training, she learned only seven symbols and used them only to make requests for specific foods.

In contrast, at the age of $2\frac{1}{2}$ years Kanzi, Matata's infant, gave evidence that he had acquired mastery of lexigrams quite spontaneously, that is, without any specific, food-reinforced, discrete-trial training regimens. His mastery had been via observational learning during the daily training sessions given to his mother. Evidence of Kanzi's mastery of lexigrams and their meanings became apparent when Matata was separated from him for purposes of breeding. Even from the first day, it was apparent that he had learned what his mother had failed to learn. He was able to use lexigrams to request items, to comment on activities as he engaged in them, and he even comprehended symbols' meanings when used by others. He comprehended hundreds of spoken English words and novel requests made of him, again without specific training (Savage-Rumbaugh et al., 1986; Savage-Rumbaugh, 1988; Savage-Rumbaugh et al., in press).

Further evidence for the bonobo's ability to learn without specific training came from Mulika, born to Matata in 1984 (Sevcik, 1989). Because her eye became infected, Mulika was separated from Matata 4 months after birth and entered the ongoing project. At 17 months of age, Mulika reliably made requests with the limited use of only 7 symbols; however, her receptive skills of both lexigrams and spoken English was determined in tests to include 70 other symbols. A review of records revealed that of those 70 lexigrams, Mulika had used 30 of them at a keyboard only once — and 2 of them not at all. Observational learning is once again implicated as a powerful, previously unappreciated form of learning in the great apes.

It is clear that for both Kanzi and Mulika, and more recently for Panbanisha, also a bonobo, and Panzee, a common chimpanzee, that competent use of word-lexigrams is most efficiently acquired if comprehension is established first. Their comprehension has come about through their observing the use of symbols by their social partners (both human and chimpanzee) and the consequences thereof. Particularly in the case of Mulika it is clear that comprehension of symbols meanings is not contingent upon actual use of the lexigrams on the keyboards that are about the laboratory. With comprehension in place, subsequent productive use of the lexigrams appears without special effort or training.

The language learning by these chimpanzees is similar to that of the human child, where comprehension precedes productive speech, but stands in sharp contrast with the language learning by Lana, Sherman, and Austin. Lana, Sherman, and Austin received training regimens to acquire specific skills with lexigrams (i.e., to request food and activities, to label items, etc.), and it was assumed that if they used their symbols, they must understand their meanings. That assumption was, however, erroneous. That chimpanzees can use lexigrams does not mean that the symbols function representationally for them. Similarly, that a person or that a digitized telephone information service "says" words is not evidence that meaning is comprehended.

Neither Sherman nor Austin comprehended symbols (i.e., their referents) without the benefit of specific training. That training emphasized teaching them to pay attention to one another and to give one another or the experimenter specific tools or foods from an array (see Savage-Rumbaugh, 1986, for a complete description of procedures with accompanying 2-hour taped documentary). After that training, which spanned several months, the symbols came to function representationally for Sherman and Austin. They could comprehend symbols' meanings when used by others to comply with requests. Shortly thereafter, they began to make statements about what it was that they were going to get from an adjoining room or refrigerator and to label activities (e.g., play, tickle, chase, play-bite, etc.) in which they were engaged, the food or drink that they were ingesting, or things that they saw from the window. Very significantly, Sherman and Austin were then able to label 17 word-lexigrams, with each being the name of a specific food or tool, as categorically being either a food or a tool, through use of two lexigrams so glossed, in a tightly controlled test situation. Such performance would not have been possible unless their symbols actually represented items not necessarily present.

Kanzi's ball-search behaviors provide a good example of his comprehension of words. He has had a long-standing penchant for balls with which to play. Daily he asks for them. Kanzi's comprehension is clearly manifested when he is told by one person, either by spoken word or by lexigram on a keyboard, at which of six or seven sites in the laboratory's 55-acre forest a ball can be found. With Kanzi then entrusted to one or two human partners who do not know where the ball is to be found, he will lead essentially without error the way to the designated site and search until the prized ball is found. Travel to the site might take 20 to 30 min. Notwithstanding, Kanzi's goal-directed travel resists all but transient distraction by events along the trail.

Corroborating evidence for the importance of rearing upon the development of observational and relational learning skills comes from recent work that entails the use of video-formatted tasks and joysticks (Rumbaugh, Richardson, Washburn, Savage-Rumbaugh, & Hopkins, 1989) for studying cognition, learning (Washburn et al., 1989), laterality ((Hopkins & Morris, 1989), and numerical competencies (Rumbaugh, Hopkins, Washburn, & Savage-Rumbaugh, 1989). In our video-formatted tasks, the subject manipulates a joystick to control the movement of a cursor on a monitor and thereby is able to work on a variety of tasks. The video task paradigm was stimulated largely by early work with two of our language-trained chimpanzees, Sherman and Austin (Savage-Rumbaugh, 1986), who learned to use the joystick by observing an experimenter perform the task for them. After only a few minutes of demonstration, they literally elbowed the experimenter from the joystick and started to use it effectively. It was clear that they had perceived the relationship between the movement of the joystick by the experimenter and the movement of the cursor on the monitor. Lana, our initial subject in the language acquisition studies (Rumbaugh, 1977), also learned to use the joystick through observation.

By contrast, neither Matata nor two cage-reared orangutans were able to learn use of the joystick tasks by observation. Only through the benefit of specific software-training programs, developed for and used successfully with rhesus monkeys (Rumbaugh, Richardson, Washburn, Savage-Rumbaugh, & Hopkins, 1989), did they learn.

Thus, only language-sophisticated subjects have learned to use the joystick by observation. All other primate subjects required operant-shaping programs. The capacity for this skill exists in each subject, but how that skill can be mastered depends on the rearing history of the subjects.

It is probably significant that the subjects that have demonstrated joystick capabilities, with or without training, are of those species that show significant positive values within the transfer index paradigm, as was discussed earlier. It is likely that subjects/species that fail to manifest such a positive correlation in TI tests will fail to do other than the most basic joystick tasks regardless of how they are trained with it.

THE TIES THAT BIND: A PERSPECTIVE OF DEVELOPMENT, REARING, AND ADULT COMPETENCIES

We view it as quite probable that only early enriched environments, and in particular those noted for concentration upon rich social commerce and relational symbolic learning, allow the chimpanzee's psychological competencies to emerge in new and novel ways — ways that might be very foreign to their species in the field or in zoos. This contention goes beyond the suggestion that subjects simply become facile learners as a result of such rearing. It is, more pointedly, that they become adroit at relational learning skills, skills that entail more than the specific reward values of a single stimulus in a discrimination-learning situation. Their learning entails the discernment of temporal and causal relationships between responses and specific consequences that ensure. Very important is the fact that they can learn as much, and possibly more, from observing the consequences of their social partners' responses as from their own behavior. Such learning skills extend to the developing chimpanzee opportunities that far exceed its motoric ability to effectively interact with the physical and social environs.

That what is learned might be unique to enriched captive settings is made clear when they are compared with those acquired in feral settings. To the degree that Matata's record is instructive, what is learned for survival in the field is not applicable to the demands of relational tasks of a laboratory context.

We propose that the developmental structures for cognition in apes and humans are quite plastic and reflect in substantial measure the essence of early environment. The structures can selectively include records of salient experiences and organize them as models for approximate replication at later times. They also can organize experiences to serve as bases for the generation of new adaptive response patterns.

Cognition appears to assume patterns that are in accord with the more complex, yet structured and important, aspects of the environment within which development occurs. If the most complex and organized aspect of the early environment is one that emphasizes language and relational learning, chimpanzees will focus upon that in a measure that competes even with their appetites to be with their own social groups. Although our young apes can go visit other animals any time they wish, they typically want to leave them — even their mother — after a short period of time to resume the various activities of language learning that characterize their lives in our laboratory. Language provides a particular — and powerful — structure for the organization of cognition during development.

The enrichment inherent in a language-steeped environment might enhance the complexity of the neural networks of the chimpanzee's brain which approximate those that provide for language acquisition in the human child. As important, however, is the probability that relatively specific, facilitating, and limiting boundaries for cognitive development are defined by various environments.

We suggest that the developmental pattern of the chimpanzee becomes organized by the language-steeped environment so that it becomes uniquely sensitive to those new experiences that serve to elaborate and refine that format. Salient events, activities, or stimuli are assimilated by each organism into its cognitive repertoire, and the structure and organization of this cognitive architecture is altered appropriately to accommodate the structure and constraints of each experience. Experiences of each new day that "fit," that are logical extensions of the individual's developing pattern, are keenly attended and responded to, for those experiences can augment or elaborate the developmental pattern's structure, and subsequently its function.

Environmental challenges that are antithetical to the structure and function of the primary developmental format are resisted or otherwise not experienced to any benefit. They do not fit. That an "old dog" can learn new tricks is, quite probably, limited to those classes of tricks for which there is an early history and an accomplished record. One probably cannot "teach an old dog new tricks" if one is talking about tricks quite foreign to the class for which it has mastery.

We suggest, then, that as the chimpanzee learns the relational demands of language, it is developing neurological networks that resemble those that were basic to human neuro-evolutionary trends and the evolution of language and attendant lateralization.

In sum, we propose that the major dimensions of human competence for language, numbers, calculations, extrapolations, and so on, are reflections of (a) genetically possible modes and levels of development, as (b) modulated by degree of environmental complexity, and as (c) topically declared and limited by the recurring themes and ever-increasing difficulty of "object lessons" encountered by the organism across the days and years of its maturation to adulthood. Because the ape is so closely related to the human, it is sensitive to the identical environments that foster psychological competence in the human child — and likely for the same reasons. Being thus influenced, the chimpanzee can become unsuited for life in the field — just like humans who mature in contexts designed by eons of civilization, culture, and educational systems. The early environment serves not only to foster relatively specific competencies, it serves to "lock out," to preclude, and increasingly so across time, the possible development of other, equally impressive dimensions of competence — the bases for which lay in infancy spent in other kinds of enriched/stimulating environments.

There is an implication in our perspective for the emergence of human culture and civilization. Our perspective implies that the first steps taken toward culture, presumably by the innovations of adults, had their maximum impact upon and through the young, who by observation and living the consequences thereof became particularly adroit in advancing those hard-earned gains in their own adulthood. Their gains, in turn, provided still better, more focused contexts whereby the intellect of their own infants were both patterned and directed. Hence, we suggest that cultural gains evolved more as a consequence of contexts within which infants grew and the achievements that they, in turn, could make as adults than as a consequence of a capacity for invention/innovation bestowed upon an individual by virtue of being an adult.

ACKNOWLEDGEMENTS

Preparation of this chapter was supported by National Institutes of Health Grant RR-00165 and by Grant HD-06016 from the National Institute of Child Health and Human Development to the Yerkes Regional Primate Research Center. Additional support was provided by the College of Arts and Sciences, Georgia State University. We thank Austin H. Riesen for his critical comments and Clyde W. Faulkner for his colleagueship.

REFERENCES

Alcock, J. (1984). *Animal behavior, an evolutionary approach.* Sunderland, MA: Sinauer Associates.
Beaton, A. (1986). *Left side, right side: A review of laterality research.* New Haven: Yale University Press.
Bennett, E. L., Rosenzweig, M. R., Morimoto, H., & Herbert, M. (1979). Maze training alters brain weights and cortical RNA/DNA ratios. *Behavioral and Neural Biology, 26,* 1–22.
Bolser, L. A., Runfeldt, S., & Morris, R. D. (1988). Handedness in language-trained chimpanzees *(Pan troglodytes)* in daily activities and assessment tasks. *Journal of Experimental and Clinical Neuropsychology, 10,* 40.
Bruner, J. (1972). Nature and uses of immaturity. *American Psychologist, 27,* 687–708.
Bryden, M. P. (1982). *Laterality: Functional asymmetry in the intact brain.* New York: Academic.
Chevalier-Skolnikoff, S. (1982). Facial expression and cognitive processes in great apes. In C. T. Snowdon, C. H. Brown, & M. R. Petersen (Eds.), *Primate communication* (pp. 392–420). New York: Cambridge University Press.
Cheney, D. L., & Seyfarth, R. M. (1990). *How monkeys see the world.* Chicago: University of Chicago Press.
Curtiss, S. (1977). *Genie: A psycholinguistic study of a modern "wild child."* New York: Academic.
Davenport, R. K., Rogers, C. W., & Rumbaugh, D. M. (1973). Long-term cognitive deficits in chimpanzees associated with early impoverished rearing. *Developmental Psychology, 9,* 343–347.
Denenberg, V. (1981). Hemispheric laterality in animals and the effects of early experience. *Behavioral and Brain Sciences, 4,* 1–50.
Dewson, J. H. (1977). Preliminary evidence of hemispheric asymmetry in auditory function in

monkeys. In S. Harnad, R. W. Doty, L. Goldstein, J. Jaynes, & G. Krautharmer (Eds.), *Lateralization in the nervous system* (pp. 63–74). New York: Academic.

Dore, F. Y., & Dumar, C. (1987). Psychology of animal cognition: Piagetian studies. *Psychological Bulletin, 102,* 219–233.

Entus, A. K. (1977). Hemispheric asymmetry in processing of dichotically presented speech and nonspeech sounds. In S. J. Segalowitz & F. A. Gruber (Eds.), *Language development and neurological theory* (pp. 63–73). New York: Academic.

Falk, D., Cheverud, J., Vannier, M. W., & Conroy, G. C. (1985). Advanced computer graphics technology reveals cortical asymmetry in endocasts of rhesus monkeys. *Folia Primatologica, 46,* 98–103.

Fobes, J. L., & King, J. E. (1982). Measuring primate learning abilities. In J. L. Fobes & J. E. King (Eds.), *Primate behavior* (pp. 289–321). New York: Academic.

Frost, G. T. (1980). Tool behavior and the origins of laterality. *Journal of Human Evolution, 9,* 447–459.

Gallup, G. G. (1987). Self awareness. In J. Erwin (Ed.), *Comparative primate biology: Volume 2B. Behavior, cognition and motivation* (pp. 3–16). New York: Liss.

Gardner, A., & Gardner, B. (1969). Teaching sign language to a chimpanzee. *Science, 165,* 664–672.

Geschwind, N., & Levitsky, W. (1968). Human brain: Left-right asymmetries in temporal speech region. *Science, 161,* 186–187.

Gluck, J. P., Harlow, H. F., & Schiltz, K. A. (1973). Differential effect of early enrichment and deprivation on learning in the rhesus monkey. *Journal of Comparative and Physiological Psychology, 84,* 598–604.

Goodall, J. (1986). *The chimpanzees of Gombe.* Chicago: University of Chicago Press.

Hamilton, C. H., & Vermeire, B. A. (1988a). Complementary hemispheric specialization in monkeys. *Science, 242,* 1691–1694.

Hamilton, C. H., & Vermeire, B. A. (1988b). Cognition, not handedness, is lateralized in monkeys. *Behavioral and Brain Sciences, 11,* 723–725.

Harlow, H. F., Gluck, J. P., & Suomi, S. J. (1972). Generalization of behavioral data between nonhuman and human animals. *American Psychologist, 27,* 709–716.

Harlow, H. F., Harlow, M. K., Rueping, R. R., & Mason, W. A. (1960). Performance of infant rhesus monkeys on discrimination learning, delayed response, and discrimination learning set. *Journal of Comparative and Physiological Psychology, 53,* 113–121.

Hayes, K. J., & Nissen, C. H. (1971). Higher mental functions of a home-raised chimpanzee. In A. M. Schrier & F. Stollnitz (Eds.), *Behavior of nonhuman primates* (pp. 59–115). New York: Academic.

Hinde, R. A., & Stevensen-Hinde, J. (1973). *Constraints on learning: Limitations and predispositions.* London: Academic.

Holloway, R. L., & de la Costa-Lareymondie, M. C. (1982). Brain endocasts asymmetry in pongoids and hominoids: Some preliminary findings on the paleontology of cerebral dominance. *American Journal of Physical Anthropology, 58,* 101–110.

Hopkins, W. D., & Morris, R. D. (1989). Laterality for visual-spatial processing in two language trained chimpanzees (*Pan troglodytes*). *Behavioral Neuroscience, 103,* 227–234.

Hopkins, W. D., Morris, R. D., & Savage-Rumbaugh, E. S. (1991). Evidence for asymmetrical hemispheric priming using known and unknown warning stimuli in two language-trained chimpanzees (*Pan troglodytes*). *Journal of Experimental Psychology: General, 120,* 46-56.

Hopkins, W. D., & Savage-Rumbaugh, E. S. (in press). Vocal communication as a function of differential rearing experience in *Pan paniscus:* a preliminary report. *International Journal of Primatology.*

Hopkins, W. D., Washburn, D. A., & Rumbaugh, D. M. (1990). Processing of form stimuli presented unilaterally in humans, chimpanzees (*Pan troglodytes*) and monkeys (*Macaca mulatta*). *Behavioral Neuroscience, 104,* 577-582.

Jason, G. W., Cowey, A., & Weiskrantz, L. (1984). Hemispheric asymmetry for a visual-spatial task in monkeys. *Neuropsychologia, 22,* 777-784.

Jerison, H. J. (1985). On the evolution of mind. In D. A. Oakley (Ed.), *Brain and mind* (pp. 1-31). London & New York: Methuen.

Krech, D., Rosenzweig, M. R., & Bennett, E. L. (1962). Relations between brain chemistry and problem solving among rats raised in enriched and impoverished environments. *Journal of Comparative and Physiological Psychology, 55,* 801-808.

Kroodsma, D. E. (1982). Learning and the ontogeny of sound signals in birds. In D. E. Kroodsma & E. H. Miller (Eds.), *Acoustic communication in birds.* (Vol. 2, pp. 1-19). New York: Academic.

LeMay, M. (1985). Asymmetries of the brains and skulls of nonhuman primates. In S. Glick (Ed.), *Cerebral lateralization in nonhuman species* (pp. 235-245). New York: Academic.

LeMay, M., & Geschwind, N. (1975). Hemispheric differences in the brains of great apes. *Brain, Behavior, & Evolution, 11,* 48-52.

Lenneberg, E. H. (1967). *Biological foundations of language.* New York: Wiley.

Levy, J. (1982). Mental processes in the nonverbal hemisphere. In D. R. Griffin (Ed.), *Animal mind—human mind* (pp. 57-73). Berlin: Springer-Verlag.

Lieberman, P. (1975). *On the origins of language.* New York: Macmillan.

MacNeilage, P. F., Studdert-Kennedy, M. G., & Lindblom, B. (1987). Primate handedness reconsidered. *Behavioral and Brain Sciences, 10,* 247-303.

Marler, P. (1970). A comparative approach to vocal learning: Song development in white-crowned sparrows. *Journal of Comparative and Physiological Psychology, 71,* 1-25.

Masterson, R. B., & Berkley, M. A. (1974). Brain function: Changing ideas in the role of sensory, motor and association cortex in behavior. *Annual Review of Psychology, 25,* 277-312.

Masterson, R. B., & Skeen, L. C. (1972). Origins of anthropoid intelligence: Prefrontal system and delayed alternation in hedgehog, tree shrew, and bush baby. *Journal of Comparative and Physiological Psychology, 81,* 423-433.

Menzel, E. W., Jr., Davenport, R. K., & Rogers, C. M. (1970). The development of tool using in wild-born and restriction-reared chimpanzees. *Folia Primatologica, 12,* 273-283.

Molfese, D. L., & Betz, J. C. (1988). Electrophysiological indices of the early development of lateralization for language and cognition, and their implications for predicting later development. In D. L. Molfese & S. J. Segalowitz (Eds.), *Brain lateralization in children: Developmental implications* (pp. 171-190). New York: Guilford.

Passingham, R. (1975). Changes in size and organization of the brain in man and his ancestors. *Brain, Behavior and Evolution, II,* 73-90.

Passingham, R. (1982). *The human primate.* New York: Freeman.

Passingham, R., & Ettlinger, G. (1974). A comparison of cortical function in man and other primates. *International Review of Neurobiology, 16,* 233-299.

Petersen, M., Beecher, M., Zoloth, S., Moody, D., & Stebbins, W. (1978). Neural lateralization of species-specific vocalizations by Japanese macaques. *Science, 202,* 324-327.

Pohl, P. (1983). Central auditory processing: Ear advantages for acoustic stimuli in baboons. *Brain and Language, 20,* 44-53.

Riesen, A. H. (1982). Effects of environments on development in sensory systems. In W. D. Neff (Ed.), *Contributions to sensory physiology* (Vol. 6, pp. 45-77). New York: Academic.

Rumbaugh, D. M. (1969). The transfer index: An alternative measure to learning set. In C. R. Carpenter (Ed.), *Proceedings of the Second International Congress of Primatology* (pp. 541-547). Basel, Switzerland: Karger.

Rumbaugh, D. M. (1970). Learning skills of anthropoids. In L. Rosenblum (Ed.), *Primate behavior: Developments in field and laboratory research* (pp. 231-245). New York: Academic.

Rumbaugh, D. M. (1977). *Language learning by a chimpanzee: The LANA project.* New York: Academic.

Rumbaugh, D. M., Hopkins, W. D., Washburn, D. A., & Savage-Rumbaugh, E. S. (1989). Lana chimpanzee learns to count by "Numath": A summary of a videotaped experimental report. *The Psychological Record, 39,* 459–470.

Rumbaugh, D. M., & Pate, J. L. (1984). The evolution of cognition in primates: A comparative perspective. In H. L. Roitblat, T. G. Bever, & H. S. Terrace (Eds.), *Animal cognition* (pp. 403–420). Hillsdale, NJ: Lawrence Erlbaum Associates.

Rumbaugh, D. M., Richardson, W. K., Washburn, D. A., Savage-Rumbaugh, E. S., & Hopkins, W. D. (1989). Rhesus monkeys (*Macaca mulatta*), video tasks and implications for stimulus-response spatial contiguity. *Journal of Comparative Psychology, 103,* 32–38.

Savage-Rumbaugh, E. S. (1986). *Ape language: From conditioned responses to symbols.* New York: Columbia University Press.

Savage-Rumbaugh, E. S. (1988). A new look at ape language: Comprehension of vocal speech and syntax. In D. Leger (Ed.), *The Nebraska Symposium on Motivation, 35* (pp. 201–255). Lincoln: University of Nebraska.

Savage-Rumbaugh, E. S., MacDonald, K., Sevcik, R. A., Hopkins, W. D., & Rubert, E. (1986). Spontaneous symbol acquisition and communicative use by two pygmy chimpanzees. *Journal of Experimental Psychology: General, 115,* 211–235.

Savage-Rumbaugh, E. S., Murphy, J., Sevcik, R. A., & Rumbaugh, D. M. (in press). Language comprehension in ape and child. *Monographs of the Society for Research in Child Development.*

Scarr-Salapatek, S. (1976). An evolutionary perspective on infant intelligence: Species patterns and individual variations. In M. Lewis (Ed.), *Origins of intelligence* (pp. 165–197). New York: Plenum.

Sevcik, R. A. (1989). *A comprehensive analysis of graphic symbol acquisition and use: Evidence from an infant bonobo (Pan paniscus).* Unpublished doctoral dissertation, Georgia State University, Atlanta.

Seyfarth, R. M., & Cheney, D. L. (1986). Vocal development in vervet monkeys. *Animal Behaviour, 34,* 1640–1658.

Seyfarth, R. M., Cheney, D. L., & Marler, P. (1980). Vervet monkeys alarm calls: Semantic communication in a free ranging primate. *Animal Behaviour, 28,* 1070–1094.

Stell, M., & Riesen, A. (1987). Effects of early environments on motor cortex neuroanatomical changes following somatosensory experience. Effects of Layer III pyramidal cells in monkey cortex. *Behavioral Neuroscience, 101,* 341–346.

Stephan, H., Bauchot, R., & Andy, O. J. (1970). Data on size of the brain and of various brain parts in insectivores and primates. In C. R. Noback & W. Montagna (Eds.), *The primate brain* (pp. 289–297). New York: Appleton–Century–Crofts.

Struhsaker, T. T. (1967). Social structure among vervet monkeys (*Cercopithecus aethiops*). *Behaviour, 29,* 83–121.

Suomi, S. J. (1982). Abnormal behavior and primate models of psychopathology. In J. L. Fobes & J. E. King (Eds.), *Primate behavior* (pp. 172–209). New York: Academic.

Turkewitz, G. (1977). Development of lateral differentiation in the human infant. *Annals of the New York Academy of Sciences, 299,* 309–317.

Wada, J., Clarke, R., & Hamm, A. (1975). Cerebral hemispheric asymmetries in humans. *Archives of Neurology, 32,* 239–246.

Warren, J. M. (1980). Handedness and laterality in humans and other animals. *Physiological Psychology, 8,* 351–359.

Washburn, D. A., Hopkins, W. D., & Rumbaugh, D. M. (1989). Video-task assessment of learning and memory in macaques (*Macaca mulatta*): The effects of stimulus movement on performance. *Journal of Experimental Psychology: Animal Behavior Processes, 15,* 393–400.

Washburn, D. A., & Rumbaugh, D. M. (in press). Rhesus monkey (*Macaca mulatta*) complex learning skills reassessed. *International Journal of Primatology.*

Witelson, S. (1977). Anatomic asymmetry in the temporal lobes: Its documentation, phylogenesis, and relationship to functional asymmetry. *Annals of the New York Academy of Sciences, 299,* 328–354.

Witelson, S. F. (1987). Neurobiological aspects of language in children. *Child Development, 58,* 653–688.

Yeni-Komshian, G. H., & Benson, D. A. (1976). Anatomical study of cerebral asymmetry in the temporal lobe of humans, chimpanzees, and monkeys. *Science, 192,* 387–389.

Young, G., Segalowitz, S. J., Corter, C. M., & Trehub, S. (Eds.). (1983). *Manual specialization and the developing brain.* New York: Academic.

7

The "Postural Origins" Theory of Primate Neurobiological Asymmetries

Peter F. MacNeilage
University of Texas at Austin

Until very recently, there has been no doubt in the minds of most people that cerebral hemispheric specializations, associated with both handedness and language, first evolved in humans. This conclusion is a comforting one for the vast majority of people, as it fits their anthropocentric view of humankind. The supposedly emergent handedness specialization often is linked to the evolution of tool construction and use, and the fact that natural language is confined to humans makes it seem reasonable that its associated neural specialization also should be confined to humans. But regardless of how this view fits with human predilections, it is becoming clear that it must be replaced with a radically different one. It looks as if other animals once again are going to mess up our tidy, self-centered view of the world (Fuller, 1949).

The "Postural Origins" theory is an initial attempt to provide a unified view of the evolution of cerebral hemispheric specialization in all primates, based on both the newly emerging evidence in other primates and well-established evidence of the nature of hemispheric specializations in humans. It is argued that not only the left-hemisphere specializations of modern humans but also the right-hemisphere specializations, revealed in visual-spatial functions, may have taken a major formative step in the development of lateralized control of whole-body postural organization, as an adaptation to the inherently asymmetrical arboreal habitat of early primates, perhaps as early as 50 million years ago. It is argued that both hand use and communication developed lateralized neural specializations under these conditions because both functions were dependent on efficient whole-body postural organization. This history is considered to be reflected in the fact that human footedness, a necessarily postural specialization, has a stronger contralateral relation to language specialization in humans than does handedness. The weak relation between handedness and language specialization in humans, especially for tasks that do not involve whole-body postural adjustments, is considered to be due to two factors: the existence of a primate heritage of preference for both hands, and the development of the capacity for ipsilateral control of the hand with the evolution of complex forms of bimanual coordination in higher primates. The evidence for these conclusions, most of which have been developed in collaboration with Bjorn Lindblom and Michael Studdert-Kennedy, and discussed in detail elsewhere (MacNeilage, 1987, in press; MacNeilage, Studdert-Kennedy, & Lindblom, 1987, 1988), is now summarized.

BACKGROUND

Posture

As posture is the central concept in this chapter, it is appropriate to begin by a definition of it. *Webster's Seventh New Collegiate Dictionary* (1971) defined posture as: "Relative arrangement of the different parts esp. of the body . . . the position or bearing of the body, whether characteristic or assumed for a particular purpose." Characteristic postures include those assumed for locomotion (e.g., bipedal, quadrupedal), rest (sitting, lying), feeding, sexual intercourse, and communication. Most communicative acts of tetrapods are associated with particular whole-body postures. Postures for a particular purpose can be thought of as situationally induced variants within the aforementioned categories and others. Virtually every movement of an animal has postural consequences, as anybody with back problems will testify. Consequently a postural control mechanism is integral to action in the most basic sense. It is argued here that this fundamental fact is a necessary background for attempts to understand the evolution of both handedness and language. It is particularly important to note that the meaning of the term *posture* is not confined to static configurations, but also applies to acts with their associated movement dynamics.

POSTURE AND PRIMATE ORIGINS

The primate order was born when, under unknown selection pressures, certain mammals converted from a primarily terrestrial to a primarily arboreal habitat—to life in the trees. This development, described by Eisenberg (1981) as a truly three dimensional experiment, had profound postural consequences. In contrast to the relatively homogeneous support provided for an animal in terrestrial, aquatic, or aerial media, the supports provided by the arboreal habitat are: "(1) discontinuous, (2) limited, and variable in width, (3) mobile, and (4) oriented at all possible angles to the gravity vector" (Cartmill, 1974, p. 45). During the course of primate evolution various postural adaptations have been made to this demanding habitat, particularly for purposes of locomotion (e.g., vertical clinging and leaping, brachiation, knuckle walking) and feeding, including various modes of manual food acquisition.

It is considered that most of the earliest true primates—the first prosimians—were small manual predators (Fleagle, 1988). Of these, many adopted a new locomotor mode of vertical clinging and leaping (Napier & Walker, 1967). Their characteristic resting and feeding posture was clinging to relatively thin vertical supports. Fig. 7.1 shows a modern prosimian, the Tarsier, in such a posture. It is clear from the figure that this posture is necessarily asymmetrical. Neither the two hands nor the two legs can be

FIG. 7.1. A prosimian (Tarsier) in typical resting posture of vertical clinging—note the postural asymmetry.

placed at the same level on the support because it is not large enough to support them both at the same level, and the animal must hang to one particular side of the support. Many early primates must have spent the great majority of their time in this asymmetrical posture, as do their modern counterparts such as tarsiers and some species of bush baby. The demands of such a posture become particularly clear when one notes that in certain species, babies, from a few days of age onward, are characteristically left in this position while the parent forages (Charles-Dominique, 1984). Given that the posture of these animals must be asymmetrical in every instance of vertical clinging, and that the animal must initiate an acrobatic leap from this position, the question arises as to whether there is selection pressure for a consistent choice of a particular asymmetry. (A systematic asymmetry in the leaping behavior of one prosimian is reported in Jouffroy & Gasc, 1984.) It is clear from Fig. 7.1 that the high side of the body bears more of the load than the low side. Is there a pressure to developing a stronger side that would characteristically be the high side?

The answer to this question may come in part from consideration of postural aspects of feeding. Vertical clingers and leapers, and other small prosimian quadrupeds, are highly specialized feeders. They are manual predators typically grasping insects and small animals with one hand, though sometimes with both. Manual predation presumably evolved because of the difficulty of oral predation under arboreal conditions. Thus, for the first time in the half billion years of their existence, a group of vertebrates changed from bilaterally symmetrical midline predation by mouth to predation with an organ (the upper limb), which on most occasions is deployed with an asymmetrical overall body movement pattern. Cartmill (1975) argued that two of the main morphological adaptations of early primates, frontal eyes and the prehensile hand, were primarily adaptations for predation.

The act of manual feeding is highly specialized in some living primates. Bishop (1964) described insect-grabbing acts that cannot be followed by the naked eye. As in the case of the vertical clinging and leaping adaptation, one might ask whether this highly specialized feeding adaptation was accompanied by selection pressure for asymmetrical function. Did both arms become equally adept at this life-supporting "smash and grab" operation (Bishop, 1964) or, by analogy with the role of the mouth in all nonprimate predators, did a single organ become favored for predation. If so, then it seems clear from Fig. 7.1 that the hand used would be the lower one—the one bearing less weight in the vertical clinging posture, and therefore less able to provide postural stability during a sudden lateral arm movement. Consequently, there would be a complementary relation between the reaching hand and the contralateral side being used for postural support.

HANDEDNESS 1: ASYMMETRIES FAVORING THE LEFT LIMB IN OTHER PRIMATES

Prosimians.   Luckily, this discussion is not entirely academic. In 1984, Jeannette Ward and her colleagues at Memphis State University initiated a series of publications on hand use in prosimians (see Table 7.1) with a study of hand preferences in reaching for food in the lesser bush baby (*Galago senegalensis*), a vertical clinger and leaper, under two conditions: (a) a condition in which they reached through holes in their wire mesh cages placed so as to require vertical posture with support by the nonreaching hand, and (b) a condition in which food was dropped on the cage floor, thus requiring a tripedal horizontal postural stance (Sanford, Guin, & Ward, 1984). The first sign to appear in the literature that posture may be an important factor in hand preference was the finding that there was a strong (left) hand preference for reaching when the animals were in their more characteristic vertical posture but not when they were in a horizontal posture. Both trends were highly reliable on retest, but hand preference was not significantly correlated across the two conditions. The relation between left-hand preference and vertical posture has been confirmed for bush babies in two other studies by Ward and her colleagues (Sanford & Ward, 1986; Larson, Dodson, & Ward, 1989).

Ward and her colleagues also have found left-hand reaching preferences in several studies of lemurs: ring-tailed lemurs (*Lemur catta*) (Milliken,

TABLE 7.1
Summary of Studies Showing Left-Hand Reaching Preferences in Prosimians

	L	*R*	*A*	
Reaching; Vertical Posture Versus Horizontal Posture. Sanford et al., 1984	14	5	6	
Reaching; Visual Discrimination. Lesser Bush Babies. Sanford & Ward, 1986	7	1	0	*B* < .05
Reaching; Lesser Bush Babies. Larson et al., 1989	7	3	0	NS
Moat Reaching. Ruffed Lemurs. Forsythe et al., 1988	5	0	0	*B* < .05
Reaching, etc. Ring-Tailed Lemurs. Milliken, et al., 1989	7	0	0	*B* < .01
Reaching; Black Lemurs. Forsythe & Ward, 1988	20	12	1	NS
Reaching; Lemurs; 6 Species. Ward et al., in press	91	65	38	*B* < .05
Reaching etc.; Slender Lorises.	8	0	0	*B* < .01

Note. L = left, R = right, A = ambidextrous; B = binomial.

Forsythe, & Ward, 1989); black lemurs (*Lemur macaco*) (Forsythe & Ward, 1988); and a group of 194 lemurs of six species and five subspecies (Ward, Milliken, Dodson, Stafford, & Wallace, in press). The importance of postural considerations in hand use in lemurs also has been established by Ward's group. Forsythe, Milliken, Stafford, and Ward (1988) reported that although a group of five ruffed lemurs did not show particularly strong left-hand reaching preferences during foraging, members of the group made 514 out of 515 extended reaches for food floating in a moat, with their left hands!

These most surprising recent findings of Ward's group are nevertheless not altogether without precedent. They were foreshadowed by an informal report by Subramoniam (1957) who noted that all eight members of a group of slender lorises (*Loris tardigradus*) virtually always used their left hands to reach for food.

As Table 7.1 shows, not all of these studies produced statistically significant excesses of left-hand preferences over right-hand preferences. But as Ward (in press) stated, the only limiting factor in this regard seems to be the size of the particular sample available for study, a problem that plagues this area of work in general.

In contrast to the eight studies summarized in Table 7.1, which have found either significant left-hand reaching preferences or strong trends toward them in prosimians, there are not even any instances of strong trends toward right-hand preferences in groups of prosimians (though Ward [in press] has noted a trend toward more right-hand preferences in older animals, particularly older females, than in younger ones). Overall, this constitutes extremely strong evidence for the widespread existence of left-hand reaching preferences in a diverse array of prosimians.

Monkeys and Apes. There are a number of studies, summarized in Table 7.2, that suggest that the left-hand reaching preference is also present in higher nonhuman primates. An extremely large-scale study reporting strong left-hand preferences in a task that involved primarily reaching was conducted recently by Hauser et al. (in press). They observed rhesus monkeys on a task in which an animal must: (a) reach and grasp a lid, (b) open the lid, and (c) hold it open while (d) reaching inside to grasp chow. They found with two different size groups (277 and 130) that over 50% of the animals preferred to make both reaches with their left hand and hold the lid open with the right hand. The next most popular mode, used on about 25% of occasions, was the mirror image of the first mode in terms of hand use.

Relatively consistent though not particularly strong left-hand reaching preferences for food thrown to animals in naturalistic settings have been reported in a number of earlier studies of Japanese macaques (*Macaca*

fuscata; Itani, 1957; Itani, Tokuda, Furuya, Kano, & Shin, 1963; Tokuda, 1969). This trend was recently noted again, by Watanabe and Kawai (in press), at statistically significant levels.

A significant left-hand preference for reaching but not for a number of other activities was observed in marmosets (*Callithrix jacchus*) by Box (1977). Left-hand preferences for a number of reaching acts, which either occurred alone or as the terminal stage of tasks that required one or more other acts, were observed in a group of 10 stumptail macaques (*Macaca speciosa*) by Beck and Barton (1972). This result, though not statistically significant in itself, was of particular interest because there was a dissociation between the left-hand reaching preferences in this group of animals and right-hand preferences for other acts, most marked when fine manipulation was required. (The right-hand preferences are discussed later.) There are also a number of studies in which a trend toward left-hand preference was observed for an expose and reach sequence required in a visual two-choice discrimination task, or in a tactile discrimination task (Ettlinger, 1961; Ettlinger & Moffett, 1964; Gautrin & Ettlinger, 1970; Milner, 1969.) The trend reached statistical significance in the Ettlinger (1961) study. Quicker learning of a tactile discrimination task by animals with left-hand preferences than those with right-hand preferences recently was observed by Horster and Ettlinger (1985), though in this study no more animals preferred the left hand than the right. Fagot, Drea, & Wallen (in press) recently reported another instance of left-hand preference in rhesus monkeys, which they attributed to spatiotactile specialization of the left hand-right hemisphere. They found that 20 of a group of 30 animals preferred their left hand in a task in which they had to search manually within an opaque box for peanuts mixed with sand and stones, while clinging with three limbs to the vertical wire netting of the cage.

Three studies deserve separate consideration because they seem to involve left-hand preferences under especially demanding visuospatial conditions. This is most obviously true of the study of King and Landau (in press) who reported highly significant left-hand preferences in a group of 18 squirrel monkeys (*Saimiri sciureus*) on two tasks that involved catching goldfish. In one task, fish were caught from a bowl and in the other they were caught in a wading pool. Median tests evaluating the level of left-hand preference in the population were significant beyond the .001 level. The postural differences between these two tasks did not seem to be important: The correlation between the amount of left-hand preference on the two tasks was beyond the .01 level. In contrast, no significant hand preference was observed in either bipedal or tripedal reaches for static targets. In addition, Fagot and Vauclair (1988a) observed left-hand preferences in baboons in a task requiring precise alignment of a window in a sliding vertical Plexiglas panel with another aperture leading to a food reward. In addition, they obtained the same trend in a group of gorillas (Fagot & Vauclair, 1988b), which suggests functional continuity between great apes and monkeys in left-hand preferences under such conditions. As in the King and Landau study, simple reaching tests did not evoke a population-level hand preference in either baboons or gorillas. It is also interesting to note that in the Beck and Barton (1972) study mentioned earlier, of the 17 reaching responses studied, two of the top four median left-hand reaching preference levels (98% and 82%) were on the two tasks requiring reaching into a moving tube.

A statistically significant left-hand reaching preference in the lesser apes has been found by Olson, Ellis, and Nadler (1990) on a task that required taking raisins from the mesh screen of the cage while in bipedal position. A nonsignificant trend toward a left-hand preference also was observed in a task in which animals picked up raisins from the cage floor.

The Meaning of the Left-Hand Preferences

In a review of studies of handedness in primates in 1987 (MacNeilage et al., 1987), it was suggested that a left-hand-right-hemisphere specialization for visually guided movement may have evolved with a complementary right-side-left-hemisphere postural control specialization in the context of the evolution of the prehensile hand in early prosimians, perhaps as early as 50 million years ago. Since then, a good deal of additional data has accumulated to support this view (studies added since the 1987 review are indicated by a superscript "2" in Tables 7.1 & 7.2). The reason that the origin of the specialization was assigned to early prosimians is that it was in these animals that the supposedly causal selection pressure for unimanual predation first arose. It is considered that at least some small predatory prosimians "represent a conservative primate pattern carried forward into the present relatively unchanged" (Eisenberg, 1981, p. 161). In addition, there is increasing evidence for the contention (MacNeilage et al., 1987) that the left-hand-right-hemisphere specialization also may be present in monkeys, as well as evidence that it also may be present in gibbons and gorillas, though in gorillas it may only be evoked under special conditions. It is supposed that the presence of this specialization in modern monkeys and apes implies its presence in ancestral monkeys and apes, as they were presumably descendents of prosimians that already had developed the specialization. The left-hand preference also may be a feature of tactile tasks, though this possibility brings up some complicated questions, beyond the scope of this chapter. (See MacNeilage et al., 1987, including Footnote 1, for a discussion of this question.)

HANDEDNESS 2: ASYMMETRIES FAVORING THE RIGHT LIMB IN OTHER PRIMATES

In the 1987 review of primate handedness studies (MacNeilage et al., 1987), evidence for right-hand preferences in some nonhuman primates suggested the existence of right-handedness for manipulation and practiced acts. This suggestion remains appropriate in the light of more recent evidence. But there has been one very important addition to this evidence. Shafer (1987) has found evidence for a generalized right-hand preference, including a right-hand preference for simple reaching in gorillas. This evidence makes this genus appear to be more like humans than any other primate taxon, at this juncture. The results on monkeys and apes, summarized in Table 7.2, will now be considered.

Monkeys. Perhaps the most important single study showing right-limb asymmetries in other primates is the study of Beck and Barton (1972). In addition to the left-hand preference for reaching for food in various tasks, already discussed, this study showed a significant right-hand preference in the same group of 10 animals for the manipulation and holding acts that preceeded or accompanied the reaching acts. The study has three outstanding features:

1. The dissociation between left-hand preferences for reaching and right-hand preferences for other tasks in this study (see MacNeilage et al., 1987 for a summary of the results on the various individual tasks) showed for the first time that different types of task could systematically evoke different hand preferences in the same members of a primate species—a pattern quite different to that typical of humans.
2. It is the only study to have tested a fairly large primate sample on a very wide range of different experimental tasks including a number that were quite demanding.
3. It was on the most highly demanding type of task from the standpoint of manipulation that the highest levels of right-hand preferences were obtained—median preference levels of 96% and 97% were observed on a task that required two single finger movements to open two embedded hasps on a box containing food.

This study was the main reason for our 1987 recommendation (MacNeilage et al., 1987) that the question of primate handedness, which was at that time a dead issue, should be reconsidered.

Another study showing a significant right-hand preference on a test involving manipulation was that of Hopkins, Washburn, and Rumbaugh (1989). Though there were only five subjects in this study, two rhesus monkeys and three chimpanzees (hence its double listing in Table 7.2), all showed significant right-hand preferences and higher right-hand perfor- mance levels on a computer-game task in which the subject must hit a moving target stimulus on an oscilloscope screen with a cursor controlled by a joystick. The authors considered this to be evidence for a manipulative specialization of the right upper limb. An analogous specialization to that suggested by the study of Hopkins et al. may be indicated by a study of Preilowski (1979). He found that all eight of a group of rhesus monkeys showed higher levels of right-hand control in a task involving control of pressure exerted between the thumb and forefinger. Interestingly, however, this ability was independent of hand preference for the task.

The most marked manual asymmetry so far recorded in a single sample of nonhuman primates was reported by Kuhl (1988). She found that every single one of a group of 30 macaque monkeys (three species) she has studied over the past 10 years (2 to 3 years per animal) in auditory discrimination tasks, spontaneously chose the right hand for response purposes. The response was of a manipulative type—pressing, holding, and releasing a key—in a situation where the animal never saw the hand. As there is evidence that monkeys have a left-hemisphere specialization for auditory function (to be discussed later), the relative contribution of auditory and motor factors to this asymmetry is not clear. Perhaps it is because this task simultaneously evokes both propensities that the limb asymmetries ob- served in this task are so extraordinarily high.

The studies of Warren (1977) and the act and reach tasks studied by Ettlinger (1961) and Milner (1969) did not involve significant right-hand preference levels as such, but a trend toward increasing levels of right-hand preferences with increasing experience in performing tasks. It is of interest that in the latter case the trend is for animals without an initial preference to develop a right-hand preference rather than for left preferences to change to right preferences.

The study of King and Landau (in press), like that of Beck and Barton (1972), is of particular interest because it also reports a dissociation of hand preferences in two different tasks in the same animals. However, in this case both tasks involved reaching. In contrast to the left-hand preference for catching goldfish, many of the same animals showed a right-hand prefer- ence in a suspended reach task in which the animal had to obtain a piece of marshmallow on a dowel while clinging vertically with three limbs to the steel mesh of the cage wall. Indirect evidence that monkeys may have an overall preference for use of the right forelimb comes from a study of 145 rhesus monkeys (Falk, Pyne, Helmkamp, & DeRousseau, 1988) in which forelimb bones were found to be significantly larger on the right side, as they are in humans (Ruff & Jones, 1981). This study replicates an earlier, smaller scale study of Dhall and Singh (1977), in which they compared muscle weights in the upper body. However, this latter study included an additional finding suggesting that suspended reaching by the right hand might be favored in Old World monkeys as well as New World monkeys (King & Landau, in press). The only exception to their finding of heavier muscles on the right side was a significantly heavier left pectoralis major, the muscle that they considered most important for forelimb suspension.

Great Apes.   At the time of the 1987 review, there was relatively little evidence available regarding handedness in the great apes. Most of the evidence was equivocal though there were some trends toward right-hand preferences in gorillas. At that time, it was suggested that the great apes might be intermediate between monkeys, with their visuospatially related left-handedness and their manipulation-related right-handedness, and humans, with their generalized right-hand preference. Subsequent information suggests that this may indeed be the case. The study of gorillas adjusting a Plexiglas screen (Fagot & Vauclair, 1988b) suggests, as was noted earlier, that this species also possesses the tendency to favor the left hand in situations with relatively high amounts of visuospatial demand. And the studies of Shafer (1987) and Heestand (1986), respectively, suggest that gorillas might possess a humanlike generalized right-hand preference at the population level and an association of this preference with a postural asymmetry favoring action on the right side.

Shafer (1987) tabulated an astonishing total of 53,750 manual acts, 48,007 of which were unimanual, in a group of 47 gorillas. All acts involving upper limb use were tabulated during the sampling periods, and allocated to 1 of 10 categories (see Table 7.3). In terms of overall hand preference, 34 gorillas preferred the right hand, 10 preferred the left, and one was ambipreferent. Computation of Z scores on overall totals of individual animals revealed 24 right-hand preferences and 10 left-hand preferences ($\chi^2 < .05$). Overall, there were more right-hand acts than left-hand acts in 9 of the 10 behavioral categories considered.

Heestand (1986) studied free behavior of 70 apes—29 gorillas, 20 chimpanzees, 8 orangutans, and 13 siamangs. She found relatively little evidence of significant hand preferences. (The number of data points in each behavioral subcategory were apparently much smaller in Heestand's study than in Shafer's [1987].) However, she found an extremely strong trend in all four species for the right side of the body (forelimb and hindlimb) to initiate locomotion. That this postural bias was related to handedness was shown by the fact that over two thirds of the significant limb preferences for other activities (mostly upper limb preferences) shown by individual animals were concordant with their locomotion initiation asymmetries, significantly more than would be expected by chance (χ^2 9.89 $p < .01$—this author's computation). Contrarily, the animals without

TABLE 7.3
Relative Use of the Right and Left Hands in a Population of 47 Gorillas

Task Category	Total Acts	R:L Ratio	Signif. R.	Signif. L.
Eat	19,070	.96	18	10
Touch Self	10,623	1.20	15	2
Manipulate Small Object	7,644	1.25	11	4
Manipulate Large Object	3,331	1.18	5	3
Touch Other	2,753	1.20	5	3
Hit/Slap	1,086	1.51	4	1
Gestures	438	1.28	–	–
Throw	133	1.46	–	–
Dig/Sift	113	1.50	–	–
Other	2,816	1.31	13	2
	48,007	M 1.29	Σ 71	Σ 25

Note. The overall ratio of right- to left-hand acts, and the number of individuals with significant preferences on each class of act are given for each task category. L = Left; R = Right. Adapted from "Patterns of Hand Preference Among Captive Gorillas" by D. Shafer, 1987. Unpublished master's thesis, San Francisco State University.

locomotor initiation asymmetries showed no obvious bias toward a particular hand preference in the other activities. The finding of a right-side preference for initiation of locomotion perhaps has a parallel in the finding of Bracha, Seitz, Otemaa, & Glick (1987) that human adult men (though not women) prefer to turn to the right during their everyday activities.

Two other studies showing right-hand preferences in gorillas should be noted, one old and one new. In a study that has been widely ignored, probably because the behavior involved is not typical of humans, Schaller (1963) reported that in eight different subgroups of gorillas there was a preference for right-hand initiation of chest-beating displays. Overall, 90 right-hand initiations were observed out of a total of 110 displays. Like the finding of Kuhl (1988) summarized earlier, this result could be interpreted in terms of a left-hemisphere communication specialization, hand preference itself, or both.

In addition to finding left-hand preferences for reaching in gibbons, Olson et al. (1990) found a significant right-hand preference in gorillas in procuring food inserted into the wire mesh screens of their cages, a task they believe involves a manipulative component. No preferences were found in orangutans.

The Evolution of Right-Handedness

Subsequent results have supported the suggestion (MacNeilage et al., 1987) that with the evolution of species less dependent on unimanual predation and the vertical clinging posture, the posturally specialized right side may have become more available for operations on the environment beyond simple prehension. This side, because of its presumed greater strength (resulting from its postural support role), may have become favored for application of force on environmental objects. In addition, the heritage of the right hand as a versatile gripping device, in its postural support role, may have fitted it for manipulative operations as well as object contact. It also may have been that the capacity of the left hemisphere for the on-line, feedback-dependent adjustments initially required for postural support may have fitted it for on-line, time-extended interactions of the right hand-body complex with environmental objects. In short, the right side may have become the operational side for most purposes. With the advent of bipedalism, the left lower limb may have taken on the role of postural support. The fact that the left lower limb in human adults tends to be larger than the right is sometimes attributed to its postural support role (Ruff & Jones, 1981).

In contrast to the left hemisphere, the right hemisphere may have been best fitted for off-line preprogramming operations leading to the execution of ballistic reaching gestures. As ballistic prehension of food became less central in primates, and foraging became more central, left-hand preference may have become less predominant, eventually dropping out for the most part in humans. However, a role of the still-existing right-hemisphere, visual-spatial specialization in manual control still can be noted in the establishment of visually based presetting conditions, for right-hand as well as left-hand reaching, in humans (Goodale, 1990).

POSTURAL ORIGIN OF A COMMUNICATIVE SPECIALIZATION?

It has been suggested that right-handedness in humans and other higher primates had its origin in a left-hemisphere specialization evolving for postural control of the body, particularly the right side of the body, associated with vertical clinging and left-handed unimanual predation in early primates. The suggestion that the left-hemisphere language specialization might also have had a postural origin is somewhat more speculative. However, the existence of a left-hemisphere communicative specialization in monkeys suggests that some type of nonlinguistic explanation for the site of the language specialization is necessary, and this is an attempt to provide one.

There are three main sources of evidence for a left-hemisphere specialization for auditory function in monkeys (recall also Kuhl, 1988) and two of these studies involved vocal stimuli. (See MacNeilage, 1987, for more details.) First, Dewson (1977) found a deficit in a short-term auditory memory task in four monkeys with lesions of the left superior temporal gyrus, but no deficits in two animals with corresponding lesions on the right side. Second, Petersen, Beecher, Zoloth, Moody, & Stebbins (1978) showed that five of six Japanese macaque monkeys were better at discriminating conspecific vocal signals when they were presented to the right ear than when they were presented to the left. However, only one of five members of other species showed a right-ear advantage on these macaque calls. Third, Heffner and Heffner (1984), using the same stimuli as Petersen et al., showed that all five monkeys with ablation of the left superior temporal gyrus (the homolog of Wernicke's Area in humans) showed a deficit in discrimination in a conditioned avoidance task, but none of five monkeys with a corresponding right-hemisphere lesion were so afflicted. It must be admitted that all three of these studies suggest a specialization for perception, not a production specialization such as one might expect if postural considerations were involved. However, as Lashley (1951), Liberman and Mattingly (1985), and others have observed regarding speech, perceptual and productive aspects of communication have too much in common to depend on entirely separate mechanisms.

Part of the argument that postural considerations are involved in the evolution of the communicative hemispheric specialization comes from an analogy with manual evolution. The importance of the postural background for hand use has been neglected because of our focus on the most distal component of manual specialization, the hands and fingers, in isolation from the arms and the rest of the body, on which hand use is often dependent. Operations involving the hands and fingers, without the requirement of specific types of postural support from the body have become relatively more important in higher primates, especially in humans. But if we are to understand evolution we must focus both on what things are like and what they were like, because past adaptations are the basis for present ones. Asymmetrical use of the hand must have arisen in the context of asymmetrical use of the body.

In considering the evolution of speech, there also has been an excessive focus on the most distal component of the motor apparatus, the vocal tract and the upper articulators. Like the hands in the manual system, this most distal component of the vocal apparatus has undergone the most elaboration in humans. The most well-known scenario for the evolution of speech production (Lieberman, 1984) postulates a change in the shape of the articulatory apparatus as the rubicon that was crossed to obtain language. The main units of speech that set it apart from other primate calls — syllables, phonemes, features — are produced primarily by activities of the articulatory apparatus. But there are two more proximal functional components of speech that are equally essential to it, the phonatory and the respiratory components. In fact, these are the systems responsible for the macaque calls for which there is apparently a specialized left-hemispheric processor. Both of these components are influenced by postural factors, particularly the respiratory component, on which the phonatory component is dependent. For example, with respect to human speech, Hixon (1973) has pointed out that: "Departures from the upright posture have marked effects on the behaviors and interactions of various respiratory parts, these effects being related mainly to the influence of gravity" (p. 111). With regard to the need to maintain a more or less constant level of alveolar air pressure during human speech, Hixon noted that:

> . . . every postural change requires a different solution to the mechanical problem of providing a given alveolar pressure. Indeed the complexity of respiratory function in speech becomes quite staggering when consideration is given to the innumerable postures in which the body is oriented and reoriented with respect to gravity. (p. 114)

No doubt similar posture-related adjustments are necessary for vocalization in the various postural contexts required in the arboreal habitat.

There also has been another bias operating in the consideration of language evolution. Because language developed to its present level in the vocal-auditory medium, there has been an excessive focus on the evolution of vocal-auditory communication in comparative studies of natural primate communication, at the expense of the other main communicative medium, the visual medium. There are two primary sources of visually communicated signals in other primates: body postural and facial. Of these, the postural source was the first dominant source in our land-dwelling ancestors. For example, MacLean (1982) described representative courtship and threat gestures of lizards in terms of actions involving most of the body. Such gestures were also typical in the earliest reptiles, the first land-dwelling vertebrates, though these creatures had neither well-developed vocal and auditory capacities nor the capacity for facial expression.

Whole-body communicative gestures continue to play an important role in other living primates. For example, in a review of communication by postures in the rhesus monkey, Hinde and Rowell (1962) identified the following postural displays: five sitting postures, six categories of attack and threat, locomotion in fear, two classes of friendly behavior, and one miscellaneous category (pacing). In addition, it is important to note the high frequency with which communicative gestures with components from different sources are integrated in primate displays. Such displays often involve a specific whole-body posture with a specific facial expression and a specific vocalization. Given this fact, is it likely that the left-hemispheric specialization for vocal communication in monkeys is only for vocal communication?

With respect to the evolution of manual specialization, it has been argued here that the characteristically asymmetrical postures accompanying hand use in the arboreal habitat of the earliest primates may have contributed to the evolution of a lateralized postural control mechanism. To the degree that whole-body postural communication was important in early primates, to the degree that it was integrated with facial and vocal communicative sources, and to the degree that vocal communicative acts themselves involved postural adjustments, communication as well as hand use may have required the services of a lateralized postural control mechanism in this new habitat.

The arguments just given form part of the basis for suggesting that the left-hemisphere specialization for vocal communication as well as right-handedness might have had a postural origin. Language and manual specialization of the typical right-handed human might then be homologous in that they had a common origin in the development of a lateralized system for control of whole-body posture in the arboreal habitat of early primates.

At present, there is no evidence for a left-hemisphere specialization for communication in living prosimians. The question has not been investigated. Nevertheless, it is suggested that the specialization present in monkeys was also present in early prosimians. There are two reasons for this suggestion. The first is that there do not seem to have been any selection pressures specific to monkeys that would have required a communicative specialization, not present in prosimians, to have evolved in monkeys. The second is that, as in the case of hand use, the asymmetrical habitat encountered by early prosimians is considered to have exerted important selection pressures toward use of a lateralized postural controller for communicative acts.

POSTURAL IMPLICATIONS OF HUMAN ASYMMETRY PATTERNS

How does our knowledge of patterns of hemispheric specialization in humans fit the view of their evolution in other primates that has been presented here? An important human functional asymmetry in any attempt to establish a connection between humans and other primates is the one reflected in footedness. Footedness in humans has received little attention, and, to the author's knowledge, there has not been a single satisfactory explanation for its existence in humans (see Peters, 1988, for a review). It often has been considered an indirect effect of handedness, although the precise basis for the relationship has not been adequately given. In addition, as shown in Table 7.4, which is a summary of a number of studies of handedness-footedness relations, there is a dissociation between the two

TABLE 7.4
Summary of Foot Preference Data in Relation to Handedness
from Several Studies

| | Ns | | Percent Foot Preference | | | |
| | | | Right-Handers | | Left-Handers | |
	R	L	% Right	% Left	% Right	% Left
Eyre & Schmeekle (1933)	184	9	100	0	33	67
Peters & Durding (1979)	56	56	95	5	50	50
Chapman et al. (1983)	248	60	96	4	33	67
Clymer & Silva (1985)	622	45	94	6	31	69
Nachshon & Denno (1987)	533	80	91	9	47	53
Maki (1990)	99	90	94	6	51	49
Means			95	5	41	59

Note. L = Left; R = Right.

preferences in about 1 in every 10 people, which also has not been satisfactorily explained. One suggestion that has been made is that footedness is a more unbiased index of some basic lateral specialization in being less subject to dextral social pressures than handedness (e.g., Chapman, Chapman, & Allen, 1983). This explanation could fit the right-handed left-footers in Table 7.4, but there is an almost equally large number of left-handed right-footers who thus would be deemed to have moved in a direction diametrically opposite to the social pressure.

The present thesis is that an understanding of footedness and its relation to other fundamental asymmetries in primates, including humans, can be gained by noting its postural significance. Footedness is obviously an indicant of postural asymmetry because use of one leg for operations on the environment requires postural support of the body with the other leg. The predominance of right-footedness in humans is considered to be consistent with the conclusion from the postural origins theory that the right side of the body has become the operational side in higher primates (consequently right-footedness is predicted in other higher primates).

There is one particularly salient finding in the literature on human footedness, which has for the most part been ignored presumably because footedness itself is not well understood. In response to contradictory evidence on the relation between various indicants of human hemispheric specializations in studies with small numbers of subjects, Searleman (1980) reassessed these relationships in a study of 373 subjects (256 right-handers and 117 left-handers). His main finding was that, ". . . surprisingly, footedness and not handedness was the single best predictor of cerebral organization for language" (p. 252). In detail, Searleman found the following;

A significant relationship between footedness and direction of ear advantage was found for left handers ($\chi^2 p < .005$), such that left handers who were left footed or mixed footed had a much higher incidence of LEA (33% and 23% respectively) than did left handers who were right footers 2.5%). . . . The relationship between footedness and direction of ear advantage, collapsed across handedness, was also significant ($\chi^2 p < .001$), with left footed and mixed footed subjects having the highest incidence of LEA. Direction of ear advantage was not significantly related to any of the other subject variables, *including handedness*. (emphasis added, p. 249)

More recently, Maki (1990), working in this author's laboratory, replicated all of Searleman's (1980) findings (including the lack of a relation between handedness and language lateralization) in a study of 197 subjects (100 right-handers and 97 left-handers). Perhaps the most surprising finding of Searleman's study was the extremely strong tendency for right-footed left-handers to show a right-ear advantage in the dichotic listening task, suggesting that their language control coincided with the control of their preferred foot. He found that 39 of 40 of these subjects showed a right-ear advantage. Maki also observed this very strong trend. She found that 39 of her 46 right-footed left-handers had a right-ear advantage.

These results are readily explainable in the context of the postural origins theory. As footedness necessarily involves a postural asymmetry, the correlation between footedness and language laterality is evidence for the claim of a fundamental relation between postural and communicative specializations. Contrarily, the lack of a close relation between language laterality and handedness — a severe problem for any theory that maintains that one evolved from the other — is not surprising from the standpoint of the postural origins theory. It is simply reflective of the fact that in primate evolution there have been two hand-brain systems that could be used — even preferred — in normal animals, only one of which is dependent on the hemisphere specialized for posture and language. In fact, it is argued elsewhere that the lack of population-level hand preferences in many studies of other primates that involve undemanding tasks is due to an approximately equal number of animals choosing each of the two systems (MacNeilage, in press). The main evidence supporting this argument is that animals choosing left and right hands for such tasks are not simple mirror images of each other but have different specific patterns of hand-use propensities. An additional factor allowing flexibility in hand-brain relationships is the evolution of complex forms of bimanual coordination in higher primates, which permit ipsilateral control of the hand via the corpus callosum. In humans, the system of choice is overwhelmingly the right-hand-left-hemisphere system, with negligible evidence of specialized use of the motor outlet of the visuospatially specialized right hemisphere. Nevertheless, the flexible evolutionary basis for hand use allows the possibility of hand-use preferences that are contralateral to the visuospatially specialized hemisphere. A study of such cases was made by Kimura and D'Amico (1989). They showed that a group of adextrals (left-handers and ambidexters) with good spatial ability showed a right-ear advantage on the dichotic listening test equivalent to that of a group of right-handers comparable spatial ability. They suggested that in the adextral group the advantage to the left hand from the right-hemisphere spatial control overrides the advantage to the right hand from left-hemisphere praxic motor control. Nevertheless, it is well accepted that in such subjects there can also be a nonnegligible component of ipsilateral control of the preferred hand from the left hemisphere, presumably via the corpus callosum. (See MacNeilage, in press, for a discussion.)

It follows from the postural origins theory that when overall hand choice and footedness go their separate ways in humans, this dissociation will be least marked for hand acts requiring whole-body postural support. Consistent with this expectation are the facts that right-footed left-handers tend to be weak left-handers (Annett & Turner, 1974; Chapman et al., 1983) and their weakness often is reflected in the choice of the right hand for acts such as swinging a bat or an axe, which involve whole-body postural control (Bryden & Steenhuis, 1989; Healey, Liederman, & Geschwind, 1986). Such left-handers were detected by the keen clinical eye of the late Norman Geschwind (1985), who informally identified seven people who wrote with their left hand on paper but with their right hand on the blackboard.

CONCLUSION: STATUS OF THE POSTURAL
ORIGINS THEORY

The postural origins theory gives a unified account of a large body of findings regarding neurobiological asymmetries in primates, both human and nonhuman. It is the only relatively comprehensive account of the evolution of neurobiological asymmetries in other primates, and how these asymmetries relate to asymmetries in humans. It is the only theory to give an account of the strongest relation between a pair of asymmetries in humans, those for language and footedness, and to attempt to give an evolutionary basis for the lack of a close relation between handedness and language laterality. Finally, it has the merit of being consistent with the Neodarwinian Theory of Evolution by Natural Selection — natural selection of adaptive functions.

NONPRIMATE ORIGINS OF PRIMATE
NEUROBIOLOGICAL ASYMMETRIES?

It is presently an open question as to whether the neurobiological asymmetries that are claimed to have developed in early primates, according to the postural origins theory, actually originated in early primates. There is a good deal of evidence for the existence of postural asymmetries and asymmetries of spatial function in other mammals (Glick, 1985) and even some evidence for an asymmetry associated with vocal communication (Ehret, 1987; see the response to Dennenberg in MacNeilage et al., 1988 for further discussion of this question). The only claim being made here is that a particularly strong impetus toward the pattern of asymmetries considered to have existed in early primates was provided by selection pressures for unimanual predation and communication in a wholly arboreal habitat, and that subsequent developments in primates consisted of modifications of these patterns.

IMPLICATIONS OF THE POSTURAL ORIGINS
THEORY FOR LANGUAGE ONTOGENY

In the context of the topic of this chapter, the postural origins theory must be regarded as deep background. However, one important implication of the theory for language development in modern hominids seems clear. Just as language must have evolved in the context of the overall organization of both cerebral hemispheres, so must it develop in that context. Consequently, one should not be misled by the modularity of language components revealed in modern adult hominids into believing that language either evolved or developed in a modular fashion. Just as it was seen to be misleading to overemphasize the recently evolving distal components of the manual and vocal systems in attempting to understand their associated neural specializations, so is it misleading to overemphasize the end product of language development in trying to understand development itself. The link between neurobiological asymmetry for language and such a lowly thing as posture may be unwelcome, but it nevertheless may be important even for the understanding of language development. Language develops in a hemisphere that gives the first spontaneous sign of its specialized role in the form of a postural asymmetry favoring the right side in neonates (Michel, 1983).

REFERENCES

Annett, M., & Turner, A. (1974). Laterality and the growth of intellectual abilities. *British Journal of Psychology, 44,* 37–46.

Beck, C. H. M., & Barton, R. L. (1972). Deviation and laterality of hand preference in monkeys. *Cortex, 8,* 339–363.

Bishop, A. (1964). Use of the hand in lower primates. In J. Buettner-Janush (Ed.), *Evolutionary and genetic biology of primates* (Vol. 2, pp. 133–255). New York: Academic.

Box, H. O. (1977). Observations on spontaneous hand use in the common marmoset (*Callithrix jacchus*). *Primates, 18,* 395–400.

Bracha, H. S., Seitz, D. J., Otemaa, J., & Glick, S. D. (1987). Rotational movement (circling) in normal humans: Sex difference and relationship to hand, foot and eye preference. *Brain Research, 411,* 231–235.

Bryden, M. P., & Steenhuis, R. E. (1989). Different dimensions of hand preference relate to skilled and unskilled activities. *Cortex, 25,* 289–304.

Cartmill, M. (1974). Pads and claws in arboreal locomotion. In F. A. Jenkins (Ed.). *Primate locomotion* (pp. 45–83). New York: Academic.

Cartmill, M. (1975). *Primate origins.* Minneapolis: Burgess.

Chapman, J. P., Chapman, L. J., & Allen, J. J. (1983). The measurement of foot preference. *Neuropsychologia, 25,* 579–584.

Charles-Dominique, P. (1984). Bushbabies, lorises and pottos. In D. Hamilton (Ed.), *The encyclopedia of mammals* (pp. 332–339). New York: Facts on File Publications.

Clymer, P. E., & Silva, P. A. (1985). Laterality, cognitive ability and motor performance in a sample of seven year olds. *Journal of Human Movement Studies, 11,* 59–68.

Dewson, J. H. (1977). Preliminary evidence of hemispheric asymmetry of auditory function in monkeys. In S. Harnad, R. W. Doty, J. Jaynes, L. Goldstein, & G. Krauthamer (Eds.), *Lateralization in the nervous system* (pp. 63–71). New York: Academic.

Dhall, U., & Singh, I. (1977). Anatomical evidence of one-sided forelimb dominance in the rhesus monkey. *Anatomischer Anzeiger, 141,* 420–425.

Ehret, G. (1987). Left hemisphere advantage in the mouse brain for recognizing ultrasonic communication calls. *Nature, 325,* 249–51.

Eisenberg, J. F. (1981). *The mammalian radiations: An analysis of trends in evolution, adaptation, and behavior.* Chicago: University of Chicago Press.

Ettlinger, G. (1961). Lateral preferences in monkeys. *Behaviour, 17,* 275–87.

Ettlinger, G., & Moffett, A. (1964). Lateral preferences in the monkey. *Nature, 204,* 606.

Eyre, M. B., & Schmeekle, M. M. (1933). A study of handedness, eyedness and footedness. *Child Development, 4,* 73–78.

Fagot, J., Drea, C., & Wallen, K. (in press). Asymmetrical hand use in rhesus monkeys (*Macaca mulatta*) in tactually and visually regulated tasks. *Journal of Comparative Psychology.*

Fagot, J., & Vauclair, J. (1988a). Handedness and manual specialization in the baboon. *Neuropsychologia, 26,* 795–804.

Fagot, J., & Vauclair, J. (1988b). Handedness and bimanual coordination in the lowland gorilla. *Brain Behavior and Evolution, 32,* 89–95.

Falk, D., Pyne, L., Helmkamp, C., & De Rousseau, C. J. Skeletal asymmetry in forelimb of *Macaca mulatta. American Journal of Physical Anthropology, 77,* 1–6.

Fleagle, J. C. (1988). *Primate adaptation and evolution.* New York: Academic.

Forsythe, C., Milliken, G. W., Stafford, D. K., & Ward, J. P. (1988). Posturally related variations in the hand preferences of the ruffed lemur (*Varecia variegata variegata*). *Journal of Comparative Psychology, 102,* 248–250.

Forsythe, C., & Ward, J. P. (1988). Black lemur (*Lemur macaco*) hand preference in food reaching. *Primates, 29,* 75–77.

Fuller, B. A. G. (1949). The messes animals make in metaphysics. *The Journal of Philosophy, 46,* 829–838.

Gautrin, D., & Ettlinger, G. (1970). Lateral preferences in the monkey. *Cortex, 6,* 287–292.

Geschwind, N. (1985). Implications for evolution, genetics and clinical syndromes. In S. D. Glick (Ed.), *Cerebral lateralization in nonhuman species* (pp. 247–278). Orlando: Academic.

Glick, S. D. (Ed.). (1985). *Cerebral lateralization in nonhuman species.* Orlando: Academic.

Goodale, M. (1990). Brain asymmetries in the control of reaching. In M. A. Goodale (Ed.), *Vision and action: The control of grasping* (pp. 14–32). Norwood, NJ: Ablex.

Hauser, M., Perry, P., Manson, J. H., Ball, H., Williams, M., Pearson, E., & Berard, J. (in press). It's all in the hands of the beholder. *Behavior and Brain Sciences.*

Healey, J. M., Liederman, J., & Geschwind, N. (1986). Handedness is not a unidimensional trait. *Cortex, 22,* 33–54.

Heestand, J. E. (1986). *Behavioral lateralization in four species of apes.* Unpublished doctoral dissertation, University of Washington, Seattle.

Heffner, H. E., & Heffner, R. S. (1984). Temporal lobe lesions and the perception of species-specific vocalizations by macaques. *Science, 226,* 75–76.

Hinde, R. A., & Rowell, T. E. (1962). Communication by postures and facial expressions in the rhesus monkey (*Macaca mulatta*). *Proceedings of the Zoological Society of London, 138,* 1–21.

Hixon, T. J. (1973). Respiratory function in speech. In F. D. Minifie, T. J. Hixon, & F. Williams (Eds.), *Normal aspects of speech, hearing and language* (pp. 73–125). Englewood Cliffs, NJ: Prentice-Hall.

Hopkins, W. D., Washburn, D. A., & Rumbaugh, D. M. (1989). A note on hand use in the manipulation of joysticks by two rhesus monkeys and three chimpanzees (*Pan troglodytes*). *Journal of Comparative Psychology, 103,* 91–94.

Horster, W., & Ettlinger, G. (1985). An association between hand preference and tactile discrimination in the monkey. *Neuropsychologia, 23,* 411–413.

Itani, J. (1957). Personality of Japanese monkeys. *Iden, 11,* 29–33.

Itani, J., Tokuda, K., Furuya, Y., Kano, K., & Shin, Y. (1963). The social construction of natural troops of Japanese monkeys in Takasakiyama. *Primates, 4,* 1–42.

Jouffroy, F. K., & Gasc, J. P. (1984). A cineradiographical analysis of leaping in an African prosimian (*Galago alleni*). In F. A. Jenkins (Ed.), *Primate locomotion* (pp. 117–141). New York: Academic.

Kimura, D., & D'Amico, C. (1989). Evidence for subgroups of adextrals based on speech lateralization and cognitive patterns. *Neuropsychologia, 27,* 977–986.

King, J. E., & Landau, V. (in press). Manual preferences in varieties of reaching in squirrel monkeys. In J. Ward (Ed.), *New evidence of primate behavioral asymmetries.* New York: Springer-Verlag.

Kuhl, P. K. (1988). On handedness in primates and human infants. *The Behavioral and Brain Sciences, 11,* 739–741.

Larson, C. F., Dodson, D. L., & Ward, J. P. (1989). Hand preferences and whole body turning biases of lesser bushbabies (*Galago senegalensis*). *Brain, Behavior and Evolution, 33,* 261–267.

Lashley, K. S. (1951). The problem of serial order in behavior. In L. A. Jeffress (Ed.), *Cerebral mechanisms in behavior* (pp. 112–146). New York: Wiley.

Liberman, A. M., & Mattingly, I. G. (1985). The motor theory of speech perception revised. *Cognition, 21,* 1–36.

Lieberman, P. (1984). *The biology and evolution of language.* Cambridge, MA: Harvard University Press.

MacLean, P. D. (1982). On the origin and progressive evolution of the triune brain. In E. Armstrong & D. Falk (Eds.), *Primate brain evolution: Methods and concepts* (pp. 291–316). New York: Plenum.

MacNeilage, P. F. (1987). The evolution of hemispheric specialization for manual function and language. In S. Wise (Ed.), *Higher brain functions: Recent explorations of the brain's emergent properties* (pp. 285–309). New York: Wiley.

MacNeilage, P. F. (in press). Implications of primate behavioral asymmetries. In J. Ward (Ed.), *New evidence of primate behavioral asymmetries.* New York: Springer-Verlag.

MacNeilage, P. F., Studdert-Kennedy, M. G., & Lindblom, B. (1987). Primate handedness reconsidered. *The Behavioral and Brain Sciences, 10,* 247–263.

MacNeilage, P. F., Studdert-Kennedy, M. G., & Lindblom, B. (1988). Primate handedness: A foot in the door. *The Behavioral and Brain Sciences, 11,* 748–758.

Maki, S. (1990). *An experimental approach to the postural origins theory of neurobiological asymmetries in primates.* Unpublished doctoral dissertation, University of Texas at Austin.

Michel, G. F. (1983). Development of hand use preference during infancy. In G. Young, S. J. Segalowitz, C. M. Corter, & S. Trehub (Eds.), *Manual specialization and the developing brain* (pp. 33–70). New York: Academic.

Milliken, G. W., Forsythe, C., & Ward, J. P. (1989). Multiple measures of hand-use lateralization in the Ring-Tailed Lemur (*Lemur catta*). *Journal of Comparative Psychology, 103,* 262–268.

Milner, A. D. (1969). Distribution of hand preferences in monkeys. *Neuropsychologia, 7,* 375–377.

Nachson, I., & Denno, D. (1987). Birth order and lateral preferences. *Cortex, 22,* 567–578.

Napier, J. R., & Walker, A. C. (1967). Vertical clinging and leaping. *Folia Primatologica, 6,* 204–219.

Olson, D. A., Ellis, J. E., & Nadler, R. D. (1990). Hand preferences in captive gorillas, orang-utans and gibbons. *American Journal of Primatology, 20,* 83–94.

Peters, M., & Durding, B. M. (1979). Footedness of left and right handers. *American Journal of Psychology, 92,* 133–142.

Petersen, M., Beecher, B., Zoloth, S., Moody, D., & Stebbins, W. (1978). Neural lateralization of species-specific vocalizations by Japanese macaques (Macaca fuscata). *Science, 202,* 324–327.

Preilowski, B. (1979). Performance differences between hands and lack of transfer of finger posture skill in intact rhesus monkeys: Possible model of the origin of cerebral asymmetry. *Neuroscience Letters,* (Suppl. 3), 589.

Ruff, C. B., & Jones, H. H. (1981). Bilateral asymmetry in cortical bone of the humerus and tibia—Sex and age factors. *Human Biology, 53,* 69–86.

Sanford, C. G., Guin, K., & Ward, J. P. (1984). Posture and laterality in the bushbaby. *Brain Behavior and Evolution, 25,* 217–224.

Sanford, C. G., & Ward, J. P. (1986). Mirror image discrimination and hand preference in the bush baby (*Galago senegalensis*). *Psychological Record, 36,* 439–449.

Schaller, G. B. (1963). *The Mountain Gorilla.* Chicago: University of Chicago Press.

Searleman, A. (1980). Subject variables and cerebral organization for language. *Cortex, 16,* 239–254.

Shafer, D. (1987). *Patterns of hand preference among captive gorillas.* Master's thesis, San Francisco State University.

Subramoniam, S. (1957). Some observations on the habits of the slender loris, (*Loris tardigradus L*). *Journal of the Bombay Natural History Society, 54,* 386–398.

Tokuda, K. (1969). On the handedness of Japanese monkeys. *Primates, 10,* 41–46.

Ward, J. P. (in press). Prosimians as animal models in the study of neural lateralization. In F. L. Kitterle (Ed.), *Cerebral lateralization: Theory and research: The Toledo Symposium.* Hillsdale, NJ: Lawrence Erlbaum Associates.

Ward, J. P., Milliken, G. W., Dodson, D. L., Stafford, D. K., & Wallace, M. (in press). Handedness as a function of sex and age in a large population of Lemur. *Journal of Comparative Psychology.*

Warren, J. M. (1977). Handedness and cerebral dominance in monkeys. In S. Harnad, R. W. Doty, J. Jaynes, L. Goldstein, & G. Krauthamer (Eds.), *Lateralization in the nervous system.* New York: Academic.

Watanabe, K., & Kawai, M. (in press). Lateralized hand use observed in the precultural behavior of the Koshima monkeys (*Macaca fuscata*). In J. P. Ward (Ed.), *New evidence of primate behavioral asymmetries.* New York: Springer-Verlag.

Webster's Seventh New Collegiate Dictionary. (1971). Springfield, MA: Merriam-Webster.

8

Developmental Changes in Nonhuman Primate Patterns of Brain Lateralization for the Perception of Speech Cues: Neuroelectrical Correlates

Dennis L. Molfese
Southern Illinois University

Philip A. Morse
Boston University, and
New England Rehabilitation Hospital

This chapter provides a review of recent evoked potential investigations that have focused on comparisons between human and nonhuman primates. Both the published literature reviewed here and the new research data from rhesus monkeys concern one aspect of auditory perception for speech and related nonspeech cues — voice onset time (VOT). This cue has long been recognized as important for the perception of human speech information (Liberman, Cooper, Shankweiler, & Studdert-Kennedy, 1967). More recently, work has emerged that ties the perception of such information to brain response patterns in humans from infancy into adulthood (Molfese & Betz, 1988). However, little information is available concerning the perception of this information by nonhuman primates. The purpose in reviewing both the human and nonhuman reports in the present article is to address the origins of human speech discrimination abilities and the cross-species similarities in brain responsiveness in this process.

ELECTROPHYSIOLOGICAL PROCEDURES

The event-related potential (ERP) recorded from the scalp is a synchronized portion of the ongoing electroencephalogram (EEG) pattern that is elicited in response to the onset of some external or internal stimulus and that reflects changes in brain electrical activity over time. These variations in brain activity are reflected by amplitude changes or fluctuations in the height of this complex waveform at different points in its time course (Callaway, Tueting, & Koslow, 1978). A critical defining feature of the ERP is that it is time locked to the onset of some event in the subject's environment, whereas the ongoing EEG activity reflects a wide range of neural activity related to the myriad of neural and body self-regulating systems as well as the various sensory and cognitive functions ongoing in the brain at that time. The ERP, because of this time-locked feature, has been shown more likely to reflect both general and specific aspects of the evoking stimulus and individual's perceptions and decisions regarding the stimulus. Moreover, this time-locking feature enables researchers to pinpoint, with some degree of certainty, portions of the electrical response that occurred while the subject's attention was focused on a discrete event (Molfese, 1983; Nelson & Salapatek, 1986).

The ERP is not an exact and stable pattern that reflects only those discrete neural events directly related to the evoking stimulus, the task, or the subject's state. Rather, it is a by-product of the brain's bioelectrical response to an event that begins at levels well below that of the cortex as the stimulus information is transformed by the sensory systems. This activity progresses through the brainstem structures, into the midbrain, and on upward into the higher centers of the brain. Such signals must travel through a variety of tissues of different densities, conductivity, and composition (e.g., neurons, glial cells, fiber tracts, cerebral spinal fluid, bone, muscle) before they reach the recording electrodes placed on the scalp. Consequently, the final version of the ERP recorded at the scalp is a composite of a variety of complex factors, some of which relate directly to the testing situation and some of which do not. Moreover, as changes occur moment by moment in these factors, changes will occur at the same time in the amplitude of the ERP waveform which reflect both these non-task-related changes as well as changes in a variety of task-related cognitive factors. Because of such changes in the ERP, which result in part from continuous changes in the physiology of the subject, many researchers collect a number of ERPs to the same stimulus within a single recording session, and sum or average these responses to calculate an averaged evoked response. It is reasoned that either the summed or the averaged response is more likely to contain the repetitive activity that reflects the processing of the stimulus from one time to the next. The non-stimulus-related activity that is not time locked to the onset of the stimulus would be expected to average out or be minimized in the summed or averaged waveform of the ERP. Additional analyses subsequently are conducted on these waveforms and include a range of options such as amplitude and latency measures performed on various peaks of the averaged ERP, area measures, and a wide range of multivariate analysis procedures.

The ERP procedure has a number of strengths which include its ability to employ identical procedures with all participants, regardless of age or species. Consequently, direct comparisons of subject responses can be made between various subject groups in terms of discrimination abilities. Although the waveshapes of the ERPs will change from infancy to adulthood and differ across different species, one can assess whether the brain responses recorded from these different populations reliably discriminate between different stimuli, subject groups, and task characteristics. Moreover, the ERP procedures can be used to obtain response information from subjects who either have difficulty in responding in a normal fashion (as in the case of individuals with brain damage) or cannot respond because of language or maturity factors (as with young infants and children). The ERPs also provide information concerning both between-hemisphere differences as well as within-hemisphere differences. Thus, they can be used to address not only left–right hemisphere differences but anterior–posterior differences as well. Finally, the procedure provides time-related information that may offer insights into when information is detected and processed.

HUMAN SPEECH PERCEPTION: VOICE ONSET TIME

Previous researchers had identified voice onset time or VOT, the temporal relationship between laryngeal pulsing and the onset of consonant release, as an important cue for the perceived distinction between voiced and voiceless forms of stop consonants such as *b* and *p* (Liberman et al., 1967). Adult listeners appear to discriminate a variety of speech sounds by the phonetic labels attached to them. For example, adults readily can discriminate between consonants from different phonetic categories, such as [ba] and [pa], whereas they perform at only chance levels when attempting to discriminate between two different [ba] sounds that differ acoustically to the same extent as the [ba-pa] difference (Lisker & Abramson, 1970). This pattern of discrimination for between-phonetic category contrasts while chance levels of discrimination are noted for within-category contrasts is referred to as "categorical perception." Studies with infants (Eilers, Gavin, & Wilson, 1980; Eimas, Siqueland, Jusczyk, & Vigorito, 1971), children (Streeter, 1976), and adult listeners (Lisker & Abramson, 1970) have demonstrated categorical perception and discrimination for a wide range of contrasts such as voicing (*ba, pa; ga, ka*) and place of articulation (*ba, da, ga*).

The classic work by Eimas et al. (1971) investigating early categorical perception in young infants, when viewed against a backdrop of reports that language perception skills were lateralized (Kimura, 1961, Shankweiler & Studdert-Kennedy, 1967; Studdert-Kennedy & Shankweiler, 1970), provided one obvious approach to studying early lateralization for specific language-related cues. Clearly, if infants possessed such skills, one would expect that these skills should be lateralized to one hemisphere, generally the left, whereas the other hemisphere (the right) would not show such abilities. Molfese (1978), in a follow-up to work by Dorman (1974), attempted to determine whether categorical discrimination of VOT could be assessed using ERP procedures and, if present, whether such discriminations were confined to one hemisphere.

Before the work could begin with young infants, Molfese (1978) first had to determine whether such effects occurred for adults. To this end, Molfese recorded ERPs from the left and right temporal regions of 16 adults during a phoneme identification task. Scalp electrodes were placed over these sites using the Jasper (1958) system. In this case, the sites were T3 and T4 referenced to linked ear leads. The adults listened to auditorily presented and randomly ordered sequences of synthesized bilabial stop consonants with VOT values of +0 msec, +20 msec, +40 msec, and +60 msec. In the +0 msec case, the onset of consonant release and vocal fold vibration occurred simultaneously, whereas in the +60 msec condition the onset of laryngeal pulsing was delayed for 60 msec after consonant release. The ERPs were recorded in response to each sound; then, after a brief delay, the adults pressed a series of keys to identify the sound they had heard. Two regions of the ERP (one component centered around 135 ms and the second occurring between 300 and 500 ms following stimulus onset) did change systematically as a function of each sound's phonetic category—a categorical discrimination effect. Stop consonant sounds with VOT values of +0 and +20 msec (sounds identified as *ba* by the listeners) were discriminated from those with VOT values of +40 and +60 msec (sounds they identified as *pa*). However, the ERPs did not discriminate between the speech sounds from the same phonetic category. That is, they could not discriminate between the two tokens from the *ba* category that consisted of different VOT times, nor could they discriminate between the two different VOT tokens from the *pa* category. Consequently, there were no differences in the waveforms between the +0 and +20 msec sounds or between the +40 and +60 msec sounds. Electrophysiological studies employing similar stimuli with a variety of different populations have replicated this finding (Molfese, 1980; Molfese & Hess, 1978; Molfese & Molfese, 1979, 1988). Surprisingly, however, in all of these studies at least one region of the ERP in which this categorical discrimination effect was noted across the different age groups occurred over the right temporal region.

Similar effects were noted with 4-year-old children in a study involving the velar stop consonants *k* and *g*. Molfese and Hess (1978) recorded ERPs from the left and right temporal scalp regions of 12 preschool-age children (mean age = 4 years, 5 months) in response to randomly ordered series of synthesized consonant-vowel syllables in which the initial consonant varied in VOT from +0 msec, to +20 msec, to +40 msec, to +60 msec. Upon analysis of the ERPs, they, like Molfese (1978), also found a categorical discrimination effect whereby one late-occurring portion of the waveform (peak latency = 444 msec) changed systematically in response to consonants from different phonetic categories but did not respond differentially to consonants from within the same phonetic category. As in the case of Molfese, this effect occurred over the right hemisphere. However, unlike the adult study by Molfese, they found a second portion of the auditory ERP that occurred earlier in the waveform, before this right-hemisphere effect, and which was detected by electrodes placed over both hemispheres. This earlier auditory ERP component also discriminated the voiced from the voiceless consonants in a categorical manner (peak latencies = 198 and 342 msec). Similar results recently have been reported by Molfese and Molfese (1988) with 3-year-old children.

This work was extended later to include newborn and older infants (Molfese & Molfese, 1979). In the work with newborn infants, Molfese and Molfese presented the four consonant-vowel syllables used by Molfese (1978) to 16 infants between 2 and 5 months of age (mean = 3 months, 25 days). ERPs again were recorded from the left and right temporal locations. Analyses revealed that one portion or component of the auditory ERP, recorded from over the right hemisphere approximately 920 msec following stimulus onset, discriminated between the different speech sounds in a categorical manner. As in the case of Molfese and Hess (1978), Molfese and Molfese also noted a second portion of the auditory ERP that was present over both hemispheres and that also discriminated between the consonant sounds categorically. The major portion of this component occurred 528 msec following stimulus onset. These results, then, paralleled the findings of Molfese and Hess in noting two portions of the auditory ERP that discriminated between the speech sounds categorically. These included a bilateral component that occurred first in the waveform, followed by a right-hemisphere lateralized component that occurred later in time and also discriminated between the sounds categorically. A final portion of the ERP waveform was found to differ between the two hemispheres across all of the different stimuli.

A second experiment described by Molfese and Molfese (1979) failed to note any such bilateral or right-hemisphere lateralized effects with a younger group of infants. In that study they tested 16 newborn infants under 48 hours of age and failed to note any categoricallike discrimination effects in their sample on the basis of group analyses. However, a recent study by D. Kurtzberg (personal communication, 1988) employing a different evoked-potential test procedure suggests that at least some younger infants may be able to discriminate between voiced and voiceless consonant sounds.

One discrepancy between the adult study of Molfese (1978) and the studies with children (Molfese & Hess, 1978; Molfese & Molfese, 1988) and infants (Molfese & Molfese, 1979) concerns the absence of a bilateral effect with the adult population studied by Molfese. At first it was speculated that such a bilateral effect might drop out with further maturation and development. However, recent work with adults (Molfese, 1980) suggests that the bilateral effect remains in adults but that the area in which this effect can be noted is more restricted. The difference, then, between the two age groups could be due to the shrinking size of the electrical fields over which the effect can be detected. As individuals age, the scalp potentials become more and more differentiated, with more differences in electrical activity being noted between even closely adjacent electrode sites.

In one such study that illustrates this point, Molfese (1980) tested a group of adults to determine whether the laterality effects noted for the VOT stimuli were elicited by only speech stimuli or whether similar electrophysiological effects could be noted for both speech and nonspeech sounds. Such a comparison would allow conclusions to be reached regarding similarities in mechanisms that might subserve the perception of materials with similar temporal delays (+0, +20, +40, +60 msec). If the right-hemisphere and bilateral categorical effects occurred for nonspeech stimuli containing comparable temporal delays, it would be clear that such effects would be due to the temporal nature of the cues rather than to their "speech" quality. Molfese used four "tone onset time" (TOT) stimuli (from Pisoni, 1977). Each TOT stimulus was 230 msec in duration and consisted of two tones. The TOT stimuli differed from each other in the onset of the lower frequency tone (500 Hz) relative to the higher frequency tone (1500 Hz). The lower tone began at the same time as the upper tone for the 0-msec TOT stimulus. However, the lower tone lagged behind the upper tone by 20 msec for the +20-msec TOT stimulus. This delay increased to 40 msec and 60 msec, respectively, for the +40- and +60-msec TOT stimuli. Both tones ended simultaneously. ERPs were recorded from 16 adults. Analyses indicated that one region of the auditory ERP centered around 330 msec and common to electrodes placed over the temporal, central, and parietal regions of the right hemisphere categorically discriminated the +0- and +20-msec TOT sounds from the +40- and +60-msec sounds. No comparable changes were noted over the left hemisphere at this latency. However, bilateral responses were noted earlier in time from the left and right parietal regions 145 msec following stimulus onset and over the central areas at 210 msec. These effects are illustrated in Fig. 8.1 in which the group-averaged ERPs are displayed for each hemisphere and each of the TOT stimuli. In the case of the right-hemisphere lateralized response, the right-hemisphere response to the 0-msec stimulus is characterized by three downward pointing or negative peaks that occur at approximately 120 msec (N120), 280 msec (N280), and 400 msec (N400). The last two peaks, N280 and N400, reach a point of equal negativity for the +0- and +20-msec stimuli.

LEFT HEMISPHERE   RIGHT HEMISPHERE

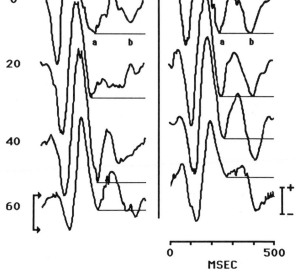

FIG. 8.1. Group-averaged ERPs recorded from electrodes placed over the left and right hemispheres of human adults in response to TOT stimuli varying in onset times from 0 msec to 60 msec. Points "a" and "b" indicate the negative peaks that varied as a function of TOT. In the right hemisphere, the 0- and 20-msec tones, the "a" and "b" peaks reached equal negativity as indicated by the horizontal line. However, the negativity for "b" increased relative to "a" for the 40- and 60-msec stimuli. Note that the "b" peak descends below the horizontal line. This difference does not hold for the left-hemisphere responses. A bilateral hemisphere effect is indicated by the smaller P60 − N110 amplitudes (indicated by the arrows at the bottom left of the AERs) for the 40- and 60-msec stimuli than for the 0- and 20-msec stimuli for both hemispheres. All ERPs begin at stimulus onset and continue for 500 msec. The calibration marker at the bottom right of the AERs is 2 uV with positive polarity (+) up.

However, the final negative peak (N400) increases its negativity for the +40- and +60-msec stimuli whereas the second negative peak, N280, does not. No such effect can be seen in the waveforms depicted for the left hemisphere at these latencies. The bilateral effect, on the other hand, can be readily observed in the ERPs from both hemispheres. In this case, the amplitude from the positive peak or point at approximately 80 msec to the negative peak at 120 msec is larger in response to the +0- and +20-msec stimuli than to the +40- and +60-msec stimuli. Interestingly, these bilateral effects were detected by electrodes placed over regions that were not sampled in the original Molfese (1978) study. Thus, the lack of bilateral effects in the original study appears to result from the use of fewer electrodes that resulted in a more restricted sampling of electrical activity across the scalp. However, when more of the scalp activity is sampled, as in the case of the infant and child studies, processing of the temporal cue appeared to involve both bilateral responses that occurred earlier in time, followed by later right-hemisphere lateralized responses.

Although one might speculate that the findings of the TOT stimuli may not be appropriately generalized to the VOT findings, a study that directly compares the two stimulus sets suggests that in fact identical responses occur to each. The work by Molfese and Molfese (1988) with 3-year-old children, employed both the VOT stimuli used by Molfese and Hess (1978) and the TOT stimuli of Molfese (1980). Here, Molfese and Molfese found that both stimulus sets produced identical right-hemisphere responses. Given the lack of differentiation of the brain's response to these speech and nonspeech signals, which vary along the same continuum, it appears that the categorical changes noted in the ERP are indeed the result of responses to temporal delays rather than to some general "speech" quality per se.

Although the right-hemisphere discrimination of the VOT cue seems paradoxical in light of arguments that language processes are carried out primarily by the left hemisphere, three developments that have emerged in the research literature within the last decade clearly support a right-hemisphere involvement in VOT discrimination:

1. Some researchers have suggested that the VOT cue is not speech specific but rather reflects the discrimination of a more basic temporal cue (Pisoni, 1977). Thus, VOT processing could be performed by nonlanguage mechanisms that reside in the other hemisphere. The lack of differences in the brain's evoked potential response to the speech and nonspeech materials that varied along a temporal dimension would support this point. Pisoni has made a similar argument based on his findings with adults in a behavioral discrimination study.

2. Clinical studies of VOT suggest that this temporal cue may be discriminated, if not exclusively, then at least in part, by the right hemisphere (for a review of this literature, see Molfese, Molfese, & Parsons, 1983). For example, Oscar-Berman, Zurif, and Blumstein (1975) noted that left-hemisphere-damaged individuals made fewer VOT-related errors than right-hemisphere-damaged patients in a dichotic identification task. This could be interpreted to indicate that the left-damaged patients, because they had an intact right hemisphere, were able to perceive and process the VOT information appropriately unlike the right-damaged patients who had sustained injury to the VOT-processing centers within the right hemisphere. Miceli, Caltagirone, Gianotti, and Payer-Rigo (1978), using a nondichotic

pair presentation task, noted that the left-brain-damaged aphasic group made fewest errors with stimuli differing in voicing but not in place of articulation whereas the right-damaged patients performed better when asked to discriminate between sounds that varied in place of articulation. Blumstein, Baker, and Goodglass (1977) also noted fewer errors for voicing contrasts than for place contrasts with left-hemisphere-damaged Wernicke aphasics. Finally, Perecman and Kellar (1981), based on their own findings that left-hemisphere-damaged patients continue to match sounds on the basis of voicing but not place, speculated that voicing could be processed by either hemisphere but that the PLACE cue was more likely to be processed by only the left hemisphere. All of these studies, then, suggest that the right hemisphere may play a more important role in the processing of related information.

3. The electrophysiological studies of Molfese and his colleagues point to several regions of the brain that appear responsive to voicing contrasts. That is, the brain's response does not appear to reflect a simple left–right difference but instead indicates a more dynamic process in which the involvement of the two hemispheres and regions within the hemispheres change across time. A summary of these findings is presented in Table 8.1.

In summary, then, four general findings have emerged from this series of VOT/TOT studies with human infants, children, and adults. First, the discrimination of the temporal delay cue common to voiced and voiceless stop consonants can be detected by electrophysiological measures – specifically, the ERPs recorded from electrodes placed on the scalp over the two hemispheres. Second, from at least 2 months of age if not before, the infant's brain appears capable of discriminating voiced from voiceless stop consonants in a categorical manner. Third, categorical discrimination across different ages appears to be carried out first by bilaterally represented mechanisms within both hemispheres and then, somewhat later in time, by right-hemisphere lateralized mechanisms. And fourth, the discrimination of the VOT cue may access more basic auditory processes that are not specific to speech per se.

NONHUMAN PRIMATE SPEECH DISCRIMINATION

As noted in the previous section, results from electrophysiological studies with human infants, children, and adults appear to parallel the findings from behavioral studies in a number of ways. From early in infancy, humans appear to discriminate between speech sounds that vary along specific acoustic dimensions in a fairly consistent fashion. In addition, however, the use of ERP procedures to study speech discrimination enabled

TABLE 8.1
Summary of Studies Investigating VOT Discrimination in Human Infants,
Children, and Adults

Study	Age	N	Stimuli	Sites	Results
Molfese & Molfese (1979)	1 Day	16	0-, 20-, 40-, 60-msec B/P	T3,T4	n.s.
Molfese & Molfese (1979)	4 Mo.	16	0-, 20-, 40-, 60-msec B/P	T3,T4	Bilateral: (400 msec–600 msec) 0-, 20-msec < > 40-, 60-msec RH: (660) msec–1,000 msec) 0-, 20-msec < > 40-, 60-msec
Molfese & Molfese (1988)	36 Mo.	12	0-, 20-, 40-, 60-msec G/K TOT	T3,T4	RH: (50 msec–220 msec) 0-, 20-msec < > 40-, 60-msec RH: (320 msec–500 msec) 0-, 20-msec < > 40-, 60-msec
Molfese & Hess (1978)	54 Mo.	12	0-, 20-, 40-, 60-msec G/K	T3,T4	Bilateral: (120 msec–180 msec, 200–460 msec) 0-, 20-msec < > 40-, 60-msec RH: (300–500 msec) 0-, 20-msec < > 40-, 60-msec
Molfese (1978)	27 Yrs	16	0-, 20-, 40-, 60-msec B/P	T3,T4	RH: (5 msec–235 msec) 0-, 20-msec < > 40-, 60-msec RH: (105 msec–175 msec) 0-, 20-msec < > 40-, 60-msec
Molfese (1980)	20 Yrs.	16	0-, 20-, 40-, 60-msec TOT	T3,C3, C4,T4 T5,P3, P4,T6	Bilateral: P3, P4 (140 msec–260 msec) 0-, 20-msec < > 40-, 60-msec Bilateral: P3, P4, C3, C4 (120 msec–190 msec) 0- 20-msec < > 40-, 60-msec RH: All Sites (320 msec–380 msec) 0-, 20-msec < > 40-, 60-msec

researchers to address questions concerning the more specific nature of the hemisphere differences reported in early behavioral and electrophysiological studies of young infants. Although clearly both hemispheres appear to be involved in the discrimination of different speech cues, the left hemisphere appears to play an additional role in the discrimination of consonant place information (Molfese & Betz, 1988), whereas the right hemisphere serves at least an additional function in the perception of temporal cues such as VOT. The early discrimination of such speech cues and the consistent involvement of the different hemispheres in humans could be used to argue that the perception of such cues is based on innately specified mechanisms that are unique to humans. On the other hand, such abilities might reflect mechanisms common to primates in general (Kuhl, 1981; Kuhl & Miller, 1975; Kuhl & Padden, 1983) or even to mammals (Adams,

Molfese, & Betz, 1987; Wilson, 1987). The research outlined as follows attempts to address this issue.

Behavioral Indices

A number of studies with nonhuman primates attempted to determine if certain types of speech perception abilities occurred in animals who do not possess the ability to produce the range of human sounds. For example, Waters and Wilson (1976) used a shock avoidance task to test rhesus monkeys on their ability to establish a voiced-voiceless boundary and to discriminate contrasts along that continuum relative to their boundary. In fact, they found that these nonhuman primates placed the boundary for [ba – pa] in the same region as adult human listeners. Moreover, they noted that the rhesus discriminated better between than within the two categories. Kuhl and Padden (1983) confirmed this finding using a more extensive set of synthetic speech stimuli that differed in voicing. Finally, categorical responding to such voice contrasts has also been reported with nonprimates such as chinchillas (Kuhl, 1981; Kuhl & Miller, 1975). A more thorough and comprehensive review of this literature is available in Harnad (1987).

Electrophysiological Indices of Categorical Discrimination of Voicing

Although several researchers have focused their attention on the study of categorical perception for voicing (and place of articulation) information in nonhuman primates, few have attempted to address the neurocortical bases underlying the perception of these speech cues. These studies reveal little about the brain organization for this process in monkeys and its comparability to that in humans, either in terms of the brain regions that might subserve such discriminative abilities or the specific manner in which the discriminations are made. If either the brain regions that subserve the speech perception functions or the organization of the speech sound categories differ between human and nonhuman primates, then speculations concerning the origins of human speech perception abilities as simple extensions of general auditory abilities common to other species will need to be revised. The electrophysiological studies outlined in the following sections were conducted in an attempt to address these issues.

The data reported concern categorical discrimination of voicing by rhesus monkeys at three different ages (1 month, 1 year, and 3 years) and how their discrimination patterns resemble and differ from those noted in humans. The gross brain organization for perception of this speech contrast is reported for each age level tested and comparisons made across the three age groups. The results from this series of studies are presented in Table 8.2.

TABLE 8.2
Summary of Studies Investigating VOT Discrimination in Rhesus Monkeys
(*Macaca Mulatta*) at 1 Month, 1 Year, and 3 Years of Age

Age	N	Stimuli	Results
1 Mo.	5	0-, 20-, 40-, 60-msec	Bilateral: (240 msec–340 msec)
			0-, 20-msec, < > 40-, 60-msec
1 Yr.	5	0-, 20-, 40-, 60-msec	RH: (340 msec–450 msec)
			0-, 20-msec < > 40-, 60-msec
3 Yr.	11	0-, 20-, 40-, 60-msec	LH: (180 msec–360 msec)
			0-, 20-msec < > 40-, 60-msec

The data for the 1-year-olds have been previously published in detail
(Morse, Molfese, Laughlin, Linnville, & Wetzel, 1987), whereas the data
for the 1-month-olds and 3-year-olds have not been reported in earlier
publications. To facilitate comparisons with the human studies, the same
speech contrasts and methods of presentation were employed with both the
humans and the rhesus monkeys.

1-Month-Olds.   In the case of the 1-month-old group, ERPs were
recorded from over the left and right temporal scalp regions (T3 and T4,
referred to linked ears, cf. Jasper, 1958) of each animal in response to the
continuum of voiced and voiceless velar stop consonants employed by
Molfese and Hess (1978).

Each infant animal was tested individually while swaddled in a blanket
held in one of the tester's laps. One region of the ERPs between 240 msec
and 340 msec (peak latency of 300 msec) following stimulus onset discriminated between the voiced and voiceless stop consonants. This change in the
ERP waveform occurred over both the left- and right-hemisphere temporal
regions as indicated by a main effect for VOT, $F(3, 24) = 3.98, p < .0195$.
Planned comparisons indicated that although the ERPs evoked by the two
voiced stimuli differed from those produced in response to the voiceless
ones, $F(1, 24) = 8.42, p < .0077$, there were no differences in the ERP
responses to consonants from the same phonetic category. The responses to
the 0-msec and 20-msec stimuli did not differ from each other, $F(1, 24) =
1.79, p < .19$, and the ERPs to the 40-msec and 60-msec sounds did not
differ, $F(1, 24) = 1.77, p < .193$. These effects can be viewed in the group
averaged ERP waveforms that are displayed in Fig. 8.2. The region affected
appears to involve the region of the ERP that occurred after the initial large
negative deflection and represents a shift from a positive peak to a
following negative peak. In Fig. 8.2 this region corresponds to the
waveform encompassed by the rectangle. Here, the amplitude in the ERP
waveform between the points marked "a" and "b" within the rectangle is
larger for the left-hemisphere (LH) ERPs elicited by the 40-msec and

ONE-MONTH-OLD RHESUS
(n = 5)

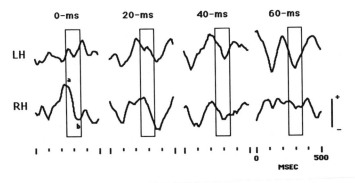

FIG. 8.2. Group-averaged ERPs collected from over the left and right hemispheres of five 1-month-old infant rhesus monkeys to a set of synthetic speech stimuli that varied in voice onset time from 0 msec to 60 msec. Calibration marker is 20 uV. Positive polarity is up.

60-msec stimuli. For the right-hemisphere (RH) ERPs, however, the vertical distance from point "a" to point "b" is larger for ERPs elicited by the 0-msec and 20-msec stimuli than for those elicited by the 40-msec and 60-msec stimuli.

1-Year-Olds. By 1 year of age, some marked differences have occurred in the ERP responses to the voicing cue. As indicated in Table 8.2, changes in the ERP waveform that appear to discriminate between the voiced and voiceless stimuli along human category boundaries are detected by electrodes placed over the right temporal (T3, T4) scalp locations of the 1-year-olds. These data are from a published report by Morse, Molfese, Laughlin, Linnville, and Wetzel (1987) in which a group of normal rhesus monkeys was compared with two other groups that were exposed to lead during different stages of prenatal and postnatal development. For the purposes of this chapter, only data from the five normal animals are represented here. Morse et al. reported a categorical discrimination effect for the ERPs recorded from over the right temporal region of the normal control animals. In this case, a systematic change was noted in the ERP waveform between 340 and 450 msec following stimulus onset that discriminated between but not within the phonetic categories. This effect can be viewed in Fig. 8.3. As in the preceding figure, the region of the ERP that varied as a function of VOT again involved the portion of the waveform following the initial large negative deflection and involved a change in amplitude from the following positive peak to a later negative point. In this

ONE-YEAR-OLD RHESUS
(n = 5)

TEMPORAL SITES

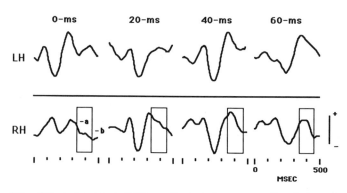

FIG. 8.3. Group-averaged ERPs collected from over the left and right hemispheres of five 1-year-old infant rhesus monkeys to a set of synthetic speech stimuli that varied in voice onset time from 0 msec to 60 msec. Calibration marker is 20 uV. Positive polarity is up.

figure, the amplitude of the ERP from point "a" to point "b" within the rectangle is smaller for the ERPs to the 0-msec and 20-msec stimuli than for the 40-msec and 60-msec stimuli. This effect appears to be the result of a prominent positive peak at approximately 370 msec for the 40- and 60-msec stimuli whereas no such peak can be noted for the 0- and 20-msec stimuli.

3-Year-Olds. Although the 1-month- and 1-year-old data fit at least in part with findings from the human data, the results from tests of the 3-year-old rhesus present a markedly different picture in terms of laterality. The 3-year-old rhesus monkeys were tested using procedures identical to those employed with the 1-year-olds. In this case, as indicated in Table 8.2, instead of the right-hemisphere effect previously reported for humans and for the 1-year-old rhesus, a left hemisphere categorical discrimination effect was noted for the 11 animals tested. A main effect for VOT, $F(3, 30) = 5.55$, $p < .0038$, and a VOT ß Hemisphere interaction, $F(3, 30) = 5.82$, $p < .0029$ identified systematic changes in the ERP waveform between 180 and 360 msec as a function of the phonetic category. Scheffe planned comparisons indicated that the ERPs to the 0-msec and 20-msec stimuli differed from those to the 40-msec and 60-msec stimuli, $F(1, 30) = 62.18$, $p < .00001$. However, although the ERPs to the 0-msec and 20-msec stimuli did not differ from each other, $F(1, 30) = .133$, $p < .72$, the ERPs to the 40-msec and 60-msec sounds did differ from each other, $F(1, 30) = 22.089$, $p < .0002$. Thus, changes in this region of the ERP indicate that the brain responses over the left hemisphere discriminate both between as well as within the different phonetic categories. This effect is illustrated in Fig. 8.4. As was the case for the 1-month- and 1-year-olds, the region of the ERP that varied as a function of VOT again involved the portion of the waveform following the initial large negative deflection or peak in the wave. To help illustrate the effects for the 3-year-olds, a horizontal line is drawn through the baselines (as determined by a 75-msec prestimulus period for each wave) for each of the left-hemisphere ERPs. The second positive peak in each wave is shaded to illustrate the region of the waves that the analyses indicated varied with changes in VOT. In this figure the shaded areas are larger for the left-hemisphere ERPs to the 0-msec and 20-msec stimuli than for the ERPs evoked by the 40-msec and 60-msec stimuli. However, as indicated by the Scheffe tests, the shaded areas for the 0-msec and 20-msec ERPs appear quite similar in size, whereas the 40-msec ERP is markedly smaller than that for the 60-msec ERP. Thus, although the 3-year-olds discriminate one phonetic category from another, they also are able to discriminate comparable acoustic differences within the second phonetic category.

In summary, by 1 month of age electrodes placed over the left and right temporal and parietal areas of both hemispheres of rhesus monkeys detect changes in the ERP patterns that appear to correspond to different human phonetic categories. By 1 year of age, this categorical discrimination effect

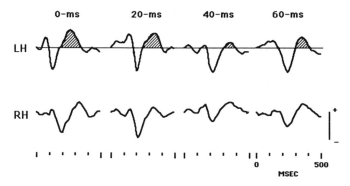

FIG. 8.4. Group-averaged ERPs collected from over the left and right hemispheres of 11 3-year-old rhesus monkeys to a set of synthetic speech stimuli that varied in voice onset time from 0 msec to 60 msec. Calibration marker is 20 uV. Positive polarity is up.

appears to be restricted to the right hemisphere. Finally, by 3 years of age, only a left-hemisphere response is noted that discriminates both between phonetic categories as well as partially within these categories.

SUMMARY AND CONCLUSIONS

The research with nonhuman primates described in this chapter has indicated that there are some indicators of speech discrimination patterns that are similar to those found in humans, whereas other features are quite dissimilar. Rhesus monkeys of all ages generated ERPs to speech stimuli varying in VOT that discriminated one phonetic category from another. This evidence of categorical discrimination would appear to be the most robust finding, holding up across human and nonhuman species. In this regard the two species are quite similar. However, with development the older rhesus (3-year-olds) begins to evidence some abilities at within-category discrimination (+40-msec vs. +60-msec) not seen in the human subjects tested with this paradigm and stimulus set.

In contrast, the patterns of cerebral lateralization evidenced in the rhesus monkey differ in several ways from that observed in humans. Although the 1-year-old rhesus monkeys displayed a right-hemisphere lateralized categorical discrimination of the VOT continuum, similar to that observed in humans of varying ages, the developmental pattern differed between the two species. Although humans at most ages tested generally display a bilateral followed by a right-hemisphere lateralized response, the rhesus display an initial bilateral response at 1 month, a right-hemisphere lateralized response at 1 year, and then a left-lateralized pattern of responding by 3 years. Furthermore, the temporal aspects of the ERP region where the speech sound discrimination occurs differed between the two species. Whereas the human ERP responses indicated both early and late ERP activity that reflected changes in VOT, the rhesus monkey's responses consistently occurred late in the waveform.

Thus, although some similarities exist between the human and nonhuman primate data for VOT discrimination and lateralization, there are enough differences to suggest that the pattern of brain mechanisms that subserve these discrimination functions in fact do differ in some important ways between the two species. Although there may be a common thread of mechanisms that subserve VOT discrimination in both human and nonhuman primates, it is at the same time clear that marked differences do separate the two species. The rhesus responses do not perfectly mirror those observed in humans. Consequently, the mechanisms that subserve these functions may in fact differ between humans and rhesus monkeys.

At what point in development these similarities and differences emerged remains unclear. The evolutionary break that gave rise to the divergence of the lineages for these two species is clearly an old one and the differences that distinguish between these two species are marked. The similarities may have preceded this break whereas the differences detected could reflect the results of this change. In the present case, it is possible that the similarities in speech perception responses between humans and rhesus monkeys may have resulted from a common evolutionary history prior to the divergence of the ancestors for these two species. Likewise, the differences reported here in the perception of speech sounds may have emerged after this evolutionary break. The differences in speech perception noted in this chapter between these two species may have occurred subsequently in the continued brain development of Old World monkeys, once they diverged from the main branch of primates that developed into *Homo sapiens.* Alternatively, they may have occurred in the continued brain development of the main branch within which *Homo sapiens* eventually emerged.

The thread that seems most common across both species is the categorical nature of the sorting of these acoustic cues. This suggests that this aspect of VOT discrimination may predate the divergence of nonhuman and human primates. The finding that chinchillas (nonprimate mammals) evidence categorical discrimination for VOT (Kuhl & Miller, 1975) further reinforces this hypothesis. The additional finding in the present series of studies of partial within-category discrimination in older rhesus monkeys suggests that this may be one aspect of auditory development in present-day rhesus monkeys that represents a further evolution (and perhaps refinement) of the Old World monkey's processing of acoustic information.

In contrast, the patterns of hemispheric lateralization and temporal features associated with the categorical processing of VOT clearly differentiate the two species. Whereas a bilateral, followed by a right-hemisphere component is generally the norm for present-day humans, the rhesus monkey varies considerably in its pattern of lateralization, depending upon age. Given the ontogenetic stability of this pattern in humans, it is tempting to speculate that this relatively robust pattern emerged in the course of human evolution following our divergence from the Old World monkey branch of primates. Similar developmental ERP studies carried out with the great apes might help to determine if this pattern of hemispheric specialization occurred relatively soon after this period of divergence, or whether the emergence of these stable patterns of lateralization for speech discrimination is a more recent developmental occurrence, perhaps related to the emergence of the specialized ability of humans to produce speech. The finding that the great apes consistently show some of the neuroanatomical asymmetries (e.g., left-hemisphere length, perisylvian region differences) that present-day humans exhibit (Geschwind & Galaburda, 1987; LeMay & Geschwind, 1975; Yeni-Komshian & Benson, 1976) raises the interesting possibility that these dynamic (ERP) aspects of hemisphere lateralization may well have emerged with the great apes, rather than awaiting the dramatic changes in the evolution of the vocal tract and the emergence of syntax and semantics.

ACKNOWLEDGEMENTS

Support for this work was provided by the National Science Foundation (BNS 8004429, BNS 8210846), the National Institutes of Health (R01 HD17860) and the Office of Research Development and Administration (2-10947), Southern Illinois University at Carbondale.

REFERENCES

Adams, C. A., Molfese, D. L., & Betz, J. C. (1987). Electrophysiological correlates of categorical speech perception for voicing contrasts in dogs. *Developmental Neuropsychology, 3,* 175–189.

Blumstein, S., Baker, E., & Goodglass, H. (1977). Phonological factors in auditory comprehension in aphasia. *Neuropsychologia, 15,* 19–30.

Callaway, E., Tueting, P., & Koslow, S. (1978). *Event-related brain potentials and behavior.* New York: Academic.

Dorman, M. (1974). Auditory evoked potential correlates of speech sound discrimination. *Perception & Psychophysics, 15,* 215–220.

Eilers, R., Gavin, W., & Wilson, W. (1980). Linguistic experience and phonemic perception in infancy: A cross-linguistic study. *Child Development, 50,* 14–18.

Eimas, P. D., Siqueland, E., Jusczyk, P., & Vigorito, J. (1971). Speech perception in infants. *Science, 171,* 303–306.

Geschwind, N., & Galaburda, A. M. (1987). *Cerebral lateralization: Biological mechanisms, associations, and pathology.* Cambridge, MA: MIT Press.

Harnad, S. (1987). *Categorical perception: The groundwork of cognition.* Cambridge, England: Cambridge University Press.

Jasper, H. H. (1958). The ten-twenty electrode system of the International Federation of Societies for Electroencephalography: Appendix to report of the committee on methods of clinical examination in electroencephalography. *Journal of Electroencephalography and Clinical Neurophysiology, 10,* 371–375.

Kimura, D. (1961). Cerebral dominance and the perception of verbal stimuli. *Canadian Journal of Psychology, 15,* 166–171.

Kuhl, P. (1981). Discrimination of speech by nonhuman animals: Basic auditory sensitivities conductive to the perception of speech-sound categories. *Journal of the Acoustical Society of America, 70,* 340–349.

Kuhl, P., & Miller, J. (1975). Speech perception by the chinchilla: Voiced–voiceless distinction in alveolar plosive consonants. *Science, 190,* 69–72.

Kuhl, P., & Padden, D. (1983). Enhanced discriminability at the phonetic boundaries for the voicing feature in macaques. *Perception & Psychophysics, 32,* 542–550.

LeMay, M., & Geschwind, N. (1975). Hemispheric differences in the brains of great apes. *Brain, Behavior & Evolution, 11,* 48–52.

Liberman, A. M., Cooper, F. S., Shankweiler, D., & Studdert-Kennedy, M. (1967). Perception of the speech code. *Psychological Review, 74,* 431–461.

Lisker, L., & Abramson, A. S. (1970). The voicing dimension: Some experiments in comparative phonetics. In (Ed.), *Proceedings of the 6th International Congress of Phonetic Sciences* (pp. 563–567). Prague: Academia.

Miceli, G., Caltagirone, C., Gianotti, G., & Payer-Rigo, P. (1978). Discrimination of voice versus place contrasts in aphasia. *Brain and Language, 6,* 47–51.

Molfese, D. L. (1978). Neuroelectrical correlates of categorical speech perception in adults. *Brain and Language, 5,* 25–35.

Molfese, D. L. (1980). Hemispheric specialization for temporal information: Implications for the perception of voicing cues during speech perception. *Brain and Language, 11,* 285–299.

Molfese, D. L. (1983). Event related potentials and language processes. In A. W. K. Gaillard & W. Ritter (Eds.), *Tutorials in ERP research: Endogenous components* (pp. 345–368). Amsterdam: North Holland.

Molfese, D. L., & Betz, J. C. (1988). Electrophysiological indices of the early development of lateralization for language and cognition, and their implication for predicting later development. In D. L. Molfese & S. J. Segalowitz (Eds.), *Brain lateralization in children: Developmental implications* (pp. 171–190). New York: Guilford.

Molfese, D. L., & Hess, T. M. (1978). Speech perception in nursery school age children: Sex and hemisphere differences. *Journal of Experimental Child Psychology, 26,* 71–84.

Molfese, D. L., & Molfese, V. J. (1979). Infant speech perception: Learned or innate. In H. A. Whitaker & H. Whitaker (Eds.), *Advances in neurolinguistics* (Vol. 4, pp. 225–238). New York: Academic.

Molfese, D. L., & Molfese, V. J. (1988). Right hemisphere responses from preschool children to temporal cues contained in speech and nonspeech materials: Electrophysiological correlates. *Brain and Language, 33,* 245–259.

Molfese, V. J., Molfese, D. L., & Parsons, C. (1983). Hemisphere involvement in phonological perception. In S. Segalowitz (Ed.), *Language functions and brain organization* (pp. 29–49). New York: Academic.

Morse, P. A., Molfese, D. L., Laughlin, N. K., Linnville, S., & Wetzel, W. F. (1987). Categorical perception for voicing contrasts in normal and lead-treated rhesus monkeys: Electrophysiological indices. *Brain and Language, 30,* 63–80.

Nelson, C. A., & Salapatek, P. (1986). Electrophysiological correlates of infant recognition memory. *Child Development, 57,* 1482–1497.

Oscar-Berman, M., Zurif, E., & Blumstein, S. (1975). Effects of unilateral brain damage on the processing of speech sounds. *Brain and Language, 2,* 345–355.

Perecman, E., & Kellar, L. (1981). The effect of voice and place among aphasic, nonaphasic right-damaged and normal subjects on a metalinguistic task. *Brain and Language, 12,* 213–223.

Pisoni, D. B. (1977). Identification and discrimination of the relative onset time of two component tones: Implications for voicing perception in stops. *Journal of the Acoustical Society of America, 61,* 1352–1361.

Shankweiler, M., & Studdert-Kennedy, D. (1967). Identification of consonants and vowels presented to left and right ears. *Quarterly Journal of Experimental Psychology, 14,* 69–63.

Streeter, L. A. (1976). Language perception of two-month-old infants shows effects of both innate mechanisms and experience. *Nature, 259,* 39–41.

Studdert-Kennedy, M., & Shankweiler, D. (1970). Hemisphere specialization for speech perception. *Journal of the Acoustical Society of America, 48,* 579–594.

Waters, R. S., & Wilson, W. A., Jr. (1976). Speech perception by rhesus monkeys: The voicing distinction in synthesized labial and velar stop consonants. *Perception & Psychophysics, 19,* 285–289.

Wilson, M. (1987). Brain mechanisms in categorical perception. In S. Harnad (Ed.), *Categorical perception: The groundwork of cognition* (pp. 387–420). Cambridge, England: Cambridge University Press.

Yeni-Komshian, G. H., & Benson, D. A. (1976). Anatomical study of cerebral asymmetry in the temporal lobe of humans, chimpanzees, and rhesus monkeys. *Science, 192,* 387–389.

9 Language Learning in the Bonobo: How and Why They Learn

E. Sue Savage-Rumbaugh
Georgia State University, and
Yerkes Regional Primate Research Center

THE BIOLOGICAL RELATIONSHIP OF MAN AND APE

The development of mind and the acquisition of language are two mental processes that seem to set *Homo sapiens* firmly apart from all other primates. Yet given the extraordinarily close genetic and morphological similarity between *Homo* and *Pan* (Sibley & Ahlquist, 1987), the apparent vast gap in mental ability represents an anomaly in the animal kingdom. *Homo* and *Pan,* by all reasonable taxonomic measures, should be in the same genus (Diamond, 1988).

There is some morphological basis for the mental difference between man and ape in that the brain of the ape is one third the size of man's (Passingham, 1982). Nonetheless, many examples may be found of persons whose brains are far below the normal size, but who display no intellectual deficit with regard to language development (Seckel, 1960). These findings have led to the assumption that there must be something about the unique structure of man's brain that has resulted in his intellectual achievements. Yet, there exist no clearly documented anatomical structures present in man's brain that are completely absent in the chimpanzee (Passingham, 1981, 1982). Man thus finds himself in the awkward position of having to acknowledge that the known physical basis of the dissimilarity between himself and the ape does not justify the degree of behavioral dissimilarity.

This raises the possibility that more of the behavioral differences between *Pan* and *Homo* may be attributable to learning than previously acknowledged. It also suggests that language may have been an "invented" behavior, rather than a biological endowment. Perhaps a small physical difference, such as the ability to engage in the controlled expiration of air, would have permitted a complex apelike intelligence to take advantage of this newfound physical ability and invent a crude language. Such an invention, perhaps primitive at first, could have been culturally transmitted across generations and likely would have exerted its own pressure for biological improvement. The invention of even a simple language would place severe biological pressures to evolve quickly upon the species that produced the invention. Members of the group who could not facilely acquire the new skill would rapidly be excluded from the larger community. It is self-evident that a behavioral-cultural invention on the order of a primitive language would allow a species to outpace other ape species very rapidly.

This hypothesis suggests that the mental gap between *Homo* and *Pan* may not be not as large as it appears and that apes might presently be biologically prepared to invent a primitive language, though mechanically compromised with regard to speech — an efficient medium of expressing it. One means of testing such a hypothesis would be to cross-rear members of *Homo* and *Pan*. Tarzan aside, there is only one feasible means of doing this, and that, of course, is for humans to rear chimpanzees.

The first such cross-species rearing project was undertaken by Hayes and Hayes (1952; Hayes, 1951) with the chimpanzee Viki. They attempted to teach Viki spoken English, but concluded that although chimpanzees could acquire many human competencies not normally found in apes, they could not learn to speak. Later studies, using modalities other than speech revealed that apes could acquire a rather large vocabulary (Gardner & Gardner, 1971; Rumbaugh, 1977). However, questions about whether words, as employed by apes, functioned as tokens to gain access to rewards, or as true symbols, clouded the interpretation of the data (Savage-Rumbaugh, Rumbaugh, & Boysen, 1980; Terrace, 1985). Initially it was assumed that apes, unlike children, could not acquire symbols observationally, but had to be rewarded for using the correct symbol (Gardner & Gardner, 1971; Premack, 1971), and often the object of note had to be shown to them before they could name it (Terrace, 1979).

LANGUAGE AND APES

Recent work has shown that these assumptions were based on the erroneous conclusion that apes could not acquire symbols through observational learning as do children. In part this erroneous conclusion arose because the first studies used either a vocal or a sign language system. In retrospect, the imitative skills required by either of these systems were beyond the capacity of young apes (Tomasello, 1990). Because the apes could not easily imitate either the words or the signs, shaping and reward of the response morphology was required. Such shaping functioned to deter comprehension and referential learning, because it stressed response topology, being "right," at the expense of communicating, and coming to understand the communications of others.

When a communication system was utilized that both simplified the topology of the response and provided extensive opportunity for observational learning, it was found that chimpanzees readily acquired symbols without reward or training (Savage-Rumbaugh, McDonald, Sevcik, Hopkins, & Rubert, 1986). Not only were printed symbols (lexigrams) learned, but comprehension of the spoken word also occurred and preceded the learning of lexical symbols.

Although animals such as dogs, sea lions, and dolphins have been trained to respond to spoken commands, there is no evidence to suggest that they are able to learn the meanings of words, as opposed to a series of motor commands (Schusterman & Gisiner, 1988). In some cases these commands are quite sophisticated. Herman, Richards, and Wolz (1984) have demonstrated that dolphins are sensitive to the order of three-word commands and that they can report whether an object is present or absent in their tank. Nonetheless, such usages should not be equated with knowing the meaning of a word and being able to use it referentially as do young children. Neither dolphins, dogs, nor sea lions are able to produce words, nor are they able to respond appropriately to a word employed in a truly novel manner. For example, a dolphin that can take a frisbee to a hoop on command cannot respond to propositional information such as "The hoop is hiding under the frisbee."[1]

Kanzi, a pygmy chimpanzee (*Pan paniscus*) was the first ape to demonstrate that observational exposure was sufficient to provide for the acquisition of lexical and vocal symbols (Savage-Rumbaugh, Sevcik, Rumbaugh, & Rubert, 1985). Three additional apes (two pygmy chimpanzees and one common chimpanzee) also have learned symbols without training, indicating that Kanzi's ability is unique neither to him nor to his species (Brakke & Savage-Rumbaugh, 1989). There is little doubt that observational learning is a more powerful method of language acquisition than is symbol training, given that the motoric responses of the system are simple enough for the ape to manage.

When words are learned observationally, those who would use an S-R conditioning response to dismiss the field of ape language, find it difficult to offer an explanation of how the behavior was acquired and what served

---

[1]It might be possible to arrange a training paradigm such that the dolphin appears to learn to respond such propositional information. Such would not negate the point being made here which is that the dolphin cannot transfer meaning from a command to a propositional statement because it has only learned a series of motor responses.

as the reward. How, for example, can an experimenter reinforce a response when what is being learned is not expressed behaviorally? When a symbol is comprehended there is often no overt cue that comprehension is occurring at the time. How is such covert behavior reinforced? If there is an intrinsic reinforcer for comprehension, what is it? How can the chimpanzee parcel out sounds from the speech stream in order to know which ones are important, or even where one word stops and another starts? Once this mysteriously is accomplished, how does the chimpanzee know which sounds to link with which referents or even that sounds have referents? How does the chimpanzee come to understand the concept that these sounds and lexigrams are being used to refer to objects and events at all? And how and why does the chimpanzee come to associate a particular sound with a particular symbol? How can a chimpanzee learn to match the sound to the picture of the real object and to the lexical symbol without being trained to do so (Savage-Rumbaugh, 1987). What motivates it to even want to learn this? Answers to these questions are fundamental to the advancement of our understanding of the bio-linguistic substrate.

STRUCTURAL THEORIES OF LANGUAGE

Studies of human learning have begun to turn to information-processing models and neural networks to explain complex behaviors for which there exists no overt measurable responses (Estes, 1978). Cognitive approaches to animal learning are tending to follow the models set by studies of human cognition (Roitblatt, 1987). Consequently, the goal of current animal studies is often that of attempting to lay bare the structure of the animal mind. The assumption underlying much of this work is that the experimental elucidation of structure will resolve the innate properties of human and animal mind by revealing how different species organize their perceptual and cognitive words. Most structural explanations treat learning as a subsidiary process. They assume that knowledge-organizing programs are innate and do not vary substantially from animal to animal within a given species.

The classical model of structural approaches is exemplified by the search for a universal grammar (UG), a grammar that will reveal the essence of man's linguistic capacity (Newmeyer, 1986). This search is founded upon the belief that once the UG is discovered, all other differences between languages will be readily explainable with a straightforward analysis of symbol input. If this view is accurate, it logically follows that there can be no similar explanation of chimpanzee language as there is no evidence that chimpanzees exhibit human language in their natural state. Consequently, any attempt to look for something analogous to UG is logically pointless.

Upon this perspective, whatever it is that a chimpanzee does, regardless of how closely it may resemble language—will not be language because the behavior can not depend on UG. That is to say, a chimpanzee cannot "learn" language, because the critical aspects of UG cannot be not learned; they are innate, and exist only in man.

It hardly needs stating that this view presumes its own conclusion and precludes all others. Although it is tempting to conclude that language must be innate, there are basic problems with this perspective that have yet to be sufficiently addressed by its proponents. First, the accepted dogma that closely related animals have no languagelike communication system is unproven. It is more accurate to state that man has yet to be able to decipher the communication systems of highly evolved mammals to any significant extent. The possibility that they have a communication system that assigns new sounds to new meanings and/or orders sounds according to the semantic relationships between them remains open. It is clear that apes may coordinate travel patterns and times through calls, as well as inform each other of the whereabouts of other animals and food resources (Ghiglieri, 1988; Tuttle, 1988).

The second problem with the innate perspective is that humans receive an enormous amount of daily input from which to learn language. The quantity and quality of this input from before birth onward makes it unlikely that there will be any aspect of language that a person did not have ample opportunity to learn. Additionally, it is true that each speaker must learn at least some aspects of all the major components of language, phonetics, semantics, and grammar (Wardhaugh, 1977). Indeed, even if some pieces of language eventually are identified as innate, it is reasonable to assert that the overwhelming majority of language is learned. In fact, so many of the components of language demonstrably require learning, one might inquire why nature would have programmed a few small innate pieces that seemingly we could have done without?

As it becomes increasingly clear that most components of language are learned, the importance of determining how language is acquired is viewed as crucial to understanding the development of mind (Fodor, 1982). Similarly, because nonhuman primates are capable of acquiring many components of language (Rumbaugh, 1986) and because they do so by processes similar to those that we employ, understanding the cognitive skills of nonhuman primates is becoming recognized as essential to understanding our own evolution. Because the life histories of such animals can be studied and documented in far greater detail than those of humans (and if need be even manipulated), it is reasonable that process-oriented attempts to understand how closely related animals acquire simple language will be found to have relevance to the development of language in humans.

PROCESS-ORIENTED THEORIES
OF LANGUAGE BEHAVIOR

The only process-oriented account that presently attempts to explain language behavior is Skinner's (1957) analysis in *Verbal Behavior*. Although this account has many virtues, it focuses upon adults and provides no developmental model of phonetics, semantics, or grammatical structure. It also fails to offer any analysis of language comprehension. What it does provide is a new vocabulary and a new way of talking about language that is strictly process oriented and avoids the error of assuming that meaning is inherent within words themselves.

Although Skinner's (1957) *Verbal Behavior* turns toward process, it offers no motivational mechanism to undergird such an account. The theory simply assumes that reinforcement is intrinsic. In other words, the child engages in behaviors that lead to language acquisition because he or she finds it reinforcing to do so. This perspective suffers, of course, from circularity and from motivational postulates that can be applied only to humans.

Unfortunately for those who would seek explanations in a procedural account, the real paradoxes of language acquisition are not addressed by *Verbal Behavior*. For example, how does the child come to determine which units are words, that is, where one word begins and another ends? How does the child come to use words reliably when they often are associated with very different consequences? How does the child make the pairing between word and consequence when each word is used a different way in a different sentence on almost every occasion? How does a child begin to understand what is said to him when parents do not set up specific invariable relationships between what they say and what they do? Even more important, how does a child learn which words are related to each other in a particular way in order that he or she may start to break the grammatical code?

It is unsatisfactory to conclude that grammar has been explained by the concepts of the "autoclitic" and the "interverbals." How is it that the child knows when and where to employ different autoclitic devices in the interpretation and/or production of novel sentences? In this regard *Verbal Behavior* seems to imply that the description of a phenomenon is equivalent to explanation. But this is not so; description is only a first step.

A PROCESS-ORIENTED INTERINDIVIDUAL ACCOUNT OF
LANGUAGE ACQUISITION IN THE CHIMPANZEE

Neither a structuralist approach, nor a behavioristic approach presently provides for an adequate description of what happens as a chimpanzee learns to produce and comprehend lexigram symbols and to comprehend novel spoken sentences (Savage-Rumbaugh, Sevcik, & Brakke, in press). Certainly, human language cannot be genetically preprogrammed in the ape, nor can the use of lexical symbols be assumed to be intrinsically reinforcing. What is needed is a process-oriented model of how chimpanzees acquire symbols.

Symbol acquisition in the chimpanzee appears to begin with the learning of routines. These are not experimentally planned routines, but rather routines that emerge out of everyday life. The chimpanzee's daily interactions with caretakers, although not experimentally programmed, can be viewed as a series of interindividual "routines," which become ever more complex and interchangeable with maturation and experience. The word *routine* is used to mean a more or less regularly sequenced set of interindividual interactions that occur in a relatively similar manner across time, or at different times. The sequence of interactions may vary, as may the words used in connection with the interaction, however each routine is carried out for a specific purpose.

For example, changing diapers, getting ready to go outdoors, taking a bath, riding in the car, looking at a book, blowing bubbles, putting items in the backpack, visiting with other apes, playing a game of tickle, traveling down various trails in the forest, are all routines. The chimpanzee may be a willing or unwilling participant within such routines. Similarly, he or she may play different roles on different occasions as participant or observer.[2]

The learning of such routines occurs regardless of whether the chimpanzee actively seeks to carry out the routine or finds it reinforcing. For example, a young chimp that is walking about, playing and climbing, and exploring its world, may be startled and irritated when someone waves a white thing in its face, pulls it down, and begins forcibly separating its body from the warm and comfortable white cloth in its groin — if it does not know what is happening to it. If, however, it recognizes that action as the "changing diaper routine," it will come over quietly and lie down when it sees the clean diaper being displayed — as a signal of the caretaker's intent.

---

[2]Bruner (1983), referring to children, has used the term "format" in a similar way and Nelson (1986) has spoken of "event knowledge" or "scripts." I have chosen to use a different term, because I am speaking of apes, not children, and it is premature to equate the processes through use of common terms. Bruner suggested that such routines teach the child their roles, with the mother first playing her role and then also that of the child and then slowly phasing herself out while still providing the child with the structure and sufficient cues to enable him or her to play their part of the role. Nelson referred to the value of such routines in generating within the child event-based knowledge regarding how the real world operates. The view offered here is not in opposition to either of these positions. Rather, it complements them by more explicitly defining how it is that such routines facilitate the comprehension of words and motivate their usage for apes.

If the caretaker always executes the diaper removal and replacement in the same calm manner, the chimp will lie still, knowing what to expect. If, however, a new caretaker comes in, and tries to hold its feet, or lifts its bottom up, and if the chimpanzee has never experienced this during previous "diaper-changing routines," it will startle and wiggle away — because it no longer finds its world predictable and is uncertain as to what the future actions of the other party will be within this routine.

Likewise, a young chimpanzee may come to learn the "preparing the milk bottle" routine, even though it only watches and does not prepare the bottle itself. Nonetheless, its knowledge of the various steps can be inferred from the manner in which it anticipates each step. For example, before the chimpanzee learns that the nipple must be placed on the bottle in order for sucking to occur, it will attempt to grab a bottle without the nipple and put it to its face, perhaps inadvertently pouring milk all over itself. Once it has recognized that the nipple must be attached to the bottle it waits patiently while this step of the routine is completed. It is important to note that the learning of routines is accomplished by even very young apes with no explicit reinforcement.

Human caretakers inevitably accompany most parts of a routine with gestural, lexical, and vocal markers directed to the ape. (They are not instructed to do so by experimental design, but rather do so as a natural extension of their tendency to behave in this fashion with young children.) All caretakers emit some verbal markers during routines, but there is great variation in whether or not they wait for the ape to respond to the marker appropriately before proceeding to the next part of the routine. These verbal markers function to signal transitions between various components of a given routine, or changes from one routine to another.

For example, let us take as a sample routine, "blowing bubbles." This routine has the following components: (a) finding the bubbles, (b) opening the bubbles, (c) getting the bubble wand out of the bubble jar, (d) blowing bubbles, and (e) watching or attempting to pop the bubbles. Both participants may take turns at any of these activities. Additionally, some components often are added by the apes themselves, such as drinking the bubbles and/or pouring the bubble liquid out on the floor. Moreover, because all routines develop spontaneously and no experimental guidance is given, they inevitably differ on each new occasion.

The way in which each caretaker uses verbal markers to denote different parts of the routine also will differ. All caretakers probably will use the keyboard symbols and English words to announce the intended activity and changes in the activity. Use of one's language system to convey intended action seems to be a fundamental component of all interindividual communicative processes.

The bubble-blowing routine typically will be announced with some statement such as "let's play with the bubbles," "let's find the bubbles," "would you like the bubbles," and so forth, while pointing to the BUBBLES lexigram. The routine may be initiated because the caretaker decides this would be fun to do, or because he or she sees the chimpanzee reaching toward a bottle of bubbles. In any case, initially, the chimpanzee makes no response to the vocal, gestural, or symbolic initiation of the routine, as though no communication had occurred. If the bubbles then are shown to the ape, it probably will attempt to open them as it is naturally curious, but it will not hold them carefully, showing no anticipation of the liquid inside. Once opened, it will taste the substance, but will do little more. However, as the caretaker announces and demonstrates different parts of the routine, the ape attends and will begin to participate, first by trying to grab the bubbles, later by repeatedly taking the wand out of the jar and replacing it, and still later by attempting to blow bubbles.

Just as parts of the routine are learned and practiced spontaneously after observing the caretaker, so do the caretaker's gestural and verbal markers come to be responded to appropriately across time. For example, once the routine is known, the initiating statement, "would you like to play with bubbles" while pointing to the lexigram, will elicit a response of looking and/or reaching toward the jar of bubbles, in place of the absence of response observed initially.

That is, as routines are learned, behavioral changes occur in the ape that suggest that the ape now knows the main components of the routine. It will look toward the bubbles when the routine is initiated, it will attempt to open the jar only while holding the jar upright, it will look for and extract the bubble wand, and, if it can not successfully blow bubbles, it will hold the bubble wand to the caretaker's mouth—thereby instigating the action the caretaker generally makes in the routine right before the bubbles are blown. It also will attempt to catch the bubbles as they pass by. More important, however, once the routine is understood, it will be initiated by the ape. At first, such initiations will be rather primitive in the sense that they will be action based and context dependent. For example, the chimpanzee may see the bottle of bubbles among other toys and pick it up and look at the caretaker. By selecting the bubbles from among other things, the chimpanzee thus has conveyed its desire to execute the "bubble-blowing" routine. Later, it may simply point to the bubbles and look at the caretaker. Still later, it will point to the BUBBLES lexigram and turn to the caretaker.

In so doing, the ape moves from being a passive observer of a routine to an active participant, to a primitive initiator, to a communicator symbolically announcing his or her intentions to another party. The process occurs very naturally, without the caretaker intentionally or knowingly structuring the transition from passive-receptive comprehension to active-productive knowledge and use. It appears to happen more rapidly with routines that are most clearly structured and effectively marked. It is important that the symbolic marker precede the routine or changes in the components of the routine. Verbal, gestural, or action markers that merely overlay a routine (such as repeatedly commenting "bubbles" while bubbles are being blown, as opposed to before they are blown) are not acquired as effectively as markers that signal changes between routines or changes within a given routine.

This transition from action to gesture to symbol is similar to that described by Locke (1980), Bruner (1983), and Nelson (1985) for children. However, it is important to note the ways in which the model being presented here differs from these accounts. They stress the role of the mother in terms of "scaffolding" and "ratcheting" the communicative process. What is emphasized here is that the process is not driven by the caretaker, but by the mutual need to coordinate interindividual interactions within routines. The verbal and nonverbal segmental symbolic markers allow such coordination to take place. It is because these symbolic markers allow the recipient to predict what is going to happen next that they are learned—though first only in the comprehension mode. Although the ape's caretaker may serve as a "scaffolder" (Bruner, 1983) or as a catalyst (Nelson, 1985), the caretaker is not the "driving force" behind language acquisition in the ape. Rather, it is the ape's desire to be able to predict more accurately what is going to happen to it next. To the extent that the caretaker's markers serve to signal this, the markers are learned receptively.

But how does an ape come to know the specific referent of a given symbolic marker? This problem, which Bruner (1983) referred to as the "Wittgensteinian dilemma," has been raised many times by those studying language acquisition in children. In brief, the dilemma is this: How does the language learner come to know to what the speaker is referring, because in nearly all settings there are multiple referents?

How can the ape ever come to learn that the caretaker is using the word *bubbles* to refer to the jar of soap bubbles and/or the bubbles themselves that are blown rather than the act of puffing air, the taste of the soapy liquid, the opening of the bottles, or the many other indeterminate referents in the situation—or even to the whole routine itself? Indeed, how does the chimp come to acquire the idea that the word *bubbles* should refer to something?

Part of the answer to this question is hidden in what happens as parts of the routine are negotiated and symbolically marked. For example, after the bubble bottle has been grasped, the caretaker may say "you open it." If this is not understood, the caretaker may place the bubble bottle in the chimp's hand and show him or her how to start opening it, and repeat the marker "you open it" thus engaging the chimp in the subroutine of opening, within the larger routine of blowing bubbles. The symbolic marker, in various forms, will continue to be repeated, along with increasingly explicit action guiders and aid until the next event in the routine is performed.

Another example is the "going outdoors routine." As this routine is initiated, the chimpanzee may be asked to retrieve a shirt to wear outdoors. After this routine is well established and the components are behaviorally anticipated by the chimp, the routine will be initiated only by symbolic vocal markers (or words). If the chimpanzee does not link these vocal markers to the next expected component of the "going outdoors routine," it will not respond. The caretaker then will produce more elaborate and direct action-based markers, such as looking toward the shirts, pointing to them, leading the chimp by the hand to the shirts, putting a shirt in the chimp's hand, and, if necessary, returning to the original action of the routine, that of putting the shirt on the chimp. Thus, the ape cannot "err." All that he or she can do is not understand the routine completely and require increasingly explicit help in carrying it out. To the extent that the routine, and its symbolic vocal and/or lexical markers, are understood and expressed, the routine is facilitated and jointly coordinated by both parties.

The symbolic marking of events utilized by the caretaker becomes expanded as the routine is learned. Caretakers now signal not only what is to happen, but what they expect the chimpanzee to do in preparation. Again, this is not part of an experimentally contrived plan, but seems to be a behavior that emerges of its own accord on the part of the caretaker as the chimpanzee gains increasing competency with symbolic markers.

When any segment of the announced routine is not understood by the chimp, that segment is broken down into smaller and smaller steps, and guidance is added, until the ape is able to carry out the appropriate set of actions with the appropriate objects, in the appropriate ways. Additionally, the symbolic markers will be broken apart into smaller units and associated with the correct parts of the routine.

As the ape comes to use symbolic markers to initiate various routines of its own, the function of the symbolic markers changes from that of signaling what the caretaker is about to do, to that of signaling what the ape is about to do. Thus, "blowing bubbles" becomes something that one or both may do, in whole or in part. Once the routine and the markers are understood to this extent, it then will become important for the ape to attend to more subtle and complex symbolic markers that specify variations on the actions and roles within a given routine, such as who is going to do what, how, and when.

The relationship of any given routine to many others also aids the development of reference. There are, for example, routines with bubbles that do not involve blowing, such as "putting the bubbles in the backpack" for the purpose of having them to play with later. During this routine, the word *bubbles* and the lexigram for *bubbles* often will be repeatedly uttered while the caretaker is looking for the bubbles and announcing to the chimp that such is the goal of their actions. Once the bubbles are found they will be placed in the backpack and not mentioned again for some time. Thus, the word *bubbles* now functions in two ways: to initiate a search for the bubble bottle, or to initiate a game with the bubble bottle. It even may be used in other routines such as "hide the bubbles" or "put the bubbles in the bathwater." In all of these instances the single commonality is the word *bubbles* and the bottle of bubbles. Thus reference as a concept, and knowledge of a specific referent comes not from a single routine, but from a group of intermeshed routines that share overlapping symbolic markers. It also comes from the application of the symbolic marker to actions that the caretaker requests of the ape, such as "helping find the bubbles." Although the ape may not know initially that it is expected to search for the bubbles, it does come to perceive that actions other than finding the bubbles do not suffice when it is asked to "find the bubbles."

Symbolic markers may be gestural, vocal, lexical, or any combination of these modalities. However, bonobos appear generally to comprehend the vocal marker before they comprehend the lexical marker. This is probably because they do not need to take their attention away from the routine to hear the verbal marker, but they do need to do so to look at a lexical or gestural marker.

Routines and symbolic markers within those routines are learned even though the chimp is only an observer, not a participant, within the routine. Kanzi, for example, never wore diapers because he was raised by his mother, Matata, until he was old enough for potty training. However, his younger sisters were reared by human caretakers and diapered. Kanzi has learned the major components of the "diaper-changing routine," even though he himself was not subjected to the indignity. He is able to fetch a diaper if asked, to take a diaper off a younger chimp, to help wipe the appropriate area, and will attempt, though awkwardly, to replace the diaper. He also helps by depositing the diapers in the trash. Attempts were not made to deliberately teach Kanzi his role in this routine. Rather, after observing numerous diaper changes directed toward siblings, Kanzi began initiating participation on his own, typically by removing a dirty diaper. Symbolic markers then were overlaid upon these events, to request that Kanzi do them properly if he was going to do them at all.

Markers, whether they are actions, gestures, or vocalizations, are thus used by caretakers during routines. Routines constantly overlap with one another, and form intermingled subsets. They are built up around activities of the day and may involve things that are of interest to the chimpanzees, such as bubbles or traveling outdoors to locations baited with food, or things that just need to be done, such as diaper changes. Some routines, such as diaper changes, may interrupt or occur in the middle of other routines. Different caretakers mark the routines somewhat differently, though all carry out the major components in a similar manner because of the external constraints of the task at hand—for example, there are a limited number of ways to blow bubbles, change diapers, or obtain M&Ms from Flatrock location.[3] As the components of these routines are learned by the apes, there are changes in their behavior that make such learning apparent. They participate in routines in an increasingly appropriate and coordinated manner.

It should perhaps be mentioned that knowledge of a routine that is not liked by the chimpanzee can result in deliberately increasingly sophisticated attempts to circumvent various aspects of the routine. However, whether cooperation, avoidance, or neither results at any given time, the routines eventually are learned. Second, the symbolic markers that signal various aspects of the routine are acquired. At first, the ape displays comprehension of these symbols only within an established routine (for example, it may recognize and use the M&M symbol on the way to Flatrock, but seem confused if the symbol is used during a game of tickle in the group room). Later, it will be observed that comprehension extends beyond the routine itself. These extensions occur naturally as a function of overlapping routines.

For example, in addition to blowing bubbles and changing diapers, there inevitably will be a need to transfer items in and out of the backpack that is carried daily in the woods. Sometimes the needed items will be bubbles or diapers; other times the bubbles and diapers that are in the backpack must be ignored in order to satisfactorily retrieve another item, such as the can opener when it is needed for the can-opening routine. If Kanzi needs a can opener, and is attempting to find one in the backpack, he likely will hear the words, "no, not the diapers" or "no, not the bubbles," as he pulls out the wrong items. If he tries to use these in place of the can opener, he will be shown why "bubbles is not what we need," and will be encouraged to look further. Thus, he will hear symbolic markers from the "bubbles routines" used in other circumstances. In this second context, they do not denote "blowing of bubbles" but rather that the bottle of bubbles is not the needed object component of the present routine. As routines overlap, so does the use of their symbolic markers. To the extent that these symbolic markers, or words, are used in many different routines, they become comprehended in an increasingly context-free manner. Evidence that such a process of decontextualization of vocal and lexical markers has occurred is obtained

---

[3]Foods are taken out to a number of special locations in the woods each day. These locations have names and the chimpanzee can ask to travel to any location they wish and obtain the food that is found there. "Flatrock" is one of these locations and the food that is found there is M&Ms.

by testing Kanzi in a formal setting that is independent of any routine in which the symbolic marker otherwise might be used. When Kanzi is able to identify the word or the lexigram, apart from any routine, and properly link it with its intended referent, referential vocabulary acquisition can be said to have taken place. The test setting has the property of being "routine free," in that any item can be a component of the test. Consequently, the fact that a test is in progress cannot signal to Kanzi that the lexigram BUBBLES, for example, is now the appropriate word to select.

Once symbolic markers are comprehended referentially across routines, they begin to be used to initiate routines. This change is an important one, for it permits the ape to initiate routines out of context and to determine, at points of change, which of many alternative routines will be engaged in next by the group. Even before symbolic vocal markers are comprehended, the ape will initiate routines simply by beginning the action components of the routine itself. For example, if Kanzi wants to blow bubbles, he may pick out the bubble bottle, open it, and begin to blow bubbles. However, commencing and carrying out such a routine without markers or signals being directed to others is successful only to the extent that others need not be involved or coordinate their behavior with Kanzi in any predictable manner. If others are involved they can cooperate only if they know the routine. For example, should Kanzi wish to play with bubbles while out in the woods, it will be necessary to retrieve them from the caretaker's backpack. If Kanzi simply walks over to the caretaker and grabs his or her backpack and starts pulling things out of it, this will be responded to in a negative manner. It is not that the caretaker does not want Kanzi to play with the bubbles, but unless he announces his intended action, the caretaker will not understand why the backpack has been taken and is being rifled through. If, however, Kanzi announces "bubbles," and points to the caretaker's backpack, he can be given the backpack with knowledge of his intended action. Everyone, including Kanzi, is comfortable because they know what is being done, and within reason, what will occur next: Kanzi will play with the bubbles and perhaps solicit the interactions of others in the bubble-blowing game. However, if the backpack is simply grabbed, no one in the group is sure what will happen next. The caretaker may get angry and try to grab it back, Kanzi may climb a tree with the backpack if he sees the caretaker is angry, everything may fall out of the backpack, and so forth, and no comfortable, coordinated, agreed-upon routine will be in place.

Thus, as the symbolic markers that initiate routines or various components of routines are comprehended, there develops a natural and spontaneous pressure to comprehend and then to produce these symbols. This pressure comes first from a desire to determine the next routine or the next component of an ongoing routine. When the next action component is engaged without a marker to signal what will be done, misunderstanding or lack of interindividual coordination can result. Lack of coordination prevents the successful execution of joint attention and sets the motivational stage for productive lexical usage. Thus, if Kanzi wants to go to Flatrock location it becomes advantageous for him to announce this intent, if he wishes the group to adopt that destination as the next travel routine. If Kanzi wishes to blow bubbles, it becomes advantageous for him to announce that intent, lest his taking of the backpack be misinterpreted as an aggressive action. The driving force that moves the ape from symbol comprehension to symbol production is the desire to exert some control over what happens or is done next. To the degree that future events entail social companions, it becomes propitious to achieve joint engagement by announcing intent. To the extent that the ape fails to do so, it has little control over what happens to it next. In a sense, this perspective is similar to that offered by Bruner (1983) when he observed that for children "the engine that drives the enterprise is not language acquisition per se, but the need to get on with the demands of culture" (p. 103). Culture, however, is a very general term, making it difficult to know just what it is that is driving the child — other than the desire to be like other human beings. In our view, it is not culture that is driving the ape, but the desire for control.

No contextual records of Kanzi's symbol usage were kept during his early acquisition. The focus at that time was not on "how" Kanzi acquired symbols, but rather on the fact that he acquired them at all without training. Each symbol he used was noted along with a code that detailed whether the communication was a request, a statement, a comment, etcetera. The current perspective as to how Kanzi learned symbols was developed in retrospect from that data base. However, data on two additional chimpanzees being reared with Kanzi support this perspective, albeit with some qualifications. Contextual data have been taken on the utterances of these animals, thus making it possible to trace the evolution of a word. Table 9.1 illustrates all of Panbanisha's usage of the word *bubbles* from the first usage at 13 months of age to the emergence of the first "comment," a usage that reflects sophisticated generalization at 21 months of age. These data reflect only Panbanisha's utterances, not those directed to her, hence they do not reveal her emerging comprehension. However, they do show clearly how her productive usage moves from routine-dependent imitation, to initiation of routines, to the use of the word to control which routine is selected by the caretakers, to "generalized comments" that finally reflect sophisticated comprehension and word usage. The progression of the word *bubbles* in Panbanisha reveals that usage need not be frequent for this progression to take place.

By contrast, another chimpanzee of a different species shows a similar but much delayed pattern (see Tables 9.2 and 9.3).

TABLE 9.1
Developmental History of Panbanisha's Usage of "Bubbles"

---

13 Months 29 Days (01/15/87)

During a game of bubbles the teacher draws Panbanisha's attention to the bubble lexigram. Panbanisha approaches and tries to say "bubbles" after the teacher, however she accidentally touches the lexigram OIL which is located next to bubbles. The teacher asks "Do you want oil or bubbles?" and Panbanisha responds by rushing over to the bubble jar and mouthing it.

Comment: Panbanisha is imitating the teacher, and saying "bubbles" as part of what is done during the bubble-blowing routine. At this early age imitation often occurred. However, Panbanisha also shows comprehension of the spoken word by mouthing the bubble jar after she hears the teacher mention bubbles.

---

16 Months 30 Days (05/18/87)

Panzee (the common champanzee coreared with Panbanisha) is playing with the keyboard, touching lexigrams that interest her. Panzee does not appear to be attempting to communicate as she activates the symbols FLATROCK and BUBBLES. However, her teacher decides to treat it as a communication and replies that they cannot go to
Flatrock, but they could play with bubbles. Panzee makes no response. However, Panbanisha observes this exchange, then goes to the keyboard, says "bubbles," and looks toward Panzee's teacher. The teacher interprets this a response to her questions and gets out some bubbles and plays with bubbles with both chimpanzees.

Comment: The bubbles routine is not yet in progress and bubbles are not present, but Panbanisha uses BUBBLES to initiate the routine. She does not initiate it completely on her own yet, but only after the teacher already has suggested the activity.

---

17 Months 2 Days (05/19/87)

Panbanisha and the teacher are seated in front of the keyboard playing with toys. The teacher is showing Panbanisha some new lexigrams. They have not been talking about bubbles. Panbanisha all at once carefully points to bubbles and looks at the teacher. The teacher interprets this as a request and looks in the backpack where she finds some bubbles for Panbanisha. The teacher notes that this is first time she has seen Panbanisha ask for bubbles.

Comment: Again, the bubble-blowing routine is not in progress, however, now the teacher has not previously mentioned bubbles. Panbanisha seems able to think of this on her own and to encode the request symbolically.

---

17 Months 5 Days (05/21/87)

Panbanisha and the teacher are getting ready to take a bath when Panbanisha spontaneously asks for bubbles. There are no bubbles present. The teacher agrees that they can play with the bubbles and begins looking through the backpack to find some bubbles. While the teacher is looking, Panbanisha comments bubbles twice, remarking on the target of the teacher's search.

Comment: Panbanisha again spontaneously requests to play with bubbles even though they are not present and the teacher has not initiated the routine. Additionally, she comments on the target of the teacher's search even though the bubbles are not visible.

(continued)

TABLE 9.1 (*continued*)

17 Months 5 Days (05/21/87)

The teacher is blowing bubbles, then stops for a little bit and looks at something else. Panbanisha says "bubbles" to ask him to continue.

Comment: This is the first time Panbanisha has used "bubbles" to ask that a routine, which is in progress, continue.

17 Months 9 Days (05/25/87)

The teacher is outdoors in the woods with Panbanisha. They are walking along the trail when Panbanisha stops and asks to play with bubbles. There are no bubbles in the backpack, so she is told that maybe she can do so later when they go back inside.

This is the first time Panbanisha has used the bubbles lexigram outdoors. Generally, though not always, bubbles has been an indoor game.

17 Months 10 Days (05/26/87)

Panbanisha is again walking with the teacher out in the woods. They are traveling through a dense scrubby area toward the raison site. It is necessary that they walk on a footbridge here because of the wet ground. Panbanisha does not want to go this way and keeps heading back toward the lab. The teacher insists they continue on to raisons but Panbanisha refuses, then says "bubbles" and looks back toward the lab. The teacher interprets this an expression of why Panbanisha wants to go back to the lab. She is told that they need to continue on now, but that they can play with bubbles when they return.

Comment: Panbanisha now uses BUBBLES to try and change the planned activity from one she does not like to one that she would rather do and one that would return her to the lab.

17 Months 15–21 Days

Panbanisha asks for bubbles on 5 occasions as she and the teacher are working with other things. Each time she seems to enjoy playing with them very much. Each of these requests is spontaneous and is not preceded by the teacher showing or talking about the bubbles. Panbanisha seems very interested in her ability to bring about the "playing with the bubbles" routine. After these 6 days, she seems to lose interest in bubbles and this word does not occur again for 2 months.

Comment: This does not mean that Panbanisha does not play with bubbles for 2 months, just that the word does not occur again in the daily notes for 2 months.

20 Months (08/17/87)

The teacher is getting ready to go outdoors. Panbanisha wants to stay inside and play. She asks for "bubbles" and then for "balloons." These are two things that usually are played with indoors. The teacher refused the request and tells Panbanisha that they are going to go on outdoors now anyway.

Comment: Again Panbanisha used BUBBLES to attempt to get the teacher to do something different than what had been announced.

20 Months (08/17/87)

As the teacher is looking through a cabinet, she comes across some bubbles and comments upon this. Panbanisha agrees, commenting "bubbles" herself. Panbanisha does not attempt to play with the bubbles, nor indicate that she wants to by reaching out for them.

Comment: This is the first usage of a comment in a situation that clearly reveals that Panbanisha does not have an interest in obtaining the bubbles.

(*continued*)

TABLE 9.1 (*continued*)

20 Months 14 Days (08/31/87)

Panbanisha is touching different words on the keyboard, seemingly practicing the activation of ones that she knows. She includes BUBBLES during this self-initiated practice session.

20 Months 24 Days (09/10/87)

Panbanisha is playing with the dogs outside the lab. She stops and activates the BUBBLES symbol and looks at the teacher. The teacher interprets this as a request to play with bubbles while also playing with the dogs. This is not something that Panbanisha has done before but something she appears to have thought of on her own. The teacher agrees and goes to the lab and retrieves some bubbles. Panbanisha then plays happily with the dogs and the bubbles for over half an hour.

20 Months 28 Days (09/14/87)

Panbanisha asks the teacher for some bubbles. The teacher has a bin of toys and bubbles are in this bin. The teacher gives Panbanisha the bubbles and she plays happily.

21 Months 5 Days (09/23/87)

Panbanisha stares at her bath water as it is foaming up very high in the sink, as the teacher has inadvertently poured in a lot of soap. It has made a very tall pile of bubbles, not the kind one blows from the bubble jar, but small foamy bubbles. Panbanisha looks at this large pile of soapy foam and comments "bubbles."

SUMMARY

The model of lexical acquisition by apes can be summarized in the following major components:

1. Routines are engaged in by caretakers as a natural part of daily life — apes learn these routines by virtue of the fact that they occur. Knowledge of components, and their sequencing, is intrinsically valuable to the chimpanzee, because of its predictive value. That is, such knowledge allows the ape to know what is going to happen next in its world. Because the behavior of others and the events in one's environment constitute an ever-changing mosaic, learning to anticipate any component of regularity that prepares one to anticipate future events becomes intrinsically valuable. In any event, routines and their components come to be learned and anticipated without extrinsic reward.

2. Routines are marked symbolically by vocal, gestural, and lexical signals. Such markers signal the onset of the routines and the different components of the routines. The chimpanzee associates these markers with the routines. As the symbolic markers are learned, the chimpanzee's behavior begins to change in that the next component of the routine will be

TABLE 9.2
Developmental History of Panzee's Use of Bubbles

14 Months 6 Days (02/05/87)

Panzee is watching as the teacher blows bubbles. The teacher draws Panzee's attention to the lexigram on the keyboard and says "bubbles" several times. Panzee then touches the BUBBLES.

Comment: This is an imitation of the teacher's behavior. At an early stage, both Panzee and Panbanisha often pointed to any lexigram that the teacher drew their attention to, as if they enjoyed imitating what the teacher said. Panzee's early imitation of bubbles differs from Panbanisha in that she shows no evidence of making a connection between the symbol and the object at this age.

14 Months 14 Days (02/13/87)

Panzee is watching as the teacher blows bubbles. The teacher holds up the bubbles symbol on a plaque and points to it. Panzee points to BUBBLES and then touches the bubble blower.

Comment: This is the first evidence that Panzee is beginning to realize that there is a correspondence between the bubbles symbol and the object.

17 Months 18 Days (05/18/87)

Panzee is exploring sounds that symbols make as she touches the keyboard. One of the symbols that she touches is bubbles.

18 Months 28 Days (05/28/87)

Panzee keeps trying to take the jar of bubbles because she wants to play with them. The teacher places her finger on the symbol and helps her say "bubbles."

Comment: Teachers have been encouraged not to use this method of instruction. However, on this occasion this teacher chose to do so in any case, believing that it might help Panzee.

21 Months 26 Days (09/26/87)

Panzee and the teacher are playing with bubbles when the teacher comments bubbles at the keyboard. Panzee then places her lips on the BUBBLES lexigram.

21 Months 26 Days (09/26/87)

Panzee again seems to be exploring the keyboard, touching a number of symbols, but not attempting to communicate. One of these symbols is BUBBLES.

22 Months 11 Days (10/11/87)

The teacher is blowing bubbles and asks Panzee if she can name bubbles. Panzee does not respond. The teacher points to the bubbles lexigram and Panzee imitates, saying "bubbles."

22 Months 21 Days (10/11/87)

Panzee and the teacher are playing with bubbles. The teacher comments "bubbles" at the keyboard. Panzee then touches BUBBLES and points to the teacher's mouth, wanting her to blow more bubbles.

Comment: This is Panzee's first real communicative use of the BUBBLES lexigram. Although it is imitative in that the teacher has said "bubbles" earlier, the imitation occurs because Panzee wants to communicate about bubbles, not just because she is imitating.

(*continued*)

TABLE 9.2 (continued)

23 Months 18 Days (11/18/87)

The teacher and Panzee are blowing bubbles. The teacher says "bubbles" then asks Panzee if she can say this also. Panzee repeats "bubbles" after the teacher.

Comment: The teacher urges Panzee to say "bubbles." Teachers are asked not to use this method as a general teaching strategy, however Panzee is far behind Panbanisha at this point and the teacher is trying to help her along just this once.

27 Months 28 Days (03/28/88)

The teacher is blowing bubbles with bubble gum and comments "bubbles" as she does so. Each time one pops Panzee wants to see her do this again and signals this by pointing to the teacher's mouth. After several times, Panzee spontaneously touches the BUBBLE lexigram to ask the teacher to blow another bubble.

27 Months 29 Days (03/29/88)

The teacher tells Panzee she is going to blow a bubble. Panzee says "bubble" after the teacher to indicate that she agrees with this idea, then waits and watches as the teacher does so.

Comment: This is the first time Panzee has used "bubbles" to indicate agreement with the teacher's intended action.

29 Months 21 Days (05/21/88)

The teacher who is playing with Panbanisha blows bubbles toward Panzee and her teacher. Panzee's teacher then picks up some bubbles and blows them for Panzee. She then queries Panzee, asking "What are we playing with?" Panzee touches the BUBBLES lexigram in reply.

Comment: This is the first time Panzee's use of "bubbles" is nonimitative.

29 Months 21 Days (05/21/88)

Panzee and her teacher are visiting various rooms in the laboratory. (They have just traveled to the observation room where others are working okn data and observing.) Panzee spontaneously says "bubbles." Her teacher agrees and looks around the observation room but finds no bubbles.

Comment: This usage is both nonimitative and independent of the normal context in which the bubble game is played. There are no bubbles present, suggesting that Panzee is able to think of them on her own, without a physical cue.

29 Months 22 Days (05/22/88)

Panzee is leaning out of her chair attempting to play with Panbanisha who is nearby. Her teacher tries to distract her from playing with Panbanisha by asking "Why don't you play with the bubbles?" In response to the question, Panzee turns and activates the BUBBLES, indicating that she understands what the teacher has said. (The teacher did not activate the lexigram; she spoke the word.)

Comment: Panzee demonstrates that she has made a connection between the spoken word and the BUBBLES lexigram.

(continued)

TABLE 9.2 (*continued*)

30 Months 3 Days (06/03/88)

The teacher is again blowing bubble-gum bubbles and Panzee is attempting to catch them before they pop. The teacher is using "bubbles" to comment upon this activity. Later after the teacher stops, Panzee says "bubble surprise," then approaches the teacher and looks closely at her mouth, waiting for her to blow bubbles again.

Comment: Panzee elects to use a modifier ("surprise") when the bubbles of interest are not soap bubbles, but bubble-gum bubbles.

30 Months 10 Days (06/10/88)

The teacher is blowing bubbles with bubble gum, but has not commented on the activity. When she stops Panzee says "bubble" to ask her to start the activity once again. She wants the teacher to blow bubbles so that she can pop them.

30 Months 10 Days (06/10/88)

A bit later Panzee stops trying to pop the bubbles and just watches the teacher blow them. While she is watching, the teacher remarks that she is going to blow a bubble. Panzee responds by saying "bubbles," to indicate her agreement.

Comment: Panzee has lost interest in obtaining bubble-gum bubbles or in popping them, only in observing their production. She now uses "bubbles" to indicate the activity she wants another to perform.

30 Months 27 Days (06/27/88)

Panzee is in woods at Scrubby Pine Nook eating melon when she spontaneously comments "Yes." The teacher asks her "Yes what?" and Panzee answers "yes bubbles." The teacher tells her that they cannot play with bubbles right now, but perhaps will get some later.

32 Months 24 Days (08/24/88)

The teacher is again blowing bubbles with bubble gum and commenting to Panzee upon this activity. This time the teacher remarks "surprise bubbles," following Panzee's earlier usage. Five minutes later, after another activity has intervened, Panzee asks the teacher to reinstate the bubble game by saying "bubbles" and looking closely at the teacher's mouth.

32 Months 31 Days (08/31/88)

Panzee starts to grab the bubbles out of a bin of play toys without asking. She is told not to grab, but to ask. She then uses the keyboard to say "bubbles." To determine how well Panzee understands the word, the teacher then lays out five photos of objects in front of Panzee and asks her if she can select the picture of bubbles. Panzee does so.

Comment: The teacher is now confident of Panzee's comprehension of bubbles to insist that she use it to communicate when she is otherwise engaged in an activity that would seem impolite.

34 Months 13 Days (10/13/88)

Panzee is by the NASA building when she begins to fuss. The teacher asks her what is wrong and she answers "bubbles" and then adds "surprise." The teacher notes that a few days earlier when they visited this building, one of the persons working there had given Panzee some bubble gum.

34 Months 22 Days (10/22/88)

Panzee is riding around in the car looking at various things when she spontaneously says "bubbles." The teacher, who interprets this as a request for bubbles, looks in the backpack and finds none, then takes Panzee back to the group room and gets some bubbles.

TABLE 9.3
Increasingly Competent Levels of Symbol Usage in Two Species of Ape

Action	Panbanisha (Pan Paniscus)	Panzee (Pan Troglodytes)
Imitative Touching	13 Months 29 Days	14 Months 6 Days
Earliest Evidence of Beginning Comprehension of the Relationship Between Spoken Word and Object, or Symbol and Object	13 Months 29 Days (Word and Object)	14 Months 14 Days (Symbol and Object)
Exploratory Touching of Different Symbols on the Board	−	17 Months 18 Days
Imitative Use to Indicate Agreement with Teacher	16 Months 30 Days	27 Months 29 Days
Imitative Use of Communicative Request During Bubble-Blowing Routine	17 Months 5 Days	22 Months 21 Days
Nonimitative Use of Bubbles in Response to Teacher's Query	−	29 Months 22 Days
Nonimitative Communicative Request in Old Context — Bubbles Are Not Being Blown But Are Present	17 Months 2 Days	−
Nonimitative Communicative Request in New Context — Bubbles Are Absent	17 Months 5 Days	29 Months 21 Days
Nonimitative Addition of Modifier to Request a Particular Type of Bubbles (Bubble Gum)	−	30 Months 3 Days
Nonimitative Use of to Alter Planned Activity	17 Months 10 Days	34 Months 22 Days
Nonimitative Use of to Comment on Actions of Teacher	20 Months	−
Practices Touching Bubbles	21 Months 5 Days	−
Nonimitative Generalized Comment in New Context		

behaviorally anticipated immediately after the symbolic marker has been produced but before the component actually has begun. This comprehension of the symbolic markers can be observed most clearly in routines that have a number of components that can be sequenced in several ways, so that the vocal, lexical, or gestural marker serves as a signal for the variable component of the routine.

3. Caretakers tend to mark both their own future actions in a routine and the actions they intend the ape to produce, particularly as the ape clearly begins to comprehend and anticipate various components of the routine. In marking aspects of the apes' own actions, the referents of symbolic markers

become clarified as action and marker must converge if the ape is to successfully carry out the intended routine or set of events.

4. Routines and their symbolic markers are naturally interdigitated because components of one routine invariably are used in a different manner in other routines. As the routines and symbolic markers overlap, the referent of these markers is made increasingly specific and becomes divorced from its original context.

5. When comprehension of symbolic vocal, gestural, and lexical markers becomes fully separated from the routine, the chimpanzee can pass formal tests of word recognition and can pair·spoken words with their lexical and photographic equivalents. He or she also can answer simple questions about these vocal and lexical symbols.

6. The comprehension of routines and the vocal and lexical markers that signal routines lead naturally to productive use. At first, production simply may be moving on to the next action component of a routine before it is marked by others, but later, the routines themselves will be announced with lexical markers. The transition from comprehension to production occurs naturally, but can be facilitated by the use of queries about intent once comprehension is in place.

This explanation of symbol learning by apes currently stops with the exposition of individual symbols. Clearly, any process-oriented account of language will need to go much further, encompassing symbol combinations and symbol-ordering rules or syntax. The chimpanzees' currently emerging competencies in sentence-processing capacity are already sufficient to demonstrate that many aspects of syntactical ordering can be accomplished by apes. It is hoped that ongoing studies of the emergence of this skill will provide the basis for expansion of the present theory to multisymbol use and eventually syntax.

ACKNOWLEDGEMENTS

The preparation of this chapter and research described herein were supported by National Institute of Child Health and Human Development grant NICHD-06016, which supports the Language Research Center, cooperatively operated by Georgia State University and the Yerkes Regional Primate Research Center of Emory University. In addition, the research is supported in part by RR-00165 to the Yerkes Primate Research Center of Emory University. This research also was supported by the College of Arts and Sciences of Georgia State University. The author wishes to thank Karen Brakke, Kelly McDonald, Jeannine Murphy, Elizabeth Rubert, Rose Sevcik, and Philip Shaw for their work with the bonobos.

REFERENCES

Brakke, K., & Savage-Rumbaugh, E. S. (1989, August). Speech comprehension in an infant bonobo (*Pan paniscus*) and chimpanzee (*Pan troglogytes*). Paper presented at the 5th annual meeting of the Language Origins Society, Austin, TX.

Bruner, J. (1983). *Child's talk: Learning to use language.* New York: Norton.

Diamond, J. M. (1988). DNA-based phylogenies of the three chimpanzees. *Nature, 332,* 685–686.

Estes, W. K. (1978). *Handbook of learning and cognitive processes: Vol. 5. Human information processing.* Hillsdale, NJ: Lawrence Erlbaum Associates.

Fodor, J. A. (1982). *The modularity of mind.* Cambridge, MA: MIT Press.

Gardner, B. T., & Gardner, R. A. (1971). Two-way communication with an infant chimpanzee. In A. M. Schrier & F. Stollnitz (Eds.), *Behavior of nonhuman primates* (Vol. 4, pp. 117–184). New York: Academic.

Ghiglieri, M. (1988). *East of the mountains of the moon: Chimpanzee society in the African rain forest.* New York: Free Press.

Hayes, C. (1951). *The ape in our house.* New York: Harper & Row

Hayes, K. J., & Hayes, C. (1952). Imitation in a home-raised chimpanzee. *Journal of Comparative and Physiological Psychology, 45,* 450–459.

Herman, L. M., Richards, D. G., & Wolz, J. P. (1984). Comprehension of sentences by bottlenosed dolphins. *Cognition, 16,* 129–219.

Locke, A. (1980). *The guided reinvention of language.* New York: Academic.

Nelson, K. (1985). *Making sense: The acquisition of shared meaning.* New York: Academic.

Nelson, K. (1986). *Event knowledge: Structure and function in development.* Hillsdale, NJ: Lawrence Erlbaum Associates.

Newmeyer, F. J. (1986). *Linguistic theory in America* (2nd ed.). San Diego: Academic.

Passingham, R. E. (1981). Primate specializations in brain and intelligence. *Symposium of the Zoological Society of London, 46,* 361–388.

Passingham, R. E. (1982). *The human primate.* Oxford, England: Freeman.

Premack, D. (1971). On the assessment of language competence in the chimpanzee. In A. M. Schrier & F. Stollnitz (Eds.), *Behavior of nonhuman primates* (Vol. 4, pp. 185–228). New York: Academic.

Roitblatt, H. L. (1987). *Introduction to comparative cognition.* New York: Freeman.

Rumbaugh, D. M. (1977). *Language learning by a chimpanzee.* New York: Academic.

Rumbaugh, D. M. (1986). Comparative psychology: Patterns in adaption. In A. M. Rogers & C. J. Scheirer (Eds.), *G. Stanley Hall Lecture Series* (Vol. 5, pp. 7–53). Washington, DC: American Psychological Association.

Savage-Rumbaugh, E. S. (1987). Communication, symbolic communication, and language: A reply to Seidenberg and Petitto. *Journal of Experimental Psychology: General, 116,* 288–292.

Savage-Rumbaugh, E. S., McDonald, K., Sevcik, R. A., Hopkins, W., & Rubert, E. (1986). Spontaneous symbol acquisition and communicative use by a pygmy chimpanzee (*Pan paniscus*). *Journal of Experimental Psychology: General, 115,* 211–235.

Savage-Rumbaugh, E. S., Rumbaugh, D. M., & Boysen, S. (1980). Do apes use language? *American Scientist, 68,* 49–61.

Savage-Rumbaugh, E. S., Sevcik, R. A., & Brakke, K. E. (in press). Symbols: Their communicative use, combination, and comprehension by bonobos (*Pan paniscus*). In L. P. Lipsitt & C. Rovee-Collier (Eds.), *Advances in infancy research* (Vol. 7). Norwood, NJ: Ablex.

Savage-Rumbaugh, E. S., Sevcik, R. A., Rumbaugh, D. M., & Rubert, E. (1985). The capacity of animals to acquire language: Do species differences have anything to say to us? *Philosophical Transactions of the Royal Society of London, B308,* 177–185.

Schusterman, R. L., & Gisiner, R. (1988). Artificial language comprehension in dolphins and sea lions: The essential cognitive skills. *The Psychological Record, 38,* 311–348.

Seckel, H. P. G. (1960). *Bird headed dwarfs.* Basel, Switzerland: Karger.

Sibley, C. G., & Ahlquist, J. E. (1987). *Journal of Molecular Evolution, 26,* 99.

Skinner, B. F. (1957). *Verbal behavior.* New York: Appleton–Century–Crofts.

Terrace, H. (1979). *Nim.* New York: Knopf.

Terrace, H. (1985). In the beginning was the "name." *American Psychologist, 40,* 1011–1028.

Tomasello, M. (1990). Cultural transmission in the tool use and communicatory signalling of chimpanzees. In S. Taylor-Parker & K. Gibson (Eds.), *Cognition and communication in animals: Developmental perspectives* (pp. 274–311). Cambridge, England: Cambridge University Press.

Tuttle, R. H. (1988). *Apes of the world: Their social behavior, communication, mentality, and ecology.* Park Ridge, NJ: Noyes Data.

Wardhaugh, R. (1977). *Introduction to linguistics.* New York: McGraw-Hill.

Weiskrantz, L. (Ed.). (1985). *Animal intelligence: Proceedings of the Royal Society.* Oxford, England: Clarendon Press.

10 Imitation, Grammatical Development, and the Invention of Protogrammar by an Ape

Patricia M. Greenfield
University of California, Los Angeles

E. Sue Savage-Rumbaugh
Language Research Center, Georgia State University and
Yerkes Regional Primate Research Center, Emory University

The conservative nature of evolution, plus wide agreement that human language has a strong innate basis (Chomsky, 1965, 1967; Goldin-Meadow, 1978; Goldin-Meadow & Mylander, 1984; Lenneberg, 1967; Lieberman, 1984), suggests that much of the genetic basis of human language must be shared not only with present-day chimpanzees but also with our common primate ancestor. There is evidence that a species of chimpanzee, *Pan paniscus,* shows more resemblance than humans or the other great apes to this common ancestor (Zihlman, Cronin, Cramer, & Sarich, 1978). *Pan Paniscus* is also closer to humans in sociosexual behavior (Savage-Rumbaugh, 1984) and prolonged maturation (Kuroda, 1989) than the other, more commonly studied chimpanzee species, *Pan troglodytes.* For these reasons, our selected species, *Pan paniscus* (also known as the pygmy chimpanzee or bonobo) is a particularly promising model for the behavioral exploration of human evolution.

Our studies of imitation and protogrammar in the bonobo or pygmy chimpanzee provide new clues to the evolutionary origins of conversational competence and grammar in human language. Although we have exposed *Pan paniscus* to a humanly devised symbol system, we have not looked merely for chimpanzee analogues of what humans do with a symbol system, but have discovered languagelike phenomena that reflect the ape's own propensities and its way of life (McNeill, 1974).

Bypassing the vocal limitations of chimpanzees and other apes, research projects beginning in the late 1960s (summarized by Hill, 1978) used visual symbol systems to take apes much further into human language than previous attempts (Kellogg, 1968). Just how far became, however, very controversial (Bronowski & Bellugi, 1970; Chomsky, 1967; Limber, 1977; Petitto & Seidenberg, 1979; Terrace, Petitto, Sanders, & Bever, 1979, 1980).

Imitation

Terrace et al. (1979, 1980) have interpreted the presence of imitation in language-trained chimpanzees as an indication that chimpanzees differ significantly from human children in their language-learning ability. Implicit in this argument is the notion that imitation reflects a rote and mechanical approach that does not characterize true human language. According to this view, imitation displays an absence of conversational competence.

However, studies of imitation in human children suggest that it serves many different pragmatic functions in a conversation (Ochs Keenan, 1977). The rarest of these is rote imitation, defined as the intention to copy another (Ochs Keenan, 1977). Examples of the various functions repetition can serve in young children's speech are presented in Table 10.1. Only in the last example in Table 10.1 is the purpose of the repetition to imitate—and even there imitation is not rote. Instead, it is meaningfully selective. In sum, imitations in children (and humans more generally) reveal the presence of conversational competence.

An analysis of chimp–human discourse shows that two pygmy chimpanzees, Kanzi and Mulika, use partial or complete repetition of others' symbols as children do: They usually do not produce rote imitations, but rather use repetition to fulfill a variety of conversational purposes (Table 10.2). This analysis follows that used with human children by Ochs Keenan (1977) and should be equally acceptable for chimpanzees. Unfortunately though, there has tended to be a double standard for assessing the linguistic competence of human children and chimpanzees (de Villiers, 1984).

Grammar

Rules through which symbols may be combined in a potentially infinite number of ways constitute grammar, often considered the sine qua non of human language (Chomsky, 1965). Apes can learn to combine two or more symbols in nonrandom ways (Fouts & Couch, 1976; Gardner, R. A., & Gardner, B. T., 1969; Patterson, 1978, 1980; Terrace et al., 1979), including the use of sign language inflections (Patterson & Linden, 1981; Rimpau, Gardner, & Gardner, 1989). However, from a linguistic point of view, combinations alone, even inflected combinations, are not sufficient to demonstrate grammar. There are, at minimum, five basic criteria that must be met before a grammatical rule can be attributed to such combinations:

TABLE 10.1
Uses of Repetition by Humans

Confirm/Agree

(Matthew, age 12 months)
Mother: *Is that the birdie?*
Matthew: *dird* (bird), pointing to it.
(Greenfield, unpublished data, 1969)

Excitement

(Twins, Toby and David, with their nanny, Jill)
Jill: *And we're going to have hot dogs.*
Toby: *Hot dogs!* (excitedly)
Jill: *And soup.*
David: *Mmm soup!*
(Ochs Keenan, 1977)

Choose Alternative

(Katie, age 14 months, with caregiver at infant daycare center. Caregiver pretends to pour tea for both of them, and they pretend to drink it.)
Caregiver: *Are you full, or do you want some more?*
Katie: *More.*
(Leddick, unpublished observation, 1989)

Imitation

(Twins, Toby and David, 2 yrs., 9 mos., with their nanny, Jill)
Jill: *Aren't I a good cook? Say "Yes, the greatest!"*
Toby: *Yes the greatest.* (Softly)
Jill: *That's right.*
David: *The greatest!* (loudly)
(Ochs Keenan, 1977)

Note. Adapted with permission from "Comparing Communicative Competence in Child and Chimp: The Pragmatics of Repetition" by P. M. Greenfield and E. S. Savage-Rumbaugh. *Journal of Child Language* (in press).

1. Each component of a combination has independent symbolic status (Brown, 1973).
2. A reliable and meaningful (semantic) relationship exists between the symbols (Savage-Rumbaugh, 1990).
3. Relations between categories of symbols are involved, not merely relations between individual symbols (Bronowski & Bellugi, 1970).
4. Some formal device, either inflection or statistically reliable order (Braine, 1976; Goldin-Meadow & Mylander, 1984), is used to relate the symbol categories.
5. Rules are productive (Savage-Rumbaugh, Sevcik, Rumbaugh, & Rubert, 1985)

    a. Utterances are *not* imitated (Petitto & Seidenberg, 1979)
    b. A wide variety of combinations is produced (Bronowski & Bellugi, 1970)
    c. Some new rules never modeled are created. (This last is not a criterion for the existence of a rule, but for the invention of a rule.)

Terrace et al. (1979) have pointed out the deficiencies of studies of chimpanzee grammar in a number of these areas. Indeed, no previous study has satisfied all of these criteria. Some researchers have trained a predetermined symbol order (without establishing that the chimpanzees were able to use the individual symbols meaningfully) (Muncer & Ettlinger, 1981; Premack, 1970; Rumbaugh, Gill, & von Glaserfeld, 1973). In other research, symbol selection was constrained experimentally through reinforced associations (Matsuzawa, 1985). In still other research, repetitive question prompts were used to generate the corpus (Gardner, B. T., & Gardner, R. A., 1975; Van Cantfort, Gardner, & Gardner, 1989). The spontaneous, creative, or communicative aspects of grammatical combination were therefore lacking to one extent or another. Still other researchers have reported data incompletely or have not systematically eliminated imitations from the analyses (Gardner, B. T., & Gardner, R. A., 1974; Gardner, R. A., & Gardner, B. T., 1969; Miles, 1990; Patterson, 1978, 1980; Patterson & Linden, 1981; Rimpau, Gardner, R. A., & Gardner, B. T., 1989; Terrace et al., 1979, 1980). Imitation leaves open the possibility that combinations may reflect productive use of grammar by humans rather than by apes (Terrace et al., 1979).

Another problem in grammatical studies of ape language is that rules for ordering two symbols often have been idiosyncratic to particular signs rather than combinations between members of two symbol categories (Fouts & Couch, 1976; Terrace et al., 1979, 1980). At the two-word stage, the stage with which we are principally concerned in our analysis of chimpanzee grammar, this limitation sometimes exists for human children as well (Braine, 1976). In mature human grammar, however, basic syntactic rules (e.g., in English, subject precedes verb) involve a large number of lexical items that can function in each syntactic category (e.g., adult subject and verb categories each contain many lexical items). We show that Kanzi's emergent syntax also involves relations between categories, each of which is composed of diverse lexical items.

Rules must not only exist independently of highly structured training settings and imitation; they must, at least in part, be determined by the ape as well as by its models. Early protohumans invented language; they did not merely learn it. To truly shed light on the evolution of grammar, it is necessary to demonstrate some capacity to invent grammatical rules.

Although claims of innovative compound words abound in the ape language literature (Fouts, 1974, 1975; Patterson, 1980; Miles, 1975; Patterson & Linden, 1981), these are by their nature one-time occurrences and ambiguous (Petitto & Seidenberg, 1979; Terrace et al., 1979, 1980); in any case, such examples belong to the lexicon rather than grammar. In contrast, we present examples of statistically reliable protogrammatical rules that an ape has invented himself.

REARING ENVIRONMENT AND SUBJECTS

The primary communication system of the present study consists of lexigrams (printed geometric symbols). (Methodological details are presented in Savage-Rumbaugh, McDonald, Sevcik, Hopkins, & Rubert, 1986.) A few informal and American Sign Language gestures also are used alone and in combination with the lexigram system.[1] Human companions use English freely (for examples, see discourse in Table 10.2). Details of procedure are presented in an earlier publication (Savage-Rumbaugh et al., 1986).

Kanzi, a bonobo chimpanzee, received his first exposure to the use of lexigrams, gextures, and human speech at 6 months of age while in the care of his mother, who was in a language-training program (Savage-Rumbaugh et al., 1986). He produced his first lexigram at age 2½ years without training. A complete record has been kept of Kanzi's semiotic productions since that time.

Mulika, his half-sister, was born when Kanzi was 3 years old. She spontaneously produced her first lexigram at 12 months of age. A complete record subsequently was kept of her semiotic usage.

In contrast to other studies that have attempted to train symbols or signs (Asano, Kojima, Matsuzawa, Kubota, & Mutofushi, 1982; Fouts, 1973; Gardner, B. T. & Gardner, R. A., 1980; Gardner, R. A. & Gardner, B. T., 1969; Kellogg, 1968; Miles, 1983; Premack, 1970; Rumbaugh et al., 1973; Savage-Rumbaugh, 1986), the purpose of this research was to determine how much language the pygmy chimpanzee could acquire in the ongoing course of normal communication similar to what human children receive. Training has been avoided assiduously, even to the point of not asking the repetitive questions typically seen in early mother-child dialogue. The chimpanzees also are raised in a more natural environment. They have not been separated completely from their mother, and they forage daily in a large forest which is replenished with food.

As reported elsewhere (Savage-Rumbaugh et al., 1986), they have begun to comprehend spoken English, and such comprehension typically precedes

---

[1]Miles (1975, 1978) reports a closely related phenomenon in language-trained *Pan troglodytes* chimpanzees: combinations consisting of a formal American-Sign-Language sign, plus a natural communication element, such as a play posture.

TABLE 10.2
Uses of Repetition by Pygmy Chimpanzees (*Pan Paniscus*)

Confirm/Agree

(Kanzi, age 5, with Kelly)
With Kanzi on her shoulders, Kelly stops at the door leading outside to comment at the lexigram board.
Kelly: *We are GOing to see the GIBBONs* (as per Kanzi's earlier request).
Kanzi: *GIBBON,* vocalizing *eh-uh* in agreement.

(Mulika, age 2, with human caregiver/researcher, Kelly)
Kelly: *#Let's see what's on TELEVISION.*
Mulika: *TELEVISION* (Then Mulika went to the video deck and gestured to it, ready for Kelly to put a tape in.)

(Kanzi, age 5, with human caregiver/researcher, Rose)
Kanzi has indicated that he is interested in looking in the refrigerator. Rose opens it and Kanzi points to a bowl of raspberries. Rose takes out the raspberries and uses the keyboard.
Rose: *We will call these FOOD.* (This is because there is not a symbol for raspberries on the keyboard.)
Kanzi: *FOOD* (He does not indicate any desire to have the raspberries, however, but goes over and looks out the window.)

Excitement

(Mulika, age 2, with human caregiver/researcher, Kelly)
Kelly: *GO A-FRAME* (informing Mulika of destination verbally and with lexigrams)
Mulika: *GO,* vocalizing excitedly

Choose Alternative

(Kanzi, age 5, with human caregiver/researcher, Rose)
Rose: *You can either PLAY or watch TV.*
Kanzi: *TV* (Kanzi watches after Rose turns it on.)

Imitation/Request

(Mulika, age 2, with human caregiver/researcher, Karen)
Mulika reaches for Karen's coke.
Karen: *COKE,* showing Mulika the lexigram
Mulika: *COKE*

Note. Italicized capital letters indicate lexigrams for the chimps, lexigrams plus spoken English for the humans; italicized small letters indicate spoken English. Adapted with permission from "Comparing Communicative Competence in Child and Chimp: The Pragmatics of Repetition" by P. M. Greenfield and E. S. Savage-Rumbaugh. *Journal of Child Language* (in press).

the onset of lexigram usage. Through formal vocabulary tests of comprehension and production (Savage-Rumbaugh, 1987; Savage-Rumbaugh et al., 1986), the researchers established the independent symbolic status of most of the lexical elements used in combinations (details are to be found in Greenfield & Savage-Rumbaugh, 1990).

IMITATION BY KANZI AND MULIKA

This analysis focuses on a month of data taken during October of 1985, when Kanzi was 5 and Mulika almost 2 years old. Table 10.2 presents qualitative examples of some of the communicative functions that repetition served for Kanzi and Mulika. Note that the functions parallel those presented in Table 10.1 for human children. In similar fashion, Kanzi and Mulika selectively repeat lexigrams produced by their conversational partners for pragmatic purposes: to confirm or agree, to express excitement, to choose an alternative, as well as to imitate. An important point is that these functions do not occur exclusively in request or instrumental situations; in the last CONFIRM/AGREE example, Kanzi confirms an identification, without wanting the identified item (FOOD). (The reader is referred to Greenfield & Savage-Rumbaugh (in press) for quantitative results and more detailed analysis.)

Terrace et al. (1979), in their treatment of imitation, pointed out that their chimpanzee, Nim, imitated more than the typical child (44%, including expansions) (Sanders, 1985). In contrast, ape language projects deemphasizing drilling and emphasizing a naturalistic communication environment have found lower rates of imitation than did Project Nim, which relied heavily on rote language drill as a teaching method (Greenfield & Savage-Rumbaugh, 1984; Miles, 1983, 1990; Patterson, 1979, 1981). Similarly, Kanzi and Mulika imitate less than Nim and do not differ from human children in this respect. Kanzi's rate of 6% immediate imitation is similar to figures for children up to age 3 years. Mulika's rate of 21% is not above the range of children between 1 and 2 years of age, just starting to talk (Goldin-Meadow & Mylander, 1984).

KANZI'S GRAMMAR

This analysis was based on 5 months of Kanzi's output, April through August 1986; Kanzi was 5½ years old. (Mulika's lexigram skills were not well enough developed for her to make frequent combinations.)

In order to assure the creativity of Kanzi's symbol combinations, we excluded all imitations (including reductions and expansions) from the analysis. We also analyzed video tapes to determine caregiver input and, hence, the possible environmental source of any rules that might develop. (See details in Greenfield & Savage-Rumbaugh, 1990.)

Following accepted methodology for studying word or sign combinations of children at the two-word stage (Brown, 1973; Goldin-Meadow, 1984; Schlesinger, 1971), we classified all two-element combinations (lexigram-lexigram and lexigram-gesture) for which contextual information was available into semantic relations such as agent-action and action-object. We used Kanzi's behavior subsequent to an utterance as the basis for judgments of semantic relations, thus resolving the problem of the subjectivity of "rich interpretation." Table 10.3 presents the distribution and examples of semantic relations; the examples also illustrate how Kanzi's behavior provided "behavioral concordance" for assigning combinations to semantic

TABLE 10.3

Distribution of Two-Element Semantic Relations in Kanzi's Corpus

Relation		Example (of Dominant Order)
Conjoined Actions[a]	92	*TICKLE BITE*, then positions himself for researcher/ caregiver to tickle and bite him
Action-Agent[a]	119	*CARRY you (gesture)*, gesturing to Phil, who agrees to
Agent-Action[a]	13	carry Kanzi
Action-Object[a]	39	*KEEP-AWAY BALLOON*, wanting to tease Bill with a
Object-Action[a]	15	balloon and start a fight
Object-Agent[a]	7	*BALLOON you (gesture)*, Kanzi gestures to Liz; Liz gives
Agent-Object[a]	1	Kanzi a balloon.
Entity-Demonstrative[a]	182	*PEANUT that (gesture)*, points to peanuts in cooler.
Demonstrative-Entity[a]	67	
Goal-Action[a]	46	*COKE CHASE;* then researcher chases Kanzi to place in
Action-Goal[a]	10	woods where Coke is kept
Conjoined Entities[b]	25	*M & M GRAPE.* Caregiver/researcher: "You want both of these foods?" Kanzi vocalizes and holds out his hand.
Conjoined Locations[b]	7	*SUE'S-OFFICE CHILDSIDE;* wanted to go to those two places.
Location-Entity[b]	19	*PLAYYARD AUSTIN;* wants to visit Austin in the play-
Entity-Location[b]	12	yard.
Entity-Attribute[b]	12	*FOOD BLACKBERRY*, after eating blackberries, to
Attribute-Entity[b]	10	request more.
Miscellaneous[b]	37	These include low-frequency relations (less than seven) such as attribute of action, attribute of location, affirmation, negation, and relations involving an instrument.
Two-Mode Paraphrase[b,c]	4	*CHASE chase (gesture)*, trying to get staff member to chase him in the lobby.
No Direct Relation[b]	6	*POTATO OIL;* Kanzi commented after researcher had put oil on him as he was eating a potato.
TOTAL	723	

Note. Italicized capital letters indicate lexigrams. Adapted with permission from "Grammatical Combination in *Pan Paniscus:* Processes of Learning and Invention in the Evolution and Development of Language" by P. M. Greenfield and E. S. Savage-Rumbaugh (1990), in S. T. Parker and K. R. Gibson (Eds.), *"Language" and Intelligence in Monkeys and Apes: Comparative Developmental Perspectives,* New York, Cambridge University Press.
[a]These relations are analyzed for their ordering regularities in the tables and text that follow. [b]These relations either lacked ordering structure or were too infrequent to be subject to such an analysis. [c]There were no purely repetitious two-symbol utterances in the two-symbol corpus. This low-frequency category contains the closest phenomenon to a repetition.

relations. To supplement this table, the 5-month corpus of Kanzi's two-element combinations consisting of two lexigrams or one lexigram and one gesture is presented as an appendix. (Methodological details concerning reliability and coding appear in Greenfield & Savage-Rumbaugh, 1990.)

Next we discuss in detail all those relations in which Kanzi used symbol order as a formal device to construct a particular semantic relationship.

Rule Learned from Environmental Models: Action Precedes Object

The variety of action-object examples presented in the appendix illustrate the second criterion of a grammatical rule: Kanzi relates two symbol categories; he combines and recombines a category of nine action lexigrams with a second category of 13 object lexigrams.

Contrary to the claim that chimpanzees cannot make verbal statements but are limited to demands or instrumental requests (Petitto & Seidenberg, 1979; Sanders, 1985), the top of Table 10.4 presents a statement (*HIDE PEANUT*) by Kanzi of his impending action. Statements are in the minority in our data (4%), but they do occur.

The second part of Table 10.4 shows the development of a symbol-ordering rule. As children often do at the two-word stage (Braine, 1976), Kanzi moves from no significant ordering tendency at the beginning of the period (first row of figures) to a statistically significant preference for the action-object ordering found in English (second row of figures) (a preference that, unlike Nim's, is not disturbed by countertrends of individual lexical items [Terrace et al., 1980]). The fact that Kanzi's caregivers show this same action-object order in even stronger form than does Kanzi (Table 10.4, last row of figures), indicates that it originated in the environmental model presented to him.

Looking at this developmental trend another way, we can say that there is significant movement away from an object-action order, toward an action-object order ($p < .01$, χ^2 test). It may be of evolutionary significance that this movement parallels a common trend in the history of language away from an object-verb order and toward the verb-object order (Nocentini, 1988).

To test whether the semantic relation between actions and objects actually was understood by Kanzi at the time of his production data, we looked at naturally occurring examples of comprehension and miscomprehension of action-object lexigram relations expressed by human caregivers during the same period of time. The results show that Kanzi not only used but understood this relationship (Greenfield & Savage-Rumbaugh, 1990). Here is an example of correct comprehension:

Caregiver/researcher: *PLAY HAT KEEPAWAY*
Kanzi grabs the hat and shakes it at caregiver/researcher.

TABLE 10.4
Kanzi's Two-Element Lexigram-Lexigram Combinations: Relations Between
Action and Object (Animate and Inanimate)[a]

Examples	Action	Object	
Inanimate Object	*HIDE*	*PEANUT*	Kanzi then hides some peanuts.
Animate Object	*GRAB*	*HEAD*	Caregiver/researcher has been biting and grabbing Kanzi's head. Kanzi gets into her lap (into position to be grabbed).

The Development of Kanzi's Lexigram Order

	Action-Object	*Object-Action*	
Early (4/10/86–4/26/86)	3	7	
Late (4/29/86–8/30/86)	31	6	$p < .00000$[b]

Kanzi's Human Caregivers' Lexigram Order

Action-Object	*Object-Action*	
51	7	$p < .00000$[b]

Note. Lexigrams are in italicized capital letters. Adapted with permission from "Grammatical Combination in *Pan Paniscus:* Processes of Learning and Invention in the Evolution and Development of Language" by P. M. Greenfield and E. S. Savage-Rumbaugh (1990), in S. T. Parker and K. R. Gibson (eds.), *"Language" and Intelligence in Monkeys and Apes: Comparative Developmental Perspectives,* New York, Cambridge University Press.

[a]Because there was evidence (to follow) that gestures were treated separately from lexigrams in Kanzi's formal rules, combinations in which an object was symbolized by a demonstrative gesture were not included in the action–object rule. However, these examples are included in the appendix.
[b]Test for significance of a proportion (one-tailed). (Bruning & Kintz, 1977).

This example is all the stronger because playing keepaway is not the obvious action to do with a hat.

The next example is of a misunderstanding that strongly indicates that Kanzi constructs action–object relations in his own mind:

Caregiver/researcher: *ICE,* commenting on a big block of ice on TV. *Someone is HIDing in the ice.*

Kanzi starts searching under the blankets. He has apparently understood the action–object relation, HIDE ICE, and is looking for the ice!

As with children, an error provides the best evidence of Kanzi's own constructions. This particular misunderstanding provides evidence for constructive comprehension of an action–object relation.

Invented Rules

A Formal Rule: Gesture After Lexigram. Kanzi's human caregivers have exposed him to the English word-order model, agent before action (Human Caregivers' order, third and fourth row of figures, Table 10.5). His own lexigram-lexigram combinations (second line of figures in Table 10.5) show signs of following this rule, but they are too infrequent for statistical reliability. However, Kanzi makes up his own rule for combining agent gesture with action lexigram: His highly significant ordering rule, "Place gesture last" (the first line of figures, Table 10.5), uses the opposite ordering strategy from that of his caregivers' English-based rule. Note that Kanzi's caregivers conform to their English-based ordering strategy even in their gesture plus lexigram utterances (third line of figures, Table 10.5).

Kanzi's rule, "Place gesture last," has considerable generality as well as originality. The remainder of Table 10.5 shows how this rule is manifest in three other semantic relations: entity-demonstrative, goal-action, and object-agent. In the case of these three relations, Kanzi's rule operates in the absence of a human model, as the human model figures in Table 10.5 show.

Although three of the relations involve a demonstrative gesture, the fourth, goal-action, involves combining a lexigram with one of several action gestures. Thus, to a limited extent, this rule involves relations between two categories, a larger category of lexigrams and a smaller category of gestures.

The rule "Place gesture last" may have been a purely arbitrary formal rule. It was not merely an artifact of lack of vocabulary on the lexigram keyboard. For example, the lexigram LIZ was always on the keyboard. It was produced in first position in LIZ HIDE (agent-action relation in appendix). However, at other times Kanzi did not use a lexigram to refer to Liz; he gestured instead (see *BALLOON you [gesture referring to Liz]* in Table 10.3). Although Kanzi could have used the lexigram LIZ in this last example, he chose to denote Liz through gesture, and, at the same time, the expression of Liz as agent moves from first position as a lexigram to second position as a gesture.

Nor was the order, gesture-after-lexigram, strictly a matter of physical convenience. In one video, Kanzi was relatively near a person and far from the lexigram board. Yet he moved to the board to touch a lexigram, then returned to gesture toward the person. In this situation, producing the gesture last involved greater physical effort and more time than producing the gesture first would have. Although this observation confirms the impression of a purely formal arbitrary rule, a defining feature of human language, there is another possibility that cannot be eliminated. Kanzi's caregivers often waited for him to confirm or behaviorally specify the meaning of a lexigram utterance; Kanzi often did this by means of a gesture.

TABLE 10.5
Kanzi's Ordering Rule: Gesture Follows Lexigram

RELATIONS BETWEEN AGENTS AND ACTIONS

Example:	Action	Agent
Kanzi:	*CHASE*	*you (demonstrative gesture)*

Kanzi says this after caregiver/researcher, suggests going to sandpile for food. Kanzi touches caregiver/researcher, who agrees to chase him there.

Kanzi's Order

	Agent-Action	*Action-Agent*	
Lexigram Action- Gesture Agent	7	116	$p = .00000$[a]
Lexigram-Lexigram	6	3	

Human Caregivers' Order

	Agent-Action	*Action-Agent*
Lexigram Action- Gesture Agent	14	0
Lexigram-Lexigram	14	0

ENTITY-DEMONSTRATIVE RELATIONS

Example:	Entity	Demonstrative
Kanzi:	*FOOD*	(demonstrative gesture)

He requests food from cooler by pushing FOOD key and then pointing to cooler.

	Demonstrative *Gesture 1st*	*Demonstrative* *Gesture 2nd*	
Kanzi	67	182	$p = .00000$[a]
Human Model	3	2	

GOAL-ACTION RELATIONS

Example:	Goal	Action
Kanzi:	*DOG*	*(go gesture)*

He then led to the dogs' pen.

	Action Gesture 1st	*Action Gesture 2nd*	
Kanzi	0	30	$p = .00000$[a]
Human Model	0	0	

OBJECT-AGENT RELATIONS

Example:	Object	Agent
Kanzi:	*BALLOON*	*You (demonstrative gesture to person)*

Kanzi gestures to researcher; she gives Kanzi a balloon.

	Agent Gesture 1st	*Agent Gesture 2nd*	
Kanzi	1	7	$p < .03$[a]
Human Model	0	0	

Note. Lexigrams are in italicized capital letters. Adapted with permission from "Grammatical Combination in *Pan Paniscus:* Processes of Learning and Invention in the Evolution and Development of Language" by P. M. Greenfield and E. S. Savage-Rumbaugh (1990), in S. T. Parker and K. R. Gibson (Eds.), *"Language" and Intelligence in Monkeys and Apes: Comparative Developmental Perspectives,* New York, Cambridge University Press.

[a]Test for significance of a proportion (two-tailed) (Bruning & Kintz, 1977).

Thus, the structure of the communicative situation may have inadvertently influenced the "gesture last" rule.

Kanzi "Teaches" his Human Caregivers an Invented Rule: Symbol Order Reflects Action Order. Kanzi frequently combined two action lexigrams (see first example in Table 10.3 and first category in Appendix). At first glance, these combinations seemed to be mere unstructured lists. Unlike the other rules discussed up to now, they lack the minimum requirements of a proposition: one predicate and one argument; conjoined action combinations simply chain two predicates. However, these combinations revealed unsuspected regularities (Table 10.6), reflecting natural action categories and preferred action orders in social play. Kuroda observed some of these same preferred behavior sequences among pygmy chimpanzees in the wild (S. Kuroda, personal communication, July 1987), as has Boehm (1988) with other species of chimpanzee, *Pan troglodytes.* Table 10.6 presents quantitative evidence that Kanzi translates regularities of action order into regularities of lexigram order.

Most important, Kanzi has not only created these symbol ordering rules for action-action sequences himself, but he has also invented the very relation of conjoined action. In 6 hours of videotape, dating 5 months before the start of the corpus, when Kanzi was already producing frequent conjoined action combinations, there was only one example of a caregiver combining the action words involved in the conjoined-action ordering rule; and that one example was a direct imitation of Kanzi. Five months later, at

TABLE 10.6
Conjoined Action Lexigram Combinations

Prefers in 1st Position	No. Times 1st	No. Times 2nd	
CHASE	19	8	$p < .04$[a]
TICKLE	29	15	$p < .04$[a]
Prefers in 2nd Position			
HIDE	2	9	$p < .04$[a]
SLAP	1	6	$p < .06$[a]
BITE	21	38	$p < .04$[a]
No Position Preference			
GRAB	5	4	
HUG	7	5	

Note. Lexigrams are in italicized capital letters. Adapted with permission from "Grammatical Combination in *Pan Paniscus:* Processes of Learning and Invention in the Evolution and Development of Language" by P. M. Greenfield and E. S. Savage-Rumbaugh (1990), in S. T. Parker and K. R. Gibson (eds.), *"Language" and Intelligence in Monkeys and Apes: Comparative Developmental Perspectives,* New York, Cambridge University Press.
[a]Test for significance of a proportion (two-tailed) (Bruning & Kintz, 1977).

the start of our corpus, in about 2 hours of videotape, there were 10 examples of conjoined-action combinations produced by caregivers; however, a caregiver was imitating Kanzi in 9 out of 10 cases. (Two caregivers were sampled in the earlier period; the same two, plus two more, were sampled in the later period.) The fact that, in virtually all instances, the caregivers imitated Kanzi's conjoined-action utterances indicates that Kanzi not only invented conjoined action meaning rules; he also taught them to his human caregivers!

A Rule for Combining Three Lexigrams

Only one three-element pattern reached sufficient productivity in the period under study to be analyzed quantitatively: the conjoined-actions-plus-agent (gesture) pattern. These combinations combined and preserved the ordering rules of their constituent two-element combinations, as children's early multiword utterances do (Braine, 1976). An example of this statistically significant pattern is CHASE BITE you (gesture). Here CHASE and BITE are ordered in accord with the conjoined-action rules (Table 10.6), while the combination also conforms to the "Place gesture last" rule (Table 10.5). Table 10.7 presents the other examples of conjoined-action-plus-agent combinations.

Strengths and Limitations of Kanzi's Grammar

Productivity. The productivity of the relations that Kanzi constructs and the fact that they consist of functional categories that cannot be reduced to preferences associated with particular words is illustrated by Kanzi's use of the lexigram AUSTIN, the name of a *Pan troglodytes*

TABLE 10.7
Kanzi's Three-Element Lexigram-Lexigram Combinations: Conjoined Actions
Plus Agent

Complete Corpus of Examples of Rule-Governed Order
CHASE BITE you (demonstrative gesture)   (3)
GRAB BITE you (demonstrative gesture)   (2)
CHASE HIDE you (demonstrative gesture)   (2)
Complete Corpus of Counterexamples to Rule-Governed Order
GRAB TICKLE you (demonstrative gesture)   (1) Rule-governed order is significantly dominant, $p < .00000$[a].

Note. Lexigrams are in italicized capital letters. Numerals in parentheses indicate frequencies.
[a]Test for significance of a proportion (one-tailed). (Bruning & Kintz, 1977).

chimpanzee also at the Language Research Center. Kanzi uses the lexigram AUSTIN in 11 different semantic relations (action-agent, action-goal, action-object, affirmation-goal, attribute-entity, conjoined locations, entity-demonstrative, entity-location, goal-agent, goal-instrument, recipient-object). (See appendix for specific utterances.)

A Difference in Symbol Order Signals a Difference in Meaning.   Even more important, Kanzi shows an incipient ability to use a difference in symbol order to signal a difference in meaning. When animate beings function as agents of action in Kanzi's lexigram-lexigram combinations, he tends to place them first. When they function as objects of action, he tends to produce them last. A chi-square test shows this difference to be significant at the .05 level. As an example, he contrasts GRAB MATATA, where Matata is grabbed, with MATATA BITE where Matata functions as agent. This is the beginning of autonomous syntax, in which symbol order signals meaning relations without the help of a disambiguating context.

Although apes have been reported to use a difference in sign order to signal or to comprehend a difference in meaning, the evidence is either anecdotal (Fouts, 1975) or partial imitation is at play (Gardner, B. T., & Gardner, R. A., 1978); in still others the extent of imitation is unknown (Patterson, 1978). Kanzi, in contrast, has shown himself consistently able to use a reversal of word order to signal a change of meaning in his spontaneous symbol combinations.

Utterance Length.   Although Kanzi had been combining lexigrams for about 3 years at the time of the grammar study, most combinations (90%) were still of only two elements and most utterances were still single symbols. This length limitation agrees with Terrace et al.'s (1979) observation of Nim. In Kanzi's case, short symbol combinations also may reflect a modality problem. Although caregivers spoke in normal English sentences, they most frequently inserted only one or two lexigrams per sentence, reflecting the mechanical difficulty of the lexigram mode in generating longer utterances. However, Kanzi does differ from Nim in that he produces *nonredundant* three-element combinations in which two two-element combinations have been linked to add new information (see also Savage-Rumbaugh et al., 1986).

CONCLUSION

Imitation in the chimpanzee, as in the human child, reveals not a lack of conversational competence (Sanders, 1985; Terrace et al., 1979) but its presence. The ability to use repetition of others to fulfill various pragmatic functions is not unique to *Pan paniscus,* but is shared with *Pan troglodytes,* as inspection of published data from Sherman and Austin shows (Greenfield & Savage-Rumbaugh, 1984, in press).

In the area of grammar, Kanzi shows the ability to learn a productive symbol-order rule governing relations between two categories of symbols. Although there have been claims that apes use English word order in constructing two-symbol combinations, this is the first time an ape has used word order that is not dependent on either partial imitation of the preceding utterance or position preferences for specific lexical items (Gardner, B. T., & Gardner, R. A., 1974; Patterson, 1978; Terrace et al., 1980). It is also the first time an ape consistently has used a difference in symbol order to signal a difference in meaning when imitated utterances have been systematically excluded.

An alternative explanation for these results might be that Kanzi's symbol combinations, with their ordering regularities, are simply learned habits. First, ignoring symbol order for the moment, we see that the combinations in the corpus (appendix) are both spontaneous (not imitated from preceding context) and encode meanings that are consistent with the conversational and extralinguistic context, including Kanzi's own behavior and goals in the situation (see Table 3). Second, no differential reinforcement was given for particular symbol orders or for particular meaning relations. Third, when an ordering rule has been modeled by caregivers (action-object combinations), the data indicate that Kanzi has acquired a generative rule, rather than specific position habits. Several lines of evidence support this point:

1. There are a large number and variety of spontaneous action-object combinations (see appendix for complete list).

2. Given lexical items appear in different positions in different ordering rules expressing different semantic relations. A good example is the lexigram BITE which is generally produced first in action-object combinations (see appendix), but is most often produced second in conjoined action combinations (Table 10.6).

3. As noted earlier, Kanzi uses a reversal of symbol order to signal a difference in meaning when he combines an action lexigram with a lexigram representing an animate being.

This evidence precludes rote association between lexigram and serial position as an explanation of the relevant symbol-ordering rule.

Kanzi also has shown the ability to invent primitive grammatical rules for ordering symbols. These are rules that cannot have been learned as "habits" or otherwise induced from information in the environment, for analysis of input indicated either that no models at all had been provided for the semantic relation in question (e.g., conjoined-action combinations) or that an opposite symbol order had been modeled by human caregivers (agent-action combinations).[2]

This type of inventive capacity has now been established for deaf children being raised without a sign-language model (Goldin-Meadow, 1978; Goldin-Meadow & Mylander, 1984), as well as for hearing children, who develop word-order regularities in their speech, despite the absence of such regularities in the input model provided by certain languages (Slobin, 1966). In the case of Kanzi, as for children, these inventions indicate an internal or innate predisposition for meaningful symbol combination structured by regularities of symbol order.

Unique among apes, Kanzi also is beginning to use ordering rules to combine two semantic relations into meaningful and rule-bound three-element combinations. The grammar of the three-element combinations was almost certainly also invented by Kanzi, for the structure is based on combining his other two invented rules, conjoined action and "place gesture last." Most interesting, Goldin-Meadow and Mylander (1984) reported that the most frequent "complex" sentence structure created by deaf children being raised without a sign-language model are conjoined action utterances. Such structures consist of two action signs, plus pointing to indicate the agent. It is striking that the most frequent complex structure created by these deaf children is also the most frequent complex structure created by a bonobo chimpanzee.

Both of Kanzi's invented rules are action-based. "Place gesture after lexigram" is a rule that orders the action mode of the symbolic communication itself. The rule may provide automaticity at the level of sequencing, freeing deliberate cognitive processes to formulate meaning relations. Automatic ordering is particularly functional where one must coordinate communication in two modes. Note Kanzi has invented a rule based on arbitrary formal (rather than semantic or pragmatic) criteria.

Kanzi also has invented a semantically and pragmatically motivated symbol-order rule — based on ordering actions in species-specific play sequences that also occur in the wild (Boehm, 1988; S. Kuroda, personal communication, July 14, 1987). This finding suggests that grammar may have evolved originally partly in response to the need to coordinate complex action sequences with conspecifics. In this way, a primitive syntactic structure would have taken advantage of an available action structure, an evolutionarily natural proposal (cf. Greenfield, in press). From a slightly different perspective, conventionalized ordering in social play has been transformed into conventionalized ordering in symbolic communication.

---

[2]Patterson and Linden (1981) report that Koko the gorilla uses a sign order (noun-adjective) that is the opposite of the model provided by human caregivers. Although examples are provided, there is no quantitative data.

In conclusion, these results suggest that the potential to invent (as well as learn) a rudimentary grammar (or protosyntax) and to use language conversationally was present approximately 5 million years ago when hominids and chimpanzees split in the phylogenetic tree.

ACKNOWLEDGEMENTS

We would like to thank Elizabeth Rubert, Jeannine Murphy, Phillip Shaw, Rose Sevcik, and Kelly McDonald for assistance in all aspects of the data collection. Thanks also to Penny Nelson for help with data analysis and to Terrence Deacon and Duane Rumbaugh for stimulating discussion. This research was supported by National Institute of Child Health and Human Development grant NICHD-06016, which supports the Language Research Center, cooperatively operated by Georgia State University and Yerkes Regional Primate Research Center of Emory University. In addition, the research is supported in part by RR-00165 to the Yerkes Regional Primate Research Center of Emory University. PMG was supported by the Bunting Institute, Radcliffe College, by a grant from the Office of Naval Research to the Bunting Institute, and by the UCLA Gold Shield Faculty Prize.

REFERENCES

Asano, T., Kojima, T., Matsuzawa, K., Kubota, K., & Mutofushi, K. (1982). Object and color naming in champanzees (*Pan troglodytes*). *Proc. Jap. Acad., 58,* 118–122.

Bloom, L. (1970). *Language development: Form and function in emerging grammars.* Cambridge, MA: MIT Press.

Boehm, C. (1988, July). *Behavior of chimpanzees at Gombe.* Paper presented at The Origin of Human Language, NATO Advanced Study Institute and Meeting of the Language Origins Society, Cortona, Italy.

Braine, M. D. S. (1976). Children's first word combinations. *Monographs of the Society for Research in Child Development, 41*(1, Serial No. 164), 1–96.

Bronowski, J., & Bellugi, U. (1970). Language, name, and concept. *Science, 168,* 669–673.

Brown, R. (1973). *A first language: The early stages.* Cambridge, MA: Harvard University Press.

Bruning, J. L., & Kintz, B. L. (1977). *Computational handbook of statistics.* Glenview, IL: Scott, Foresman.

Chomsky, N. (1965). *Aspects of the theory of syntax.* Cambridge, MA: MIT Press.

Chomsky, N. (1967). Human language and other semiotic systems. *Semiotica, 25,* 31–44.

de Villiers, J. (1984). Limited input? Limited structure. Commentary on Goldin-Meadow & Mylander. *Monographs of the Society for Research on Child Development, 49*(3–4, Serial No. 207), 122–129.

Fouts, R. S. (1973). Acquisition and testing of gestural signs in four young chimpanzees. *Science, 180,* 978–980.

Fouts, R. S. (1974). Capacities for language in great apes. In R. H. Tuttle (Ed.), *Socioecology and psychology of primates: Proceedings of the 19th International Congress of Anthropological and Ethnological Sciences* (pp. 371–390). Chicago: Aldine.

Fouts, R. S. (1975). Communication with chimpanzees. In I. Eibl-Eibesfeld & G. Kurth (Eds.), *Hominisation and verhalten* (pp. 137–158). Stuttgart, Germany: Gustav Fisher.

Fouts, R. S. & Couch, J. B. (1976). Cultural evolution of learned language in chimpanzees. In E. Simmel & M. Hahn (Eds.), *Communicative behavior and evolution* (pp. 141-161). New York: Academic.

Gardner, B. T., & Gardner, R. A. (1974). Comparing the early utterances of child and chimpanzee. In A. Pick (Ed.), *Minnesota symposium on child psychology* (Vol. 8, pp. 3-23). Minneapolis: University of Minnesota Press.

Gardner, B. T., & Gardner, R. A. (1975). Evidence for sentence constituents in the early utterances of child and chimpanzee. *Journal of Experimental Psychology: General, 104*(3), 244-267.

Gardner, B. T., & Gardner, R. A. (1978). Comparative psychology and language acquisition. *Annals of the New York Academy of Science, 309,* 37-76.

Gardner, B. T., & Gardner, R. A. (1980). Two comparative psychologists look at language acquisition. In K. Nelson (Ed.), *Children's language* (Vol. 2, pp. 331-369). New York: Gardner Press.

Gardner, R. A., & Gardner, B. T. (1969). Teaching sign language to a chimpanzee. *Science, 165,* 654-672.

Goldin-Meadow, S. (1978). A study in human capacities. *Science, 200,* 649-651.

Goldin-Meadow, S., & Mylander, C. (1984). Gestural communication in deaf children: The effects and noneffects of parental input on early language development. *Monographs of the Society for Research in Child Development, 49*(3-4, Serial No. 207), 1-120.

Greenfield, P. M. (1969). Unpublished data.

Greenfield, P. M. (in press). Language, tools, and brain: The ontogeny and phylogeny of hierarchically organized sequential behavior. *Behavioral and Brain Sciences.*

Greenfield, P. M., & Savage-Rumbaugh, E. S. (1984). Perceived variability and symbol use: A common language-cognition interface in children and chimpanzees (*Pan troglodytes*). *Journal of Comparative Psychology, 96*(2), 201-218.

Greenfield, P. M., & Savage-Rumbaugh, E. S. (1990). Grammatical combination in *Pan paniscus*: Processes of learning and invention in the evolution and development of language. In S. T. Parker and K. R. Gibson (Eds.), *"Language" and intelligence in monkeys and apes: Comparative developmental perspectives* (pp. 540-578). New York: Cambridge University Press.

Greenfield, P. M., & Savage-Rumbaugh, E. S. (in press). Comparing communicative competence in child and chimp: The pragmatics of repetition. *Journal of Child Language.*

Hill, J. H. (1978). Apes and language. *Annual Review of Anthropology, 7,* 89-112.

Kellogg, W. N. (1968). Communication and language in home-raised chimpanzee. *Science, 162,* 423-427.

Kuroda, S. (1989). Developmental retardation and behavioral characteristics in the pygmy chimpanzees. In P. G. Helthe and L. A. Marquardt (Eds.), *Understanding chimpanzees* (pp. 184-193). Cambridge, MA: Harvard University Press.

Leddick, K. (1989). Unpublished observation. Department of Psychology, UCLA.

Lenneberg, E. H. (1967). *Biological foundations of language.* New York: Wiley.

Lieberman, P. (1984). *The biology and evolution of language.* Cambridge, MA: Harvard University Press.

Limber, J. (1977). Language in child and chimp? *American Psychologist, 32,* 280-293.

Matsuzawa, T. (1985). Use of numbers by a chimpanzee. *Nature, 315,* 57-59.

McNeill, D. (1974). Sentence structure in chimpanzee communication. In K. Connolly & J. Bruner (Eds.), *The growth of competence* (pp. 75-94). New York: Academic Press.

Miles, H. L. W. (1975). The relationship of natural communications and the use of sign language in two chimpanzees. Paper presented at the American Anthropological Association, San Francisco.

Miles, L. W. (1978). Natural communications and sign combinations in the use of sign language by chimpanzees. In D. Chivers & J. Herbert (Eds.), *Recent advances in primatology: Vol. 1. Behavior.* London: Academic Press.

Miles, H. L. (1983). Apes and language: The search for communicative competence. In J. De Luce & H. T. Wilder (Eds.), *Language in Primates* (pp. 43–61). New York: Springer-Verlag.

Miles, H. L. W. (1990). The cognitive foundations for reference in a signing orangutan. In S. T. Parker and K. R. Gibson (Eds.), *"Language" and intelligence in monkeys and apes: Comparative developmental perspectives* (pp. 511–539). New York: Cambridge University Press.

Muncer, S. J., & Ettlinger, G. (1981). Communication by a chimpanzee: First-trial mastery of word order that is critical for meaning, but failure to negate conjunctions. *Neuropsychologia, 19,* 73–78.

Nocenti, A. (1988, July). *Roots of language: The forbidden experiment.* Paper presented at The Origin of Human Language, NATO Advanced Study Institute and Meeting of the Language Origins Society, Cortona, Italy.

Ochs Keenan, E. (1977). Making it last: Repetition in children's discourse. In S. Ervin-Tripp & C. Mitchell-Kernan (Eds.), *Child Discourse* (pp. 125–138). New York: Academic.

Patterson, F. G. (1978). The gestures of a gorilla: Language acquisition in another pongid. *Brain and Language, 5,* 72–97.

Patterson, F. G. (1979). *Linguistic capability of a low-land gorilla.* Unpublished doctoral dissertation, Stanford University, Stanford, CA.

Patterson, F. G. (1980). Innovative uses of language by a gorilla: A case study. In K. Nelson (Ed.), *Children's language* (Vol. 2, pp. 497–561). New York: Gardner Press.

Patterson, F. G. (1981). Ape language. *Science, 211,* 86–87.

Patterson, F., & Linden, E. (1981). *The education of Koko.* New York: Holt, Rinehart, & Winston.

Petitto, L. A., & Seidenberg, M. S. (1979). On the evidence for linguistic abilities in signing apes. *Brain and Language, 8,* 162–183.

Premack, D. (1970). A functional analysis of language. *Journal of the Experimental Analysis of Behavior, 14,* 107–125.

Rimpau, J. B., Gardner, R. A., & Gardner, B. T. (1989). Expression of person, place, and instrument in ASL: Utterances of children and chimpanzees. In R. A. Gardner, B. T. Gardner, & T. E. Van Cantfort (Eds.), *Teaching sign language to chimpanzees* (pp. 240–268). Albany: State University of New York Press.

Rumbaugh, D. M., Gill, T. V., & von Glasersfeld, E. C. (1973). Reading and sentence completion by a chimpanzee. *Science, 182,* 732–733.

Sanders, R. J. (1985). Teaching apes to ape language: Explaining the imitative and nonimitative signing of a chimpanzee (*Pan troglodytes*). *Journal of Comparative Psychology, 99*(2), 197–210.

Savage-Rumbaugh, E. S. (1984). *Pan paniscus* and *Pan troglodytes.* In R. L. Susman (ed.), *The pygmy chimpanzee: Evolutionary biology and behavior* (pp. 395–413). New York: Plenum.

Savage-Rumbaugh, E. S. (1986). *Ape language: From conditioned response to symbol.* New York: Columbia University Press.

Savage-Rumbaugh, E. S. (1987). A new look at ape language: Comprehension of vocal speech and syntax. In D. W. Leger (Ed.), *Comparative perspectives in modern psychology: Nebraska Symposium on Motivation, 1987* (Vol. 35, pp. 201–255). Lincoln: University of Nebraska Press.

Savage-Rumbaugh, E. S. (1990). Language acquisition in a non-human species: Implications for the innateness debate. In C. Dent & P. Zukow, (Eds.), *The idea of innateness: Effects on language and communication research* [Special issue]. *Developmental Psychobiology, 23,* 599–620.

Savage-Rumbaugh, E. S., McDonald, K., Sevcik, R. A., Hopkins, W., & Rubert, E. (1986).

Spontaneous symbol acquisition and communicative use by pygmy chimpanzees (*Pan paniscus*). *Journal of Experimental Psychology: General, 115,* 211–235.

Savage-Rumbaugh, E. S., Sevcik, R. A., Rumbaugh, D. M., & Rubert, E. (1985). *Philosophical Transactions of the Royal Society of London, B#308,* 177–185.

Schlesinger, I. M. (1971). Production of utterances and language acquisition. In D. Slobin (Ed.), *The ontogenesis of grammar: A theoretical symposium* (pp. 63–101). New York: Academic Press.

Slobin, D. I. (1966). The acquisition of Russian as a native language. In F. Smith & G. A. Miller (Eds.), *The genesis of language: A psycholinguistic approach* (pp. 129–148). Cambridge, MA: MIT Press.

Terrace, H. S., Petitto, L. A., Sanders, R. J., & Bever, T. G. (1979). Can an ape create a sentence? *Science, 206,* 891–900.

Terrace, H. S., Petitto, L. A., Sanders, R. J., & Bever, T. G. (1980). On the grammatical capacity of apes. In K. Nelson (Eds.), *Children's Language* (Vol. 2, pp. 371–496). New York: Gardner Press.

Van Cantfort, T. E., Gardner, B. T., & Gardner, R. A. (1989). Developmental trends in replies to Wh-questions by children and chimpanzees. In R. A. Gardner, B. T. Gardner, & T. E. Van Cantfort (Eds.), *Teaching sign language to chimpanzees* (pp. 198–239). New York: State University of New York.

Zihlman, A. L., Cronin, J. E., Cramer, D. L., & Sarich, V. M. (1978). Pygmy chimpanzee as a possible prototype for the common ancestor of humans, chimpanzees, and gorillas. *Nature, 275,* 744–746.

APPENDIX:
Corpus of Kanzi's Spontaneous Two-Element Combinations (Two Lexigrams or Lexigram plus Gesture), April–August 1986

Conjoined Actions
Bite chase 2*
Bite grab 2
Bite hide
Bite hug
Bite slap 2
Bite tickle 13
Carry go(g)
Chase bite 6
Chase go(g)
Chase hide 7
Chase hug 4
Chase tickle 2
Come(g) chase
Come(g) hide
Grab bite 4
Grab slap
Hide chase 2
Hide come(g) 3
Hug bite 6

Hug chase
Slap grab
Slap keep-away
Tickle bite 21
Tickle chase 3
Tickle grab
Tickle hide
Tickle slap 3

Action-Agent
Bite you(g) 18
Carry you(g) 9
Chase dog
Chase dog(g)
Chase you(g) 53
Grab you(g) 4
Hide Austin 2
Hide you(g) 7
Hug you(g) 4
Keep-away you(g) 2

Slap you(g) 10
Tickle you(g) 8

Agent-Action
Liz hide
Matata bite
Matata chase
Mulika bite
Mulika chase
Penny tickle
You(g) carry 2
You(g) chase 5

Action-Goal
Chase Austin
Chase banana
Chase food
Chase grouproom
Chase M&M
Chase melon

Chase mushroom-trail
Chase sourcream
Chase tree
Go Austin

Goal-Action
Austin come(g)
Austin go(g) 8
Ball chase(g)
Ball go(g)
Blueberry come(g)
Childside bite
Childside chase
Childside go(g)
Clover go(g)
Coke chase
Colonyroom bite
Dog go(g)
Food chase
Gibbon carry
Grouproom open 2
Ice go(g)
Juice hug
M&M chase 2
M&M go(g)
Melon go(g)
Orange open(g)
Outdoors chase 2
Peanut go(g) 2
Play-yard slap
Potato go(g)
Strawberry go(g)
Surprise chase
Surprise come(g)
Surprise go(g) 2
Sweet-potato go(g)
Tool-room come(g)
Trailer go**
Water come(g)
Water go(g)

Action-Instrument
Chase ball
Tickle ball

Instrument-Action
Ball chase
Water chase

Action-Attribute
Chase bad
Chase one
Chase two
Hide three

Attribute-Action
Bad chase
One hide

Action-Object
Bite ball 3
Bite cherry
Bite coke
Bite food
Bite orange-drink 2
Bite tomato 2
Carry ball
Chase that(g)
Grab Austin
Grab head
Grab Kanzi 2
Grab Matata
Grab that(g) 2
Hide Austin
Hide peanut
Hug ball
Keep-away balloon
Keep-away clay 4
Keep-away that(g)
Slap ball 9
Slap that(g)
Tickle ball

Object-Action
Ball slap 7
Ball tickle 3
Surprise hide 2
That(g) grab
That(g) keep-away
Water hide

Action-Recipient
Give(g) Kanzi

**Action-
   Volitional Object**
Hug surprise

**Volitional Object-
   Action**
Juice hide
Milk hug
Orange-juice hug
Raisin hug

Affirmation-Goal
yes Austin

Agent-Object
You(g) surprise

Object-Agent
Ball you(g)
Balloon you(g) 2
Juice you(g)
Peach you(g)
Playyard you(g)
Surprise you(g)

Attribute-Entity
Austin that(g)
Austin tv
Coke water
Egg food
Good mushroom
Ice water
Surprise ball
Surprise food 2
Sweet-potato food

Entity-Attribute
Food banana
Food blackberry 3
Food grape
Food melon
Food orange
Food surprise 2
Surprise balloon
Surprise carrot
Videotape(g) Austin

Comitative-Action
That(g) come

Conjoined Entities
Bread banana

Bread juice
Cheese blackberry
Grape yogurt
Hamburger peanut
Hotdog cereal
Ice oil
Ice tv
Juice banana
Juice orange-drink
M&M egg
M&M grape 2
Melon orange-drink
Orange-drink melon 2
Orange-drink peanut
Peanut hamburger
Peanut jelly
Potato bread
Potato burrito
Sourcream ball
Tomato potato
Water ice 2

Conjoined Locations
Austin gibbon
Austin peanut 2
Austin Sue's-office
Sue's-office childside
Staff-office grouproom
Melon orange-drink

Demonstrative-Entity
That(g) apple 3
That(g) banana 5
That(g) blackberry
That(g) blueberry
That(g) bread
That(g) carrot 2
That(g) cheese
That(g) coke
That(g) food 6
That(g) grape 2
That(g) hamburger
That(g) hotdog
That(g) ice 3
That(g) jelly 2
That(g) juice 4
That(g) kiwi 3
That(g) kool-aid 2

That(g) lettuce
That(g) melon 6
That(g) milk
That(g) orange-drink 2
That(g) peach 2
That(g) peanut
That(g) raisin 4
That(g) sourcream 2
That(g) surprise
That(g) tomato 6
That(g) yogurt 2

Entity-Demonstrative
Apple that(g)
Austin that(g)
Ball that(g) 2
Balloon that(g) 2
Banana that(g) 8
Blackberry that(g) 4
Blueberry that(g) 7
Bread that(g)
Burrito that(g) 3
Butter that(g)
Carrot that(g) 4
Cherry that(g) 2
Coke that(g) 9
Egg that(g) 4
Food that(g) 8
Grape that(g) 10
Hamburger that(g) 2
Ice that(g)
Jelly that(g) 6
Juice that(g) 10
Key that(g)
Kiwi that(g) 5
Kool-aid that(g) 3
Light that(g)
M&M that(g) 2
Melon that(g) 6
Milk that(g) 2
Oil that(g) 2
Onion that(g)
Orange-drink that(g) 10
Orange-juice that(g) 2
Peach that(g) 14
Peanut that(g) 7
Potato that(g) 10

Raisin that(g)
Sourcream that(g) 3
Strawberry that(g) 12
Surprise that(g) 7
Tomato that(g) 2
TV that(g) 2
Water that(g) 3

Effect-Negative Cause
Bad mushroom-trail

Entity-Affirmation
Blueberry yes(g)

Entity-Location
Austin playyard
Austin tv
Banana peanut
Food grouproom 2
Ice grouproom
Peanut Austin
Peanut trailer
Playyard outdoors
Water ice 2
Water playyard

Location-Entity
Bread jelly 2
Group-room water
Kool-aid strawberry
Logcabin food
Mushroom-trail
  mushroom
Playyard Austin 4
Playyard ball(g)
Playyard Matata
Sandpile tomato
Staff-office water 2
Sue's-office Sue
Trailer dog
Trailer peanut 2

Goal-Agent
Austin you(g)

Goal-Instrument
Austin key
Child-side key

Instrument-Object
Can-opener milk
Knife(g) kiwi

Location-Agent
Playyard you(g)

Location-Comitative
Grouproom Matata

Attribute-Location
Childside playyard

Staff-office playyard

Nonexistence-Entity
No balloon
No coke

Possession-Entity
You(g) burrito

Recipient-Object
Austin balloon(g)

Object-Recipient
Egg Austin
Hotdog Austin
Peanut Kanzi

Transport-Location
Vehicle trailer***

2-Mode Paraphrase
Chase chase(g)
Bad bad(g) 3

*Frequencies are denoted by a numeral following the example. If there is no numeral, the frequency is one.
**He wants to go to the trailer.
***He is not describing a vehicle trailer, but wants to go in a car (vehicle) to the mobile-home (trailer), a location.

Note: The six lexigram combinations bearing "no direct relation" to each other are not included in the appendix, as they are not comprehensible without context. An example, with context, is presented at the end of Table 3.

III

Language Acquisition in Children

This part of the book contains six chapters that elucidate behavioral, social, cognitive, motor, neural, and logical factors deemed to be of high relevance to the ontogeny of normal language acquisition in children. The work presented includes both experimental studies and observations concerning the emergence and/or elicitation of language behavior in structured laboratory situations which provide insights into how meaning is mapped onto utterances.

In chapter 11, Charles Catania provides his views on behavioral mechanisms that may have operated to influence the evolution of language. Catania's central argument is that language developed in the social context of hominid evolution due to the functional effects that the utterances of the speaker had upon the listener. As the author puts it: "What we transmit in language is the verbal behavior itself, and its primary function is to get someone else to do something. By talking, we change each other's behavior." Further, ". . . [language] evolved as a form of social control, in a progression from vocal releasers to varied verbal functions shaped by social consequences. . . ." Catania also describes the results of experimental studies carried out by him and his colleagues to investigate contingency-shaped and rule-governed behaviors as these factors relate to the control that language exerts upon the guidance of behavior. The empirical work reviewed covers research that examines the ontogeny of rule-governed behavior and the relevance of equivalence classes in ". . . extending verbal control that already has been established."

Next, Andrew Lock discusses the relevance of both social context and social practices for development of the cognitive skills necessary to establish and maintain meaningful discourse. Lock describes observations made by him, in structured laboratory situations, of interactions between children, under 2 years of age, and their mothers. He analyzes the relevance of the social interactions (e.g., looking at pictures in a photo album) for the development of memorial skills. As with other contributors to this volume, Lock grapples with the issue of how infants "make sense of the world." According to the author, the world of the infant is organized through a process of social construction. Lock's view on this issue is as follows: "Now, the first step in understanding how a socially constructive account of development can be essayed is not to appeal to individually pregiven cognitive mechanisms that underwrite cognition, but to focus on the infant's immediate experiences, and ask how these are engineered so as to become imbued with sense (while recognizing that immediate experience is underwritten by a vast array of individual cognitive power)." Further, ". . . This socially constituted 'perception of the world' constitutes the world an infant will come to talk about. The tactics that adults employ in constituting the structures of that perception likewise play a role in informing the processes whereby speaking is constructed." In many ways, Lock's analysis of how meaning comes to be established is similar, both operationally and conceptually, to the notion of "routine" described earlier in this volume by Savage-Rumbaugh.

In the following chapter, Kathy Hirsh-Pasek and Roberta Michnick Golinkoff review their work on early language comprehension. The authors describe the "preferential looking paradigm" and how it can be used to study what infants understand about language. Hirsh-Pasek and Golinkoff present results from three examples of their empirical work that used the preferential looking paradigm. The data from the first of the studies suggest that the infants ". . . seem to have an operating principle that guides them to look for 'packages,' " — constituents beyond the single word — in the input language that they hear. Results from their second investigation suggest that infants with no more than two working words in their vocabulary are aware of word order and are cognizant of positional cues. Their third study investigated the sensitivity of infants to the ". . . syntactic environments in which verbs are used." Their findings revealed that girls just under 2.5 years of age ". . . make use of the syntactic information in the input to decide whether the familiar verb they are hearing is being used transitively or intransitively." Further, the data from this last study support the idea that 28-month-old children can employ syntactic markers to identify the class of a verb. Hirsh-Pasek and Golinkoff also detail the ways that their paradigm can be employed to ask some of the classic questions concerning when in development necessary aspects of language comprehension are established.

Stephen Crain and Rosalind Thornton next describe their studies de-signed to explain: ". . . How the adult grammar is achieved on the basis of the linguistic input available to the learner." They employ a technique termed elicited production. The authors outline the logical problem of acquisition: ". . . the data available underdetermine what the learner comes to know. As a solution to this problem, current linguistic theory supposes that the constraints that characterize the final state also characterize the initial state. That is, the constraints are not learned; rather they are innately specified as part of universal grammar. . . ." The authors indicate the logical necessity of this observation is that innate features should appear in every natural language and children should conform to ". . . constraints early in the course of language development." Crain and Thornton detail experiments designed to test whether children exhibit structure-dependent or structure-independent forms regarding the formation of questions. Their results suggest structure dependence exists. The data therefore argue for the innateness of the grammatical form. Other studies of young children support the notion that they appropriately employ contractions when they should, without apparently having to learn this constraint. The authors also describe their studies of elicited production relating to long-distance wh-movement and rightward contraction. These data, too, are consistent, in their view, with a universal grammar interpretation of language acquisition.

In the next chapter, Esther Thelen provides an overview of the emergence of speech in the larger context of the development of motor behavior. Thelen uses dynamical systems theory as a framework for explicating how prespeech sounds eventually are transformed into understandable utterances. The author argues that there exist three extant processes that operate in parallel to underpin the development of speech. These are, respectively, biases for natural categories of sound, perceptual biases, and selection biases that match natural sound and motor output. Thelen asserts that a "hard-wired" system does not drive the motor coordination necessary for production. Rather, she suggests that movement and its coordination is determined by preferences inherent in the system. Such system preferences in turn are configured by what are known in dynamical systems terms as attractors. Thelen suggests that as development of the speech system proceeds, ". . . even small changes in anatomy, for example, potentially can engender new attractor states." Further, Thelen asserts that novel behavioral configurations can be achieved in the context of a dynamical systems framework because elements in the system can be assembled and reassembled. The solutions for assembling necessary configurations is called a phase shift. Further, the use of a dynamic systems analysis leads to the conclusion that complex human perceptual-motor systems are nonlinear. That is, ". . . [such systems] can preserve coordinative outcome under a range of boundary conditions, yet when certain critical boundary values are reached, they spontaneously reorganize." Thelen employs dynamical systems theory to analyze how elements of language, observed over a developmental trajectory, emerge as a function of the interaction between the child and his or her physical and social environment.

In the final chapter of this section, Ursula Bellugi and Karen van Hoek compare the acquisition of spoken and signed language. The authors describe their research with deaf children who learn American Sign Language (ASL) as their mode of communication. Bellugi and van Hoek outline the similarities and differences between the formal structure (e.g., grammar) and representation (e.g., the use of space to represent syntax) of the two types of language. They document the problems faced by the learner of ASL in terms of their need to achieve a mapping of spatial perception, memory, and spatial transformation (using a visual channel) to develop understanding. Bellugi and van Hoek demonstrate the importance of the left hemisphere for language, either spoken or visuo-spatial, by documenting the existence, in left-hemisphere lesioned, congenitally deaf signers, of sign language aphasias. They also report on a rare neurodevelopmental disorder, Williams Syndrome, in which an experiment of nature helps to further elucidate the orthogonality of language and other cognitive functions. Investigations of such children offer a window into brain function that both challenges many contemporary theoretical views and informs neuroscientists concerning the normal development of brain mechanisms that may subsume language development.

11 The Phylogeny and Ontogeny of Language Function

A. Charles Catania
University of Maryland

Turn to any definition of the word *language* and the odds are high that it will be framed in terms of the metaphor of communication. Here is one dictionary example: "The aspect of human behavior that involves the use of vocal sounds in meaningful patterns and, when they exist, corresponding written symbols to form, express, and communicate thoughts and feelings. . . . Any method of communicating ideas. . . . The transmission of meaning, feeling, or intent" (Morris, 1969, p. 736).

The dictionary definitions are indeed consistent with general usage. Ask undergraduates to say what the functions of language are and communication certainly will be high on their list. If they are pressed to say what is communicated, they are likely to invoke feelings or ideas. Our culture places high value on being understood, on expressing one's emotions, on conveying one's feelings. These are all variations on the metaphor of communication. In many contexts it is appropriate to speak of language in such terms. But too much is left unstated in that metaphor and it is easy to pass over the properties that remain implicit. What functions are served by communicating one's feelings or thoughts to someone else? What selective advantages do such practices have?

A LANGUAGE METAPHOR

According to the metaphor, which Reddy (1979) has called the *conduit* metaphor, language is a vehicle for transferring something from one individual to another (cf. Lakoff & Johnson, 1980). The metaphor pervades our everyday talk: We *get something across* to someone; we *put our ideas into* words; our words are *filled with emotion,* or they *carry meaning;* sometimes we *weigh* them, and sometimes we find them *hollow;* a paragraph can be *packed with information* or have substantial *thought content,* or it can consist of *empty* words.

It is easy to see why the metaphor is so appealing, especially in contemporary human environments. Not only does sound travel from speaker to listener in face-to-face dialogue; we transmit speech patterns via lasers, fiber optics, or radio waves, and we transform and preserve it in a variety of recording media (including written texts). But according to this metaphor of communication, it is not merely the physical by-products of speech that we transmit. Rather, the sounds of speech carry something. They are containers, and the things they purport to deliver from speaker to listener have been variously called meanings, thoughts, ideas, intentions, feelings, information, and so on.

It is clear, however, that the metaphor has serious limitations. Consider, for example, the magnetic patterns produced on a tape by the recorded voice of a speaker. The speaker may have expressed feelings or said something meaningful, but those feelings or meanings cannot exist merely in the magnetic patterns on the tape. Where are they when the tape is not being played? Even when the tape is played the original speaker is not recreated; all that is produced is a facsimile of the speaker's voice. The only point at which meanings or feelings can reenter the account is if a listener is present who reacts to the playback. It would of course be proper to talk about the listener as appreciating or not appreciating the speaker's feelings, or as understanding or misunderstanding what the speaker meant. But if the feelings or meanings were not present in the magnetic patterns on the unplayed tape, it is appropriate to ask about the sense in which it can be said that the feelings or meanings truly were transmitted from speaker to listener (cf. Catania, 1984, p. 222).

One crucial element is the behavior of the listener. If communication is to be successful, the speaker and the listener must already hold something in common: They must share similar verbal histories (this point is consistent with the origins of the words *common* and *communication,* which are close etymological relatives). In this limited sense, the listener cannot receive from the speaker anything other than what the listener already has.

Note that the question is not about transmission per se. It would be frivolous to debate whether or not a listener can receive a speaker's words. If that did not happen, there would be no spoken language. Obviously, verbal patterns are transmitted from speaker to listener over other media as well, and the transmission often involves transformation and storage of these patterns, as in the example of the tape recording. (In recognition of such transformations, *verbal* here refers to language in general, whether the interaction involves speech, gesture, writing, or some other modality, whereas *vocal* refers specifically to the speech modality.)

The transformations demonstrate that modality is not critical. For example, once formal relations between spoken and written language have been learned, whether in terms of alphabets, syllabaries, or ideographs, verbal patterns can be preserved in transformation at least at the level of these units even if other details are lost. Thus, it makes sense to speak of transmitting such patterns as words or sentences, because these are verbal entities defined in terms of such language units.

The metaphor of communication only enters the account as a problem when the verbal patterns are said to carry something. The feelings, meanings, or information that are said to be carried typically are regarded as distinct from the transmitted patterns; they survive physical changes, such as magnetic encoding on tape or geometric transformation in a written transcript. But they cannot be equated with the verbal patterns that carry them — they are not mere words — and thus their status is ambiguous.

The reason that the metaphor is a matter of concern is that it has entered ubiquitously into accounts of both the phylogenic and the ontogenic origins of natural language. If the metaphor is problematic, then so too will be accounts based upon it. The present treatment offers accounts of language phylogeny and ontogeny that do not appeal to the metaphor. Given the magnitude of the subject matter, these accounts necessarily will be incomplete. Whether they are seen as painted in broad strokes or simply as sketchy will depend on the reader. In any case, they may suggest useful directions for further inquiry.

THE PRIMARY FUNCTION OF LANGUAGE

The central argument of the present account is that the primary function of language is simpler than the one suggested by the metaphor of communication. What we transmit in language is the verbal behavior itself, and its primary function is to get someone else to do something. By talking, we change each other's behavior. Verbal behavior allows one to do things via the mediation of another organism. Sometimes what gets done involves nonverbal effects, as when we ask someone to move something or to bring something to us; sometimes it involves verbal effects, as when we change what someone else has to say about something.

The argument for the primacy of this function is that other functions gain their significance only through it. Is there some more important reason we might describe our feelings to others than that they may then treat us differently? Is there some more important reason we might give information to others than that they may then act upon it? Is there some social function more powerful or more general than changing what another individual does that could have provided the selective contingencies under which human language evolved? The argument does not question whether transmitting information or describing feelings are functions of language; rather, it is that these are secondary functions that can become important only if they sometimes make a difference, by changing the behavior of others. Why is changing another's behavior more important than, say, transmitting information? The answer is that there is no point to transmitting information that the other does not act upon; and if the other acts on the information, the behavior of the other has been changed.

If the primary function of language is that it is an efficient way in which one individual can change the behavior of another, it follows that this behavior is quintessentially social and can emerge only in organisms whose behavior is already sensitive to social contingencies. Discriminating the behavior of other organisms, whether of one's own or of other species, has clear selective advantages. Consider, for example, the relation between predator and prey. A predator that can distinguish whether or not it has been noticed by its prey has a distinct advantage over one that cannot; an advantage also accrues to a prey that can distinguish whether or not it has been noticed by its predator.

Discriminations of the behavior of others are at the heart of our human concept of intentionality (cf. Dennett, 1987): We say we understand someone's intentions when our discriminations of the various properties of that individual's past and current behavior enable us to act appropriately with respect to what that individual will do in the future. In fact, if discriminating one's own behavior is taken as a special case of discriminating the behavior of others (e.g., Bem, 1967), it can be argued that this topic encompasses all of the phenomena considered under the rubric of intentionality. Judgments of the intentions of others are, above all, social judgments, and it takes no special assumptions about the selective contingencies that must have operated on both intraspecific and interspecific social behavior to see that such contingencies could shape well-prepared capacities for social discriminations.

Behavior is a joint function of phylogenic contingencies, those that have operated during the evolution of species in ancestral environments, and ontogenic contingencies, those that have operated during the interaction of organism and environment within its own lifetime (cf. Dawkins, 1982; Skinner, 1966). We know that some interspecific social discriminations have a substantial phylogenic component. For example, discriminations of predator behavior by prey are especially likely to be shaped phylogenically, because prey usually have little opportunity in their own lifetimes to learn relevant discriminations involving the behavior of their predators; it is too late to learn after one has been caught (cf. Bolles, 1970).

We therefore should not be surprised if phylogenic contingencies involving the important social consequences of maternal-infant interactions and of mate or kin selection also have shaped some social discriminative skills that do not have to be learned or that are learned with particular ease. In any case, the stage is set for verbal behavior once intraspecific social discriminative stimuli have become important to the members of a species, because the organism so discriminating has become a potential listener. (It is of interest that many of the problems in teaching symbol use to our highly social primate relatives arise because the primates are more likely to attend to the behavior of their human handlers than to the inanimate apparatuses in the context of which symbolic materials are presented [cf. Savage-Rumbaugh, 1986].)

STRUCTURE AND FUNCTION

The main concern in what follows is language function, and it may be important to note that issues of function are often orthogonal to those of structure (cf. the corresponding distinction between physiology and anatomy in biology; Catania, 1984, pp. 353–356). This account deals only in passing with language structure, productivity, and other topics that have been central to some treatments. For the present purposes, it matters little what form languages take, provided the appropriate behavior is available to both speaker and listener.

Structure is a property that language shares with nonverbal behavior. Thus, it may be useful to consider analogous relations in nonverbal cases. Locomotion, for example, has a grammar (e.g., Gallistel, 1980). The coordinations involved in walking or in flying are complex, and new structural relations may be introduced by novel situations such as the partial immobilization of a limb (e.g., cf. Provine, 1982, on the effects of induced wing asymmetries on wing coordination in the chick). Such cases demonstrate that motor programs determined phylogenically may restrict some properties of human bipedal locomotion or avian flight. Nevertheless, these structural constraints cannot determine when and where a human walks or a bird flies. To deal with such functional aspects of behavior, it is necessary to take ontogenic contingencies into account; we must attend to the interactions between behavior and environment.

Now let us return to the verbal case. "There's a person walking" and "There's a bird flying" are sentences with similar structures, but whether the speaker happens to say one or the other is determined by aspects of the speaker's situation that are orthogonal to those structures. If the bird was on the ground while the person was in the air, the sentences might have become "There's a bird walking" and "There's a person flying." Such correspondences between events and what is said about them are established and maintained by verbal communities. Even if it were shown conclusively that the acquisition of grammatical structure by children proceeds under definable phylogenic constraints, that structure would not determine when children spoke or what they talked about. Evidence is presented later showing that what someone says can be shaped by its consequences. The present case is not weakened if it turns out that, despite such evidence, constraints operate on the shaping of some properties of verbal behavior (e.g., its grammatical structure). If universals of language have evolved, their place in the present account is analogous to that of motor programs in accounts of the determinants of the topography of nonverbal behavior.

As for productivity, it is not a sufficient defining property of language even though it might make significant contributions to it. One type of occasion for productivity occurs when different dimensions of behavior are occasioned jointly by different events, as when a physical object determines the noun and an action determines the verb of a sentence. Such cases are to be understood in terms of novel conjunctions of such events, but these events need not be verbal. Just as a human may utter a sentence that has never been uttered before, a bird may fly a path that has never been flown before; and if one wing is injured, the bird may fly that path with wing and feather adjustments that it had never made before. The integration of the components of each involves complex coordinations (cf. Catania & Cerutti, 1986; Fentress, 1978), and the properties of these coordinations (e.g., grammatical or physiological constraints) remain issues of structure.

PHYLOGENIC PROBLEMS

"The power of communication between members of the same tribe by means of language has been of paramount importance in the development of man; and the force of language is much aided by the expressive movements of the face and body" (Darwin, 1872/1965, p. 354). Even Darwin was caught up by the metaphor of communication. But a crucial feature of his analyses of the expression of emotion was that they did not appeal to language. The point is significant for any account of the phylogenic origins of language. Darwin confirmed with a variety of examples that many nonhuman organisms, and especially primates, were highly competent at expressing pleasure, anger, fear, and other emotions. Why then should language have evolved, if its main function was the expression of emotions? Within a given species, evolutionary contingencies rarely create new systems that duplicate functions already well served by existing systems. Why would it be important to tell others how we feel if we could do just as well by showing them, through facial expression, posture, or other behavior?

Suppose then that for emotions we substitute feelings, or ideas, or information? Consider the wordless thought, the wordless feeling, the wordless idea. Consider any one of these at a time before anything quite like a word even existed yet. If only one individual has it, how is that one able to give it to another? And what good does it do the other to receive it? What is the point of transmitting information that the other cannot act upon? In what way do these two have a selective advantage over others of their species who do not share their thoughts or feelings or ideas?

This is not to say that they could not interact in other ways. If one makes a particular call in the presence of a predator that the other does not see and the other then behaves appropriately with respect to that predator (e.g., Gouzoules, Gouzoules, & Marler, 1984), the selective advantage is obvious. But in this case what is transmitted is the predator call and what is communicated is the presence of the predator, not a thought or a feeling or an idea.

We learn to talk about our feelings, but the words we use are taught to us by the same verbal communities that provide us with all the other words of our language. This teaching can be accomplished only on the basis of what is publicly shared by the speakers and listeners of the language. How then can the words for private events such as feelings and thoughts and ideas be taught? The difficulties created by positing a language of private events that is not based on the public practices of the verbal community or that assumes that these events have special nonphysical properties distinguishing them from public ones have been discussed in philosophical terms by Wittgenstein (1958) and in psychological terms by Skinner (1945).

Their arguments often have been misunderstood. They do not deny the private; instead, they point out some necessary limitations on the language of private events following from the fact that common vocabularies can only be based on what is public, that is, on what is mutually accessible to and therefore shared by speakers and listeners. If a private feeling does not have a public correlate, how can anyone ever tell when anyone else has it? If one cannot tell, how can one ever teach the other the word for it?

These difficulties are multiplied if a language of private feelings, thoughts, or ideas is assumed to provide the roots of language as well as the core of contemporary verbal practices. A plausible account of language origins must be able to deal simultaneously with the behavior both of speakers and of listeners, because verbal behavior cannot occur if speakers exist without listeners or listeners without speakers. For some aspect of the speaker's behavior to provide a selective advantage, appropriate behavior must already be available on the listener's part; similarly, for some aspect of the listener's behavior to provide a selective advantage, appropriate behavior must already be available on the speaker's part. They (or their descendants) eventually may come to "share their thoughts," that is, to speak of private events, but what they share of private events must be anchored in public ones.

Other problems of language phylogeny arise because early human vocal language has left few traces. It would be begging the question to assume that it emerged full-blown. It presumably evolved in a series of historical stages and not in an abrupt and unique creation. Furthermore, each stage must have provided a selective advantage, or at least must not have conferred a disadvantage, but we should not expect to find all of these earlier stages in contemporary behavior (cf. Dawkins, 1982, pp. 38, 104). Though each stage had to be superior to its predecessors, many predecessors will not have survived.

Consider intraspecific competition when extreme members of a population have some selective advantage. For example, once capture by predators has shaped fast escape in a population, we should not expect to find many slow runners in it, even if that speed provided a selective advantage at an earlier time when it was fast relative to the population mean (a complementary selection would operate on speed or on other aspects of hunting in the predator population). The evolution of the horse provides a striking example (Simpson, 1951). If we cannot count on the survival of intermediate cases when selection has produced changes in single dimensions of behavior such as speed or size or sensory capacity, what then when we try to deal with language, a class of behavior with multiple and complexly interacting dimensions?

LANGUAGE ORIGINS

A detailed treatment of the history of theories of language origin is provided in Catania (1985), and is not recapitulated here (the evolutionary scenario presented in the following also draws heavily from that source). Early theories of language origin gave picturesque names to the several hypotheses of language origin that dominated debate from the eighteenth century through the twentieth century. For example, the onomatopoetic *bow-wow* theory was based on the imitation of animal cries, the *pooh-pooh* theory saw the origins of speech in interjections such as grunts of pain, the *yo-he-ho* theory assumed language began with the coordinated sounds of those working together at strenuous tasks, and the *sing-song* theory advocated love songs and rhythmic chants as the source of language. These accounts, concerned with the sorts of behavior that might have been the precursors of speech, typically had little to say about the functions of language.

More recent theories also have looked at relations between language and behavior of other sorts: for example, tying the origins of language to the parallel development of tool use by hominids or, with the acceptance of gestural languages as examples of verbal behavior, exploring analogies between vocal and manual dexterity. But correlations of verbal behavior with such activities as tool making, agriculture, or the mastery of fire are not strictly relevant to this account, again because they do not address the question of language function.

The argument so far has been that language could not have evolved as a vehicle of communication. The scenario that follows assumes instead that it evolved as a form of social control, in a progression from vocal releasers to varied verbal functions shaped by social consequences (cf. Jaynes, 1977, pp. 126–138). It is one of several options; alternative or parallel paths might be developed in such other contexts as maternal-infant interaction or mate selection. Recognizing these other possibilities, let us nevertheless start with a band of preverbal hominids in which a minimal repertory of fixed action patterns elicited by vocal releasers is already established (see Provine, 1986, for an example of a visual releaser in contemporary human behavior).

Such classes of behavior exist among many mammalian and avian species, as when vocal calls affect the behavior of conspecifics (e.g., Kroodsma & Miller, 1982). For example, some cries occasioned by predators produce freezing or flight or attack; others in different circumstances are correlated with feeding or with sexual behavior. Predator calls may vary with kind of predator, and the response to the call may depend on who the caller is and who the listener is (e.g., Seyfarth, Cheney, & Marler, 1980). That complexity is no problem: The more complex the properties of known calls of existing species, the easier it is to grant more sophisticated cases shaped by phylogenic contingencies.

Assume the calls of a primate leader once determined the behavior of members of its band as reliably as a releaser elicits a fixed action pattern. At first the vocabulary of releasers was limited to just a few calls, not yet qualifying as verbal behavior but with relatively simple effects corresponding to those of utterances such as "come" or "go" or "stop." Over many generations, perhaps millenia, a more extensive repertory of more varied calls was differentiated. If the details of these calls were weakly determined phylogenically, this rudimentary verbal control later could be supplemented by variations produced by ontogenic contingencies (evolutionary precedent is available in other species: e.g., in the ontogenic elaboration of phylogenically predisposed bird song). For example, a dominant speaker might learn to attack a listener who does not respond in the characteristic way, thereby punishing disobedience (many contemporary contingencies continue to maintain the effectiveness of verbal control by reinforcing the following of instructions and punishing deviations from it).

Perhaps here or perhaps at a later stage of the scenario, the increasing complexity of verbal behavior and of the contexts within which it occurred must have reached the point at which some calls occasionally were combined. Their several forms then could evolve into verbs, nouns, and various modifiers: "stop," "run," "dig" eventually must have been supplemented by "catch rabbit," "build fire," "plant seed," "watch infant," "sharpen blade," and so on. This is a critical step about which it would be desirable to say more, but though we cannot say much about how it came about, we at least can be confident that the combination of verbal units vastly expanded the potential effects of verbal behavior. (If we are tempted to argue for the priority of form over function or function over form in this progression, it may be useful to be reminded that comparable issues in biology were resolved by instead relating both form and function to evolutionary contingencies.)

So far we have at least one speaker, probably a dominant male, a relatively restricted repertoire of vocal releasers, and a population of listeners responding to the items in the leader's vocal repertoire in consistent and characteristic ways. The vocal control had social functions that gave the group a competitive edge relative to other similar groups: keeping the group together during movement; coordinating aggression or flight in encounters with other groups; and so forth. Other kinds of vocal control presumably also evolved in interactions between mothers and their offspring, between mates, and within various subgroups of the hominid social unit. (The present account follows the leader–follower track rather than alternative scenarios in which these other types of interactions assume a more dominant role, in part because of its obvious implications for the nature of leadership in contemporary religious, political, social, and intellectual institutions; other scenarios also might place more emphasis on reciprocities that do not enter into the present account: cf. de Waal, 1989.)

For the leader and the leader's successors, attentive listeners were a prerequisite for exerting verbal control. When the leader's verbal behavior changed the listener's behavior, this change was presumably a consequence that could reinforce the leader's verbal behavior. Thus, the importance to the leader of having an audience was built in early. For the others, the listeners or followers, access to the leader and thus to the leader's instructions was similarly important; the verbal community could not survive as a group if it was not. Obedience produced consequences, including some arranged by the leader, that helped to maintain obedience, but some of the leader's control over the audience still may have had a primarily phylogenic basis, in that the effectiveness of verbal control may have depended on the leader's commanding look or the leader's quality of voice or those other individual aspects we sometimes call charismatic.

This verbal control was asymmetrical, and the individual differences thus implied made some members of the band more susceptible to it than others. Insofar as it involved responses to particular calls as well as verbal control in general, some calls became effective only for particular individuals. The singling out of verbal control over individuals by distinctive calls was the beginning of the language evolution leading to names (much later in human prehistory, when sources of verbal control had become more diffuse, keeping one's name secret became a way to escape from its power: cf. Frazer, 1922/1951, pp. 284–289).

These properties of verbal control are consistent with superstitions about the magic of words and with observations about insidious controlling effects of verbal behavior in contemporary culture. And if speculations on the origins of language in song were off the mark only in that they did not invoke song as the original language of verbal control, then perhaps some of the power of music lies in its earlier verbal functions, even if those functions now have become vestigial (this account has emphasized the language of command, which brings to mind military marches, but lullabies and serenades are consistent with scenarios respectively involving mother-infant interactions and mate selection). If the musical properties of voice were once the critical features of phylogenic verbal control and that control gradually was supplanted by ontogenic control, the latter may have evolved around nonmusical dimensions of vocal stimuli, such as what we now call vowels and consonants.

Once verbal behavior had expanded to an extensive repertory including arbitrary as well as phylogenically determined calls, idiosyncratic repertories developed by particular leaders were ordinarily lost to later generations until some ways of establishing this verbal behavior in the leaders' successors had evolved. The next step in this evolution, perhaps long in coming, was the repetition by the follower of the leader's verbal behavior (the repetition presumably began in an overt vocal form, but the argument also can be made in terms of covert behavior; cf. Jaynes [1977], in which verbal control is extended by the listener's auditory hallucinations of the speaker's utterances).

Repetition by the listener became especially critical as verbal behavior became more complex. Its significance, however, was not merely that it initiated relevant vocal behavior in those who were to become the leader's successors (and thereby became a way in which behavior could replicate itself). That contingency would have had relatively remote effects and by itself might not have been sufficient to maintain ontogenic features of vocal repertories over generations. A more important and immediate consequence was that repetition of the leader's utterances established conditions under which the leader could give instructions to be followed in the leader's absence, at later times and in other places. In effect, control was gradually transferred from the leader's verbal behavior to the listener's own repetition of it. The extended social organization this allowed maintained the advantages of verbal control. It expanded the influence of the leader and allowed coordinated human groups to expand beyond the range of the human voice. It also created the precursors of human verbal memory (but that is another story).

The maintenance of idiosyncratic verbal repertories across generations had an additional effect. Not only could particular human languages be established, but they also could begin to change arbitrarily; dialects could begin to emerge. It is reasonable to assume that during this stage critical periods in the mastery of language became a mechanism by which groups maintained their integrity against intrusions from outsiders, that is, as a sort of social isolating mechanism, perhaps related to mechanisms of kin selection. Dialect differences may have provided a simple basis for reducing the verbal control that could be exerted by outsiders, and it must have operated especially effectively when human travel was more limited than it has become in recent times.

In contemporary human communities native speakers still can be distinguished from relative newcomers to a language on the basis of accent, and local dialects as well as differences in national languages remain the basis of major social and political distinctions. The continuing power of such determinants of human social groupings testifies to deeply rooted phylogenic origins. (It may be worth noting that these phylogenic contingencies work against structural features with generality across languages; this poses problems for accounts of language universals, which often fail to consider the phylogenic contingencies that might have produced them.)

To the extent that increases in population over human evolution gave competitive advantages to groups that were efficient in food procurement or production and were coordinated in combat, the pressure for more powerful verbal control led to further refinements. Once leaders were able to instruct the verbal behavior of listeners who could in turn instruct the nonverbal behavior of others, the prerequisites for human religious and political institutions were firmly in place. The invention of writing, perhaps initially a matter of record keeping, further removed verbal control from the behavior of individual leaders. The behavior of a substantial proportion of the present human population of the world is influenced by records of the verbal behavior of past generations (e.g., to mention only a few, the *Koran, Das Kapital,* the *Analects of Confucius,* the *Torah,* and the *New Testament*).

We have not dealt with the ways in which the leader's verbal behavior is shaped by contingencies. Verbal control will not be advantageous if the speaker's instructions have little relation to the circumstances confronted by the group. Thus, another part of the story must deal with the contingencies that shape the speaker's verbal behavior (cf. Catania, Shimoff, & Matthews, 1989).

Furthermore, if verbal behavior begins as social control, control does not stop at nonverbal behavior. Once verbal behavior is established, one individual can instruct what another says as well as what the other does. Giving a definition or stating a fact or asking a question is an instruction with respect to verbal behavior just as much as giving an order or making a request is an instruction with respect to nonverbal. Speaking affects the behavior of others whether or not it has the grammatical character of the imperative; to the extent that a declarative makes another behave with respect to some object or event, it includes an implicit "look" or "see" or "listen." We cannot judge whether a particular instance of verbal behavior is an instruction on the basis of its grammatical form; consistent with our initial assumptions, in many senses all utterances are ways of telling someone else what to do.

CONTINGENCY-SHAPED AND RULE-GOVERNED BEHAVIOR

One implication of the listener's repetition of the speaker's verbal behavior in our phylogenic account is that verbal control gradually can shift from what someone else says to what one says to oneself. This account is consistent with what we know about contemporary human behavior. To elaborate on this point, it is necessary to consider the distinction between rule-governed and contingency-shaped behavior. For these purposes, a rule is simply an instance of verbal behavior that determines what someone does.

A fundamental property of behavior is its sensitivity to its consequences. Much research on nonhuman learning has concentrated on how behavior changes when its consequences change. Behavior determined by its consequences is called contingency-shaped. For example, the rate and temporal patterning of a pigeon's pecks at a key are determined by the schedule according to which its pecks produce food. The rate is higher when food deliveries depend on number of responses than when they depend on elapsed time, and different temporal patterns emerge when number and time requirements are constant than when they vary from one food delivery to the next. The behavior of nonhuman organisms is sensitive to such contingencies between responses and their consequences, in the sense that it changes consistently when these contingencies change.

Human behavior, however, is often rule-governed rather than contingency-shaped; to the extent that it is determined directly by verbal behavior, it is determined only indirectly by its consequences (Skinner, 1969). To the extent that consequences are involved, they operate not on specific instances of behavior but rather on the higher-order class of behavior called rule-following. Such behavior is necessarily less sensitive to its consequences than behavior that is contingency-governed; it does not change easily when contingencies change. One result is that human schedule performances typically differ qualitatively from those maintained by nonhuman organisms.

It is paradoxical that verbal behavior can make human behavior less rather than more sensitive to its consequences. We usually assume that verbal behavior is beneficial, but in these instances it can instead get in the way. This is the sense in which we may speak of verbal behavior as insulating behavior from its consequences. Concerns about what happens when people simply do what they are told or blindly obey orders are concerns about rule-governed behavior.

These properties of rule-governed behavior have been explored experimentally (e.g., Catania, Matthews, & Shimoff, 1982; Matthews, Catania, & Shimoff, 1985; Shimoff, Matthews, & Catania, 1986). In one study, student's presses on left and right buttons occasionally produced points later exchangeable for money. Lights above the buttons lit alternately, indicating which button was operative. A number-based schedule (variable ratio) operated for the left button and a time-based schedule (variable interval) for the right. Between periods of responding, the student filled in "guess sheets" with sentences to be completed, such as "The way to earn points with the left button is to": Guess sheets were returned with points awarded for guesses. The points were used to shape the student's verbal behavior, that is, they were awarded for successively closer approximations to particular statements about contingencies or performances (cf. Greenspoon, 1955).

The nonverbal performance, button pressing, was determined not by the contingencies arranged for pressing, but rather by the student's verbal behavior. For example, statements that points depended on slow left pressing and fast right pressing, when shaped, reliably produced corresponding pressing rates, slow left and fast right, despite the fact that the actual schedules respectively produce high and low rates in contingency-shaped performances. Shaping performance descriptions was more consistently effective than shaping contingency descriptions (e.g., "The left button produces points after a random number of presses"), depending mainly on whether verbal behavior was available to the student relating performance to contingencies; and shaping verbal behavior was more consistently effective than establishing verbal behavior by instructions (telling the student what to say about the performance). Pressing rates typically conformed to the shaped verbal behavior even when such responding reduced the student's net earnings (as with low rates given a number-based schedule).

In other words, when verbal behavior is involved, initiated either by the experimenter through instructions or by the human responder through private talk, human behavior becomes rule-governed rather than contingency-shaped. Shaping what people say about their own behavior appears to be a more effective way to change their behavior than either shaping their behavior directly or telling them what to do (cf. Luria, 1961; Vygotsky, 1934/1986; Zivin, 1979). Once nonverbal behavior has come to be determined by verbal behavior, it appears sensitive to contingencies only indirectly, to the extent that changing contingencies may lead to changes in the corresponding verbal behavior.

Clearly there must be points at which human behavior makes direct contact with contingencies. Many skilled motor performances presumably do not allow verbal mediation (consider the role of verbal behavior in tying shoelaces). In some performances that begin with large instructional components (e.g., as in learning to drive a stick-shift car), verbal behavior eventually seems to drop out, at which point the performance is sometimes called automatic. And perhaps verbal behavior itself is ordinarily contingency-shaped even though much nonverbal behavior is ordinarily rule-governed. If so, contingencies may generate verbal behavior that in turn produces nonverbal behavior consistent with natural consequences. Behavior may become sensitive to its consequences because the individual has developed a good verbal formulation of contingencies; in this case the sensitivity, mediated by verbal behavior, is indirect (this point is relevant to the problem of where the leader's verbal behavior comes from in our phylogenic scenario).

THE ONTOGENY OF RULE-GOVERNED BEHAVIOR

Ontogeny does not recapitulate phylogeny (cf. Gould, 1977). Thus, we cannot expect to trace the evolution of language by following the development of language in the child. It is nevertheless of interest to ask about the ontogeny of rule-governed behavior. The research on rule-governed behavior described so far was conducted with adults (mainly undergraduates), but developmental data are also available.

Recall that schedule performances of humans differ qualitatively from those of nonhuman organisms. This performance difference has been studied with children of various ages (Bentall, Lowe, & Beasty, 1985; Lowe, Beasty, & Bentall, 1983). The tasks used were simple ones in which responses such as button presses produced simple consequences, such as snacks or opportunities to hear music, according to various schedules. In most cases, the schedule was fixed interval: A consequence was arranged for the first response after a fixed duration had elapsed since the start of the interval. The characteristic nonhuman performance is an increasing rate as time passes within each interval. The performance of verbally competent human adults, however, typically consists of one of two patterns: either a high steady rate or a long pause about equal to the scheduled interval.

For children under 2 years of age, performance is completely contingency-governed, in the sense that it is not distinguishable from performances of nonverbal organisms such as pigeons or rats. For children between about 2 and 4 or 5 years of age, performances are transitional, with variable properties that apparently are related both to contingency-governed and to rule-governed behavior. Children older than 5 years typically produce performances with the relatively stereotyped properties that characterize adult rule-governed performances. Other studies show that verbal behavior is involved in the development of the rule-governed performances: Inter-mediate-age children who do not show rule-governed behavior on their own with these schedules do so when they are given some simple verbal instructions about the performance (Bentall & Lowe, 1987).

The effects of shaped verbal behavior on nonverbal schedule perfor-mances also can be demonstrated with children. The advantage of this procedure is that the direction of effect is unambiguous: First comes the change in verbal behavior, produced experimentally by shaping, and then follows the change in the nonverbal behavior. For example, one experiment with 4- to 6-year-olds (Catania, Lowe, & Horne, 1990) arranged reinforcing consequences that consisted of the successive lighting up of the lamps in an eight-lamp column; when the complete column was lit, the child earned a present, a small box later exchangeable for pictures to be pasted in the child's scrapbook and a toy that the child could select from a "treasure chest." The child occasionally talked about the presents with a hand puppet (Garfield the cat), who appeared from time to time through a small curtained aperture at the side of the equipment console.

Initially, the child could light the lamps in the column by pressing one of two windows in front of a computer monitor. When a window showed a star, presses worked according to a random-ratio or RR schedule (after a random number of responses); when it showed a tree, presses worked according to a random-interval or RI schedule (after a random time). Technically, an RR 10 schedule during "star" alternated with an RI 10-sec schedule during "tree," in a multiple schedule with 60-sec components. As is typical only for verbal humans, even at this age the two schedules did not produce different response rates.

After some sessions, Garfield appeared in periods between schedule components and began asking the child "how the game worked." During this time, lights in the column were lit depending on what the child said (usually accompanied by an enthusiastic reaction from Garfield); this method was used to shape what the child said about the performance. The child was never told what to say or what to do. The verbal shaping procedure was adapted to each child's vocabulary. For example, fast and slow usually meant different things to the child than to the experimenter (e.g., fast or slow hand movements toward the windows rather than rates of pressing); it was therefore usually simpler to shape alternatives such as "press a lot without stopping" and "press and wait." Although performance was more variable than with adults, successful shaping of verbal behavior (e.g., "the star [tree] works when you press it fast [slow]") typically was accompanied by corresponding rates of pressing. As with adults, verbal behavior produced corresponding rate changes even when those changes were opposed to the usual effects of the schedule contingencies (e.g., the child who came to say "With the star you press and wait" produced relatively low rates when the star was present even if the schedule that operated in the presence of the star was random-ratio, which produces relatively high rates in nonverbal organisms). As another demonstration of the primacy of the verbal behavior, successful reversal of the verbal behavior in an individual child also was accompanied by reversal of response rates.

How does this effect of the child's own verbal behavior on its subsequent nonverbal behavior begin? A phylogenic origin should not be rejected out of hand, though it is perhaps too wild a speculation to attribute it to a phylogenic history similar to that in our evolutionary scenario. As for possible ontogenic sources, one exists in the correspondence training that is likely to be a part of the child's early verbal environment (e.g., Risley & Hart, 1968). Differential consequences are based on agreement between saying and doing as children are taught to report their own behavior, to make and keep promises, and so on. But the demonstration of agreement between a child's verbal and nonverbal behavior does not establish that one class of behavior is produced by the other (cf. Baer, Detrich, & Weninger, 1988; Matthews, Shimoff, & Catania, 1987).

EQUIVALENCE CLASSES

Another possibility is that these properties of verbal behavior depend in some way on the phenomenon of equivalence classes. The concept of equivalence classes emerges from arbitrary matching-to-sample procedures (Sidman, Rauzin, Lazar, & Cunningham, 1982). For example, if a pigeon learns to peck a circle given a green sample and a square given a red circle, the pigeon will not respond appropriately if it is given circles or squares as samples and must peck either green or red. This is a symmetry test (given "if

A then B," test "if B then A"). Along with symmetry, equivalence relations also include the properties of reflexivity (identity matching, or "if A then A") and transitivity ("if A then B" and "if B then C" implies "if A then C").

So far, the development of equivalence relations seems to be a special characteristic of the performances of verbally competent humans. After learning arbitrary matches, language-competent humans pass these tests without additional training but language-disabled retarded children do not (Devaney, Hayes, & Nelson, 1986). It remains an open question whether preverbal infants must acquire verbal behavior before they can master equivalences, or whether equivalences are a prerequisite for their verbal behavior. (But see also McIntire, Cleary, & Thompson, 1987, in which macaques passed reflexivity, symmetry, and transitivity tests after completing a procedure designed to teach them responses that qualified as "names" for each of the two classes of stimuli used in the matching task. In interpreting this experiment, a position at one extreme is to accept the "naming" as an instance of verbal behavior in the macaque; a position at the other is to argue that the naming procedure reduced all performances during the tests to explicitly taught response chains.)

Equivalence classes do not appear to be reducible to stimulus control relations, in which a stimulus sets the occasion on which a response has consequences. Stimulus control relations are unidirectional, but equivalence classes require bidirectionality. For example, the relation between a red traffic light and stepping on the brakes is not reversible. But that between the red light and the word *stop* is. Symmetries exist in the relations among verbal responses and nonverbal events. We can produce a pencil upon hearing the word *pencil* and we can produce the word *pencil* upon seeing the writing implement. These kinds of equivalences are what make verbal behavior symbolic. Unlike nonverbal events, verbal events can function both as stimuli and as responses (lever presses and key pecks are not analogously interchangeable with lights and tones). Verbal behavior can be defined in terms of such equivalences (Catania, 1986).

Equivalences are relevant to the present account because they may play a significant functional role in extending verbal control that already has been established. For example, suppose parents already have taught a child to obey the words *stop* and *go* while crossing at an intersection and the child then learns that a red traffic light is equivalent to the word *stop* and a green one to the word *go*. It would be important to know whether the behavior of stopping and going will transfer from the words to the traffic light colors.

An experiment with a 5-year-old demonstrates an analogous example of transfer of function across members of an equivalence class (Catania, 1986; Catania, Horne, & Lowe, 1989). Essentially, it involved first establishing slow responding given star as a stimulus and fast responding given tree, and then using a matching procedure to establish wiggly line as equivalent to star and box as equivalent to tree. The question was then whether the respective slow and fast rates would transfer without further training to wiggly line and box.

The experiment was conducted in a setting similar to that on rule-governed behavior described earlier. Stimuli were presented on a video monitor behind response windows on which the child could press. Reinforcing consequences were arranged via the column of lights and verbal interactions with the child were mediated by the Garfield hand puppet. First, the child was taught to respond relatively slowly during star and relatively quickly during tree; the procedure was similar to that of the other experiment, except that rate differentiating rather than interval and ratio schedules were used (technically, a RI 10-sec schedule that made consequences available only for slow responding was used to produce low rates in the presence of one stimulus and a RI 10-sec schedule that made consequences available only for fast responding was used to produce high rates in the presence of a second stimulus). Even with these rate differentiating schedules performance was insensitive to the schedule contingencies, and verbal intervention was necessary to establish a rate difference. During this stage, the child came to say "star slow" and "tree fast."

Later, in a procedure arranged during sessions that alternated irregularly with those of the rate differentiation, the child learned arbitrary matching. A sample appeared in a middle window. A press on on this window turned on comparisons on a random three of four windows in a square array around the middle window (cf. Sidman, 1987). A press on the comparison that was arbitrarily designated as the match to the sample lit a column light; any other press terminated the trial. With star, tree, and circle as comparisons, the child learned to match star comparison to wiggly line sample, tree comparison to box sample, and circle comparison to zigzag lines sample (this third arbitrary match involved shapes not used in the rate procedure).

A verbal intervention on some trials early during this procedure greatly facilitated acquisition of matching; when the sample appeared, Garfield pointed to it and said "See this one"; when the comparisons appeared, Garfield then said "Which one goes with this one?"

By this point, the child had learned the rate combinations star-slow and tree-fast, and had mastered the arbitrary matching of wiggly line-star and box-tree to a level of better than 95% accuracy. Transfer was demonstrated when wiggly line and box were substituted for star and tree in the rate procedure: The child responded at the same slow rate to wiggly line as to star, and at the same high rate to box as to tree. During the transfer test, the child also called the wiggly line "slow" and the box "fast."

In subsequent matching of these shapes without feedback, the child demonstrated that star and wiggly line had become members of one equivalence class whereas tree and box had become members of another by performing at about 95% accuracy in an identity test (star-star; tree-tree) and a symmetry test (wiggly line-star; box-tree); a transitivity test was not possible because each class included only two stimuli.

The question already has been raised whether equivalences are a prerequisite for verbal behavior or verbal behavior makes possible the mastery of equivalences. In the preceding example, the verbal labels "slow" and "fast" presumably had a role in the transfer of function. Yet we might be reluctant to speak of a child's utterance as a verbal label unless it already exhibited the properties of equivalence. For example, the verbal competence of a child who could say the word *star* on seeing the form but who could not pick out the form on hearing the word might be suspect on the grounds of this failure of symmetry. In other words, language cannot be invoked as a prerequisite for equivalences if equivalences are implicit in the criteria for language. Perhaps there is a third alternative: that with respect to verbal behavior and equivalence relations, neither is a prerequisite for the other, but rather both are different facets of a single human competence.

DISCRIMINATING ONE'S OWN BEHAVIOR

More relevant for the present purposes is that the equivalence relation has features compatible with the verbal control that characterizes rule-governed behavior. For example, the reciprocity of speaker and listener that entered into the earliest stages of our evolutionary scenario already involved symmetrical elements. What was spoken word and heard response for one individual was necessarily heard word and spoken response for the other.

The verbal control observed in rule-governed behavior may occur because descriptions of one's own behavior necessarily involve the development of equivalences between one's saying and one's doing. In other words, equivalence relations may tie verbal and corresponding nonverbal behavior together so that a change in the former also pulls along the latter. Thus, strengthening correspondences between saying and doing may help verbal contingencies to override nonverbal ones. But even if this is not the case, equivalences remain relevant to verbal control because the phenomenon of transfer of function sets the stage for the unlimited extension of verbal control to new classes of behavior.

Discriminations of one's own behavior are critical to complex verbal behavior, and a case can be made that propositional language would be impossible without such discriminations. The importance of such discriminations is fairly obvious in cases like "I am pleased to tell you X" versus "I am sorry to tell you X"; it is clear that consistent usage of such phrases must depend on discriminating the circumstances under which one may be saying "X." But similar dependencies exist in a variety of simpler constructions.

Consider saying either "This is a book" or "This is not a book." If "is" and "is not" are about anything, they are about the relation between the word *book* and whatever "this" is. To use "is" and "is not" appropriately, we must not only be able to distinguish between saying "book" and saying something else; we must also be able to distinguish between saying "book" when a book is present and saying it when one is not. In other words, even in these constructions our proper use of some words depends on our awareness of the rest of what we are saying. (This is the most important property of the verbal class called autoclitic [cf. Skinner, 1957].)

If discriminations of one's own behavior necessarily are involved even in such fundamental constructions, then such discriminations must have become established early in the evolution of complex utterances. Given this implicit role of awareness of one's own behavior, it is interesting to speculate that the capacity to discriminate properties of one's own behavior is a prerequisite for natural language. It is consistent with this view that deictic expressions develop early in the acquisition of language in children (e.g., Wales, 1986); deictic terms involve distinctions that are relative to the speaker, as in *here* versus *there* or *this* versus *that,* and they therefore also entail discriminations of properties of one's own behavior.

This account opened by questioning the metaphor of communication, and it therefore may be fitting to close it by returning to that metaphor. Consider first what must have happened as verbal control increased in complexity with the expansion of human groups. As a consequence of contact with different and conflicting speakers, it must have become important for listeners to discriminate among the various sources of verbal control. In particular, if direct verbal control of the listener by the speaker was at some point supplanted by indirect control via the listener's repetition of the speaker's utterance, listeners eventually must have learned to discriminate themselves from others as the sources of verbal behavior.

This is one more case in which discriminations of one's own behavior may have been significant. It is one thing to respond directly to what someone else has said; it is another to respond to one's own repetition of the other's utterance; it is still another to distinguish that repetition from a novel utterance of one's own. Discrimination of such sources of verbal control may have marked the beginnings of those processes we speak of as consciousness or self-awareness (cf. Jaynes, 1977). Organisms that have reached this point are ones that may be ready to talk to each other about their thoughts and their hopes and their feelings.

REFERENCES

Baer, R. A., Detrich, R., & Weninger, J. M. (1988). On the functional role of the verbalization in correspondence training procedures. *Journal of Applied Behavior Analysis, 21,* 345–356.

Bem, D. J. (1967). Self-perception: An alternative interpretation of cognitive phenomena. *Psychological Review, 74,* 183–200.

Bentall, R. P., & Lowe, C. F. (1987). The role of verbal behavior in human learning: III. Instructional effects in children. *Journal of the Experimental Analysis of Behavior, 47,* 177–190.

Bentall, R. P., Lowe, C. F., & Beasty, A. (1985). The role of verbal behavior in human learning: II. Developmental differences. *Journal of the Experimental Analysis of Behavior, 43,* 165–181.

Bolles, R. C. (1970). Species-specific defense reactions and avoidance learning. *Psychological Review, 77,* 32–48.

Catania, A. C. (1984). *Learning* (2nd ed.). Englewood Cliffs, NJ: Prentice-Hall.

Catania, A. C. (1985). Rule-governed behavior and the origins of language. In C. F. Lowe, M. Richelle, D. E. Blackman, & C. Bradshaw (Eds.), *Behavior analysis and contemporary psychology* (pp. 135–156). Hillsdale, NJ: Lawrence Erlbaum Associates.

Catania, A. C. (1986). On the difference between verbal and nonverbal behavior. *The Analysis of Verbal Behavior, 4,* 2–9.

Catania, A. C., & Cerutti, D. (1986). Some nonverbal properties of verbal behavior. In T. Thompson & M. D. Zeiler (Eds.), *Analysis and integration of behavioral units* (pp. 185–211). Hillsdale, NJ: Lawrence Erlbaum Associates.

Catania, A. C., Horne, P., & Lowe, C. F. (1989). Transfer of function across members of an equivalence class. *The Analysis of Verbal Behavior, 7,* 99–110.

Catania, A. C., Lowe, C. F., & Horne, P. (1990). Nonverbal behavior correlated with the shaped verbal behavior of children. *The Analysis of Verbal Behavior, 8,* 43–55.

Catania, A. C., Matthews, B. A., & Shimoff, E. (1982). Instructed versus shaped human verbal behavior: Interactions with nonverbal responding. *Journal of the Experimental Analysis of Behavior, 38,* 233–248.

Catania, A. C., Shimoff, E., & Matthews, B. A. (1989). An experimental analysis of rule-governed behavior. In S. C. Hayes (Ed.), *Rule-governed behavior: Cognition, contingencies and instructional control* (pp. 119–150). New York: Plenum.

Darwin, C. (1965). *The expression of the emotions in man and animals.* Chicago: University of Chicago Press. (Original work published 1872)

Dawkins, R. (1982). *The extended phenotype.* San Francisco: Freeman.

Dennett, D. C. (1987). *The intentional stance.* Cambridge, MA: MIT Press.

Devaney, J. M., Hayes, S. C., & Nelson, R. O. (1986). Equivalence class formation in language-able and language disabled children. *Journal of the Experimental Analysis of Behavior, 46,* 243–257.

de Waal, F. (1989). *Peacemaking among primates.* Cambridge, MA: Harvard University Press.

Fentress, J. C. (1978). *Mus musicus,* the experimental orchestration of selected movement patterns in mice. In G. M. Burghardt & M. Bekoff (Eds.), *The development of behavior: Comparative and evolutionary aspects* (pp. 321–342). New York: Garland.

Frazer, J. G. (1951). *The golden bough* (abridged ed.). New York: Macmillan. (Original work published 1922)

Gallistel, C. R. (1980). *The organization of action.* Hillsdale, NJ: Lawrence Erlbaum Associates.

Gould, S. J. (1977). *Ontogeny and phylogeny.* Cambridge, MA: Harvard University Press.

Gouzoules, S., Gouzoules, H., & Marler, P. (1984). Rhesus monkey (*Macaca mulatta*) screams: Representational signalling in the recruitment of agonistic aid. *Animal Behaviour, 32,* 182–193.

Greenspoon, J. (1955). The reinforcing effect of two spoken sounds on the frequency of two responses. *American Journal of Psychology, 68,* 409–416.

Jaynes, J. (1977). *The origin of consciousness in the breakdown of the bicameral mind.* Boston: Houghton Mifflin.

Kroodsma, D. E., & Miller, E. H. (Eds.). (1982). *Acoustic communication in birds: Vol. 2. Song learning and its consequences.* New York: Academic Press.

Lakoff, G., & Johnson, M. (1980). *Metaphors we live by.* Chicago: University of Chicago Press.

Lowe, C. F., Beasty, A., & Bentall, R. P. (1983). The role of verbal behavior in human learning: Infant performance on fixed-interval schedules. *Journal of the Experimental Analysis of Behavior, 39,* 157–164.

Luria, A. R. (1961). *The role of speech in the production of normal and abnormal behavior.* New York: Liveright.

Matthews, B. A., Catania, A. C., & Shimoff, E. (1985). Effects of uninstructed verbal behavior on nonverbal responding: Contingency descriptions versus performance descriptions. *Journal of the Experimental Analysis of Behavior, 43,* 155–164.

Matthews, B. A., Shimoff, E., & Catania, A. C. (1987). Saying and doing: A contingency-space analysis. *Journal of Applied Behavior Analysis, 20,* 69–74.

McIntire, K. D., Cleary, J., & Thompson, T. (1987). Conditional relations by monkeys: Reflexivity, symmetry, and transitivity. *Journal of the Experimental Analysis of Behavior, 47,* 279–285.

Morris, W. (Ed.). (1969). *The American heritage dictionary of the English language.* Boston: Houghton Mifflin.

Provine, R. R. (1982). Preflight development of bilateral wing coordination in the chick (*Gallus domesticus*): Effects of induced bilateral wing asymmetry. *Developmental Psychobiology, 15,* 245–255.

Provine, R. R. (1986). Yawning as a stereotyped action pattern and releasing stimulus. *Ethology, 72,* 109–122.

Reddy, M. J. (1979). The conduit metaphor. In A. Ortony (Ed.), *Metaphor and thought* (pp. 284–324). New York: Cambridge University Press.

Risley, T. R., & Hart, B. (1968). Developing correspondence between the nonverbal and verbal behavior of preschool children. *Journal of Applied Behavior Analysis, 1,* 267–281.

Savage-Rumbaugh, E. S. (1986). *Ape language.* New York: Columbia University Press.

Seyfarth, R. M., Cheney, D. L., & Marler, P. (1980). Vervet monkey alarm calls: Semantic communication in a free-ranging primate. *Animal Behaviour, 28,* 1070–1094.

Shimoff, E., Matthews, B. A., & Catania, A. C. (1986). Human operant performance: Sensitivity and pseudosensitivity to contingencies. *Journal of the Experimental Analysis of Behavior, 46,* 149–157.

Sidman, M. (1987). Two choices are not enough. *Behavior Analyst, 22,* 11–18.

Sidman, M., Rauzin, R., Lazar, R., & Cunningham, S. (1982). A search for symmetry in the conditional discrimination of Rhesus monkeys, baboons, and children. *Journal of the Experimental Analysis of Behavior, 37,* 23–44.

Simpson, G. G. (1951). *Horses.* New York: Oxford University Press.

Skinner, B. F. (1945). The operational analysis of psychological terms. *Psychological Review, 52,* 270–277.

Skinner, B. F. (1957). *Verbal behavior.* New York: Appleton-Century-Crofts.

Skinner, B. F. (1966). The phylogeny and ontogeny of behavior. *Science, 153,* 1205–1213.

Skinner, B. F. (1969). An operant analysis of problem solving. In B. F. Skinner, *Contingencies of reinforcement* (pp. 133–171). New York: Appleton-Century-Crofts.

Vygotsky, L. (1986). *Thought and language.* Cambridge, MA: MIT Press. (Original work published 1934)

Wales, R. (1986). Deixis. In P. Fletcher & M. Garman (Eds.), *Language acquisition* (2nd ed.) (pp. 401–428). New York: Cambridge University Press.

Wittgenstein, L. (1958). *Philosophical investigations* (3rd ed.). New York: Macmillan.

Zivin, G. (Ed.). (1979). *The development of self-regulation through private speech.* New York: Wiley.

12 The Role of Social Interaction in Early Language Development

Andrew Lock, PhD
*Department of Psychology, Massey University,
Palmerston North, New Zealand*

This chapter is concerned with infants under the age of 2 years. All of them are able to get some things done in communion with their caretakers, and most of the older ones are able to use "words" as part of that doing. Yet it is unlikely that any of them have a mental representational system that could be called a "language system." These children are viewed here as being engaged in activities that create, or provide them with, abilities that eventually may be theorized into academic discourse as *enabling* "language," but not as *having* "language." Crudely, the children discussed here are engaged with their parents in doing things. Out of these doings they eventually do become able to act in ways that make a sensible discourse possible in terms of cognitive modules grappling with the features of some mental object called "Language," setting the parameters of emerging grammatical systems, and so on.

The perspective of this chapter is inherently social. It is concerned with elucidating how infants are inducted into the social practices of the cultures they are born into. It regards these practices as having a history, and as providing the resources out of which infants are able to come to make sense of the worlds they live in. It holds that these practices have a constitutive and constructive role to play in development, in that, first, they act to constitute the world as composed of possible discourse topics, and, second, are integral to constructing the ways in which human cognitive skills come to function in constituting and maintaining our discourses as sensible to each other. Before saying more about this perspective in the abstract, it is perhaps useful to move to some concrete examples of development in situ.

MEMORY AS A SOCIALLY CONSTITUTED SKILL

"Memory" is a skill that is actively constructed in the course of receiving instruction about ways of conducting dialogues with other people. Edwards and Middleton (1988) have reported on the way mothers and young children begin to talk to each other when they are looking at family photograph albums. They argued that this social practice creates particular memory skills, in that, partly, it makes particular events memorable.

Looking at photographs, and sustaining dialogues around that looking, is a quite complicated social activity. First, photographs rarely are taken by children, and so the pictures they capture are not ones that correspond to the child's view (or potential source of memory) of the occasion they preserve. Thus, young children, even if they have perfect (photographic?) memories will find it difficult to relate a photographic representation of an event to their own memorial representation. Second, we know from two decades of research into the cognitive bases of memory that retrieval is affected by encoding. Events that make no sense are unlikely to be recalled because, making no sense, it is unlikely they were encoded. Few cognitive psychologists ask, though, where "making sense" comes from. Edwards and Middleton (1988) would claim that, in contemporary Western cultures at least, the forms of discourse centered around photograph albums function, at one level, to provide frames of reference that function to structure the child's perspective on what is and what is not interesting in the world.

Photographs usually are taken on what count for significant events in the adult culture. Without this adult importation of cultural significance into a child's life, events like "going on holiday," "my brother's wedding," and "your birthday" are just another day to a child. Culturally useful encoding strategies are only going to be elaborated as events are constituted as culturally significant through the child's continual immersion in the discourses that make up the life of its culture. Thus, talking about photographs not only will help a child interrogate its own memory, but simultaneously will inculcate an entire perspective as to what in future will count as memorable, that is, to be paid attention to and encoded.

In the case of much younger adult-infant "dialogues," one does not see such high-level social structuring of memory skills as noted by Edwards and Middleton (1988) being carried out, but even more basic ones (and, further, it is possible to detect more subtle subcultural variations in how this social marking of what is to count as memorable is transacted). Adults construct discourses with young infants not only on the basis of their presupposition that infants do have recollections, but also in ways that reflect and embody their own presuppositions as to what is culturally "important" in the child's memory.

The following illustrative examples are in fact very mundane, and it can be difficult to notice their developmental significance or cultural "importance." But the claim here is that they are of massive significance: first, in the emerging subculture of the adult-infant relationship; second, in how that subculture is embedded in the wider culture in which it is situated; and, third, in the construction of the skills the infant will need to participate in the practices and discourses of these cultures.

The following are some examples of what one mother said to her 18-month-old son in a videotaped interaction with him, centered around books and toys, in our "laboratory" in Lancaster:

Example 1. "It's like the clock at home." Here she is showing the child a clockwork toy, and focusing his attention on the key that winds it up.

Example 2. "It's a snake. Remember the one you had at the fairground once?" Now she is showing him a different toy, but still relating what he sees to another temporally displaced context.

Example 3. "He's got boots on, hasn't he? They look like Daddy's shoes." At this point they are looking at a picture book, and again she betrays her presupposition that her infant understands a lot of what she is saying, that her words serve to bring to his mind, as the picture does in hers, a remembered event.

Example 4. Still looking at the book, she says: "Ooh, it's a red car, isn't it, like the one we saw in the garage when we got petrol this morning."

What is going on here is that the infant's memorial skills are not being left to mature by chance. His mother is constitutively exercising them for him. His access to what we as psychologists call his memory is being constructed as they interact around what they are jointly looking at. Unless asked to remember, he might not: He might stay context bound. In all the aforementioned examples, left to his own devices, the infant might not be motivated to exercise what we call "his memory," to see (literally) this event in front of him as having any connection to an event that can be accessed only through the directive and depictive content of his mother's words (and, later, it is claimed that the mother's strategy not only is acting in a constitutive manner with respect to her child's memory skills, but is changing, inter alia, his experience of objects and events as he perceives them).

There is nothing inherently significant about having seen a red car getting petrol in the morning. This is not the significance of what his mother is doing. Rather, its significance lies in the fact of her having an unarticulated grasp that the event they presently share perceptually links to another event in their recently shared past perception, and does so in a way that her infant may well be able to grasp/perceive (having lived with him for 18 months she will have, as all mothers do, an inarticulable but detailed grasp of, or "feel" for, what he can manage). In doing this she, unawares, provides assistance to what, in the discourse of professional psychology, we term the structuring of her child's memory skills.

These examples flesh out something of the perspective being adopted here, emphasizing that it gives a prime importance to social interaction. At the same time, however, this perspective does not imply that biological factors play an insignificant role in human development. Rather, it seeks to locate human biology in its social context. Thus, it is undeniable that human infants are endowed biologically with capacities that enable them to elaborate skills beyond those their simian relatives, at present, have been shown capable of. However, it also must be recognized that these skills have been selected for in an environment that is not solely a natural one, but one elaborated and sustained by human social practices. If memory (or language) refers to anything beyond the discourses in which it is currently employed, then its "real" existence as a cultural institution has had to have been elaborated and conserved in human life over aeons of time: Memory and language have been constituted out of human practices.

THE SOURCES OF SOCIAL CONSTRUCTIVISM AS A PERSPECTIVE ON INFANCY

As outlined here, this perspective has its roots in the work of Macmurray (1957, 1961), Vygotsky (1962, 1978, 1981), and G. H. Mead (1934). Macmurray's view of development is that, essentially, human babies do not exist as individuals in their own right: "[The human infant] cannot, even theoretically, live an isolated existence; . . . he is not an independent individual. He lives a common life as one term in a personal relation. Only in the process of development does he learn to achieve a relative independence, and that only by appropriating the techniques of a rational social tradition" (Macmurray, 1961, p. 50). In Macmurray's view, then, infants' psychological functioning is divided between themselves and informed adults. Unlike other animals, we humans are biologically "inadequate," in that we cannot sustain our life by biological "givens," but must rely on culturally given thoughts and intentions.

This mode of life is to be distinguished from an organic one. Organisms have motivations, or drives, and are provided with at least the rudiments of consummatory actions. By contrast, the human infant's motivations are structured through intention, where "the intention is the mother's, necessarily; the motives, just as necessarily, are the baby's own" (Macmurray, 1961, p. 51). Macmurray stated further:

> All this may be summed up by saying that the unit of personal existence is not the individual, but two persons in personal relation; and that we are persons

not by individual right, but in virtue of our relation to one another. The personal is constituted by personal relatedness. The unit of the personal is not the "I," but the "You and I." (p. 61)

Consider, for example, the mother of a 6-month-old infant boy who has to structure her interaction with him around a formboard, because she is in our laboratory, and this is what we have told her to do. She has, perforce, her own motives to interact with her child during his waking life. In this situation, however, the structure of her motives is being specified by us, but she, as an adult, is competent to take our instructions into her plans, and elaborate ways of going ahead for herself, for she has adult skills. Her infant, however, possesses few skills of his own. In fact, when watching what he does, we, as observers, are almost forced to conclude that he does not know how to structure any actions for himself in this situation. His mother needs to do this for him. He actually finds picking up the pieces of the form board a very difficult task; and putting them in their right holes really looks impossible for him. Further, it appears he cannot even conceive the goal of putting them in any hole. When we watch what happens during the session, however, he not only picks up pieces, but gets three into the right holes with little difficulty.

Yet, when we look closely at what the infant does, it is quite clear that he is not really doing much of anything at all. It looks as if he is motivated to pick the pieces up, yet they do not stand very proud of the board, and he does not appear to have the skill to grasp them (and it is not always easy for adults to get hold of small, "fiddly" objects either). But mother "hangs" the pieces over the holes, and over the edge of the board, making them easier to grasp. And in doing this, she sometimes places a piece in such a fashion next to the hole it should occupy, that, with a fortuitous swipe on his part, it goes straight in. Then, "Ooh, look, you've got it in, aren't you clever."

For "picking up the pieces," she seems to be structuring a goal the child has into one he can complete successfully. For "putting in the pieces" she is doing this, and more: She actually is creating the goal and giving some structure to it at the same time. She is specifying and structuring the child's motivations for him, by creating a framework for action that is structured and specified by her (and eventually, as investigators, our) intentions. Her intentions really are structuring the course of his actions. The child does not get the pieces in their holes, but then neither does she: "They" get them in, working together as a dyad.

Infants' motives gain their structuring, then, from the intentions that animate an adult's structuring of their infant's actions during the course of acting, or playing games, with them: "I" create "this" as something for "you" to do, and once "we" have done that, "we" can use it as the basis for constructing something new to do.

This interactive paradigm for conceptualizing development more often is associated with the work of the Russian psychologist Vygotsky than the philosophy of Macmurray. Both Vygotsky and Macmurray posited a view of language development as rooted in the social process of communication, a vehicle whereby communication is structured into conventional, rather than idiosyncratic, form. In Macmurray's (1961) view, "Long before the child learns to speak he is able to communicate, meaningfully and intentionally, with his mother. In learning language, he is acquiring a more effective and more elaborate means of doing something which he already can do in a crude and primitive fashion" (p. 60).

For Vygotsky, the notion of "doing something one can already do" had a more precise meaning, and he gave it a central role in his account of human development. For him, on the one hand, human development is the gaining of control of what one can already do; and on the other, another apparent paradox, much of what one can already do one cannot be said to do at all, because other people, not you, are responsible for "your" being able to do it. Much of what one can do already exists as what he termed an *intermental* ability, not an *intramental* one.

Both these writers' views find an echo in the symbolic interactionism espoused by George Herbert Mead (1934):

> Meaning can be described, accounted for, or stated in terms of symbols or language at its highest and most complex stage of development (the stage it reaches in human experience), but language simply lifts out of the social process a situation which is logically or implicitly there already. The language symbol is simply a significant or conscious gesture. (p. 79)

In Mead's symbolic interactionism, meaning is regarded as objectively present in social interaction, having as its locus the triadic relationship among a gesture, the response of another to it, and the result of the social act so initiated. And being objectively present, it is there irrespective of whether the participants whose interaction brings it about are aware of it. In addition, social interaction is constitutive not only of objective meaning, but also of the vehicles of that meaning. For example, gestures are constituted by another acting on the basis of some activity thereby elevating that activity to gestural, communicative status. Gestures are not pregiven signals linked to pregiven meanings, as ethologists might describe them in animals; they are distilled in the ongoing course of interaction itself.

DEALING WITH LANGUAGE DEVELOPMENT AS A PROCESS OF SOCIAL CONSTRUCTION

Developing infants are faced with the problem of making sense of their experience of the world. This problem can be conceived as having two temporal components. First, a "here-and-now," what one immediately sees, hears, feels, etcetera: Recent research on the perceptual abilities of even very young infants shows them to be quite good at perceiving the immediate world, of making sense of it as "real" (e.g., see Bremner [1988] for a review). But second, to make sense of it as "humanly real," what is perceived in the here and now has to be informed by "information" that is not immediately present. Only then can what is presently perceived be "recognized" (that is, apprehended in terms of nonimmediate information), and so be seen as "making sense." Now, the first step in understanding how a socially constructive account of development can be essayed is not to appeal to individually pregiven cognitive mechanisms that underwrite recognition, but to focus on the infant's immediate experiences, and ask how these are engineered so as to become imbued with sense, (while recognizing that immediate experience is underwritten by a vast array of individual cognitive power). Such an essaying would go something like the following.

In our "laboratory" at Lancaster, Service, Lock, and Chandler (1989) found that mothers tailored their performance of the components of the act of picking up an infant to their knowledge of their child's familiarity with the routine. With 6- to 9-month-old infants, mothers tended to perform the pick-up components singly — look, vocalize, then form a pick-up offer. For example:

Example 5.
Joanne is 9 months, 0 days of age:
The mother looks at Joanne.
Joanne looks at her mother.
The mother says "Jojo."
Then forms a pick-up offer.
Joanne raises her arms.
Her mother places her hands under the child's armpits.
She lifts Joanne up.

With older infants, mothers more frequently combined the components — they looked, vocalized, and gestured simultaneously. For example:

Example 6.
Daniel is 18 months, 7 days of age:
His mother stands up and looks at him.
Daniel looks toward her.
She says "Are you coming?" and gestures.
Daniel raises his arms.
His mother makes contact.
Then lifts him up.

The temporal structuring of these mothers' interactions with their infants reflects their understanding of their infants' differing competencies and the developmental changes that are fostered by the changing structures of interacting. Young infants are deficient in their comprehension of the interactions in which they participate, and these deficiencies are one of the factors that make it difficult to sustain interactions with them. By contrast, with an older infant, one may act on the knowledge gained from previous interactions that the infant both knows, as they both perceive them and participate with them in the here-and-now, something about how adults act and how what they are doing, at this particular moment, is related to what they are about to go on to do. Further, one may expect that the older infant knows something of how the particular act is related to what has been going on before it (that is, some contexts of interaction make being picked up likely): None of this can be presupposed with the younger infant.

An infant's motives gain their structuring, then, from the intentions that animate the way an adult tries to structure the infant's actions during the course of acting, or playing games, with them. But, at the same time, the point here is that the immediate perceptual world of the infant also is gaining a structure, such that what they "see" affords different courses of continued actions. Thus, through social interaction, infants come to live in different worlds, different *Umwelts* (cf. von Uexkull, 1982/1940). And the claim here is that even more subtle aspects of social interaction play a fundamental role in the structuring of these developmental changes.

For example, we also found (Service et al., 1989) that adults vary in the extent to which they mark the components of the act of picking up infants. Some mothers consistently act in the "sequential" manner noted earlier, whereas others coalesce the components into a single moment, not signaling gesturally that they intend to pick up, but moving in on the infant with a sweep of the arms, often without gaining the infant's attention, and saying for example, "Come on then, let's go and see Teddy." These differences were found to be associated with different general strategies used in playing with toys. Mothers who marked the components of the pick-up interaction selected fewer toys to show their infants, and then used these toys as the focus for sustained interactions, pointing out different parts of them, and using them as "pieces" that could be related to other objects so as to create something new to be talked about (see later discussion). By contrast, mothers who did not mark pick-up components selected more toys over the observational period, and tended to hand them to their infants and leave them to explore them without any sustained interaction being focused around them, there thus being little demonstration of the relations between parts and wholes.

I have argued elsewhere (Lock, Service, Brito, & Chandler, 1989) that these differences are also characteristic of the ways different adults interact with older infants, and are correlated with different paths infants take into the elaboration of their early "language" abilities. The following dialogue is from the same mother who provided Examples 1 through 4 earlier of context hopping. Both it, and the nonverbal techniques deployed with it to sustain and direct her 18-month-old child's attention (that are not transcribed here), can be seen as contributing to the construction of the child's analytic skills. This set of maternal utterances comes from looking at a picture book:

Example 7.
It's a hen.
There's a beak.
And two feet.
And there's a hen with lots of little chicks.
There's a tree.
And how many leaves have you got on the tree?
One, two, three. . . . sixteen leaves and sixteen little birds sitting on the branch.
And look at these little birds here.
There are two big ones, and there are two more big ones, and there are two very big ones and there's some little ones and they've got . . . , do you see where their eyes are? Do you?
Where's the birdy's eye?
Get her eye.
That's right.
And where's her nose?
Yes.
And where's her mouth?

The point here is that the child's perception of the pictures is being directed in an analytic way. Here's a hen, a whole object, but look, it has parts within it, and other things (chicks) that go with it. Trees have parts, called leaves and branches, and birds can sit on trees, can't they: That's what you are looking at; notice them?

The process of analysis underlying the understanding that things have names in a context-free way is being given a socially engineered workout here. It also is in the context hopping that was being made to happen in Examples 1 through 4. Similarly, a lot of the play she directs is concerned with the relationships that can exist between objects, that is, how objects can be regarded as parts of larger wholes:

Example 8.
Show it to Teddy.
Example 9.
Put it on the saucer.
Example 10.
Put that bug into the bucket.

Example 11.
Are you going to get the snake to catch this bubble?

Further, she juggles objects and contexts in a more sophisticated way than in dealing with pictures in a book, with the result that symbolic play is engineered:

Example 12.
Would you like a cup of tea?
Yes, go on, it's a nice little cup.
You have some. (Child pretends to drink.)
Give it to Teddy.
Go on, give Teddy a drink. (Child holds cup to Teddy's lips.)

Here she gets the infant to put two objects not just in conjunction within the present perceptual world, but in a conjunction that only makes sense through their relation to something that is not immediately present: The "tea" is imaginary, and must be brought in from absent contexts to inform present action. This is quite a complicated activity: One object (the cup) is to be related to another (tea) which has to be lifted out of absent contexts (and lifted out of absent objects to be put in this one), and then both the cup and its imaginary contents have to be regarded as a whole and placed in relation to a third, and not just Teddy, but the right part of Teddy—his mouth. And then, look, Mummy can be substituted for Teddy, and the cup can be related to yet another object newly constituted whole:

Example 13.
Shall I have a drink?
OK, put the cup on the saucer.
Yes, that's very proper now, isn't it?

By contrast, a different mother, using the same book as in Example 7, gives her 18-month-old daughter a very different experience:

Example 14.
What's that one?
Yeah, chickens.
Oh look, ducks.
And a birdie.
There's another birdie.
See the other bird there, Kate.
Hey look, a butterfly.
Flowers.
See the flowers.
And a bee.
Look at the bee.

And a rabbit.
Hmmm, bunny rabbit.

There is no emphasis on the world as being composed of wholes that may be dissociable into parts; of parts that can be related to wholes; of disembedding events from their given context and reembedding them in remembered ones so as to establish similarities between scenarios. This lack of emphasis is carried over into play with objects:

Example 15.
Ooh, look, isn't he pretty (giving a small, furry animal)?
Yes, he's pretty, isn't he?
Do you like him? (Child hugs toy.)
Yes, he's nice, isn't he?
(Child drops toy.)
Ooh, and look at this one (getting a spinning top from the box).
Look, look, it's lovely, isn't it? No?
Well, what about this, then (retrieving a yo-yo).
It's a yo-yo. You have it.
Yes, it's nice, isn't it?
(Child drops yo-yo, and so the "interaction" continues over 8 minutes, incorporating 32 new or re-presented toys).

These two quite differently structured forms of interacting represent one dimension on which the social experience of Western, suburban infants can

FIG. 12.1. There are 10 differences between Figures A and B. They are not easily found; nor, in the absence of linguistically mediated communication, would it be easy to convey to another what the nature of the task to be carried out was.

FIG. 12.2. Here the marks analogically represent an adult's pointing finger. The finger can dart from A to B, both highlighting that there are differences to be found, and making them apparent.

vary. In terms of the effects of these different forms upon the infant's perception of its immediate world, then the sorts of "spot-the-difference" visual puzzles illustrated in Figs. 12.1 and 12.2 provide good metaphors. The markers on Fig. 12.2 stand for both the way that some adults employ their fingers to direct an infant's attention to the parts of wholes and the results of their doing this for the nature of the child's perception: Parts of objects or events can be made to stand out from others as the infant perceives them.

The "sense" of the world the infant comes to perceive is structured into his or her act of perception in terms of the spatial relation of parts to wholes — and the projects these relations afford — and the temporal relations that have been condensed into the phenomena that are perceived: That is not just "a" cup, but it is one like Daddy's, that got broken yesterday, that is fragile, that can have tea in it, that can then be fed to Teddy or be put on a saucer, etcetera, all at once.

SOCIAL INTERACTION AND ITS CONTRIBUTION TO "LANGUAGE"

This socially constituted "perception of the world" constitutes the world an infant will come to talk about. The tactics that adults employ in constituting the structure of that perception likewise play a role in informing the processes whereby speaking is constructed. First, the analytic skills that Bates and her colleagues (Bates, Benigni, Bretherton, Camaioni, & Volterra, 1979) isolated as among the prerequisites for speech are embedded in the "illuminating" fingers and gestures of marking adults. Lock et al. (1989) provided some data indicating that infants who show what Nelson (1973) called a "referential" style of early language use have experienced a marked style of social interaction, whereas those showing what she called the "expressive" style do not. Second, context hopping has the essential character that underwrites both symbolism and reference. Third, part-whole relations, as played out by illuminating fingers, and context hopping are involved in coming to understand names as names.

The general point, then, is that the resources contributing to the child's communicative development are made apparent to the child by the structural nature of the communicative acts the adult and infant engage in. This development can be characterized as a two-stage process. To begin with, the meanings that the child must come to control exist in the joint actions between adult and child: They are objectively given in social interaction. Second, the structure of the social interaction affects the clarity of these "objectively givens," and this clarity in turn affects the ease with which an infant comes to control them, exploit them, and construct the skills that underlie their emerging cognitive abilities.

Finally, then, the view portrayed here supports, but would reconceptualize, the point made about this period by Bates, Bretherton, and Snyder (1988) that: "*Modules are not born; they are made.* An independent and ultimately 'impenetrable' use of grammar is slowly constructed, piece by piece, practiced endlessly until it becomes as effortless and routine as any other fully acquired perceptual-motor skill" (p. 284). In this present perspective, for "use of grammar" read "use of language." Further, the social nature of constructing and practicing perceptuomotor skills is emphasized. Human sociocultural practices are not just another factor aiding and abetting the process of development, but are integral to it: The social actions of an already enculturated other act to construct the functional cognitive abilities of each and every one of us.

REFERENCES

Bates, E., Benigni, L., Bretherton, I., Camaioni, L., & Volterra, V. (1979). *The emergence of symbols: Cognition and communication in infancy.* New York: Academic Press.

Bates, E., Bretherton, I., & Snyder, L. (1988). *From first words to grammar: Individual differences and dissociable mechanisms.* New York: Cambridge University Press.

Bremner, J. G. (1988). *Infancy.* Oxford, England: Basil Blackwell.

Edwards, D., & Middleton, D. (1988). Conversational remembering by mothers and children: A study of scaffolded learning. *Journal of Social and Personal Relationships, 5,* 3–25.

Lock, A., Service, V., Brito, A., & Chandler, P. (1989). The social structuring of infant cognition. In G. Bremner & A. Slater (Eds.), *Infant development.* London: Lawrence Erlbaum Associates.

Macmurray, J. (1957). *The self as agent.* London: Faber & Faber.

Macmurray, J. (1961). *Persons in relation.* London: Faber & Faber.

Mead, G. H. (1934). *Mind, self and society.* Chicago: University of Chicago Press.

Nelson, K. (1973). Structure and strategy in learning to talk. *Monographs of the Society for Research in Child Development 48* (Serial No. 149).

Service, V., Lock, A., & Chandler, P. (1989). Individual differences in early communicative development. In S. von Tetzchner, L. Siegel, & L. Smith (Eds.), *The social and cognitive aspects of normal and atypical language development.* New York: Springer-Verlag.

von Uexkull, J. (1982). The theory of meaning. *Semiotica, 42,* 25–82. (Original work published in 1940.)

Vygotsky, L. S. (1962). *Thought and language.* Cambridge, MA: MIT Press.

Vygotsky, L. S. (1978). *Mind in society.* Cambridge, MA: Harvard University Press.

Vygotsky, L. S. (1981). The genesis of higher mental functions. In J. V. Wertsch (Ed.), *The concept of activity in Soviet psychology.* Armonk, NY: M. E. Sharpe.

13 Language Comprehension: A New Look at Some Old Themes

Kathryn Hirsh-Pasek
Temple University

Roberta Michnick Golinkoff
University of Delaware

> . . . it seems to me that, if anything far-reaching and real is to be discovered about the actual grammar of the child, then rather devious kinds of observations of his performance, his abilities, and his comprehension will have to be obtained, so that a variety of evidence may be brought to bear on the attempt to determine what is in fact his underlying linguistic competence at each stage of development. Direct description of the child's actual verbal output is no more likely to provide an account of the real underlying competence in the case of child language than in the case of adult language . . . Not that one shouldn't start here, perhaps, but surely one shouldn't end here. . . . (Chomsky, 1964, p. 36)

In the last 25 years, many researchers have heeded the call to look for those "devious" measures that would uncover the child's language knowledge through comprehension even before the child could produce language. New assessments of comprehension have been pioneered that have been highly informative (see Golinkoff, Hirsh-Pasek, Cauley, & Gordon, 1987, for a review). Generally speaking, however, many of these efforts have been plagued with methodological difficulties. In the commonly used picture-pointing technique, for example, young children often are puzzled by attempts to depict dynamic episodes in a static representation (Friedman & Stevenson, 1975; Cocking & McHale, 1981). In tasks that require children to act out commands like "Make the cat chase the dog," young children often are disposed to act on the dog without regard to the particular request at hand. Whether or not the child understands the structure in question, these tests can be viewed as tests of compliance rather than of comprehension. Thus, although there have been a number of attempts to describe early language comprehension, our methods have constrained us. First, most of the methods can be used only with older children (greater than 28 months of age) who are already language users. Second, the field has created measures that are better at assessing the comprehension of nouns than at assessing the comprehension of verbs or other linguistic descriptions of actions and events.

This chapter is yet another attempt to address the issue of early language comprehension. The first part of the article presents the "preferential looking paradigm": a new way of assessing language comprehension in children as young as 12 months of age (Golinkoff & Hirsh-Pasek, 1981; Golinkoff et al., 1987). The second part presents three representative studies of language comprehension that begin to reveal the organizational principles that young children use as they comprehend their language input. Finally, in the third part of the article we present an interactive framework for looking at the process of language comprehension. Within this framework, we can ask several questions such as: (a) Why does the preferential-looking paradigm seem to provide a more sensitive metric of early capabilities than previous measures? (b) what might findings generated in this paradigm tell us about language comprehension? and (c) how might these results provide some answers to often asked questions in language development?

The Preferential Looking Paradigm

The paradigm was adapted from one that Spelke (1979) used to study intermodal perception. In the language version, the infant is seated on her mother's lap, midway between two television monitors (see Fig. 13.1). Between the two monitors is a central speaker that plays a linguistic stimulus that "matches" or is consistent with only one of the displays. Also between the two monitors is a light that comes on during the 3-sec intertrial interval to direct the child's attention toward the center. The infant's task is to choose the video screen that "goes with" or matches the linguistic message.

The rationale of the experiment is that children will be drawn to look at a screen that is consistent with a linguistic message rather than a screen that is inconsistent with that message—if, indeed, they understand the language used. In general, the video sequences that children see contain contrastive scenes of people engaging in dynamic events. Every attempt is made to balance the videos for perceptual salience. For example, colors and size of characters are kept constant and the frequency and quality of movement is balanced. Although total control is, of course, impossible to achieve, it is difficult to attribute positive results to perceptual factors. This is because the linguistic stimulus is counterbalanced across subjects to match each

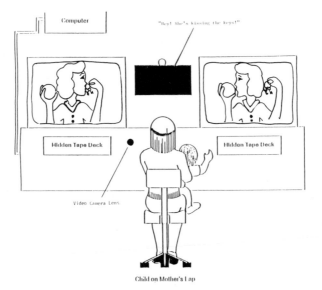

Computer

"Hey! She's kissing the keys!"

Hidden Tape Deck   Hidden Tape Deck

Video Camera Lens

Child on Mother's Lap

FIG. 13.1.   Schematic depiction of the preferential looking paradigm.

member of a pair of video displays. For example, a given child sees two simultaneous video scenes, one of which displays Cookie Monster tickling Big Bird whereas the other displays Big Bird tickling Cookie Monster. This child will hear the linguistic stimulus, "Look, Cookie Monster is tickling Big Bird!", however, a child in the other half of the design will hear "Look! Big Bird is tickling Cookie Monster!" In all the studies that have yielded positive results, the results are always obtained across both halves of the design.

Thus, the independent variables in this design are the linguistic stimuli (always complete grammatical sentences), the side of the match (counterbalanced across tapes and subjects), and sometimes age. The dependent variables in this paradigm are: (a) the amount of visual fixation time to the matching versus the nonmatching screen, and (b) the latency or time to look at the matching or the nonmatching screen. Latency is calculated from the time that children look at the center light between the two screens until they look toward one of the video screens. The design of one of the experiments is depicted on Table 13.1. Because all of the experiments to be described use this method, the following section describes a typical design in some detail.

When the procedure begins, the picture on each screen comes on alone before the pictures on the two screens come on together. In the first "sequential trial," the child sees the left screen come on with a scene of a girl kissing some keys while she holds a ball in the foreground. This lasts for 6 sec while the right screen is blank. During this presentation, the child hears a nondescript audio like, "What is she doing?" During the 3-sec intertrial

TABLE 13.1
Standard Design for Comprehension Studies in the Preferential Looking Paradigm — Example from Experiment 1: The Perception Of Constituent Structure

Left Screen	Audio	Right Screen
Sequential Trials for Stimulus Familiarization		
Girl kissing ball while dangling keys in foreground	"Oh, what's going on?"	Blank
Blank	{Center light} "Hey, what's going on?"	Blank
Blank	"Look! What is she doing?"	Girl kissing keys while holding ball in foreground.
Simultaneous Trial for Calculation of Stimulus Salience		
Blank	{Center light} "Wow, what's happening!"	Blank
Girl kissing ball . . .	"What are they doing?"	Girl kissing keys . . .
Test Trials		
Blank	{Center light} "Hey, she's kissing the keys!"	Blank
Girl kissing ball . . .	"Wow, she's kissing the keys!"	Girl kissing keys . . .
Blank	{Center light} "Where is she kissing the keys?"	Blank
Girl kissing ball . . .	"Oh! She's kissing the keys!"	Girl kissing keys . . .

Note. Video events are 6 sec long; intertrial intervals when both screens are blank, 3 sec.

interval, the infant's attention is drawn to a center light that remains on for the duration of the interval. Next, the right screen shows a picture of a girl kissing a ball while dangling keys in the foreground. The left screen is blank and the child again hears the nondescript audio, "What is she doing?" The right screen goes off and the center light appears once more. Notice that the child has now learned that stimuli are delivered on both screens. In the last of the familiarization trials, both of these scenes come on together and the child hears, "Hey, what are they doing?" This "simultaneous trial" accomplishes two things: It shows the child that stimuli will be delivered simultaneously on both screens; and it provides the opportunity to assess whether one screen is preferred over the other when language cannot be used to guide visual fixations.

With the familiarization complete, Trials 4 and 5 comprise the test trials in which children hear the linguistic stimulus, "Hey, she's kissing the keys. Where is she kissing the keys?" or "Hey, she's kissing the ball. Where is she kissing the ball?" This linguistic stimulus comes on during the 3-sec intertrial interval when the center light is on and is restated again in the test trial. All of these experiments use at least four different stimulus pairs of the particular structure that the experiment is designed to test.

Experimental Controls.   A number of controls have been built into the procedure. First, as Fig. 13.1 shows, the mother wears a visor over her eyes so that she cannot see the stimuli and unwittingly influence the looking patterns of her infant. Second, the observers who are recording the eye fixations from behind the screens are blind to the experimental condition being run. Reliability for the measurement of visual fixation has now been obtained in three ways: between two on-line observers, between two off-line observers coding from videotape taken of subjects during testing, and between one on-line and one off-line observer. In all conditions, reliability exceeds .90 (see Naigles, Hirsh-Pasek, & Golinkoff, 1989).

The third control built into these designs is that the actors or objects are in constant motion so that the child cannot use activity alone to provide a strategic solution to the mapping between the language and the scene. Fourth, as stated earlier, every attempt is made to balance the colors, shapes, and degree of activity that appear on both screens. Fifth, a number of factors are counterbalanced in these designs. The tapes are shown in both video decks so that half the subjects see the matches in one pattern and the other half see the opposite pattern. Also, half the subjects in an experiment hear an audio tape that matches one member of a video pair; for the other half of the subjects, the audio matches the opposite member of the pair. Sixth and finally, the Delaware and Temple laboratories often each run half of the design. This practice enables us to replicate our findings before considering any result firm.

Procedure.   Children come into the laboratories and play with the experimenter before testing begins. During that time, the mother fills out a vocabulary inventory (Rescorla, 1985) that provides a fairly complete record of the child's productive vocabulary. The mothers also report on the kinds of sentences that the children use so that they can be crudely assigned as one-word speakers or as more advanced speakers.

Rationale for the Procedure.   To summarize, then, the preferential looking paradigm presents two simultaneous scenes on television monitors with a centrally placed linguistic stimulus that goes with or describes only one of the scenes. Following Spelke (1979), the underlying rationale of this research is that children will prefer to watch a video event that matches a linguistic stimulus over an event that does not match the stimulus. It could be argued that this rationale contradicts much of the developmental research, which shows that infants prefer to watch novel or discrepant stimuli over familiar stimuli (see Cohen, DeLoache, & Strauss, 1979). Note that even if infants did look at the discrepant stimulus (the nonmatch), this would constitute evidence for comprehension. That is, consistent looking patterns toward the nonmatch would signify that the child comprehended the target utterance, evaluated the two video choices, and preferred to match the visual event discrepant from the linguistic stimulus. In none of the studies so far conducted has there been a consistent preference for the nonmatch.

There may be an additional reason why infants and toddlers in this task do prefer the matching screen. Tasks that require subjects to find the correspondence between visual and auditory stimuli are fundamentally different than those that require discrimination in a single modality. One could argue that the preferential looking paradigm in a sense duplicates the language-learning situation children find themselves in: namely, figuring out what in the environment is being commented upon.

THREE REPRESENTATIVE STUDIES

To date, the method has been used in a series of experiments that are beginning to shed light on the organizational principles that young children use to interpret their language input. This chapter reports on just three of these. Experiment 1 focused on whether infants hear an utterance as a string of individual words or rather as a string that is organized in some way. Experiment 2 probed the kind of organization that infants might perceive in the input by testing whether infants are sensitive to word order in active reversible sentences. Finally, Experiment 3 asked whether these infants and toddlers could even go beyond attention to word order to note the syntactic markers that differentiate sentences that are formed from transitive versus intransitive verbs.

Experiment 1: The Perception of Constituent Structure. Experiment 1 was designed to assess whether infants are sensitive to constituent structure. The design of this experiment appears on Table 13.1. It is fashioned after an experiment by Sachs and Truswell (1978) that asked whether young children could follow two-word commands like "tickle book" and "kiss keys." The reasoning behind the Sachs and Truswell experiment was as follows: If young speakers can correctly carry out two-word commands—especially bizarre ones like "kiss keys"—then they must realize that words in a string form units to specify particular relationships. If, on the other hand, children are focusing on individual words in the input and are using familiarity or semantic probability to carry out these commands, then they should fail to carry out a set of bizarre commands.

A number of experiments support the latter view. These experiments conclude that children use their knowledge of individual lexical items or of event probability to interpret sentences. For example, in a study by Chapman and Miller (1975), children presented with sentences such as "Baby feeds Mommy," interpret it as "Mommy feeds Baby."

Other results are compatible with a one-word-at-a-time, or a "building-block" theory of early comprehension (Bloom & Lahey, 1978). Most notably Slobin (1973, 1985) posited a set of operating principles by which children would, for example, pay attention to the last word heard in a string.

Returning to the Sachs and Truswell (1978) study, the children ranged in age from 16 to 24 months, with a mean of 19.6 months. Thus, the children at the upper limit of the age range already were producing two-word speech. Their results suggest that all of the children were able to carry out some of the unusual commands and that this ability increased with age.

This preferential looking adaptation of Sachs and Truswell (1978) task is considerably less demanding in that it did not require that the subjects carry out the bizarre commands. Further, subjects consisted of only those infants whose mothers reported in a telephone interview that their children could comprehend the names of the 12 nouns in the videos were subjects. Comprehension of the verbs was not assessed. The 16 infants (half boys and half girls) were 13 to 15 months of age (mean age = 14 months) with an average productive vocabulary of 25 words.

All children heard both more likely ("She's pushing the plant.") and less likely ("She's kissing the keys.") statements. As in the example previously described, when the woman is kissing the keys, the ball is held in the foreground. When the woman is kissing the ball, the keys are dangled in the foreground. Thus, the action of kissing, and the objects (keys and a ball) are visible on both screens.

The logic of the present experiment is identical to that of Sachs and Truswell's (1978). If children organize their input into packages of words that map onto relationships in the environment, then the linguistic stimulus, "She's kissing the keys," should direct attention toward the interactive scene in which the woman is kissing the keys. If, however, the independent word-by-word hypothesis is correct, infants should distribute their attention equally between the two screens. If the strategy of focusing selectively on the last word is correct, the infants should actually look at the incorrect screen because the object represented by the last word is foregrounded on the nonmatching screen.

The results of this study are presented in Table 13.2. It seems as if these

TABLE 13.2
Experiment 1: The Perception of Constitutent Structure — Mean Visual Fixation
Time (in sec) to the Match and Nonmatch Displayed by Stimulus (n = 32)

	Stimulus Event				
	Eating — Cookie or Banana[a]	Smelling — Boat or Shoe	Tickling — Phone or Book	Kissing — Ball or Keys	Mean
Match	3.38	3.11	2.47	2.66	2.90
Nonmatch	1.97	2.18	2.22	2.29	2.16

[a]The auditory stimulus was counterbalanced such that half the children heard "She's eating the cookie," and half heard "She's eating the banana."

infants, who are all in the one-word stage of language production, are predisposed to organize their input into packages of words that represent relationships. The mean visual fixation time to the match was 2.90 sec and to the nonmatch, 2.16 sec (p < .05). This result is upheld for both likely and unlikely combinations. As Sachs and Truswell (1978) were quick to point out, this propensity to organize the input is not evidence of a grammatical capability. Yet, to induce a grammar the child must be able to identify sequences of words that "hook together" to convey some unit of meaning. Thus, this result suggests that even very immature speakers have taken the first step in the language-learning process: They seem to have an operating principle that guides them to look for "packages" — constituents beyond the single word — in the input language that they hear.[1]

Experiment 2: The Comprehension of Word Order.   The next question, then, is whether infants go beyond noticing phrasal constituents to noticing some of the organizational patterns that make up the grammar of their language. The world's languages use two major devices for representing meaning relations such as who does what to whom. At one extreme, English relies heavily on the order of words in a sentence to specify meanings. Thus, the sentence, "Brutus killed Caesar," means something historically different than the sentence, "Caesar killed Brutus." At the other extreme are languages like Turkish with relatively free word order that use inflectional markings to denote particular case role relations (Slobin & Bever 1982, 1985).

Because English is predominantly a word-order language and because the majority of psycholinguistic studies are carried out with English-speaking

---

[1]To secure these results we currently are running a control condition in which children hear the audio "See the keys!" Such a control is designed to rule out the possibility that infants are focusing solely on the word *keys* and picking the scene in which the keys are involved in the interactive event.

children, children's sensitivity to word-order relations has been studied extensively (see Golinkoff et al., 1987). Thus far, the results from these studies are equivocal (Hirsh-Pasek, Golinkoff, de Gaspe Beaubien, Fletcher & Cauley, 1985; Atkinson, 1986). Some studies find that toddlers are not even sensitive to whether a sentence contains scrambled or normal word order (Wetstone & Friedlander, 1973). Others suggest that children—at least by age 24 months—do show some sensitivity to word order when they are asked to carry out commands (Roberts, 1983) or point to pictures (Golinkoff & Markessini, 1980).

It was hypothesized that in a less taxing comprehension paradigm, infants would attend to word order. Especially for English, attention to word order is critical for deciphering the mapping between the input language and events in the environment. Golinkoff et al. (1987) had already shown that 28-month-old children, producing two- and three-word speech, demonstrated the comprehension of word order in the preferential-looking paradigm. To ask whether children who were not yet producing ordered speech could nonetheless use word order in comprehension, new videotapes were created with Big Bird and Cookie Monster serving as the actors (Hirsh-Pasek et al., 1985). For example, on one screen, Big Bird washed Cookie Monster while Cookie Monster waved Big Bird away. The roles were reversed on the other screen with Cookie Monster doing the washing. Then they were asked either, "Where is Cookie Monster washing Big Bird?" or the reverse, "Where is Big Bird washing Cookie Monster?" The design for one block of trials in this experiment is outlined in Table 13.3. Subjects first received training to ensure that they knew the characters' names.

The design of these tapes preclude any explanation of word-order comprehension that has to do with semantic strategies or pragmatic factors. Both characters were equally likely to perform the action portrayed and both characters were highly animated. Furthermore, no experimenter intervened to provide the stimuli to the child as is usually the case in other tests of comprehension. Thus, there were no subtle inadvertent cues available to the child for how to solve this word-order problem.

Forty-eight infants, ages 16 to 18 months (mean age = 17.5 months), most of whom were in the one-word stage of language production, participated in this experiment. Half of the subjects were tested in the Philadelphia laboratory and half were tested in the Delaware laboratory. Subjects in the two labs heard the reverse audio and saw the events on the tapes in the opposite order. Half of each sample were boys and half were girls. The results across the four active reversible verbs on the dependent variable of total visual fixation are presented on Table 13.4. Infants demonstrated a significant looking preference for the matching screen over the nonmatching screen. This effect held for the dependent measures of visual fixation ($M = 2.85$ sec vs. 2.09 sec) and latency ($M = 1.42$ sec vs.

TABLE 13.3
The Structure of the Stimulus Videotapes for the Verb "Tickle"
in the Word-Order Experiment

Tape 1	Audio	Tape 2
	Sequential Trials for Stimulus Familiarization	
Cookie Monster (CM) tickles Big Bird (BB) while Big Bird holds a box full of toys.	"Who's tickling?"	Blank screen
Blank screen	"Who's tickling?"	BB tickles CM while CM holds a box full of toys.
	Simultaneous Trial for Calculation of Stimulus Salience	
CM tickles BB	"They're tickling!"	BB tickles CM
	Test Trials	
CM tickles BB	"Look! CM is tickling BB! Where is CM tickling BB?"	BB tickles CM
CM tickles BB	"Hey, CM is tickling BB! Find CM tickling BB!"	BB tickles CM

[a]For ease of exposition, intertrial intervals (when both screens are blank) have been omitted. "Feed," "wash," and "hug" had the identical structure with side of match counterbalanced. The side of the first scene during the sequential trials also was counterbalanced across the verbs.

TABLE 13.4
Boys and Girls' Mean Visual Fixation Times (in sec) to the Match Versus the
Nonmatch for the 4 Stimuli in the Word-Order Experiment

Sex	Stimuli				
	Hug	Tickle	Feed	Wash	Means
Girls					
Match	2.49	3.25	2.75	2.89	2.84
Nonmatch	1.98	2.01	2.02	1.95	1.99
Boys					
Match	2.09	3.23	3.88	2.19	2.85
Nonmatch	2.78	1.82	1.77	2.43	2.20

1.82 sec). The results are consistent across both laboratories and post hoc analyses ensure that the results hold equally for subjects producing only one word at a time and for subjects who have just started to put words together.

As inspection of the means for boys and girls reveals, there was an interaction in the data between sex, stimulus, and match–nonmatch. The girls uniformly preferred the match across the four verbs whereas the boys preferred the match on only the middle two verbs. Post hoc tests indicated, however, that on the first and last verbs where the boys appeared to prefer the nonmatch, these differences were not statistically significant. Other than post hoc explanations of differences in attention span, it is unclear why the boys should have failed on the first and last verbs. It should be noted that when sex differences have emerged in other studies in this paradigm it is invariably the case that girls outperform boys.

The fact that infants watched the matching screen significantly more than the nonmatching screen suggests that infants, some of whom have only two words in their productive vocabularies, are attentive to word order or positional cues in their language. The ability to organize the input through word order is critical for the acquisition of grammar. If one endorses a theory of acquisition that turns on distributional analysis (e.g., Maratsos & Chalkley, 1980), sensitivity to word order permits the child to notice classes that appear in different positions. If one favors a competition model (Bates & MacWhinney, 1987), the child must detect word-order cues because these are among the major competitors for how languages encode meaning relations. Finally, if one supports the parameter theory of linguistic development (see Roeper & Williams, 1987), word-order cues provide the input that can trigger settings for head-initial versus head-final languages or for configurational versus nonconfigurational languages. Indeed, such findings beg for cross-linguistic validation on children learning languages that do not rely as heavily on word order as does English, for example, Hungarian.

The finding that word order is comprehended is interesting, but it is not conclusive evidence that the child is using a syntactic system. For one thing, these results do not speak to whether the child has syntactic categories such as "sentence subject" or semantic categories such as "agent." Further, attention to word order may be one instantiation of a more general cognitive ability to notice temporal order. The last study to be described provides more secure evidence that young learners—at least by the time that they are 2 years of age—may be comprehending and using a syntactic system.

Experiment 3: Children's Comprehension of Subcategorization Frames. The third and final experiment to be described examined toddler's knowledge of subcategorization frames around verbs; that is, are young language learners sensitive to the kinds of syntactic environments in which verbs are used? These different environments direct listeners to one meaning over another. Can toddlers go beyond general organizing principles (such as attention to word order) to use information that is unquestionably language specific?

This study was done in collaboration with Drs. Lila Gleitman, Henry Gleitman, and Letitia Naigles (Hirsh-Pasek, Naigles, Golinkoff, Gleitman, & Gleitman, 1988). It focused on the critical division between the types of sentence frames generally used with transitive verbs ("X blixes Y") and intransitive verbs ("X and Y blix"). It also capitalized on Jackendoff's (1986) and Bowerman's (1983) suggestion that within the class of motion verbs, transitive verbs often signal causative action and intransitive verbs signal noncausative action.

In this task the videos again made use of Cookie Monster and Big Bird (see Table 13.5). On the left screen, for example, children saw Cookie Monster turning Big Bird by pushing him around with his hands (a causative action). On the right screen, they saw Cookie Monster and Big Bird turning together. During the familiarization trials, children heard a nondescript audio like, "Look, turning!" that labeled the action but applied equally to both screens. During the test trials, however, half of the subjects heard a transitive sentence, "Look, Cookie Monster is turning Big Bird"; whereas the other half heard an intransitive sentence, "Find Cookie Monster and Big Bird turning." Two of the verbs were familiar ones (*turn* and *bend*) and two were unfamiliar (*flex* and *squat*), as assessed by parental

TABLE 13.5
The Structure of the Stimulus Videotapes in the Subcategorization Experiment[a]

Tape 1	Audio	Tape 2
Sequential Trials for Stimulus Familiarization		
Big Bird (BB) is pushing Cookie Monster (CM) into a squatting position	"See? Squatting!"	Blank screen
Blank screen	"Look! Squatting!"	BB and CM are squatting side by side
Simultaneous Trial for Calculation of Stimulus Salience		
BB pushes CM into a squatting position	"See, squatting!"	BB and CM are squatting side by side
Test Trials[b]		
BB pushes CM into a squatting position	"Find BB squatting CM!"	BB and CM squatting side by side
BB pushes CM into a squatting position	"Look at BB squatting CM!"	BB and CM squatting side by side

[a]Three additional verbs, constructed along the identical lines, made up the rest of the stimulus tape. The side of the first appearance of a sequential trial was counterbalanced as was the side of the matching screen. For ease of exposition, the intertrial intervals when both screens are blank, are not shown. [b]The linquistic stimulus is from the transitive condition; the same videotapes were used for the intransitive condition except for the test trials. Here subjects heard, "Find Big Bird and Cookie Monster squatting!"

interview. Notice that to solve the problem presented in this task, the children must know that the verb *turn* can be used either transitively or intransitively and that the frame surrounding the verb determines which aspect of the verb is being referred to. It is also of note that recent research by Rispoli and Bloom (1988) suggests that this task should be quite taxing for young learners. Their findings indicate that very few children produce the same verb in both a transitive and an intransitive frame. Further, most of the transitive frames used by children involve an animate actor and an inanimate object or recipient of the action.

The subjects in this study were 96 children equally divided into three age groups, 18 to 21 months, 22 to 25 months, and 26 to 30 months, in a between-subject design with half of the children in the transitive condition and half in the intransitive condition. The 32 infants in the 18 to 21 age month group showed no preference for the matching screen when they heard either the transitive or the intransitive audios (see Table 13.6). The "middle age" group at 24 months began to show some trend toward the comprehension of transitive frames with the result being controlled by the girls who looked longer at the matching screen ($M = 2.91$ sec) than at the nonmatching screen ($M = 2.00$ sec). In this middle group, even the girls showed no preference for the match when they heard the intransitive audio ($M = 2.74$ sec for the matching screen and 2.69 sec for the nonmatching screen). Finally, by age 28 months, both the boys and the girls looked longer at the matching screen than at the nonmatching screen in the transitive condition ($M = 3.54$ sec and 2.25 sec, respectively) while still showing a random looking pattern in the intransitive condition ($M = 3.08$ sec for the match versus 2.68 sec for the nonmatch).

TABLE 13.6

Boys' and Girls' Mean Visual Fixation Times (in sec) to the Matching Versus the Nonmatching Screen for the Older (28.9 Months) and the Middle (24.5 Months) Age Groups Across the Two Conditions in the Original Subcategorization Study

			Stimuli	
Age	*Sex*	*Audio*	*Match*	*Nonmatch*
Older				
(26–30 months)	Boys ($n = 8$)	Transitive	3.66	2.087*
	($n = 8$)	Intransitive/original	2.91	2.65
	Girls ($n = 8$)	Transitive	3.43	2.42**
	($n = 8$)	Intransitive/original	3.25	2.71
Middle				
(22–25 months)	Boys ($n = 8$)	Transitive	2.37	2.85
	($n = 15$)	Intransitive/original	2.53	2.35
	Girls ($n = 8$)	Transitive	2.91	2.00*
	($n = 8$)	Intransitive/original	2.74	2.69

*$p < .05.$ **$p < .01.$

The most interesting results from this study, however, emerge from a follow-up experiment that varied the intransitive audio within the two older groups. In the follow-up experiment, an additional 16 subjects were run in a condition in which they heard the intransitive sentence, "Big Bird is turning WITH Cookie Monster." Even though the order of the nouns in this condition parallels that heard in the transitive condition with the noun arguments appearing on either side of the verb ("Big Bird is turning Cookie Monster"), both sexes at 28 months of age significantly preferred the noncausative video as the match for the linguistic stimulus ($M = 3.06$ sec for the match and 2.37 sec for the nonmatch, respectively). In the control trials, they showed no preference for the causative over the noncausative video (see Table 13.7).

Thus, the subcategorization study provides developmental evidence that, by just under 2.5 years of age, young (female) learners make use of the syntactic information in the input to decide whether the familiar verb they are hearing is being used transitively or intransitively. They seem to realize the power the subcategorization frame has in influencing the meaning of the verb. In fact, to further secure the result, another group of 28-month-olds demonstrated that they could use the frame in which a verb is nested to figure out the meaning of an unfamiliar verb. This is what Landau and Gleitman (1985) dubbed the syntactic bootstrapping hypothesis (see also, Naigles, Gleitman, & Gleitman, in press). Finally, this result suggests that 28-month-olds are not just attending to word order as a strategy for figuring out sentence meaning. Rather, in the WITH condition ("Big Bird is turning with Cookie Monster"), these toddlers attended to a syntactic marker—specifically the preposition *with*—to determine verb class. If order alone had determined their choice, they should have watched the transitive event because the "with" condition mirrors the order of the transitive frame.

TABLE 13.7
Mean Visual Fixation Times (in sec) to the Matching Versus the Nonmatching Screen for the Older Children (28.9 Months) in the Intransitive "With" Condition and in the Control Condition That Checked for a Visual Preference for "Cause" Over "Noncausal" Actions

	Visual Event	
Audio	*Match*	*Nonmatch*
Intransitive "With"	3.06	2.24**
	Cause	*Noncause*
Control	2.65	3.16

**p < .01.

Discussion

Taken together, these studies begin to shed light on the kinds of organizational strategies that young learners are imposing on the input that they hear. By the tender age of 14 months, in the beginning of the one-word stage, infants act as if they expect to hear constituent packages (Experiment 1). By 17 months of age, still in the one-word stage, infants, as shown in Experiment 2 — the Big Bird/Cookie Monster word-order study — are attentive to word order in active reversible five-word sentences. Finally, by 28 months of age, these nascent speakers are sensitive to the kinds of syntactic information that specify verb classes and relationships between verb classes and environmental events.

As in all psychological experimentation it would be ideal to obtain converging evidence for these findings. For example, it would be useful to test subjects' language comprehension with a separate, unrelated paradigm. To date, however, other comprehension paradigms do not permit investigators to look for evidence for linguistic structures at these young ages. It is possible, however, to relate performance in the paradigm at a younger age with performance on other language tasks at a later age. Multiple assessments of this nature are planned for future research.

Given that the preferential looking paradigm provides at least preliminary evidence for these linguistic sensitivities, it becomes incumbent upon us to ask: (a) why these early abilities are evident in the preferential looking paradigm; (b) what these findings might tell us about early language comprehension; and (c) how these findings might address some long-standing issues in language development.

Answers to these questions can only be forthcoming if we adopt a broader view of the language comprehension process than has been held in the past. It is commonly accepted, at least implicitly, that language comprehension is not merely the comprehension of language per se. Rather, language comprehension is the process by which we derive a mental representation by culling from a number of different, parallel and interactive sources — some linguistic (lexical and syntactic) and some nonlinguistic (such as the interpretation of the social or environmental context). In fact, these sources ordinarily do not disagree with each other, but rather, enable children to use their coalition to guide comprehension. That is, more often than not, young children hearing linguistic information are in a familiar situation in which the knowledge that they hold in their scripts for an event (Nelson, 1985), the social and environmental contexts, and the syntax and lexical choices all converge on the same interpretation. It is rare that speakers try to confuse the young child by talking about something totally new or by putting the syntactic information in conflict with the contextual cues that the child is witnessing.

Comprehension is an interactive process that involves finding correspondences or coalitions between these sources (see Fig. 13.2). Indeed, theories like Bloom and Lahey's (1978), Just and Carpenter's (1987), and McClelland's (1987), among others, have suggested a multifaceted view of language comprehension. The proliferation of bootstrapping theories is testimony to the importance of these sources and to the correlations between them. Yet, many who study language through comprehension lose sight of the interactive nature of the process. For example, studies that focus on the comprehension/production debate (Chapman & Miller, 1975; Straight, 1985) often fail to discuss what they mean by comprehension or, for that matter, production. The failure to discuss the meaning of comprehension is an important omission because the tests used to assess comprehension are grounded in an implicit theory of how the process works.

Consequently, studies that focused on syntactic comprehension sometimes adopted a narrow view of the comprehension process by testing for comprehension in situations devoid of other, normally contributing information sources like social context or general knowledge. Many of the natural sources for comprehension are omitted or are put into conflict with the syntactic system. Children may respond in such tasks, but may not demonstrate the upper limits of their knowledge.

In contrast, the preferential looking paradigm neither omits the contribution of sources like prosody, or social context, nor puts them into conflict. As such, linguistic ability may be revealed in the preferential looking paradigm because the necessity for the child to call upon nonlinguistic skills to respond is much reduced. Thus, in answer to the first question posed, why language skills appear so much more advanced in this

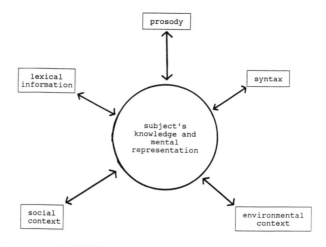

FIG. 13.2. The process of language comprehension.

paradigm, there are two answers: (a) The method makes fewer response demands on subjects than other comprehension paradigms, and (b) the view of language comprehension that underlies this task does not pit sources ordinarily used in language comprehension against each other. This task does not ask whether children prefer a semantic interpretation over a syntactic one as in sentences like "Baby feeds Mommy." It simply asks whether children can attend to word order when the other available cues will not enable them to solve the problem posed in the task.

The positive findings on language comprehension presented earlier open up a large Pandora's box. For example, it now becomes important to ask how the various sources of input (e.g., prosody, syntax, semantics) contribute to language comprehension. The coalition view also forces one to ask whether all of these sources are weighted equally (they are probably not and it probably varies across contexts and age), and it compels one to look at the kinds of information that each source contributes to the language comprehension task. Yet, adopting this view of comprehension as a framework for future studies enables the field to address the other two questions posed previously. First, what does language qua language contribute to the language comprehension process? Remember that in young children, some accounts (see, e.g., Chapman, 1978) rely exclusively on the probability of events with very little reliance on language. To this question we now can say that language contributes a good deal to the comprehension process. The preferential looking paradigm forces children to use language to solve the task. Without some knowledge of syntax or precursors to syntax, children could not figure out which of the two screens was being described by the accompanying linguistic message. Further, this result obtains even with the relatively complex stimuli (both linguistic and nonlinguistic) used in our experiments. Such findings have consequences for theories that describe the acquisition of grammar. Without some of these capacities for the interpretation of the input, few theories could explain how children induce the grammar of their language.

Second and last, how might the findings from this paradigm help resolve some of the longstanding issues in language development? Consider, for example, the comprehension/production debate. These results provide compelling evidence that the comprehension of syntactic forms precedes production of those forms in speech. The answer to this debate again raises more questions than it answers. Why does comprehension appear so early? What is the developmental course of the apparent capacities children are revealing? One potential response to these questions will undoubtedly be grounded in some view of language comprehension. In comprehension, children receive organized prosodic and syntactic packages. They need to recogize the input rather than to engage in the recall and assembly that is required to produce parallel constructions (Bloom, 1974; Boom & Lahey,

1978). Comprehension requires only the unpackaging of organized information rather than the generation of that package. Comprehension requires the activation of lexical choices rather than the making of decisions among competing lexical choices. The bottom line is that even though comprehension and production might share the types of sources that feed each system, these sources are used and weighted differently.

In sum, then, there are some "devious" ways to look at language development through comprehension. To do so, however, requires adopting and exploring a broad view of what it means to comprehend language. Such a view results in the development of assessments in which children can use a number of sources to support their interpretations: Crucial sources of information are neither omitted nor put in conflict with one another. Thus, by building tasks that are sensitive to the many variables at work in comprehension, we optimize children's ability to demonstrate what they can do with linguistic stimuli and how linguistic stimuli potentially contribute to the comprehension process.

The preferential looking paradigm may allow for the discovery of a number of linguistic sensitivities that young learners bring to the task of grammatical acquisition. Although this method seems to be providing a measure of young children's developing language skills, however, it is by no means a panacea. Not all subjects tested completed the experiment and not all experiments conducted within this paradigm succeeded. For example, the 18-month-olds in Experiment 3 showed no evidence of comprehending the transitive and intransitive sentences, even though subjects of the same age responded well in tests of word-order comprehension (Experiment 2). Further, the origins of observed early linguistic sensitivities are still open to debate. All that is known is that these sensitivities to input must be in place early to guide acquisition.

The development of complex processes like language (at least grammar) depend crucially on the child's ability to extract certain kinds of information from the input. Whether the child is acquiring language under a competition theory (Bates & MacWhinney, 1987) or a parameter theory (Hyams, 1986), the studies described begin to search for the sensitivities to the input that might ensure language learning. Future studies hopefully will yield an even clearer picture of which sensitivities are important for early language learning and when and how these sensitivities develop. What is clear is that regardless of whether their source is linguistic or cognitive, such sensitivities are necessary as children try to make sense of their language input.

ACKNOWLEDGEMENTS

The research reported in this article was supported by the following grants: HD15964 and HD19568 to both authors from the National Institute of Child Health and Human Development; a James McKeen Cattell Sabbatical Award and a John Simon Guggenheim Memorial Fellowship to Golinkoff; and a Spencer Foundation grant to Hirsh-Pasek.

REFERENCES

Atkinson, M. (1986). Learnability. In P. Fletcher & M. Garman (Eds.), *Language acquisition: Studies in first language development* (pp. 90–108). Cambridge, MA: Cambridge University Press.

Bates, E., & MacWhinney, B. (1987). Competition, variation, and language learning. In B. MacWhinney, B. (Ed.), *Mechanisms of language acquisition* (pp. 157–194). Hillsdale, NJ: Lawrence Erlbaum Associates.

Bloom, L. (1974). Talking, understanding, and thinking. In R. L. Schiefelbusch & L. L. Lloyd (Eds.), *Language perspectives—Acquisition, retardation, and intervention* (pp. 285–312). Baltimore: University Park Press.

Bloom, L., & Lahey, M. (1978). *Language development and language disorders.* New York: Wiley.

Bowerman, M. (1983). Evaluating competing linguistic models with language acquisition data: Implications of developmental errors with causative verbs. *Quaderna di Semantica, 3,* 5–66.

Chapman, R. S. (1978). Comprehension strategies in children. In J. F. Kavanaugh & W. Strange (Eds.), *Speech and language in the laboratory, school, and clinic* (pp. ???–???). Cambridge, MA: MIT Press.

Chapman, R. S., & Miller, J. F. (1975). Word order in early two- and three-word utterances: Does production precede comprehension? *Journal of Speech and Hearing Research, 18,* 355–371.

Chomsky, N. (1964). Formal discussion. In U. Bellugi & R. Brown (Eds.), The acquisition of language. *Monographs of the Society for Research in Child Development, 29* (1, Serial No. 92).

Cocking, R. R., & McHale, S. (1981). A comparative study of the use of pictures and objects in assessing children's receptive and productive language. *Journal of Child Language, 8,* 1–13.

Cohen, L. B., DeLoache, J., & Strauss, M. S. (1979). Infant visual perception. In J. Osofsky (Ed.), *Handbook of infant development* (pp. 393–438). New York: Wiley.

Friedman, S., & Stevenson, M. (1975). Developmental changes in the understanding of implied motion in two-dimensional pictures. *Child Development, 46,* 775–778.

Golinkoff, R. M., & Hirsh-Pasek, K. (1981). *A new approach to language comprehension.* Unpublished grant proposal to National Institute of Child Health and Human Development.

Golinkoff, R. M., Hirsh-Pasek, K., Cauley, K., & Gordon, L. (1987). The eyes have it: Lexical and syntactic comprehension in a new paradigm. *Journal of Child Language, 14,* 23–45.

Golinkoff, R. M., & Markessini, J. (1980). "Mommy sock": The child's understanding of possession as expressed in two-noun phrases. *Journal of Child Language, 7,* 119–136.

Hirsh-Pasek, K., Golinkoff, R. M., de Gaspe Beaubien, F., Fletcher, A., & Cauley, K. (1985, October). *In the beginning: One-word speakers comprehend word order.* Paper presented at the Boston Child Language Conference, Boston.

Hirsh-Pasek, K., Naigles, L., Golinkoff, R. M., Gleitman, L., & Gleitman, H. (1988, October). *Syntactic bootstrapping: Evidence from comprehension.* Paper presented at the Boston Child Language Conference, Boston.

Hyams, N. (1986). *Language acquisition and the theory of parameters.* Dordrecht, Holland: Reidel.

Jackendoff, R. (1986). *Semantics and cognition*. Cambridge, MA: MIT Press.

Just, M. A., & Carpenter, P. (1987). *The psychology of reading and language comprehension*. Boston: Allyn & Bacon.

Landau, B., & Gleitman, L. R. (1985). *Language and experience: Evidence from the blind child*. Cambridge, MA: Harvard University Press.

Maratsos, M., & Chalkley, M. A. (1980). The internal language of children's syntax: The ontogenesis and representation of syntactic categories. In K. Nelson (Ed.), *Children's language* (Vol. 2, pp. 127–214). ???.

McClelland, J. (1987). *The case for interactionism in language processing* (Tech. Rep. No. ONR-87-1). Pittsburgh: Carnegie Mellon University.

Naigles, L., Gleitman, L., & Gleitman, H. (in press). Acquiring the components of verb meaning through syntactic evidence. *Cognitive Psychology*.

Naigles, L., Hirsh-Pasek, K., & Golinkoff, R. M. (1989, October). *Comprehension of the passive by two-year-olds*. Paper presented at the Boston Child Language Conference, Boston.

Naigles, L., Hirsh-Pasek, K., Golinkoff, R., Gleitman, R., & Gleitman, H. (1987, October). *From linguistic form to meaning: Evidence for syntactic bootstrapping by two-year olds*. Paper presented at the Boston Child Language Conference, Boston.

Nelson, K. (1985). *Making sense: The acquisition of shared meaning*. Orlando, FL: Academic.

Rescorla, L. (1985, April). *Identifying language delay at age 2*. Paper presented at the meeting of the Society for Research in Child Development.

Rispoli, M., & Bloom, L. (1988). The conceptual origins of the transitive/intransitive distinction. Unpublished manuscript, University of California, Berkeley.

Roberts, K. (1983). Comprehension of production of word order in stage I. *Child Development, 54*, 443–449.

Roeper, T., & Williams, E. (Eds.). (1987). *Parameter setting*. Dordrecht, Holland: Reidel.

Sachs, J., & Truswell, L. (1978). Comprehension of two-word instructions by children in the one-word stage. *Journal of Child Language, 5*, 17–24.

Slobin, D. I. (1973). Cognitive prerequisites for the development of grammar. In C. A. Ferguson & D. I. Slobin (Eds.), *Studies of child language development* (pp. 175–207). New York: Holt, Rinehart & Winston.

Slobin, D. I. (1985). Cross-linguistic evidence for the language-making capacity. In D. I. Slobin (Ed.), *The crosslinguistic study of language acquisition, Vol 2* (pp. 1157–1256). Hillsdale, NJ: Lawrence Erlbaum Associates.

Slobin, D. I., & Bever, T. (1982). Children use canonical sentence schemas: A crosslinguistic study of word order and inflections. *Cognition, 12*, 229–265.

Spelke, E. (1979). Perceiving bimodally specified events in infancy. *Developmental Psychology, 15*, 626–636.

Straight, S. (1985). The importance and irreducibility of the comprehension/production dialectic. In G. McGregor (Ed.), *Language for hearers*. Oxford, England: Pergamon.

Wetstone, H., & Friedlander, B. (1973). The effect of word order on young children's responses to simple questions and commands. *Child Development, 44*, 734–740.

14 Recharting the Course of Language Acquisition: Studies in Elicited Production

Stephen Crain
University of Connecticut

Rosalind Thornton
Massachusetts Institute of Technology

A central goal of research on language acquisition is to explain the course of development: how the adult grammar is achieved on the basis of the linguistic input available to the learner. The knowledge that the learner brings to that task (including procedures for learning) often is called the language acquisition device (LAD). The linguistic input from parents and others is called the primary linguistic data (PLD). On the basis of these data, the LAD hypothesizes a series of grammars, the last of which is the adult grammar, or "final state." The entire process is represented schematically in Example 1:

Input (PLD) → LAD → Final State   (1)

Because language acquisition takes several years to complete, one thing to be explained is how child grammars change over time. The experiments presented in this chapter focus on one experimental design that has proven to be particularly useful in charting the time course of children's acquisition of syntax — the technique of elicited production. The syntactic constructions investigated in these experiments are not evident in children's spontaneous speech and, in some cases, have been found to pose difficulties for them in the usual tests of comprehension such as figure manipulation and picture verification. The technique of elicited production yields a new perspective on children's acquisition, one that is more in keeping with the precepts of current linguistic theory. Before turning to the laboratory, however, it is useful to consider several issues about the nature of language acquisition and note how these issues are resolved in current theory. As in any science, the data that warrant attention largely depend on the basic tenets of the theory itself. The present article focuses on children's knowledge of several syntactic phenomena that are central to the theory of Transformational/ Generative Grammar.

There are basic observations about children's linguistic development that any theory of acquisition must address. Prominent among these is the fact that every normal child converges on a grammatical system that is nearly equivalent to everyone else's, despite the considerable latitude in linguistic experience. The universality of language acquisition stands in striking contrast to the more limited attainment of cognitive skills of comparable complexity, such as the ability to perform arithmetic calculations. Another, perhaps less obvious, fact is that every child comes to know facts about the language for which there is no corresponding input. To appreciate this claim about "the poverty of the stimulus," it is necessary to consider how conceptions of the PLD and the properties of the final state have changed in recent years within the Generative framework.

LANGUAGE ACQUISITION IN THE ABSENCE OF EXPERIENCE

In the 1960s and early 1970s, the final state of language acquisition was viewed as a complex system of phrase structure rules and transformational rules. Researchers in language acquisition conceived the course of language development to be a gradual, piecemeal accrual of both kinds of rules. Developmental change was characterized as stepwise advancement from compact grammars with just a few rules, to more and more expansive grammars, with many rules. The PLD was the source for rules that were not yet contained in the learner's current grammar. It was assumed that learners induced new rules by hearing sentences in situations that indicated what meanings should be assigned to them. In other words, the PLD was (and still is) seen to consist of utterance/meaning pairs. At that time, it also was believed that wrong turns taken by the learner could be set right on the basis of the input. So, for example, if the learner produced a nonadult utterance in some situation or assigned a nonadult meaning to some utterance, these problems could be pinpointed and the relevant adjustments could be made, enabling the learner to converge on the adult grammar.

Despite the appeal of this early picture of acquisition, several changes in linguistic theory undermined it. Conceptually there was a shift from postulating a final state that incorporated a large number of rules to one that now contains, instead, a limited number of rules and principles that interact in an intricate fashion. There has been a corresponding shift in the conception of the initial state of the LAD. The linguistic rules and principles that belong to the initial state are referred to as Universal Grammar.

Recently, there has been a concerted effort to handle linguistic phenomena that involve the "movement" of constituents by a single rule: "Move alpha."[1] Some measure is needed, as a consequence, to prevent highly general rules like "Move alpha" from *overgenerating,* that is, from producing constructions that do not occur in the target language. The measure that is taken is to hold overgeneration in check with negative statements, or *constraints.* Constraints spell out the circumstances in which the general rules and principles are not operative.[2] It generally is assumed that the constraints are part of the initial state (Universal Grammar). The reasoning turns on two observations: (a) the fact that constraints are negative, and (b) the fact that the PLD does not contain "negative evidence." Together, these observations conspire to create what often is called "the logical problem of language acquisition."

To understand the logical problem of language acquisition, it is useful to introduce some notation. To begin, a language is seen as the acquisition of a mapping between an unbounded set of utterances and their potential meanings. This is represented in Example 2:

> < utterance1, meaning1 >   (2)
> < utterance2, meaning2 >
> < utterance3, meaning3 >
> •
> •
> •

Another aspect of the mapping is the information encoded in constraints. Roughly, constraints fall into two classes. One type of constraint informs the learner that an utterance, although grammatical, cannot have a particular interpretation. Consider the interpretations that can be given to the pronoun *he* in the sentences in Example 3:

(a)   John thinks he is clever.   (3)
(b)   He thinks John is clever.
(c)   After he came in, John said something clever.

Note that in the first sentence ("John thinks he is clever") the pronoun can be interpreted as referring to the individual named by the proper name *John.* However, in the second sentence ("He thinks John is clever") *he* cannot be *John.* The third sentence shows that this constraint on corefer-

---

[1]Sections entitled Structure Dependence, *Wanna* Contraction, and Long-Distance Wh-Movement discuss movement in the formation of Wh-questions.

[2]A word of clarification is in order. For a constraint to have the desired effect, it need not contain a negative term. Expressions such as "must" and "always" also serve to constrain the language that otherwise would be generated by the highly general principles and rules (Fodor & Crain, 1987).

ence does not depend solely on the fact that the pronoun appears before the proper name; in Example 3(c) *he* comes before *John,* yet coreference is possible. Coreference is ruled out in the second example because the pronoun and the proper name are in a particular structural relationship.[3] This type of constraint on interpretations can be represented in the notation of utterance/meaning pairs as follows:

$$< \text{utterance, *meaning} > \qquad (4)$$

Another class of constraints informs the learner that certain forms of expression are not permissible in the grammar. Consider the paradigm in Examples 5 and 6:

(a)   Who do you want to help?   (5)
(b)   Who do you wanna help?

(a)   Who do you want to help you?   (6)
(b)   *Who do you wanna help you?

Every adult is implicitly aware that contraction is permitted in Example 5(b), but not 6(b). (The reason for this is discussed later in the section entitled *Wanna* Contraction.) On the assumption that the input to children consists only of the grammatical sentences in the paradigm (and their associated meanings), it is difficult to see how children could learn where contraction is not admissible. To make matters worse, children might well be tempted to produce ungrammatical utterances like Example 6(b) on analogy with the grammatical ones, if these were not ruled out by some aspect of Universal Grammar. Knowledge of negative facts of this kind can be represented as follows:

$$< \text{*utterance, meaning} > \qquad (7)$$

To summarize the discussion so far, Universal Grammar views the task of language learning as the acquisition of mappings of utterances and meanings. The adult mappings (final state) include knowledge of certain restrictions on the meanings that can be mapped onto utterances as well as restrictions on the utterances that can be used to express meanings. This

---

[3]In terms of current theory, the pronoun in Example 3(b) "c-commands" the proper name. That part of the theory that deals with coreference relations is Binding Theory. Binding Theory contains a constraint called Condition C that disallows coreference between a proper name (or any "referring" expression) and any noun phrase that c-commands it. One NP c-commands another if there is a path between them that goes up to the nearest branching node above the first, and then down to the second. Children's knowledge of Condition C of the Binding Theory was investigated by Crain and McKee (1985), who found that children as young as 3 years correctly "rejected" coreference in sentences like Example 3(b) 87% of the time, but accepted coreference in sentences like Example 3(c) equally often.

knowledge is encoded in constraints. The problem for the learner is that there are no data available in the environment corresponding to the kinds of negative facts that constraints account for. In the case of *wanna* contraction, for example, the learner would seem to require information about which utterances do not occur in the target language. In the literature on language learnability, this kind of input is called "negative evidence." It is widely accepted, however, that negative evidence is not systematically available to children (see Brown & Hanlon, 1970; Fodor & Crain, 1987; Grimshaw & Pinker, 1989; Wexler & Culicover, 1980).

The argument from the "poverty of the stimulus" can now be properly appreciated: The adult grammar contains a set of constraints; but constraints are negative statements, and the only apparent source of data by which constraints could be learned (negative evidence) is not available. The situation confronting the language learner is depicted in Example 8.

$$\text{Input} \rightarrow \text{LAD} \rightarrow \text{Final State} \tag{8}$$

$$<u,m> \qquad <u,m>$$
$$<u,*m>$$
$$<*u,m>$$

In other words, the logical problem of language acquisition is that the data available underdetermine what the learner comes to know. As a solution to this problem, current linguistic theory supposes that the constraints that characterize the final state also characterize the initial state. That is, the constraints are not learned; rather, they are innately specified as part of Universal Grammar (the LAD). This circumvents the problem of learning negative facts without negative evidence.

There are two empirical consequences of this innateness hypothesis that deserve further comment. First, any principle that is innate should appear in every natural language (except where it is "unlearned" on the basis of exposure to available utterance/meaning pairs). A second consequence of innateness is the expectation that children should adhere to constraints early in the course of language development. Some explanation would clearly be called for if a putatively innate property is not respected in the language of children until well after the relevant lexical items have been learned. The purpose of the experiments reported in this chapter is to investigate young children's knowledge of several purportedly innate constraints on what can be said, including the constraint on *wanna* contraction. The experiments test children's knowledge of one aspect of the mapping of utterance/meaning pairs for which there is no corresponding input: <*utterance, meaning>.

EXPERIMENTAL RESEARCH: THE ELICITED
PRODUCTION TASK

Until recently, the literature on children's development of syntax relied almost exclusively on data from children's spontaneous speech and on the results of experimental tests of children's comprehension of sentences. There have been only a handful of elicited production studies (e.g., Bellugi, 1971; Hamburger & Crain, 1982; Tager-Flusberg, 1982). This is somewhat surprising because the method of elicited production is a more direct way to tap children's linguistic competence. Correct combinations of words are not likely to come about by accident; as long as children's productions are appropriate and closely attuned to the context, even a single successful production of the target utterance is a compelling argument for linguistic competence.

Despite these virtues, it is clear why researchers have rarely sought to elicit production data from children. As Ferreiro, Othenin-Girard, Chipman, and Sinclair (1976) put the problem: "Experiments in which children are asked to produce utterances seem on the whole to be free of the hazards of comprehension studies. However, once again, we come up against an obstacle that is due to the nature of language itself: how to construct a situation that will obligatorily give rise to a certain sentence pattern? No such situations exist: thanks to the very rules that make language what it is, perfectly adequate and grammatically correct descriptions in many different forms can be given for any event or situation" (p. 231). Notwithstanding this caveat, it has proven possible to elicit certain target structures by careful adherence to two methodological principles. First, the presuppositions associated with the construction must be satisfied; otherwise, children will not produce anything like the construction that is targeted. In addition, one must ensure that the experimental situations are not amenable to simpler, alternative ways of expressing the same message. In other words, the contexts that are devised should be uniquely felicitous for the construction under investigation. By observing these prerequisites, the studies presented in the next section explore several linguistic phenomena that have significant bearing on language learnability in the absence of experience.

Structure Dependence

Perhaps the most fundamental constraint in the Generative framework is structure dependence (Chomsky, 1971). It is a basic tenet of the theory that all grammatical principles are structure dependent. Roughly, a linguistic hypothesis is structure dependent if it applies to abstract properties of sentences, such as constituent structure. A structure-independent hypothesis, on the other hand, operates on sentences construed as strings of words, rather than on their structural representations. Because structure-independent hypotheses apply to ordered strings, they invoke linear relations like "first," "left-most," and so on. This contrasts with structure-dependent properties, which invoke structural relations like "main clause," "subordinate clause," and "subject NP." According to the innateness hypothesis, then, children invariably should apply structure-dependent principles in the course of language acquisition, even if their linguistic experience is limited such that it is also amenable to structure-independent hypotheses.

The paradigm case of structure dependence is the formation of yes/no questions. A linear (structure-independent) strategy for generating yes/no questions might be as follows:

Move the *first* "is" (or "can", "will", etc.) to the front
of the sentence.   (9)

This principle produces correct question forms for many simple declarative sentences, as in Example 10. As Chomsky (1971) pointed out, what is so striking about the constraint of structure dependence is that it rules out hypotheses that appear to be computationally simpler than is necessary to capture the facts about question formation in simple sentences.

John is tall.	Is John tall?	(10)
Mary can sing very well.	Can Mary sing very well?	

Given the reasonable assumption that children encounter simple sentences first, at least some children might be expected to adopt the structure-independent hypothesis in Example 9, were it not precluded by Universal Grammar. Notice, though, that these children would produce incorrect question forms when they began to ask more complex questions, for instance, questions that contain a relative clause. Consider Example 11 below. Applying the structure-independent rule to it results in the ungrammatical question in Example 12. The correct question form in Example 13 comes from the application of a structure-dependent rule that treats *the man who is running* as a single constituent. It is this constituent, the entire subject noun phrase, that must be inverted with the first auxiliary verb in the main clause, to give the correct question form. This transformational operation is called Subject/Auxiliary inversion.

The man who is running is bald.	(11)
*Is the man who __ running is bald?	(12)
Is the man who is running __ bald?	(13)

In order to test whether children give structure-independent responses such as Example 12, an elicited production procedure was devised to evoke complex yes/no questions from children. The procedure was to preface a

declarative like Example 11 with the carrier phrase "Ask (someone) if . . . ,"
as in Example 14.

Ask Jabba if the man who is running is bald.   (14)

In a study by Crain and Nakayama (1987), 30 3- to 5-year-old children
responded to requests like Example 14 by posing yes/no questions to Jabba
the Hutt, a figure from "Star Wars" who was being manipulated by one of
the experimenters. Following each question, Jabba was shown a picture and
would respond "yes" or "no." This game was used to see whether children
would produce incorrect question forms like Example 12 in response to
prompts that contained a relative clause, such as Example 14.

The outcome was exactly as predicted: Children never produced incorrect
question forms like Example 12. Thus, a structure-independent strategy was
not adopted in spite of its simplicity and in spite of the fact that its
application would yield a correct form for many sentences. The findings of
this study, then, lend support to one of the central claims of Universal
Grammar, that the initial state of the language faculty contains structure
dependence as an inherent property. It is worth underscoring the point that
system-internal constraints such as structure dependence are efficacious in
forestalling wrong turns that a learner might otherwise take. These constraints obviate the need for negative evidence which would be required if
learners did in fact produce ungrammatical question forms.

On the methodological side, two further characteristics of the data should
be noted. First, 60% of children's responses overall were precisely the
utterances that were targeted, and 80% of the responses by the older
children were grammatical variations of the targeted utterances. In short,
this technique was quite successful at narrowing down children's responses
within manageable limits, and narrowing them down to ones that are telling
with respect to language learnability.

Wanna Contraction

The elicited production paradigm also proved to be a useful tool in
exploring children's knowledge of the constraint on *wanna* contraction. The
task in this study required children to ask "Wh-questions," that is, questions
that begin with a Wh-phrase such as *who, which one, what,* and so on.
Wh-questions are interesting because it is hypothesized that they involve the
"movement" of a Wh-phrase from its original location (in the underlying
syntactic representation: D-structure) to sentence-initial position. It is
further hypothesized that a record of the movement is maintained in the
form of a *trace* that remains at the site of extraction. For example, in
Example 15(a) the Wh-phrase *who* has been extracted from its original
position, as the object of the verb *help*. By contrast, the Wh-phrase in

Example 16(a) has been moved from its original position as subject of the infinitival clause, leaving a trace *t* behind, between *want* and *to*.

   (a)   Who do you want to help t?   (object extraction)   (15)
   (b)   Who do you wanna help?

   (a)   Who do you want t to help you?   (subject extraction)   (16)
   (b)   *Who do you wanna help you?

The inadmissibility of contraction in Example 16(b) is assumed to derive from principles of Universal Grammar that prohibit two words from contracting together when a Wh-trace intervenes. In Example 15(b) the Wh-phrase *who* has been moved from object position, so the trace that is left behind does not block contraction. On the assumption that children are not informed about where contraction is illicit, it has been proposed that the principle underlying the grammatical constraint on *wanna* contraction is an innate component of Universal Grammar. This leads us to expect children's adherence to the constraint early in the course of language acquisition. To test this prediction, it was critical that children exhibit a preference to contract *want* and *to*. This was a reasonable expectation, though, given the findings of previous research that have led to the proposal that both children and adults use reduced forms whenever possible (Chomsky, 1981; Hammouda, 1988). In the present case, a preference for reduced forms would be revealed in the frequency count of contracted forms in extracting from the object position of the infinitival clause, as in Example 15(b). Comparing this result with the proportion of contracted forms in extracting from subject position, as in Example 16(b), would indicate whether or not children's grammars contained the putatively universal constraint on *wanna* contraction.[4]

Two experimenters were needed to elicit the relevant Wh-questions. One solicited the child's help in finding out information about rats. The child's help was sought in this task because the rat (a puppet) in the experimental workspace was too timid to talk to grown-ups. The protocols for the *wanna* contraction paradigm set up situations with three different characters, one of which becomes the focus for eliciting a question. By setting an array of characters in front of the child, the pragmatics of the situation demand that the child ask a "full" question such as "Who do you want to eat the cookie?", instead of a partial question such as "Who do you want?" Example 17 is typical of the protocols used to elicit questions that involve

---

[4]Although children's systematic control of this subtle contrast could appear in spontaneous production data, the crucial situations probably occur quite rarely in children's experience, so it is difficult to gather data in sufficient quantity to reach firm conclusions. By contrast, the elicitation technique can be used to generate an ample database to examine these contrasts for any child.

extraction from the subject of the infinitival clause (where contraction is not permissible in the adult grammar).

Experimenter: There are three guys in this story; Cookie Monster, a dog, and this baby. One of them gets to take a walk, one gets to take a nap, and one gets to eat a cookie. And the rat gets to choose who does each thing. So, *one* gets to take a walk, right? Ask Ratty who he wants.   (17)
Child: *Who do you want to take a walk?*
Rat: I want the dog to take a walk.

Both subject and object extraction questions were elicited from 21 children, who ranged in age from 2 years, 10 months to 5 years, 5 months (mean = 4 years, 3 months). The results were clearly in accord with the theory of Universal Grammar. Nineteen children successfully produced full Wh-questions. In the object extraction questions by these children, where contraction is possible in the adult grammar, 59% contained contracted forms. By contrast, in asking subject extraction questions, only one child's utterances contained any contracted forms. In short, the data provide strong presumptive evidence that children are guided by the universal constraint that sanctions contraction in certain contexts and not others.

Long-Distance Wh-Movement

Another elicited production study investigated children's knowledge of a different kind of Wh-question: "long-distance" questions with extraction of the Wh-phrase from a tensed subordinate clause. These questions are subject to another constraint, called Subjacency. For one thing, the Subjacency constraint prohibits Wh-phrases from moving in one fell swoop over two sentence boundaries.[5] An example of this kind of illegal maneuver is illustrated in Example 18. Rather, the Wh-phrase must pass through the intermediate COMP position in transit to its final destination. This movement of the Wh-phrase from COMP to COMP is depicted in Example

---

[5]More specifically, Subjacency prohibits the direct (nonstop) movement of constituents across more than one NP or S. In some instances, violations of the Subjacency constraint result in ill-formed linguistic expressions, that is <*utterance, meaning> pairs. For example, the sentence in (i) violates Subjacency because the Wh-phrase *what* crosses both NP and S in a single bound.

(i)   *[$_{Comp}$ What [$_S$do you believe [$_{NP}$the claim that Cookie Monster eats t?

The violation of Subjacency in (i) cannot be "saved" by COMP to COMP movement, because movement to the nearest COMP crosses both NP and S. Although the intended meaning of the utterance in (i) is clear, it cannot be expressed in these words. Thus, the Subjacency constraint results in another negative fact that can be represented in the notation of utterance/meaning pairs as <*utterance, meaning>.

19.[6] Note that legal derivations of long-distance Wh-movement require two traces, one at the original extraction site, and one in the intermediate COMP.

*[Comp What [s do you think [Comp [s Cookie Monster eats t? (18)

[Comp What [s do you think [Comp t [s Cookie Monster eats t? (19)

Note that on the surface the ill-formed derivation in Example 18 cannot be distinguished from the well-formed derivation in Example 19. This is because the trace in the intermediate COMP position is not phonetically realized in English. However, in other languages such as dialects of German and Romani (McDaniel, 1986), a copy of the fronted Wh-phrase may appear in this position. A surprising outcome of the present study was the finding that several children learning English produced similar questions (see later examples).

Another constraint on long-distance Wh-questions is illustrated in Examples 20 and 21. A comparison of the examples shows that the complementizer *that* is optional if the Wh-phrase originated in object position of the embedded clause. Notice, however, that the complementizer must be omitted if the Wh-phrase originated in subject position, as in Example 21.[7] If the complementizer is not omitted, the sentence is ungrammatical (although it can be easily understood). In the notation developed earlier, children's knowledge of this constraint would be represented as < *utterance, meaning >.

(a) What do you think pigs eat t? (20)
(b) What do you think that pigs eat t?

(a) What do you think t eats pigs? (21)
(b) *What do you think that t eats pigs?

An elicited production study was designed to investigate children's knowledge of this constraint. This study called for only a slight modification of the game used in the *wanna* contraction study, so both studies were administered

---

[6]Long-distance extraction from infinitival clauses as in *wanna* contraction must proceed from COMP to COMP, in order to conform to the requirements of Subjacency. The trace left in the intermediate COMP has no bearing on the *wanna* contraction facts, however.

[7]The complementizer *that* must be absent in Example 21(b) in order for the trace to be "properly governed," according to the Empty Category Principle of Universal Grammar, which requires empty categories to be properly governed (Chomsky, 1981, 1986). In subject extraction cases like Example 21(b), "proper government" is a structural relationship that must hold between the trace of Wh-movement at the original extraction site and the trace left in the intermediate COMP as the Wh-phrase made its way to the sentence-initial COMP. The presence of a complementizer in the intermediate COMP position nullifies proper government, in violation of the Empty Category Principle.

in one session to the same 21 children. To elicit questions like Examples 20 and 21, the rat was asked by the child to make a series of guesses, for example, about what pigs like to eat, what Cookie Monster likes to eat, what the child had hidden in a box, and so forth. Protocols such as Example 22 were designed to elicit both subject and object extraction questions.

Experimenter: In this game the rat has to guess what Cookie Monster eats, and what is in the box, OK? But before we let the rat guess, let's make sure we know the answers ourselves. (*Experimenter whispers, so the rat supposedly can't hear*) Cookie Monster eats . . .   (22)
Child: *Cookies*
Experimenter: In the box there are . . .
Child: *Marbles*
Experimenter: Good, let's ask about Cookie Monster first. *We* know that Cookie Monster eats cookies, right? Ask the rat what *he* thinks.
Child: *What do you think Cookie Monster eats?*
Rat: I think Cookie Monster eats ants.
Experimenter: Ants! That's a silly rat! Well, let's see what the rat says about the next one. Let's ask about the box. *We* know that there are marbles in the box, right? Ask the rat what *he* thinks.
Child: *What do you think's in that box?*
Rat: A watermelon?

It is worth noting that the experimenter's lead-in ("We know what Cookie Monster likes to eat. Ask the rat what he thinks") contains several clues about the question that is being targeted, including several words that could be of service to the child in forming long-distance questions. Note, however, that the experimenter's lead-in does not itself contain a long-distance question. This must be constructed by the child on the basis of the available cues, a feat of astronomical proportions unless the critical structures were accessible in the child's grammar.

Unfortunately, children consistently chose to delete complementizers in their Wh-questions in this study, presumably due to their penchant for reduced forms. Therefore, their knowledge of the contrast between Examples 20 and 21 could not be ascertained. Nevertheless, the situations were successful in eliciting long-distance questions.[8] Questions with extraction

---

[8]Analysis of children's spontaneous productions reveal relatively few instances of long-distance movement. Apparently, only 16 instances of long-distance Wh-movement appear in the Brown corpus of Adam (MacWhinney & Snow, 1985) between the ages of 2 and 4 years (de Villiers, Roeper, & Vainikka, 1990). Moreover, all of Adam's long-distance questions are instances of object extraction. By contrast, the children in this study produced questions of

from both subject and object position were elicited from 19 of the 21 child subjects, who ranged in age from 2 years, 10 months to 5 years, 5 months (mean = 4 years, 3 months).[9]

Another finding was quite unexpected. Some children's productions of long-distance questions contained a Wh-phrase in the intermediate COMP, as well as in sentence-initial COMP position.[10] Questions with the medial-Wh occurred with both extraction from object and subject. Some illustrations are given in Example 23.[11]

> What do you think what Cookie Monster eats? (K.P. 5;0)   (23)
> Who do you think who Grover wants to hug? (T.A. 4;9)
> What do you think what the baby drinks? (M.W. 3;3)
> What do you think what's in that box? (M.W. 3;3)
> What do you think really what's in that can? (K.R. 3;9)

These questions with a medial-Wh indicate that children's phrasal structure includes the COMP position, because this position is "filled" by the extra Wh-phrase. As in dialects of German and Romani, the grammars of these children allow the trace to be phonetically realized. Finally, because this fortuitous error demonstrates that children move Wh-phrases COMP to COMP in long-distance questions, it demonstrates their adherence to the Subjacency constraint.[12]

---

both types and, based on the frequency of grammatical errors (e.g., resumptive pronouns), it would appear that children actually have less difficulty with subject extraction than with object extraction. An asymmetry in this direction is reported in the aphasia literature, and in the literature on reading disability.

[9]The one child who failed to produce any long-distance questions was 3 years, 7 months of age. Another child produced only two of the targeted structures, but each of the remaining 19 children produced at least five long-distance questions.

[10]Children only used medial-Wh questions when extracting from tensed clauses. In the study of extraction from infinitival clauses, children never asked corresponding questions with a medial-Wh, such as "Who do you want *who* to help you?" This contrast appears to hold true in languages that allow a medial-Wh.

[11]To our knowledge, this error has not been reported in the literature. This is hardly surprising, however, given the infrequence of long-distance Wh-questions in young children's spontaneous speech. Nevertheless, the medial-Wh form is quite systematic in the speech of children who generate it. This is evidence that it is truly the product of their grammars, and does not reflect performance limitations.

[12]A follow-up study was conducted on a child who consistently used medial-Wh questions. In addition to questions beginning with "who" or "what," other Wh-phrases like "which Smurf" and "which animal" were evoked. The results confirm the hypothesis that the medial-Wh is an overt "trace" of long-distance movement. The following sentences are illustrative of this child's Wh-questions:

(i) Which Smurf do you think *who* is in the can?
(ii) Which animal do you think *what* says "woof woof"?

These examples show that the medial-Wh bears only the syntactic features of a Wh-trace, and does not exhibit other properties marked on the full Wh-phrase, such as Smurfhood.

Experiment on Rightward Contraction

In the experiment on long-distance movement, children often produced utterances like Example 24.

Who do you think's in the box?   (24)

cf. *Who do you wanna help you?

Sentences like this represent an apparent counterexample to the generalization that the trace of Wh-movement blocks contraction. Example 24 is clearly a well-formed sentence, so contraction must be admissible. It appears, however, that contraction takes place across the trace of a Wh-phrase, in violation of the constraint that prohibited *wanna* contraction in certain sentences (see *Wanna* Contraction section).

This apparent conflict between principles has received critical attention in the literature. A particularly insightful explanation was offered by Bresnan (1971), who proposed that contraction occurs to the left in some cases and to the right in others. According to Bresnan, *wanna* contraction is an instance of leftward contraction; contraction of *want* and *to* is inhibited whenever a trace is to the left of *to*. By contrast, Bresnan argued that *is* contracts with material to its right, despite orthographic appearances to the contrary; *is*-contraction is permitted when the trace of a Wh-phrase appears to the left of *is*, as indicated in Example 25.

Who do you think t is in the box?   (25)

An orthography that conformed with Bresnan's proposal would represent *is*-contraction as in Example 26, with *is* contracting onto the word *in*.

Who do you think s'in the box?   (26)

The following examples provide further support for Bresnan's (1971) treatment of *is*-contraction. These examples show that when the trace of a Wh-phrase intervenes between *is* and material to its right, contraction is inhibited.

(a)   Do you know what that is doing t up there?   (27)
(b)   Do you know what that's doing up there?

(a)   Do you know what that is t up there?   (28)
(b)   *Do you know what that's up there?

If it could be shown that children are treating Example 24 as an instance of rightward contraction, this would reinforce the conclusion that children respect the prohibition on contraction across a Wh-trace. It is important to establish, then, that children know that *is*-contraction cannot occur if a trace intervenes between *is* and a lexical item that follows it.

To test this aspect of children's linguistic knowledge, a study was devised to encourage children to formulate questions like those in Examples 27 and 28. As in the previous studies, the prediction of universal grammar is that children will not produce ungrammatical questions such as Example 28(b), despite the absence of relevant evidence from the environment. The target productions were evoked using protocols such as those in Example 29. Notice that the experimenter is careful not to use contracted forms, so as not to provide any clues about where contraction is and is not permitted.

Experimenter: Ask Ratty if he knows what that is doing up there.   (29)
Child: *Do you know what that's doing up there?*
Rat: It seems to be sleeping.
Experimenter: Ask Ratty if he knows what that is up there.
Child: *Do you know what that is up there?*
Rat: A monkey.

Twelve children were tested. They ranged in age from 2 years, 11 months to 4 years, 5 months, with an average age of 3 years, 8 months. The findings are completely in accord with the expectations of linguistic theory. Questions involving rightward contraction were elicited from all of the children, and there was not a single instance of contraction where it is ruled out in the adult grammar. It is reasonable to conclude that children's questions with contraction in the previous experiment should not be counted as violations of the constraint prohibiting contraction across a trace. By overriding their strong tendency to use reduced forms wherever their grammars permit, the present study offers further evidence of children's early knowledge of a linguistic principle for which they have no corresponding experience.

CHARTING A NEW COURSE FOR LANGUAGE ACQUISITION

Recent advances in linguistic theory have led to an increase in the amount of linguistic knowledge that is hypothesized to be innately specified. A linguistic property is seen to be a good candidate for being innate if it appears universally, and if it is mastered in the absence of evidence for it in the linguistic input. It is also reasonable, though it is not logically necessary, to expect innate properties to emerge early in linguistic development. These considerations make it important to understand why language acquisition appears to take so long and why children appear to take so many wrong turns in the course of development.

Much of the evidence for gradual acquisition comes from longitudinal studies of children's spontaneous productions. Transcripts of children's speech seem to suggest that complex syntactic structures (such as long distance Wh-questions) are mastered quite late. This is surprising given the strong assistance they receive from Universal Grammar. Of course, the absence of a construction in children's spontaneous speech is not incontrovertible evidence of its absence in their grammars, presumably because the crucial situations that call for complex constructions occur only rarely.

Children's apparent failures to stay on course also have been uncovered, however, in tests of their comprehension of complex sentences, using tasks such as figure manipulation and picture verification. These recalcitrant data also can be questioned, because the interpretation of imperfect performance in any psycholinguistic experiment is complicated by the existence of a variety of factors extraneous to syntax. Successful comprehension requires children to parse the test sentence, to plan and execute an appropriate response, to accommodate any unmet presuppositions, and so on. Unless it can be shown that the difficulties children encounter are not attributable to one or more of these factors, it is premature to attribute children's imperfect performance to their lack of syntactic knowledge. It has been demonstrated in several studies that failure to control the nonsyntactic demands of experimental tasks were the source of children's errors, since the errors disappeared or were greatly reduced in tasks that simplified these additional burdens on language processing (Crain & Fodor, in press; Hamburger & Crain 1982, 1984).

These observations point out the need for additional sources of data in assessing young children's syntactic knowledge. Focusing on the methodology of elicited production, this chapter offers evidence of children's early mastery of several complex linguistic phenomena, including purportedly innate constraints. The evidence substantiates the claim that children's comprehension failures in previous research were due to performance limitations, and did not reflect their grammatical competence. If the results of the present research are any indication, young children have a great deal more linguistic knowledge under their belts than they exhibit in the usual tests of comprehension or in their spontaneous productions. The findings of these studies, therefore, paint a new picture of the course of linguistic development, one that is more in keeping with current linguistic theory.

ACKNOWLEDGEMENTS

This research was supported in part by a Program Project Grant to Haskins Laboratories from the National Institute of Child Health and Human Development (HD-01994). Special thanks go to Charlotte Madison and the teachers and children at the University of Connecticut Child Labs, Storrs, CT. We also would like to thank Janet Dean Fodor, Henry Hamburger, Cecile McKee, Mineharu Nakayama, Jaya Sarma, and Donald Shankweiler for their contributions to the research reported here.

REFERENCES

Bellugi, U. (1971). Simplification in children's language. In R. Huxley & E. Ingram (Eds.), *Language acquisition: Models and methods* (pp. 95–119). London: Academic.

Bresnan, J. (1971). Contraction and the transformational cycle. Bloomington, IN: Indiana University Linguistics Club.

Brown, R., & Hanlon, C. (1970). Derivational complexity and order of acquisition in child speech. In J. R. Hayes (Ed.), *Cognition and the development of language* (pp. 11–54). New York: Wiley.

Chomsky, N. (1971). Problems of knowledge and freedom. New York: Pantheon.

Chomsky, N. (1981). *Lectures on government and binding.* Dordrecht, Holland: Foris.

Chomsky, N. (1986). *Knowledge of language: Its nature, origin, and use.* New York: Praeger.

Crain, S., & Fodor, J. D. (in press). Competence and performance. In E. Dromi (Ed.), *Language and cognition: A developmental perspective.* Norwood, NJ: Ablex.

Crain, S., & McKee, C. (1985). Acquisition of structural restrictions on anaphora. In S. Berman, J.-W. Choe, & J. McDonough (Eds.), *Proceedings of the North Eastern Linguistic Society* (Vol. 16, pp. 94–111). Amherst, MA: GLSA.

Crain, S., & Nakayama, M. (1987). Structure-dependence in grammar formation. *Language, 63,* 522–543.

de Villiers, J., Roeper, T., & Vainikka, A. (1990). The acquisition of long-distance rules. In L. Frazier and J. de Villiers, (Eds.), *Language processing and language acquisition.* Dordrecht, Holland: Kluwer Academic Publishers.

Ferreiro, E., Othenin-Girard, C., Chipman, H., & Sinclair, H. (1976). How do children handle relative clauses? *Archives de Psychologie, XLV* (3), 229–266.

Fodor, J. D., & Crain, S. (1987). Simplicity and generality of rules in language acquisition. In B. MacWhinney (Ed.), *Mechanisms of language acquisition: Proceedings of the 20th Annual Carnegie-Mellon Conference on Cognition* (pp. 35–64). Hillsdale, NJ: Lawrence Erlbaum Associates.

Grimshaw, J., & Pinker, S. (1989). Positive and negative evidence in language acquisition. (Reply to: The child's trigger experience: "Degree-0" learnability. Target article by D. Lightfoot). *Behavioral and Brain Sciences, 12*(2), 334.

Hamburger, H., & Crain, S. (1982). Relative acquisition. In S. Kuczaj II (Ed.), *Language development 1: Syntax and semantics* (pp. 245–274). Hillsdale, NJ: Lawrence Erlbaum Associates.

Hamburger, H., & Crain, S. (1984). Acquisition of cognitive compiling. *Cognition, 17,* 101–136.

Hammouda, S. (1988). *Learnability issues in the acquisition of the dative alternation in English.* Unpublished doctoral dissertation, University of Connecticut, Storrs.

MacWhinney B., & Snow, C. (1985). The child language data exchange system. *Journal of Child Language, 12,* 271–296.

McDaniel, D. (1986). *Conditions on Wh-chains.* Unpublished doctoral dissertation, City University of New York.

Tager-Flusberg, H. (1982). The development of relative clauses in child speech. *Papers and Reports on Child Language Development, 21,* 104–111.

Wexler, K., & Culicover, P. (1980). *Formal principles of language acquisition.* Cambridge, MA: MIT Press.

15 Motor Aspects of Emergent Speech: A Dynamic Approach

Esther Thelen
Indiana University

The utterance of even a simple one-syllable word requires the coordination in time and space of over 70 muscles and 8 to 10 different body parts, ranging from the diaphragm to the lips. The acquisition of language is considered the preeminent achievement of human cognition, and motor coordination and control of the articulators is an essential component of this developmental landmark.

In this chapter, I view the motor aspects of early speech in the larger context of early motor development. There has been considerable research on infant prespeech and its transition to referential language by scholars interested in early language. I approach this transition from a somewhat different perspective by assuming that speech motor skills develop by the same general principles as other motor skills. Thus, I attempt to embed what is known about prespeech in a more general theoretical framework of the organization and the nature of change in the motor system.

To do this, I briefly introduce a theoretical perspective that addresses how complex systems like the human motor system change over time. These principles of *dynamical systems* are very general and can be applied both to the assembly of behavior in real time, that is, how the articulators cooperate to produce phonemes, syllables, and words, as well as to the emergence of behavior in ontogenetic time, that is, how infants progress from vegetative to speech sounds. Dynamical systems are especially powerful because they focus not just on the products or end states, but on the processes that give rise to new forms in behavior and development.

The overall argument of the chapter is that there are three ongoing, parallel, and interacting processes by which the prespeech sounds of the infant are transformed into intelligible speech. First, there are natural categories of sounds that emerge when the oral, facial, respiratory, and ingestive apparatus at particular stages of anatomical and functional maturation are combined and activated. Second, perceptual biases make infants sensitive to certain features of the sound and visual environment and to the proprioception of their own vocal behavior. And third, infants select from the universe of possible natural categories of sounds by matching their own motor output to the sounds and sights of the natural language environment. The core assumption here is that speech coordination is in principle no different from other motor skills that arise as the actor continually matches the task requirements with the self-organizing capabilities of the perception-action system.

WHAT IS COORDINATION?

Movements are considered to be coordinated when the activities of the participating elements are related to one another in space and time in an ordered and regular way. For speech, this means that the lips, tongue, jaw, vocal apparatus, and diaphram all must work together precisely to produce a rapid stream of phonemes with sufficient invariance to be understood as natural language. In the development and control of skilled actions such as speech, the central nervous system must deal with a fundamental dualism. At the same time that the final gesture must have a functional acoustic or topological invariance (the aria or the pas de deux is always immediately recognizable), it is also true that actions are never performed twice in exactly the same way. The muscles and joints of the effector systems can be assembled in a potentially enormous number of combinations, yet the motor performance always has both a commonality or invariant aspect and a task-specific flexibility (Bernstein, 1967).

As mentioned previously, vocal language requires that the speaker produce a stream of phonemes with sufficient invariance to be perceived by the listener with high accuracy over a wide variety of speaker contexts, such as eating, chewing gum, a stuffy nose, and so on, and acoustic environments, such as noisy cocktail parties, which may call for enhanced articulation or phonation. Recent research on adult speech coordination suggests that the central nervous system accomplishes this remarkable feat of preserving the acoustic stream in the face of continually variable task demands by planning at the level of the task rather than prescribing the specific participating elements (Fowler, Rubin, Remez, & Turvey, 1980). For example, Kelso, Tuller, V-Bateson, and Fowler (1984) had speakers produce single utterances, /baeb/ or /baez/, in a series of trials during which the jaw was occasionally and unpredictably tugged downward while moving upward toward the final /b/ or /z/. The acoustic output of the perturbed trials could not be distinguished from the control trials. Speakers compensated relatively immediately (within 20–30 msec) for the mechanical disturbance to the jaw in a task-specific manner. For the /baeb/ syllable, when lip closure is crucial, subjects increased the upper lip activity and had normal tongue activity. For the /baez/ syllable, where the final sound is produced by tongue-palate constriction, subjects increased tongue activity, but not lip activity.

This experiment and others like it (see Abbs, Gracco, & Cole, 1984) demonstrate an essential cooperativity of the speech articulators that allows a higher level goal (the output syllable) to be accomplished by a variety of task-specific routes. The speed of these compensations is an order of magnitude smaller than those associated with traditional reaction time processes, suggesting that this flexibility must be at a relatively "low" level of organization. Thus, once the speaker plans for the intended acoustic goal, the subunits can be rapidly adjusted to the demands of the task.

A DYNAMICAL SYSTEMS INTERPRETATION OF COORDINATED ACTION

This duality of invariance and flexibility that characterizes all natural actions means that coordination cannot be accomplished by highly specific "hard-wired" connections to the motor effectors. Instead, dynamical theories view motor systems as belonging to a larger class of complex systems that produce patterned behavior (Kelso, Holt, Kugler, & Turvey, 1980; Kugler, Kelso, & Turvey, 1980; Schöner & Kelso, 1988). There is increasingly wide interest in physics, chemistry, mathematics, and biology in the behavior of systems made up of very many component parts that change over time (see, e.g., Kelso, Mandell, & Shlesinger, 1988). Under certain energetic conditions, those of thermodynamic nonequilibrium, such systems can produce pattern and order in a seemingly spontaneous manner. Crystals, clouds, laser lights, and fluid flow patterns are all examples of order emerging from the dynamic interplay of the elements alone. There is no need to invoke a template, prescription, or code specifying the pattern, and indeed in these physical systems, no one would do so.

In complex biological systems, however, it commonly is assumed that strict genetic, neural, or cognitive codes are needed to produce coherent behavior. Yet, as we have seen in the example of speech production, such an assumption is insufficient to explain both topological stability and task flexibility. Principles derived from the more general study of pattern formation in complex systems (see Haken, 1983) increasingly are being applied to a large variety of physiological, neurobiological, and cognitive systems. These principles are especially powerful for characterizing real-time motor behavior and its changes in ontogenetic time (Kelso & Tuller, 1984; Thelen, Kelso, & Fogel, 1987).

For real-time actions, a dynamical approach to coordinated movement can be summarized as follows, with a particular reference to the coordinated movements of speech:

1. All perceptual-motor activities require the cooperation of many anatomical elements and physiological processes. When these elements are assembled in a specific task context, they produce spatially and temporally ordered behavior that has a unitary and cohesive character. Complex systems compress the many "degrees of freedom" of the participating units into patterns with far fewer degrees of freedom.

Speech, for example, is produced by a complex set of articulator elements (velum, tongue, lips, jaw, etc.), activated by an even more complex central nervous system, and operating within the ongoing physiological processes of the body. A simple utterance, or even a convoluted sentence, is a vast simplification of the high dimensionality of the cooperating units.

2. The resulting movement solution is not predetermined or prewired, but is constructed from the available elements for a specific task. The same task may be accomplished by a variety of means and from different initial conditions, depending on the particular assembly of subunits. Movement solutions are therefore not instantiated a priori but arise in the process of functional action.

In speech, as mentioned earlier, the question is how the linguistically invariant task — produce a relevant target speech element — can be accomplished from a variety of initial conditions, which include the ongoing speech context and expected and unexpected perturbations in the speech apparatus. This equifinality of outcome can happen only if the subunits can be flexibly assembled (Kelso, Saltzman, & Tuller, 1986; Saltzman, 1986, 1989).

3. The system may prefer some movement configurations under certain conditions, however, because they are energetically efficient or specially learned. It is a general characteristic of complex dynamic systems to settle into such a preferred configuration within a particular set of boundary conditions. This configuration, known in dynamic terminology as an *attractor,* acts as a kind of magnet, drawing the system into that state from many initial positions and even when perturbed. The attractor state itself may display complex behavior, including cyclicity and deterministic chaos (e.g., Gleick, 1987).

The boundary conditions for the attractor are determined by the organism, the environment, and the task. Some movement attractors, such as locomotion or speech, may be very stable and look hard-wired. However, even small changes in the boundary conditions, wearing high-heeled shoes or chewing gum, for example, may elicit new coordinative adaptations.

This has several important implications for the acquisition of speech sounds. First, given the anatomy of the vocal tract, the ranges of motion of the participating articulators, and the respiratory activation of the vocal apparatus, certain sounds and combinations of sounds may be more easily produced than others. The system more readily settles in to these attractors, and they are hard to perturb. Other productions — coordinative ensembles — may be possible, but more difficult, and yet others, nearly impossible.

In a recent paper adopting a dynamical view, Mohanan (1989) called such preferred vocal combinations *universal attractors*. He noted that certain phonological forms occur in nearly all languages (these are general features such as changing nasal vowels to the place of the following consonants and deleting final consonants). Such universal attractors arise because there are constraints on the vocal outcome that are inherent in the production system and are not language specific. Mohanan further proposed that linguistic grammars are built only within the bounds of these universal attractors, that is, that languages can both evolve and develop only as they work within these preferred spaces.

During development, these speech sound attractors can shift as the boundary conditions change through growth, use, and experience in a vocal environment. As I suggest later, the universal prespeech sounds of infants may be phonological attractors of considerable stability, given the organic constraints. Nonetheless, dynamical systems predicts that even small changes in anatomy, for example, potentially can engender new attractor states.

4. Dynamical systems can produce such novel behavioral configurations in response to changing boundary conditions because the elements are free to reassemble. Such a new solution is known as a *phase shift*. Phase shifts occur when the internal cohesiveness of the subunits is disrupted because the internal or external conditions are changed and the system seeks a new attractor or level of stability. Thus, the particular combinations of muscles and joints used for overground walking when wearing tennis shoes are not functional when the heel is lifted inches off the ground by high-heeled pumps, and new muscle forces and timing must be used to accomplish the same task. That the system reassembles in response to the distance of the heel from the ground alone illustrates that it is sensitive to this change in one element. Parameters of the system that are unspecific and even outside the organism can reorganize the system in specific ways (Schöner & Kelso, 1988).

Thus, dynamic systems such as the human perceptuo-motor system are essentially *nonlinear*. They can preserve a coordinative outcome under a range of boundary conditions, yet when certain critical boundary values are reached, they spontaneously reorganize.

5. Finally, it is important to emphasize that coordinated movement patterns are continually assembled and modulated by dynamic perceptual information. The motor field is determined by the ongoing demands and conditions of the outside world and the actors' perceptions of their own movements. We see later how this dynamic coupling between perception and action may be the key to the acquisition of speech.

DEVELOPMENT AS A DYNAMICAL PROCESS

The same principles that apply to the assembly of coordinated movement may be generalized to systems that change over an expanded time scale (Thelen, 1988, 1989b). The basic premise of a dynamical view of development is that the appearance of new behavioral forms is an emergent rather than a prescriptive process. Developing organisms are also systems with many elements and subsystems that cooperate to produce patterned behavior and that change over time. New forms in ontogeny arise from the process of the interactions of the changing organic subsystems and the changing relations between the organism and the task environment. Because complex systems are nonlinear, new forms are the natural consequences of the phase shifts and bifurcations that occur as these changes disrupt the stability of the current state. The resulting behavior at any point in ontogenetic time thus is assembled "softly" as a function of maturational status and the task context. Like the assembly of motor patterns, no a priori formula, schema, or maturational clock is needed to script the acquisition of new and more complex behavior. Form emerges in interaction.

In dynamic terminology, ontogeny can be envisioned as a series of emerging and dissolving attractor states, or stable phases, which are preferred, but not obligatory places where the organism "wants" to be. In early development, behavior may represent the output of an intrinsic dynamics, that is, motor configurations that result from the assembly of components within a current energy status and without a large influence from an intentional set or task boundary conditions. For example, well-defined newborn infant state behavior, spontaneous movement patterns, and early affectlike expressions have been characterized as such dynamic attractors: stable configurations emerging from the current neuromuscular and physiological condition of the infant (Fogel & Thelen, 1987; Thelen et al., 1987; Wolff, 1987). As infants mature, demands from the social and physical world increasingly interact with these intrinsic dynamics to make old solutions unstable and shift the system into cascading new forms. Thus, a smile configuration, initially produced by intrinsic dynamics, becomes increasingly bounded by the tasks of social and object interaction. With this new stability, the old attractor configuration dissolves. Infants no longer smile only when drowsy, but direct their smiles to social partners (Fogel & Thelen, 1987). As development proceeds, preferred solutions become increasingly stable, reflected in their ease of use, accuracy, and efficiency, yet the system retains flexibility to add new configurations as tasks demand.

NEW FORMS EMERGE IN DIALOGUE WITH THE PERIPHERY

What are the forces that disrupt stable solutions during ontogeny and cause the system to seek new levels of adaptive complexity? The processes of somatic growth alone can effect phase shifts. As structures grow, relationships among parts change. Because of the nonlinear nature of cooperative systems, even a small anatomical change can cause massive structural and functional reverberations (Gould, 1977; Thelen & Fisher, 1982). Anatomical changes in infants' vocal apparatus, for example, are essential for speech to emerge.

This dynamic approach assumes, in addition, that ordered behavior is a reflection not just of the anatomical construction of the nervous system and body parts, but also of the organic substrate interacting within the constraints and demands of the world. What this suggests for development is that this intimate interaction between the organism and the environment actually may drive developmental change. Here I follow the recent work of Edelman (1987) in suggesting that stable patterns of coordinated activity are selected from the intrinsic dynamics of the developing organism as it acts and interacts with its environment. This presumes that in early life, more patterns are generated than eventually are used. Some become stable and are retained; other behavioral combinations are lost. What determines this selection is a fit between the action and the demands of the periphery.

To accomplish this selection process, infants must be sensitive to the multiple sensory consequences of their own actions, and must use that information to further select and refine behavioral patterns. Edelman (1987) provided a theory of how this might happen that is consistent with what is known about neural architecture and development. In brief, as a result of prenatal epigenetic processes, the brain at birth is organized into highly overlapping, individually variant networks or neuronal groups. Especially important is that the local networks receiving input from a particular sensory modality have multiple and redundant connections with other local areas. In this way, every motor action generates multiple and simultaneous sensory maps that are linked, in parallel, to form higher order global maps. In other words, both the movement and its visual, proprioceptive, auditory, and tactile consequences continuously converge and are correlated. As each slightly different variant of a movement combination is generated in presumably slightly different contextual conditions, the resulting features are fed back into this global mapping so that they may become associated with their motor responses. This type of reiterated feature correlation process alone can produce stable categories of action; certain elements become reliably associated with each other. Computer simulations of such systems show learning and generalization by this reentry procedure without an explicit instructor and without traditional reinforcement mechanisms (e.g., Kuperstein, 1988, among others). The action categories self-assemble because of the dynamic interplay of the components. How such a process can account for the transition from prespeech to speech is the subject of the next section.

PHASE SHIFTS IN THE TRANSITION FROM PRESPEECH TO SPEECH

The vocal behavior of infants in their first year or so shows a typical stagelike developmental course, which in dynamic terms can be seen as a series of phase shifts in qualitative output modes. Oller (1980, 1986) has characterized infant vocalizations as they progress toward the basic units of human speech, well-formed syllables. (The construct of stages is used here, as in other developmental domains, to denote a period where a behavioral mode predominates, but may not be exclusively performed.) During the first 2 months, or "phonation stage," infants produce "comfort sounds." These have speechlike phonation, resembling vowel sounds but of lower frequency and not fully resonant, and they lack the consonant-vowel combination of speechlike syllables. The "gooing" stage emerges at 2 to 3 months of age. "Gooing" infants retain the quasi-resonant vowellike sounds of the first stage combined with articulated sounds from the back of the vocal cavity. These gutteral articulations may be precursors to consonants, but they also are not fully formed. The third stage is the "expansion stage" of age 4 to 6 months. Here infants produce a variety of new sounds like raspberries, squeals, growls, yells, whispers, isolated vowellike sounds, and immature syllables. True, well-formed syllables appear in the "canonical stage," usually quite suddenly at 7 to 10 months of age. This stage is characterized by true babbling, or the production of reduplicated syllables such as [mamama] or [dadada] with articulated consonants and fully resonant vowels. Finally, infants may engage in "variegated babbling" before using language, that is, combinations of different syllable types.

It is clear that these stages represent increasing levels of coordination and control of the speech articulators. But what processes lead to this particular sequence of patterned behavior? What changes disrupt the stability of one phase and cause the system to shift into new modes? What is the relationship between the trajectory of prespeech behavior and the onset of true speech and language? These developmental outcomes can be understood as the dynamic coalescence of three parallel, continuous underlying processes.

Process 1: Changes in the Anatomy and Control of the Vocal Motor Apparatus

The lips, tongue, and palate of the newborn infant are sufficiently mature to allow for sucking, swallowing, and simple phonation, but many structural and functional changes must take place before words and phrases can be uttered. Compared to adults and older children, infants have a relatively small mouth cavity and a large, relatively immobile tongue. Their lips are shorter, smaller, and less mobile. The soft palate incompletely separates the nose from the pharanx, and the jaw and larynx are more cartilagenous and mobile. Infants also have a characteristic firm fat pad on their cheeks which restricts mobility. During development, the soft palate moves forward and downward, closing off the air stream from pharynx to nose, and the relationship between the palate and its extrinsic muscles also changes. The tip and blade of the tongue rapidly elongate and the extrinsic musculature develops. The lips and mouth show a larger range of motion and the fat pad gradually decreases in size (Bosma, 1972; Fletcher, 1973). It is interesting to note that the anatomical changes in the oral cavity are believed to be largely function driven. In particular, the movements of the relatively large tongue in sucking, crying, and swallowing exert mechanical stresses on the relatively fragile palate and underdeveloped muscles of the jaw, thereby molding the oral cavity and its supporting muscles.

Functional changes accompany this anatomical remodeling. The abrupt sphincterlike closing of the pharynx associated with crying in newborns gives way to a differentiated action in phonation. The movements of the palate also become finer. Development of the intrinsic muscles of the tongue allow for diverse and rapid movements, much finer and more discriminating than the whole-tongue thrusting characteristic of newborns. Similarly, the lips become more articulated (Fletcher, 1973). Speech requires voluntary control of respiration: the ability to produce uninterrupted inspirations, to slow the breathing rate, to increase lung air pressure, and to keep a volume of unexpired air in the lungs. Infants begin to acquire such control at about 2 months of age (McKenna, 1986). In sum, the integrated structure-function ensemble of the newborn, admirably adapted for sucking and swallowing, undergoes anatomical and neural differentiation and reintegration for the production of speech sounds.

The vocal behavior of infants in their first 6 months or so likely reflects primarily these organic changes. Koopmans-van Beinum and van der Stelt (1986) analyzed the early sounds of two infants in terms of changing patterns of phonation and articulation. What is apparent from Fig. 15.1 is an increasing participation of more well-differentiated elements in the vocal act. At first, sound output is simply the expression of air through the vocal chamber. Next, phonation is interrupted, but without any articulation, resulting in "gooing" noises. In the expansion stage, the rather sudden

AGE IN WEEKS	01-05	06-09	10-14	15-19	20-26	27-
PHONATION:						
HIGH FUNDAMENTAL FREQ.	X					
CREAKY	X	X				
SHORT	X	X	X	X	X	X
FLAT	X	X	X	X	X	X
FALLING INTONATION	X	X	X	X	X	X
ASPIRATED		X	X	X	X	X
RISING INTONATION		X	X	X	X	X
GLOTTAL STOPS IN SERIES		⊗1	X	X	X	X
COMPLEX INTONATION			X	X	X	X
VARIATIONS IN LOUDNESS				X	X	X
VARIATIONS IN DURATION					X	X
RHYTHMIC SERIES						⊗3
ARTIC. POSITION:						
PHARYNX	X	X				
RAISED VELUM		X				
CLOSED MOUTH		X				
ARTIC. MOVEMENT:			⊗2	X	X	X
PHARYNX			X	X	X	X
VELUM			X	X	X	X
UVULA			X	X	X	X
BACK OF THE TONGUE			X	X	X	X
LOWER JAW			X	X	X	X
MIDDLE OF THE TONGUE				X	X	X
TONGUE TIP				X	X	X
LIPS				X	X	X
REPETITIVE ARTIC. MOV.						⊗3

FIG. 15.1. Phonation and articulation in the sound production of two infants in the first months of life. The number circles indicate the onset of (1) gooing, (2) expansion, and (3) babbling. From Koopmans - van Beinum & Van der Stelt (1986). (Reprinted with permission).

emergence of articulatory control over a number of oral structures leads to a rapid increase in the sound types produced. Babbling appears when infants repeat these articulatory movements in rapid sequence.

From a dynamical perspective, these stages can be seen as attractors which stabilize and destabilize over time. When newborns expire air through their vocal chambers, they produce a natural resonance which is a function of the particular structural features of the oral cavity, its current configuration, and the air pressure of the expired breath. Without intention, the system "settles" into a vocal output with a characteristic frequency and temporal envelope. When the infant is relatively relaxed, these are interpreted as "comfort noises." Under different energy constraints, for example if the infant shifts from a relaxed state to high distress, increased muscle tension and respiratory movements cause the system to seek another stable attractor, crying, with a different output topography. Comfort noises may be thought of as precursors to vowels in that they share certain energy constraints in the vocal tract.

The first developmental phase shift occurs when infants are able to simply interrupt a single cycle of respiration, often in association with particular affective states or social situations. The system then seeks another stable output mode, gooing, which may replace or coexist with the first attractor. The next phase shift into the expansion stage occurs with the acquisition of some articulatory ability in the jaw, tongue, lips, pharynx, and palate. This allows the system to settle into many different stable resonant states, depending again, on the particular configuration of the oral apparatus and the energy delivered to the system from the respiratory cycle.

The expansion stage is important because it demonstrates that the oral structures can spontaneously organize and reorganize into many different coordinative modes or multistable attractors from the cooperativity of many elements. But equally significant is that the production of this wide variety of sounds, from growls and squeaks to raspberries, gives infants the opportunity to explore, both motorically and perceptually, this large universe of possible vocal states, the places where the system can and prefers to settle.

The progressive stabilization and destabilization of these system attractor states is well illustrated by the developmental profile of phonation and articulation of one infant collected by Koopmans-van Beinum and van der Stelt (1986) (see Fig. 15.2). This shows the predominance of comfort sounds in the first weeks, a rapid shift to interrupted phonation in week 8, a surprising reoccurrence of uninterrupted phonation at 15 weeks, which the authors claim was associated with much exploration of pitch and loudness, and the slow acquisition of articulatory movements. Sequenced articulations did not begin until nearly 6 months of age.

I have suggested here that the changes through the expansion stage are driven primarily by organic development: function-driven anatomical re-

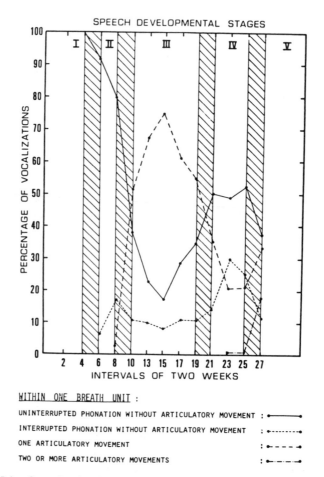

FIG. 15.2. Speech developmental stages summarized for one infant showing the increase and decline of particular sound types. The shaded areas indicate transitions to a new stage. From Koopmans - van Beinum & Van der Stelt (1986) (Reprinted with permission).

modeling, increasing respiratory control, and the neural differentiation of the articulator segments. There is evidence that additional processes are necessary for the shift into the canonical babbling stage, a shift where the system's "natural dynamics" are appropriated by the demands of a linguistic environment and a new "linguistic dynamics" emerges.

Process 2: Sensitivity to the Linguistic Environment

Much converging evidence indicates that from their earliest days, infants are exquisitely sensitive to the human voice and, in particular, to the qualities of natural language (see review by Fifer & Moon, 1989). Newborn infants can distinguish speech from nonspeech, and prefer speech to nonspeech. Infants only a few hours to a few days old prefer female over male voices, prefer their mothers' voices to that of strangers, and listen-longer to a story read aloud by their mothers before their birth than to a novel story. Recently DeCasper, Maugais, Lecanuet, Granier-Deferre, and Busnel (1986) reported different heart rate responses in 34-week-old fetuses to familiar stories read by their mothers or strangers than to unfamiliar stories. Mehler et al. (1988) found that 4-day-old infants prefer to listen to spoken passages in their mothers' native language. Not only do fetuses apparently attend to some language-relevant acoustic features in utero, they are seemingly influenced by this experience both before and after birth.

The sound-attentuating properties of the uterine environment make it likely that the prosodic elements of speech and their modulation are the most salient for the fetus and newborn (Fifer & Moon, 1989). The universality of adults' use of "baby talk" or "motherese" when talking to young infants suggests that these musical qualities of speech continue their importance in early infancy. Caregivers dramatically change their speech when talking to infants: Speech is simplified, segmented, and notably slowed in tempo. Adults limit their repertoire to a few repeated words or syllables delivered in a high pitch and with much greater pitch modulation than in normal adult speech (Fernald & Simon, 1984; Papousek & Papou-sek, 1986). Although caregivers make these adjustments without conscious intent, motherese indeed may match the perceptual and motoric abilities of young infants. For example, gooing vocalizations resemble musical tones and infants continually explore pitch modulations. By age 4 months, infants prefer to listen to motherese (Fernald, 1985), with the patterns of intonation being especially salient (Fernald & Kuhl, 1987). The implications of this match between the social vocal environment and the infant's reception and production are further explored later.

A large body of research shows that in addition to their sensitivity to prosody, infants can distinguish many phonetic contrasts of speech at a very young age (see Jusczyk, 1981, 1989). There has been a long debate on whether young infants' abilities to perceive speech sounds graded on acoustic dimensions categorically, that is, as two dichotomous phonemes, is evidence of innate special language-processing devices. The discovery of categorical perception in a number of nonhuman species made it more likely, however, that this processing is at the psychophysiological level rather than in specially evolved and dedicated speech mechanisms (Kuhl, 1986). That categorical perception may be an incidental consequence of the organization of the auditory system rather than from human phylogenetic design does not diminish that there is a match between the abilities of the infant and the language environment. Whatever the source, this multiple matching is an essential element in the processes of acquiring coordinative categories.

Jusczyk (1989) and his colleagues present compelling evidence that infants continue to pay attention to and process language-specific sounds throughout infancy. During the first 6 months, infants are able to distinguish between phonetic distinctions occuring outside their native language, but they begin to lose this ability after the first half of the year. By 6 months of age, they show preferences for listening to languages with the same prosodic structure as their native language, and by age 9 months, they can distinguish their native language on the basis of phonetic content. Indeed, their perceptual sensitivity develops in advance of their ability to produce language-specific phonemes.

Finally, studies of early hemispheric specialization confirm infants' receptiveness to language-relevant aspects of the environment. At birth or within a few weeks of birth, infants showed asymmetrical auditory evoked potential responses to speech versus a musical tone, pure tone, or noise (Molfese, Freeman, & Palermo, 1975). In dichotic listening tasks, 2- to 4-month-old infants recovered more quickly from habituation to syllables presented to the right ear and musical notes to the left ear than the reversed conditions. Recently Molfese and Molfese (1985; see also chapter 8 of this volume) reported that lateralized responses to speech stimuli predicted language test scores at age 3 years, suggesting that the early discrimination ability was related to later language development.

Thus, young infants are producing sounds from the spontaneous movements of their oral structures, and they are perceiving both the motoric and aural consequences of these sounds. At the same time, they are uniquely sensitive to the language environment that has surrounded them since before birth. How, then, do language-specific motor categories arise?

REENTRY MULTIMODAL MAPPING

Recall that there is strong anatomical evidence for highly overlapping and redundant interconnections between the local areas receiving sensory information in all modalities both from external world and from self-activity (Edelman, 1987). Infants show behavioral manifestations of these overlapping maps from birth in the form of coordination between sensory modalities and between perception and motor actions (see reviews by Meltzoff, 1986; Sullivan & Horowitz, 1983). Especially relevant for speech coordination are newborns' abilities to coordinate head and facial actions with audition and vision. A number of studies confirm head turning toward a sound (e.g. Clifton, Morrongiello, Kulig, & Dowd, 1981). Even more dramatic is the demonstration that newborn infants as young as 42 min old will imitate adult mouth-opening and tongue-protruding gestures when presented in a facilitative fashion (Meltzoff, 1986; Meltzoff & Moore, 1983). These apparently innate abilities mean than infants will be predisposed to direct their gaze to the source of a sound and that they can, as Meltzoff (1986) put it, "apprehend the equivalence between human actions they see and human actions they themselves can produce, whether they see them or not" (p. 256).

Edelman's (1987) theory predicts that with a system primed to perceive the intermodal equivalencies of everyday experience (voices usually have a visual source who moves; self-produced vocalizations have both proprioceptive and auditory consequences, etc.) and sufficient repetition, the intercorrelation of sensory and motor maps in itself can lead to stable perceptual and motor categories that "fall out" as the dynamic result of this reiteration process. Such categories are clearly evident by 4 or 5 months of age. At this age, infants prefer to look at events that correspond to the sounds they are hearing (Spelke, 1979). More specifically, infants already associate the visual components of speech with their auditory correlates. In a number of experiments where infants were given the choice of looking at speakers whose mouth movements were concordant or discrepant with syllables played to the infants, they consistently preferred the match (Dodd, 1979; Kuhl & Meltzoff, 1982, MacKain, Studdert-Kennedy, Spieker, & Stern, 1983). In addition, infants preferred to look at the parent (mother or father) whose voice they were hearing (Spelke & Owsley, 1979).

Striking evidence of a perception-production match has been reported by Kuhl (1986, 1989). Four-month-old infants imitated the pitch contours of the female talkers, alternating their vocalizations with the speaker. When Kuhl (1989) presented 12- to 18-week-old infants with either the vowel /a/, /i/ or /u/, she found that the infants produced vowel sounds themselves that resembled the modeled vowel both acoustically and perceptually. Further evidence of perceptual categorization at around 5 to 6 months of age is Kuhl's demonstration that infants could recognize vowels and syllables as similar when they were spoken by male, female, and children talkers. Even more remarkable is that by age 6 months, infants perceived phonetically "good" vowels as better exemplars of the vowel category than poor ones (Kuhl, 1986).

DYNAMIC ASSEMBLY OF THE MOTOR ASPECTS OF SPEECH

From a dynamical perspective, the behavioral output at any point in time is the condensation of the multiple underlying structures and processes by a particular context or task demand. These elements themselves may have unique ontogenetic trajectories. Because the stability of complex systems is

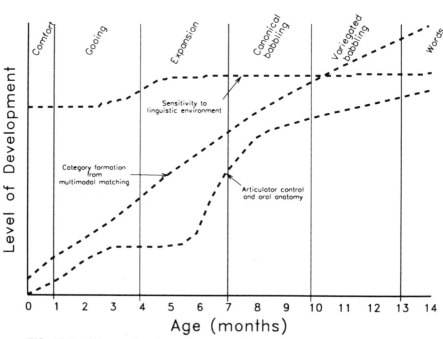

FIG. 15.3. Scheme for the emergence of stable "stages" of sound types based on the interaction of three parallel processes. Because the system is nonlinear, discrete qualitative forms arise from continuous processes.

exquisitely dependent on the states of the components, a small change in one component can drive the emergence of qualitatively new forms.

Fig. 15.3 presents a hypothetical account of how the interaction of the three continuous processes described earlier can lead to the observed stages of early vocalization. Infants' sensitivity to their vocal environment and their ability to continuously correlate their own production and reception is high at birth (and perhaps before) due to their neural anatomy, the highly redundant and overlapping networks established in the brain prenatally. This ability forms the basis of category formation throughout development (Edelman, 1987). As a result of this continuous process, more and more categories — auditory-motor, auditory-visual, auditory-auditory, motor- visual — emerge as stable attractors simply from infants' exposures to their own and others' language behavior. The common features of the articulation-sound match or of the vowel /a/ spoken by mom, dad, and the babysitter coalesce, and as infants have more experience hearing and producing sounds, the initial broad intermodal equivalencies become progressively more differentiated to match the real world. At the same time, the vocal apparatus matures and changes, leading to more articulatory control. Articulation seems to become especially accelerated around 4 to 6 months of age.

At each point in time, the infant's vocal output is the system compression of these neural and anatomic elements determined by the child's task context or energetic state. The comfort and gooing stages represent the natural resonances when expirations of moderate frequency move through the oral cavity with or without glottal interruptions. The acceleration of articulatory control allows the infant to explore a wide range of such natural resonances, which emerge when the infant can begin to modulate pitch and articulation. Thus, the change in this one parameter gives rise to a new, multistable phase. This expansion stage presumably gives the infant a large universe of correlated auditory and proprioceptive feedback.

The phase shift into canonical babbling is a result of a critical scaling point in the ongoing category formation from multimodal matching. Infants now select from the universe of vocal sounds they produce those that begin to match those sounds they hear in their language environment, but again, within the constraints of the other ongoing processes. Canonical babbling approximates fully resonant, reduplicated syllables, but with the most simple articulation: /mamama/, /dadada/, /babababa/. It is as though once infants are able to match their vocal output to the syllabic categories they have been hearing for 6 months, the system assembles into the energetically least costly attractor state, rhythmic repetition of easily formed phoneme combinations. The apparent universality of the /mama/ /dada/ syllables in early babbling gives credence to the notion that infants are attempting speechlike sounds within the confines of where the system "wants to be" at that particular neural and anatomical status.

Canonical babbling is important first because infants have reduced their universe of vocal output both in frequency and articulation range (squeals and raspberries are not normally part of social discourse). It is also important because it represents the initial sequencing of syllable combinations and approximates the rhythmic structure of speech. Although the kinematic aspects of babbling have not been studied, they would likely resemble the underlying organization of adult speech as a cyclic attractor. Dynamical systems often exhibit cyclicity as a result of their particular assembly and use of energy — a swinging pendulum is a straightforward physical example, but cyclicity is also characteristic of very many biological systems. For example, Kelso, Vatikiotis-Bateson, Saltzman, and Kay (1985) asked adult speakers to produce utterances with normal prosody but substituting a simple syllable /ba/ or /ma/ for the real syllable as their lip and jaw movements were monitored. A phase plane analysis, a continuous plot of the position of a speech articulator versus its velocity, revealed an underlying cyclic topography where the peak velocity and displacement were related in a lawful way despite differences in the rate and stress of the syllables. Many other naturally repeating movements exhibit this cyclic regularity, including leg movements in newborn and even premature infants

(Thelen, Kelso, & Fogel, 1987). This suggests that cyclic repetition is a natural and preferred state for neuromuscular systems under certain constraints, and may thus "fall out" in infants as a consequence of a certain degree of articulator maturation.

Finally, babbling appears to reflect a qualitative shift in hemispheric specialization. It is commonly believed that in the left hemisphere language and speech share common motor capacities, likely involving timing and sequencing of moving segments. Although the evidence is still somewhat equivocal, there are suggestive links between lateral specialization for hand use and the onset of babbling. Ramsay (1984, 1985), for example, found that unilateral hand preference was much stronger on the first week of duplicated babbling than for preceding weeks, but that there was considerable fluctuation in preference in the following 14 weeks of testing. MacNeilage, Studdert-Kennedy, and Lindblom (1984; see also, MacNeilage, 1986) believed that speech and hand use are related more in their need for bilateral hemispheric coordination than in simple lateralization of function. In this view, the critical developmental event may be the coordination between the hemispheres via the corpus callosum. Bresson et al. (1977) found evidence of a right-hand bias in collaborative reaching (two hands cooperating) at age 21 to 28 weeks, an age coincident with babbling onset, but Ramsay and Willis (1984) did not find this hand preference, and in addition noted that collaborative reaching actually declined with babbling onset. Bates, O'Connell, Vaid, Sledge, and Oakes (1985) interpreted these and their own fluctuating correlations between handedness and language as evidence of the dynamic and nonlinear relation between these skills. This is to be expected if indeed skills are assembled "on-line" from many components and are highly sensitive to their task and competing demands. (A similar dynamical model of laterality development is suggested in Thelen, 1989b.)

The most compelling support that babbling emerges from the confluence of increasing articulator control and processes of multimodal matching comes from studies of deaf infants. Oller and Eilers (1988) recently compared the phonological characteristics of the vocal behavior of 9 hearing-impaired infants with 21 normally hearing infants. None of the deaf infants had started canonical babbling by age 10 months, the latest age of onset in the normal infants. Some hearing-impaired children did produce canonical syllables in the second year, but one profoundly deaf child with no cochleas, and who presumably could not profit by the auditory amplification provided to the infants, did not produce canonical syllables even by 3 years of age.

It is noteworthy that these deaf infants did produce both gooing sounds and the precanonical vocalizations characteristic of the expansion stage at ages comparable to the hearing children. In principle, the hearing-impaired children should have no retardation of articulation control mediated by brain maturation. Nonetheless, it is essential for infants to hear language to select canonical sound types from the universe of possible noises they can utter. Visual and/or amplified sound provided sufficient, but impoverished stimuli to some hearing-impaired infants for these syllable types to eventually coalesce, but the process was delayed. The shift into spoken language requires that infants categorize the natural dynamics of the vocal tract into the coordinative structures characteristic of what they hear.

This intermodal matching may reflect the characteristics of the infant's particular linguistic community as early as the babbling stage. Boysson-Bardies and colleagues (Boysson-Bardies, Sagart, & Durand, 1984; Boysson-Bardies, Sagart, Halle, & Durand, 1986) found that observers could use prosodic cues of 8-month-old infants to correctly distinguish infants from French-speaking homes from those of Cantonese or Arabic parents. In addition, these authors could detect language-specific patterns in the spectral analyses of infant babbling samples similar to those generated by female speakers of the same language. Infants could be reliably categorized into their language groups by these patterns.

In the final prespeech stage of variegated babbling, infants expand canonical babbling through increasing articulator recruitment and continued reentry multimodal mapping. In this stage, a variety of mature syllable types and language-appropriate prosody may be combined. Infants often sound as if they are speaking true language when they mimic syllables and prosody, but it may be many months before words are used and combined in referential language. Once the motor aspects of speech no longer limit the emergence of spoken language, further development depends on the continued interaction of the child's self-organizing abilities and the rich language environment.

CONCLUSION: FROM SPEECH TO LANGUAGE

This dynamical systems account of motor behavior shares many features with the approaches of Bates (1979; Bates & MacWhinney, 1987), Lieberman (1984), and Lindblom, MacNeilage, and Studdert-Kennedy (MacNeilage, 1986; MacNeilage, Studdert-Kennedy, & Lindblom, 1984; Studdert-Kennedy, 1983), among others, on the ontogenetic and phylogenetic origins of language. These authors rejected the notion of a privileged and dedicated language device: hard-wired circuitry encoding the logical structure of human grammars that specifically evolved in *Homo sapiens* and directs the learning of vocal language. Rather they saw language having arisen phylogenetically from the coalescence and modification of multiple existing parts such as hemispheric specialization for feeding, tool use, and gestures, expansion of cortical association areas, anatomic remodeling of the oral cavity and vocal tract, changing control of respiration and swallowing, modifications of the perceptual apparatus, and above all, a functional drive to communicate.

Dynamical theory suggests that such complex systems will self-organize into behavioral regimes where the system is "comfortable" given the status of the components. The constraints of the system may dictate that some solutions are extremely stable, and indeed appear to be hard-wired. For example, phonemes are universally the building blocks of human language. Phonemes originated, according to Lindblom (1988), as a compromise between sounds that were easiest to produce and those offering maximal discriminability. A survey of a large language data base showed a relation between the number of vowel types in the language system and the complexity of the vowel types. Only languages with a large number of vowel types used elaborated vowel articulation; small systems used only basic types. Languages naturally appropriate the energetically least costly vowels and add the more difficult sounds only when they are needed for discrimination. Lindblom concluded that vowel and consonant phonetic values evolved "in response to universal, nonlinguistic articulatory and perceptual constraints" (p. 9). Nonetheless, phoneme attractors are so stable as to assume linguistic function.

Dynamical theory also would predict that when the constraints are loosened, the system would be free to assemble in a variety of task-appropriate ways. That the development of vocal behavior proceeds in normal infants in a predicable sequence argues for strong organic constraints in the first year, likely in the anatomical and neural components. However, children can learn language in the second year in what Bates and MacWhinney (1987) called "radically different ways" (p. 159). This can best be explained by language itself as a dynamic assembly of many subsystems whose development is heterochronic and asynchronous. In any child at any point in time, the functional need to communicate assembles the system based on the status of these subsystems in a context-sensitive and nonlinear way. That children have idiosyncratic "styles" of language learning means that the paths to the final stable attractor states are themselves not strongly constrained. Fogel and Thelen (1987) have argued for identical processes underlying nonvocal communicative gestures in the first year.

Although the skills of talking and walking are constructed from very different component subsystems, the same principles can be applied to their developmental course (Thelen, 1989a; Thelen, Ulrich, & Jensen, 1989). Like vocal behavior, locomotion is dynamically assembled from subsystems that themselves are changing over time rather than being scripted from a maturational or cognitive device. Although the final state is extremely stable, it is "softly assembled" and thus, always context sensitive. And most important, the acquisition of both skills is function driven. New forms arise from the continual interplay between the receptive organism and the social and physical world.

ACKNOWLEDGEMENTS

Preparation of this article was supported by research grant (HD 22830) from the National Institute of Child Health and Human Development and a Research Scientist Development Award (KO2 MH718) from the National Institutes of Mental Health. I thank Kim Oller and Peter Jusczyk for their kind suggestions.

REFERENCES

Abbs, J. H., Gracco, V. L., & Cole, K. J. (1984). Control of multimovement coordination: Sensorimotor mechanisms in speech motor programming. *Journal of Motor Behavior, 16,* 195–231.

Bates, E. (1979). The emergence of symbols: Ontogeny and phylogeny. In W. A. Collins (Ed.), *Children's language and communication* (pp. 121–155). Hillsdale, NJ: Lawrence Erlbaum Associates.

Bates, E., & MacWhinney, B. (1987). Language, variation, and language learning. In B. MacWhinney (Ed.), *Mechanisms of language acquisition* (pp. 157–193). Hillsdale, NJ: Lawrence Erlbaum Associates.

Bates, E., O'Connell, B., Vaid, J., Sledge, P., & Oakes, L. (1985, April). Language and hand preference in early development. Paper presented at the meeting of the Society for Research in Child Development, Toronto.

Bernstein, N. (1967). *Co-ordination and regulation of movements.* New York: Pergamon.

Bosma, J. F. (1972). Form and function in the infant's mouth and pharynx. In J. F. Bosma (Ed.), *Third symposium on oral sensation and perception: The mouth of the infant* (pp. 3–27). Springfield, IL: Thomas.

Boysson-Bardies, B. de, Sagart, L., & Durand, C. (1984). Discernible differences in the babbling of infants according to target-language. *Journal of Child Language, 11,* 1–15.

Boysson-Bardies, B. de, Sagart, L., Halle, P., & Durand, C. (1986). Acoustic investigations of cross-linguistic variability in babbling. In B. Lindblom & R. Zetterstrom (Eds.), *Precursors of early speech* (pp. 113–126). New York: Stockton Press.

Bresson, F., Maury, L., Pieraut-Le Bonniec, G., & de Schonen, S. (1977). Organization and lateralization of reaching in infants: An instance of asymmetric functions in hands collaboration. *Neuropsychologia, 15,* 311–320.

Clifton, R., Morrongiello, B., Kulig, J., & Dowd, J. (1981). Developmental changes in auditory localization in infancy. In R. N. Aslin, J. R. Alberts, & M. R. Peterson (Eds.), *Sensory and perceptual development: Influence of genetic and experimental factors* (pp. 141–160). New York: Academic.

DeCasper, A. J., Maugais, R., Lecanuet, J-P., Granier-Deferre, C., & Busnel, M-C. (1986, November). Familiar and unfamiliar speech elicit different cardiac responses in human fetuses. Paper presented at the meeting of the International Society for Developmental Psychobiology, Annapolis, MD.

Dodd, B. (1979). Lip reading in infants: Attention to speech presented in- and out-of-synchrony. *Cognitive Psychology, 11,* 478–484.

Edelman, G. M. (1987). *Neural Darwinism*. New York: Basic.

Fernald, A. (1985). Four-month-old infants prefer to listen to motherese. *Infant Behavior and Development, 8,* 181-195.

Fernald, A., & Kuhl, P. (1987). Acoustic determinants of infant preference for motherese speech. *Infant Behavior and Development, 10,* 279-293.

Fernald, A., & Simon, T. (1984). Expanded intonation contours in mothers' speech to newborns. *Developmental Psychology, 20,* 104-113.

Fifer, W., & Moon, C. (1989). Early voice discrimination. In C. von Euler, H. Forssberg, & H. Lagercrantz (Eds.), *Neurobiology of early infant behaviour* (pp. 277-286). Basingstoke, England: Macmillan.

Fletcher, S. G. (1973). Maturation of the speech mechanism. *Folia Phoniatrica, 25,* 161-172.

Fogel, A., & Thelen, E. (1987). The development of expressive and communicative action in the first year: Reinterpreting the evidence from a dynamic systems perspective. *Developmental Psychology, 23,* 747-761.

Fowler, C. A., Rubin, P., Remez, R. E., & Turvey, M. T. (1980). Implications for speech production of a general theory of action. In B. Butterworth (Ed.), *Language production: Vol. 1. Speech and talk* (pp. 373-420). New York: Academic.

Gleick, J. (1987). *Chaos: Making a new science.* New York: Viking.

Gould, S. J. (1977). *Ontogeny and phylogeny.* Cambridge, MA: Harvard University Press.

Haken, H. (1983). *Synergetics: An introduction* (3rd ed.). Heidelberg, Germany: Springer-Verlag.

Jusczyk, P. W. (1981). The processing of speech and non-speech sounds by infants: Some implications. In R. N. Aslin, J. R. Alberts, & M. R. Petersen (Eds.), *Development of perception* (pp. 192-215). New York: Academic.

Jusczyk, P. W. (1989, September). Developing phonological categories from the speech signal. Paper presented at the meeting of the International Conference on Phonological Development, Stanford, CA.

Kelso, J. A. S., Holt, K. G., Kugler, P. N., & Turvey, M. T. (1980). On the concept of coordinative structures as dissipative structures: II. Empirical lines of convergence. In G. E. Stelmach & J. Requin (Eds.), *Tutorials in motor behavior* (pp. 49-70). New York: North Holland.

Kelso, J. A. S., Mandell, A. J., & Shlesinger, M. F. (1988). *Dynamic patterns in complex systems.* Singapore: World Scientific.

Kelso, J. A. S., Saltzman, E. L., & Tuller, B. (1986). The dynamical theory on speech production: Data and theory. *Journal of Phonetics, 14,* 29-60.

Kelso, J. A. S., & Tuller, B. (1984). A dynamical basis for action systems. In M. S. Gazzaniga (Ed.), *Handbook of cognitive neuroscience* (pp. 321-356). New York: Plenum.

Kelso, J. A. S., Tuller, B., V-Bateson, E., & Fowler, C. A. (1984). Functionally specific articulatory cooperation adaptation to jaw perturbations during speech: Evidence for coordinative structures. *Journal of Experimental Psychology: Human Perception and Performance, 10,* 812-832.

Kelso, J. A. S., Vatikiotis-Bateson, E., Saltzman, E. L., & Kay, B. (1985). A qualitative dynamic analysis of reiterant speech production: Phase portraits, kinematics, and dynamic modeling. *Journal of the Acoustical Society of America, 77,* 266-280.

Koopmans-van Beinum, F. J., & van der Stelt, J. M. (1986). Early stages in the development of speech movements. In B. Lindblom & R. Zetterstrom (Eds.), *Precursors of early speech* (pp. 37-50). New York: Stockton Press.

Kugler, P. N., Kelso, J. A. S., & Turvey, M. T. (1980). On the concept of coordinative structures as dissipative structures: I. Theoretical lines of convergence. In G. E. Stelmach & J. Requin (Eds.), *Tutorials in motor behavior* (pp. 3-47). New York: North Holland.

Kuhl, P. K. (1986). Infants' perception of speech: Constraints on characterizations of the initial state. In B. Lindblom & R. Zetterstrom (Eds.), *Precursors to early speech* (pp. 219–244). New York: Stockton Press.

Kuhl, P. K. (1989). Infants' acquisition of speech: Evidence of an early understanding of auditory-articulatory correspondences. In J. Erber, R. Menzel, H-J. Pfluger, & D. Todt (Eds.), *Neural mechanisms of behavior* (pp. 153–154). Stuttgart, Germany: Thieme.

Kuhl, P. K., & Meltzoff, A. (1982). The bimodal perception of speech in infancy. *Science, 218,* 1138–1141.

Kuperstein, M. (1988). Neural model of adaptive hand-eye coordination for single postures. *Science,* 239, 1308–1311.

Lieberman, P. (1984). *The biology and evolution of language.* Cambridge, MA: Harvard University Press.

Lindblom, B. (1988, June). Some remarks on the origin of the "phonetic code." Paper presented at the Symposium on Developmental Dyslexia: Aspects on Memory Functions, Sequencing and Hemispheric Interactions, Stockholm, Sweden.

MacKain, K. S., Studdert-Kennedy, M., Spieker, S., & Stern, D. (1983). Infant intermodal speech perception is a left hemisphere function. *Science, 219,* 1347–1349.

MacNeilage, P. F. (1986). Bimanual coordination and the beginnings of speech. In B. Lindblom & R. Zetterstrom (Eds.), *Precursors of early speech* (pp. 189–201). New York: Stockton Press.

MacNeilage, P. F., Studdert-Kennedy, M. G., & Lindblom, B. (1984). Functional precursors to language and its lateralization. *American Journal of Physiology, 246,* (*Regulatory, Integrative, and Comparative Physiology, 15,* R912–914).

McKenna, J. J. (1986). An anthropological perspective on the Sudden Infant Death Syndrome (SIDS): The role of parental breathing cues and speech breathing adaptations. *Medical Anthropology, 10,* 9–53.

Mehler, J., Jusczyk, P. W., Lambertz, G., Halsten, N., Bertoncini, J., & Amiel-Tison, C. (1988). A precursor of language acquisition in young infants. *Cognition, 29,* 143–178.

Meltzoff, A. N. (1986). Imitation, intermodal representation, and the origins of mind. In B. Lindblom & R. Zetterstrom (Eds)., *Precursors to early speech* (pp. 245–265). New York: Stockton Press.

Meltzoff, A. N., & Moore, M. K. (1983). The origins of imitation in infancy: Paradigm, phenomena, and theories. In L. P. Lipsitt & C. K. Rovee-Collier (Eds.), *Advances in infancy research* (Vol. 2, pp. 265–301). Norwood, NJ: Ablex.

Mohanan, K. P. (1989, September). Universal attractors in phonology. Paper presented at the International Conference on Phonological Development, Stanford, CA.

Molfese, D. L., Freeman, R., & Palermo, D. (1975). The ontogeny of lateralization for speech and nonspeech stimuli. *Brain and Language, 2,* 356–368.

Molfese, D. L., & Molfese, V. J. (1985). Electrophysiological indices of auditory discrimination in newborn infants: The bases for predicting later language development? *Infant Behavior and Development, 8,* 197–211.

Oller, D. K. (1980). The emergence of the sounds of speech in infancy. In G. Yeni-Komshian, J. Kavanagh, & C. Ferguson (Eds.), *Child phonology: Vol. 1. Production* (pp. 93–112). New York: Academic.

Oller, D. K. (1986). Metaphonology and infant vocalizations. In B. Lindblom & R. Zetterstrom (Eds.), *Precursors of early speech* (pp. 21–36). New York: Stockton Press.

Oller, D. K., & Eilers, R. E. (1988). The role of audition in infant babbling. *Child Development, 59,* 441–449.

Papousek, H., & Papousek, M. (1986). Structure and dynamics of human communication at the beginning of life. *European Archives of Psychiatry and Neurological Sciences, 236,* 21–25.

Ramsay, D. S. (1984). Onset of duplicated syllable babbling and unimanual handedness in infancy: Evidence for developmental change in hemispheric specialization? *Developmental Psychology, 20,* 64–71.

Ramsay, D. S. (1985). Fluctuations in unimanual hand preference in infants following the onset of duplicated syllable babbling. *Developmental Psychology, 21,* 318–324.

Ramsay, D. S., & Willis, M. P. (1984). Organization and lateralization of reaching in infants: An extension of Bresson et al. *Neuropsychologia, 22,* 639–641.

Saltzman, E. L. (1986). Task dynamic coordination of the speech articulators: A preliminary model. *Experimental Brain Research, Series 15,* 129–144.

Saltzman, E. L. (1989). A dynamical approach to gestural patterning in speech production. *Ecological Psychology, 1,* 333–382.

Schöner, G., & Kelso, J. A. S. (1988). Dynamic pattern generation in behavioral and neural systems. *Science, 239,* 1513–1520.

Spelke, E. S. (1979). Perceiving bimodally specified events in infancy. *Developmental Psychology, 15,* 626–636.

Spelke, E. S., & Owsley, C. J. (1979). Intermodal exploration and knowledge in infancy. *Infant Behavior and Development, 2,* 13–27.

Studdert-Kennedy, M. (1983). On learning to speak. *Human Neurobiology, 2,* 191–195.

Sullivan, J. W., & Horowitz, F. D. (1983). Infant intermodal perception and maternal multimodal stimulation: Implications for language development. In L. P. Lipsitt & C. K. Rovee-Collier (Eds.), *Advances in infancy research* (Vol. 2, pp. 183–239). Norwood, NJ: Ablex.

Thelen, E. (1988). Dynamical approaches to the development of behavior. In J. A. S. Kelso, A. J. Mandell, & M. F. Shlesinger (Eds.), *Dynamic patterns in complex systems* (pp. 348–369). Singapore: World Scientific.

Thelen, E. (1989a). Evolving and dissolving synergies in the development of leg coordination. In S. Wallace (Ed.), *Perspectives on the coordination of movement* (pp. 259–281). Amsterdam: Elsevier North Holland.

Thelen, E. (1989b). Self-organization in developmental processes: Can systems approaches work? In M. Gunnar & E. Thelen (Eds.), *Systems and development: The Minnesota Symposia in Child Psychology* (Vol. 22, pp. 77–117). Hillsdale, NJ: Lawrence Erlbaum Associates.

Thelen, E., & Fisher, D. M. (1982). Newborn stepping: An explanation for a "disappearing reflex." *Developmental Psychology, 18,* 760–775.

Thelen, E., Kelso, J. A. S., & Fogel, A. (1987). Self-organizing systems and infant motor development. *Developmental Review, 7,* 39–65.

Thelen, E., Ulrich, B. D., & Jensen, J. L. (1989). The developmental origins of locomotion. In M. Woollacott & A. Shumway-Cook (Eds.), *The development of posture and gait across the lifespan* (pp. 25–47). Columbia: University of South Carolina Press.

Wolff, P. H. (1987). *The development of behavioral states and the expression of emotion in early infancy: New proposals for investigation.* Chicago: University of Chicago Press.

16 Linguistic and Spatial Development: Dissociations Between Cognitive Domains

Ursula Bellugi
The Salk Institute for Biological Studies, La Jolla, CA

Amy Bihrle
The Salk Institute for Biological Studies,
and University of California, San Diego

David Corina
The Salk Institute for Biological Studies, La Jolla, CA, and
University of Calfornia, San Diego

THE STRUCTURE OF AMERICAN SIGN LANGUAGE

To investigate language and its formal architecture, as well as its representation in the brain, in this chapter we examine properties of languages in different modalities (spoken and signed). Research over the past decade has specified the ways in which the formal properties of languages are shaped by their modalities of expression, sifting properties peculiar to a particular language mode from more general properties common to all languages (Bellugi, 1988; Bellugi & Klima, 1982; Klima & Bellugi, 1979). American Sign Language (ASL) exhibits formal structuring at the same levels as spoken languages and similar kinds of organizational principles (constrained systems of features, rules based on underlying forms, recursive grammatical processes). Yet research shows that at all structural levels, the form of an utterance in a signed language is deeply influenced by the modality in which the language is cast (Bellugi, 1980).

American Sign Language has been forged into an autonomous language with its own internal mechanisms for relating visual form with meaning. ASL has evolved linguistic mechanisms that are not derived from those of English (or any spoken language), thus offering a new perspective on the determinants of language form (Bellugi & Studdert-Kennedy, 1980; Klima & Bellugi, 1979). ASL shares underlying principles of organization with spoken languages, but the instantiation of those principles occurs in formal devices arising out of the very different possibilities of the visual-gestural mode (Bellugi, 1988). We consider briefly spatial aspects of the structure of ASL at different linguistic levels—the layered structure of phonology, three-dimensional morphology, and the spatially organized syntax.

Phonology Without Sound.   Research on the structure of lexical signs has shown that, like the words of spoken languages, signs are fractionated into sublexical elements. The elements that distinguish signs (handshapes, movements, places of articulation) are in contrasting spatial arrangements and co-occur throughout the sign. For example, the signs SUMMER, UGLY, and DRY are made with the same handshape and movement at three different spatial locations (shown in Fig. 16.1-a).

Vertically Arrayed Morphology.   The grammatical mechanisms of ASL elaborately exploit the spatial medium and the possibility of simultaneous and multidimensional articulation. Like spoken languages, ASL has devel-

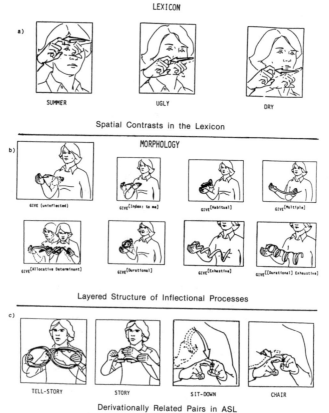

FIG. 16.1.   Linguistic contrasts in American Sign Language.

oped grammatical markers that serve as inflectional and derivational morphemes; these are regular changes in form across syntactic classes of lexical items associated with systematic changes in meaning. Some sample inflections on the single sign GIVE are shown in Fig. 16.1-b, including inflections for person, number, distributional aspect, temporal aspect, for example, conveying the meanings "give to me," "give regularly," "give to them," "give to certain ones at different times," "give over time," "give to each," "give over time to each in turn." Fig. 16.1-c shows sample derivationally related pairs of signs in ASL; verbs and their formationally related noun pairs, distinguished only by subtle features of movement. In ASL, families of sign forms are related via an underlying stem: The forms share a handshape, a location, and a local movement shape. Inflectional and derivational processes represent the interaction of the stem with other features of movement in space (dynamics of movement, manner of movement, directions of movement, spatial array, and the like) all *layered* with the sign stem.

Spatially Organized Syntax.   Languages have different ways of marking grammatical relations among their lexical items. In English, it is primarily the *order* of the lexical items that marks the basic grammatical relations among verbs and their arguments; in other languages, it is the morphology of case marking or verb agreement that signals these relations. ASL, by contrast, specifies relations among signs primarily through the manipulation of sign forms in *space*. Thus in sign language, space itself bears linguistic meaning. The most striking and distinctive use of space in ASL is in its role in syntax and discourse. Nominals (nouns or noun phrases) introduced into ASL discourse may be associated with specific arbitrary points in a horizontal plane of signing space. In signed discourse, pointing again to a specific locus clearly "refers back" to a previously mentioned nominal, even with many other signs intervening. The ASL system of verb agreement, like its pronominal system, is also in essence spatialized. Verb signs for a large class of verbs move between the abstract loci in signing space, bearing obligatory markers for person (and number) via spatial indices, thereby specifying subject and object of the verb, as shown in Fig. 16.2-a. This spatialized system thus allows explicit reference through pronominals and agreement markers to multiple, distinct, third-person referents. The same signs in the same order, but with a reversal in direction of the verb's movement, indicate different grammatical relations. Furthermore, sentences with signs in different temporal orders still can have the same meaning, because grammatical relations are signified spatially. Coreferential nominals are indexed to the same locus point, as is evident in complex embedded sentences, such as shown in Fig. 16.2-b. Different spaces may be used to contrast events, to indicate reference to time

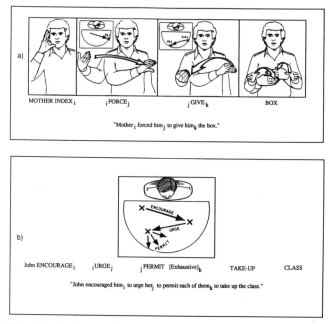

FIG. 16.2. Syntactic spatial mechanisms in American Sign Language. (a) A spatially organized sentence in ASL showing nominal establishment and verb agreement; and (b) Spatial reference diagram for multiclausal sentence.

preceding the utterance, or to express hypotheticals and counterfactuals. This pervasive use of space for referential indexing, verb agreement, coreference, and grammatical relations is clearly a unique property of visual-gestural systems.

American Sign Language is thus markedly different in surface form from English, and from spoken languages in general. The inflectional and derivational devices of ASL, for example, make structured use of space and movement, nesting the basic sign stem in spatial patterns and complex dynamic contours of movement. ASL is also different from spoken languages in the extent and degree of "motivatedness" between meaning and form. ASL signs for basic level objects, for example, themselves are sometimes globally iconic, their form resembling some aspect of what they denote. At the morphological and syntactic levels also, there is often some congruence between form and meaning. Spoken languages are not without such direct clues to meaning (for example, reduplication processes that provide direct methods of reflecting meaning through form), but in sign languages such transparency is certainly more pervasive. ASL thus bears striking traces of its representational origins, but at the same time is a fully grammaticized system, constituting an autonomous language.

Universals of Signed Languages. The effort to understand how language modality may determine linguistic form has led to studies in the realm of cross-linguistic comparisons between signed languages (Fok, Bellugi, & Lillo-Martin, 1986; Fok, Bellugi, van Hoek, & Klima, 1988). There are many different natural signed languages, just as there are different spoken languages. Signed languages appear to spring up wherever there are communities (and generations) of deaf people. The signed language that developed among deaf people in Great Britain, for example, is mutually incomprehensible with American Sign Language — the two languages differ from one another at all linguistic levels. It is of importance to examine the surface differences between signed and spoken languages, in terms of the ways in which languages exploit the resources of their transmission modalities to express grammatical information. The grammatical mechanisms of ASL exploit elaborately the spatial medium and the possibility of simultaneous and multidimensional layering. ASL is a heavily inflective language; moreover, the forms of its inflections are unique to the spatial medium (Klima & Bellugi, 1979). Its rich system of grammatical markers (for person, many distinctions of number, grammatical aspect, and recursive operations) are concurrently layered with the sign stem, providing an unusual three-dimensional morphology; in this respect, English and ASL differ. Whereas English relies heavily on order of lexical items in its syntax, ASL relies primarily on spatially organized syntax. Although the principles underlying the grammar of ASL are universal to both spoken and signed language, aspects of its surface patterning might be universal to the visual-spatial modality.

Investigations of Chinese Sign Language recently have begun to address this question of the effect of modality on the surface form of signed languages (Fok, Bellugi, & Klima, in press; Fok et al., 1988). Chinese Sign Language (CSL) was selected because of the contrasts between the two spoken languages used in America and Hong Kong, the countries where ASL and CSL developed. Particularly important is the fact that spoken Chinese has essentially no grammatical inflections. If CSL, like ASL, turns out to be a heavily inflecting language, that could not be attributed to influence from spoken Chinese, but it would support the view that inflection is the form of patterning favored by the visual modality. Studies of CSL therefore provide a direct way of examining both the independence of signed language from spoken language, and the issue of the relationship between modality of transmission and the surface form of language that results.

A number of studies have examined memory and processing of CSL, the formal properties of CSL, and contrasts in processing CSL and ASL by American and Chinese hearing and deaf subjects (Fok, Bellugi, & Klima, in press; Fok et al., 1986; Fok et al., 1988; Klima & Bellugi, 1979). The results show, first of all, that ASL and CSL are indeed independent, unrelated signed languages, and that they differ in ways analogous to the differences found between spoken languages. Differences are found at each of the major structural levels — phonology, morphology, and syntax. Certain handshapes, locations, and movements occur in one sign language but not in the other. Indeed, just as there are differences in the way a French person and an American pronounce /t/ or /d/, there are consistent, fine-grained "phonetic" differences between CSL and ASL even when they use the same handshapes. Just as the possibilities for word formation are constrained differently in different spoken languages, signs within a sign language exhibit formational constraints specific to their individual sign languages. Thus, signed languages are constrained not merely by motor limitations on handshapes, locations, and movements, nor by general visual constraints. Rather, they are constrained in ways that are far less predictable, and that are language specific.

Nevertheless, the studies also find that CSL bears the imprint of the visual modality in its surface grammatical patterning. CSL, like ASL, has developed its own grammatical inflections that co-occur with the sign stem, and uses spatial contrasts for its syntax. Fig. 16.3 shows aspects of grammatical patterning in CSL, including families of derivationally related signs showing layered contrasts; verb inflections in CSL marked by manipulations of spatial endpoints; CSL classifiers, and their form under some spatially realized inflections.

Thus, studies of CSL show that it exhibits the same principles of grammatical patterning as ASL, although they are completely distinct, mutually unintelligible signed languages. As in ASL, the grammatical patterning that has arisen in CSL is heavily conditioned by the modality in which the language has developed. Both American and Chinese Sign Languages are predominantly multilayered with respect to form — with differences in levels of grammatical structure mirrored by differences in layers of form, making complex use of space in the service of syntax. In summary, we find that languages in the visual-spatial modality are subject to language-specific, linguistic constraints on form, analogous to those found in spoken languages; at the same time, the special resources of the modality have a profound effect on the surface patterning in both signed languages.

THE ACQUISITION OF A SPATIALLY ORGANIZED LANGUAGE

Signed languages are based upon the same universal linguistic principles as spoken languages; however, their surface forms are heavily influenced by

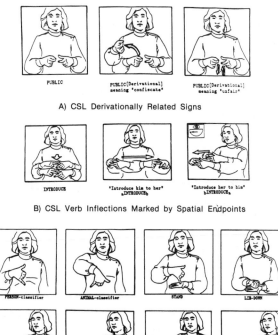

A) CSL Derivationally Related Signs

B) CSL Verb Inflections Marked by Spatial Endpoints

C) CSL Classifiers and Related Forms

FIG. 16.3. Studies of Chinese Sign Language grammatical structure.

their roots within the visuospatial medium. The young deaf child is faced with the dual task in sign language of spatial perception, memory, and spatial transformations on the one hand, and processing grammatical structure on the other, all in one and the same visual event. The change in transmission system (from the ear to the eye, from the vocal apparatus to the hands) could be expected to have a profound influence on acquisition. Deaf children who are acquiring ASL as a native language thus provide a privileged testing ground for the investigation of language-specific determinants of language acquisition.

Numerous studies have been done examining the acquisition of specific grammatical subsystems in ASL by deaf children of deaf parents. These include studies of pronominal reference, verb agreement, verbs of motion and location, derivational processes, compounding, aspects of spatially organized syntax, and discourse, among them Petitto (1983), Launer (1982), Supalla (1982), Meier (1982), Loew (1982), Lillo-Martin, Bellugi,

Struxness, & O'Grady (1985), Lillo-Martin (1986), and Newport and Meier (1986). Many of the domains that these studies examine are areas in which, because of its spatialized underpinnings, the acquisition of ASL might be expected to take a different course than the acquisition of a spoken language like English.

Pronominal Reference in a Spatial Language.   The system of personal pronouns in ASL is dramatically different from the system of pronouns evolved in spoken languages. Deixis in spoken languages is considered a verbal surrogate for pointing. In ASL, however, deixis *is* pointing. The pronominal signs in ASL are, in fact, the same as pointing gestures that hearing people use to supplement their words nonverbally. This transparency of meaning could be expected to lead to ease of acquisition of such forms by young deaf children learning ASL as compared with spoken languages.

The problems children have in learning terms that "shift" with speaker and addressee (such as *I* and *you*) are well known and well documented for spoken languages (Clark, 1978). Some, though not all, children temporarily "reverse" the meanings of the pronouns, using *you* to refer to themselves, and using *I* and *me* to refer to the addressee. The hearing child's problems with the shifting nature of such arbitrary strings of sounds as *you* and *me* is readily understandable. In contrast, one might expect that, because of their transparent nature, the learning of the sign equivalents of pronominal reference in ASL would be early and error-free. In ASL, the pronoun signs are exactly the same as the pointing gestures one would use to indicate self and addressee. Given such obvious gestures, easy acquisition would seem to be a foregone conclusion. However, it has been found that deaf signing children make errors in pronominal reference exactly analogous to those made by hearing children learning English and at the same ages, affording a dramatic example of similarities between the acquisition of spoken and signed languages, despite striking differences in language modality (Bellugi & Klima, 1982, 1990; Petitto, 1983).

Petitto (1983) found that deaf children display precisely the same progression, at the same ages, as do hearing children learning pronominal reference systems in spoken languages. The indexical form first appears as a pointing gesture. It then disappears from the child's repertoire for a period of several months. When it reappears, it is as a pronominal sign that is integrated into a linguistic system but marked by some systematic errors. These errors, and their resolution, occur exactly on target with those observed in children learning spoken languages, at the same ages. Particularly striking is the fact that some deaf children make errors of reversal, using the sign YOU (pointing at addressee) for self-reference, and the sign

ME (pointing at self) for reference to the addressee. This is exactly analogous to hearing children's confusions concerning the use of the English pronouns *I* and *you*. It appears to make little difference, then, whether pronominal terms are symbolized by arbitrary streams of sound segments, as in spoken language, or by pointing signs that are indistinguishable in form from pointing gestures, as in sign language. These studies provide evidence for discontinuity in the transition from prelinguistic gesture to linguistic system, even when the two are identical in form and share a single channel of expression. This is evidence that the transition from gesture to sign requires a reorganization of the child's linguistic knowledge and shows that the function of a gesture as a linguistic unit, rather than the iconicity of its form, may determine the course of acquisition.

Spatialized Verb Agreement.   How do children acquire a morphological system that is grammaticized, but that nevertheless displays a large amount of iconicity? Does the iconicity of ASL signs or grammatical processes give children a special way into language learning? A study of the acquisition of verb agreement was conducted, focusing on deaf children of deaf parents ranging in age from 1 year, 6 months to 3 years, 9 months. The order in which agreement forms were acquired, and the kinds of errors that the children made, indicated strongly that verb agreement is acquired as a morphological system, rather than as a mimetic or analogic system (Meier, 1982). Just as do children learning spoken languages, deaf children learning ASL as a first language produce a variety of overgeneralizations, as the children begin producing inflected forms with regularity. Children provide agreeing forms for verbs that do not take agreement in the adult language, such as SPELL, SAY, and LIKE, among others (see Fig. 16.4). These forms cannot be interpreted as mimes or spatial analogues of the referenced actions. They are morphological overregularizations, ungrammatical in the adult language, entirely analogous to English-speaking children's provision of *goed* and *holded* for past tense.

The evidence indicates that the child does not make use of the iconic potential provided by the visuospatial mode to enter the grammatical system. Rather, he or she begins with uninflected signs, and then systematically analyzes the morphologically complex forms, analyzing which verbs do and do not undergo agreement, what arguments are marked, and whether the markers are optional or obligatory. All of these aspects are worked out by signing children by approximately age 3 years, at which time the ASL system for marking verb agreement is stabilized and mastered, comparable to the emergence of aspects of inflectional morphology in spoken languages, despite the differences in form.

*SPELL$^{[X:'to me']}$ / SPELL   *SAY$^{[X:'to you']}$ / SAY

*LIKE$^{[X:'to it']}$ / LIKE

FIG. 16.4.   Overgeneralization of verb inflections by young deaf children of deaf parents.

Spatially Organized Referential Framework for Syntax and Discourse. The integration of verb agreement with the spatial reference system in ASL syntax and discourse is highly complex, involving the use of abstract spatial loci for referential indexing, for verb agreement, and for coreference, within both fixed and shifting spatial referential frameworks. Deaf children begin by using uninflected verbs and relying on the order of signs to specify grammatical relations, even when this is ungrammatical in the adult language (Newport & Meier, 1986). Even when they have acquired the regularities of agreement morphology, integrating it with the spatial reference framework for syntax and discourse represents additional levels of complexity. In a spoken language like English, the intended reference of lexical pronouns is often unclear. The spatial mechanisms used in ASL, by contrast, require that identity of reference be maintained across arbitrary points in space that are not lexical units. When deaf children first attempt to specify pronominal indices and verb agreement to arbitrary locus points in space, they sometimes incorrectly index all verbs for different referents to a single locus point, as if "stacking" them at a single point in space. And yet, studies of comprehension of nominal establishment and verb agreement shows good mastery by the age of 3 years (Bellugi, 1988). By the age of 5 years, deaf children give spatial indices to nominals and pronominals, and use the appropriate agreement with most verbs; they have begun to master aspects of complex spatial integration across sentences as well.

Recent studies in the acquisition of ASL have focused on the development of discourse structure. Discourse cohesion in ASL involves the use of spatial coindexing of referents across sentences, combining verb agreement and pronominal reference with the maintenance of an array of referential loci throughout the discourse. The studies of deaf children's development of discourse cohesion and the spatial reference system have found that the spatially realized aspects of discourse structure (establishment and maintenance of referential loci) develop in parallel with those aspects of discourse structure that are not manifested spatially (e.g., identification of characters, the choice between nominals and pronominals in making reference, maintenance of topic). Furthermore, these studies indicate that the overall system, including the spatialized reference system, develops in the same way and on the same timetable as the equivalent system in hearing children acquiring English (van Hoek, Norman, & O'Grady-Batch, 1989).

Thus, across a range of linguistic subsystems, the deaf child, like his hearing counterpart, extracts discrete components of the language presented to him. Furthermore, the evidence suggests that even when the modality and the language offer possibilities that seem intuitively obvious or transparent (e.g., pointing for pronominal reference), deaf children ignore this directness and analyze the language input as part of a formal linguistic system. Studies of the acquisition process have found that deaf and hearing children show a strikingly similar course of development if exposed to a natural language at the critical time. These data thus dramatically underscore the biological substrate of the human capacity for creating linguistic systems. Such findings powerfully show how language, independent of its transmission mechanisms, emerges in the child in a rapid, patterned, and—above all—linguistically driven manner.

SPATIAL LANGUAGE AND SPATIAL SCRIPT

The focus throughout these studies has been the relationship between language and other cognitive domains, as revealed by the study of languages in the visuospatial modality—signed languages. We now turn to studies of the acquisition of a different kind of visual language: written language. Many studies by now have shown that deaf children exposed to ASL as a primary language acquire sign language in accordance with the same developmental milestones and at the same rate as the acquisition of comparable spoken languages, as mentioned earlier. Some of these children, however, have difficulty learning to read English fluently. It seems likely that the primary problem is that the child who is born deaf has little or no access to the spoken language around him. This raises an important question: How does a deaf child approach the task of learning a written representation of a spoken language he has never heard?

A number of ongoing studies are investigating this question with respect to different scripts, focusing on the acquisition of alphabetic script by American deaf children or on the acquisition of logographic script by Chinese deaf children, as well as comparisons across the two groups (see Fok & Bellugi, 1986). Taken together, these studies compare deaf signing children (acquiring ASL or CSL) with hearing children (speakers of English or Chinese), and examine the interaction between primary language modality — spoken or signed — and orthographic structure — alphabetic or logographic — in the child's entry into script.

Alphabetic Script.   Aspects of the interaction between ASL and other linguistic systems in the deaf child's environment (signing, fingerspelling, and script) in preschool deaf children of deaf parents have been examined in a number of studies (O'Grady, van Hoek, & Bellugi, in press; Padden, in press; Padden & LeMaster, 1984). In one study, American preschool deaf children's ASL signing, fingerspelling, and attempts at writing were contrasted (O'Grady et al., 1990). The deaf children were given picture books containing pictures of 40 common items, and were asked to sign, fingerspell, and write the name for each item.

By the age of 3 years, all the deaf children knew the correct ASL signs for nearly all the items, performing nearly at ceiling in their primary language. The 3-year-olds, however, were incapable of writing letters or words, and often produced scribbles. By the age of 4 years, most of the deaf children wrote actual English letters, but frequently these were random combinations of letters. Some of the scribbles of the youngest children proved insightful in terms of their attempts to make connections across linguistic systems. One child volunteered that what he had scribbled for the picture of a duck and for the picture of a pie were in fact based on the forms of the corresponding ASL signs (Fig. 16.5-a). He made the ASL sign DUCK, pointed to the handshape, and then pointed to the "writing," indicating that the two were intended to be the same. For "pie," the child first drew a square, and showed that he was illustrating the first handshape of the sign. He then made another drawing and indicated that he was illustrating one hand moving across the other. Thus his written responses (or more appropriately, his graphic representations) involved invented forms for representing the handshape and/or movement of the ASL sign, providing explicit evidence that he was attempting to connect the written language with his native language, ASL.

Another study examines responses from school-age children on the written naming task described previously, finding clear and consistent differences between contrasting deaf and hearing groups (Bellugi, Tzeng, Klima, & Fok, 1989; Fok, van Hoek, Klima, & Bellugi, in press). First-grade hearing children frequently base their early attempts at spelling on

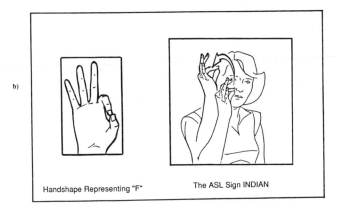

FIG. 16.5. American deaf children's "borrowing" from American Sign Language principles.

phonological analysis of words. Their spellings indicate a strong tendency toward using letter names to orthographically represent sounds of words (e.g. "n-d-n" for *Indian,* "p-n-o" for *piano,* responses starting with *g* or *j* for *chair*) and otherwise spelling by ear ("n" for *knife*). Deaf children, on the other hand, were quite uninfluenced by pronunciation. By the first and second grades, almost a third of the deaf children's responses were entirely correct. However, their mistakes differed from those made by hearing children in several ways. There were systematic elements in the deaf children's spelling patterns, derived from the orthographic system itself, without reference to sound. The errors sometimes reflect awareness of the visual form of English words, in terms of number and shape of letters, preservation of doubling of letters (even with the wrong letters), and so forth. Even when all the letters were correct, they were sometimes in the wrong order (e.g., crossing syllable boundaries as in "bota" for *boat* or "alppe" for *apple*). It also was found that deaf children at all grade levels were more likely to provide correct silent letters than were hearing children (e.g., "k" in *knife* or "c" in *duck*), further evidence of their essentially visual nonphonological approach.

As with the preschool deaf children in the study cited earlier, there were instances in which school-age deaf children attempted to connect their written responses to their primary language, ASL. As an example, many of the incorrect written responses of the young deaf children to *Indian* began with the letter *f,* whereas the common incorrect response to *fork* began with the letter *w.* Children "explained" their responses by showing the ASL signs INDIAN and FORK, which are made with the ASL handshapes also used for *f* and *w* in fingerspelling (see Fig. 16.5-b). These results suggest that deaf children who do not have access to the phonological forms of the spoken language nonetheless bring to bear a visual approach to the entry into writing English, and even at times make attempts to connect the orthographic system to their native sign language, ASL.

Visuospatial Script.   Unlike the English alphabetic script, the Chinese writing system is opaque with respect to the script/speech relationship and is emphatically spatial in the layout of every logographic symbol. The principles underlying the two contrasting orthographies (Chinese and English) are radically different in degree of sound to symbol correspondence, in numbers of distinct units, and in spatial organization (Tzeng & Hung, 1988). Fok and Bellugi (1986) investigated the beginning stages of writing in deaf and hearing Chinese children in four Hong Kong schools using the same picture-naming task as with the American children reported earlier. In other studies, American school-age deaf and hearing children's written English was contrasted with comparable deaf and hearing Chinese children's written Chinese (Fok & Bellugi, 1986; Fok, van Hoek et al., in press). The deaf children who took part in these studies were congenitally and profoundly deaf, had learned a sign language as a primary form of communication, and were in schools for the deaf in the United States or Hong Kong. The stimulus for eliciting written responses was the picture book used in the studies described previously.

Clear differences were found between the deaf and hearing children with respect to their basic approach to learning and using the Chinese writing system. Although the opportunities for using a phonological approach to writing are less direct in Chinese than English, the Chinese hearing children did bring their knowledge of the sound structure of the language into play in that some of their written errors are based on homophones in the spoken language, typically taking the form of substitutions of one character for another having similar pronunciation but no visual similarity. The deaf Chinese children in the study made no errors of this sort; rather, their errors frequently involved substitution of characters or components of characters that were visually similar to the correct character. The most revealing types of errors were those involving invented character forms (e.g., nonexisting Chinese characters). Often, target and error pairs made by deaf and hearing children alike were strikingly similar in spatial architecture and spatial organization. Even when the invented characters were unrelated to the target, they were invariably well-formed characters showing sensitivity to the implicit rules of spatial architecture.

Some of the errors made by the deaf children appeared to be based on principles of CSL, combining elements in ways that would be appropriate in CSL sign formation devices but not in written Chinese (Fok, van Hoek et al., in press). Some deaf children created nonsense "compound" characters, added movement "squiggles" to characters, and used size and shape characters to name objects as would be appropriate in CSL but not in written Chinese. The children extract rules of their primary language, CSL, and apply them to another form of visuospatial language, that of written Chinese script (Fok & Bellugi, 1986).

Comparisons of all four groups of children—deaf and hearing Americans, deaf and hearing Chinese—learning two different scripts suggest that the linguistic knowledge and predispositions the children bring to the task of learning play a large role in the early stages of acquiring and processing script, but that the nature of the script system determines the ways in which they may manifest. Hearing children rely on phonological representations, but in different ways in each of the two scripts. Deaf children in both countries take a visual approach to script and bring knowledge of their native sign languages to bear on the task, despite the fact that neither writing system has any intrinsic connection with either signed language. However, the Chinese writing system clearly appears to offer a greater opportunity for deaf children to draw on knowledge of their native language; the visual-spatial nature of the script affords a more intimate connection with the children's native visual-spatial language.

THE INTERPLAY BETWEEN SPATIAL LANGUAGE AND SPATIAL COGNITION

The study of the acquisition of a spatial language, and of the interaction between a spatial primary language and domains related to language, raises several important questions with respect to the interaction between language and other cognitive functions, particularly spatial cognitive functions. Some of these are being addressed in separate studies. In a spatially organized language, there may be a special and important relationship between the acquisition of language and the development of its non-linguistic spatial cognitive substrate. As Newport and Meier (1986) put it, "it has sometimes been suggested that spatial representation is conceptually difficult for the child, and therefore is a cognitively complex medium in which to signal linguistic functions" (pp. 916–917). On this view, the acquisition of morphological devices in ASL should occur somewhat later than the acquisition of formally similar devices in spoken languages, where spatial representation is not involved.

In fact, the available evidence suggests that spatial representation itself does not constrain the acquisition process, insofar as it has been found that the acquisition of the grammatical devices of ASL occurs on a strikingly similar timetable to the acquisition of spoken language devices that are formally similar. Separate studies now are comparing the acquisition of discourse functions (spatially marked anaphoric reference and discourse organization) across hearing and deaf children in the same sets of tasks (Bellugi, 1988; Lillo-Martin, Bellugi, Struxness, & O'Grady, 1985; van Hoek, Norman, & O'Grady-Batch, 1989). The findings suggest that even acquisition of discourse structures that are primarily spatially marked occurs on the same timetable as the acquisition of equivalent structures by hearing children acquiring English.

Separability.   Recent studies have focused on the developmental course for the acquisition of the spatial cognitive underpinnings that may form the prerequisites for the mastery of linguistic system (Bellugi, O'Grady et al., 1990; Reilly, McIntire, & Bellugi, 1990). The purpose of these investigations is to determine whether the development of spatially organized syntax is yoked to the development of those aspects of spatial cognition that could be considered a nonlinguistic substrate to sign. The results indicate that deaf children who have early exposure to a spatialized linguistic system perform at the same level as hearing children on spatial cognitive tasks. Some studies, reported later, suggest that there may even be some enhancement of certain spatial nonlanguage abilities, in children with early experience with a spatial linguistic system.

Spatial Analysis of Dynamic Displays.   The importance of spatial contrasts in sign language prompted an investigation of the ability to process nonlinguistic spatial displays in deaf and hearing children (Bellugi, O'Grady et al., 1990). An experiment was designed to assess the spatial abilities that children bring to bear in analyzing movements in space; the experiment was carried out with deaf and hearing children in four Hong Kong schools. The deaf children had been exposed to both a visuospatial primary language (Chinese Sign Language) and a visuospatial script (Chinese kanji or logographs). In order to extract movement in a direct way, a technique was used that highlighted movement patterns as dynamic patterns of light, using a small light-emitting diode attached to the fingertip (Poizner, 1981). Sixty invented (nonexisting) Chinese characters were presented as moving patterns of light, created by videotaping (in a darkened room) a person "writing" the characters in the air, so that only the pattern of a small moving light was visible on the screen (Fig. 16.6). Deaf and hearing children in Grades 1, 4, and 8 were asked to watch each point light display and write down the separate strokes of the nonsense character represented as a continuous flow of movement. Fig. 16.6 presents responses from deaf and hearing children in the first grade on a sample item. The hearing children tended to produce continuous squiggles; the deaf children were significantly better at remembering, analyzing, and decoding the movement in space into discrete components.

The same experiment has been conducted with hearing and deaf American subjects who have no knowledge of Chinese characters; again the deaf are significantly better than the hearing subjects (Bellugi, Tzeng, Klima, & Fok, 1990). It appears that this task taps special abilities for spatial analysis on the part of deaf children. Deaf children exposed to a visuospatial language may bring markedly enhanced spatial abilities to this task (Fok & Bellugi, 1986). Moreover, these results are consistent with studies by Neville, using correlations between electrophysiological indices and behavior, suggesting that attention to peripheral visual space is superior in deaf signing subjects (and may be mediated by different neural systems) than in hearing subjects (Neville, 1988; Neville, Schmidt, & Kutas, 1983).

DISSOCIATION BETWEEN LANGUAGE AND SPATIAL COGNITION IN DEAF SIGNERS

ASL displays complex linguistic structure comparable to that found in spoken languages, but conveys much of its structure by manipulating

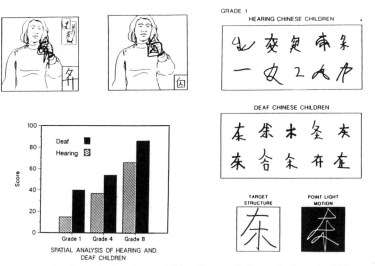

FIG. 16.6. Deaf and hearing children's spatial analysis of Chinese nonsense characters.

spatial relations, thus exhibiting properties for which each of the hemispheres of hearing people shows a different predominant functioning. The study of deaf signers with unilateral (left or right) cerebral lesions offers a unique vantage point for understanding the organization of higher cognitive functions in the brain, and how modifiable that organization may be (Bellugi, 1983; Bellugi, Poizner, & Klima, 1989; Poizner, Klima, & Bellugi, 1987). The broad aim of these studies is to investigate the relative contributions of the cerebral hemispheres with special references to the interplay between linguistic functions and the spatial mechanisms that convey them in profoundly deaf people whose primary mode of communication is a visuospatial language.

Impaired Language Capacities in Left-Lesioned Signers.   In a series of studies, researchers have intensively analyzed deaf signers with unilateral brain damage, either to the left hemisphere or to the right hemisphere (Bellugi, Klima, & Poizner, 1988; Bellugi, Poizner, & Klima, 1983, 1989, in press; Klima, Bellugi, & Poizner, 1988; Poizner et al., 1987). The signers with left-hemisphere damage showed frank sign language aphasias (and relatively preserved nonlanguage spatial functions). One left-hemisphere-damaged signer was agrammatic for ASL. Her signing was severely impaired, halting and effortful, reduced often to single sign utterances, and completely without the syntactic and morphological markings of ASL. Her lesion was typical of those that produce agrammatic aphasia for spoken language. The other two left-hemisphere-damaged signers had fluent sign aphasias, but differed in the nature of their impairments. A second left-lesioned signer was completely *grammatical* in her poststroke signing, although she made selection errors in the formational elements of signs, producing the equivalent of phonemic paraphasias in sign language. Her signing although grammatical was sometimes vague, as she often omitted specifying who or what she was referring to. She also had a marked sign comprehension loss. Interestingly, this marked and lasting comprehension loss would not be predicted from her lesion if she were hearing. Both major language-mediating areas (Broca's area and Wernicke's area) were intact. Her lesion was in the inferior parietal lobe, an area known to function for higher order spatial analysis. The third left-hemisphere-damaged signer had many grammatical errors; in fact, he was *paragrammatical*. He made selection errors and additions within ASL morphology, and erred in the spatialized syntax and discourse processes of ASL. Thus, differential damage within the left hemisphere produced sign language impairments that were not uniform, but rather cleaved along lines of linguistically relevant components.

Quite remarkably, considering the spatial nature of sign language, the signers with right-hemisphere damage were not aphasic. They exhibited fluent, grammatically correct, virtually error-free signing, with good range of grammatical forms, no agrammatism, and no signing deficits. Furthermore, the left-hemisphere-damaged subjects, but not those with right-hemisphere damage, were impaired in tests of ASL structures at different linguistic levels. Importantly, this preserved signing was in the face of marked deficits shown by the right-hemisphere-damaged signers in processing nonlanguage spatial relations. Across a range of tests, the signers showed the classic visuospatial impairments seen in hearing subjects with right-hemisphere damage.

Impaired Spatial Cognition in Right-Lesioned Signers. Selected tests that are sensitive distinguishers of visuospatial performance in left-versus right-hemisphere-damaged hearing subjects were administered, including drawing, block design, selective attention, line orientation, facial recognition, and visual closure (Poizner, Kaplan, Bellugi, & Padden, 1984). The drawings of the right-hemisphere-damaged subjects tended to show severe spatial disorganization, whereas those of the left-hemisphere-damaged subjects did not. The right-hemisphere-damaged subjects were not able to indicate perspective; several neglected the left side of space, and one right-hemisphere-damaged subject even added unprompted verbal labels on the drawings. The drawings of the left-hemisphere-damaged subjects in general showed superiority, with overall spatial configurations preserved. The two groups of deaf signing patients differed across the range of visuospatial tasks administered, with right-hemisphere-damaged subjects reflecting gross spatial disorganization. These nonlanguage data show that the right hemisphere in deaf signers can develop cerebral specialization for nonlanguage visuospatial functions. The right-hemisphere-lesioned subjects in general showed severe left-sided neglect and were seriously impaired in nonlanguage visuospatial capacities, but their signing was still fluent and remarkably unimpaired. Fig. 16.7 shows results of right- and left-hemisphere-lesioned deaf subjects on a visuospatial task (block design) in which right-lesioned subjects are severely impaired, and on a language task (the ASL equivalent of "rhyme") in which left-lesioned subjects show impairment relative to controls and right-lesioned subjects. The right-lesioned subjects (but not the left) showed no impairment in any of the grammatical aspects of their signing; however, their impairments were vividly apparent in spatial mapping, which is considered next.

Dissociation Between Spatial Syntax and Spatial Mapping. The patients' impairments in the use of space differ according to whether differentiated points in space are used syntactically or are used to give relative positions in space (Poizner et al., 1987). Patients were asked to describe the physical layout of their living quarters from memory; in this

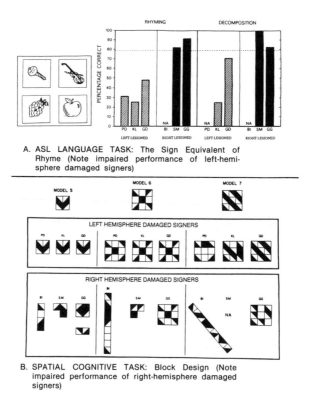

A. ASL LANGUAGE TASK: The Sign Equivalent of Rhyme (Note impaired performance of left-hemisphere damaged signers)

B. SPATIAL COGNITIVE TASK: Block Design (Note impaired performance of right-hemisphere damaged signers)

FIG. 16.7. Dissociation between spatial language and spatial cognition in deaf signers.

task, signing space is used to describe space and actual spatial relations are thus significant. The descriptions given by the right-lesioned signers were grossly distorted spatially. These patients were able to enumerate all the items in the room, but displaced their locations and even distorted spatial relations among them. In contrast, the left-hemisphere-damaged subjects' room descriptions sometimes were linguistically impaired (matching their linguistic breakdown in other domains) but without spatial distortions.

Where space is used in ASL to represent syntactic relations, however, the pattern was reversed. One left-hemisphere-damaged subject showed impairment of spatial syntax: He had a disproportionately high ratio of nouns to pronouns and tended to omit verb agreement (both pronouns and verb agreement involve spatial indexing in ASL). Furthermore, when he did use spatial syntactic mechanisms, he sometimes failed to maintain the correct agreement. For all three right-lesioned signers, spatially organized syntax was correct and appropriate; indeed, all three even used the left side of signing space in syntax. Thus, even within signing, the use of space to represent *syntactic* relations and the use of space to represent *spatial* relations may be differentially affected, with the former disrupted by left-hemisphere damage and the latter by right-hemisphere damage (Bellugi, Klima, & Poizner, 1988).

Analysis of the patterns of breakdown of a visuospatial language in deaf signers thus allows new perspectives on the nature and determinants of cerebral specialization for language. These data show that hearing and speech are not necessary for the development of hemispheric specialization: Sound is not crucial. In these deaf signers, it is the left hemisphere that is dominant for sign language. The subjects with damage to the left hemisphere showed marked sign language deficits but relatively intact capacity for processing nonlanguage visuospatial relations. The subjects with damage to the right hemisphere showed much the reverse pattern. Thus, not only is there left-hemisphere specialization for language functioning, there is a complementary right-hemisphere specialization for visuospatial functioning. The fact that much of the grammatical information is conveyed via spatial manipulation appears not to alter this complementary specialization. These results have broad implications for the neurological basis of the separation and interaction between language and spatial cognition.

Thus, studies of patterns of impairment due to localized lesions in deaf signers reveal that patients with damage to the left hemisphere show marked sign language deficits but preserved nonlanguage visuospatial capacities, and patients with damage to the right hemisphere show the reverse pattern. Furthermore, linguistic components of sign language are found to be selectively impaired, depending on the locus of the left-hemispheric lesions. These results suggest that the human capacity for creating complex linguistic systems with a specific syntactic organization has a strong innate component, and moreover, that the left hemisphere in humans may have an innate predisposition for language, independent of language modality.

DISSOCIATIONS BETWEEN LANGUAGE AND SPATIAL COGNITION IN WILLIAMS SYNDROME

Studies of the behavioral effects of focal lesions in deaf signing adults have contributed to knowledge of brain/behavior relationships. We report on a new direction of studies with a specific neurodevelopment disorder, Williams Syndrome, which also promises to augment knowledge of the relationships between cognitive domains and their underlying neural substrate. Although patterns of spared and impaired cognitive processes are observed following acquired focal lesions, it is unusual to find such sharp cleavages in development. Although it is well known that specific language deficits can exist without accompanying spatial cognitive deficits in development, the opposite pattern, in which linguistic abilities are selectively spared, is rare and has been little studied. Research shows that Williams Syndrome, which results in distinctive physical characteristics (e.g., specific facial features, heart defects), gives rise to a neuropsychological profile that is highly discontinuous from normal, and in which linguistic functioning is selectively spared in the face of severe spatial impairment and general mental retardation (Bellugi, Bihrle, Jernigan, Trauner, & Doherty, 1990). This fractionation of higher cortical functioning provides us an unusual opportunity to explore some of the central issues of cognitive neuropsychology. We have thus begun a program of studies of linguistic and cognitive functioning, studies of brain structure using magnetic resonance imaging, and brain function using neurophysiological measures, as well as studies of the neurobiological basis for the syndrome (Bellugi, Marks, Bihrle, Jernigan, & Culler, 1987; Bellugi, Marks, Neville, & Jernigan, 1987).

Cognitive Deficits in Williams Syndrome.   In studies so far, we have been examining six adolescent Williams Syndrome subjects across a range of neuropsychological tests, assessing general cognitive, linguistic, and visual spatial functioning (Bellugi, Marks, Bihrle, & Sabo, 1988; Bellugi, Sabo, & Vaid, 1988). The Williams Syndrome adolescents, with chronological ages ranging from 10 to 18 years, all have histories of delayed language and motor milestones, have IQs ranging from 41 to 64, attend special classes for the educable or trainable mentally retarded, and are unable to function normally in daily life. Despite unusually preserved linguistic capacities, all of the Williams Syndrome subjects tested are severely impaired on tests of general cognitive functioning. The subjects are uniformly unable to perform tasks reflecting the attainment of concrete operations, skills that are easily mastered by normal children by the ages of 7 to 8 years. The Williams Syndrome subjects fail across the board on tasks reflecting knowledge of conservation (two-dimensional space, number, substance, continuous and discontinuous quantity, and weight), seriation, and multiple classification, underscoring aspects of their severe cognitive deficits.

Peaks and Valleys in Spatial Cognition.   Whereas specific deficits of spatial cognition often are encountered with specific localized lesions, mental retardation generally is thought of as a nonspecific pervasive disorder resulting in across-the-board deficits. Recent studies, however, suggest that Williams Syndrome results in an uneven profile of deficits and preservations, with a particularly striking deficit in spatial cognition (Bellugi, Sabo, & Vaid, 1988; Bihrle, Bellugi, Delis, & Marks, 1989). Williams Syndrome subjects demonstrate gross deficiencies on a host of visuoconstructive tests. On a drawing task, the Williams Syndrome subjects make some effort to represent the features of the target, but they completely fail to organize the features into functional objects. Furthermore, there is a complete lack of spatial orientation, perspective, and closure. Although the Williams Syndrome subjects produced very poor drawings, they often spontaneously described the object they were drawing with great detail and accuracy. For example, in the course of drawing a bicycle, one subject labeled the parts represented (wheel, handlebar, pedals, seat, basket, wheel protectors, chain) and explained the functional significance of these parts ("it has wheel protectors like this and that; the wheel protectors are against dirt and rust"). Fig. 16.8 shows the Williams Syndrome subjects' grossly impaired drawings as well as their impaired performance on a block design task. The figure also presents the contrast between two age- and IQ-matched children, one Williams and one Down, in drawings of a bicycle. Although the Down Syndrome child's drawing is highly simplified, it shows good form and closure, in contrast to the disparate parts displayed in the Williams Syndrome child's drawing.

The Williams Syndrome subjects demonstrate a similar impairment on other visuoconstructive tasks. For example, on the Developmental Test of Visual-Motor Integration the Williams Syndrome subjects were required to copy a set of figures, ranging from straight lines and circles to more complex three-dimensional figures, from a model. The adolescents achieved scores typical of 5-year-old children. They demonstrated particular difficulty with items that required the integration of component parts to form a whole (e.g., a triangle formed by the arrangement of smaller circles). This difficulty was most apparent on a drawing task that requires the subject to copy a hierarchical figure: a global form comprised of numerous smaller, local forms (e.g., a large *A* made up of smaller *M*s). The Williams Syndrome subjects, like unilateral right-hemisphere-damaged adults, were more accurate at representing local features relative to the global configuration (Bihrle et al., 1989). The parallel between Williams Syndrome subjects and right-hemisphere-damaged patients is particularly intriguing because there is no evidence of space-occupying lesions in Williams Syndrome (Bellugi, Marks, Bihrle et al., 1987).

On visuospatial tests that do not involve motor manipulation, the Williams Syndrome subjects also demonstrate sharp cleavages in functioning. For example, on a test considered to be a relatively pure measure of spatial processing (Benton Line Orientation test), the Williams Syndrome subjects were severely impaired. Yet, these same subjects demonstrated a surprising ability to discriminate among unfamiliar faces on a complex visuoperceptual test (Benton Test of Facial Recognition). The Williams Syndrome subjects characteristically responded easily and correctly on this visuoperceptual test, suggesting that this preservation may be a hallmark feature of the disorder.

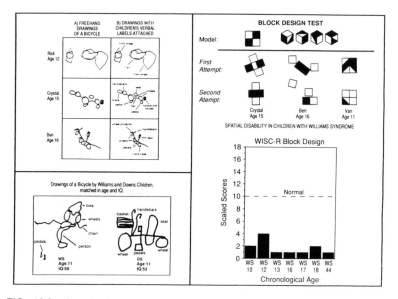

FIG. 16.8.   Impaired spatial cognition in Williams Syndrome children.

Selective Preservation of Grammatical Abilities.   In contrast to the Williams Syndrome children's impaired levels of nonlinguistic cognitive functioning, they demonstrate surprisingly good linguistic abilities in spontaneous speech and on formal language measures. Samples of the children's spontaneous utterances were obtained from conversation, interviews, and narrative elicitation tasks. The Williams Syndrome children are so loquacious, social, and interactive that the amount of spontaneous language elicited in a test session is considerable. The following is a language sample from a 17-year-old Williams Syndrome girl who has an IQ of 50, who was describing to her father her experience of having a magnetic resonance image of her brain: "There is a huge magnetic machine. It took a picture inside the brain. You could talk but not move your head because that would ruin the whole thing and they would have to start all over again. After it's all done they show you your brain on a computer and they see how large it is. And the machine on the other side of the room takes pictures from the computer. They can take pictures instantly. Oh, and it was very exciting!"

Despite marked cognitive deficits, the children's expressive language is elaborate and generally grammatically correct. The older Williams Syndrome children's expressive language is complex in terms of morphological and syntactic structures including full passives, embedded relative clauses, a range of conditionals, and multiple embeddings. Their sentences are complex and the syntax correct, although there are occasional errors of overgeneralization of morphology and pronoun usage.

The children also demonstrate impressive abilities on a range of formal language tests assessing vocabulary, morphology, and syntax. They have relatively preserved lexical semantic abilities, complex expressive morphology and syntax, as well as good metalinguistic skills. Age-equivalent scores on tests of both expressive language (e.g., the Gardner test) and receptive language (e.g., the Peabody Picture Vocabulary Test-Revised) were consistently higher than mental ages for the six Williams Syndrome subjects tested. Furthermore, they show a remarkable ability to define words, and to perform metalinguistic tasks, such as grammaticality judgments and self-correction, indicating that their linguistic abilities include awareness of grammatical structure.

Their scores on formal tests of grammatical knowledge are far higher than their scores on nonlanguage cognitive tasks and are in advance of what one would expect from their mental ages. Fig. 16.9   illustrates one aspect

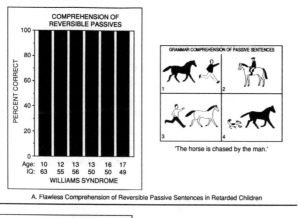

A. Flawless Comprehension of Reversible Passive Sentences in Retarded Children

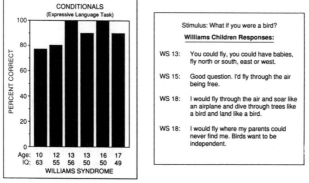

B. Grammatically Correct Responses to Conditional Sentences

FIG. 16.9.   Preserved grammatical abilities in Williams Syndrome children.

of their good linguistic functioning. The children are unable to handle Piagetian tasks of conservation, argued to be a prerequisite to acquisition of certain linguistic structures, for example, passives. However, the children routinely produce full passive sentences and their comprehension of semantically reversible passive sentences (e.g., "The horse is chased by the man") is flawless. The children perform well on other types of linguistic tasks such as responses to conditional sentences (e.g., one child responded to "What if you were a bird?" with: "I would fly through the air and soar like an airplane, and dive through the trees like a bird . . . ," see Fig. 16.9-b). Note in particular the excellent grammatical structure of the sentences of Williams Syndrome children in responding to conditional questions. This disproportionate sparing of language in the face of other cognitive impairments is highly unusual (the more typical pattern is the reverse), and is particularly impressive considering the delayed onset of language development. The dissociation between language and nonlinguistic cognitive capacities is quite dramatic and is consistently found across the children examined.

Linguistic abilities appear to be an island of sparing in Williams Syndrome, in the face of severe general cognitive deficits, particularly in the spatial cognitive domain. What is intriguing is that in Williams Syndrome, fractionations in higher cortical functioning occur in the absence of identifiable focal damage and in the background of general mental deficiency. Ongoing neuroanatomical studies using magnetic resonance imaging reveal that specific cerebral subsystems may develop in anomalous ways in Williams Syndrome, and these unique neuroanatomical features may relate to the behavioral features of the disorder (Bellugi, Bihrle et al., 1990; Jernigan & Bellugi, 1990). Further investigation of the neuropsychology and neuroanatomy of Williams Syndrome may aid in an understanding of the separability and interrelationship among components of cognition, and ultimately, their representation in the brain.

CONCLUSIONS

We have focused on the issue of separability between linguistic and nonlinguistic cognitive domains through an examination of the interplay and dissociations between language and spatial cognition. The linguistic development of young deaf children who are acquiring a language in the visual-spatial modality provides a privileged testing ground for addressing the relationship between these two domains. The spatialized structure of American Sign Language might be expected to have a profound impact on the course of language development; what is found in fact is that deaf children's acquisition of ASL proceeds on exactly the same timetable, and with the same developmental milestones, as hearing children's acquisition of spoken languages such as English. Moreover, there is no evidence that the necessity of developing spatial cognitive abilities in any way delays linguistic development in the deaf signing child; on the contrary, the evidence points to a selective *enhancement* of spatial processing abilities in deaf signing children.

Studies of brain-damaged signers have provided strong evidence for the independence of linguistic and spatial cognitive domains, even in a spatially organized language. Here we have argued that the left hemisphere shows specialization for language, regardless of the modality in which the language is cast. Damage to the left hemisphere produces sign language aphasias comparable to those observed in hearing subjects, whereas damage to the right hemisphere results in impairment of spatial abilities, but importantly, produces no impairment of language. Converging evidence from developmental studies and studies of brain-damaged signers indicates strongly that language, even in the visual-spatial modality, develops and breaks down independently from nonlinguistic spatial cognition.

A separate line of evidence for the dissociability of language and spatial cognition comes from studies of a rare neurodevelopmental disorder, Williams Syndrome. In Williams Syndrome, there appears to be a relative sparing of linguistic (in particular, grammatical) abilities in the face of severely impaired spatial and nonlinguistic cognitive functioning. These findings suggest that cleavages in higher cortical functioning may occur in development even in the absence of focal lesions. These studies of deaf signers and Williams Syndrome subjects provide powerful vehicles for delineating the components of cognition and their underlying neural bases, and should contribute to an understanding of some central issues of cognitive neuroscience that tie cognitive functions to brain organization.

ACKNOWLEDGEMENTS

This research was supported in part by grant HD13249, HD26022, DC00146, DC00201, and NS22342 from the National Institutes of Health to the Salk Institute for Biological Studies. We thank Edward S. Klima, Ovid Tzeng, Daisy Hung, and Lucinda O'Grady for their help in these studies. Karen van Hoek has been instrumental in particular in many of the studies reported here. We are also very grateful to the subjects and their families who participated in these studies. Illustration drawings copyright, Ursula Bellugi, The Salk Institute for Biological Studies, La Jolla, CA 92037.

APPENDIX

Notational conventions used for American Sign Language in this chapter:

SIGN Words in capital letters represent English glosses for ASL signs. The gloss represents the meaning of the unmarked, unmodulated, basic form of a sign out of context.

SIGN[“Exhaustive”] Morphological processes may be indicated by the specification of grammatical category of change or by the meaning of the inflected form.

ASL Spatialized Syntax: As part of the spatialized syntax of ASL, a horizontal plane in signing space is used for abstract spatial loci. Nouns, indexible verbs, pronouns, classifiers, size and shape specifiers can be associated with abstract spatial loci, and these are indicated by subscripts.

$_i$SIGN$_j$ Subscripts from the alphabet are used to indicate spatial loci. Nouns, pronouns, and verbs of location are marked with a subscript to indicate the locus at which they are signed (INDEX$_a$, BOY$_a$, AT-X$_a$) in planes of signing space. Inflected verbs are marked with an initial subscript to mark origin location, and/or a final subscript indicate the endpoint location ($_a$GIVE$_b$). Subscripts indicate abstract reference as well as coreference.

REFERENCES

Bellugi, U. (1980). The structuring of language: Clues from the similarities between signed and spoken language. In U. Bellugi & M. Studdert-Kennedy (Eds.), *Signed and spoken language: Biological constraints on linguistic form* (pp. 115–140). Dahlem Konferenzen. Weinheim/Deerfield Beach, FL: Verlag Chemie.

Bellugi, U. (1983). Language structure and language breakdown in American Sign Language. In M. Studdert-Kennedy (Ed.), *Psychobiology of language* (pp. 152–176). Cambridge, MA: MIT Press.

Bellugi, U. (1988). The acquisition of a spatial language. In F. Kessell (Ed.), *The development of language and language researchers, essays in honor of Roger Brown* (pp. 153–185). Hillsdale, NJ: Lawrence Erlbaum Associates.

Bellugi, U., Bihrle, A., Jernigan, T., Trauner, D., & Doherty, S. (1990). Neuropsychological, neurological and neuroanatomical profile of Williams Syndrome. *American Journal of Medical Genetics, 6,* 115–125.

Bellugi, U., & Klima, E. S. (1982). The acquisition of three morphological systems in American Sign Language [Keynote Address, Child Language Research Forum, Stanford University]. *Papers and Reports on Child Language Development, 21,* K1–35.

Bellugi, U., & Klima, E. S. (1990). Properties of visual spatial languages. In S. Prillwitz & T. Vollhaber (Eds.), *Sign language research and application: Proceedings of the International Congress, 1990* (pp. 16–25). Hamburg, Germany: Signum-Verlag.

Bellugi, U., Klima, E. S., & Poizner, H. (1988). Sign language and the brain. In F. Plum (Ed.), *Language, communication, and the brain* (pp. 39–56). New York: Raven.

Bellugi, U., Marks, S., Bihrle, A., Jernigan, T., & Culler, F., (1987, November). *Neuropsychological and neurobiological account of a metabolic disorder.* Presented at the meeting of the Society for Neurosciences, New Orleans, LA.

Bellugi, U., Marks, S., Bihrle, A. M., & Sabo, H. (1988). Dissociation between language and cognitive functions in Williams Syndrome. In D. Bishop & K. Mogford (Eds.), *Language development in exceptional circumstances* (pp. 177–189). London: Churchill.

Bellugi, U., Marks, S., Neville, H., & Jernigan, T. (1987, April). *Brain organization underlying unusual language and cognitive functions.* Paper presented at the meeting of the Western Psychological Association, Long Beach, CA.

Bellugi, U., O'Grady, L., Lillo-Martin, D., O'Grady, M., van Hoek, K., & Corina, D. (1990). Enhancement of spatial cognition in deaf children. In V. Volterra & C. J. Erting (Eds.), *From gesture to language in hearing and deaf children* (pp. 278–298). New York: Springer-Verlag.

Bellugi, U., Poizner, H., & Klima, E. S. (1983). Brain organization for language: Clues from sign aphasia. *Human Neurobiology, 2,* 155–170.

Bellugi, U., Poizner, H., & Klima, E. S. (1989). Language, modality and the brain. *Trends in Neurosciences, 10,* 380–388.

Bellugi, U., Poizner, H., & Klima, E. S. (1990). Mapping brain function for language: Evidence from sign language. In G. M. Edelman, W. E. Gall, & M. Cowan (Eds.), *Signal and sense: Local and global order in perceptual maps* (pp. 521–543). New York: Wiley.

Bellugi, U., Sabo, H., & Vaid, J. (1988). Spatial deficits in children with Williams Syndrome. In J. Stiles-Davis, M. Kritchevsky, & U. Bellugi (Eds.), *Spatial cognition: Brain bases and development* (pp. 273–298). Hillsdale, NJ: Lawrence Erlbaum Associates.

Bellugi, U., & Studdert-Kennedy, M. (Eds.). (1980). *Signed and spoken language: Biological constraints on linguistic form.* Dahlem Konferenzen. Weinheim/Deerfield Beach, FL: Verlag Chemie.

Bellugi, U., Tzeng, O. J. L., Klima, E. S., & Fok, A. (1989). Dyslexia: Perspectives from sign and script. In A. M. Galaburda (Ed.), *From reading to Neurons.* (pp. 137–172). Cambridge, MA: MIT Press/Bradford Books.

Bihrle, A. M., Bellugi, U., Delis, D., & Marks, S. (1989). Seeing either the forest or the trees: Dissociation in visuospatial processing. *Brain and Cognition, 11,* 37–49.

Clark, E. V. (1978). Awareness of language: Some evidence from what children say and do. In A. Sinclair, R. J. Jarvella, & W. J. M. Levelt (Eds.), *The child's conception of language* (pp. 17–43). Berlin: Springer-Verlag.

Fok, Y. Y. A., & Bellugi, U. (1986). The acquisition of visual-spatial script. In H. Kao, G. van Galen, & R. Hoosain (Eds.), *Graphonomics: Contemporary research in handwriting* (pp. 329–355). Amsterdam: North Holland.

Fok, Y. Y. A., Bellugi, U., & Klima, E. S. (in press). Sign and script processing in Chinese. In H. Kao (Ed.), *Proceedings of the International Congress of Psychology.* Sydney, Australia.

Fok, Y. Y. A., Bellugi, U., & Lillo-Martin, D. (1986). Remembering in Chinese signs and characters. In H. Kao & R. Hoosain (Eds.), *Linguistics, psychology, and the Chinese languages* (pp. 177–202). Hong Kong: University of Hong Kong.

Fok, Y. Y. A., Bellugi, U., van Hoek, K., & Klima, E. S. (1988). The formal properties of Chinese languages in space. In M. Liu, H. C. Chen, & M. J. Chen (Eds.), *Cognitive aspects of the Chinese language* (pp. 187–205). Hong Kong: Asian Research Service.

Fok, Y. Y. A., van Hoek, K., Klima, E. S., & Bellugi, U. (in press). The interplay between visuospatial script and visuospatial language. In D. Martin (Ed.), *Advances in cognition, education and deafness.* Washington, DC: Gallaudet University Press.

Jernigan, T., & Bellugi, U. (1990). Anomalous brain morphology on magnetic resonance images in Williams Syndrome and Down Syndrome. *Archives of Neurology, 47,* 529–533.

Klima, E. S., & Bellugi, U. (1979). *The signs of language.* Cambridge, MA: Harvard University Press.

Klima, E. S., Bellugi, U., & Poizner, H. (1988). Grammar and space in sign aphasiology. *Aphasiology, 2,* (¾) 319–328.

Launer, P. (1982). Acquiring the distinction between related nouns and verbs in American Sign Language. Unpublished doctoral dissertation, City University of New York.

Lillo-Martin, D. (1986). Parameter setting: Evidence from use, acquisition, and breakdown in American Sign Language. Unpublished doctoral dissertation, University of California, San Diego.

Lillo-Martin, D., Bellugi, U., Struxness, L., & O'Grady, M. (1985). The acquisition of spatially organized syntax. *Papers and Reports on Child Language Development* (pp. 74–81) Palo Alto, CA: Stanford University Press.

Loew, R. C. (1982). Roles and reference. In F. Caccamise, M. Garretson, S. U. Bellugi (Eds.), *Teaching American Sign Language as a second foreign language* (pp. 40–58). Silver Spring, MD: National Association of the Deaf.

Meier, R. (1982). Icons, analogues, and morphemes: The acquisition of verb agreement in American Sign Language. Unpublished doctoral dissertation, University of California, San Diego.

Neville, H. J. (1988). Cerebral organization for spatial attention. In J. Stiles-Davis, M. Kritchevsky, & U. Bellugi (Eds.), *Spatial cognition: Brain bases and development* (pp. 327–341). Hillsdale, NJ: Lawrence Erlbaum Associates.

Neville, H. J., Schmidt, A., & Kutas, M. (1983). Altered visual evoked potentials in congenitally deaf adults. *Brain Research, 266,* 127–132.

Newport, E., & Meier, R. (1986). Acquisition of American Sign Language. In D. I. Slobin (Ed.), *The cross linguistic study of language acquisition* (pp. 881–938). Hillsdale, NJ: Lawrence Erlbaum Associates.

O'Grady, L., van Hoek, K., & Bellugi, U. (1990). The intersection of signing, spelling, and script. In W. Edmondson & F. Karlsson (Eds.), *SLR '87: Papers from the Fourth International Symposium on Sign Language Research* (pp. 224–234). Hamburg: SIGNUM-Verlag.

Padden, C. (in press). The acquisition of fingerspelling in deaf children. In P. Siple & S. Fischer (Eds.), *Theoretical issues in sign language research.* Chicago: University of Chicago Press.

Padden, C. A., & LeMaster, B. (1984). An alphabet on hand: The acquisition of fingerspelling in deaf children. *Sign Language Studies, 47,* (2), 161–172.

Petitto, L. A. (1983). From gesture to symbol: The relation between form and meaning in the acquisition of ASL. *Papers and Reports on Child Language Development, 22,* 100–107.

Poizner, H. (1981). Visual and "phonetic" coding of movement: Evidence from American Sign Language. *Science, 212,* 691–693.

Poizner, H., Kaplan, E., Bellugi, U., & Padden, C. (1984). Visual-spatial processing in deaf brain-damaged signers. *Brain and Cognition, 3,* 281–306.

Poizner, H., Klima, E. S., & Bellugi, U. (1987). *What the hands reveal about the brain.* Cambridge, MA: MIT Press/Bradford Books.

Reilly, J., McIntire, M., & Bellugi, U. (1990). Faces: The relationship between language and affect. In V. Volterra & C. Erting (Eds.), *From gesture to language in hearing and deaf children.* (pp. 128–141). New York: Springer-Verlag.

Supalla, T. (1982). Structure and acquisition of verbs of motion and location in American Sign Language. Unpublished doctoral dissertation, University of California, San Diego.

Tzeng, O. J. L., & Hung, D. L. (1988). Orthography, reading, and cerebral functions. In D. DeKerckhove & C. J. Lumsden (Eds.), *The alphabet and the brain: the lateralization of writing* (pp. 273–290). Berlin: Springer-Verlag.

van Hoek, K., Norman F., & O'Grady-Batch, L. (April, 1989). *Spatial and nonspatial referential cohesion in the development of American Sign Language narrative.* Paper presented at the Stanford Child Language Research Forum, Palo Alto, CA.

IV

Acquisition by Instruction in the Language Delayed

In this, the final section of the book, there are four chapters that address the issue of how language can be acquired by children who are language impaired. Basic to all of the work presented is an assumption that in order to intervene, clinicians must have an operational grasp of the essentials of the acquisition processes. The different chapters address both theoretical and clinical issues in the context of innovative empirical studies to gain knowledge about ways to effectively teach language to populations of language-delayed and retarded children.

In chapter 17, Keith Nelson outlines his ideas concerning different language-learning models and different ways to intervene in order to teach language. He describes a language-acquisition model, rare-event learning mechanism (RELM), which assumes that at any point in the acquisition process most of the information available is ignored. He further argues that at critical junctures in the developmental process, rare or infrequent sequences of events, essential for language learning, are noticed and acquired by the child. Such selective engagement sets the occasion for what Nelson terms *selective storage*. Nelson also defines and describes other postulated selective mechanisms that are essential for acquisition: retrieval, analysis, monitoring and consolidation, imitation, and elicitation. He provides an example of how different children could boot strap the acquisition of passive sentences and describes how the RELM model could account for the observed behavior. Nelson next describes internal psychological factors that could influence language acquisition. He assesses the potential role of affect and provides a description of how networks of knowledge could be linked. Nelson also outlines the conversational circumstances that may influence language advances. In this regard, the author highlights the role of growth recasts in language acquisition. He asserts that structural changes subsumed ". . . under the term *recast* include addition of new structural elements, delation of structural elements, changes that respond to a perfectly grammatical sentence by the child, as well as those that expand or correct an utterance of a child." The author also elucidates how nonconversational training might influence particular language advances.

Next, Mary Ann Romski and Rose A. Sevcik describe their research on language learning in children and young adults who do not speak and have been diagnosed as being mentally retarded. The authors suggest that one reason that some mentally retarded children do not exhibit productive language is that the auditory vocal routes are impaired. If alternate systems are employed, Romski and Sevcik argue, it may be possible to teach language to such individuals. Romski and Sevcik used a computer-based symbol system, in a mealtime context, to augment other modes of communication with their subject population. The visual-graphic system is based upon the lexigram system developed by the Rumbaughs (see chapters 6, 9, & 10). The authors indicate that: "For subjects who come to the task with little comprehension of speech, the development of symbol comprehension skills consistently preceded symbol production skills indicating that they learned symbols in the way a typical child first learns words, that is, by establishing comprehension skills." Romski and Sevcik indicate that their work has focused in the main upon gaining an understanding of how symbol acquisition occurs in their retarded subjects. Thus, the major comparisons between their subjects and normal children is in the realm of early linguistic development. The authors do point out, however, that their subjects, using the computer-based symbol system, have ". . . attained levels of augmented language abilities heretofore unrealized in this population. . . ." Romski and Sevcik assert that their research supports the conclusion that instructional success, with the language impaired, is contingent upon the interaction between what a learner brings to the teaching situation in terms of communication and speech skills and the altered modality used for instruction.

In the following chapter, Mabel L. Rice discusses "teachability factors" associated with children who have been diagnosed as having a specific language impairment (SLI). Such children exhibit a profile of social, intellectual, and sensory function that is age appropriate but have language skills below expectation. Rice outlines the research literature that has focused upon a description and analysis of the problems shown by SLI children. Although not much is known about the lexical development of SLI children, Rice feels that this aspect of their linguistic development may be a critical factor in the deficits observed. The author suggests that a general explanatory model for SLI must account for: language delay relative to normal social and cognitive development, problems with morphology and word learning, and the social and long-term risks associated with academic achievement. Rice describes studies carried out by her at the Language Acquisition Preschool (LAP). The teaching strategies used at the LAP are ". . . an eclectic combination of techniques to enhance the salience and meaningfulness of linguistic input largely drawn from the adult interaction literature. . . ." Two of Rice's major conclusions are: (a) Difficulty in verb learning is a central issue in SLI, and (b) language acquisition is hampered by social reactions that impair motivational mechanisms necessary for language learning.

In the final chapter, James E. McLean and Lee Snyder-McLean report on their intervention research with subjects who are diagnosed as severely to profoundly retarded. Results from a series of investigations revealed the existence of different types of individuals regarding their a priori demonstration of the ability to have an intent to effect another person. Based upon their research findings, the authors identified a taxonomy that includes six different levels of communicative intent. Although many of the subjects studied demonstrated strong communication repertoires in terms of ". . . conventional distal gestures . . ." they did not evidence ". . . oral or symbolic communicative forms." Most important, McLean and Snyder-McLean found that their nonverbal subjects ". . . only indicated referents — they did not represent them." The authors assert that when nonhandicapped children reach a similar stage of communicative behavior they rapidly achieve spoken symbolic forms. In their subjects, the behavior observed is consonant with the hypothesis that there is ". . . an arrest of the normal developmental processes at the point of transition from prelinguistic to linguistic communication." Further, McLean and Snyder-McLean argue that treatment models for the severely retarded should emphasize the teaching of ". . . socially functional messages in interactive contexts with responsive people. . . ." This is the case because such a strategy leads to ". . . good acquisition rates and improved generalization." McLean and Snyder-McLean assert that such training should target acquisition of communicative behavior that has "effects on receivers." The result will lead to increased reinforcement of interaction between the child and those with whom he communicates.

17 On Differentiated Language-Learning Models and Differentiated Interventions

Keith E. Nelson
The Pennsylvania State University

In philosophy, linguistics, and psychology it often is assumed that good theoretical work should keep a clear distance from applied teaching and intervention settings. The assumption of this article and of its associated program of research is that just the opposite strategy pays off—good theoretical work can be grounded in data collected from applied settings (cf. Anderson, 1987). A second central orientation for this chapter is that both applied and theoretical work need finer differentiation than we have so far seen. In order to achieve the kind of differentiated theories and differentiated interventions argued for, it is essential to recognize that many key questions are open rather than settled. This position is close to that of Elizabeth Bates and her colleagues with respect to dissociable mechanisms in language acquisition (Bates, Bretherton, & Snyder, 1988; see also chapter 2 of this volume). Premature closure, the treatment of important questions as if a little bit of rhetoric and data settle them when neither argumentation nor data have been conclusive, can seriously hamper progress in intervention and theory. Accordingly, a third theme for this chapter is that many key issues in language acquisition remain open. A final theme concerns the process of language acquisition itself: We argue that advances in development can occur very rapidly if the child has access to even a little bit of the right evidence. To account for this phenomenon a rare-event learning mechanism (RELM) is hypothesized and described.

A good illustration of an open question in language acquisition comes from the work of Fillmore (1988) on second-language acquisition. Her work reminds us that we need to pay attention not only to when children learn language but also to when they do not, even though the circumstances seem to be favorable. Fillmore has looked at American nursery schools where the teachers speak English and most of the children are well along in English as a first language, but where a few children have learned Korean, Chinese, Spanish, or some other language as a first language, and have virtually no English. Over the course of 9 months of daily participation in nursery school, some of the latter group of children make substantial progress in English as a second language. Others, whose first-language skills in Korean, Spanish, or another language are quite good, make essentially no progress in either speaking or understanding English, despite some 700 hours in an environment rich in opportunities for participation in English-language conversations. Fillmore's research reminds us forcefully that a simple description of the environment in terms of the dominant language, or even of relative frequencies of syntactic constructions, is at best a crude one.

In order to put Fillmore's (1988) findings into perspective, note that even 7 hours of language interaction may be enough to stimulate significant advances in preschool children's sign language (Maxwell, 1983), spoken language (Nelson, 1977a), or reading and writing (Bissex, 1980; Soderbergh, 1977). So, there is a paradox—massive interaction sometimes means minuscule learning, but little interaction sometimes means alot of learning. This paradox holds for children across a wide range of cognitive capacities. To understand why input time and learning rates can be paradoxically related, we need differentiated descriptions, pinpointing those pieces of input that actually go into the child's long-term representations. These encodings of language are a small percentage of the apparent input.

There are many steps in processing, from initial attention through various passes in working memory and various passes into and out of long-term storage, along with the assembling of examples for comparison, and the abstraction of patterns for repeated testing against evidence in the examples. By the end of this chapter, we will have looked at many of these processing steps in light of what we know about children's language environments and how they exploit their environments. For the moment, we note only that our goal is to build a model of what the child brings to language acquisition, what the relevant language environment may be for a particular child, and how children use their emotional, social, and cognitive resources to take advantage of environments.

RELM: A LANGUAGE-ACQUISITION MODEL THAT DIFFERENTIATES BY VARIATION ACROSS CHILDREN, BY DEVELOPMENTAL STAGES, AND BY PROCESSING STEPS

The acquisition model presented here is open and evolving, with ample room for gradually filling in more about biological contributions, individual differences, and cultural variations, as new information becomes available. The model is concerned with how children use input and how they act with others. It also is concerned with the processing steps that bring current input into contact with the built-in constraints and acquired networks of representations. The model can be applied to sign language, reading, and writing, as well as speech and all subdomains of language. The model of RELM in this chapter elaborates on earlier versions (Nelson, 1980, 1981, 1982, 1987, 1988) with respect to both processing steps and individual differences.

A key assumption is that, at any developmental stage, children ignore challenging linguistic structures in much of the input that they encounter but select certain infrequent, or rare, sequences of events to guide them toward the acquisition of new structures. Within these rare-event sequences, efficient and powerful processing allows a little bit of conversational evidence to serve as the base for important language advances.

To emphasize these qualities in language learning, the model is labeled a rare-event learning mechanism—RELM. When the learner fully engages RELM to analyze a particular structure, a few relevant conversational sequences may be enough for its acquisition. For a period, RELM gives a high priority to processing all information relevant to this structure and actively seeks this information. "Hot spots" of analysis thus are seen as being central to the acquisition process. The next sections of this chapter provide an account of some of the many processing steps involved in selective analysis and acquisition of any new language structure. Fig. 17.1 schematizes the process.

Selective Engagement

In the acquisition process for any new language structure the first hypothesized stage entails the cognitive system selectively "attending to" certain word strings that do not match current structural descriptions; these strings initially are coded as mismatches or discrepancies from the current system. For example, a child may form a hot spot for analysis of English auxiliary use. She then may selectively (though subconsciously) attend to tag questions and passives as interesting, but initially uncodable, input strings worth storing for comparison with her current descriptions of auxiliary use. Once the discrepancies between new and current usage have been coded, the descriptions can be refined, and refined again through many cycles, until all essential details of input strings are coded. Thus, in acquiring tag questions and passive sentence structure the child eventually will code precisely which pronouns and which auxiliaries are deployed in contrasts such as "Isn't he?" versus "Aren't they?", and "They are helping him" versus "He is being helped by them." The selective engagement or "attention" (cf. Bates & MacWhinney, 1987) of the child's system—usually at a subconscious level—

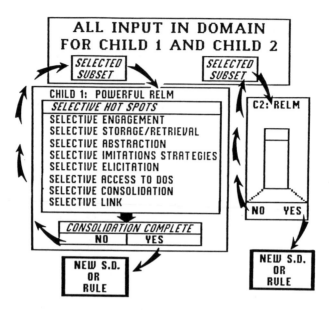

FIG. 17.1. Language learning according to RELM involves each child selectively processing and analyzing only a small subset of the overall input encountered by the child. At any developmental point, a selected set of tentative new rules or structural descriptions (S.D.s) under acquisition remain in hot spot status until abstraction and consolidation have been completed.

works on structural details in coordination with storage, retrieval, and comparison processes (cf. Demetriou, 1988; Fischer & Pipp, 1984; Nelson, 1987, 1988, 1989, 1990; Nelson, Loncke, & Camarata, in press; Rumelhart, & McClelland, 1986a, 1986b; Sternberg, 1984).

Selective Storage

In each instance of learning a new language structure, the learner's comparison system selectively focuses on mismatches within particular foci of analysis. Selected input strings are stored at several levels. Discrepancy tagging is the first level. When this process is applied, the child's system has noticed only that an input string is discrepant from any retrieved structural description; the input string then is tagged for storage in connection with the closest available structural description. So, for example, the child who can retrieve a structural description for "The alligator chased the tigers" might selectively tag as discrepant "The tigers were chased by the alligator, weren't they?" The learner's system at this point does not know how to describe the discrepancies between the input and the available structural description for a simple active sentence. However, by selectively storing in gestalt form of all or part of the discrepant sentences together with related sentences for which a full structural description is available, the child sets the stage for further rounds of selective attention, storage, and analysis (see Fig. 17.1).

Notice that, here again, the processing power of the system is applied very selectively. There is no broad claim that every input string that the child attends to is stored in complete form. Similarly, in contrast to simulations of language learning by Pinker (1984) and Wexler and Cullicover (1980), the model does not assume massive, extended, mainframe-computerlike retrieval by which the child can compare exhaustively all strings to all established rules and tentative rules. Instead, the model makes the limited claim that for selected foci young children and many older learners have the inclination and cognitive power to store some complete input strings for which a full structural description is not yet available together with selectively retrieved prior input strings and input descriptions that are "similar" — in ways to be specified and clarified by the learning mechanism's further examples and analyses in the future. Selective processes are the key words here.

When the child abstracts new levels of structural description for to-be-acquired forms, the child's selective tagging and storing keeps pace. This means that the more specific the child's tentative structural description, the more specific the memory tags and therefore the later retrieval will be. What the child is able to do, even by age 18 months or so, is to set up files in long-term memory that can be addressed according to particular structural details of interest. Accordingly, a child who is working out the final details of, say, passive tag questions and who encounters a new example will be able to (a) store the input string along with a fairly precise structural description, (b) retrieve related holistically stored input strings from earlier rounds of analysis, and (c) retrieve any previously stored structural descriptions concerning relevant details of auxiliary choice, positive or negative valence, by-clause, pronoun choice, and word order. By relying on a system that can be selective and efficient in storage, the child is able to tolerate considerable dispersion — across time and conversations — of the needed examples for working out a particular new structural description. Later, under the Variations on a Theme section, more detail is provided on how a child's current level and style might feed into successive rounds of hot spot storage, retrieval, and analysis of new language structures.

Selective Retrieval

As indicated earlier, the learner who tags a new input string as a mismatch with current structural descriptions will be able to retrieve previously stored examples related to the same kind of mismatch. Learners assemble within a short-term processing space ("working memory plus") a series of related examples, on which they perform systematic pattern analyses. Due to parallel processing within the learning system, complex searches, complex pattern analyses, further storage, and ongoing conversation can co-occur or alternate at very high speeds (cf. Bock, 1982; MacWhinney, 1987; Nelson, 1987a, 1980, 1982, 1987, 1988; McClelland & Rumelhart, 1986; Rumelhart & McClelland, 1986a, 1986b).

Selective Analyses in Working Memory

The learning system places patterns of input strings together in working memory according to similarities in their available structural descriptions and similarities in the gaps or discrepancies in these structural descriptions. Selective processing enters here in several ways. First, processing time is limited so that only a limited number of comparisons can be carried out on any assembled set of structural descriptions, wholistically stored input strings, and fragments of stored input strings (cf. Shiffrin, Murnane, Gronland, & Roth, 1989). Second, within the limited number of comparisons possible, analysis will concentrate on hot spots or tentatively abstracted foci of a particular developmental stage or substage. Thus, a child might search through several different examples of well-described active sentences along with less fully described, but semantically similar passive examples, ignoring all aspects of the sentences that do not relate to working out the *by*-clause, or other details of the active–passive distinction. On another occasion, using similar sets of sentences for comparison, the child might actively seek comparisons that concern the way in which modifier types are combined to produce complex noun phrases such as, "The big muddy alligator."

Selective Hypothesis Monitoring and Consolidation

In the period following the establishment of a new structural hypothesis, the child will be particularly attentive to input strings that appear related to the hypothesis. The child will compare strings looking for matches and mismatches, just as has been described previously. When input strings perfectly match with the available structural description, then during this period of intensive monitoring special record keeping will occur in long-term memory to determine how often the structural descriptions are successful. In many cases this will result in holistic storage of matching input strings. Naturally, any mismatches also will be noted and will result in further rounds of attention, retrieval, storage, analysis, and monitoring. These processing rounds will recur until a reasonable criterion of success is achieved or until the structural hypothesis is revised or dropped. Although authors such as Wexler and Cullicover (1980) stress distinctions between grammaticality and ungrammaticality, it seems likely that the child makes match–mismatch comparisons across a wide range of different types of hypothesis. Both in an individual child and across children the same kind of evidence may be used to generate quite different hypotheses. To the extent that this is true, a model of language acquisition actually becomes a series of related models with different children eventually achieving similar success by different paths. These different paths include differences in attention, in use of evidence, and in style of analysis, comprehension, production, and discourse (Bates et al., 1988; Ferguson, 1988; Nelson, 1987; Nelson et al., 1989; Nelson, Loncke, & Camarata, in press).

We must stress that it is important not to put the cart before the horse. If we endow the child with powerful structural descriptions before the child has begun to abstract its own structural descriptions, then we misrepresent the process of language acquisition and we underestimate the powers of attention, monitoring, memory, and analysis that even young preschool children bring to bear on language acquisition. These same abilities can be applied to the acquisition of any other complex, rule-governed, emotionally laden, communicative system (cf. chapter 2 of this volume; Calvin, 1990). Within a domain, additional domain-specific abilities or mechanisms also may play a role in acquisition, as Chomsky (1968, 1982), Fodor (1984), and Gardner (1983) have argued, and as discussed later under the section Selective Domain Organizing Supports. However, there are extensive data and good reasons to believe that a child initially organizes any domain in a flexible and somewhat idiosyncratic fashion (Bissex, 1980; Denninger, 1983; Macken & Ferguson, 1983; Maxwell, 1983; McTear, 1984; Nelson & Bonvillian, 1978; Nelson & Nelson, 1978). As the child's mastery of a system develops, domain-specific "modules" and "faculties" (that is, neural networks subtending domain-specific representations and processing routes) gradually emerge along with increased automaticity of processing. Thus, in accord with the general arguments of Bates, Thal, and Markman (chapter 2 of this volume) and Bates et al. (1988), the developmental literature as well as the literature on the loss of skills in aphasia (Bonvillian, Nelson, & Charrow, 1976; Sacks, 1987, see also, chapters 2 & 16 of this volume) points toward relatively low levels of domain specificity early in acquisition, but increasingly higher levels of domain-specific organization and storage as mastery and overlearning are achieved. In short, for the most part, acquisition success in a domain causes modularization, not the reverse. Further discussion of domains and their emergent organization can be found in Nelson (1991).

MacWhinney (1988) described normal children's language acquisition as "richly buffered" (p. 98). Nelson and others agree, arguing that most children receive an input "cushion" for first language so rich that it obscures the high power of the child's information-processing capacities (Nelson, 1977a, 1977b, 1980, 1981, 1987, 1988). Only when a child is given thin, but adequate, interaction experience in a communication system can we arrive at reasonable estimates of the limits of the child's attention, storage, retrieval, and analytic capacities. Similarly, when children acquire an atypical mode of communication, such as drawing or written or signed language, with the ease that we usually see in spoken first-language acquisition—that is, on the basis of limited, though fluent interactions with adults or older children who are expert in the particular mode—then we see that the learning mechanism is indeed flexible, open, and capable of remarkable feats of selective analysis, storage, retrieval, hypothesis formation and construction, and hypothesis monitoring and consolidation (Bissex, 1980; Maxwell, 1983; Pemberton & Nelson, 1987; Soderbergh, 1977). In each case, we may suppose, powerful and selective processes necessary for learning first are applied to a few of the structural details of a communication exchange system; then, with those first details in place, the child goes through round after round of actively seeking new foci or hot spots for engagement and analysis until gradually the complete system is worked out. Late stages of acquisition within any subdomain may involve considerable reanalysis and reorganization for flexible and creative use of rules that had been consolidated at an earlier stage (Bowerman, 1985; Demetriou, 1988; Nelson, 1987; Nelson & Nelson, 1978). Children with mild to severe delays in language learning may have less "buffering" in terms of intact processing capacities and/or their exposure to easy-to-process input (cf. Camarata & Nelson, 1988, in press; Heimann & Nelson, 1991; MacWhinney, 1988; Nelson, 1977a, 1988; Rice, 1988; chapters 18 & 19 of this volume).

Selective Imitation Strategies

From the earliest stages of language learning, different children display dramatically different tendencies to imitate—from no immediate imitation to immediate imitation in more than half of their conversational turns. These differences in imitation frequency must affect how children allocate their processing resources in working memory. More research is required to sort out the short-term and long-term consequences of reliance on imitative strategies. Nelson, Baker, Denninger, Bonvillian, & Kaplan (1985) observed that for early language stages the advantages and disadvantages of heavy imitation are about equal, but after the age of 2 years, the child's further progress on language is likely to be slowed by a strong proclivity for immediate imitation. These authors and many others, although taking widely differing perspectives on how imitative style interacts with other stylistic components that children bring to language learning, agree that imitative strategies have learning consequences (Bates, et al., 1988; Meltzoff & Gopnik, 1989; Nelson & Bonvillian, 1978; Speidel & Nelson, 1989).

Selective Elicitation

Children do not process "input sources" the way computer simulations do. Rather, they enter interactions, pursue goals, and plan actions or utterances that elicit certain kinds of language behaviors from others. Differences among children in their elicitation strategies can influence substantially the tone and content of cycles of interaction between language learners and their conversational partners (Ferguson, 1988; Macken & Ferguson, 1983; Shatz, 1987).

Selective Domain Organizing Supports

Children are remarkably flexible in their modes of learning language, from sign to text to speech to combined modes. Their ease of learning language in each mode can be supported by a number of different systems.

Production Constraints/Supports. Consider the "articulation" of linguistic messages in three modes: spoken, signed, and written. Whenever a learning child interacts with a fluent producer of a given language mode, the child is aided by the fact that the number of differentiated movement patterns and the number of resulting expressive components are limited. The child and the expert partner share essentially the same constraints. These support efficient organization of the output systems, but they do not eliminate the need for an extensive period of learning. In fact, there are some remarkable parallels in learning stages and processes between early spoken or signed phonological systems and later progress in syntax and discourse (Lindblom, MacNeilage, & Studdert-Kennedy, 1984; Macken & Ferguson, 1983; Maxwell, 1983; Nelson, 1977a, 1982, 1987; Nelson & Nelson, 1978; see also, chapter 15 of this volume).

Possible Subdomain-Specific Physiological Supports. In the absence of differentiated and rigorous work on how children learn language through particular episodes of interaction, many theorists have argued that subdomain-specific biological supports are the only reasonable explanation of children's language-learning success. At present, these proposals have the double limitation of vagueness and lack of persuasive data. Perhaps future work will provide stronger support for claims of innate underpinnings for basic semantic reference (Macnamara, 1982), templates underlying syntactic rule detection (Chomsky, 1968), systems of principles with crucial parameter values (Chomsky, 1980, 1982), or principles for organizing and interrelating stored information (Slobin, 1985).

Selective Linking and Integrating Networks of Knowledge (LINK)

Children tend to actively seek patterns of meaning cutting across domains and subdomains that many investigators and theorists have found convenient to keep separate. All children show this tendency for linking and integrating networks of knowledge (LINK). In early stages of language acquisition such link tendencies are better supported, on the whole, than tendencies to organize language tightly into subdomains, such as discourse and syntax (Bates et al., 1988; Maxwell, 1983; Nelson, 1991; Nelson et al., 1985).

These LINKs help to account for the relative ease of movement across far from fixed domain boundaries in the creation of metaphor, simile, analogy, and pantomime by young children, older children, and adults. As LINK networks grow extensive, overlearned, and accessible, they increasingly facilitate learning to learn, creativity, and on-line flexible adjustments of referential communication to changing goals, partners, and settings.

INPUT DEFICITS AND PROCESSING DEFICITS THAT NECESSITATE DETOURS TO ACHIEVE PROGRESS IN LANGUAGE ACQUISITION

Here it will be informative to discuss a few illustrations of partial detours around processing deficits as they fit into the RELM framework. The selected cases in no way represent the full range of language disorders, a topic beyond the scope of this chapter.

Technology-Augmented Progress in Communication in Retarded Individuals

In adolescents and adults who repeatedly have been assessed as severely retarded and whose combined receptive and productive vocabulary is under 20 words, it is highly likely that learning mechanisms are impaired. Nevertheless, with computer-augmented systems for pairing arbitrary visual lexigrams or text-plus-lexigram keys with social and food contingencies, surprising gains in symbolic communication have been achieved. When the computer-augmented system also triggers synthetic or prerecorded speech upon selection of certain keys (lexigram-plus-text), even stronger gains in comprehension and in subject-initiated communication have been reported (Romski & Sevcik, 1989; see also chapter 18 of this volume).

From the viewpoint of the RELM model, these technology-augmented conditions offer exceptional supports (domain organizing supports [DOS]) to severely retarded individuals in their language acquisition. These supports operate to constrain symbol choices in both storage and retrieval to a small number (typically 4 to 20). In addition, by means of augmented "speech," retarded individuals gain the power to trigger complex spoken phrases or sentences without having to activate and execute their own speech strings. Thus, such capacities as remain in the retarded individual's "thinly buffered" cognitive repertoire still may be put to effective use for abstraction, storage, and retrieval of components of a limited but highly useful message set. These are exciting conclusions. Moreover, there is a strong potential for new variations on technology augmentation to extend even further the communicative repertoire of retarded individuals and others with severe communication difficulties.

Input Shifts and Output Shifts that Bypass Specific Sensory and Motor Deficits and Facilitate Communicative Development in RELM-Intact Children

The RELM model posits considerable flexibility in the modes of language and in the patterns of input that can be successfully employed as bases for acquisition of a language system. The model fits well the successful acquisition of sign language from fluent sign partners, not only for children with normal hearing but also for severely hearing-impaired children. In our own work with computer-plus-teacher interactive systems in special education, we have found that software allowing text keys to be patterned in exploration phases into sentences that trigger meaningful graphics can help profoundly deaf children and autistic children and children with palsy or other serious motor impairments (Heimann & Nelson, 1991; Nelson, Prinz, Prinz, & Dalke, in press) in their acquisition of first language and text skills. Simple head movements, for example, can be linked to cursor movement and on-screen text key selection, allowing motorically limited children to make decisions and create text sentences just as rapidly as children without motor deficits.

The limit of language mastery for these children with sensory or motor deficits is set by a limit in the fluency of their human or computer partner.

In the case of sign language acquisition by deaf children of hearing parents, a shift in input patterns, so that these children receive 1 or 2 hours per week of interaction with fluent deaf signers, typically provides sufficient uptake for steady progress in sign language (Nelson, 1987, 1990). This finding reminds us of the consideration raised both in the introduction to this chapter and in the RELM model—a small quantity of high-quality input may provide all the processing opportunities that a rare event acquisition mechanism needs to achieve language fluency.

New Possibilities for Bypassing Individual Differences in Processing and Organizing Sequential Language

The RELM model is heuristic in the sense that its flexibility invites consideration of what would happen if some entirely new way of presenting speech were arranged for language learners. Technology now allows relatively easy manipulation of speech rate, format transitions, redundant voices, and redundant parallel presentation of graphic sequences portraying the meanings of spoken sentences. For children with deficits such as those considered earlier, it may be possible to find newly effective computer-assisted presentations that carry more redundancy and different speech rates than any child encounters without technology.

Similarly, for children who are diagnosed as having no other deficits than language delay it could be theoretically and practically of great interest to see what happens when communicative rates and redundancies are varied over new ranges through computer-assisted presentations. These children with specific language impairment (SLI) have been classified in laboratory tasks as impaired on both verbal and nonverbal material when very rapid sequences need to be comprehended or produced. Tallal and Curtiss (1990) reviewed these impairments. One telling example is that at rates of serial presentations of 250 msec per each of three tones, SLI children remember well, but at faster rates, such as 75 msec/tone, these children remember the stimuli much less well than normal children. This outcome invites the question whether an input set of sentences containing challenges to child's current language level would be processed more effectively if input speech were computer slowed. It would be consistent with the RELM model if SLI children built up representations of structural relations in syntax and phonology that at first could only be successfully retrieved and used when rates were close to the computer-slowed rates during learning. But with those representations in place the child might be able to automatize or otherwise enhance certain steps in processing in order to encode speech strings at normal speeds.

The next section of this chapter provides more explicit illustration of how a normal child's current system might influence the pathway to mastery of new syntactic structures.

VARIATIONS ON A THEME: HOW TWO DIFFERENT CHILDREN COULD BOOTSTRAP OR "DARWIN-STRAP" THEIR WAY TO ACQUIRING PASSIVE SENTENCES

Rounds of Analysis for a 2-Year-Old with Adequate Structural Descriptions Already in Place for Copula, Auxiliary, Past, Present, and Progressive Tenses, and Simple and Active Sentences

Round 1.   Passives enter hot spot status, they are noticed by the system as some unspecified mix of known and unfamiliar structures. There is fragmentary storage only at this point.

Round 2.   Gestalt storage of three passives in long-term memory, plus associated context. Associated context is assumed to be stored with all other sentences encoded into long-term memory.

Round 3.   Analysis in working memory of a new passive, aided by retrieval of three gestalts, leading to retrieval tags connecting all four examples and further tagging of all four as discrepant from active declarative.

Round 4.   A new passive enters working memory analysis, aided by retrieval of Round 3 information, leading to abstraction of a partial structural description of prototypical passives stored as a tag with all passives considered in this round.

Round 5.   Six more passives are given the same kind of processing attention seen in Round 4, leading to a build-up in long-term memory of further exemplars, their contexts, and their partial structure descriptions. Processing of the sixth passive in this round in working memory leads to a full structural description for prototypical passives that is stored in connection with the exemplar set used to "crack the code" for passives.

Round 6.   Through analytic rounds extending for several years, further subtleties in the structural descriptions of nonprototypical and prototypical passives are acquired (cf. Marchman, Bates, Burkardt, & Good, 1990).

Rounds of Analysis for an 8-Year-Old with No Passive Representations But with Adequate Structural Descriptions for All Verb Tenses and Most Prepositional Phrases, Appropriate Selection Restrictions for Most Verbs, and Extensive Long-Term Networks of Related Gestalts for Most of the Syntactic System

Round 1. Passives enter hot spot status for the first time. (This occurs so late in development for this child simply because no passives in salient contexts have been encountered before.)

Round 2. Six passives are stored as gestalts and also in redundant fashion as discrepancies from most prepositional phrases and from active sentences.

Round 3. One more passive enters working memory from ongoing conversation. By relying on rapid parallel search, many related structural descriptions plus supporting gestalts also enter comparisons in working memory and trigger abstraction of prototypical passive structure. In addition, relying on constraints already in the syntactic system, hypotheses are set up about probable behavior of nonprototypical passives. The 8-year-old's system has "learned how to learn" and proceeds actively.

Round 4. In 1 or 2 weeks, the Round-3 hypotheses about subtleties of passive structure and use are actively tested against data, leading to consolidation of a revised set of structural descriptive representations in long-term memory. Passives go off hot spot status. By relying on a more extensive set of established exemplars than that available to the 2-year-old and on structures retrieved from a long-term store that is searched more rapidly, this 8-year-old illustrates the rapid, rare-event learning of language structures.

The RELM model assumes for the aforementioned examples that the systematic structures are emergent, and that at each round of analysis there is a comparison and competition among multiple structural hypotheses. In this respect the account is similar to the Darwinian metaphor for developmental change proposed by Bates, Thal, and Marchman (see chapter 2 of this volume). They stress "continuity in the mechanisms, motives, and representations that underlie the evaluation and development of language." In addition, the RELM model is compatible with the notions of Calvin (1990) that: (a) a "Darwinian Machine" competition in subconscious serial buffers leads to the selection of the best candidate structure in terms of its current fit with available language data; and (b) essentially the same cognitive and competitive processes that occur in language development underlie the selection of nonverbal ballistic movement and other non-linguistic behaviors.

The child's pathway to higher levels of competence in discourse and semantics as well as syntax are affected by the child's current linguistic and cognitive levels. In addition, many other factors influence individual routes—a topic addressed in the next section.

INTERNAL PSYCHOLOGICAL CIRCUMSTANCES THAT INFLUENCE OR FAIL TO INFLUENCE PARTICULAR LANGUAGE ADVANCES

It is rather bizarre that the literature on children's acquisition of communication has so little to say about linkages between rules and representations in syntax, semantics, phonology, and pragmatics on the one hand and various systems of emotional or social rules and representations on the other. Let us briefly consider the kinds of information that may be included in a future, more richly differentiated account of communicative development. Take the example of affective state as raised by the research of Lois Bloom (see chapter 5 of this volume). Far from inhibiting or making less efficient the retrieval of the representations needed to learn a new word or to produce an already learned word appropriately in context, rich emotional access is likely to be highly supportive of language learning and language expression. The kinds of intersubjectivity between child and social partner that many investigators (e.g., Trevarthen, 1979) have discussed should certainly be part of any systematic account to how various language rules and forms come to be understood and used. For some language impairment and disorders, there may be a severe disability in language expression but no other obvious impairment in language or cognition. Nevertheless, the expressive disabilities may in part involve difficulties in establishing usual relationships between social-emotional systems and cognitive and language systems.

Stage-Front Versus Behind-the-Scenes Processing

Some children occasionally engage in episodes of actively and consciously manipulating and varying rules, phrases, and sentences in the languages they are learning. Other children show no such activity. Language acquisition models must account for language mastery by the full range of language learners. Accordingly, it seems appropriate to assume that most children most of the time do their language analyses and their abstractions of new language structures "behind the scenes" of conscious attention. As we see later, there are interactional strategies that adults can adopt to set the stage for language progress. Such strategies indirectly facilitate behind-the-scenes processing of relevant language structures; they accomplish this by drawing the child's conscious attentions to shared verbal meaning and shared social-emotional engagement.

Other Internal Events

Other internal processes may contribute to individual differences in what children do in conversation and what they learn from particular conversations. Many of these processes were considered in the first section (RELM) of this chapter. By way of further illustration, consider the internal event of retrieving information from long-term memory just after an adult has spoken to a child. The child's cognitive system presumably will find it easier to work out new language structures if retrieval is rapid, parallel, and efficient in yielding prior utterances and structural descriptions closely related to the adult utterances that the child has just encountered. Finally, when the child is alone there may be individual differences in "off-line," delayed retrieval and analyses of examples encoded from prior conversations (cf. Bowerman, 1985; Calvin, 1990; MacWhinney, 1987). What counts in developmental progress for all individuals in language are cognitive comparisons among the rare events, selected out of the total stream of language exemplars.

CONVERSATIONAL CIRCUMSTANCES THAT INFLUENCE OR FAIL TO INFLUENCE PARTICULAR LANGUAGE ADVANCES

In the past 20 years, many studies have tried to draw conclusions about the influence of input on children's language advances. Here we deal only with studies well enough designed to support reasonable conclusions about the influence of input on children's language advances.

Growth Recasts to Language-Impaired Children

In order to determine if language-impaired children have gained a particular new structure through intervention, it is essential to demonstrate that: (a) they initially lack structure, (b) they receive opportunities for learning, and (c) they generalize the newly acquired structure to everyday conversational exchanges. In a recent study, Camarata and Nelson (1988, in press) met these criteria using a technique labeled *growth recasts* to stimulate acquisition of new language structures by impaired children.

Growth recasts in this work are replies by adult therapists or speech pathologists to utterances that a child has just produced. Specifically, a reply to a child's utterance is a recast if it: (a) maintains the basic meaning and basic references to events of the child's utterance, (b) occurs immediately (within 3 seconds of the child's utterance), and (c) includes syntactic changes. The recast is a *growth recast* if it includes syntactic structures beyond the child's current level. Because the adult utterance carries the same meaning, but differs from the child's utterance structurally, the child can compare the two structures. Each growth recast thus provides an opportunity for growth in the sense that some of the particular structures incorporated in the adult recast are beyond the child's language system. For example, if a child says "The boy rolled the ball," an adult might provide the growth recast, for a child lacking the passive, by saying "Yes, the ball was rolled by the boy." For each child studied (Camarata & Nelson, 1988, in press), recasting effectively triggered introduction of new language structures into their spontaneous language (cf. Scherer & Olswang, 1984). Moreover, in comparison with a behaviorally oriented imitation procedure, recasting required fewer target presentations for acquisition to occur.

In contrast to recasting, most language training for language-impaired children occurred outside conversational contexts. And for the most part, such out-of-context training has not generalized to spontaneous use of new language forms, in ordinary conversational settings.

This general conclusion may seem surprising if one looks at the published conclusions of many authors who have reported on training studies with language-impaired children. After all, within the stripped-down context of training, it is common for investigators to observe that repeatedly asking a child to pay attention and produce a form such as "in," "sock," or "ing," etcetera, does lead to a clear-cut increase in the frequency of using the form with training materials. However, the possible advantages of making a form and its production highly salient, often observed, and often rewarded may be more than offset by the disadvantages of out-of-context, nonconversational training conditions (Nelson, 1988).

From a theoretical perspective, frequent presentation and imitation in no way guarantees occurrence of the needed encodings and comparisons held to lie behind incorporation of new forms, rules, and principles into the language system. Instead, stropped-down training may lead to encoding and retrieval from training-specific production systems.

Growth Recasts to Children Who are Progressing Normally in Language Acquisition

An extensive chain of naturalistic and experimental studies now converge on the conclusion that growth recasts can suffice to trigger the acquisition of a wide range of new syntactic structures by children. There is no similar convergent pattern of evidence supporting other conversational circumstances as effective triggers. But new triggers should be sought and tested. As Bates et al. (1988) and Nelson (1977a, 1977b, 1980, 1981, 1982, 1988) argued, experimentally convergent work is an essential way of testing whether naturalistically identified potential triggers can be effective and efficient in inducing language advances.

Once we have a more fully differentiated account of how particular kinds of recasts facilitate particular kinds of syntactic advances, we may be able to draw inferences about the processing that children follow in exploiting the information in growth recasts. Similarly, when other triggering conversational events are established, accounts of how these triggers function at particular stages of language acquisition for particular language forms should lead to more refined models of the emergence of new language structures in the child's system. We then may be in a position to translate our empirically based models into effective language intervention strategies for language-impaired children.

Next, we consider the relatively small body of evidence bearing on some more differentiated questions about how recasts are placed in discourse and the degree of challenge that they provide to particular children's current language levels.

Which Utterances Receive Recasts?

As the aforementioned definition of recasting illustrates, recasting always departs from exact imitation of a child's utterance. Beyond that, however, the recasts can vary from modifications of complete and grammatically correct sentences, to slight corrections, to reorderings of utterances, to relatively major corrections or expansions of the child's utterances, to shorter replies that provide recasting through deletion of many elements present in the child's utterance. In terms of providing opportunities for the child to compare similarities and differences between his or her own utterance with its underlying rules and an adult recast, all of these varieties of recast may have an impact on the child's language progress.

The first empirical outcome to be considered here is that when children produce utterances containing a structural error, adults are more likely to provide imitations or recasts than when children make no error. Observe that findings stated in this form are relatively undifferentiated—they do not specify the particular kind of error in the children's utterances, and they do not differentiate between various kinds of imitations or recasts. Reports by Hirsh-Pasek et al. (1984) and Penner (1987) are couched in these broad terms. If different kinds of adult recasts play different roles in the child's analysis of new language forms, then these rather general analyses may obscure important processing steps in the child's working out of new language structures. For example, theoretical and empirical work by Nelson and his colleagues (Nelson, 1978, 1980, 1981, 1987, 1988, 1989; Nelson, Denninger, Bonvillian, Kaplan, & Baker, 1984) suggests that exact imitations play a very different role than growth recasts.

Bohannon and Stanowicz (1988, 1989) examined which utterances by children elicit imitations and which utterances elicited recasts. They found for 2-year-old children that: (a) well-formed utterances elicit relatively more exact imitations by their parents and other adults than ill-formed sentences, and (b) utterances containing semantic, phonological, or syntactic errors are more likely to elicit recasts that replace elements in the child's utterance or that add new elements to the utterance. In short, there is specific and differential contrast in the pattern of replies that adults give children's utterances: Not only do utterances that contain errors elicit a higher percentage of recasts, but these recasts can be further differentiated into those that do and those that do not carry correct exemplars matched to the child's error. An error by the child either in syntax or in phonology was followed in 36% of the cases by a recast in parental speech. Similarly, but even more dramatically, an error by the child in semantics (for example, *dog* for *cow*) was followed by a correcting parental recast in 89% of cases. These results are for sentences by the children containing only one error. Bohannon and Stanowicz argued that this kind of pairing of a single error within a subdomain of language, such as syntax, with an adult recast that provides an opportunity to observe the correct exemplar constitutes one ideal learning situation. In terms of either the RELM model or the competition model (Bates & MacWhinney, 1987), the child is given a clear opportunity to compare her own handling of a certain structure with an adult's handling of that same structure. If the child's attention is already on the appropriate meaning and nonverbal context of the utterance, analysis of the structural contrast between the child's utterance and the adults's may be facilitated.

It is important to note though that many learning opportunities arise even when the child had made no error in her own sentence. For example, in Bohannon and Stanowicz's (1988, 1989) data (parent and nonparent considered together), adults provide recasts to 13% of children's well-formed, error-free sentences. Which of these adult replies could provide learning opportunities to the child? A more differentiated analysis of data is needed to answer this question. The particular kinds of recasts that would provide learning opportunities are growth recasts presenting structures that the child has yet to acquire. However, in order to specify which recasts are growth recasts, it would be necessary to analyze each child's current level of language proficiency. The next subsection presents evidence concerning this level of differentiation.

Further Demonstrations and Experimental Studies That Growth Recasts Facilitate the Acquisition of New Language Structures

In a series of studies, Nelson and his colleagues (Baker & Nelson, 1984; Baker, Pemberton, & Nelson, 1985; Nelson, 1977b, 1982, 1987; Nelson et al., 1984; Pemberton & Watkins, 1987) have used baseline and intervention procedures to allow controlled tests of the hypothesis that growth recasts facilitate the acquisition of new language structures. Children only received intervention, and control structures were tracked, when both target and control structures were known to be lacking in the child's language systems at the onset of intervention. For example, if a child specifically lacked relative clauses, then the child might receive growth recasting that introduced relative clauses; a child who says, "The boy small" could be given the recast, "The boy who is sitting is small". Similarly, a child who says, "The horse chased the dog," and who lacks passives might receive the recast, "The dog was chased by the horse." In these studies recasts were given both for utterances that contained an error, and for utterances that were perfectly well formed but lacked the target structure. Children who received growth recasts for such structures as modals, future-tense verbs, complex noun phrases, relative clauses, passives, and tag questions acquired these structures in about 6 hours of conversation of which growth recasts comprised less than 10% of the adult utterances. These are differentiated outcomes in the sense that particular children who lacked particular language structures before interventions and who received intervention targeted specifically to the absent structures acquired those structures but not the untargeted control ones during the period of intervention.

Further steps in differentiating would be appropriate in both experimental and observational work. Steps in these directions are presented next.

Differentiated Levels of Challenge Between Children's Utterances and Growth Recasts

Another kind of differentiation that would help to fill out the picture theoretically and in terms of intervention strategies for language-impaired children would be to specify the gap in levels of complexity between a child's utterances and the growth recasts. On the basis of past analyses, it appears that we often have underestimated the level of challenge that children can accommodate. Children 30 months of age who are close to normative levels in the complexity of their language system have been shown in growth-recasting studies to acquire passives (cf. Horgan, 1978, on passive acquisition between ages 5 and 11 years), tag questions, and relative clauses many steps in complexity above their current language systems (Baker & Nelson, 1984; Baker et al., 1985; Nelson, 1977b, 1987, 1988; Nelson et al., 1984).

Learning the "Unlearnable"

In recent years, some linguists have argued that particular syntactic structures are "unlearnable" if they are both rare in the child's overall input and complex: Maturationally governed, innate biological constraints and principles are held to underlie acquisition of such structures (Lightfoot, 1989). The experimental studies discussed earlier cast doubt on these lines of argument, because results show that 30- to 36-month-old children learn rare and complex target structures rapidly when the targets are recast to be easily noticed and processed. Matched-control children who encounter the same structures — passives, tag questions, and relative clauses — only very rarely and not as recasts do not acquire the structures. Thus, good processing opportunities rather than maturational status determine whether rapid learning takes place. The RELM escapes the apparent unlearnability problem for structures rare in the overall "impoverished" input set (cf. Chomsky, 1968, 1980, 1982; Lightfoot, 1989) by taking dramatically effective advantage, when they do occur, of certain *doubly rare* instances in naturalistic conversation — those instances (e.g., growth recast sequences) that both present a clear challenge to the child's current level and facilitate processing and encoding.

Differentiating Conversational Sequences into Deeper Levels

Most analyses of conversations in the literature, intended to assess "input" to children, are highly undifferentiated accounts of what adults say to children under what circumstances. The majority of studies go no deeper than Level 1 or 2 in Table 17.1: They say nothing about the child's utterances, but simply tabulate different categories of adult speech, usually broad undifferentiated categories such as questions, declaratives, or repetitions. The more differentiated accounts discussed earlier at least move into a two-layer analysis of conversational exchange: A prior utterance is considered in relation to a reply.

As we move down Table 17.1 toward the more differentiated descriptions, a clear agenda for rigorous future research emerges. What we would like to know about children's utterances that contain errors is what particular conversational sequences help the child to notice, analyze, abstract, and consolidate new language structures that will, in effect, repair the errors. An adequate description would specify what kinds of adult

TABLE 17.1
Levels of Analysis of Adult and Child Conversational Exchanges

Level	Type of Analysis
1	Child Utterances Unanalyzed. Adult Noncontingent Categories Analyzed: e.g., Dclaratives, Auxiliary-Fronted Questions
2	Child Utterances Unanalyzed. Adult Contingent Categories Analyzed: e.g., Exact Immediate Imitation, Recasts – Undifferentiated by Complexity
3	2-Layer Simple Cross-Classifications: Child Preceding Utterance Categories, Cross-Classified by Adult Reply Categories
4	a. Level 2, Cross-Classified by Children's Rates of Language Learning b. Level 3, Cross-Classified by Children's Rates of Language Learning
5	2-Layer Complex Cross-Classification: Child Preceding Utterance Categories, Cross-Classified by Adult Reply Categories Without Challenges, and Adult Reply Categories With Challenges to Individual Child OR Adult Preceding Utterance Categories Without Challenges, and Adult Preceding Utterance Categories With Challenges, Cross-Classified by Child Reply Categories
6	Many-Turn, Many-Layer Analyses of Utterance → Reply → Reply, Cross-Classified by Error Type/No Error and Challenges/Replies to Challenges, Degree of Challenge, Degree and Rate of Acquisition of Challenge Structures

utterances, carrying which levels of challenge to the child's error, and placed where in the conversational sequences, contribute to the child's learning.

For children who have produced utterances that contain no error, opportunities for learning may arise from growth recasts or other conversational sequences that present challenges to the child's current level of language. It would be rewarding to see some investigations go three, four, five, or more layers deep into conversation as part of a differentiated account. For example, adult utterances may set up a topic in an initial turn of conversation. The next turn may give the child the chance to display her current level of language. In the next turn, the adult may provide a growth recast or repetition of what the child has just said. If it is a growth recast, the child then may provide clues that she understood the adult utterance by attempting to reproduce or elaborate it. In the next turn after that, further acknowledgment, confirmation, elaborations, new structural contrasts, and so forth, may occur.

Further Differentiations of Rare-Event Processing

As we have seen previously, all recasts have the property of maintaining the basic event reference of a prior utterance, yet syntactically redisplaying or recasting the meaning. Growth recasts do this "at growth potential," that is, above the child's current level. When the child succeeds in encoding at least part of the growth recast into long-term memory, a rare *coalescence* of conditions occurs. This coalescence happens only in a rare minority of conversational opportunities. In discussions earlier in this chapter, the following contributing conditions were emphasized: (a) a base utterance followed immediately (within 3 sec) by a recast; (b) shared reference and shared nonverbal context for utterance and recast; and (c) the child's attention to the base utterance, as inferred from the fact that the child produced it, or the utterance occurred in a story to which the child closely attended.

Here we differentiate further conditions that seem likely to facilitate successful encoding and processing of rare-event sequences leading to acquisition of new syntactic and discourse structures: (a) prosody cues correlated with phrasal structure (cf. Morgan, 1986); (b) rates of language (sign, speech, or text) compatible with the child's sequential processing capacities; (c) additional nonverbal and verbal priming of target-relevant information from long-term memory, both before the base utterance and after the recast; (d) immediately after the recast, relatively few processing demands that compete with target-relevant retrieval, comparison, abstraction, and storage; (e) structural recasts of the targets by more than one partner and with some variety in priming contexts (cf. Salomon, Perkins, & Globerson, in press); and (f) adaptation of interaction to the child's cognitive motivational and social style, including comfortable emotional-social rapport with the current conversational partner(s) (cf. earlier discussions on internal states) and including subtle support from the partner for the child's self-esteem and initiative-taking (cf. Lepper et al., in press).

CONCLUSION

The following are synopses of the issues we have discussed:

1. Highly detailed and precise models of how some children smoothly learn language and how others fall behind are needed.

2. Theorists and practitioners alike need to acknowledge and orient to key open questions on acquisition and on strategies for helping language-impaired children in acquisition.

3. An important set of open questions concerns which aspects of the input are influential at particular stages in the child's acquisition of particular new language structures, and how the influential components of the input are processed by the child.

4. Theoretical models of language acquisition must deal with actual rather than invented input sets, and with data demonstrating clear-cut acquisition of new language structures by particular children at particular developmental stages. A powerful strategy for improving models of development, then, is to study instances of substantial change intensively. As part of this strategy, investigators could profitably collect data on precisely what input contributes to such change and on the steps along the path to a substantial structural change. As Bates and MacWhinney (1987) observed: "In short, we cannot assume that the data input to the learner is the same for every child—even though it may look the same from our point of view" (p. 19).

An analogy with another field of study may be helpful. Studying the "life history" of a tornado, from formation to disappearance, proved not very revealing when undifferentiated techniques of tracking broad weather fronts were applied. But hand throwing instrument packages into the path of a newly formed tornado yielded fine-grained, differentiated, developmental data. Similarly, to understand how newly forming language structures are acquired, data collections needs to focus on clear-cut instances of language advance and on the conversational circumstances that support such instances. It may be easier to choose a random sunny day and to analyze whatever data happen along for possible tornadoes or possible language advances, but that is no substitute for intensive, precisely focused study of particular phenomena.

5. Methods of investigation must be adapted to the questions they address. For example, for many of the theoretical questions concerning how the child uses input to make progress in syntax, the standard and most often used, but least differentiated method is very weak: Brief cross-sectional transcripts, no matter how many times they are coded and run through computer-based analyses and simulations, will provide only limited bases for detailed theorizing or intervention. Instead, such transcripts must be supplemented by many intensive data bases that specify both available input and the child's own utterances at a density many times greater than that usually reported. Moreover, such intensive sampling needs to be combined with convergent, closely related experimental designs.

This volume includes an impressive range of creative, and revealing, and, to use the term that Hirsh-Pasek and Golinkoff favor, "devious" methods of studying language acquisition. To reveal the heart of language acquisition, these devious methods must be coordinated in highly differentiated ways to answer highly differentiated questions. Questions such as "How does the child find in input, initially represent, retrieve, analyze, abstract, and consolidate passive structures?" need to replace broad questions such as "Is language innate?" or "Does input matter?" Similarly, methods and data analyses that differentiate by the child's language level, cognitive level, quality and quantity of input should replace investigations that create undifferentiated data by collapsing variation on most or all of these factors.

6. A rare-event learning mechanism, RELM, is presented here in its most recent form. The model is an evolving one. By explicitly addressing individual differences in many aspects of language processing, the model accommodates language-impaired as well as normal children. Biological constraints on learning and organizing language subdomains and an overall language system also are incorporated as a domain-organizing system. However, it is argued that these constraints operate at many levels, that they permit language acquisition in many flexible modes (sign, text, speech, etc.), and that their form is still highly speculative. As open questions go, the nature of built-in constraints remains one of the most open in the field.

7. Too often intervention procedures and theoretically oriented descriptive and simulated studies have counted each input occurrence of a structure as an important event. But only a few examples in a typical conversation really contribute to language growth. These *rare* examples are *encoded* examples that enter a sequence of comparison and analysis for the abstraction of new structures.

8. A goal for future treatment of language-impaired children should be to develop specific approaches, differentiated according to the child's impairments and according to the input that the child already is encountering. Current literature and current clinical procedures almost never give differentiated data in both these areas for individuals.

9. Many children may be "impaired" only in the input they encounter. Given proper assessment such children could be expected to profit richly from conversationally embedded intervention techniques such as growth recasting. In growth recasting targets for acquisition are presented as recasts to utterances that the child has just produced, as in the following exchange. Child: "The porpoises is jumping." Adult: "Yes, the porpoises are jumping, aren't they?" Six hours or less of growth recasting have produced substantial syntactic gains.

10. The RELM model proposes that acquisition can be very rapid, if the input is optimal and if the child's learning mechanism gives strong selective priority to particular new structures, discrepant from the language structures already in the child's language system. Work on techniques such as growth recasting show that sufficient conditions for triggering rapid, rare-event style learning can be created in conversational contexts. For speech pathologists, therapists, teachers, and parents, there are grounds for some optimism in these developments. It may be feasible to develop mixed models of intervention that are primarily, but not exclusively, conversational in nature so that most intervention materials have a high probability of receiving processing and analysis by RELM. The new language structures then would be encountered primarily in conversation and might be readily

generalized across conversational settings, rather than being restricted (like most prior intervention results) to the specific people and contexts involved in training. Here we suspect that "less is more." Each targeted language structure could receive fewer presentations than in traditional imitation training and yet be acquired more efficiently.

11. The search for differentiated treatments of language-impaired children and differentiated models of the learning process underlines the fundamental complimentarity rather than the opposition between applied and theoretical work. Each can advance by focusing on open questions and by seeking answers through diverse, finely differentiated methods and strategies. Anderson (1987) has presented similar arguments not only for language acquisition but for cognitive science research in general.

12. Research on language acquisition and intervention should be aided by recognizing that questions in science are never completely closed or completely separate. As Bates and her colleagues (Bates et al., 1988) argued in a recent book: "Eccentricity should always be the argument of last resort in science. We think that it is better scientific policy to assume that any phenomenon can be shown to belong to a more general family of facts. This approach is particularly wise when we are dealing with biological processes that had to evolve from simpler beings" (p. 298).

ACKNOWLEDGEMENTS

Preparation of this chapter and conduct of reviewed studies on recasting and language processing was supported by a variety of grants: Grants G008302959 and G0008430079 from the U.S. Department of Education, a grant from The Hasbro Children's Foundation, National Science Foundation Grants BNS-8013767 and INT-8722794, and Grant R01 DC00508 from the Public Health Service.

Many thanks to Joy Struble and Jeanie Ghaner for assistance on the manuscript and to my colleagues in this volume and at the conference for constructive comments.

REFERENCES

Anderson, J. R. (1987). Methodologies for studying human knowledge. *Behavioral and Brain Sciences, 10,* 467–477.

Baker, N., & Nelson, K. E. (1984). Recasting and related conversational techniques for triggering syntactic advances by young children. *First Language, 5,* 3–22.

Baker, N. D., Pemberton, E. F., & Nelson, K. E. (1985, October). *Facilitating young children's language development through stories: Reading and recasting.* Paper presented at the Boston University Conference on Language Development, Boston.

Bates, E., Bretherton, I., & Snyder, L. (1988). *From first words to grammar*. London: Cambridge University Press.

Bates, E. L., & MacWhinney, B. (1987). Competition, variation, and language learning. In B. MacWhinney (Ed.), *Mechanisms of language acquisition* (pp. 157-194). Hillsdale, NJ: Lawrence Erlbaum Associates.

Bissex, G. L. (1980). *GNYS AT WRK: A child learns to read and write*. Cambridge, MA: Harvard University Press.

Bock, K. (1982). Toward a cognitive psychology of syntax: Information processing contributions to sentence formulation. *Psychological Review, 89,* 1-47.

Bohannon, N., & Stanowicz, L. (1988). The issue of negative evidence: Adult responses to children's language errors. *Developmental Psychology, 24,* 684-689.

Bohannon, N., & Stanowicz, L. (1989). Bidirectional effects of repetition in conversation: A synthesis within a cognitive model. In G. Speidel & K. E. Nelson (Eds.), *The many faces of imitation in language learning* (pp. 121-150). New York: Springer-Verlag.

Bonvillian, J. D., Nelson, K. E., & Charrow, V. R. (1976). Language and language-related skills in deaf and hearing children. *Sign Language Studies, 12,* 211-250.

Bowerman, M. (1985). Beyond communicative adequacy: From piecemeal knowledge to an integrated system in the child's acquisition of language. In K. E. Nelson (Ed.), *Children's language* (Vol. 5, pp. 369-398). Hillsdale, NJ: Lawrence Erlbaum Associates.

Calvin, W. H. (1990). *The cerebral symphony*. New York: Bantam.

Camarata, S., & Nelson, K. E. (1988, June). *Remediating language disorders: Treatments and targets*. Paper presented at University of Wisconsin-Madison Symposium on Research in Child Language Disorders, Madison, WI.

Camarata, S., & Nelson, K. E. (in press). Treatment efficiency as a function of target selection in the remediation of child language disorders. *Clinical Linguistics & Phonetics*.

Chomsky, N. (1968). *Language and mind*. New York: Harcourt Brace Jovanovich.

Chomsky, N. (1980). *Rules and representations*. New York: Columbia University Press.

Chomsky, N. (1982). *Some concepts and consequences of the theory of government and binding* [Linguistic Inquiry Monograph 6]. Cambridge, MA: MIT Press.

Demetriou, A. (Ed.). (1988). *The neo-Piagetian theories of cognitive development: Toward an integration*. Amsterdam: Elsevier.

Denninger, M. S. (1983). *Developmental and individual differences in children's categorization of emotional stimuli*. Unpublished doctoral dissertation, The Pennsylvania State University, University Park.

Ferguson, C. A. (1988). Individual differences in language learning. In M. L. Rice & R. L. Schiefelbusch (Eds.), *The teachability of language* (pp. 187-198). Baltimore: Brookes.

Fillmore, L. W. (1988). In M. Rice & R. Schiefelbusch (Eds.), *Teachability of language* (pp. 311-332). Baltimore, MD: Brookes.

Fischer, K. W., & Pipp, S. L. (1984). Processes of cognitive development: Optimal level and skill acquisition. In R. J. Sternberg (Ed.), *Mechanisms of cognitive development* (pp. 45-80). New York: Freeman.

Fodor, J. A. (1984). *The modularity of mind*. Cambridge, MA: MIT Press.

Gardner, H. (1983). *Frames of mind*. New York: Basic.

Heimann, M., & Nelson, K. E. (1991, April). *Increasing language skills in autistic children through more computer instruction: A pilot study*. Paper presented at the meeting of the Society for Research in Child Development, Seattle, WA.

Hirsh-Pasek, K., Treiman, R., & Schneiderman, M. (1984). Brown & Hanlon revisited: Mothers' sensitivity to ungrammatical forms. *Journal of Child Language, 11,* 81-88.

Horgan, D. (1978). The development of the full passive. *Journal of Child Language, 5,* 65-80.

Lepper, M. R., Aspinwall, L. G., Mumme, D. L., & Chabay, R. W. (in press). Self-perception and social-perception processes in tutoring: Subtle social control strategies of expert tutors.

In J. M. Olson & M. P. Zanna (Eds.), *Self inference processes: The Ontario Symposium on Personality and Social Psychology* (Vol. 6). Hillsdale, NJ: Lawrence Erlbaum Associates.

Lightfoot, D. (1989). The child's trigger experience: Degree-0 learnability. *Behavioral and brain sciences, 12,* 321-375.

Lindblom, B., MacNeilage, P., & Studdert-Kennedy, M. (1984). Self-organizing processes and the explanation of phonological universals. In B. Butterworth, B. Comrie, & O. Dahl (Eds.), *Explanations for language universals* (pp. 181-204). The Hague, Netherlands: Mouton.

Macken, M. A., & Ferguson, C. A. (1983). Cognitive aspects of phonological development: Model, evidence, and issues. In K. E. Nelson (Ed.), *Children's language* (Vol. 4, pp. 256-282). Hillsdale, NJ: Lawrence Erlbaum Associates.

Macnamara, J. (1982). *Names for things.* Cambridge, MA: MIT Press.

MacWhinney, B. (1987). The competition model. In B. MacWhinney (Ed.), *Mechanisms of language acquisition* (pp. 249-308). Hillsdale, NJ: Lawrence Erlbaum Associates.

MacWhinney, B. (1988). Competition and teachability. In M. L. Rice & R. L. Schiefelbusch (Eds.), *The teachability of language* (pp. 63-104). Baltimore: Brookes.

Marchman, V. A., Bates, E., Burkhardt, A., & Good, A. (1990). *Functional constraints on the acquisition of the passive* (Tech. Rep. No. 89-10). University of California, San Diego.

Maxwell, M. (1983). Language acquisition in a deaf child of deaf parents: Speech, sign variations and print variations. In K. E. Nelson (Ed.), *Children's language* (Vol. 4, pp. 283-314). Hillsdale, NJ: Lawrence Erlbaum Associates.

McClelland, J. L., & Rumelhart, D. E. (1986). *Parallel distributed processing* (Vol. 2). Cambridge, MA: MIT Press.

McTear, M. (1984). *The development of conversational ability in children.* London: Academic.

Meltzoff, A. N., & Gopnik, A. (1989). On linking nonverbal imitation, representation, and language learning in the first two years of life. In G. E. Speidel & K. E. Nelson (Eds.), *The many faces of imitation* (pp. 23-51). New York: Springer-Verlag.

Morgan, J. L. (1986). *From simple input to complex grammar.* Cambridge, MA: MIT Press.

Nelson, K. E. (1977a). Aspects of language acquisition and use from age two to age twenty. *Journal of the American Academy of Child Psychiatry, 16,* 584-607.

Nelson, K. E. (1977b). Facilitating children's syntax acquisition. *Developmental Psychology, 13,* 101-107.

Nelson, K. E. (1980). Theories of the child's acquisition of syntax. A look at rare events and at necessary, catalytic, and irrelevant components of mother-child conversation. *Annals of the New York Academy of Sciences, 345,* 45-67.

Nelson, K. E. (1981). Toward a rare-event cognitive comparison theory of syntax acquisition. In P. S. Dale & D. Ingram (Eds.), *Child language: An international perspective* (pp. 229-240). Baltimore: University Park Press.

Nelson, K. E. (1982). Experimental gambits in the service of language acquisition theory: From the Fiffin Project to operation input swap. In S. A. Kuczaj (Ed.), *Language development: Syntax and semantics* (pp. 159-199). Hillsdale, NJ: Lawrence Erlbaum Associates.

Nelson, K. E. (1987). Some observations from the perspective of the rare event cognitive comparison theory of language acquisition. In K. E. Nelson (Ed.), *Children's language* (Vol. 6, pp. 289-331). Hillsdale, NJ: Lawrence Erlbaum Associates.

Nelson, K. E. (1988). Strategies for first language teaching. In M. Rice & R. L. Schiefelbusch (Eds.), *Teachability of language* (pp. 263-310). Baltimore: Brookes.

Nelson, K. E. (1989). Indirect aspects of communicative gains: Toward fuller accounts of sequence and process. *American Journal on Mental Retardation, 93,* 20-26.

Nelson, K. E. (1991). Varied domains of development: A tale of LAD, MAD, SAD, DAD, and RARE and surprising events in our RELMs. In F. Kessel, M. H. Bornstein, & A. J.

Sameroff (Eds.), *Contemporary constructions of the child: Essays in honor of William Kessen* (pp. 123–142). Hillsdale, NJ: Lawrence Erlbaum Associates.

Nelson, K. E., Baker, N. D., Denninger, M., Bonvillian, J. D., & Kaplan, B. J. (1985). *Cookie* versus *do-it-again:* Imitative-referential and personal-social-syntactic-initiating language styles in young children. *Linguistics, 23,* 433–454.

Nelson, K. E., & Bonvillian, J. D. (1978). Early semantic development: Conceptual growth and related processes between 2 and 4 ½ years of age. In K. E. Nelson (Ed.), *Children's language* (Vol. 1, pp. 467–556). New York: Gardner Press.

Nelson, K. E., Denninger, M. M., Bonvillian, J. D., Kaplan, B. J., & Baker, N. D. (1984). Maternal input adjustments and non-adjustments as related to children's linguistic advances and to language acquisition theories. In A. D. Pellegrini & T. D. Yawkey (Eds.), *The development of oral and written languages: Readings in developmental and applied linguistics* (pp. 31–56). New York: Ablex.

Nelson, K. E., Heimann, M., Abuelhaija, L. A., & Wroblewski, R. (1984). Implications for language acquisition models of children's and parents' variations in imitation. In G. E. Speidel & K. E. Nelson (Eds.), *The many faces of imitation in language learning* (pp. 305–324). New York: Springer-Verlag.

Nelson, K. E., & Nelson, K. (1978). Cognitive pendulums and their linguistic realization. In K. E. Nelson (Ed.), *Children's language* (Vol. 1, pp. 223–286). Hillsdale, NJ: Lawrence Erlbaum Associates.

Nelson, K. E., Loncke, F., & Camarata, S. (in press). Integrating research on development and deafness. In M. Marschark & D. M. Clark (Eds.), *Psychological perspectives on deafness.* Hillsdale, NJ: Lawrence Erlbaum Associates.

Nelson, K. E., Prinz, P. M., Prinz, E. A., & Dalke, D. (in press). Processes for test and language acquisition in the context of microcomputer-videodisc instruction for deaf and multi-handicapped children. In D. S. Martin (Ed.), *Advances in cognition, education and deafness.* Washington, DC: Gallaudet College Press.

Pemberton, E. F., & Nelson, K. E. (1987). Using graphic recasting and modeling to foster young children's drawing ability. *Visual Arts Research, 23,* 29–41.

Pemberton, E. F., & Watkins, R. V. (1987). Language facilitation through stories: Recasting and modeling. *First language, 7*(1), 1–15.

Penner, S. (1987). Parental responses to grammatical and ungrammatical child utterances. *Child Development, 58,* 376–384.

Pinker, S. (1984). *Language learnability and language change.* Cambridge, MA: Harvard University Press.

Rice, M. L. (1988). Synthesis/commentary: Teaching and learning strategies. In M. L. Rice & R. L. Schiefelbusch (Eds.), *The teachability of language* (pp. 351–355). Baltimore: Brookes.

Romski, M. A., & Sevcik, R. A. (1989). An analysis of visual-graphic symbol meanings for two nonspeaking adults with severe mental retardation. *Augmentative and Alternative Communication, 5,* 109–114.

Rumelhart, D. E., & McClelland, J. L. (1986a). On learning the past tenses of English verbs. In J. L. McClelland & D. E. Rumelhart (Eds.), *Parallel distributed processing* (Vol. 2, pp. 216–271). Cambridge, MA: MIT Press.

Rumelhart, D. E., & McClelland, J. L. (1986b). *Parallel distributed processing* (Vol. 1, pp. 216–271). Cambridge, MA: MIT Press.

Sacks, O. (1987). *The man who mistook his wife for a hat.* New York: Harper & Row.

Salomon, G., Perkins, D. N., & Globerson, T. (in press). Partners in cognition: Extending human intelligence with intelligent technologies. *Educational Researcher.*

Scherer, N. J., & Olswang, L. B. (1984). Role of mothers' expansions in stimulating language production. *Journal of Speech and Hearing Research, 27,* 387–396.

Shatz, M. (1987). Bootstrapping operations in child language. In K. E. Nelson (Ed.), *Children's language* (Vol. 6, pp. 1–22). Hillsdale, NJ: Lawrence Erlbaum Associates.

Shiffrin, R. M., Murnane, K., Gronlund, S., & Roth, M. (1989). On units of storage and retrieval. In C. Izowa (Ed.), *Current issues in cognitive processes* (pp. 25–67). Hillsdale, NJ: Lawrence Erlbaum Associates.

Slobin, D. I. (1985). Crosslinguistic evidence for the language-making capacity. In D. I. Slobin (Ed.), *The crosslinguistic study of language acquisition* (Vol. 2, pp. 1157–1256). Hillsdale, NJ: Lawrence Erlbaum Associates.

Soderbergh, R. (1977). *Reading in early childhood: A linguistic study of a preschool children's gradual acquisition of reading ability.* Washington, DC: Georgetown University Press.

Speidel, G. E., & Nelson, K. E. (Eds.). (1989). *The many faces of imitation in language learning.* New York: Springer-Verlag.

Sternberg, R. J. (1984). Mechanisms of cognitive development: A componential approach. In R. J. Sternberg (Ed.), *Mechanisms of cognitive development* (pp. 163–186). New York: Freeman.

Tallal, P., & Curtiss, S. (1990). Neurological basis of developmental language disorders. In A. Rothenberg (Ed.), *Brain and behavior in child psychiatry* (pp. 93–110). Heidelberg, Germany: Springer-Verlag.

Trevarthen, C. (1979). Communication and cooperation in early infancy: A description of primary intersubjectivity. In M. Bullowa (Ed.), *Before speech: The beginning of interpersonal communication* (pp. 321–347). Cambridge, England: Cambridge University Press.

Wexler, K., & Cullicover, P. W. (1980). *Formal principles of language acquisition.* Cambridge, MA: MIT Press.

18 Patterns of Language Learning by Instruction: Evidence from Nonspeaking Persons with Mental Retardation

Mary Ann Romski
Department of Communication, Georgia State University,
Language Research Center, Georgia State University, and
Emory University

Rose A. Sevcik
Language Research Center, Georgia State University
and Emory University

The majority of children with mental retardation encounter some degree of difficulty acquiring a first language regardless of the etiology of their cognitive disability (Bensberg & Sigelman, 1976; Keane, 1972; Rosenberg, 1982). Two broad patterns of language acquisition impairments, based on oral language production skills, can be distinguished in children with mental retardation.

The first pattern is observed in youngsters who acquire oral language, albeit slowly, but exhibit varying degrees of impairment in the semantics, syntax, pragmatics, and/or phonology of their spoken language comprehension and/or production. For these youngsters, the process of how they acquire spoken language, the similarities and differences between their acquisition and that of normally developing youngsters, and the conditions that facilitate their language learning have been the focus of investigation for some time now (see Rosenberg, 1982, for a review).

The second global pattern is displayed by youngsters with mental retardation who do not acquire oral language production skills. In general, these persons are those with the lowest IQ levels (Sheehan, Martyn, & Kilburn, 1968). They are, by description, more dissimilar than similar and frequently exhibit accompanying disabilities that may include, though are not limited to, cerebral palsy, sensory impairments, or maladaptive behaviors (Guess & Horner, 1978; Snell, 1987).

More specifically, this group of youngsters with mental retardation typically have some amount of life-span experience. Their case histories clearly report that they have had considerable one-to-one direct speech and language intervention aimed at remediating their spoken language difficulties. Often, they have made little or no significant progress with spoken language or have reached a plateau in communicative skill development. It is the language-learning process exhibited by this particularly challenging group of individuals that is the focus of this chapter.

Since the early 1970s, alternative approaches for teaching language to individuals with mental retardation who have not learned to speak have been explored (see Bonvillian & Nelson, 1982; Lloyd & Karlan, 1984; Romski & Sevcik, 1988a; Romski, Sevcik, & Joyner, 1984; Schiefelbusch, 1980, for reviews). Three main efforts, the use of American Sign Language (ASL) by individuals with hearing impairments, ape language research, and advances in computer technology, converged and served as an impetus for the initial explorations of nonspeech communication systems as a route for teaching language (Romski, Lloyd, & Sevcik, 1988; Schiefelbusch & Hollis, 1979). For almost two decades now, manual signs and visual-graphic symbols have been used to augment or to replace spoken language in instruction for nonspeaking persons with mental retardation. There remains, however, limited empirical evidence or theory about the process by which these individuals acquire an alternative language system to speech. How their acquisition of these systems compares to that of typical or other atypical children learning oral language is also largely unstudied.

INSTRUCTION VIA OTHER MODALITIES

Although typical children begin to use words almost effortlessly, by definition the individuals described in this research do not. They require specialized instruction to do so. Because, for this subject group, spoken language has not been a successful avenue for communicative development, initial productive language skills must be established through instruction via another modality (i.e., manual signs or visual-graphic symbols). An understanding of the process of language acquisition by these youngsters, then, must take into account the modality in which the language is presented as well as the instructional conditions that are employed within the chosen modality. Thus initially, a demonstration of the modality's as well as the instructional strategy's viability as teaching tools are crucial to the investigative process with the population.

Modalities. A major theme found within the early work in nonspeech communication suggested that the auditory/vocal modality may be at the root of the language-learning difficulty for this group of individuals. Thus, one could argue that if the modality in which the language system was presented and produced was altered, an individual would acquire language production skills. In a few cases, such a hypothesis was correct and when the modality was changed, a subgroup of individuals acquired productive language skills rapidly. A shift in modality alone did not result, however, in the emergence of language and communication skills for every child with retardation who did not learn to speak. What became apparent was the ways in which each modality altered various aspects of the signal (see Romski et al., 1984, for a discussion).

As an arbitrary system that employs an auditory channel for input and a vocal channel for output, speech is temporally based, dynamic, and forms a rapidly fading signal that exists only in the sender's and receiver's memories for recall (Hockett, 1960). Unaided symbol sets (e.g., manual signs) share some of the signal characteristics of speech. The structure of the signal is transitory in form and frequently involves movement or change; thus, the symbols may be considered dynamic. When used without speech accompaniment, the modality of both input (visual) and output (manual) differs from speech. Like speech, however, the communicator must produce the message utilizing recall memory. Aided symbols differ from speech and from unaided symbols in terms of the characteristics of the signal and in the individual's response. Graphic symbols are structured along spatial dimensions and remain fixed or static. The user relies on recognition memory to select a symbol for communication. Unaided and aided systems alter a number of signal dimensions that may contribute to, or account for, the differences in the subsequent outcome of an instructional process.

Instruction.   In the broadest sense of the term, Bruner (1966) defined instruction as an effort to assist or to shape growth patterns. Because the long-term goal of language instruction is to facilitate linguistic competence, one traditionally accepted model for spoken language growth by persons with mental retardation, the developmental model, employs information from child language acquisition and devises instructional strategies therefrom (Ruder & Smith, 1984). Although information about the sequence of acquisition provides a general and appropriate framework within which a child with severe oral language disabilities should progress, it is frequently difficult to devise specific teaching procedures based on phenomena that occur spontaneously in nondisabled children. As well, typical children learn to speak early in life and the youngsters who are the focus of this instruction do not. Nonhuman primate research provides another model that uses typical development as its guide yet is formed from methods and findings gained via the use of a nonspeech communication system (Romski, 1989; Romski & Savage-Rumbaugh, 1986).

Two instructional tactics have been employed, based on a nonhuman primate model, in successive longitudinal symbol acquisition studies conducted at the Language Research Center (Romski & Sevcik, 1988b; Romski, Sevcik, & Pate, 1988). Both tactics, a laboratory-based experience and a loosely structured naturalistic experience, employed arbitrary visual-graphic symbols, lexigrams, presented on computer-linked communication boards to teach initial comprehension and production of a basic vocabulary. In each study, symbol acquisition and use patterns, as well as factors that may have affected the instructional outcomes, were examined. The 16 subjects in these two studies all functioned within the moderate or severe range of mental retardation. They ranged in chronological age from 6 years, 4 months to 20 years, 2 months (mean = 13 years, 3 months). Each subject began the instruction with at least primitive intentional communication skills, less than 10 productive spoken words, and comprehension skills that ranged from no comprehension of speech to speech comprehension skills comparable to the performance of a 4-year-old child on standardized measures.

Laboratory-Based Experience. In the earlier of the two studies, three institutionalized young adults received laboratory-based instructional experience with symbols displayed on a computer-linked communication system for a consistent, though limited, period of time each day. Multiple discrete trials were presented within a request-based paradigm to establish symbol-referent associations (e.g., the lexigram for SODA corresponded to a can of Diet Coke).

This form of instructional experience facilitated the learning of at minimum 20 symbols by each of the three young adults. Two of the individuals had come to the language-learning task with little or no comprehension of spoken language and did not independently work out the correspondence between a symbol and a food. Once the specific relationships between the symbols and their referents were mastered, they learned additional symbols rapidly. Symbol comprehension, however, did not emerge early in the learning process. Along with subject-initiated symbol usage, it was one of the cumulative results of the productive instruction (see Romski, Sevcik, & Pate, 1988, for a complete description of this study). The learning process for these young adults, then, consisted of acquiring component parts (i.e., requesting, labeling, comprehending) that built upon each other and resulted in a complex of interrelated symbol skills.

Loosely Structured Naturalistic Experience. Although typical children easily employ their language skills in multiple environments with varied partners, children with mental retardation do not (Zigler & Hodapp, 1986). Thus, an important and desirable outcome of language instruction is that it results in generalized language learning and use in natural settings (Warren & Rogers-Warren, 1985). Although the laboratory-based discrete trial training model was effective and permitted an analysis of the process of acquiring symbols when production was emphasized, the stationary computer-based system and massed trial procedures did not easily transfer to naturalistic settings such as homes and classrooms. Recent commercial technological advances in portable communication systems, coupled with innovative findings from the nonhuman primate research conducted within the Language Research Center laboratory, provided a model in which communication in natural settings could be facilitated directly.

In the second long-term investigation, a loosely structured naturalistic communicative experience was employed to examine the computer-based symbol-learning processes of 13 school-age youngsters who resided at home and attended a public school educational program for students with moderate or severe cognitive disabilities. Initially, subjects were assigned to either a home or school instructional condition. In both settings, symbol use was modeled within a mealtime context by the child's adult communicative partners, and the subjects were encouraged to use symbols when communicative opportunities arose. When a symbol was touched on the portable communication system, a synthetic equivalent of the word was produced by a speech synthesizer. Thus, the visual-graphic symbol was always paired with the spoken (albeit electronic) word. As well, for partner interpretation and convenience, the printed English word equivalent of the symbol appeared in reduced size above the symbol. At systematically sampled intervals throughout the school year, nonparticipant observers coded the subjects' communicative use of their symbols in either the home or school setting through the use of the communication coding scheme (CCS) (see Romski & Sevcik, 1988b, for a detailed description of the CCS). Investigators also assessed symbol comprehension and production skills apart from the communicative context.

Rather than adopting the new symbol system as their sole form of communication, the youngsters incorporated its use within their already extant communicative repertoires. Symbol usage was comparable across the home and school conditions suggesting that the initial setting and partners were not the dominant factor in early instructional success. Although the subjects continued to rely on unintelligible vocalizations to gain the attention of their partners, they employed symbols to encode specific messages once the partner's attention was engaged. As shown in Table 18.1, the outcome was a rich multimodal system of communication that incorporated extant as well as instructed communicative skills to, for example, request items and information, and answer questions directed to them (Romski & Sevcik, 1988b, 1989). Although the majority of their symbol communications consisted of single symbol utterances, 10 of the youngsters (77%) began to generate spontaneous symbol combinations that were employed to convey more complex semantic information than single symbol usage. For example, they might produce communications in the form of MORE JUICE, CHOCOLATE MILK GOOD, or PLEASE HELP

TABLE 18.1
Examples of One Subject's Communicative Interactions

Example 1: John (J) and his mother (M) having an after-school snack in the dining room.

J	[1L4S] {FINISHED}.
J	[1VOS] XX]
=	Trying to approximate the spoken word "finished".
M	No, you/'re not.
M	You/'re tease/ing me.
=	While Mom is in the kitchen, Jon picks up a pencil.
J	[1L2S] {PENCIL}.
M	Still have your pencil?
=	Mom is still in the kitchen.
J	[3A2S] {PENCIL} {GESTURE}.
=	Jon then shows the observer his pencil.

Example 2: Jon (J), his sister (P), and his mom (M) making a grocery list.

P	What else should I get at the grocery store?
P	Can you tell me what they/'ve got at the grocery store?
J	[3D2S] XX {MAGAZINE}.
P	Well that/'s what
M	Yes Patti I/'ll have to agree with that.
P	I bet I know what kind of magazine too.
M	Every time we go in we get a magazine about [L] {BIKE} don't we?
J	[3DOS] XX {BIKE}.
M	Yes you do.
M	When we go to the grocery store Jon head/3s right for the [L] {MAGAZINE} rack and look/3s at the [L] {BIKE} and talk/3s Mom into get/ing them half the time.
P	Jon, what should I get for Valerie to drink when I go to the grocery store?
P	What should I get for Valerie to drink?
J	[3D2S] XX {JUICE}.
P	Juice.
P	That/'s right.
P	I sure will.
=	Jon laughs.

Note. All transcripts are presented in *Systematic analysis of language transcripts* (SALT) format (Chapman & Miller, 1985). Codes are from the Communication Coding Scheme (CCS) (see Romski & Sevcik, 1988b).

(Wilkinson & Romski, 1989). Just as typical children appear to use their first 50 words as a base, the core symbol vocabulary also served as a building block for the emergence of more advanced linguistic information that was employed in a meaningful and functional fashion.

Because the synthetic English word always accompanied visual symbol use, the approach permitted the communicative partners to integrate symbols into the spoken utterances they directed to the youngsters as well. They embedded symbol usage within their verbal communications that averaged 4.27 morphemes in length as illustrated in Table 18.2. Partners were sensitive to the sophistication of the youngster's speech comprehension and adjusted the amount of symbol input accordingly; that is, partners of

TABLE 18.2
Examples of Partner-Augmented Input to the Children

Example 1: A mother (M) talking to her son (B) during dinner.

M   [L] {NAPKIN}.
M   It/'s on the other side of the plate.
B   [3C2S] XX {points to napkin}.
M   Yeah.

Example 2: In the school lunch room, a teacher (T) is talking to her student (J).

T   Let's go get some [L] {ICE CREAM}.
T   But first you need to use your [L] {NAPKIN} {PLEASE}.
=   J uses his napkin.
T   OK, let's get the [L] {ICE CREAM}.

Note. All transcripts are presented in *systematic analysis of language transcripts* (SALT) format (Chapman & Miller, 1985). Codes are from the communication coding scheme (CCS) (see Romski & Sevcik, 1988b).

children who understood very little speech employed symbols in their communications to the youngsters more often than did partners whose youngsters understood spoken words. Home and school partners, however, integrated the symbols into their communications in different ways. Home partners were more likely to employ single symbols not embedded within a spoken utterance whereas school partners tended to embed symbols within the final word position of a spoken utterance. School partners also recast their student's symbol usages, an approach not observed in the home partners' use (Sevcik, Romski, & Watkins, 1989). Recasting may be a strategy teachers already employ with students and, in this case, they may have expanded its use to language instruction (see Nelson, chapter 17 of this volume).

Vocabulary assessment measures provided a structured test format in which information was gained about the subject's understanding of symbol/referent relationships removed from the context of their use. Subjects who came to the task with speech comprehension skills readily learned to comprehend and produce the majority of their symbol vocabulary. For their remaining vocabulary items, these subjects were more likely to only comprehend an item than to only produce it. For subjects who came to the task with little comprehension of speech, the development of symbol comprehension skills consistently preceded symbol production skills indicating that they learned symbols the way a typical child first learns words, that is, by establishing comprehension skills.

Apart from the skills that were the focus of instruction (i.e., comprehension and production of symbols), two striking by-products emerged from the vocabulary assessment data. After a year of participation, the intelligibility of five youngsters' audiotaped vocal responses to photographs of known objects and events improved so as to make one third of their spoken word approximations intelligible to a speech-language pathologist naive to the question of interest (Romski, Plenge, & Sevcik, 1988). As well, in structured assessments, seven participants evidenced recognition of printed English words independent of the symbol with which it was paired. In both cases, the spoken or written words were those that corresponded to the symbols they had learned in the communicative use context though they had not received any explicit instruction concerning the relationships between the symbols and their spoken or written word equivalents.

PATTERNS OF INSTRUCTED LANGUAGE LEARNING

Both instructional approaches, the laboratory-based experience and the loosely structured naturalistic experience, facilitated the growth of symbol comprehension and production skills in individuals who had previously encountered great difficulty learning language. Despite the differing instructional focuses of each approach, two rather clear patterns of acquisition have emerged across the studies as outlined in Table 18.3. The first, described as a "beginning learning pattern" consists of a slow acquisition of single symbols in comprehension and production. The second pattern, categorized as an "advanced learning pattern," involves rapid acquisition and use of vocabulary in the comprehension and production modes. For advanced learners, this vocabulary base then was extended with the emergence of symbol combinations and evidence of additional symbolic skills (e.g., recognition of printed English words). Of the 16 subjects who participated in these two studies, 6 exhibited the beginning pattern whereas the remaining 10 subjects displayed the advanced learning pattern.[1]

One approach for disentangling these patterns is to explore the types of skills that may influence the results of instruction. *Extant skills* are, by definition, those that the individual brings to the instructional process, whereas *instructed skills* are those skills that the individual acquires or learns as a result of the teaching process. Instructed skills may be affected by, and interact with, the extant characteristics of the subject. Together, extant and instructed skills contribute to an individual's symbol learning and use patterns.

Extant Skills.   The typical child develops first words in the context of already present communication skills, such as pointing and vocalizing (e.g., Bates, 1979). Though the subjects in these two studies have not exhibited

---

[1]It is important to note that the subjects who exhibited beginning learning patterns were distributed across the subjects who resided at home and those who resided in a state institution for persons with mental retardation.

TABLE 18.3
Patterns of Communicative Acquisition

Beginning Learning Pattern	Advanced Learning Pattern
slow vocabulary learning	fairly rapid vocabulary learning
small cumulative vocabulary	large vocabulary (> 50 symbols)
limited generalization	generalized use
	emergence of symbol combinations, spoken word production, printed English recognition

oral language skill, they were all intentional communicators who had developed some gestural and/or vocal skills that were successful, in a limited sense, for communication in familiar contexts.

Despite the absence of a formal, independent means of oral communication, these school-age subjects often successfully conveyed messages to their communicative partners prior to the introduction of augmented language instruction (Romski, Sevcik, Reumann, & Pate, 1989). Although vocalizations were not effective for conveying specific messages, they continued to consistently employ the vocal modality more often than any other mode. Albeit characterized as nonspeaking, about half of their observed communications consisted of vocalizations, of varying phonetic complexity, that were unintelligible to a naive listener but had the consistent effect of gaining a familiar partner's attention. The remainder of their communications consisted of idiosyncratic gestures, physical manipulation of another person, or some combination of these methods.

Although on the surface these skills appear to be similar to the early intentional communication skills of typical children prior to the emergence of their first words, it is important to note that these youngsters have relied on these communication methods for an extended period of their childhood. Such prolonged experience with restricted communication skills may have resulted in an elaborated application of these skills during communicative interactions.

Bloom (1983) argued that the three domains of form, content, and use must be integrated for the transition from prelinguistic to linguistic communication to be complete. Although all of these individuals displayed some extant communication skills prior to the onset of instruction, they had not made independently the transition from communication to intelligible words. They did not readily add linguistic content or form to their communications and thus their expressions were limited and difficult for partners to interpret.

Though often overlooked, spoken language comprehension skills play an extremely important role in early language learning. It is presumed that typical children have some speech comprehension skills upon which they attach their first spoken words (Huttenlocher, 1974). Although the majority of individuals with mental retardation come to the language instruction task with at least a single-word speech comprehension base upon which they can then bootstrap their way into the linguistic world, there are some individuals who do not have such an advantage (Romski & Sevcik, 1988b, 1989; Romski, Sevcik, & Pate, 1988). Because nonspeaking children are exposed to speech input during the course of their development, a determination of the extent to which they have developed speech comprehension abilities can provide important information about the language base upon which they can build productive symbol skills.

The extant speech comprehension skills of the 16 subjects in these two studies have been determined via traditional testing techniques. Three standardized assessments, the Peabody Picture Vocabulary Test–Revised (PPVT; Dunn & Dunn, 1981), the Assessment of Children's Language Comprehension (ACLC; Foster, Giddan, & Stark, 1983), and the Test of Auditory Comprehension of Language–Revised (TACL; Carrow-Woolfolk, 1985), have been employed to characterize their language comprehension skills. Subjects were classified as comprehenders or noncomprehenders based on their initial performance on the PPVT. Comprehenders then were also administered the ACLC and the TACL to obtain a complete profile of their comprehension skills. All comprehenders evidenced advanced patterns of symbol learning whereas the noncomprehenders comprised the beginning group.

Because the individuals who have participated in these studies are among those who, in general, encounter difficulties with standard language assessment methodologies, it is feasible that the scores and subsequent classifications may be an underestimation of the extent of their speech comprehension abilities. Standard measures typically focus on the comprehension of black and white line drawings and require the child to select an alternative from among a set of three, four, or five items. These measures may not be sensitive enough to capture subtle or inconsistent forms of contextual understanding that may predate performance on more traditional measures. Recent methodological innovations for assessing the complex speech comprehension abilities of young normally developing children (Hirsh-Pasek & Golinkoff, chapter 13 of this volume) may provide inroads for further delineating the extant speech comprehension abilities of individuals who have been difficult to assess via traditional methods.

In her 1975 monograph, Nelson suggested that typical children who produce little speech may be relying on an internal processing of the language that they hear in order to advance their linguistic competence. For subjects classified as advanced learners, the relationship between a word and its referent was established during their life experience. After a viable productive route was provided, these extant skills served as a foundation upon which they could build a relationship between the visual-graphic symbols they were now acquiring and already established understandings of spoken words. They readily abstracted the rule that each symbol represents one real-world item by pairing the symbol with the synthetic spoken word that was produced when the symbol was activated. They learned symbols rapidly and consistently generalized their use. The beginning subjects, on the other hand, evidenced little, if any, comprehension of speech at the onset of the study. They had no base of word understanding with which to link these new symbol meanings. Thus, they were beginning at an earlier point in the acquisition process as their initial step was to establish the relationship between a symbol and its referent. Because they did not understand the meaning of the spoken word, they had to rely on the cues inherent in the communicative context to learn the meaning of the visual symbol.

Similar data have been reported from chimpanzees (*Pan troglodytes*) and bonobos (*Pan paniscus*). Kanzi and Mulika, the bonobos who have evidenced comprehension of speech, learned symbols rapidly and used them flexibly without explicit training to do so. Sherman and Austin, common chimpanzees who did not comprehend spoken words, were able to learn symbols only with specific intensive instruction (Savage-Rumbaugh, 1986, 1987; Savage-Rumbaugh, McDonald, Sevcik, Hopkins, & Rubert, 1986; Sevcik, 1989; see also chapter 9 of this volume).

Although normally developing children proceed through the very early stages of comprehension rapidly (Benedict, 1979; Huttenlocher, 1974), investigations with individuals who have severe spoken language comprehension impairments illustrate the complexity of the early learning process and the critical role extant speech comprehension and communication skills the child brings to the task can play in facilitating early symbol acquisition (Romski, Sevcik, & Pate, 1988). In and of themselves these extant skills are not sufficient to produce the desired expressive language outcomes. They do, however, present the subject who brings them to the instructional task with an obvious learning advantage over those individuals who come to the symbol-learning task without them. Although those learners still can acquire the relationship between a symbol and its referent, the process is a slower and more formidable one, but as confirmed by these varied subjects, an achievable one.

Instructed Skills.   One critical aim of instructional investigations must be to clarify both what and how a child is learning given the specific instructional experience and the skills he or she brings to the language-learning task. Language instructional studies with youngsters characterized as nonspeaking usually have placed an higher emphasis on teaching productive symbol skills than on teaching comprehension skills (Romski & Sevcik, 1988a). Presumably, this focus has dominated because symbol production is perceived as allowing children to have an immediate and visible effect upon their environment. Although functionally it may seem reasonable to highlight symbol-use instruction, an approach that also stresses the role of the child as a listener shifts the emphasis away from symbol production alone and, like the process observed in typically developing children, permits the child to observe and to absorb the communicative process prior to actually taking on the role of speaker (e.g., Huttenlocher, 1974).

In the long-term study that focused on symbol use in natural communicative contexts, "advanced learners" accurately produced symbols from the onset of instruction and easily assumed both expressive and receptive communicative roles. "Beginning learners," on the other hand, typically learned to comprehend symbols before they began to reliably produce them. If accurate production had been the only criteria for performance during the early phases of instruction, these subjects may have been judged to be unsuccessful in the symbol-learning task.

The focus of instruction, then, obviously effects the outcomes reported. Again, in this case, an examination of productive skills alone would not have revealed a viable route of acquisition for some novice learners. Progress and results must be considered in terms of the child's ability to participate in receptive and expressive communicative exchanges with partners in everyday settings. Instruction that focuses on communicative use in everyday settings necessitates the measurement of multiple dimensions of behavior, including the child's patterns of symbol use and the extent of his or her abstracted symbol knowledge. Specifically, information about with whom and how the child is communicating, the functions that the child's communications serve, their successfulness, and the discourse skills (e.g., turn taking, topic maintenance) displayed contribute to a broad profile of symbol acquisition and use. As well, because the communicative partners are essential participants within the instructional framework, a measure of their own communicative behavior and of their perceptions of the child's performance add another key aspect to the emerging communicative profile. Although the patterns of communicative symbol use in functional contexts provide one dimension of detail about learning, they do not aid in ascertaining what the youngsters know about the meanings of the symbols they are using apart from a contextual framework. Measurement in structured tasks designed to assess these symbol skills are necessary as well. When communicative interaction is the focus of instruction, assessing what the children learn about the symbols they use permits the investigator to identify patterns of how they have abstracted symbol meaning from the instructional context. These findings then must be interpreted within the broad complex of linguistic/cognitive skills demonstrated so as to yield an extensive portrayal of emerging symbolic communicators.

By-Products of Instruction. Apart from the skills that were the specific goal of instruction (i.e., the comprehension and production of symbols), additional types of symbolic processing emerged in the repertoires of subjects with "advanced learning patterns." Sidman (Sidman, 1970; Sidman & Cresson, 1973) reported the successful use of a mediated-transfer paradigm as one approach by which to establish simple reading skills in speaking children with severe retardation. In this study, youngsters were able to independently extract spoken words and/or print from the available stream of communicative information. Given their age and previous experience, the visual-graphic symbol was likely the vehicle that triggered this transfer by providing the advanced nonspeaking learner with an entry point to more developmentally sophisticated symbolic skills.

With the establishment of receptive and productive symbol knowledge and use, it was also now possible to assess the emergence of a range of cognitive and linguistic functions in the youngsters. In a recent examination of symbol category structure with advanced school-age subjects, superordinate-level lexigrams (i.e., FOOD, DISH, and FUN) were taught by means of a sorting task. After learning the superordinate category symbol meanings, the subjects, on a Trial 1 test, successfully sorted previously acquired lexigrams (e.g., ICE CREAM, FORK, BASEBALL) into bins labeled with the appropriate categorical symbol (Sevcik, Abrahamsen, & Romski, 1990).

The outcomes of instruction also have provided an opportunity to investigate some neurolinguistic correlates of symbol acquisition and use. Using auditory evoked potential methods, symbol-experienced youngsters evidenced bilateral processing of acquired symbols in the frontal lobe. Waveforms also were classified correctly in terms of the meaningfulness of the stimuli (i.e., known, unknown) with greater than 80% accuracy using discriminant function analyses (Molfese, Morris, & Romski, 1990).

CONCLUSION

Individuals with retardation who learn language by instruction within other modalities highlight the degree to which early language skills are teachable. Like research in other areas of atypical development (Berko-Gleason, 1982; Cicchetti & Pogge-Hesse, 1982; Menn & Olber, 1982), the augmented language development of children with mental retardation and severe oral language disabilities shares some commonalities with the process through which typical, as well as other atypical, children proceed as they learn to speak. Careful examination of their learning patterns enhances our understanding of some of the intricacies of very early language development such as the critical role early speech comprehension skills play in the emergence of children's first productive words. These components of acquisition may be more subtle within the usual developmental process because the typical child developing language is such an adept learner.

Because the subjects who were the focus of this research came to the language-learning task with severely limited expressive vocabularies, instructional investigation has, to date, concentrated on examining the patterns of very early symbol acquisition. Consequently, comparisons between these subjects' development and that of typical children can be made only at the stages of early linguistic development. These subjects, however, have attained levels of augmented language abilities heretofore unrealized in this population, making new avenues of investigation feasible in the future. The later emergence of symbol combinations in advanced subjects suggests that, like typical and atypical oral language learners, symbol-experienced subjects may advance through at least some of the subsequent stages of language development.

The instructional process itself, then, can be a powerful tool for the investigation of a broad range of symbolic skills. Once children have a core symbol vocabulary upon which they can build, new, previously unavailable, language-learning opportunities become accessible to them. As well, the acquisition of visual-graphic symbols provide an occasion to examine how, from a neuropsychological viewpoint, these youngsters process linguistically relevant material.

The participants in these studies had failed to learn language via other modalities and instructional strategies. Past theories about alternative communication systems have attributed effective instructional outcomes to the multiple advantages of an altered input and output signal and the effect those advantages have on the design of instructional approaches (see Romski, Lloyd, & Sevcik, 1988, for a review). Our findings support a perspective that emphasizes the interaction of the subject's extant communication and speech comprehension skills with the modality and the instructional approach when accounting for an individual's ability to make use of instruction via altered modalities. Future investigations will challenge the limits of the available instructional technologies and of the individuals themselves.

ACKNOWLEDGEMENTS

An earlier version of this article was presented at the NICHD Conference BIOBE-HAVIORAL FOUNDATIONS OF LANGUAGE DEVELOPMENT, Leesburg, Virginia, June 12-15, 1988. The preparation of this manuscript and the research described within was funded by grant NICHD-06016, which sustains the Language Research Center cooperatively operated by Georgia State University and the Yerkes Regional Primate Research Center of Emory University. Additional support is provided by the College of Arts and Sciences, Georgia State University and by RR-00165 to the Yerkes Center. The authors gratefully acknowledge the children and adults who participated in these studies as well as their families, Clayton County school personnel, and the residents and staff of the Developmental Learning Center of Georgia Regional Hospital, Atlanta, for their enthusiastic cooperation during the conduct of the studies reported in this article.

REFERENCES

Bates, E. (1979). *The emergence of symbols: Cognition and communication in infancy.* New York: Academic.

Benedict, H. (1979). Early lexical development: Comprehension and production. *Journal of Child Language, 6,* 183–200.

Bensberg, G., & Sigelman, C. (1976). Definitions and prevalence. In L. L. Lloyd (Ed.), *Communication assessment and intervention strategies* (pp. 33–72). Baltimore: University Park Press.

Berko-Gleason, J. (1982). Converging evidence for linguistic theory from the study of aphasia and child language. In L. Olber & L. Menn (Eds.), *Exceptional language and linguistics* (pp. 347–356). New York: Academic.

Bloom, L. (1983). Of continuity and discontinuity, and the magic of language development. In R. Golinkoff (Ed.), *The transition from prelinguistic to linguistic communication* (pp. 79–92). Hillsdale, NJ: Lawrence Erlbaum Associates.

Bonvillian, J., & Nelson, K. (1982). Exceptional cases of language acquisition. In K. Nelson (Ed.), *Children's language* (Vol. 3, pp. 322–391). Hillsdale, NJ: Lawrence Erlbaum Associates.

Bruner, J. (1966). *Towards a theory of instruction.* Cambridge, MA: Harvard University Press.

Carrow-Woolfolk, E. (1985). *The test of auditory comprehension of language-revised.* Allen, TX: DLM Teaching Resources.

Chapman, R., & Miller, J. (1985). *Systematic analysis of language transcripts.* Madison: University of Wisconsin.

Cicchetti, D., & Pogge-Hesse, P. (1982). Possible contributions of the study of organically retarded persons to developmental theory. In E. Zigler & D. Balla (Eds.), *Mental retardation: The developmental-difference controversy* (pp. 277–318). Hillsdale, NJ: Lawrence Erlbaum Associates.

Dunn, L., & Dunn, L. (1981). *Peabody Picture Vocabulary Test-Revised.* Circle Pines, MN: American Guidance Service.

Foster, R., Giddan, J., & Stark, J. (1983). *Assessment of children's language comprehension.* Palo Alto, CA: Consulting Psychologists Press.

Guess, D., & Horner, R. (1978). The severely and profoundly handicapped. In E. L. Meyen (Ed.), *Exceptional children and youth: An introduction* (pp. 218–268). Denver: Love Publishing.

Hockett, C. (1960). The origin of speech. *Scientific American, 203,* 88–96.

Huttenlocher, J. (1974). The origins of language comprehension. In R. L. Solso (Ed.), *Theories in cognitive psychology: The Loyola symposium* (pp. 331–368). Hillsdale, NJ: Lawrence Erlbaum Associates.

Keane, V. (1972). The incidence of speech and language problems in the mentally retarded. *Mental Retardation, 10,* 3–8.

Lloyd, L., & Karlan, G. (1984). Nonspeech communication symbols and systems: Where have we been and where are we going? *Journal of Mental Deficiency Research, 28,* 3–20.

Menn, L., & Olber, L. (1982). Exceptional language data as linguistic evidence: An introduction. In L. Olber & L. Menn (Eds.), *Exceptional language and linguistics* (pp. 3–14). New York: Academic.

Molfese, D., Morris, R., & Romski, M. A. (1990). Semantic discrimination in nonspeaking youngsters with moderate or severe retardation: Electrophysiological correlates. *Brain and Language, 38,* 61–74.

Nelson, K. (1975). Structure and strategy in learning to talk. *Monographs of the Society for Research in Child Development, 38* (Serial No. 149).

Romski, M. A. (1989). Two decades of ape language research *ASHA, 31,* 81–82.

Romski, M. A., Lloyd, L. L., & Sevcik, R. A. (1988). Augmentative and alternative communication issues. In R. L. Schiefelbusch & L. L. Lloyd (Eds.), *Language perspectives: Acquisition, retardation and intervention* (2nd ed., pp. 343–366). Austin, TX: Pro-Ed.

Romski, M. A., Plenge, T., & Sevcik, R. A. (1988). *Intelligibility rating scale.* Unpublished manuscript.

Romski, M. A., & Savage-Rumbaugh, E. S. (1986). Implication for language intervention research: A nonhuman primate model. In E. S. Savage-Rumbaugh (Ed.), *Ape language: From conditioned response to symbol* (pp. 355–374). New York: Columbia University Press.

Romski, M. A., & Sevcik, R. A. (1988a). Augmentative and alternative communication: Considerations for individuals with severe intellectual disabilities. *Augmentative and Alternative Communication, 4,* 83–93.

Romski, M. A., & Sevcik, R. A. (1988b). Augmentative communication system acquisition and use: A model for teaching and assessing progress. *NSSLHA Journal, 16,* 61–75.

Romski, M. A., & Sevcik, R. A. (1989, April) *Language learning via computer-based instruction by nonspeaking youngsters with mental retardation.* Paper presented at the biannual meeting of the Society for Research in Child Development, Kansas City, MO.

Romski, M. A., Sevcik, R. A., & Joyner, S. E. (1984). Nonspeech communication systems: Implications for language intervention with mentally retarded children. *Topics in Language Disorders, 5,* 66–81.

Romski, M. A., Sevcik, R. A., & Pate, J. L. (1988). The establishment of symbolic communication in persons with mental retardation. *Journal of Speech and Hearing Disorders, 53,* 94–107.

Romski, M. A., Sevcik, R. A., Reumann, R., & Pate, J. L. (1989). Youngsters with moderate or severe retardation and severe spoken language impairments I: Extant communicative patterns. *Journal of Speech and Hearing Disorders, 54,* 366–373.

Rosenberg, S. (1982). The language of the mentally retarded: Development, processes, and intervention. In S. Rosenberg (Ed.), *Handbook of applied psycholinguistics* (pp. 329–392). Hillsdale, NJ: Lawrence Erlbaum Associates.

Ruder, K., & Smith, M. (1984). *Developmental language intervention: Psycholinguistic applications.* Baltimore: University Park Press.

Savage-Rumbaugh, E. S. (1986). *Ape language: From conditioned response to symbol.* New York: Columbia University Press.

Savage-Rumbaugh, E. S. (1987). A new look at ape language: Comprehension of vocal speech and syntax. *Nebraska Symposium on Motivation, 35,* 201–255.

Savage-Rumbaugh, E. S., McDonald, K., Sevcik, R. A., Hopkins, W., & Rubert, E. (1986). Spontaneous symbol acquisition and communicative use by a pygmy chimpanzee (*Pan paniscus*). *Journal of Experimental Psychology: General, 112,* 211–235.

Schiefelbusch, R. L. (1980). *Nonspeech language and communication: Analysis and intervention.* Baltimore: University Park Press.

Schiefelbusch, R. L., & Hollis, J. (1979). *Language intervention from ape to child.* Baltimore: University Park Press.

Sevcik, R. A. (1989). *A comprehensive analysis of graphic symbol acquisition and use:*

Evidence from an infant Bonobo (Pan Paniscus). Unpublished doctoral dissertation, Georgia State University, Atlanta.

Sevcik, R. A., Abrahamsen, A., & Romski, M. A. (1990). *Superordinate level symbol learning and categorization.* Manuscript in preparation.

Sevcik, R. A., Romski, M. A., & Watkins, R. (1989, November). *Augmented and spoken linguistic input to nonspeaking children with mental retardation.* Paper presented at the annual meeting of the American Speech-Language-Hearing Association, St. Louis.

Sheehan, J., Martin, M., & Kilburn, K. (1968). Speech disorders in retardation. *American Journal of Mental Deficiency, 73,* 251–256.

Sidman, M. (1970). Reading and auditory-visual equivalences. *Journal of Speech and Hearing Research, 14,* 5–13.

Sidman, M., & Cresson, O. (1973). Reading and crossmodal transfer of stimulus equivalences in severe retardation. *American Journal of Mental Deficiency, 77,* 515–523.

Snell, M. (1987). *Systematic instruction of persons with severe handicaps.* Columbus, OH: Merrill.

Warren, S., & Rogers-Warren, A. (1985). *Teaching functional language.* Baltimore: University Park Press.

Wilkinson, K., & Romski, M. A. (1989, November). *The emergence of visual-graphic symbol combinations in children with mental retardation using an augmented communication system.* Paper presented at the annual meeting of the American Speech-Language-Hearing Association, St. Louis.

Zigler, E., & Hodapp, R. (1986). *Understanding mental retardation.* New York: Cambridge University Press.

19 Children with Specific Language Impairment: Toward a Model of Teachability

Mabel L. Rice
Department of Speech-Language-Hearing
University of Kansas

Children's language development is universal, effortless, spontaneous, rule-governed, grammatically complex, and robust in the face of wide variations in environmental input. This characterization of language acquisition has become axiomatic in the contemporary literature. Explanatory models focus on accounting for this scenario. Yet this characterization is not completely accurate. The all-important qualifier is that it applies to most children.

In fact, a significant proportion of children do not acquire oral language in an effortless manner. A consideration of why this is so demonstrates that whereas language is a robust human skill, it is at the same time remarkably vulnerable. Language acquisition rests on a multilevel foundation of prerequisite competencies. Among the most obvious are adequate sensory, social, and intellectual skills.

These requirements are readily apparent when considering children who are hearing impaired, autistic, or mentally retarded, all of whom have concomitant verbal language limitations. In these cases communication problems are secondary to other handicapping conditions. In the 1987–1988 school year, 23% of handicapped children were reported to have speech and/or language problems (Annual OSEP Report to Congress, 1989). This estimate is probably somewhat conservative, given the current tendency to redefine children's language problems as learning disabilities when they reach the elementary grades (Snyder, 1984).

There is also a group of children whose only apparent developmental delay occurs in the domain of oral language. For these children, the communication problem is primary. Prevalence estimates for the latter group vary considerably, but 3% to 5% of preschoolers typically is reported (Leske, 1981; Rescorla, 1989; Silva, 1980; Stevenson & Richman, 1976). Given an estimated resident U.S. population of 10,879,000 children ages 3 to 5 years (Annual OSEP Report to Congress, 1989), approximately 543,950 young children are at risk for specific language impairment (SLI). This risk is also apparent in the fact that disorders of language development constitute the single largest handicapping condition in early childhood. Of the preschool children who received special education services in school year 1986, 69%, or 184,727 of the 265,814 children served, were categorized as speech-language impaired (Annual OSEP Report to Congress, 1988).[1]

When children cannot learn language on their own, they must be taught. The teachability of language depends on three factors: (a) the extent to which language, or specific dimensions of language, can be learned through teaching; (b) the extent to which a student is capable of and interested in applying requisite intellectual processes to the task, such as on-line processing, categorizing, storing, accessing and retrieving linguistic information, and establishing interrelated networks of linguistic information; and (c) the extent to which the chosen teaching approach can align the first two factors in a sociocultural context (Rice & Schiefelbusch, 1989). Therefore, the notion of teachability highlights the interface between the biobehavioral foundations of language (what a student brings to the task) and the human linguistic product, the language system, and the sources of environmental input.

The teachability issue takes us beyond the bounds of current models and descriptions of language acquisition, into the demands of first-language instruction. In order to teach language, the practitioner must accomplish three major goals. One is to identify the specific tasks to be taught and the sequence in which to teach them. The second is to design an intervention program. The third is to place the teaching activities in a broad context of social policy. In doing so, the practitioner must go far beyond the available basic literature, and take risks usually avoided by theoreticians and empirical scholars. For example, in order to identify the tasks and sequencing (i.e., what to teach and when to teach it), a language teacher must adopt certain general principles of language acquisition, identify specific components of the process, decide which components are likely keys to successful teaching, and assume a particular direction of the cause–effect relations among components.

---

[1]The importance of early intervention with handicapped children is recognized by the passage of Public Law 99-457, which mandates that special education services be provided to children ages 3 to 5 years by 1991. Furthermore, these services are to be offered in a least restrictive environment, that is, one with a maximal opportunity for enhancing a child's development, preferably in the context of normally developing peers.

Because we do not yet have a secure body of scientific knowledge on these matters, language teachers must gamble with such knowledge as we have. A sound teaching program requires a creative synthesis of the existing literature, and a willingness to explore beyond the limits of current scientific knowledge. A teacher must bet that a particular linguistic skill is the key to others, that teaching one skill will facilitate others, and that key skills are likely to generate other untaught skills. Furthermore, the teacher must make strong assumptions about causal relationships. Whether to teach linguistic skills first or more general cognitive skills, such as object categorization, depends on the language teacher's sense of which determines which. Finally, the language teacher must place the entire teaching exercise in the sociocultural context, keeping firmly in mind that people, not linguistic skills, are being taught, persons who in turn will use communication abilities in their home and community social settings. Language teachers cannot afford to teach all linguistic rules (an impossibly time-consuming task, even if all the rules were known), nor to overlook cognitive precursors, nor to lose sight of socially and culturally determined communication needs.

These practical realities of language teaching will illuminate the vulnerable aspects of the human language capacity, as well as the specific processing demands intrinsic to acquisition and the finely tuned interaction between environmental input and language development. Each of these aspects has been relatively overlooked in current explanatory accounts, yet they are essential dimensions of a complete model of language development.

This chapter addresses the teachability factors with regard to children with SLI. These youngsters, whose primary problem of development is language acquisition, inform us about its special demands. The discussion is laid out in the following manner. The literature describing SLI children is summarized. From this summary defining characteristics of these children are identified: delayed onset of language relative to social and cognitive skills, particular problems with morphology and word learning, and social/academic consequences. These characteristics then serve as organizing observations for a discussion of language intervention issues. In a final section the outline of a model of SLI is presented, with associated implications for language intervention.

CHILDREN WITH SPECIFIC LANGUAGE IMPAIRMENT: AN OVERVIEW

Definition.   Children with SLI demonstrate an asynchronous developmental profile, with age-appropriate levels of social, intellectual, and sensory development, but below age expectations for language development. Conventional diagnostic procedures address the following exclusionary criteria: performance on nonverbal intelligence tests within or better than normal range, social interactions appropriate for developmental level, and normal hearing and vision. Determination of a language deficit usually is accomplished by a combination of formal testing and observations of spontaneous language patterns and use.

Leonard's (1987) description of SLI children captured the nature of their limitations: These children "are much less skilled than their peers in such acts as extracting regularities in the speech they hear, registering the conversational contexts in which these regularities occur, examining these regularities for word-referent associations and evidence of phonological and grammatical rules, and using these associations and rules to formulate utterances of their own" (p. 33).

Investigations of SLI children typically employ a comparative group design, in which a group of SLI children at a particular age level is compared with two control groups, one of children of the same chronological age and the other of children matched for language development. The linguistic match is usually, but not always, on the basis of mean length of utterance (MLU). For example, a frequently studied group is 5-year-old SLI children, whose MLU-matched comparison group has a mean age of about 3 years (e.g., Rice, Buhr, & Nemeth, 1990; Rice, Buhr, & Oetting, in press). The advantage of this design is that it allows for determination of language deficits relative to age expectations, and possible specific differences relative to general language level. Therefore, it is possible to make some inferences about the contributions of general developmental level, as indexed by age, in comparison to general language level, as indexed by MLU. A variety of language skills have been investigated within this design, along with a number of related conceptual abilities.

The Language of SLI Children.   Although the current knowledge base is limited, some general observations can be made (for more complete literature reviews, see Johnston, 1988; Leonard, 1987, 1988). The language skills of SLI children are much like those of younger normally developing children. Early semantic development is delayed. A hallmark characteristic is the late appearance of first words (Rescorla, 1989); typically, SLI children's performance on vocabulary tests is below age expectations (Leonard, 1988). SLI children's early lexical types (Leonard, Camarata, Rowan, & Chapman, 1982) and semantic relations (Freedman & Carpenter, 1976; Leonard, Bolders, & Miller, 1976) are appropriate for their MLU levels. Likewise, major syntactic categories and sentence-level combinatorial rules resemble those of younger MLU-matched children (Morehead & Ingram, 1973).

There is also evidence of some particular linguistic problems for SLI children, relative to their MLU-matched comparison groups. The best substantiated difference is that of grammatical morphemes. Most observations are of the set of 14 morphemes studied by Brown (1973). English-speaking SLI children have particular difficulty with bound morphemes such as regular past tense and third-person singular inflections, and with the free closed-class morphemes of articles and auxiliaries (Leonard, 1989a). Italian-speaking SLI children have parallel problems with certain grammatical morphemes (Leonard, Sabbadini, Leonard, & Volterra, 1987; Leonard, Sabbadini, Volterra, & Leonard, 1988).

Furthermore, SLI children do not appear to "outgrow" their problems with morphology. Instead, a common error in the speech of older SLI children is the omission of obligatory grammatical morphemes (e.g., Weiner, 1974), even in the context of otherwise complex structures such as conjunction, complementation, and relativization. Gopnik & Crago (in press) provided a detailed description of the grammatical deficits of SLI adults, who were members of the same family.

Although phonological disorders often are overlooked in descriptions of SLI children, it must be recognized that phonology and other aspects of language impairment seem to covary to some extent. For example, Tallal, Ross, and Curtiss (1989) reported that in their sample of 90 SLI children, about 60% had some type of speech articulation deficit. Conversely, in a sample of 114 children identified as having phonological disorders, about 40% had some problems with language comprehension and 75% had some difficulties with language production (Shriberg, Kwiatkowski, Best, Hengst, & Terselic-Weber, 1986). The interaction of speech and language production is not surprising, insofar as a child who, for example, omits final sibilants also will be scored as omitting regular plurals, third-person singular agreement, and contractible copula and auxiliaries. The possible interaction of phonology and comprehension of morphemes and words is not attributable to a production problem, however. It is not clear how phonological problems interface with other aspects of language acquisition in the case of SLI children, but it is an issue much in need of careful study. Although in this chapter the emphasis is on morphology and the lexicon, it should be kept in mind that phonological processes also may be implicated in some unknown fashion for some but certainly not all of the SLI children.

Lexical Development.   Relatively little is known about the lexical development of SLI children. Yet this aspect of language may prove to be central to their difficulties. The limited evidence available suggests that their early lexical development, during the one-word stage, closely parallels that of their younger, language-matched peers (see Leonard, 1988, for a review). On the other hand, the SLI children, by virtue of their greater age, have more experience with the world, and presumably, also have greater conceptual sophistication, insofar as that is captured by nonverbal intelligence tests. The discrepancy between their experiential base and conceptual knowledge, and their lexical development, suggests that although conceptual knowledge may be necessary, it is not sufficient for learning new words.

Instead, their slower rate of word acquisition suggests special mapping problems in moving from nonlinguistic concepts to the linguistic categories evident in word meanings. Bowerman (1989) argued that children are sensitive to the regularities inherent in their native language and use this sensitivity to infer the boundaries of lexical categories. She went on to suggest that "it is possible that some children experience special difficulties in bridging the gap between nonlinguistic understanding and the formation of semantic categories" (p. 162). She identified several potential sources of difficulty: One is a problem of attention which impairs a child's ability to notice relevant similarities and differences; another is an inability to hypothesize the appropriate grouping principles; and a third is an inability to automatize obligatory distinctions. These possibilities call for further investigation.

One way to begin to explore the lexical acquisition processes of SLI children is to focus on the initial comprehension of novel lexical items. Normally developing children are able to infer much about a new word's possible meaning on the basis of a single encounter, in a "fast mapping" (Carey, 1978). The notion of fast mapping has been extended to quick incidental learning (QUIL) of words (Rice, 1990). The conventional scenario for word learning is an adult pointing to an object, as he or she turns to the child, makes eye contact, and says the object's name. Although this pairing of referent and word surely would be helpful for youngsters, it does not seem to be necessary. Instead, normally developing children can "pick up" new words embedded in conversational comments about ongoing events around them. In other words, for most children, even as young as 3 years of age, it is not necessary for the referent of a new word to be singled out in some way that focuses attention on it for word learning to take place.

QUIL processing of new words has been demonstrated in studies employing video stimuli (Rice, Buhr, & Nemeth, 1990; Rice, Buhr, & Oetting, in press; Rice & Woodsmall, 1988). The stimuli are developed by dubbing animated programs off broadcast television. The programs are simple stories without dialogue or voice-over narration. Scripts are prepared for voice-over narration that tell a simple story with a description of the events and characters. The stories feature selected novel words. The children watch the programs individually with the instructions to "watch carefully." There is no interaction with the adult. Whatever learning takes place is accomplished by the child as an observer. At the end of viewing, the children's comprehension of new words is measured by means of a picture-pointing task.

Normally developing 3- and 5-year-old children are able to match referents with new words after only two viewings of a 12-min video. In the first study, the magnitude of the effect was about 2 new words, out of 20 novel words, for the 3-year-olds and 5 new words for the 5-year-olds. This is a remarkable accomplishment, given the on-line processing demands of this very naturalistic setting. The effect was limited to object and attribute words, such as *gramophone* and *malicious;* actions (verbs) or affective state terms were not learned (Rice & Woodsmall, 1988). In another study (Rice, Buhr, & Oetting, in press), with 10 new words, the 3-year-olds learned 1.6 new words and the 5-year-olds learned 3.13 new words.

On the other hand, 5-year-old SLI children demonstrate only a very modest quick incidental learning ability. They do indicate some initial comprehension of the new words, as compared to a control group, but the mean number of new words is only 1.5 out of a possible 20 (Rice, Buhr, & Nemeth, in press) and just less than 1 out of a possible 10 (Rice, Buhr, & Oetting, 1990). In the first study, the SLI children's performance was significantly lower than their MLU-matched comparison group, as well as significantly lower than their chronological matches. In the second, their means were lower than the MLU group, although not at a level of statistical significance, and their performance was significantly lower than the age-matched group.

From one perspective, these findings are not surprising. They document that SLI children are slow word learners, a conclusion also evident in their poor performance on vocabulary tests. What the findings contribute is that at least part of the problem lies in on-line processing mechanisms that are independent of general vocabulary development, as indexed by Peabody Picture Vocabulary Test–Revised (PPVT-R), and general linguistic development, as indexed by MLU. The first conclusion is supported by the fact that PPVT-R scores do not predict the comprehension of the new words for SLI or normally developing children. The second conclusion is drawn from the poorer performance of the SLI children relative to their MLU-matched younger comparison group.

A two-edged question emerges from the QUIL phenomenon. How do normally developing preschoolers manage such an impressive feat, and why do SLI children fail? Intrinsic to the processing demands of quick word learning is the ability to parse the incoming speech stream, in order to identify the novel word, its possible grammatical class, and its possible referent (cf. Rice, 1990). Perhaps this is one source of the problems of SLI children. To test that possibility, narratives for video stimuli were prepared in which a strategic pause was inserted before the target word. The new word also was moved to the end of the sentence, to increase its salience.

Two conditions were run, one with and one without an inserted pause. The subjects were 5-year-old SLI children, with a comparison group of age-matched children and another of younger language-matched children. The findings indicated no advantage for the pause condition for the SLI children. Presumably, if the problems of the SLI children were attributable to an inability to parse the novel word, the pause condition should have enhanced their performance.

There are several plausible explanations for why SLI children did not benefit from this rather obvious cue. One is that their problem is not one of segmentation, but rather is one of hypothesizing the appropriate referent, along the lines suggested by Bowerman (1989). Another explanation is that the segmentation cues are influenced by the children's grammar, in particular, their limited morphology. And it is, of course, possible that some combination of these processes impedes word acquisition. At any rate, it would be too simplistic to conclude that SLI children have problems in word acquisition because they cannot determine word boundaries in the incoming stream of speech.

There are some interesting hints about other mechanisms at work in QUIL that warrant further study. One intriguing possibility is that normal children may call upon similar word meanings to help with the quick match with likely referents (cf. Rice, 1990). If so, the SLI children may be handicapped by a limited lexicon, insofar as they would have fewer words to serve as possible analogs for the novel word, or problems with extracting the regularities of the current lexicon in order to make an analogy in the first place. This possibility parallels the conclusion of Kail and Leonard (1986), that the apparent word-finding problems of elementary school-age SLI children are attributable to restricted elaboration of lexical storage instead of problems with long-term memory, per se. They hypothesized that the representation of words in semantic memory of SLI children is less elaborate than that of their age peers, which in turn makes it more difficult for them to retrieve targeted words. In order to evaluate either of these possibilities, we need much more information about the lexicons of SLI children, and how semantic entries are linked with each other.

Another factor implicated in the QUIL findings is the role of the grammatical frame for the new word. In the Rice and Woodsmall (1988) study, one reason that attribute words, but not action and affective words, were learned may have been that attribute words always appeared consistently in a prototypic sentence context, of article-attribute-noun. This explanation is supported by the finding that the same lexical items in the pause study (Rice, Buhr, & Oetting, in press) were not as readily mapped as in the earlier study. Furthermore, this difference was apparent only for the SLI children. In the pause study, the attribute words did not appear in the article-attribute-noun frame but instead were moved to the end of the sentence, in a predicate adjective slot. The implication is that SLI children find it easier to hypothesize a new word's possible meaning if the new word is presented in a canonical sentence frame. Presumably the predictability of the sentence frame would reduce the distributional analysis demands for inference of the grammatical class of the novel word (cf. Maratsos & Chalkley, 1981). Given the close (but imperfect) correspondence of grammatical class and meanings, a child could deduce quickly that a word preceded by an article is most likely to refer to an object or person in the scene, or that a word preceded by an article and followed by a noun refers to an attribute of the noun (object or person), a possibility first demonstrated by Brown (1957) and later by Katz, Baker, and MacNamara (1974).

In the case of SLI children, with their particular problems with morphology, the available grammatical cues may be restricted, relative to their age- and language-matched peers. For example, SLI children have particular problems with articles (Beastrom & Rice, 1986). To the extent that lexical mapping is guided by grammatical cues, the SLI children would be handicapped by their limited grammar, and, to the extent that their grammar had specific gaps not predicted by their MLU, these children would have problems of word acquisition beyond those predicted by their delayed language. The end result would be the opposite of bootstrapping. Instead of using one area of language to build another, SLI children would be left without a solid strap to hang onto.

Another interesting outcome of the studies is that none of the preschool children, either the 3- and 5-year-old normally developing children or the 5-year-old SLI children, were able to make quick referential matchings for the action words (verbs; Rice, Buhr, & Nemeth, 1990; Rice & Woodsmall, 1988). The verbs used in the studies referred to simple actions, such as *trudge*. There were both transitive and intransitive verbs, with no apparent effect for transitivity, insofar as no verbs were acquired. The difficulty with verbs is as predicted by Gentner (1982), who argued that the meanings of verbs are more difficult to map than those of nouns, in part because "the category corresponding to nouns is at its core conceptually simpler or more basic than those corresponding to verbs and other predicates" (Gentner, 1982, p. 301; cf. Maratsos, Chapter 3 of this volume).

It could be that the reason no quick mapping of verbs was evident was because the response measure, pointing to static rather than moving pictures, was biased against the action components of verbs. That interpretation was explored in a follow-up study (Rice, Buhr, & Oetting, in preparation), in which a video comprehension assessment technique was developed to parallel the format of the four-picture choice of the experimental comprehension task, which was in turn modeled on the PPVT-R. In this video test, children view a four-way split screen and point to the pictured object or event that corresponds to a named word. Preliminary analyses reveal no apparent difference between video and static picture assessment, based on within-subject comparisons of the two methods. This finding holds for SLI as well as normally developing 3- and 5-year-olds. Hence, the lack of verb mapping in this quick incidental learning situation does not appear to be attributable to a methodological artifact.

The question of how children learn verbs is of central significance in current accounts of children's syntactic development (e.g., Bowerman, 1989; Gleitman, 1989; Pinker, 1989a, 1989b). Although the studies discussed earlier were not designed to explore verb distinctions to clarify competing accounts of syntactic development, they do address critical issues. How children construe a scene and how they formulate some guesses about the referent for the verb are processes at the heart of much of the debate over the acquisition of syntax. Because a discussion of verbs would go somewhat afield from our immediate topic, it will be deferred to a later section. Suffice it to note here that the issue of how SLI children map verb meanings is of paramount importance for an account of their grammatical limitations, and the available evidence is scanty.

Causal Factors.   Efforts to identify causal factors for SLI have been inconclusive. Leonard (1987) reviewed the evidence for three accounts: One is that the communicative environment of SLI children is inadequate; the second is that SLI children have limited auditory processing abilities; and the third is that these children have subtle deficiencies with nonverbal representational ability. He concluded that none of these three provides satisfactory accounts of the language profiles of SLI children.

Each of the accounts fails on the basis of at least two of the three major challenges to any explanatory accounts. The first challenge is to demonstrate differences between SLI children and comparison groups of children. All three putative causal factors meet this challenge, relative to age-matched peers, although the evidence is mixed for the third account. On the one hand, SLI children sometimes score lower than comparison groups on selected nonverbal tests. On the other hand, they do score within normal range on nonverbal tests of intelligence. Therefore, advocates of the nonverbal representational deficit account must explain this discrepancy. For example, Johnston (1982) argued that the nonverbal intelligence tests tap into a lower order of representational ability, more dependent on perceptual instead of conceptual abilities. This explanation, however, runs counter to traditional psychometric interpretation.

The second challenge is to disambiguate cause-and-effect relationships. The first account fails this challenge. Although parents of SLI children do not interact with their children in the same way as do parents of normally developing children of the same age, the adjustments are appropriate accommodations to the more limited linguistic competencies of the SLI children. Therefore, the differences are expected consequences of a child's limited linguistic ability, not a causal determinant of those abilities. The second account is also vulnerable to this challenge, insofar as the auditory processing tasks often draw upon linguistic knowledge. The third account, that of limited nonverbal representation, has similar problems, in that children may perform poorly on symbolic play tasks because they have limited access to verbal labels, or fail to solve cognitive problems because they have limited access to verbal mnemonics.

The third challenge is to tie the purported causal mechanisms to particular language limitations. Again, all three accounts fail this challenge. In regard to the first, any adjustments or deficits in input do not account for the specific linguistic problems evidenced by SLI children. In regard to the second, although some vagaries are evident in SLI children's performance on acoustic processing tasks, the pattern of the differences does not predict the particular linguistic problems of SLI children. In the case of the third account, that of nonverbal representational ability as the possible source of the SLI children's limitations, when differences have been identified, such as limited performance on haptic recognition tasks, it is difficult to explain how they would account for the specific linguistic problems of interest.

More recently, Leonard (1989a, 1989b) proposed that SLI children have particular limitations in perceiving and hypothesizing linguistic features with low phonetic substance. This limitation, in effect, would act as a filter to distort incoming speech information in a principled way, such that SLI children would have problems with the unstressed elements of English morphology. This account meets the challenge of linking the proposed causal mechanism to the observed pattern of linguistic problems. It does not, however, completely account for the pervasive problems with the unstressed features of English that the SLI children demonstrate. For example, Watkins and Rice (in press) investigated 5-year-old SLI children's use of verb particles and prepositions. If low-phonetic substance alone were operative, there should be no difference between the two grammatical classes, insofar as the same unstressed words, such as *on,* can appear as either a particle or preposition. That prediction, however, was not supported. Particles were particularly difficult for SLI children relative to their age- and language-matched controls. Furthermore, there was evidence that the children had acquired prepositions as a general grammatical class, whereas particles were still being mastered on a word-by-word basis. Thus, the SLI children's problems with particles and prepositions seemed to be deeper than implied by an inability to process unstressed elements. Instead, as acknowledged by Leonard, semantic and syntactic limitations are also implicated.

There is growing interest in a possible genetic basis for SLI (cf. Ludlow & Cooper, 1983). Gopnik and Crago (in press) argued that individuals with

SLI, at least in the one family they studied, demonstrate missing linguistic features that are manifestations of an underlying genetic deficit. Other studies (e.g., Tallal et al., 1989; Tomblin, 1989) report a higher risk for SLI in families of SLI children than in matched-control families. In a study of 51 SLI second-graders, Tomblin (1989) reported an average frequency of immediate family members with a history of clinical treatment for language impairment of 22.9% for the families of SLI children versus 2.9% for the 136 control families. Brothers of SLI children were especially at risk, with the probability of a language impairment 30 times that of the brothers of the control children. In their samples of 90 4-year-old SLI children and 60 control children, Tallal et al. (1989) found 41.5% frequency of impairment in first-degree relatives for the SLI children compared with 18.5% for the control group, a statistically significant difference. These findings are similar to earlier reports of familial aggregations of SLI, and related studies of individuals with speech impairment (e.g., Parlour, 1990).

Although evidence for family clusters is consistent with a model of genetic factors, it is not confirmatory, as discussed by Tomblin (1989). Possible environmental contributions also may be implicated in the family groupings. Another possibility is that genetic contributions to SLI are indirect consequences of related mechanisms, such as neural development or functioning.

Academic Consequences.   Although the causal factors remain elusive, there is convincing evidence of widespread consequences of SLI. Follow-up studies (see Weiner, 1985, and Parlour, 1990 for summaries) reveal that the majority of young children with early language deficits maintain some degree of language problem. Furthermore, these children are at risk for academic achievement and social acceptance. In particular, a finding replicated across a number of studies is that SLI children encounter problems with reading. The Tallal et al. (1989) study indicates that school failure also runs in families, with 14.9% of the SLI mothers (as compared to 1.9% of the controls) held back in school sometime before the eighth grade, and 24.3% of the SLI fathers (vs. 7.4% of the control fathers).

It could be argued that the available follow-up studies present an overly pessimistic picture because they capture the consequences of earlier educational practices, ones of more than a decade ago, that have been revised in light of contemporary gains in knowledge. That possibility is countered by the preliminary findings of a longitudinal study in progress, in which preschool and kindergarten SLI children are being followed into the elementary grades. Thirty-six kindergarten children met the criteria for identification as SLI. These children attend a variety of schools in two midwestern cities. One year later, 17 of the 35 children available at follow-up were not in regular first grade, but were instead in special "developmental" first grades, designed to provide tutorial experiences in preparation for the regular first-grade curriculum. All of these children tested within normal range or above on nonverbal tests of intelligence, and did not present with other significant developmental problems. In contrast, all of the control group of 31 normally developing children were promoted to regular first grade (H. Catts, personal communication, January, 1991). This early identification of SLI children as "at risk" for academic achievement suggests that factors other than low academic performance are involved in the teachers' judgements, insofar as children usually are not exposed to a formal reading curriculum until first grade.

Social Consequences. SLI children have been described as poor communicators, relative to their normal peers (e.g., Fey, 1986). On a number of pragmatic measures, such as clarification responses and the use of cohesive discourse devices, language-impaired children perform below their age peers, on a level more like their younger language peers (Lahey, 1988). Johnston (1988) concluded that although SLI children demonstrate "interactional strengths," their limited grammatical resources lead to difficulty constructing cohesive texts, repairing conversational breakdowns, and modifying speech to fit the social situation.

The social consequences of limited verbal skill are evident in the classroom interactions of young children. In a series of ongoing studies, the social interactions of SLI children in a preschool classroom are being observed (Hadley & Rice, in press; Rice, Hadley, & Wilcox, in preparation; Rice, Sell, & Hadley, in press). Observations are collected during play time, a 45-min period during which children are free to select their own activities, interact with whom they choose, and to move about freely in the classroom. The children are 3 to 5 years of age, equally distributed across three groups, SLI, normally developing, and children learning English as a second language. There are usually two or three adults in the room during the observation time. The social interactions of the children are coded on-line by an observer in the classroom (Rice, Sell, & Hadley, 1990). The targeted behaviors are initiations and responses, with initiation defined as a verbal attempt to begin an interaction with another person. Responses can be verbal or nonverbal. In effect, the coding captures who is talking to whom, and who initiated the interaction.

The results of two studies (Hadley & Rice, in press; Rice, Sell, & Hadley, in press) reveal that the social interactions of these young children are significantly influenced by the children's facility with communication skills. Normal children were the preferred partner for all children's social interactions. Conversely, children with limited communication skills are ignored more often by their peers and are in turn less responsive to initiations directed to them. Children with speech articulation problems and limited intelligibility, a subset of the SLI children, shortened their responses. SLI children are more likely to initiate interactions with adults and less likely to initiate interactions with their normally developing peers.

The general impression is that even as young as 3 years of age children are sensitive to relative differences in verbal facility, and begin to make adjustments in their social interactions. Children with less skill develop compensatory strategies, such as reliance on adults for mediation of social interactions and to meet their needs. What is particularly striking is that the social consequences are evident on the basis of communication skill alone, insofar as the SLI children in this preschool setting do not have visible handicaps, they do not differ by race or socioeconomic status, their general social demeanor is appropriate, and their intellectual resources are commensurate with their peers. Furthermore, the apparent sensitivity to linguistic repertoires is evident in children conventionally regarded as too young for metalinguistic awareness.

Limited social interaction as a consequence of limited language may lead to yet another outcome. It is possible that classroom teachers arrive at the impression that SLI children are socially immature, insofar as they are not completely (i.e., verbally) integrated into the social interactions of their peers. In a longitudinal study underway, in which we are following the "graduates" of the Language Acquisition Preschool into the kindergarten setting (Rice, Hadley, & Wilcox, in preparation), we have encountered anecdotal reports from teachers suggesting that this might be the case. Teachers, as well as other adults, may extrapolate from the general correlation of verbal, social, and intellectual status, to the stronger assumption that an individual child's verbal ability predicts his or her intellectual abilities or social maturity. A study is in progress to explore this possibility (Alexander, Rice, & Hadley, in preparation). It may turn out that from the very outset the academic achievement of SLI children is jeopardized by a social corollary of their language limitations.

Summary.   To summarize these observations of SLI children, the picture that emerges is one of children with particular difficulties with language acquisition, such that they have limited language relative to their chronological peers yet have similar social and cognitive resources. In addition to a generally delayed emergence of language, they seem to have specific problems with morphology and probably with word acquisition. There is no apparent single causal factor, although SLI does tend to cluster in families. There are, however, social and academic consequences of a delay in early language acquisition, such that these children have restricted verbal interactions with their peers and are at risk for limited academic achievement.

THE NEED FOR A COMPREHENSIVE MODEL
OF THE SLI CHILD

How can we integrate these various observations about SLI children into a coherent model meaningful for planning language intervention? Leonard (1989b) drew upon Gardner's (1983) theory of multiple intelligences to propose that these children are examples of an individual difference in language ability (i.e., they are limited in language ability in much the same way that others may be poor in musical, spatial, or bodily kinesthetic abilities). He emphasized that such youngsters are not "damaged goods" but are simply less proficient language learners than most. He went on to conclude that an individual-differences perspective (my term, not his) would not lead to significant changes in current clinical practices, in the assessment, diagnostic, or treatment methodologies.

The multiple-intelligences account of SLI is appealing, and perhaps is true. However, it comes very close to a restatement of the descriptive definition of SLI children as those with particular problems with language acquisition. A more significant limitation is that it does not capture the expectation that all children have robust language-learning capacities, in contrast with other areas of skill, such as musical talent, which is regarded as a special occurrence in some individuals. Pinker's (1984) rather colorful way of putting it is that "there is virtually no way to prevent it [language acquisition] from happening short of raising a child in a barrel" (p. 29). That expectation, in turn, is probably a contributor to the social and academic consequences of delayed acquisition of language, in part because other children, teachers, and the very organization of the educational system presume certain language skills at certain age levels.

In order to be feasible, therefore, an account of children with SLI must take into account the following facts:

1. The onset of language is delayed relative to general cognitive and social development.
2. Particular problems are evident with morphology and word learning.
3. There are immediate social consequences, and long-term risk for academic achievement.

The challenge for the development of a comprehensive model is to determine how these three features, an asynchrony between language and general development, particular linguistic problems, and the overlaid factors of social adjustments and academic failures, fit together, how they interact to influence language acquisition, and how they evolve over the course of a child's development. Furthermore, the model should provide specific directions for language intervention.

APPLICATION OF WHAT IS KNOWN ABOUT THE SLI CHILD TO LANGUAGE INTERVENTION

These three features of SLI children guide the work underway at the recently established Language Acquisition Preschool (LAP) at the University of Kansas. LAP is designed to facilitate language development in three groups of preschool children: SLI children, normally developing peers, and children learning English as their second language, with approximately equal numbers of children in each of the groups. Detailed description of the program can be found in Rice and Wilcox (1990a). Documentation of the program's effectiveness is reported in Rice and Wilcox (1990b). The purpose of this section is to draw upon what has been learned in LAP to illustrate some training issues that follow from what we know about SLI and normally developing children. Readers interested in a review of the training literature are referred to Fey (1986) and Leonard (1981).

Asynchronous Development of Language and Cognitive/Social Skills. Given that the intellectual and social resources of these youngsters are basically intact, the LAP classroom setting was designed to be appropriate for young children's general development. The High Scope Curriculum (Hohmann, Bonet, & Weikart, 1978), widely used in preschool classrooms, was adapted for use. At the same time, it was assumed that in order to facilitate language acquisition, SLI children would require a setting in which linguistic forms and patterns were highlighted and made more salient than in the usual give and take of a classroom setting. In effect, the entire setting is socially engineered to maximize opportunities for verbal interactions and to draw attention to targeted linguistic forms in a naturalistic, unobtrusive manner.

The assumption is that in order to be maximally effective, language teaching must be matched to a child's cognitive abilities, immediate interests, and social needs. These are best elicited in the spontaneous interactions of a group of children. This assumption is evident in a recent shift from teacher-directed instruction to situationally embedded, learner-driven language teaching. These principles are extrapolated from the normative language acquisition literature. Johnston (1985) summarized them in the admonitions to fit the content to the child's cognitive interests and abilities, focus on linguistic forms, and provide language that is socially functional.

The assumption that meaningful language facilitation opportunities are determined by the context and by the child's participation ruled out a designated "language-teaching time." Instead, many of the facilitation activities are embedded in a play center time, during which the children are free to choose their activities and to change activities as they prefer. One sometimes disconcerting consequence of this approach is that children can and do walk away from an adult intent on providing special linguistic input, if the interaction is not of interest to the child. Language pathology students in training find the method to be challenging to learn, but over the past 3 years more than 30 of them have managed to do so.

The actual teaching strategies are an eclectic combination of techniques to enhance the salience and meaningfulness of linguistic input, largely drawn from the adult–child interaction literature (cf. Nelson, 1989). The intent is to increase the probability that a child will recognize a discrepancy between his or her own linguistic system and that of the adult, will identify the difference, and will be able to make adjustments toward approximation of the adult system. On the input side, the adults in LAP are trained in the use of recasts, expansions, and repetitions of what a child says, thereby providing the children with plenty of models for targeted linguistic forms and constructions, on the assumption that such techniques are likely to keep the input within the child's sphere of interest and relevant to the child's linguistic system (Nelson, 1989).

There is also, in LAP, judicious use of corrective feedback, that typically consists of something like the adult saying "you said *two ball* — hmmm, I say *two balls.*" These feedback loops are used carefully, though, to avoid pushing a child into a nonresponsive mode, a risk to be discussed later. Another way that contrastive evidence is presented is in the form of modeled interactions. The most likely setting for this is in the dramatic play area, when children play with toys and act out real-world scripts, such as a visit to a fast-food restaurant. Appropriate verbal routines are modeled, often by child models, and there may be a discussion contrasting how to say it with how not to say it. In a similar fashion, book-reading activities often include discussions about the characters' dialogue, or how to describe events or things.

Perhaps because they see this behavior modeled by the adults, the other children, especially the normally developing models, also provide corrective feedback to the SLI and the English as a second language (ESL) children, in the form of spontaneous commentary about how something is said or what is said. For example, a normally developing child said to an SLI child: "It's not *lunny*. It's *sunny,*" after the SLI child misarticulated the word *sunny* during the opening discussion of the weather. Another example is when a normal model asked an SLI child, "Why do you always say *me* do it?", with an emphasis on the *me*. Although this is not a frequent occurrence, it does seem to be a highly salient experience for the SLI children, who typically listen to but do not immediately respond to such feedback. This phenomenon also suggests a rather unusual level of metalinguistic awareness for preschool children, which may in part be due to the presence of the ESL children who use their native language as well as English in the classroom.

Children in LAP are not pressured to respond. The ESL children made it very clear that much language learning can be accomplished in a passive way, as they work out comprehension of English. The LAP ESL children enter without any English. They typically take 3 to 4 months before they begin to use English in the classroom. During that time they interact socially, especially with the adults in the room, but seldom speak in English (cf. similar observations reported by Tabors, 1987). Transition from the silent period seems to coincide with their first uses of word combinations in English. They go on to master English at or near age-level expectations, usually by the end of the first year. These observations of the ESL children suggest that it is not necessary to expect frequent responses from the SLI children in order to ensure learning, a conclusion that has not been weakened by any counterevidence.

The major pedagogical conclusion to be drawn from LAP is that language intervention that takes into account the cognitive and social integrity of SLI children recognizes the advantages of naturalistic, group-based, child-centered teaching in a minimally restrictive environment with normally developing peers. This approach, however, is incomplete without a sense of what to target as linguistic goals.

Morphology and Word Learning as Targeted Linguistic Problems. It is the choice of the particular items to teach, the order in which to introduce them, and the extent to which goals overlap at the level of individual items that force the clinician to fill in large gaps not addressed in the formal literature on language intervention (cf. Rice, 1980, chapter 6 for a discussion of some of the gaps relative to teaching of word meanings). In LAP, as in most clinical settings, the determination of what to teach an SLI child is based on the child's performance on standardized language tests and on a transcript of a sample of a child's spontaneous utterances (cf. Kelly & Rice, 1986). Observations are subdivided into the conventional linguistic categories of phonology, syntax, morphology, semantics, and pragmatics. Therapy goals then are selected from within these categories.

Given that many SLI children demonstrate problems with morphology, in particular verb inflections, and vocabulary development, these two areas often are targeted for instruction. Without clear theoretical guidelines for how to integrate morphology and the lexicon, the usual teaching strategy is to approach the two goals somewhat independently, with some activities designed to highlight verb inflections, and other activities to teach targeted lexical items. Any overlap in the two activities is more serendipitous than planned.

It must be acknowledged that the efforts of language pathologists are generally successful. SLI children, particularly if training begins in the preschool years, do benefit from language instruction. They learn new morphemes and vocabulary items, often at a rate that exceeds that of the normally developing children (cf. Leonard, 1981). For example, for 17 SLI children enrolled in LAP an average of 2.8 semesters, the mean gain on the PPVT-R was 13.3 standard score points, almost a full standard deviation (15). In comparison, normally developing peers enrolled for the same time period gained an average of 2.1 points. The greatest gain by an SLI child was 35 standard score points, more than 2 standard deviations. Virtually every SLI child improved in receptive vocabulary.

Evidence of success, however, does not rule out the need to identify the particular factors that contribute to the success, nor does it ensure maximally effective teaching techniques for all domains of language competence. Furthermore, the effects of language intervention must be very robust to generalize to new settings (cf. Fey, 1988) and to offset the social and academic consequences of SLI (to be discussed in the next section).

EXTENSION OF THE NORMATIVE LITERATURE: THE TEACHING OF VERBS

Recent developments in linguistic theory and developmental psycholinguistics suggest that it would be valuable to consider verbs as a linguistic category to target for training. Verbs are a bridge between syntax and lexicon, and the semantics of verbs influences the acquisition of verb inflections. In the following discussion, some conclusions from the language acquisition literature (greatly oversimplified in the interest of brevity) are listed, along with accompanying remarks about their relevance for understanding the nature of SLI and for language training.

Conclusion 1: Verbs Control Verb Argument Structure

A central postulate of current grammatical theory (cf. Bresnan, 1982) is that many of the facts about grammar are interpretable in terms of properties of the verb. Not all verbs can appear in all sentences, but instead the verb controls which arguments can be expressed, and the means of grammatical encoding of the expressed arguments. Pinker (1989b) provided the following examples:

John fell.
*John fell the floor.

John dined.
*John dined the pizza.

John devoured the pizza.
*John devoured.

John ate.
John ate the pizza.

John put something somewhere.
*John put something.
*John put somewhere.
*John put. (pp. 3–4)

Among the clinical implications of this conclusion are the following:

Implication 1.1.   There is more to teaching verbs than establishing the relation between label and referent. From Pinker's (1989b) examples, it is clear that speakers cannot solve the problem of how to get their ideas into language solely on the basis of finding words to match their meanings and then stringing them together. *Dined, devoured,* and *ate* all can refer to the same scene, yet *dined* does not allow a direct object, *devoured* does, but does not allow its omission, and *ate* allows either object or no object. One implication of this fact is that teaching verbs as labels for events, in isolation from the sentence frame, would not solve a child's problems in figuring out how to use the verbs in sentences.

Implication 1.2.   On the other hand, there is more to teaching syntax than establishing the linear alignment of the words, such as subject-verb-object. Instead, careful attention must be paid to verb subcategories that share properties of verb-argument structures. For example, some verbs can alternate between grammatical settings whereas others cannot. Examples of alternation are such pairs as *Sally made the ball bounce/Sally bounced the ball; Sally made the baby burp/Sally burped the baby.* Not all verbs that appear in the *make X verb* structure can alternate. For example, *Sally made the children laugh/*Sally laughed the children* (Pinker, 1989b, p. 49). The fact that children make errors and say sentences like **Sally laughed the children* is evidence for their understanding of the alternation rule, an indication that the rule is productive, just as *breaked* suggests a productive application of the regular past-tense rule. What is not known is whether or not SLI children make these kinds of errors, a point we return to shortly.

These examples suggest that teaching such an apparently straightforward syntactic structure as subject-verb-object, with examples such as *Sally bounced the ball,* and *Sally made the ball,* would overlook the important ways in which *Sally made the ball bounce* are related to each. What would also be needed is training to develop the rules governing the alternation of *Sally bounced the ball* and *Sally made the ball bounce.* Pinker (1989b, Chapter 7) argued that learning the alternation rules is enhanced by the presence of contrastive pairs. If so, it would be important to contrast the verbs *bounce* and *burp* with *laugh,* to ensure that the child understood the meanings of the verbs, how they are used in surface sentence structures, and how *bounce* and *burp,* but not *laugh,* form a set of verbs equivalent in that they allow for alternation in the two different sentence frames.

Conclusion 2: There is a Logical Problem Evident in Accounts of How Children Could Learn Verb/Argument Structure

The logical problem is addressed in the debates about the learnability of language (cf. Bowerman, 1989; Pinker, 1984, 1989a, 1989b). The problem arises from the need to reconcile three observations (cf. Baker, 1979; Pinker, 1989a, 1989b). One is that rules for sentence formation appear to be arbitrary. There are reasonable ways to extend the rules that are not allowed, as indicated by the previous examples. The second observation is that children overgeneralize their linguistic rules along the lines of plausibility not grammaticality. They make mistakes, of the same sort as the possible, but not allowable ungrammatical sentences. The third observation is that adults do not seem to provide negative evidence; that is, they do not point out to a child which sentences are not allowed, and they seldom correct the children's grammatical errors. The children seem to be able to solve the problem on the basis of positive evidence (hearing correct use of the language) alone, an enormously impressive accomplishment. The vexing problem is how they retreat from their errors, how they arrive at the less-than-all-possible applications of the rules.

Before moving on to consideration of possible ways in which children can overcome the learnability problem, it is appropriate to consider the clinical implications of the apparently limited role of negative evidence in normally developing children's language acquisition.

Implication 2.1. As described earlier, the teaching techniques used in LAP, as in most clinical settings, consist of much use of modeling the correct forms (positive evidence), along with judicious instances of corrective feedback (negative evidence). The assumption is that although negative evidence is apparently not necessary for normally developing children's acquisition of language, it can be helpful for SLI children, if used in a manner that respects their social and cognitive needs and abilities. That assumption is, in turn, based on the conclusion that SLI children, unlike their normally developing peers, are evidently unable to extract linguistic regularities from the input on the basis of positive evidence alone. For example, even into adolescence, some SLI youngsters tend to omit grammatical morphemes (cf. Fletcher & Peters, 1984; Weiner, 1974). On the learnability account, omissions would seem to be "benign," insofar as omitted morphemes could be learned on the basis of positive evidence alone (cf. Baker, 1979), a prediction not met by SLI children.

The possible benefit of negative evidence, presumably, would be attributable to provision of cues that help a child identify discrepancies between his or her linguistic system and the targeted rules (cf. Birdsong's 1989 discussion of the role of negative evidence in second-language instruction). This assumption is much in need of formal investigation. Do SLI children benefit from negative feedback? Are the benefits tied to the level of linguistic learning, such that negative feedback is most helpful when a child is at the earliest stages of rule inference, or later, when there are some indications of emerging rules? What kinds of negative evidence would be most helpful for a child who omits past-tense markings — simple explicit comparisons of "you say *go,* but I say *went*"?, for irregular past but not regular?, only if the child has tried to indicate past relations in other ways, such as using phrases like "the other day" to indicate past events?, or only if the child has use of past-tense inflections on a few but not all verbs? A host of possible questions about the provision of positive and negative evidence in training settings has yet to be addressed. Answering these questions is crucial to sorting out the complex interactions of input and acquisition that are central to the teaching mission.

Implication 2.2. Another clinical implication of the learnability problem is the assumption that children are not conservative language learners, because they generate plausible novel forms. Although there is evidence of normally developing youngsters' ability to generate novel verbs (cf. Pinker, 1989b), little evidence is available regarding the ability of SLI children to do so. In an extensive case study of the spontaneous utterances of three SLI preschoolers, very few errors of this type were noted (Bode & Rice, in preparation). On the other hand, SLI children do overregularize irregular verb inflections for past tense, indicating that they can extract "rules," or regular patterns, from the language they hear. Yet the pattern of their verb learning has yet to be described, and may well be more conservative than that of their peers, a possibility that we return to below.

Conclusion 3: Normally Developing Children Rely on a Combination of Semantic and Syntactic Bootstrapping to Acquire Verb Argument Structures

The means by which most children resolve the learnability problem seems to involve an intricate interaction of semantic and syntactic knowledge. Pinker (1984, 1989a, 1989b) hypothesized that children can draw upon subtle distinctions of verb meanings to determine the subcategories evident in allowable alternations of verb argument structures, in a semantic bootstrapping operation. For example, he argued that verbs involving a "cause of a change of physical state," such as *open,* and *melt* would show the *made X verb/verbed X* alternation discussed earlier, whereas verbs of "internally caused acts" such as *laugh* would not allow for such alternation. (For a critique of how well this account addresses the learnability problem, see Bowerman, 1989.) According to Pinker, these meaning distinctions are learned as part of learning what the verb refers to, by means of event-category labeling.

Taking a different perspective, Gleitman and her colleagues (Gleitman, 1989) argued that often there is not enough information available in the event scene for a child to make the relevant distinctions, or that alternative ways of interpreting a scene may allow for different verb choices. For example, scenes of *giving* also entail *getting.* In order to figure out the scene, Gleitman concluded, a child must call upon an understanding of how *give* or *get* appears in verb/argument structures. In other words, Gleitman turned the semantic bootstrapping account on its head, to hypothesize that instead of using verb meanings to figure out syntax, children draw upon syntax to infer the referents in a scene that match the verb, in a syntactic bootstrapping of lexical insights.

Although they emphasize opposing directions of influence, both Gleitman (1989) and Pinker (1984, 1989a, 1989b) agreed that a child probably relies on a combination of syntactic and semantic bootstrapping to figure out the riddles of linguistic structure. The specifics of how children manage to do this are not worked out, of course, but it seems that they are able to play off the close association of syntax and semantics even at the earliest stages of language acquisition to acquire abstract rules of sentence structure and to match the domains of the rules to the constraints of their native language.

Implication 3.1.   Application of this conclusion to SLI children implies that they may be caught in a very limiting Catch-22 situation. If their word-learning aptitude is impaired, they will have fewer lexical resources to draw upon for learning syntax. On the other hand, if their ability to infer linguistic structures is limited, they will be unable to call upon syntactic bootstrapping operations to infer the appropriate referent or relation for a novel verb. In effect, they may not have enough linguistic resources to serve as straps for a bootstrapping operation. To the extent that this is the case, the linguistic delays of the SLI children would not be surprising; what would be surprising is the amount of language acquisition that they do exhibit in spite of limited resources.

Implication 3.2.   The means by which young children learn the meanings of verbs is central to much of the theorizing about how children acquire syntax. The little information available about normally developing children suggests that verbs are more difficult to learn than objects or attributes, as summarized earlier. That observation does not, however, explain verb learning. What is needed is information about how children identify hypothesized features of verb meanings, such as "cause a change of physical state" versus "internally caused acts," and how such distinctions could be cued by grammatical context. Comparative information from SLI children would provide valuable clues about the nature of their lexical and syntactic limitations. For example, SLI children were less likely than their age-matched peers to prefer a change-of-state interpretation for a novel verb (Kelly & Rice, in preparation). They also made more errors in their labeling of novel activity scenes. These two findings suggest a possible linkage between their semantic interpretation strategies and their lexical limitations.

A question arises as to how errors attributable to inaccurate reference (choosing the wrong meaning for a word) can be differentiated from syntactic overgeneralizations, a problem inherent in analyses of children's spontaneous speech errors. Comprehension studies, in which features of the event scene and linguistic cues are carefully controlled, as well as the procedures of the QUIL studies described earlier, offer experimental techniques appropriate to the question (cf. Gleitman, 1989).

Conclusion 4: Children's Early Verb Learning is Conservative and Localized

In the initial stages of word learning, new verbs are learned one at a time, as labels for events (cf. Pinker, 1989b). At first, emerging verbs are not treated as equivalent in the sense of an abstract grammatical class (cf. Bloom, Lifter, & Hafitz, 1980).

Implication 4.1.   The clinical implications of this conclusion are straight-forward. The initial teaching setting should involve an activity scene, with appropriate verb labels provided. For example, Slobin (1985) proposed that a scene of fundamental import for language learning is the manipulative activity scene, involving "a basic causal event in which an agent carries out a physical and perceptible change of state in a patient by means of direct body contact or with an instrument under the agent's control" (p. 1175). A second implication is that an initial stage of learning verb stems, the uninflected forms, is appropriate with later teaching efforts focusing on verb regularities.

Some cautions, however, are in order. As Gleitman (1989) noted, activity scenes themselves often are open to varying interpretations. It may be necessary, therefore, for the clinician to ensure that the child's interpretation is in line with the intended one. If the clinician labeled the scene as *give*, it is important to know if the child reads it as *take*. In turn, the initial verb labels must be relatively quickly incorporated into morphological subcategories relevant for syntactic rules. Therefore, it would be expedient to choose similar verbs when individual items are chosen for teaching. For example, verbs of continuing action, such as *walk*, which can be marked for the progressive tense, *-ing*, could be grouped together.

Conclusion 5: Verb Semantics Exert a Major Influence on the Learning of Verb Inflections

Slobin (1985) asserted that the first scenes to receive grammatical marking are those that are prototypical, such as the manipulative activity scene. This scene is the first one marked for transitivity in those languages that do so, such as Hungarian, Polish, and Turkish. Bloom et al. (1980) reported that the first use of verb inflections in English, such as the progressive *-ing* and the past tense *-ed*, is selective and not generalized across all possible verbs. Initially, individual verbs tended to be used with only one inflection. For example, *go* was likely to be inflected with *-ing* but not with *-ed; find* with *-ed* but not *-ing*.

Implication 5.1. One implication of this conclusion is that, contrary to the usual clinical practice, the training of verb inflections would not be maximally effective without taking into account the verb stems. Current practice is to select a verb that matches the activity scene, in line with Implication 4.1, and attach the targeted verb inflection to that stem. In other words, selection of the verb stem usually is secondary to the available materials and/or activities. In fact, the verb stems usually are not recorded, with documentation focusing on the percentage of correct uses of the verb inflections. What is needed is detailed information about the possible interaction of verb meanings with verb inflections in the case of SLI children. Are their problems with verb morphology evident only with some classes of verbs and not with others? A hint in this direction is revealed in the finding of Johnston and Kamhi (1984) that SLI children were more likely than their MLU matches to use verbs describing self-movement actions, such as *come, go, walk, run, fly,* and *sit.* Do they move beyond early patterns of restricted use of verb inflections to more general, productive uses of morphemes in a manner similar to normally developing children or do their morphological rules remain constrained to specific stems? (A question encountered in the following section, as well.) Is teaching more effective with some combinations of stems and inflections than with others? Is there evidence for general principles that could guide the matching of verbs and inflections at various levels of teaching?

Conclusion 6: Children Use Pro-verbs, such as *Do, Go,* and *Get,* as General All-purpose Verbs

Bloom et al. (1980) reported that unlike the more descriptive verbs, action pro-verbs occurred with more than one inflection. In effect, this set of verbs seemed to be productive with regard to verb morphology early on. Bloom et al. pointed out that there is also evidence that Wh-question forms are first learned with pro-verbs (Wootten, Merkin, Hood, & Bloom, 1979). The pro-verbs are interesting in that they need not specify a particular predicate in the manner evident in the earlier examples of verb/argument control. Instead, they can stand for a variety of more specific verbs. It seems that children may first learn at least some of the structures of language with these all-purpose general verbs.

Implication 6.1.   An obvious implication for training follows Implication 5.1 discussed earlier, regarding the selection of verbs to use for teaching verb inflections. Bloom et al.'s (1980) findings suggest that the first choice for verb stems should be the general all-purpose verbs.

Implication 6.2.   Evidence parallel to the normative findings is emerging from studies of SLI children. Bode and Rice (in preparation) and Watkins and Rice (in preparation) report that SLI children rely on a few general all-purpose verbs in their initial verb lexicon. Furthermore, these verbs are more likely to be inflected than less-frequently-used verbs, suggesting that SLI children proceed in a conservative manner, linking verb inflections to stems at the level of individual items instead of broad classes. Consistent with these findings are those of Fletcher and Peters (1984) who report that 5-year-old SLI children had a more restricted verb vocabulary than their normal chronological age peers as indicated by differences in frequency of verb types.

A general reliance on pro-verbs would be a reasonable strategy for these youngsters, as a way of developing a functional language system, while avoiding the complications of the verbs with more specific verb argument restrictions. It is also a strategy that probably could be managed on the basis of conservative learning from positive evidence (i.e., by using the verbs in linguistic contexts highly similar to ones they encounter in linguistic input). Any problems of semantic mapping could be finessed by the imprecise reference of the pro-verbs, supplemented by the cues evident in the situation. On the other hand, such a strategy would have obvious limitations if it did not lead to a productive system of specific verb argument structures and linguistic rules governing alternative ways of expressing similar meanings. Furthermore, inflectional acquisition could be hindered as well, to the extent that inflections are limited to individual verbs.

Concluding Remarks.   As the preceding conclusions attest, even in such an oversimplified exposition, there are interesting theoretical debates about the role of verbs in children's language acquisition and an emerging empirical data base in the normative literature. Investigation of how SLI children learn verb meanings and associated linguistic structures would have clear implications for the teaching situation. It may well be that problems with verb learning are central to the observed difficulties that SLI children have with grammatical morphemes, in the case of verb inflections, and in other, as yet unrecognized, problems with linguistic structures. Likewise, it would be helpful to know if the word-learning problems of SLI children are general, or if they have specific difficulty with verb learning.

SOCIAL ADJUSTMENTS AND ACADEMIC FAILURES

Although SLI children seem to be limited in their ability to infer linguistic categories, they are not handicapped in their sensitivity to social relationships. The findings from LAP reveal that they make some subtle but significant adjustments in their interactions with their peers, adjustments that in turn restrict their opportunities for the use of language in meaningful contexts that can contribute to further language learning.

This sensitivity to their limited language is not necessarily conscious, and is probably not so much metalinguistic as social, insofar as 5-year-old SLI children have limited ability to make grammaticality judgements (Fujiki, Brinton, & Dunton, 1987). Perhaps SLI children can monitor others' comprehension of their utterances, much as normal children can (Revelle, Wellman, & Karabenick, 1985), but lack the normal range of metalinguistic strategies or perhaps the persistence needed to resolve difficulties in listener comprehension (Brinton, Fujiki, & Sonnenberg, 1988).

It may well be that such social awareness has an impact on the motivational mechanisms that underlie language acquisition. Little is known of these mechanisms in normally developing children. It generally is presumed that successful language acquisition is inherently a positive influence, such that the more language children have, the more positive their social interactions, and the more reason they have to expand their linguistic repertoire. It may well work in an opposite spiral with SLI children. By the time they are sensitive to their limitations, typically already by the age of 3 years, they may conclude that they are less capable than their peers, with a subsequent diminishment of self-esteem and reduced tolerance for failure in communication interactions, which in turn would lead to fewer opportunities to practice emerging skills in interactions with their peers. The upshot would be that they would become more quiet, more passive in communicative interactions, and more restricted in their communicative repertoire. This prediction seems to be borne out in observations underway in kindergarten settings, in which the social interactions of SLI children are being recorded (Rice, Hadley, & Wilcox, in preparation).

This scenario would further suggest that at least some of SLI children's academic failures may be attributable to early negative experiences in social interactions. These failures contribute to a SLI child's reluctance to interact with others, and, as a consequence, classroom teachers may perceive the SLI child as socially immature and further restrict the child's social and academic experiences. This is not to diminish the probable cognitive consequences of limited language. The combined negatives of the social consequences and the academic risk would be a heavy load for a child to overcome without a lot of help.

The key to intervention seems to be to break the negative chain early on, when the children are preschoolers and are developing their social identities. In order to develop confidence in their communicative abilities, they must have opportunities to interact with their peers, their normally developing chronological age mates. In other words, they must be in a least restrictive environment, along the lines of the LAP model, or elaborate steps must be taken to ensure that teaching includes opportunities to observe other children in naturalistic interactions with peers.

Many questions are in need of further investigation, such as: What is the nature of the relation between communication abilities and social interactions—is it some sort of threshold effect, such that if a child attains a certain skill level, social interactions follow, or is it a graded relation? How do the children judge the communicative competence of others in social interactions? Are SLI children marginal members of peer social networks? Can SLI children develop compensatory strategies to enhance their social acceptability? Informal observations in LAP indicate that the ESL children seem to be able to do so, but the SLI children are less successful. Are some kinds of language skills more crucial to social interactions than others? Can socially relevant peer interaction skills be trained, and if so, what are the most effective methods?

To begin answering some of these questions, the specific ways in which language, social development, and academic achievement interact during a child's progression from preschool into kindergarten and elementary school warrant further study. The special circumstances of SLI children suggest that language development may play a more crucial role in early socialization than is recognized in current accounts of children's social development.

Efforts to mitigate the social and academic consequences cannot stop with the child, however. Instead, it may be necessary to buffer the child from the expectations of the adults in our society. For example, parents may be impatient with their child's limited communication skill and inadvertently contribute to a social withdrawal. Likewise, classroom teachers may expect too much too soon in the way of language skills. A comprehensive language intervention program would address these possibilities, as well as provide teaching for the child.

These clinical implications are being explored in the LAP classroom. The preliminary indication is that they can be readily incorporated into teaching plans and activities, and the staff judges that they benefit the children and families. Definitive evaluation of their efficacy awaits formal investigation.

CONCLUSIONS

In the interest of integrating the preceding discussion into a coherent model of language teaching for the SLI child, it is posited that:

1. Language problems are at the core of the SLI child's difficulties.
2. For many SLI children, problems learning the lexicon are evident.
3. Central to many of the language limitations is a particular problem with mastery of verbs, with their associated grammatical morphemes.
4. The basic problem of language acquisition is overlaid with social reactions that interfere with motivational mechanisms needed for language learning.
5. The combination of language-learning problems and negative social consequences create a high degree of academic risk for SLI children.

From this model, clear clinical guidelines follow:

1. Provide language intervention in the most naturalistic manner possible, in which it is feasible to observe a child's use of language in functionally meaningful contexts and to incorporate those contexts in the teaching.

2. Prioritize the teaching goals as follows: Social initiations, lexical development starting with pro-verbs, then specific verbs and verb argument structures, and then grammatical morphemes and other features of formal syntax. This prioritization does not imply that training must focus exclusively on these goals in a rigid sequence. Instead, it suggests that it is important to recognize the priority of the lexicon in establishing syntactic rules, and the need to prevent the development of counterproductive social strategies.

3. Include in an intervention program parent counseling/involvement and consultation with teachers. The intent here is to buffer the child from the social and academic consequences of limited communication skills as much as possible. At the same time, the parents and teachers can, with appropriate intervention, become agents for improvements in a child's language.

The central points of this chapter are that the problems of SLI children present interesting complexities with major social and academic consequences, and that appropriate intervention strategies must take these complexities into account. Even though our knowledge base is far from complete, it is possible to provide intervention that bridges the gaps. At the same time, the search for information and insights to develop theoretical models with clinical relevance will increase the probability that our remediation efforts will be successful.

ACKNOWLEDGEMENTS

Preparation of this chapter was supported by National Institutes of Health Award R01 NS26129 to the author.

Special appreciation is expressed to Susan Kemper, Larry Leonard, Diane Frome Loeb, Clifton Pye, R. L. Schiefelbusch, Michael Studdert-Kennedy, and two anonymous reviewers for comments on earlier drafts. In addition, appreciation is due to Kim Wilcox, who, as Co-Director of the Language Acquisition Preschool, has contributed substantively to the ideas expressed here.

REFERENCES

Alexander, A., Rice, M. L., & Hadley, P. A. (in preparation) *Teacher judgements of the intellectual and social status of SLI children.*

Baker, C. L. (1979). Syntactic theory and the projection problem. *Linguistic Inquiry, 10,* 533–581.

Beastrom, S., & Rice, M. (1986, November). *Comprehension and production of the articles "a" and "the".* Paper presented at the Convention of the American Speech-Language-Hearing Association, Detroit.

Birdsong, D. (1989). *Metalinguistic performance and interlinguistic competence.* Berlin: Springer-Verlag.

Bloom, L., Lifter, K., & Hafitz, J. (1980). Semantics of verbs and the development of verb inflection in child language. *Language, 56,* 286–412.

Bode, J. V. & Rice, M. L. (in preparation). *Verbs and verb inflections in the spontaneous language of SLI preschoolers.*

Bowerman, M. (1989). Learning a semantic system: What role do cognitive predispositions play? In M. L. Rice & R. L. Schiefelbusch (Eds.), *The teachability of language.* (pp. 133–169). Baltimore: Brookes.

Bresnan, J. (Ed.). (1982). *The mental representation of grammatical relations.* Cambridge, MA: MIT Press.

Brinton, B., Fujiki, M., & Sonnenberg, E. A. (1988). Responses to requests for clarification by linguistically normal and language impaired children in conversation. *Journal of Speech and Hearing Disorders, 53,* 383–391.

Brown, R. (1957). Linguistic determinism and parts of speech. *Journal of Abnormal and Social Psychology, 55,* 1–5.

Brown, R. (1973). *A first language: The early stages.* Cambridge, MA: Harvard University Press.

Carey, S. (1978). The child as word learner. In M. Halle, J. Bresnan, & G. Miller (Eds.), *Linguistic theory and psychological reality* (pp. 264–293). Cambridge, MA: MIT Press.

Fey, M. E. (1986). *Language intervention with young children.* San Diego: College Hill.

Fey, M. E. (1988). Generalization issues facing language interventionists: An introduction. *Language, Speech, and Hearing Services in Schools, 19,* 272–281.

Fletcher, P., & Peters, J. (1984). Characterizing language impairment in children: An exploratory study. *Language Testing, 1,* 33–49.

Freedman, P., & Carpenter, R. (1976). Semantic relations used by normal and language-impaired children at Stage 1. *Journal of Speech and Hearing Research, 19,* 784–795.

Fujiki, M., Brinton, B., & Dunton, S. (1987). A grammatical judgment screening test for young elementary school-aged children. *Language, Speech, and Hearing Services in Schools, 18,* 131–143.

Gardner, H. (1983). *Frames of mind: The theory of multiple intelligences.* New York: Basic.

Gentner, D. (1982). Why nouns are learned before verbs: Linguistic relativity versus natural partitioning. In S. Kuczaj (Ed.), *Language development: Vol. 2. Language, thought, and culture* (pp. 301–334). Hillsdale, NJ: Lawrence Erlbaum Associates.

Gleitman, L. (1989). *The structural sources of verb meaning* [Keynote address]. Papers and Reports on Child Language Development. Stanford University, Stanford, CA.

Gopnik, M., & Crago, M. B. (in press). Familial aggregation of a developmental language disorder. *Cognition.*

Hadley, P. A., & Rice, M. L. (in press). *Journal of Speech and Hearing Disorders.*

Hohmann, M., Bonet, B., & Weikart, D. P. (1978). *Young children in action.* Ypsilanti, MI: High Scope Press.

Johnston, J. R. (1982). Interpreting the Leiter IQ: Performance profiles of young normal and language-disordered children. *Journal of Speech and Hearing Research, 25,* 291–296.

Johnston, J. R. (1985). Fit, focus, and functionality: An essay on early language intervention. *Child Language Teaching and Therapy, 1*(2), 125–134.

Johnston, J. R. (1988). Specific language disorders in the child. In N. Lass, L. McReynolds, J. Northern, & D. Yoder (Eds.), *Handbook of speech-language pathology and audiology* (pp. 685–715). Toronto: Decker.

Johnston, J. R., & Kamhi, A. (1984). *The same can be less: Syntactic and semantic aspects of the utterances of language-impaired children. Merrill-Palmer Quarterly, 30,* 65–86.

Kail, R., & Leonard, L. B. (1986). Word-finding abilities in language-impaired children. *Monographs of the American Speech-Language-Hearing Association* (No. 25).

Katz, N., Baker, E., & MacNamara, J. (1974). What's in a name? A study of how children learn common and proper names. *Child Development, 45,* 469–473.

Kelly, D. J., & Rice, M. L. (1986). A strategy for language assessment of young children: A combination of two approaches. *Language, Speech, and Hearing Services in Schools, 17,* 83–94.

Kelly, D. J., & Rice, M. L. (in preparation). *SLI preschoolers' description of change-of-state versus motion scenes.*

Lahey, M. (1988). *Language disorders and language development.* New York: Macmillan.

Leonard, L. B. (1981). Facilitating linguistic skills in children with specific language impairment. *Applied Psycholinguistics, 2,* 89–118.

Leonard, L. (1987). Is specific language impairment a useful construct? In S. Rosenberg (Ed.), *Advances in applied psycholinguistics: Vol. 1. Disorders of first-language development* (pp. 1–39). New York: Cambridge University Press.

Leonard, L. B. (1988). Lexical development and processing in specific language impairment. In L. L. Lloyd & R. L. Schiefelbusch (Eds.), *Language perspectives: Acquisition, retardation and intervention* (2nd ed.). Austin, TX: Pro-Ed.

Leonard, L. B. (1989a). Language learnability and specific language impairment in children. *Applied Psycholinguistics, 10,* 179–202.

Leonard, L. B. (1989b, November). *Specific language impairment as a clinical category.* Paper presented at the Convention of the American Speech-Language-Hearing Association, St. Louis.

Leonard, L., Bolders, J., & Miller, J. (1976). An examination of the semantic relations reflected in the language usage of normal and language disordered children. *Journal of Speech and Hearing Research, 19,* 371–392.

Leonard, L., Camarata, S., Rowan, L., & Chapman, K. (1982). The communicative functions of lexical usage by language impaired children. *Applied Psycholinguistics, 3,* 109–125.

Leonard, L., Sabbadini, L., Leonard, L., & Volterra, V. (1987). Specific language impairment in children: A cross-linguistic study. *Brain and Language, 32,* 233–252.

Leonard, L., Sabbadini, L., Volterra, V., & Leonard, J. (1988). Some influences on the grammar of English- and Italian-speaking children with specific language impairment. *Applied Psycholinguistics, 9,* 39–57.

Leske, M. C. (1981). Speech prevalence estimates of communicative disorders in the U.S. *American Speech and Hearing Association, 23,* 229–237.

Ludlow, C. L., & Cooper, J. A. (Eds.). (1983). *Genetic aspects of speech and language disorders.* New York: Academic.

Maratsos, M. P., & Chalkley, M. A. (1981). The internal language of children's syntax: The ontogenesis and representation of syntactic categories. In K. E. Nelson (Ed.), *Children's language* (Vol. 2, pp. 127–214). New York: Gardner Press.

Morehead, D., & Ingram, D. (1973). The development of base syntax in normal & linguistically deviant children. *Journal of Speech and Hearing Research, 16,* 330–352.

Nelson, K. (1989). Strategies for first language teaching. In M. L. Rice & R. L. Schiefelbusch (Eds.), *The teachability of language* (pp. 263–310). Baltimore: Brookes.

Parlour, S. F. (1990). *Familial risk for articulation disorder: A 28-year follow-up.* Unpublished doctoral thesis, University of Minnesota.

Pinker, S. (1984). *Language learnability and language development.* Cambridge, MA: Harvard University Press.

Pinker, S. (1989a). *Learnability and cognition: The acquisition of argument structure.* Cambridge, MA: MIT Press.

Pinker, S. (1989b). Resolving a learnability paradox in the acquisition of the verb lexicon. In M. L. Rice & R. L. Schiefelbusch (Eds.), *The teachability of language* (pp. 13–62). Baltimore: Brookes.

Rescorla, L. (1989). The language development survey: A screening tool for delayed language in toddlers. *Journal of Speech and Hearing Disorders, 54,* 587–599.

Revelle, G. L., Wellman, H. M., & Karabenick, J. D. (1985). Comprehension monitoring in preschool children. *Child Development, 56,* 654–663.

Rice, M. (1980). *Cognition to language: Categories, word meanings and training.* Baltimore: University Park Press.

Rice, M. L. (1990). Preschoolers' QUIIL: Quick incidental learning of words. In G. Conti-Ramsden & C. Snow (Eds.), *Children's language* (Vol. 7, pp. 171–196). Hillsdale, NJ: Lawrence Erlbaum Associates.

Rice, M. L., Buhr, J., & Nemeth, M. (1990). Fast mapping word learning abilities of language delayed preschoolers. *Journal of Speech and Hearing Disorders, 55,* 33–42.

Rice, M. L., Buhr, J., & Oetting, J. (in preparation). *Measurement of word comprehension: Pictures versus video.*

Rice, M., Buhr, J., & Oetting, J. (in press). Specific language impaired children's quick incidental learning of words: The effect of a . . . pause. *Journal of Speech and Hearing Research.*

Rice, M. L., Hadley, P. A., & Wilcox, K. (in preparation). *Transition of SLI children into kindergarten.*

Rice, M. L., & Schiefelbusch, R. L. (1989). (Eds.) *The teachability of language.* Baltimore: Brookes.

Rice, M. L., Sell, M.A., & Hadley, P. A. (1990). The social interactive coding system (SICS): An on-line, clinically relevant descriptive tool. *Language, Speech and Hearing Services in Schools, 21,* 2–14.

Rice, M. L., Sell, M. A., & Hadley, P. A. (in press). *Social interactions of speech and language-impaired children. Journal of Speech & Hearing Research.*

Rice, M. L., & Wilcox, K. (1990a). *Language acquisition preschool: A model preschool for language disordered children and ESL children* (Grant No. G008630279). Washington, DC: Final Report to U.S. Department of Education, Office of Special Education Programs.

Rice, M. L., & Wilcox, K. (1990b). *Classroom-based language acquisition preschool: Language intervention.* Unpublished manuscript. Department of Speech-Language-Hearing, University of Kansas, Lawrence.

Rice, M. L., & Woodsmall, L. (1988). Lessons from television: Children's word learning when viewing. *Child Development, 59,* 420–429.

Shriberg, L., Kwiatkowski, J., Best, S., Hengst, J., & Terselic-Weber, B. (1986). Characteristics of children with phonological disorders of unknown origin. *Journal of Speech and Hearing Disorders, 51,* 140–161.

Silva, P. A. (1980). The prevalence stability, and significance of developmental language delay in preschool children. *Developmental Medicine and Child Neurology, 22,* 768–777.

Slobin, D. I. (1985). Cross-linguistic evidence for the language-making capacity. In D. I. Slobin (Ed.), *The cross-linguistic study of language acquisition: Vol. 2. Theoretical issues* (pp. 1157–1256). Hillsdale, NJ: Lawrence Erlbaum Associates.

Snyder, L. (1984). Developmental language disorders: Elementary school age. In A. Holland (Ed.), *Language disorders in children* (pp. 129–158). San Diego: College Hill.

Stevenson, J., & Richman, N. (1976). The prevalence of language delay in a population of three-year-old children and its association with general retardation. *Developmental Medi-*

cine and Child Neurology, 18, 431–441.

Tabors, P. O. (1987). *The development of communicative competence by second language learners in a nursery school classroom: An ethnolinguistic study.* Unpublished doctoral dissertation, School of Education, Harvard University.

Tallal, P., Ross, R., & Curtiss, S. (1989). Familial aggregation in specific language impairment. *Journal of Speech and Hearing Disorders, 54,* 167–173.

Tomblin, J. B. (1989). Familial concentration of developmental language impairment. *Journal of Speech and Hearing Disorders, 54,* 287–295.

United States Department of Education (1988). Annual Report to Congress on the implementation of the Education of the Handicapped Act. Office of Special Education and Rehabilitative Services, Washington, D. C.

United States Department of Education (1989). Annual report to Congress on the implementation of the Education of the Handicapped Act. Office of Special Education & Rehabilitative Services, Washington, DC.

Watkins, R. U., & Rice, M. L. (in press). *Verb particle and preposition acquisition in language-impaired preschoolers.* Journal of Speech and Hearing Research.

Watkins, R. U., & Rice, M. L. *Verbs of SLI Children.*

Weiner, P. (1974). A language-delayed child at adolescence. *Journal of Speech and Hearing Disorders, 39,* 202–212.

Weiner, P. (1985). The value of follow-up studies. *Topics in Language Disorders, 5,* 78–92.

Wootten, J., Merkin, S., Hood, L., & Bloom, L. (1979, April). *Wh-questions: Linguistic evidence to explain the sequence of acquisition.* Paper presented to the Biennial Meeting of the Society for Research in Child Development, San Francisco.

20

Communicative Intent and Its Realizations Among Persons with Severe Intellectual Deficits

James E. McLean and Lee Snyder-McLean
Bureau of Child Research
University of Kansas Parsons Research Center

From the early 1960s to the middle 1970s, clinical interventions in the communication repertoires of persons with severe intellectual deficiencies were directed by a model that merged behaviorism and descriptive linguistics. This model maintained a historical clinical bias toward speech as the primary mode in which communication was to be sought (McLean, 1983), and it generated systematic modeling and reinforcement procedures to attain phonological, morphological, and syntactic forms in the speech mode (Gray & Ryan, 1973; Guess, Sailor, & Baer, 1974; Kent, 1974; McLean, Yoder, & Schiefelbusch, 1972; Ruder & Smith, 1974; Sloane & MacAulay, 1968; Waryas & Stremel, 1973).

The behavioral-linguistic focus on speech and linguistic forms for intervention in cases of severely deficient language was formalized in a "remedial model" (Guess, Sailor, & Baer, 1977). The rationale argued that the desired "end behavior" of language (i.e., linguistic forms at all levels) should be directly trained even when clients were nonverbal. The justification was that, at that time, there were no adequate empirical bases from which to identify behavioral prerequisites for spoken linguistic forms. Even the remedial programs that targeted nonspeech communicative forms in those earlier times developed their target matrices from standard linguistic forms and rule systems. For example, Carrier (1974) developed a systematic treatment program for nonverbal children with mental retardation using, as the response mode, tangible symbols of the type used by Premack (1970) in his work with chimpanzees. Though it targeted nonspeech response forms, Carrier's program was directed toward the acquisition of a repertoire of tangible symbol-morpheme strings (including function words and some

481

inflectional morphemes) whose order was controlled by the rules of standard English syntax.

RECENT REVISIONS OF THE INTERVENTION MODEL

As waves of revisionism swept over child language theory during the 1970s, the clinical intervention model began to change. The cognitivizing of semantics and syntax (Bloom, 1970; Bowerman, 1973, 1974; Slobin, 1973) was translated into clinical programs that sought to target semantic and syntactic forms to match children's knowledge base (MacDonald & Horstmeier, 1978; Miller & Yoder, 1972, 1974; Muma, 1978). The socialization of language accomplished by the revitalization of pragmatic perspectives (Bates, 1976; Bates, Camaioni, & Volterra, 1975; Bruner, 1975; Dore, 1975; Moerk, 1977; Searle, 1969) also began to influence clinical efforts with children and youth with severe language deficiencies. Specifically, targeted language forms were chosen according to social functions as opposed to linguistic structure (Fay & Schuler, 1980; MacDonald, 1982; McClowry, Guilford, & Richardson, 1982; McLean, Snyder-McLean, & Sack, 1985; Prizant & Duchan, 1981; Seibert & Hogan, 1982). In addition, treatment programs and procedures were relocated from isolated, one-on-one training environments into milieus that more closely approximated natural communication environments (Halle, 1982, 1984; Halle, Marshall, & Spradlin, 1979; Hart & Rogers-Warren, 1978; Peck & Schuler, 1983; Snyder-McLean, Solomonson, McLean, & Sack, 1984; Warren & Rogers-Warren, 1985).

The studies of language acquisition among nonhandicapped children that explicitly described the prelinguistic stage processes of both sensorimotor and sociocommunicative behavior (Bates, 1976; Bates, Benigni, Bretherton, Camaioni, & Volterra, 1979; Bates et al., 1975; Moerk, 1977) resulted in the most recent revisions in clinical intervention models. Specifically, the developmental research on nonhandicapped children detailed the prelinguistic period of development and provided a revised perspective for assessment and treatment programs for persons with severe language deficiencies. These data describe a three-stage macroprocess that begins with what Bates et al. (1975) called "perlocutionary" acts. In perlocutionary acts, an infant's motor acts are focused on an object and reflect no awareness of an adult receiver; however, these motor acts are assigned communicative significance by the adult. The developmental process then was observed by Bates et al. to include "illocutionary" motor acts that featured a "dual focus" because the infant's eye gaze shifted between an object and adult and, therefore, reflected an infant's intentions to have effects on an adult receiver. The third stage identified in developmental data featured the emergence of linguistic forms in the oral mode and was termed the "locutionary" stage by Bates et al. Such data were useful as a heuristic for designing assessment and treatment taxonomies and matrices for children and youth with severe handicaps who are beyond developmental ages and who remain nonverbal (McLean & Snyder-McLean, 1988; McLean, Snyder-McLean, & Cirrin, 1981; McLean, Snyder-McLean, & Sack, 1982; Musselwhite & St. Louis, 1982; Prizant & Duchan, 1981; Seibert & Hogan, 1982; Wetherby & Prutting, 1984).

Thus, in the most recent revisions of the clinical model, the philosophical base has shifted from purely linguistic phenomena to the psycho-communicative process. A psycho-communicative model does not ignore linguistic behavior. It does, however, define the function of communicative form in terms of its social effects on other people rather than by the semantic and syntactic relationships it might reflect. Thus, a phrase might be described as a request for an object or for attention as opposed to being first considered as an action label + object label, or a verb + noun. Such revisions allow treatment specialists to consider the communicative value of nonlinguistic acts such as gestures and combinations of gestures and intonated vocalizations. In these most recent revisions of the clinical model, taxonomies and matrices from developmental data plot out logical and socially valid sets of communication goals that might be sought for individuals with severe language deficits who remain nonverbal.

APPLICATIONS OF THE REVISED MODEL AT THE PARSONS RESEARCH CENTER

This chapter describes a decade-long series of demonstration, training, and research projects to develop a more process-oriented approach to enhancing the sociocommunicative repertoires of persons with severe mental retardation who are nonverbal in their normal communicative environments. A total of 41 subjects who presented severe developmental disabilities have been studied. All studies were directed at testing the applicability of assessment and treatment models that reflect the philosophical revisions and the developmental data emanating from the mainstream of child language research. This article presents findings both from clinical demonstration efforts and from the data obtained in three descriptive research studies. More detailed accounts of these individual studies are found elsewhere (Cirrin & Rowland, 1985; McLean & Snyder-McLean, 1987, 1988; McLean, McLean, Brady, & Etter, 1991; McLean et al., 1981; McLean et al., 1982, 1985).

INITIAL APPLICATIONS OF THE REVISED
CLINICAL MODEL

The first applications of this revised clinical model were in a demonstration project and a personnel preparation project, both funded by the U.S. Department of Education. The focus of both projects was to apply the taxonomies emanating from mainstream child language as heuristic guides to the treatment and assessment of children and youth with severe developmental disabilities. For purposes of these projects, the authors assumed responsibility for two secondary level, special education classrooms, each with an enrollment of eight students with severe mental retardation. These classrooms were located in a "special purpose school" that served the residents of a 300-bed state residential institution for persons with mental retardation.

Students who participated in this study were all severely or profoundly mentally retarded, using the AAMD classification system (Grossman, 1973), and ranged in age from 12 to 16 years at the start of these projects. All students were ambulatory, with functional hearing and vision; but all were functionally nonverbal. That is, none was ever observed or reported to use any oral or nonoral symbolic language form in any naturally occurring communication context. Further, students enrolled in these two classrooms were specifically identified by the speech and hearing department of the institution as making minimal or no progress in past and current language-training programs.

Experimental Clinical Procedures

Rationale.   Initial observations of the students in these two classrooms (in interactions with adults in their environment) revealed considerable differences in their respective communicative repertoires. Some students were relatively proactive and interacted with both objects and people. Others, however, were passive, sought isolation, and emitted high levels of self-stimulatory acts. All 16 adolescents also showed relatively low rates of communication.

Treatment efforts on these experimental clinical projects reflected two major goals. The first was to increase the rates of spontaneous communication produced by these students through the creation of highly responsive, social communication environments. The second was to describe and document the specific differences observed in the communicative performances of various members of this group. Specifically, it was hypothesized that these differences might be described, and ordered along the stage-process continuum that characterizes prelinguistic communication development among nonhandicapped infants and toddlers.

Assessment Procedures.   Toward this end, initial assessment identified students who were producing illocutionary communication acts and those who communicated at only a perlocutionary level (Bates et al., 1975). The assessment procedure was very similar to a language sample, except that nonverbal communicative behaviors rather than language were sampled. The assessment consisted of an unscripted interaction between the client and a familiar adult. To increase the probability that some communicative behavior would be observed, the interaction context was baited with various novel objects that produced interesting visual and auditory events (e.g., a battery-operated facial brush, an adult toy consisting of a wave-producing supply of oil and colored water encased in a rectangular plastic block) and a variety of highly preferred but inaccessible food and drink items (e.g., cookies in a jar with a very tightly screwed-on lid, an empty glass when the adult had a pitcher of Kool Aid). These interactive sessions were videotaped and later judged by the project staff for the presence of any illocutionary (intentional) communicative acts. In judging communicative intentionality, the behavioral criteria identified by Bates et al. and Sugarman-Bell (1978) were applied: (a) the coordination of person–object visual regard, (b) directionality of signal behavior toward the adult as receiver, and (c) persistence or cessation of signaling behavior contingent on receiver response. These assessment sessions were not specifically controlled for time but were terminated when clients had been given an opportunity to interact with each object or food item offered. Typically, sessions ran for 15 to 20 min.

FINDINGS FROM CLINICAL PROJECTS

Two major findings emerged. First, members of this group of severely to profoundly handicapped subjects could be dichotomized by the perlocutionary-illocutionary distinction borrowed from speech-act theory (Austin, 1962; Searle, 1969) by Bates and her colleagues to describe two stages of prelinguistic development among nonhandicapped infants and toddlers. That is, by applying the behavioral criteria offered by Bates et al. (1975) and Sugarman-Bell (1978), we identified a few members of the subject group who apparently did not intend to have effects on other people and thus could be considered to be operating at a perlocutionary level. Other members of the group appeared to have clear and robust intentions to have effects on other people and thus could be considered to be operating at an illocutionary level.

Second, in treatment that featured interactive social contexts and responsive adult receivers, even the most passive subjects who displayed only perlocutionary behavior at the outset of the demonstration project acquired a limited repertoire of illocutionary communicative signals, and produced these signals spontaneously in specific (usually food-related) communication contexts.

Because additional behavior differences were observed within these two levels of communicative performance among these subjects, it is possible to make further distinctions. Specifically, it is possible to distinguish two levels of perlocutionary communication and three levels of illocutionary communication.

At the perlocutionary stage, for example, there appeared to be a qualitative difference between subjects whose signals were simply reflexive reactions to internal or external stimuli, and those whose signals were proactive, purposeful attempts to have some effect on the environment. Though both groups failed to meet behavioral criteria for presence of communicative intentions, the proactive group's purposeful motor acts on objects and people provided responsive adults with behavior to which they could better assign communicative significance. For example, even though a "reaching" act might be singly focused on an object and not reflect any awareness of, or attention to, a responsive receiver, adults could quickly interpret such an act as a "request" for the object. Among members of the reactive group, however, it was more difficult to assign meaning to reflexive motor acts. For example, reflexive startles or cries in response to a moving toy object were ambiguous in that they could signal notice, fright, desire for the toy, or a rejection of the item. With these potentially important differences in their relative communicative potential recognized, perlocutionary subjects were classified as either reactive perlocutionary or proactive perlocutionary.

Among students who emitted communicative behavior that could be judged to be intentional attempts to have effects on others (illocutionary acts), three different subsets of subject groups could be identified. Each subset was based on the specific behavioral forms used by its members. One subset used what the authors labeled *primitive illocutionary acts*. These were proactive motor acts on a person or object accompanied by a coordinated person–object scheme. That is, subjects would alternate their visual attention between the object and the adult and would direct their signal behavior toward the adult. For example, a subject might reach out toward an unattainable object and then look at the adult, or might place an adult's hand on an object and look at him or her. The authors observed groups of subjects who used no communicative forms other than these primitive illocutionary acts.

A second group of illocutionary subjects appeared to be qualitatively different from those described previously. These subjects also used some primitive motor schemes as illocutionary acts, but they also used motor acts that were members of the "gestural complex" (give, show, request, and point) identified by Bates et al. (1975). This group was labeled *conventional illocutionary* because such communicative forms seemed to represent a qualitative shift to socially specialized communicative signals that reflected some external influence and modeling. Members of this conventionalized group also tended to issue some vocalizations along with their gestures. It is important to note that these vocalizations did not achieve the status of conventional words.

A third subset of subjects from the demonstration group was observed to respond to needs to communicate by using not only primitive acts and conventional gestures, but also manual signs or single, spoken words. Members of this subset were labeled *referential locutionary* because they had begun to move into quasi-linguistic forms of communicative signals. It is important to note that such symbolic forms were not observed in natural contexts, but were emitted by some subjects during the specifically interactive episodes featured in the assessment protocols being used.

In summary, the authors' clinical experience indicated that the mere determination of the presence of communicative intentions, although important, did not account for the heterogeneity observed among a sample of nonverbal subjects with severe mental retardation. First, perlocutionary subjects were observed to be of two types, reactive and proactive. Second, subjects demonstrating illocutionary behavior varied in their intentional communicative acts and could be differentiated as primitive, conventional, or referential in their form levels. At this point, then, there was an obvious need to more definitively analyze the intentional communicative acts of persons with severe mental retardation. To this end, a line of descriptive research was initiated.

PRELIMINARY RESEARCH WITH STUDENTS WITH SEVERE INTELLECTUAL DEFICITS

These studies are part of a larger, ongoing research program on the relationships between sociocommunicative performances of these subjects and their performances on a battery of sensorimotor and symbolization tasks.

Subjects and Settings

The studies were conducted in a university research facility situated on the grounds of a 300-bed residential institution for persons with mental retardation located in the midwest United States. The communicative assessment protocols (described later) were administered in a small laboratory-testing room furnished with a table and two chairs and closed cabinets containing various manipulable materials and food items. The interactions between an adult experimenter and the subject were videotaped from an adjacent observation room through one-way mirrors.

STUDY 1

Subjects

Study 1 involved 15 subjects who had been previously involved in the authors' clinical demonstration and training projects. These 15 subjects (11 boys and 4 girls) ranged in age from 10 to 18 years. All were classified as severely or profoundly mentally retarded (313 or 314, using the AAMD severity classification system [Grossman, 1973]). In addition, at the time of this study, all were producing some illocutionary (having communicative intentions) acts.

Procedures

To provide a more standardized procedure than the interactive sampling in the clinical projects, scripted interaction protocols were developed to evoke a range of communicative acts under relatively naturalistic conditions. These protocols consisted of a series of standardized interactive episodes presented to the subject as she or he interacted with the experimenter. The objects used in these episodes were known to be highly motivating for the subjects and included visual and auditory stimulus events as well as food-related items. Each episode presented the subject with a particular communication "problem" or demand situation. Sessions typically required about 20 min to complete; and each subject was assessed twice within a 2-week period.

A total of 13 different episodes or communicative tasks were included in the protocol. These were comprised of nine tasks designed to evoke requests for items or actions from the experimenter. These included requests for certain items, requests for help in a task, and requests that an activity cease. For example, an experimenter might eat from a container of Cheetos but "forget" to offer any to the subject; an experimenter might activate an electronic toy or game for a few seconds and then turn it off; or the experimenter might offer a subject a choice of small toy objects and then give him or her an item other than the one selected. One task was designed specifically to invite communicative acts that directed a receiver's attention to some item or event. In such episodes, for example, a staff confederate might knock on the outside of the observation window and the experimenter seem not to notice. Three other interactive episodes were designed.

Two were designed to evoke greetings and good-byes and one to evoke a request for the attention of the experimenter for communication. In this latter episode, for example, the experimenter would pretend not to notice a subject's request for an item. A tap on the experimenter's arm and the reissuance of the request gesture was a typical response for the "evocative" function. These 13 tasks were presented in varying sequences during the course of the interaction and the same set was presented during a second assessment session.

Videotapes of the sessions were transcribed for: (a) the occurrence of intentional communicative acts (ICAs), (b) the topographic form of each ICA, and (c) the apparent intent of each ICA. (Details regarding the specific coding system and associated interobserver reliability obtained in this study are presented in Cirrin & Rowland, 1985; McLean et al., 1981.) Based on their performance in these two sessions, subjects were classified into one of three subject groups, reflecting the highest level of communicative act produced by each subject. These groups were those identified in the previous clinical projects, that is, primitive illocutionary, conventional illocutionary, and referential/locutionary.

Results

Of the 15 subjects who completed this study, 7 were at the primitive illocutionary level (P subjects), 6 demonstrated conventional illocutionary level responses (C subjects), and 2 demonstrated referential/locutionary level responses (R subjects). Respectively, then, the P subjects were limited to direct motor acts on objects or people; C subjects used both direct motor acts and conventional gestures; and R subjects, in addition to using direct motor acts and gestures, sometimes used single manual signs or, in rare cases, single words. Both the overall rate of ICAs and the types of intended speaker functions of the observed ICAs varied between the P group and the C and R groups.

Fig. 20.1 shows the details of the apparent communicative intent mapped by severely mentally retarded subjects in Study 1. Characteristics were similar in all three studies. Subjects at the primitive signal level used their ICAs primarily to request preferred objects, to request the actions of adults in obtaining these objects, or to protest some ongoing action of the adult. By contrast, subjects who used higher level, conventional gestures or referential words or signs, in addition to requesting objects and adult actions, also used ICAs to point out (to the adult) various objects present in the testing room, as well as the scripted "window-tapping" event. In the broadest sense, these subjects were indicating objects or events for the joint attention of themselves and the adult interactor. Responses of this type made the conventional and referential subjects quite different from their

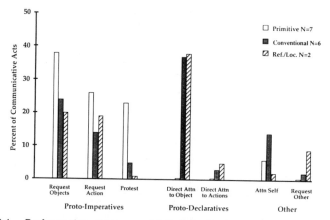

FIG. 20.1. Performative classes exhibited in Study 1 (Cirrin & Rowland, 1985; McLean et al., 1981).

primitive-level peers, who indicated only referent objects and actions directly related to their immediate desires to consume food or to manipulate interesting objects.

Bates and her colleagues (Bates et al., 1975) marked these contrasting functions of prelinguistic behavior among young, nonhandicapped children as *proto-imperatives* and *proto-declaratives*. The proto-imperatives were those ICAs that requested specific objects or facilitative actions from the receiver. The proto-declaratives were those ICAs that directed a receiver's attention to an interesting or unexpected object or event.

Application of this proto-imperative/proto-declarative dichotomy to the subjects of this study revealed that the subjects who used only primitive-level communicative signals issued only proto-imperative ICAs in that all of their acts were judged to be intended to attain immediately desired consequence. Such judgments were made by considering the context of the act, the repetition of the response if its apparent intent had not been met by the receiver, or the cessation of the act contingent on a receiver response of a certain type. In contrast to the primitive-level group's issuance of only proto-imperatives, however, subjects in the groups that used either conventional or referential level signal forms, in addition to making requests, also directed the receiver's attention to the self and to other objects or events. In Table 20.1, the ICAs from Study 1 have been collapsed into appropriate proto-imperative and proto-declarative classes and the table offers a comparison of performative classes across subject types. This comparison shows a covariance in the occurrence of proto-declarative type ICAs with the level of the signal form used. The primitive-level subjects issued no ICAs that reflect a proto-declarative intent. On the other hand, subjects using higher signal levels all issued ICAs judged to direct a receiver's

TABLE 20.1
Percentages of Imperative and Declarative Type Communication Functions for
Three Subject Groups in Study 1

| | Subject Group | | | | | | | | |
| | Primitive Illocutionary | | | Conventional Illocutionary | | | Referential/ Locutionary | | |
	Imp.	Dec.	Other	Imp.	Dec.	Other	Imp.	Dec.	Other
Study 1	87%	0	13%	43%	38%	19%	40%	43%	17%

Note. Percentages are based on the total number of ICAs produced across two sampling sessions. Adapted from "Form and Function of Communicative Behaviour Among Persons with Severe Developmental Disabilities" by J. McLean and L. Snyder-McLean, 1987, *Australia and New Zealand Journal of Developmental Disabilities, 13*(2), pp. 83–98.

attention to objects or events in the interactive environment. Such a skewed distribution between proto-imperatives and proto-declaratives is not typical among nonhandicapped children. Even at their most unskilled levels of communication, nonhandicapped children show both proto-imperative and proto-declarative functions (Bates et al., 1975).

STUDY 2

Subjects

Because most of the Study 1 subjects had participated in the 3-year clinical demonstration project discussed earlier, it was important to know whether this pattern would obtain with comparable subjects with whom the authors had no clinical history. Therefore, Study 2 replicated and extended Study 1 with a new sample drawn from the same subject population. Accordingly, 18 new subjects were selected for Study 2. These subjects were drawn from the same residential facility in which Study 1 subjects lived. Like Study 1 subjects, these subjects all were diagnosed as severely or profoundly mentally retarded and all demonstrated at least some illocutionary level communication. These subjects ranged in age from 8 to 21 years and included 11 males and 7 females.

Procedures

One possible explanation for the failure of P subjects to produce any proto-declarative ICAs in Study 1 was that the protocol included only one task designed to evoke this type of communication. Further, in the loose structure of this procedure, the experimenter might simply have provided more unscripted opportunities for proto-declaratives in interacting with the higher level (and generally more sociable) C and R subjects. Finally, many of the tasks presented in the first protocol violated some of the rules of human social interaction and, thus, might have been judged by subjects to reduce the probability of responsiveness on the part of the receiver. That is, one would not really eat Cheetos in front of a person if it was permissible for that person to have some of the Cheetos; nor would an experimenter really be unaware of the sound of another person tapping on the one-way window. Thus, the way in which several tasks were presented might have inhibited the communicative behavior of some subjects.

The procedures used in Study 2 were designed to address these concerns. First, to create a more socially appropriate need for communication, several tasks were modified so the experimenter, because of preoccupation or forgetfulness, might reasonably be unaware of the subject's "problem" in an interaction or of the novel entity or event presented in the proto-declarative tasks. Further, a second version of the protocol was created, using slightly different tasks and materials, so the tasks presented in the second testing session would represent novel communication problems for the subjects. Finally, to assure that the subject recognized the "problem" in each task, and had some history of successful experience with each situation, a brief period of turn taking was built into each task before the test trial was presented. For example, before slipping an unexpected shoe into a can of Cheetos, several successful exchanges of the Cheeto can containing only Cheetos were carried out. Similarly, before "forgetting" to give the subject a magnetic key needed to operate a mechanical toy, a brief turn-taking activity was instituted in which the experimenter returned both the toy and the needed key to the subject.

Beyond these modifications to increase the social realism of the tasks, the number of tasks designed to evoke proto-imperatives was reduced to six; and the number of tasks designed to evoke proto-declaratives was increased to three. In addition, each protocol was scripted more tightly so the order of presentation and number of times each item could be presented were not left to the discretion of the experimenter. These sessions were videotaped and coded in the same manner as the Study 1 sessions. Table 20.2 shows the composition of the protocols used in Studies 1, 2, and 3, in terms of the number of tasks designed to evoke each type of communicative function.

Results

The results of Study 2 were consistent with those of Study 1 in that the same three subsets of subjects (i.e., primitive, conventional, and referential) were observed in the sample group. The same general covariance in the rates and functions of the ICAs produced by these subjects was observed, except that

TABLE 20.2
Task Composition of Communication Assessment Protocols Used
in Studies 1, 2, and 3

Type of Task[a]	Number of Tasks Included in Protocol		
	Study 1	Study 2	Study 3
Imperative/Request Object or Action	9	6	6
(Food-Related)	(4)	(2)	(2)
Non-Food-Related)	(3)	(2)	(3)
Other: Protest; Choice)	(2)	(2)	(1)
Declarative/Request Attention to Referent	1	3	4[b]
Other	3	2	3
(Greeting)	(2)	(2)	(2)
(Evocative/Request Attention to Self)	(1)	(0)	(1)
	—	—	—
Totals	13	11	13

Note. Adapted from "Form and Function of Communicative Behaviour Among Persons with Severe Developmental Disabilities" by J. McLean and L. Snyder-McLean, 1987, *Australia and New Zealand Journal of Developmental Disabilities*, 13(2), pp. 83–98.
[a]Tasks are defined in terms of the type of communicative function they were designed to evoke. Complete copies of each protocol are available from the authors on request. [b]Two tasks involve proximal referents; two tasks involve distal referents.

one P subject in Study 2 issued an ICA judged to have a declarative function, whereas no P subject in Study 1 did. To present the overall trends in these two studies, the results from each are summarized in the following tables. For both studies, Table 20.3 shows the distribution of subjects studied across the three ICA form-level classification groupings; Table 20.4 shows the rate of ICA production for subjects in each group; and Table 20.5 summarizes distributions of proto-imperative and proto-declarative communicative functions observed for each form-level group in both studies.

STUDY 3

Again, this study of communicative form and function (McLean et al., 1991) was conducted within the framework of a larger program of research. The goal of these studies was to provide a better understanding of how these two aspects of expressive communication performance (form and function) relate to different aspects of sensorimotor and symbolization ability in severely mentally retarded adults, and, critically, to individual subject responsiveness to different treatment procedures.

TABLE 20.3

Subjects in Study 1 and Study 2: Communication Forms of Severely
to Profoundly Mentally Retarded Persons

| | | | Sex | | Communication Form Level[a] | | |
	N	CAs	M	F	P	C	R
Study 1	15	10–18 years	11	4	7	6	2
Study 2	18	8–21 years	11	7	2	8	8
Totals	33		22	11	9	14	10

Note. Subject samples are as follows: all residents of state hospital for the mentally retarded; all diagnosed severely or profoundly mentally retarded (AAMD classification); all ambulatory with functional vision and hearing; and all producing some illocutionary communication acts. Adapted from "Form and Function of Communicative Behaviour Among Persons with Severe Developmental Disabilities" by J. McLean and L. Snyder-McLean, 1987, *Australia and New Zealand Journal of Developmental Disabilities, 13*(2), pp. 83–98.

[a]Communication Form Levels: P = primitive illocutionary (No point or spoken/signed words); C = conventional illocutionary (distal point and/or ≤ 5 words/signs); R = referential locutionary (> 5, nonritualized words/signs).

TABLE 20.4

Rate of ICA Production by Three Subject Groups

| | Mean Number of ICAs Produced[a] | | |
	Primitive Illocutionary	Conventional Illocutionary	Referential/ Locutionary
Study 1 [26 Tasks]	31.57 (5–46)[b]	38.17 (13–90)	134.5 (60–209)
Study 2 [22 Tasks]	16 (9–23)	33.25 (14–59)	42.88 (18–76)
Combined Studies	28.11	35.36	61.2

Note. Adapted from "Form and Function of Communicative Behaviour Among Persons with Severe Developmental Disabilities" by J. McLean and L. Snyder-McLean, 1987, *Australia and New Zealand Journal of Developmental Disabilities, 13*(2), pp. 83–98.

[a]ICAs = Intentional Communicative Acts. Numbers represent the mean total number of ICAs produced across two sampling sessions representing a total of approximately 40 min of structured interaction time. [b]Numbers in parentheses represent the range of rates for each group.

TABLE 20.5

Percentages of Imperative and Declarative Type Communication Functions
for Three Subject Groups

| | Subject Group | | | | | | | | |
| | Primitive Illocutionary | | | Conventional Illocutionary | | | Referential/ Locutionary | | |
	Imp.	Dec.	Other	Imp.	Dec.	Other	Imp.	Dec.	Other
Study 1	87%	0	13%	43%	38%	19%	40%	43%	17%
Study 2	88%	9%	3%	55%	36%	9%	49%	42%	9%

Note. Percentages are based on the total number of ICAs produced across two sampling sessions. Adapted from "Form and Function of Communicative Behaviour Among Persons with Severe Developmental Disabilities" by J. McLean and L. Snyder-McLean, 1987, *Australia and New Zealand Journal of Developmental Disabilities, 13*(2), pp. 83–98.

Subjects

Subjects in this study included eight adults with severe to profound mental retardation. These subjects ranged in age from 23 to 37 years, and included 5 men and 3 women. Seven resided in the same institution in which the previous 33 subjects lived; and one subject was still living at home with his natural parents. Of the seven institutional residents, length of institutionalization ranged from 10 to 28 years.

Subjects selected for this study included individuals who presented communication skills that could be described as prototypic of two of the earlier subject groupings, specifically, the primitive and conventional groups. In reviewing data from the previous studies and developing criteria for identifying potential subjects who would be prototypic of subjects observed in earlier studies, it was determined that two previous subject groups could be differentiated on a more meaningful (and less pejorative) dichotomy than primitive and conventional. Specifically, the motor acts that served as the most common communicative signals for previous P subjects all involved some physical contact with the receiver or referent or both. The communicative repertoires of previous C subjects, however, included at least one distal gesture (the distal point), and most typically also included a distal request gesture. Therefore, previous subject group labels of *primitive* and *conventional* were replaced with the labels *contact gesture* and *distal gesture*.

This distinction does not represent a true dichotomy, but a continuum of communication abilities on which contact and distal gestures are the two extremes. However, for Study 3, potential subjects who might be considered prototypic of individuals functioning at the two ends of this continuum were sought. Therefore, the following subject selection criteria were developed:

CONTACT SUBJECTS: Use of contact gestures to communicate; No distal point, signs or words observed; May use one proximal ($\leq$ 6 in.), noncontact gesture.

DISTAL SUBJECTS: Use of distal point and at least one other conventional distal gesture to communicate; Use of less than five nonecholalic words, signs, or symbols.

Potential subjects were identified through interviews with direct-care and professional staff. The first of two protocols then was administered to each potential subject and the first four subjects who met the criteria for each subject group were selected, based on their performance in this one protocol.

Procedures

The procedures for this study were similar to the previous two studies. However, some changes were made in the content and administration of the two interactive protocols. These changes were: (a) inclusion of more tasks designed to evoke proto-declaratives (direct attention to other); (b) the inclusion of both proximal and distal novel events in these proto-declarative tasks; and (c) the addition of more specific rules governing the experimenter's verbal behavior during the session, to control this as a potential variable influencing rate or type of subject communication. Table 20.2 shows the composition of these protocols. Before these revised protocols were administered to the eight primary subjects, a social validation study was conducted to evaluate the effectiveness of these assessment procedures. Results of that study indicated that the tasks in the two revised protocols effectively evoked the types of intentional communication targeted, when administered to more communicatively competent mentally retarded individuals.

Results

The general patterns observed in the two earlier studies are also apparent in the third study. Specifically, even with the larger number of proto-declarative tasks, including four involving proximal referents, the Contact subjects did not produce any ICAs coded as being in the proto-declarative category (e.g., direct attention to, or comment on, item or event). However, proto-declarative functions represent from 37% to 75% of the ICAs coded for the four Distal subjects across these two protocols.

These new subjects also replicated previous findings that higher level communicators (Distal subjects in Study 3) tend to produce higher rates of ICAs than lower level communicators (Contact subjects), under the same interactive conditions. In Study 3, Contact subjects produced a mean of 49 ICAs across these two interactive protocols, compared to a mean of 140 for Distal subjects. There is considerable individual variation on this measure, however, and some overlap in the rate data for these two subject groups.

SUMMARY OF RESEARCH FINDINGS

Six Levels of Communicative Intentionality and Conventionality Observed in Severely Handicapped Individuals

This chapter has traced an ongoing program of research to better describe the heterogeneity in communication skills first observed in a clinical sample of severely mentally retarded adolescents who were nonverbal. The evolution of a classification system has been explained. This system distinguishes two levels of perlocutionary communication (reactive and proactive), and two levels of illocutionary communication (contact and distal). Illocutionary acts that are beyond gesture levels become locutionary acts in this system and occur primarily in the form of single words or manual signs. This latter stage is identified as being emerging locutionary, and is contrasted with communicative repertoires that reflect syntactic structures and inflectional morphemes currently classified as fully locutionary. The varying relationships between levels of communicative intentionality and its differential realization forms can be summarized in a six-level taxonomy. This taxonomy, including definitions and examples for each level, is presented in Table 20.6.

The authors' research, involving 41 severely handicapped adolescents and young adults to date, suggests that the presence or absence of intentional communicative acts can be judged reliably among such persons. Further, this research suggests that taxonomies derived from speech act theory and data on communicative acquisition among young, nonhandicapped children can serve as a heuristic for the study of communicative behaviors in persons with severe developmental disabilities.

Beyond Communicative Intent: Covariance of Communicative Form and Function

The fact that the communicative functions produced by these subjects consistently covaried with their overall level of communicative form seems

TABLE 20.6

Cumulative Continuum of Communicative Acts Among Subjects with Severe to Profound Mental Retardation

Class and Emergent Stage	Type of Signal	Description	Examples
Reactive Perlocutionary	Facial, Vocal, or Motor Act	Client's reactive responses to internal and external stimuli serve as signals to others who assign communicative significance to these acts	Smiles/Laughs/Screams/Cries; Puts hands to ears/mouth; Mouths objects
Proactive Perlocutionary	Purposeful Motor Act	Client's goal-oriented motor acts on objects and/or people in the environment serve as signals to others who assign communicative intents to these acts	Reaches or moves toward object/person; looks at out-of-reach object/person; manipulates or attempts to activate object
Contact Illocutionary	Contact Gesture	Client uses physical contact gestural acts to signal communicative intentions to others. Begins to coordinate his/her signal with checks of receiver attention; sometimes emits attention-getting acts	Shows object; Gives object; Gestural Naming, e.g., combs hair with comb, sitrs with spoon, drinks from empty cup; Tugs at other person; Takes other's hand and places on object to request help; Touches object of interest/need
Distal Illocutionary	Distal Gesture	Client uses distal gestural acts with appropriately intonated vocalizations to achieve a full range of communicative functions	Point, Request, Greeting, Bye, and "Don't Know" gestures; accompanies gestures with vocalizations

			Examples
Emerging Locutionary	Symbols and Single Words	Client produces communicative acts that are comprised of single or serial symbols or words using speech or nonspeech mode. Generally, form = function and lexicon $\leq$ 5 words/symbols; still rely on gestures and vocalizations to convey meaning	
Locutionary Communication	Grammatical Non-oral or Oral True-Signs	Client produces utterances in Oral or Nonoral mode. Utterances have syntactic structure and grammatical morphemes. Truly referential language—same form used for different functions; Lexicon > 5 words	

Other Communicative Acts

	Examples
Socially unacceptable and idiosyncratic gestures and other motor acts. These often emerge in Perlocutionary Stage and are assigned communicative intent by others. Many continue on into later stages, perhaps with communicative intentions underlying them (e.g., protest, get attention, get desired object)	Hitting; Hand flapping; Tantrums; Other Stereopathies

Note. Source: McLean & Snyder-McLean (1987); Labels for emergent stages taken from Austin (1962); Bates (1976); and Bates et al. (1975).

worthy of note. Specifically, the ICAs by subjects using primitive/contact gesture acts were predominantly proto-imperatives. In fact, most of the Contact gesture subjects never produced any communicative act that could be coded as a proto-declarative (i.e., intended to direct the attention of another to, or comment on, some object or event). By contrast, subjects in the conventional/distal and referential/emerging locutionary groups all produced relatively high rates of declarative acts. This covariance of communication form and function among persons with severe developmental disabilities is consistent with the findings of other investigators. Studies of children with autism (Curcio, 1978; Wetherby & Prutting, 1984) have shown that these children's communicative acts are also predominantly imperatives, with a complete lack of any pointing or commenting. Smith and Von Tetzchner (1986) found that 2-year-old Down Syndrome children produced significantly fewer declarative acts than a group of MA-matched, nonhandicapped children. These findings seem particularly important in light of research that shows that nonhandicapped children's earliest communicative acts show a full range of both imperative and declarative communicative functions (Bates et al., 1975; Coggins, Olswang, & Guthrie, 1987). In fact, declarative functions are the prevalent type among nonhandicapped children in unstructured interactions with adults.

An explanation of the proto-imperative, proto-declarative differential cannot be offered at this point in this research. Simply to consider the primitive/contact gesture subjects as less social than their conventional/distal and referential peers and, thus, less desirous of the dyadic interactions produced by proto-declarative acts is a temptation that must be rejected. Many members of the Contact gesture group did seek proximity to, and interaction with, adults. Some issued proto-imperative acts at high rates and, thus, demonstrated full awareness of the responsiveness of the interactive adult in the sampling sessions.

The authors' observations at this time suggest that the subjects at the more primitive levels of communicative signaling are highly egocentric. This egocentrism might be identified in skewed desires for objects and events that have a primary and direct sensory impact on them (e.g., food items and objects), that afford direct manipulations, and that provide sensory feedback. Pervasive egocentrism also could signal a seriously diminished ability to perceive another person's perspective on the world. Thus, an unexpected event (such as an alligator dangling from the ceiling or a car moving behind an adult interactor) might not trigger an awareness that the event was unseen by the other, or that such events might also be interesting or important to another person. Such a deficit in presuppositional ability could have serious effects on all levels of communicative behavior, including the need to signal unambiguously, the need to interact according to rules of cooperativeness, and the need to wait and fill turns in an interaction. Indeed, those subjects at contact gesture communication levels in the studies reported here, do appear to be deficient in these dyadic interaction skills. They are often difficult to maintain in interactive episodes and typically tend to show a strong preference for contexts that feature food and drink as opposed to contexts focused on items that produce only auditory and visual stimuli as consequences. Additional research is needed to explicate the possible variables involved in the impoverished communicative performance of the contact gesture users in the reported studies.

DISCUSSION

The results summarized have produced new perspectives on the strengths and the limitations of the communicative systems of nonverbal persons with severe mental retardation. It has been gratifying to find that many of these nonverbal subjects do have robust levels of communicative intent. It also has been gratifying to find that the stage processes suggested by the levels observed in their communicative behaviors could be described using the same taxonomies applied to communication-acquiring, nonhandicapped young children. Specifically, persons with severe handicaps demonstrate the emergence of communicative intentions with the same moves from single focus to coordinated object–person schemes seen among nonhandicapped children. They also demonstrate signaling behavior that moves from direct motor acts on objects and people, to contact gestures, and on to distal gestures that reflect distancing between both speaker and receiver and sign and referent. Finally, although many subjects with severe to profound mental retardation showed communicative function classes limited to proto-imperatives, many others showed communicative intentions that included proto-declarative performatives.

It is in the mechanics of communication that the severe limitations among these subjects with severe to profound retardation are apparent. Specifically, both Contact and Distal subjects in these studies issued communicative acts that served only to indicate referents, not represent them. As such, these ICAs were functional only in contexts where the referents were present and could be pointed to, or otherwise indicated. To confirm this lack of responses to indicate absent referents, the authors recently reviewed the extant data on Distal subjects and found no ICA in which an absent referent was represented by a pantomime or other symbolic form. It should be noted that the interactive sessions in these studies were not specifically designed to set up conditions in which critical referents were missing from the communicative context. However, this condition does occur naturally in several of the scripted communicative tasks (e.g., the "forgotten" key to reactivate a toy). Bates, Bretherton, Shore, and McNew (1983) also have noted the absence of "naming" pantomimes in the prelinguistic communicative acts of young, nonhandicapped children. Their report describes the emergence of such pantomimes at the same time that words were evident in a sample of nonhandicapped children.

It is highly likely that many severely handicapped children who remain nonverbal have communicative intentions that cannot be accommodated by their gestural communication systems. The fact that many subjects in the studies reported here demonstrated motor naming with objects (Escalona, 1973) while interacting with common objects in their environments, offers some indication that the communicative use of pantomimes might be taught. However, in these studies involving contexts in which communicative acts were both invited and responded to, no such pantomimical gestures were used to mark an absent referent. Overall, many questions remain about the nature and the possible limits of the symbolization abilities of these persons.

One further point should be made about the fact that these individuals indicate referents rather than represent them. Persons who can only directly indicate referents are seriously diminished in their ability to interact with others. Such ICAs are often ambiguous. For example, in the face of only indicative gestures, research procedures required the experimenters to respond to such gestures first as though they were intended to direct attention to the indicated referent. It was only after the experimenters responded to such gestures by directing their attention to the indicated referent that they could begin to infer any other communicative intent. For example, if after an experimenter directed attention to an indicated referent, a subject persisted in his or her gesture, one could conclude that the ICA was intended to accomplish more than just "direct attention," and go on to test other hypotheses regarding intent. Sometimes, these subjects would recast an ICA by issuing another gesture. Often, however, they (Contact subjects particularly) simply went on to indicate another desired object or food item. Thus, people operating with gestures that only indicate referents generally attain their communicative intentions by perlocutionary means. That is, receivers make contextually supported guesses as to the significance of an indicated referent and construct a meaning to be assigned to the ICA. They then depend on the gesturer's subsequent behavior to judge the accuracy of these guesses. One might assume that the relative inefficiency of such mechanics spurs nonhandicapped children to seek better and higher symbolic forms by which to encode their intentions and meanings more explicitly. The fact that persons with severe mental retardation often do not move beyond this relatively unsatisfactory level of communication status is, of course, the bane of the clinician and scientist alike.

The final understanding of both the potential and the limitations of language learning and communication among such people must be sought in experimental clinical efforts that are interpreted in a context that includes a careful and detailed account of the communicative behaviors with which clients enter the clinical program. Professionals eventually must be able to judge the effects of clinical interventions in terms of the abilities that were available and apparent in the pretreatment behaviors of both successful and failing clients. It is the authors' hope that detailed behavioral inventories such as these reported here will contribute to such comparison processes.

CONCLUSIONS

These studies suggest several conclusions. The data show that many of the subjects in this study had robust communicative repertoires expressed in conventional distal gestures, but showed no movement into oral or symbolic communicative forms. Further, these nonverbal subjects only indicated referents—they did not represent them. Research shows that, when non-handicapped children reach this same level and type of communicative behavior, they rather quickly move on into spoken, symbolic forms (Bates et al., 1979; Sugarman-Bell, 1978). The performances observed among the adolescent and young adult subjects in these studies reflect an arrest of the normal developmental processes at the point of transition from prelinguistic to linguistic communication. Whether this arrest can be overcome with treatment remains to be answered. At the least, however, the data confirm a hypothesis that prelinguistic communication and linguistic communication are separate learning domains (Bloom, 1983). Thus, a first conclusion is that the underlying cognitive or social requirements of a functional nonsymbolic communicative system may not support the acquisition of a symbolic linguistic communicative system.

The aspects of the cognitive domain that are insufficient for linguistic learning among these subjects cannot be detailed at this time. Assessments of cognitive holdings obtained in studies by these authors (McLean et al., 1981; McLean et al., 1990) indicate that the cognitive deficits among distal gesture-using subjects are not apparent in the sensorimotor domains of object permanence, means to ends, or schemes for relating to objects. However, subjects from these studies were deficient in both motor and verbal imitation and the symbolic function of naming. Because these nonverbal subjects also only indicated referents and did not represent them, there are indications that symbolization ability may be involved.

These data do not support a conclusion that linguistic or, at least, symbolic forms of communication cannot be acquired by persons with severe handicaps. In fact, several training programs are reporting success in training nonspeech, symbolic forms of communication for persons who have not spontaneously acquired linguistic forms (see, for example, Romski & Sevcik, chapter 18 of this volume). Perhaps the impoverished and noninteractive environments in which many persons with severe to profound retardation live and learn is a critical factor in their developmental arrest. On the other hand, the severe limitations observed in both Contact and Distal adult subjects strongly suggest that, although communicative intentions and the most basic of cooperative social interaction repertoires are deeply placed in the neurostructures of the human primate, their realizations depend on the behavioral products of neurostructures that may not be available to all persons with severe to profound mental retardation of varying etiologies. Thus, there is a need for intervention programs to fully assess and describe the communicative behavior with which students enter instruction on symbolic communication—be it in speech or nonspeech systems. The finding that the communicative system with which a student enters symbolic instruction can be related to varying outcomes of such instruction would be an important contribution to both clinical designs and to knowledge about language and mental retardation.

Other conclusions relate to the philosophy and procedures of treatment to alleviate the serious deficits in communicative effectiveness experienced by persons with severe mental retardation. Students who are limited to indicating referents leave receivers with the burden of attempting to identify and assign the full performative functions the speaker intended for the communicative act. Further, such basically low-level responses are not readily accepted from students who are in their adolescent or adult years. However, these same communicative forms are well tolerated by adults interacting with young, communication-acquiring infants. Thus, treatment might include procedures to help adults and peers who interact with nonverbal persons with severe handicaps to learn to better recognize, accept, and respond to gestural communication from individuals who are beyond typical developmental ages. In turn, such treatment suggests that initial efforts with clients with severe developmental disabilities should focus on assuring that their gestural repertoires are robust and reflect both conventional gestural forms and conventional social functions. Certainly, efforts to teach alternative (nonspeech) symbol systems are strongly indicated by these data. Such an approach would counter philosophies of the past, which focused on spoken, linguistic behavior regardless of the client's communicative behavior at entry into treatment.

Similarly, the current treatment model should emphasize pragmatic targets (e.g., requests for items, actions, and attention) as opposed to the structural linguistic relationships (e.g., agent + action + object) which dominated past treatment approaches. This emphasis on pragmatics has had important impact on training procedures. The authors' experience and the data from research (e.g., Halle, 1982, 1984; Hart & Risley, 1975;

Warren & Kaiser, 1986; see also, Romski & Sevcik, chapter 18 of this volume) suggest that teaching socially functional messages in interactive contexts with responsive people results in good acquisition rates and improved generalization potential.

Current behavioral treatment procedures target communicative behavior that has effects on receivers. The reinforcing consequences evoked in interactive contexts, then, involve responses of receivers that reflect the effects requested in the communicative act (e.g., "Help me," "Give me," and "Look") and are followed by consequences in which receivers respond to these requests. Such treatment trends are supported by the studies reported in this chapter in that the experimental protocols that presented communicative needs were successful in evoking appropriate nonverbal acts from subjects. Responsiveness to the intent of a subject's indicative act resulted in the cessation of the act. Contrarily, a receiver's failure to respond often evoked a reissuance or revision of the communicative act (McLean et al., 1990). Such differential responses to receiver responsiveness indicates that these subjects were well aware of the consequences they sought by their communicative acts.

Finally, it might be concluded that the philosophy and data from studies of language acquisition among nonhandicapped children has provided a guide for gaining better understanding of the communicative status and needs of fellow beings who have severe developmental disabilities.

ACKNOWLEDGEMENTS

The research described in this article was supported in part by grants 5-P30-HD-02528-21 and 1-P01-HD-18955-01 from the National Institutes of Health/National Institute of Child Health and Human Development.

REFERENCES

Austin, J. L. (1962). *How to do things with words.* London: Oxford University Press.

Bates, E. (1976). *Language and context.* New York: Academic.

Bates, E., Benigni, L., Bretherton, I., Camaioni, L., & Volterra, V. (1979). *The emergence of symbols: Cognition and communication in infancy.* New York: Academic.

Bates, E., Bretherton, I., Shore, C., & McNew, S. (1983). Names, gestures and objects: Symbolization in infancy and aphasia. In K. Nelson (Ed.), *Children's language* (Vol. 4, pp. 59–123). Hillsdale, NJ: Lawrence Erlbaum Associates.

Bates, E., Camaioni, L., & Volterra, V. (1975). The acquisition of performatives prior to speech. *Merrill–Palmer Quarterly, 21,* 205–226.

Bloom, L. (1970). *Language development: Form and function in emerging grammars.* Cambridge, MA: MIT Press.

Bloom, L. (1983). Of continuity and discontinuity, and the magic of language development. In R. M. Golinkoff (Ed.), *The transition from prelinguistic to linguistic communication* (pp. 79–92). Hillsdale, NJ: Lawrence Erlbaum Associates.

Bowerman, M. F. (1973). *Learning to talk: A cross-linguistic comparison of early syntactic development, with special reference to Finnish*. London: Cambridge University Press.

Bowerman, M. F. (1974). Discussion summary: Development of concepts underlying language. In R. L. Schiefelbusch & L. L. Lloyd (Eds.), *Language perspectives: Acquisition, retardation and intervention* (pp. 191–209). Baltimore: University Park Press.

Bruner, J. S. (1975). From communication to language—A psychological perspective. *Cognition, 3,* 255–287.

Carrier, J. (1974). Application of functional analysis and a non-speech response mode to teaching language. *American Speech and Hearing Monograph No. 18,* Washington, DC.

Cirrin, F. M., & Rowland, C. M. (1985). Communicative assessment of nonverbal youths with severe/profound mental retardation. *Mental Retardation, 23,* 52–62.

Coggins, T. E., Olswang, L. B., & Guthrie, J. (1987). Assessing communicative intents in young children: Low structured observation or elicitation tasks? *Journal of Speech and Hearing Disorders, 52,* 44–49.

Curcio, F. (1978). Sensorimotor functioning and communication in mute autistic children. *Journal of Autism and Childhood Schizophrenia, 8,* 281–292.

Dore, J. (1975). Holophrases, speech acts and language universals. *Journal of Child Language, 2,* 21–40.

Escalona, S. K. (1973). Basic modes of social interaction: Their emergence and patterning during the first two years of life. *Merrill–Palmer Quarterly of Behavior and Development, 19*(3), 205–232.

Fay, W. H., & Schuler, A. L. (1980). *Emerging language in autistic children*. Baltimore: University Park Press.

Gray, B., & Ryan, B. (1973). *A language program for the nonlanguage child*. Champaign, IL: Research Press.

Grossman, H. J. (1973). *Manual on terminology and classification in mental retardation*. Washington, DC: American Association on Mental Deficiency.

Guess, D., Sailor, W., & Baer, D. M. (1974). To teach language to retarded children. In R. L. Schiefelbusch & L. L. Lloyd (Eds.), *Language perspectives—Acquisition, retardation and intervention* (pp. 529–564). Baltimore: University Park Press.

Guess, D., Sailor, W., & Baer, D. M. (1977). A behavioral-remedial approach to language training for the severely handicapped. In E. Sontag (Ed.), *Educational programming for the severely and profoundly handicapped* (pp. 360–377). Reston, VA: The Council for Exceptional Children.

Halle, J. W. (1982). Teaching functional language to the handicapped: An integrative model of natural environment teaching techniques. *Journal of the Association for the Severely Handicapped, 7,* 29–37.

Halle, J. W. (1984). Arranging the natural environment to occasion language: Giving severely language-delayed children reasons to communicate. *Seminars in Speech and Language, 5*(3). New York: Thieme-Stratton.

Halle, J. W., Marshall, A. M., & Spradlin, J. E. (1979). Time delay: A technique to increase language use and facilitate generalization in retarded children. *Journal of Applied Behavior Analysis, 12,* 431–439.

Hart, B., & Risley, T. R. (1975). Incidental teaching of language in the preschool. *Journal of Applied Behavior Analysis, 13,* 407–432.

Hart, B., & Rogers-Warren, A. (1978). The milieu approach to teaching language. In R. Schiefelbusch (Ed.), *Language intervention strategies* (pp. 193–235). Baltimore: University Park Press.

Kent, L. R. (1974). *Language acquisition program for the severely retarded.* Champaign, IL: Research Press.

MacDonald, J. D. (1982). Communication strategies for language intervention. In D. P. McClowry, A. M. Guilford, & S. O. Richardson (Eds.), *Infant communication: Development, assessment and intervention* (pp. 83–146). New York: Grune & Stratton.

MacDonald, J. D., & Horstmeier, D. S. (1978). *Environmental Language Intervention Program.* Columbus, OH: Merrill.

McClowry, D. P., Guilford, A. M., & Richardson, S. O. (1982). *Infant communication: Development, assessment, and intervention.* New York: Grune & Stratton.

McLean, J. E. (1983). Historical perspectives on the content of child language programs. In J. Miller, D. E. Yoder, & R. Schiefelbusch (Eds.), *Contemporary issues in language intervention* (pp. 115–126). Rockville, MD: American Speech-Language-Hearing Association.

McLean, J. E., McLean, L. K. S., Brady, N. C., & Etter, R. (1991). Communication profiles of two types of gesture using nonverbal persons with severe to profound mental retardation. *Journal of Speech and Hearing Research, 34,* 294–308.

McLean, J., & Snyder-McLean, L. (1987). Form and function of communicative behavior among persons with severe developmental disabilities. *Australia and New Zealand Journal of Developmental Disabilities, 13,* 83–98.

McLean, J., & Snyder-McLean, L. (1988). Application of pragmatics to children and youth classified as severely mentally retarded. In R. L. Schiefelbusch & L. L. Lloyd (Eds.), *Language perspectives: Acquisition, retardation and intervention* (pp. 255–288). Austin, TX: Pro-Ed.

McLean, J., Snyder-McLean, L., & Cirrin, F. (1981, November). *Communication performatives and representational behaviors in severely mentally retarded adolescents.* Miniseminar conducted at the annual meeting of the American Speech-Language-Hearing Association, Los Angeles.

McLean, J., Snyder-McLean, L., & Sack, S. (1982). *A transactional approach to early language training: A mediated program for inservice professionals.* Columbus, OH: Merrill.

McLean, J. E., Snyder-McLean, L., & Sack, S. (1985, November). *Communicative performances in standardized contexts by severely mentally retarded adolescents.* Poster session presented at the American Speech-Language-Hearing Association Convention, Washington, DC.

McLean, J. E., Yoder, D. E., & Schiefelbusch, R. L. (Eds.). (1972). *Language intervention with the mentally retarded: Developing strategies.* Baltimore: University Park Press.

Miller, J., & Yoder, D. (1972). A syntax teaching program. In J. McLean, D. Yoder, & R. Schiefelbusch (Eds.), *Language intervention with the retarded* (pp. 191–211). Baltimore: University Park Press.

Miller, J. F., & Yoder, D. E. (1974). An ontogenetic language teaching strategy for retarded children. In R. L. Schiefelbusch & L. L. Lloyd (Eds.), *Language perspectives: Acquisition, retardation and intervention* (pp. 505–528). Baltimore: University Park Press.

Moerk, E. L. (1977). *Pragmatic and semantic aspects of early language development.* Baltimore: University Park Press.

Muma, J. R. (1978). *Language handbook: Concepts, assessment, and intervention.* Englewood Cliffs, NJ: Prentice-Hall.

Musselwhite, C. R., & St. Louis, K. W. (1982). *Communication programming for the severely handicapped: Vocal and non-vocal strategies.* Houston: College Hill.

Peck, C. A., & Schuler, A. L. (1983). Classroom-based language intervention for children with autism: Theoretical and practical considerations for the speech and language specialist. *Seminars in Speech and Language, 4*(1), 93–103.

Premack, D. (1970). A functional analysis of language. *Journal of the Experimental Analysis of Behavior, 14,* 107–125.

Prizant, B., & Duchan, J. (1981). The functions of immediate echolalia in autistic children. *Journal of Speech and Hearing Disorders, 46,* 241–249.

Ruder, K. F., & Smith, M. D. (1974). Issues in language training. In R. L. Schiefelbusch & L. L. Lloyd (Eds.), *Language perspectives: Acquisition, retardation and intervention* (pp. 565–606). Baltimore: University Park Press.

Searle, J. R. (1969). *Speech acts: An essay in the philosophy of language.* London: University Press.

Seibert, J. M., & Hogan, A. E. (1982). A model for assessing social and object skills and planning intervention. In D. P. McClowry, A. M. Guilford, & S. O. Richardson (Eds.), *Infant communication: Development, assessment and intervention* (pp. 21–54). New York: Grune & Stratton.

Sloane, H. N., & MacAulay, B. D. (1968). *Operant procedures in remedial speech and language training.* Boston: Houghton Mifflin.

Slobin, D. I. (1973). Cognitive prerequisites for the development of grammar. In D. I. Slobin & C. Ferguson (Eds.), *Studies of child language development* (pp. 175–208). New York: Holt, Rinehart & Winston.

Smith, L., & Von Tetzchner, S. (1986). Communicative, sensorimotor, and language skills of young children with Down Syndrome. *American Journal of Mental Deficiency, 9*(1), 57–66.

Snyder-McLean, L., Solomonson, B., McLean, J., & Sack, S. (1984). Structuring joint action routines: A strategy for facilitating communication and language development in the classroom. *Seminars in Speech and Language, 5*(3). New York: Thieme-Stratton.

Sugarman-Bell, S. (1978). Some organizational aspects of pre-verbal communication. In I. Markova (Ed.), *The social context of language* (pp. 49–66). New York: Wiley.

Warren, S. F., & Kaiser, A. P. (1986). Incidental language teaching: A critical review. *Journal of Speech and Hearing Disorders, 51,* 291–299.

Warren, S., & Rogers-Warren, A. (1985). *Teaching functional language: Generalization and maintenance of language skills.* Austin, TX: Pro-Ed.

Waryas, C., & Stremel, K. (1973). *On the preferred form of the double object construction.* Unpublished manuscript, Parsons Research Center, Parsons, KS.

Wetherby, A., & Prutting, C. (1984). Profiles of communicative and cognitive social abilities in autistic children. *Journal of Speech and Hearing Research, 27*(3), 364–377.

Author Index

A

Abbs, J. H., 341, 359
Abrahamsen, A., 441, 445
Abramsonm, A. S., 191, 206
Abuelhaija, L. A., 418, 419, 427
Acredolo, L., 41, 59
Adams, A. K., 104, 108, 111
Adams, C. A., 198, 206
Ahlquist, J. E., 209, 233
Albury, D., 129, 136
Alcock, J., 145, 153, 160
Alexander, A., 460, 476
Allen, J. J., 182, 184, 186
Amiel-Tison, C., 351, 361
Anderson, J. A., 36, 62
Anderson, J., 399, 424
Andy, O. J., 151, 163
Annett, M., 184, 185
Asano, T., 239, 252
Aslin, R. N., 15, 25, 28
Aspinwall, L. G., 421, 425
Atkinson, M., 309, 319
Augustine, St., 100, 111
Aurelius, G., 19, 26
Austin, J. L., 485, 499, 505

B

Baer, D. M., 481, 506
Baer, R. A., 279, 283

Bakeman, R., 129, 136
Baker, C. L., 467, 468, 476
Baker, E., 197, 206, 455, 467, 468, 478
Baker, N. D., 406, 417, 418, 419, 424, 427
Ball, H., 171, 187
Barrett, M. D., 91, 92, 100, 105, 111, 113
Barsalou, L. W., 106, 112
Bartlett, E., 95, 112
Barton, R. L., 171, 172, 173, 174, 175, 185
Bates, E. L., 32, 35, 36, 37, 38, 39, 40, 41, 42, 43, 44, 45, 46, 52, 54, 56, 58, 59, 60, 61, 63, 64, 65, 92, 112, 118, 125, 132, 136, 299, 311, 318, 319, 356, 357, 358, 359, 399, 401, 405, 407, 408, 411, 416, 417, 422, 434, 435, 436, 436, 443, 482, 485, 487, 490, 491, 499, 500, 501, 503, 505
Bauchot, R., 151, 163
Bauer, P., 44, 60
Beastrom, S., 455, 477
Beasty, A., 277, 284, 285
Beaton, A., 150, 160
Beck, C. H. M., 171, 172, 173, 174, 175, 185
Beckwith, R., 128, 129, 130, 132, 133, 136, 137
Beecher, B., 179, 188
Beecher, M., 150, 162
Beehgly-Smith, M., 39, 60
Beilin, H., 37, 60

Bellugi, U., 32, 39, 62, 64, 65, 84, 88, 236, 237, 238, 252, 326, 337, 363, 364, 367, 369, 370, 372, 374, 376, 377, 378, 379, 380, 381, 383, 384, 385, 388, 390, 391, 392

Bem, D. J., 266, 283

Benedict, H., 22, 25, 92, 93, 95, 112, 114, 439, 443

Benigni, L., 35, 36, 39, 41, 45, 52, 59, 65, 92, 112, 125, 132, 136, 229, 482, 505

Bennett, E. L., 154, 160, 162

Bensberg, G., 429, 443

Benson, D. A., 149, 164, 205, 207

Bentall, R. P., 277, 278, 284, 285

Berard, J., 171, 187

Berkley, M. A., 150, 162

Berko, J., 52, 60

Berko-Gleason, J., 441, 443

Bernstein, N., 340, 359

Bertoncini, J., 351, 361

Berwick, A., 30, 60

Best, C. T., 17, 25

Best, S., 451, 479

Betz, J. C., 149, 162, 189, 199, 206, 207

Bever, T., 308, 320

Bever, T. G., 52, 58, 62, 236, 238, 239, 241, 243, 249, 250, 254

Bickerton, D., 29, 60, 84, 87

Bierwisch, N., 98, 112

Bihrle, A. M., 384, 385, 388, 390, 391

Birdsong, D., 468, 477

Bishop, A., 168, 186

Bissex, G. L., 400, 405, 406, 425

Bloom, L., 37, 42, 60, 80, 86, 87, 91, 112, 118, 119, 121, 123, 124, 127, 128, 129, 130, 132, 136, 137, 252, 307, 313, 316, 317, 319, 320, 437, 443, 470, 471, 472, 477, 480, 482, 503, 505, 506

Blumstein, S., 196, 197, 206, 207

Bock, K., 404, 425

Bode, J. U., 468, 472, 477

Boehm, C., 247, 251, 252

Bohannon, N., 417, 425

Bolders, J., 450, 478

Bolles, R. C., 266, 284

Bonet, B., 462, 477

Bonvillian, J. D., 405, 406, 407, 417, 425, 427, 430, 443

Booth, R., 129, 136

Borer, H., 8, 11, 25, 29, 30, 45, 60

Bosler, L. A., 150, 160

Bosma, J. F., 8, 25, 347, 359

Bowerman, M. F., 50, 60, 86, 87, 89, 92, 94, 96, 100, 112, 319, 406, 414, 425, 452, 454, 456, 467, 469, 477, 482, 506

Bowman, L. L., 101, 114

Box, H. O., 171, 172, 186

Boysen, S., 48, 62, 210, 232

Boyssen-Bardies, B., 357, 359

Bracha, H. S., 177, 186

Brady, N. C., 483, 393, 507

Braine, M. D. S., 67, 70, 74, 80, 81, 87, 109, 112, 237, 238, 243, 248, 252

Brakke, K. E., 211, 215, 232

Branigan, G., 24, 25

Braunwald, S. R., 92, 112

Bremner, J. G., 293, 299

Brentano, F., 119, 137

Bresnan, J., 334, 337, 465, 477

Bresson, F., 356, 359

Bretherton, I., 35, 36, 38, 39, 40, 41, 42, 43, 45, 52, 59, 60, 65, 92, 112, 125, 132, 136, 299, 399, 405, 408, 416, 424, 425, 482, 501, 505

Brinton, B., 473, 477

Brito, A., 294, 300

Bronowski, J., 236, 237, 238, 252

Brookes, S., 92, 111

Broughton, J., 118, 137

Brown, J., 119, 137

Brown, R. N. D., 67, 78, 79, 80, 87, 88, 118, 125, 137, 241, 252, 325, 337, 451, 455, 477

Brownell, C., 41, 60

Brugman, C., 69, 88

Bruner, J. S., 37, 60, 104, 111, 112, 132, 137, 152, 160, 215, 218, 223, 232, 431, 443, 482, 506

Bruning, J. L., 246, 247, 252

Bruskin, C., 41, 63

Bryden, M. P., 150, 160, 184, 186

Buhr, J., 450, 452, 453, 454, 455, 479

Bull, C. H., 21, 27

Bullock, D., 102, 104, 108, 111, 113

Burkhardt, A., 411, 426

Busnel, M. C., 351, 359

C

Callaway, E., 189, 206

Caltagirone, C., 196, 207

Calvin, W. H., 405, 412, 414, 425

Camaioni, L., 35, 36, 37, 39, 41, 45, 52, 59, 65, 92, 112, 125, 132, 136, 299, 482, 485, 487, 490, 491, 499, 500, 503, 505
Camarata, S., 60, 402, 405, 406, 414, 415, 425, 427, 450, 478
Campbell, R., 118, 137
Capatides, J., 128, 130, 137
Carey, S., 54, 61, 95, 99, 112, 452, 477
Carney, A. E., 21, 27
Carpenter, K. L., 56, 61
Carpenter, P., 316, 320
Carpenter, R., 450, 477
Carrier, J., 481, 506
Carrow-Woolfolk, E., 438, 443
Cartmill, M., 168, 186
Caselli, C., 41, 65
Cassidy, K. W., 17, 26
Catania, A. C., 264, 267, 268, 270, 275, 276, 278, 279, 280, 284, 285
Cauley, K., 301, 302, 309, 319
Cazden, C. B., 71, 88
Cerutti, D., 268, 284
Chabay, R. W., 421, 425
Chalkley, M. A., 23, 27, 67, 68, 69, 70, 82, 88, 311, 320, 455, 478
Chandler, P., 293, 294, 300
Chapman, J. P., 182, 184, 186
Chapman, K., 450, 478
Chapman, L. J., 182, 184, 186
Chapman, R. S., 307, 316, 317, 319, 434, 443
Charles-Dominique, P., 168, 186
Charrow, V. R., 405, 425
Cheney, D. L., 153, 160, 163, 271, 285
Chevalier-Skolnikoff, S., 152, 160
Cheverud, J., 149, 161
Chipman, H., 326, 337
Chomsky, N., 6, 11, 25, 29, 30, 35, 61, 84, 88, 93, 112, 134, 137, 235, 236, 252, 301, 319, 326, 327, 329, 331, 337, 405, 407, 408, 419, 425
Churchland, P. S., 36, 50, 61
Cicchetti, D., 441, 443
Cirrin, F. M., 483, 489, 490, 503, 506, 507
Clark, E. V., 56, 61, 99, 101, 112, 134, 137, 370, 391
Clarke, R., 149, 163
Cleary, J., 280, 285
Clifton, R., 352, 359
Clymer, P. E., 182, 186
Cocking, R. R., 301, 319
Coggins, T. E., 500, 506

Cohen, L. B., 41, 61, 123, 137, 306, 319
Cole, K. J., 341, 359
Conroy, G. C., 149, 161
Cooper, F. S., 189, 191, 206
Cooper, J. A., 457, 478
Corina, D., 52, 62, 391
Corrigan, R., 39, 61, 123, 137
Corter, C. M., 149, 164
Cottrell, G., 52, 62
Couch, J. B., 236, 238, 253
Cowey, A., 150, 161
Crago, M. B., 451, 457, 477
Crain, S., 45, 61, 118, 133, 138, 323, 324, 325, 326, 328, 336, 337
Cramer, D. L., 235, 255
Cresson, O., 441, 445
Cronin, J. E., 235, 255
Culicover, P., 30, 49, 65, 93, 115, 325, 337
Culler, F., 384, 391
Cullicover, P. W., 403, 405, 428
Cunningham, S., 279, 285
Curcio, F., 41, 46, 61, 500, 506
Curtiss, S., 153, 160, 410, 428, 451, 458, 480

D

Dale, P., 42, 61
Dalke, D., 409, 427
D'Amico, C., 184, 187
Danto, A., 119, 126, 137
Darwin, C., 5, 25, 268, 284
Davenport, R. K., 153, 154, 160, 162
Davis, B. L., 20, 22, 24, 25
Dawkins, R., 266, 270, 284
de Boysson-Bardies, B., 359
DeCasper, A. J., 351, 359
de Gaspe Beaubien, F., 309, 319
de la Costelareymondie, M. C., 148, 161
Delis, D., 384, 385, 388, 391
Dell, G., 56, 61
DeLoache, J., 306, 319
Demetriou, A., 402, 406, 425
Demopoulos, W., 124, 139
Denenberg, V., 154, 160
Dennett, D. C., 26, 284
Denninger, M. K., 405, 406, 417, 425, 427
Denno, D., 182, 188
De Rousseau, C. J., 175, 186
de Saussure, F., 5, 6, 25, 108, 112
de Schonen, S., 356, 359

Detrich, R., 279, 283
Devaney, J. M., 280, 284
de Villiers, J., 236, 252, 332, 337
de Waal, F., 272, 284
Dewson, J. H., 150, 160, 179, 186
Dhall, U., 175, 186
Diamond, J. M., 209, 232
Diehl, R. L., 16, 26
Dixon, R. M. W., 70, 82, 88
Dobzhansky, T. G., 11, 25
Dodd, B., 353, 359
Dodson, D. L., 169, 170, 187, 188
Doherty, S., 384, 390
Donahue, M., 24, 25
Dore, F. Y., 152, 161
Dore, J., 42, 61, 92, 112, 482, 506
Dorman, M., 192, 206
Dowd, J., 352, 359
Doyle, W., 21, 27
Drea, C., 171, 172, 186
Dromi, E., 92, 93, 94, 100, 103, 105, 113
Druss, B., 17, 26
Duchan, J., 482, 483, 508
Dumar, C., 152, 161
Dunn, L., 438, 443
Dunton, S., 473, 477
Durand, C., 357, 359
Durding, B. M., 182, 188

E

Edelman, G. M., 345, 352, 353, 354, 360
Edwards, D., 37, 61, 288, 300
Ehret, G., 185, 186
Ehrlich, S., 96, 113
Eilers, R. E., 21, 27, 191, 206, 356, 361
Eimas, P. D., 15, 25, 191, 206
Eisenberg, J. F., 166, 173, 186
Eldredge, N., 33, 61
Ellis, J. E., 171, 173, 177, 188
Elman, J. L., 36, 58, 61
Enright, M., 123, 135, 139
Entus, A. K., 149, 160
Escalona, S. K., 41, 60, 502, 506
Estes, W. K., 212, 232
Etter, R., 483, 493, 507
Ettlinger, G., 148, 162, 171, 172, 175, 186, 187, 238, 254
Ewing, G., 124, 137
Eyre, M. B., 182, 186

F

Fagen, J., 123, 135, 139
Fagot, J., 171, 172, 173, 176, 186
Falk, D., 149, 161, 175, 186
Fantz, R., 123, 138
Farrar, J., 133, 139
Farrar, M., 118, 139
Fauconnier, G., 117, 121, 127, 138
Fay, W. H., 482, 506
Fenson, L., 39, 41, 60, 61
Fentress, J. C., 268, 284
Ferguson, C. A., 405, 407, 425, 426
Fernald, A., 351, 360
Ferreiro, E., 326, 337
Fey, M. E., 459, 462, 465, 477
Fiess, K., 124, 137
Fifer, W., 351, 360
Fillmore, L. W., 399, 400, 425
Fischer, K. W., 39, 61, 102, 113, 402, 425
Fisher, D. M., 345, 362
Fleagle, J. C., 167, 186
Fletcher, A., 309, 319
Fletcher, P., 468, 472, 477
Fletcher, S. G., 347, 360
Fobes, J. L., 151, 161
Fodor, J., 37, 45, 58, 61, 98, 99, 113, 119, 127, 138, 213, 232, 323, 325, 336, 337, 407, 425
Fogel, A., 342, 344, 345, 356, 358, 360, 362
Fok, A., 374, 379, 391
Fok, Y. Y. A., 367, 374, 376, 377, 379, 391
Foley, W., 37, 46, 61
Forsythe, C., 170, 186, 188
Foster, R., 438, 443
Fouts, R. S., 236, 238, 239, 249, 252, 253
Fowler, C. A., 340, 360
Fragaszy, D., 47, 65
Franklin, M. B., 92, 112
Frazer, J. G., 273, 284
Freedman, P., 450, 477
Freeman, R., 352, 361
French, L., 96, 113
Friedlander, B., 309, 320
Friedman, S., 301, 319
Frost, G. T., 147, 161
Fujiki, M., 473, 477
Fuller, B. A. G., 165, 186
Furuya, Y., 172, 187

G

Galaburda, A. M., 205, 206
Galanter, E., 117, 126, 138
Gallistel, C. R., 267, 284
Gallup, G. G., 154, 161
Gardner, A., 155, 161
Gardner, B., 155, 161, 210, 232, 236, 238, 239, 249, 250, 253, 254, 255
Gardner, H., 44, 65, 405, 425, 461, 477
Gardner, R. A., 210, 232, 236, 238, 249, 250, 253, 254, 255
Gasc, J. P., 168, 187
Gathercole, V. C., 101, 113
Gautrin, D., 172, 186
Gavin, W., 191, 206
Gelman, R., 95, 115
Gelman, S. A., 95, 113, 115
Gentner, D., 67, 68, 81, 88, 455, 477
Gerard, A. B., 41, 63, 99, 113
Geschwind, N., 149, 161, 162, 184, 186, 187, 205, 206
Ghiglieri, M., 213, 232
Gianotti, G., 196, 207
Giddan, J., 438, 443
Gill, T. V., 238, 239, 254
Gilmore, L. B., 155, 163
Gisiner, R., 211, 233
Glasersfeld, E. C., 239, 254
Gleick, J., 342, 360
Gleitman, H., 311, 314, 319, 320
Gleitman, L. R., 15, 25, 311, 314, 319, 320, 456, 469, 470, 471, 477
Glick, S. D., 177, 185, 186
Globerson, T., 421, 427
Gluck, J. P., 153, 161
Goad, H., 11, 25
Gold, E., 49, 50, 61
Goldin-Meadow, S., 235, 237, 241, 251, 253
Goldsmith, S., 42, 64
Golinkoff, R. M., 41, 62, 133, 135, 138, 301, 302, 305, 309, 311, 312, 319, 320
Gonzales, A., 73, 88
Good, A., 411, 426
Goodale, M., 178, 187
Goodall, J., 152, 161
Goodglass, H., 197, 206
Goodman, N., 99, 113
Goodwyn, S., 41, 59
Gopnick, M., 451, 457, 477

Gopnick, A., 39, 41, 62, 92, 113, 118, 133, 138, 407, 426
Gordon, L., 301, 32, 309, 319
Gould, S. J., 9, 25, 31, 32, 33, 34, 59, 61, 62, 277, 284, 345, 360
Gouzoules, H., 269, 284
Gouzoules, S., 269, 284
Gracco, V. L., 341, 359
Granier-Deferre, C., 351, 359
Grasse, P. P., 7, 25
Gray, B., 481, 506
Green, S., 19, 25
Greenfield, P. M., 37, 62, 92, 113, 134, 138, 237, 240, 241, 242, 243, 244, 246, 247, 250, 251, 253
Greenspoon, J., 276, 284
Grimshaw, J., 67, 70, 83, 88, 325, 337
Gronlund, S., 404, 428
Grossman, H. J., 484, 488, 506
Gruendel, J., 92, 95, 105, 114
Guess, D., 429, 443, 481, 506
Guilford, A. M., 482, 507
Guin, K., 169, 188
Guthrie, J., 500, 506

H

Hadley, P. A., 459, 460, 474, 476, 477, 479
Hafitz, J., 128, 137, 470, 471, 472, 477
Haken, H., 341, 360
Halle, J. W., 482, 504, 506
Halle, P., 357, 359
Halsten, N., 351, 361
Hamburger, H., 118, 133, 138, 326, 336, 337
Hamilton, C. H., 150, 161
Hamm, A., 149, 163
Hammouda, S., 329, 337
Hanlon, C., 325, 337
Hannan, T. E., 46, 62
Harding, C., 41, 62
Hare, M., 52, 62
Harlow, H. F., 152, 153, 161
Harlow, M. K., 152, 153, 161
Harnad, S. R., 15, 26, 29, 62, 199, 206
Harris, M., 92, 111
Harris, P., 38, 62
Hart, B., 279, 285, 482, 504, 506
Hauser, M., 171, 187
Hayes, C., 210, 232
Hayes, K. J., 146, 161, 210, 232

Hayes, S. C., 280, 284
Healey, J. M., 184, 187
Heestand, J. E., 171, 176, 187
Heffner, H. E., 179, 187
Heffner, R. S., 179, 187
Heimann, M., 406, 409, 418, 419, 425, 427
Helmkamp, C., 175, 186
Hengst, J., 451, 479
Herbert, M., 154, 160
Herman, L. M., 211, 232
Hess, T. M., 192, 193, 194, 196, 198, 200, 207
Hill, J. H., 235, 253
Hinde, R. A., 153, 161, 180, 187
Hinton, G. E., 36, 62
Hirsh-Pasek, K., 17, 26, 125, 135, 138, 301, 302, 305, 309, 311, 312, 319, 320, 416, 425
Hixon, T. J., 180, 187
Hockett, C., 431, 443
Hodapp, R., 432, 445
Hogan, A. E., 482, 483, 508
Hohmann, M., 462, 477
Holland, J. H., 58, 62
Hollis, J., 430, 444
Holloway, R. L., 148, 161
Holmgren, K., 19, 26
Holt, K. G., 341, 360
Holyoak, K. J., 58, 62
Hood, L., 42, 60, 124, 137, 472, 480
Hopkins, W. D., 150, 151, 155, 157, 161, 163, 171, 174, 187, 211, 232, 239, 240, 254, 439, 444
Horgan, D., 42, 62, 418, 425
Horne, P., 278, 280, 284
Horner, R., 429, 443
Horowitz, F. D., 352, 362
Horster, W., 172, 187
Horstmeier, D. S., 482, 507
Hung, D. L., 376, 393
Hutchinson, J., 48, 63, 95, 99, 100, 114
Huttenlocher, J., 52, 62, 113, 437, 439, 440, 443
Hyams, N., 319, 320

I

Ingram, D., 11, 25, 450, 478
Itani, J., 172, 187
Ito, T., 56, 62

J

Jackendoff, R., 110, 113, 119, 138, 319
Jacob, F., 11, 26
Jacob, M., 48, 64
Jakobson, R., 21, 26, 111, 113
Jalling, B., 19, 26
Jason, G. W., 150, 161
Jasper, H. H., 192, 206
Jaynes, J., 271, 273, 283, 284
Jensen, J. L., 358, 362
Jerison, H. J., 147, 162
Jernigan, T., 384, 388, 390, 391, 392
Jewett, J., 129, 139
Johnson-Laird, P., 129, 139
Johnson, M., 263, 285
Johnston, J., 38, 39, 62
Johnston, J. R., 450, 456, 459, 462, 472, 477, 478
Jones, D., 92, 111
Jones, H. H., 175, 178, 188
Jouffroy, F. K., 168, 187
Joyner, S. E., 430, 431, 444
Jusczyk, P. W., 15, 17, 25, 26, 191, 206, 351, 352, 360, 361
Just, M. A., 316, 319

K

Kail, R., 454, 478
Kaiser, A. P., 505, 508
Kamhi, A., 472, 478
Kano, K., 172, 187
Kaplan, B. J., 41, 46, 65, 406, 417, 427
Kaplan, E., 381, 392
Karabenick, J. D., 473, 479
Karlan, G., 430, 443
Karmiloff-Smith, A., 94, 96, 113
Katz, J. J., 98, 113
Katz, N., 455, 478
Kawai, M., 171, 172, 188
Kay, B., 355, 360
Keane, V., 429, 443
Keil, F. C., 99, 113
Kellar, L., 197, 207
Kellogg, L., 48, 62
Kellogg, W. N., 48, 62, 235, 239, 253
Kelly, D. J., 464, 478
Kelso, J. A. S., 340, 341, 342, 343, 344, 355, 356, 360, 362
Kemler Nelson D. G., 17, 26
Kempler, D., 42, 62

Kennedy, L., 17, 26
Kent, L. R., 481, 507
Kent, R. D., 18, 26
Kilborn, K., 56, 62
Kilburn, K., 429, 445
Killeen, P. R., 16, 26
Kimura, D., 184, 187, 191, 206
King, J. E., 151, 161, 171, 172, 175, 176, 187
King, M., 33, 62
Kinsbourne, M., 132, 138
Kintz, B. L., 246, 247, 252
Klein, W., 56, 62
Klima, E. S., 32, 62, 64, 84, 88, 363, 367, 370, 374, 379, 380, 383, 390, 391, 392
Kluender, K. R., 16, 26
Kojima, T., 239, 252
Koopmans-van Beinum, F. J., 19, 26, 348, 349, 350, 360
Koslow, S., 189, 206
Krech, D., 154, 162
Kroodsma, D. E., 152, 162, 271, 284
Kubota, K., 239, 252
Kuczaj, S. A. II, 91, 113
Kugler, P. N., 341, 360
Kuhl, P. K., 15, 26, 171, 175, 177, 178, 187, 198, 199, 205, 206, 351, 353, 360, 361
Kulig, J., 352, 359
Kuno, S., 47, 62
Kuperstein, M., 346, 361
Kuroda, S., 235, 251, 253
Kutas, M., 379, 392
Kwiatkowski, J., 451, 479
Kyratzis, A., 107, 109, 113

L

Labov, W., 101, 113
Lachter, J., 52, 58, 62
Lack, D., 7, 26
Lahey, M., 137, 307, 316, 317, 319, 459, 478
Lakoff, G., 75, 87, 88, 89, 98, 106, 113, 263, 285
Lamandella, J. T., 32, 62
Lambertz, G., 351, 361
Lancaster, J., 29, 62
Landau, B., 314, 320
Landua, V., 171, 172, 175, 176, 187
Langacker, R., 37, 46, 63

Larson, C. F., 169, 187
Lashley, K. S., 179, 187
Laughlin, N. K., 200, 201, 207
Launer, P., 369, 392
Lazar, R., 279, 285
Lecanuet, J. P., 351, 359
Leddick, K., 237, 253
Lehmann, W. P., 5, 26
Leinbach, J., 52, 63
LeMaster, B., 374, 392
LeMay, M., 148, 149, 162, 205, 206
Lempert, H., 132, 138
Lenneberg, E. H., 21, 26, 147, 162, 235, 253
Leonard, J., 450, 478
Leonard, L. B., 450, 454, 456, 457, 461, 462, 465, 478
Lepper, M. R., 421, 425
Leske, M. C., 448, 478
Levitsky, W., 149, 161
Levy, E., 109, 113
Levy, J., 150, 162
Liberman, A. M., 22, 26, 179, 187, 189, 191, 206
Lieberman, P., 29, 32, 34, 63, 147, 162, 179, 187, 235, 253, 357, 361
Liederman, J., 184, 187
Lifter, K., 118, 124, 137, 470, 471, 472, 477
Lightbown, L., 42, 60
Lightfoot, D, 30, 63, 419, 426
Lillo-Martin, D., 367, 369, 370, 378, 391, 392
Limber, J., 236, 253
Lindblom, B., 14, 19, 20, 24, 26, 162, 166, 174, 177, 187, 188, 356, 357, 358, 361, 407, 426
Linden, E., 236, 238, 239, 251, 254
Linnville, S., 200, 201, 207
Lisker, L., 191, 206
Lloyd, L. L., 430, 442, 443, 444
Lock, A., 103, 113, 132, 138, 218, 232, 293, 294, 299, 300
Locke, J. L., 10, 12, 20, 21, 26
Loew, R. C., 369, 392
Loncke, F., 402, 405, 427
Lowe, C. F., 277, 278, 280, 284, 285
Lucariello, J., 91, 92, 105, 107, 109, 113, 114
Lucas, D., 123, 135, 139
Ludlow, C. L., 457, 478
Luria, A. R., 277, 285
Lyons, J., 70, 88, 89, 91, 97, 98, 113

M

MacAulay, B. D., 481, 508
MacDonald, J. D., 482, 507
MacKain, K. S., 353, 361
Macken, M. A., 21, 22, 27, 28, 405, 407, 426
MacLean, P. D., 180, 187
Macmurray, J., 290, 292, 300
MacNamara, J., 37, 63, 67, 70, 78, 79, 83, 88, 96, 114, 407, 426, 455, 478
MacNeilage, P. F., 19, 20, 22, 24, 25, 26, 162, 166, 173, 174, 177, 178, 183, 184, 187, 188, 356, 357, 361, 407, 426
MacWhinney, B., 37, 46, 52, 54, 58, 59, 60, 63, 311, 318, 319, 332, 337, 357, 358, 359, 401, 404, 405, 406, 414, 417, 422, 425, 426
Maki, S., 182, 183, 188
Mandell, A. J., 341, 360
Mandler, J. M., 99, 113, 119, 123, 138
Manson, J. H., 171, 187
Maratsos, M. P., 23, 27, 67, 68, 69, 70, 74, 80, 82, 83, 84, 88, 109, 114, 311, 320, 455, 478
Marchman, V. A., 46, 52, 63, 64, 411, 426
Markessini, J., 309, 319
Markman, E. M., 48, 63, 95, 96, 99, 113, 114
Marks, S., 384, 385, 388, 391
Marler, P., 152, 153, 162, 163, 269, 271, 284, 285
Marshall, A. M., 482, 506
Martin, M., 429, 445
Marwick, H., 19, 27
Mason, W. A., 152, 161
Masterson, R. B., 150, 162
Masur, E., 133, 138
Mather, P. L., 12, 26
Matsuzawa, K., 239, 252
Matsuzawa, T., 238, 253
Matthews, B. A., 275, 276, 279, 284, 285
Mattingly, I. G., 22, 26, 179, 187
Maugais, R., 351, 359
Maury, L., 356, 359
Maxwell, M., 400, 405, 406, 407, 408, 426
Mayr, E., 7, 8, 27
McCall, R., 119, 132, 138
McClelland, J. L., 36, 50, 52, 63, 64, 316, 320, 402, 404, 426, 427
McClowry, D. P., 482, 507
McCune, L., 22, 27

McCune-Nicolich, L., 41, 63, 118, 138
McDaniel, D., 331, 337
McDonald, J., 52, 63, 211, 232
McDonald, K., 163, 232, 239, 240, 254, 439, 444
McGhee, P., 119, 132, 138
McHale, S., 301, 319
McIntire, K. D., 280, 285
McIntire, M., 378, 392
McKee, C., 324, 337
McKenna, J. J., 347, 361
McLean, J., 482, 483, 489, 490, 491, 493, 494, 499, 503, 507, 508
McLean, J. E., 481, 483, 507
McLean, L. K. S., 483, 493, 507
McNeill, D., 235, 253
McNew, S., 39, 42, 59, 60, 501, 505
McRoberts, G. W., 17, 25
McShane, J., 92, 94, 114
McTear, M., 405, 426
Mead, G. H., 290, 292, 300
Mehler, J., 351, 361
Meier, R. P., 21, 27, 32, 63, 369, 370, 371, 372, 377, 392
Meltzoff, A. N., 39, 41, 47, 62, 63, 92, 113, 118, 138, 353, 361, 407, 426
Menn, L., 22, 24, 27, 441, 444
Menzel, E. W., Jr., 154, 162
Merkin, S., 472, 480
Merriman, W. E., 95, 101, 114
Mervis, C., 58, 64, 118, 138
Miceli, G., 196, 207
Michel, G. F., 185, 188
Middleton, D., 288, 300
Miles, H. L. W., 238, 239, 241, 253, 254
Miles, L. W., 239, 253
Miller, E. H., 271, 284
Miller, G., 117, 119, 122, 126, 138
Miller, J., 21, 28, 198, 199, 205, 206, 434, 443, 478, 507
Miller, J. D., 15, 26
Miller, J. F., 307, 316, 319, 482, 507
Miller, R., 21, 28, 46, 63
Miller, R. T., 92, 112
Milliken, G. W., 169, 170, 186, 188
Milner, A. D., 171, 172, 175, 188
Moerk, E. L., 482, 507
Moffett, A., 172, 186
Mohanan, K. P., 343, 361
Molfese, D. L., 149, 162, 189, 190, 192, 193, 194, 196, 198, 199, 200, 201, 206, 207, 352, 361, 441, 444

Molfese, V. J., 192, 193, 194, 196, 198, 207, 352, 361
Moody, D., 150, 162, 179, 188
Moon, C., 351, 360
Moore, K., 47, 63
Moore, M. K., 353, 361
Morehead, D., 450, 478
Morgan, J. L., 421, 426
Morimoto, H., 154, 160
Morisset, C., 42, 61
Morris, R., 441, 444
Morris, R. D., 150, 157, 160, 161
Morris, W., 263, 285
Morrongiello, B., 123, 139, 352, 359
Morse, P. A., 200, 201, 207
Moscovitch, M., 119, 138
Mozer, M., 52, 63
Muma, J. R., 482, 507
Mumme, D. L., 421, 425
Muncer, S. J., 238, 254
Murnane, K., 404, 428
Murphy, J., 155, 163
Musselwhite, C. R., 483, 507
Mutofushi, K., 239, 252
Mylander, C., 235, 237, 241, 251, 253

N

Nachson, I., 182, 188
Nadler, R. D., 171, 173, 177, 188
Naigles, L., 305, 311, 312, 314, 319, 320
Nakayama, M., 328, 337
Napier, J. R., 167, 188
Nelson, C. A., 190, 207
Nelson, K. E., 42, 52, 63, 91, 92, 94, 95, 96, 98, 103, 104, 105, 107, 108, 109, 113, 114, 118, 123, 139, 215, 218, 232, 299, 300, 316, 320, 400, 401, 402, 404, 405, 406, 407, 409, 410, 414, 415, 416, 417, 418, 419, 424, 425, 426, 428, 430, 443, 444, 463, 478
Nelson, R. O., 280, 284
Nemeth, M., 450, 452, 453, 455, 479
Neville, H. J., 379, 384, 391, 392
Newmeyer, F. J., 212, 232
Newport, E. L., 21, 27, 32, 63, 370, 372, 377, 392
Nicolich, L., 41, 63
Nisbett, R. E., 58, 62
Nissen, C. H., 146, 161
Nocenti, A., 243, 254
Norman, F., 373, 376, 377, 378, 393

O

Oakes, L., 39, 60, 356, 359
Oatley, K., 129, 139
Ochs Keenan, E., 236, 237, 254
O'Connell, B., 40, 41, 45, 60, 63, 64, 356, 359
Oetting, J., 450, 452, 453, 454, 455, 479
O'Grady, L., 374, 378, 391, 392
O'Grady, M., 370, 378, 391, 392
O'Grady, W., 36, 37, 46, 63
O'Grady-Batch, L., 373, 376, 377, 378, 393
Olber, L., 441, 444
Oller, D. K., 18, 19, 20, 21, 27, 346, 356, 361
Olson, D. A., 171, 173, 177, 188
Olswang, L. B., 415, 427, 500, 506
Oscar-Berman, M., 196, 207
Otanes, S., 72, 73, 88
Otemaa, J., 177, 186
Othenin-Girard, C., 326, 337
Otomo, K., 21, 27
Oviatt, S., 125, 139
Owsley, C. J., 353, 362
Oyama, S., 7, 27

P

Padden, C. A., 374, 381, 392
Padden, D., 198, 199, 206
Padden, D. M., 15, 26
Palermo, D., 352, 361
Papousek, H., 351, 361
Papousek, M., 351, 361
Parlour, S. F., 458, 478
Parsons, C., 196, 207
Passingham, R. E., 147, 148, 149, 152, 162, 209, 232
Pate, J. L., 150, 151, 163, 432, 437, 439, 444
Patterson, F. G., 236, 238, 239, 241, 249, 250, 254
Payer-Rigo, P., 196, 207
Pearson, E., 171, 187
Peck, C. A., 482, 507
Pemberton, E. F., 406, 418, 419, 424, 427
Penner, S., 416, 427
Perdue, C., 56, 62
Perecman, E., 197, 207
Perkins, D. N., 421, 427

Perry, P., 171, 187
Peters, A., 43, 63
Peters, J., 468, 472, 477
Peters, M., 181, 182, 188
Petersen, M., 150, 162, 179, 188
Petitto, L. A., 115, 236, 238, 239, 241, 243, 249, 250, 254, 255, 369, 370, 392
Piaget, J., 27, 38, 63, 123, 139
Pieraut-Le Bonniec, G., 356, 359
Pinker, S., 30, 49, 52, 56, 57, 58, 63, 64, 67, 70, 78, 83, 84, 88, 90, 93, 114, 325, 337, 403, 427, 456, 461, 465, 466, 467, 468, 469, 470, 479
Pipp, S. L., 402, 425
Pisoni, D. B., 15, 25, 28, 196, 207
Plenge, T., 436, 444
Plunkett, K., 52, 64
Pogge-Hesse, P., 441, 443
Pohl, P., 150, 162
Poizner, H., 32, 64, 84, 88, 378, 380, 381, 383, 391, 392
Preilowski, B., 171, 175, 188
Premack, D., 210, 232, 238, 239, 254, 481, 508
Pribram, K., 117, 126, 138
Prince, A., 49, 52, 56, 57, 58, 64
Prinz, E. A., 409, 427
Prinz, P. M., 409, 427
Prizant, B., 482, 483, 508
Provine, R. R., 267, 271, 285
Prutting, C., 483, 500, 508
Putnam, H., 91, 98, 100, 102, 104, 114
Pylyshyn, Z., 58, 61, 124, 139
Pyne, L., 175, 186

Q

Quine, W. V. O., 99, 100, 114

R

Ramer, A. L. H., 112
Ramsay, D. S., 41, 61, 356, 361, 362
Raqib, A., 129, 136
Rauzin, R., 279, 285
Reddy, M. J., 263, 285
Reichenbach, H., 75, 88
Reilly, J., 378, 392
Remez, R. E., 340, 360
Rescorla, L. A., 92, 95, 100, 114, 134, 139, 305, 320, 448, 450, 479

Reumann, R., 437, 444
Revelle, G. L., 473, 479
Reznick, S., 42, 61, 64
Rice, M. L., 406, 427, 448, 450, 452, 453, 454, 455, 457, 459, 460, 462, 464, 468, 470, 472, 474, 476, 477, 478, 479, 480
Richards, D. G., 211, 232
Richardson, S. O., 482, 507
Richardson, W. K., 157, 163
Richman, N., 448, 479
Riesen, A. H., 147, 154, 162, 163
Rimpau, J. B., 236, 254
Risley, T. R., 279, 285, 504, 506
Rispoli, M.,313, 320
Roberts, K., 48, 64, 309, 320
Roeper, T., 11, 27, 30, 64, 311, 320, 332, 337
Rogers, C. M., 153, 154, 160, 162
Rogers-Warren, A., 432, 445, 482, 506, 508
Roitblatt, H. L., 212, 232
Romski, M. A., 409, 427, 430, 431, 432, 433, 434, 435, 436, 437, 438, 449, 441, 442, 444, 445
Rosch, E., 58, 64
Rosenberg, S., 429, 444
Rosenzweig, M. R., 154, 160, 162
Ross, C., 21, 27
Ross, R., 451, 458, 480
Roth, M., 404, 428
Roth, P., 133, 139
Rothbart, M., 129, 139
Rovee-Collier, C., 123, 135, 139
Rowan, L., 450, 478
Rowell, T. E., 180, 187
Rowland, C. M., 483, 489, 490, 506
Rubert, E., 155, 163, 211, 232, 233, 237, 239, 240, 254, 255, 439, 444
Rubin, P., 340, 360
Ruder, K. F., 431, 444, 481, 508
Rueping, R. R., 152, 161
Ruff, C. B., 175, 178, 188
Ruff, H., 123, 139
Rumbaugh, D. M., 48, 64, 146, 150, 151, 153, 155, 157, 160, 161, 162, 163, 171, 174, 187, 210, 211, 213, 232, 233, 237, 238, 239, 254, 255
Rumelhart, D. E., 36, 50, 52, 63, 64, 402, 404, 426, 427
Runfeldt, S., 150, 160
Ryan, B., 481, 506
Ryan, J., 37, 64

S

Sabbadini, L., 451, 478
Sabo, H., 385, 391
Sachs, J., 306, 307, 320
Sack, S., 482, 483, 507, 508
Sackett, G., 129, 139
Sacks, O., 405, 427
Sagart, L., 357, 359
Sailor, W., 481, 506
Salapatek, P., 190, 207
Salomon, G., 421, 427
Saltzman, E. L., 342, 355, 360, 362
Sampson, G., 98, 100, 101, 102, 103, 104,
    115
Sanders, R. J., 236, 238, 239, 241, 243,
    249, 250, 254
Sanford, C. G., 169, 188
Sarich, V. M., 235, 255
Savage-Rumbaugh, E. S., 48, 64, 146, 150,
    155, 156, 157, 161, 163, 210, 211, 212,
    215, 232, 233, 235, 237, 239, 240, 241,
    242, 243, 244, 246, 247, 250, 253, 254,
    255, 267, 285, 431, 439, 444
Scarr-Salapatek, S., 152, 163
Schachter, P., 72, 73, 88
Schaller, G. B., 177, 188
Scherer, N. J., 415, 427
Schiefelbusch, R. L., 430, 444, 448, 479,
    481, 507
Schiltz, K. A., 153, 161
Schlesinger, I. M., 37, 64, 67, 78, 80, 88,
    241, 255
Schmeekle, M. M., 182, 186
Schmidt, A., 379, 392
Schneiderman, M., 416, 425
Schoner, G., 341, 343, 356, 362
Schuler, A. L., 482, 506, 507
Schusterman, R. L., 211, 233
Schwartz, S. P., 91, 115
Searle, J. R., 119, 120, 139, 482, 485, 508
Searleman, A., 182, 183, 188
Seckel, H. P. G., 209, 233
Segalowitz, S. J., 149, 164
Seibert, J. M., 482, 483, 508
Seidenberg, M. S., 115, 236, 238, 239, 243,
    254
Seitz, D. J., 177, 186
Sejnowski, T. J., 36, 50, 61
Selfridge, O. G., 58, 64
Sell, M. A., 459, 479
Service, V., 293, 294, 300

Sevcik, R. A., 155, 163, 211, 215, 232, 233,
    237, 239, 240, 254, 255, 409, 427, 430,
    431, 432, 433, 435, 436, 437, 438, 439,
    441, 442, 444, 445
Seyfarth, R. M., 153, 160, 163, 271, 285
Shafer, D., 171, 174, 176, 188
Shallice, T., 56, 64
Shankweiler, D., 189m 191, 206, 207
Shannon, B., 98, 104, 115
Shattuck-Hufnagel, S., 23, 27
Shatz, M., 407, 428
Sheehan, J., 429, 445
Shiffrin, R. M.,404, 427
Shimoff, E., 275, 276, 279, 284, 285
Shin, Y., 172, 187
Shlesinger, M. F., 341, 360
Shore, C., 39, 40, 41, 42, 44, 45, 59, 60,
    64, 501, 505
Shriberg, L., 451, 479
Sibley, C. G., 209, 233
Sidman, M., 279, 281, 285, 441, 445
Sigelman, C., 429, 443
Silva, P. A., 182, 186, 448, 479
Simmons, H., 21, 28
Simon, T., 351, 360
Simpson, G. G., 270, 285
Sinclair, H., 37, 64, 326, 337
Singh, I., 175, 186
Siqueland, E. R., 15, 25, 191, 206
Sithole, N. W., 17, 25
Skeen, L. C., 150, 162
Skinner, B. F., 214, 233, 266, 269, 276,
    283, 285
Sledge, P., 356, 359
Sloane, H. N., 481, 508
Slobin, D. I., 37, 64, 111, 115, 251, 255,
    307, 308, 320, 408, 428, 470, 479, 482,
    508
Smiley, P., 52, 62, 113
Smith, J., 37, 62, 92, 113
Smith, L., 500, 508
Smith, M. D., 431, 444, 481, 508
Smolensky, P., 36, 50, 64
Snell, M., 429, 445
Snow, C., 332, 337
Snyder, L., 37, 38, 39, 40, 42, 43, 45, 46,
    59, 60, 64, 65, 299, 399, 405, 408, 416,
    424, 425, 447, 479
Snyder-McLean, L., 482, 483, 389, 490,
    491, 493, 494, 495, 499, 503, 507, 508
Soderbergh, R., 400, 406, 428
Solomonson, B., 482, 508

Somervill, S., 119, 140
Sonnenberg, E. A., 473, 477
Speidel, G. E., 407, 428
Spelke, E. S., 302, 305, 320, 353, 362
Spieker, S., 353, 361
Spradlin, J. E., 482, 506
Stafford, D. K., 170, 186, 188
Stanowicz, L., 417, 425
Stark, J., 438, 443
Stark, R. E., 18, 19, 27
Stebbins, W., 150, 162, 179, 188
Steenhuis, R. E., 184, 186
Stein, N., 129, 139
Steklis, H. D., 29, 62
Stell, M., 154, 163
Stemberger, J., 56, 65
Stephan, H., 151, 163
Stern, D. N., 19, 27, 353, 361
Sternberg, R. J., 402, 428
Stevensen-Hinde, J., 153, 161
Stevenson, J., 448, 479
Stevenson, M., 301, 319
St. Louis, K. W., 483, 507
Stoel-Gammon, C., 21, 27
Straight, S., 316, 320
Strauss, M. S., 306, 319
Streeter, L. A., 191, 207
Stremel, K., 481, 508
Struhsaker, T. T., 153, 163
Struxness, L., 370, 378, 392
Studdert-Kennedy, D., 191, 207
Studdert-Kennedy, M. G., 15, 23, 24, 26,
  27, 162, 166, 174, 177, 187, 188, 189,
  191, 206, 207, 353, 356, 357, 361, 362,
  363, 391, 407, 426
Subramoniam, S., 170, 188
Sugarman, S., 41, 65, 132, 139
Sugarman-Bell, S., 485, 503, 508
Sullivan, J. W., 352, 362
Sullivan, M., 123, 135, 139
Suomi, S. J., 153, 161, 163
Supalla, T., 369, 392

T

Tabors, P. O., 464, 479
Tager-Flusberg, H., 326, 337
Tallal, P., 410, 428, 451, 458, 480
Taraban, R., 52, 63
Taylor, C., 126, 139
Taylor, M., 95, 115
Tees, R. C., 17, 28

Terrace, H. S., 210, 233, 236, 238, 239,
  241, 243, 249, 250, 255
Terselic-Weber, B., 451, 479
Thagard, P. R., 58, 62
Thal, D., 39, 42, 43, 44, 60, 65
Thelen, E., 20, 27, 342, 344, 345, 356, 358,
  360, 362
Thompson, D. W., 8, 27, 34, 65
Thompson, T., 280, 285
Tokuda, K., 172, 187, 188
Tomasello, M., 118, 133, 139, 210, 233
Tomblin, J. B., 458, 480
Trauner, D., 384, 390
Trehub, S., 149, 164
Treiman, R., 416, 425
Trevarthen, C., 19, 27, 413, 428
Truswell, L., 306, 307, 320
Tueting, P., 189, 206
Tuller, B., 340, 342, 360
Turkewitz, G., 149, 163
Turner, A., 184, 185
Turvey, M. T., 340, 341, 360
Tuttle, R. H., 213, 233
Tzeng, O. J.L., 374, 376, 379, 391, 393

U

Ulrich, B. D., 358, 362

V

Vaid, J., 356, 359, 385, 391
Vainikka, A., 332, 337
Van Cantfort, T. E., 238, 255
Vander Linde, E., 123, 139
Van der Stelt, J. M., 19, 26, 348, 349, 350,
  360
van Hoek, K., 367, 373, 374, 376, 377, 378,
  391, 392, 393
Vannier, M. W., 149, 161
Van Valin, R., 37, 46, 61
Vatikiotis-Bateson, E., 340, 355, 360
Vauclair, J., 171, 172, 173, 176, 186
Vermeire, B. A., 150, 161
Vigorito, J., 15, 25, 191, 206
Vihman, M., 21, 22, 27, 28
Visalberghi, E., 47, 65
Volterra, V., 35, 36, 37, 39, 41, 42, 45, 52,
  59, 60, 65, 92, 112, 125, 132, 136, 299,
  451, 478, 482, 487, 490, 491, 499, 500,
  503, 505
von Glasersfeld, E. C., 238, 254

Von Tetzchner, S., 500, 508
von Uexkull, J., 294, 300
Vygotsky, L. S., 104, 115, 134, 140, 277, 285, 290, 292, 300

W

Wada, J., 149, 163
Waddington, C. H., 12, 13, 28
Wales, R., 283, 285
Walker, A. C., 167, 188
Wallace, M., 170, 188
Wallen, K., 171, 172, 186
Walley, A. C., 15, 28
Wanner, E., 15, 25
Ward, J. P., 169, 170, 186, 187, 188
Wardhaugh, R., 213, 233
Warren, J. M., 149, 150, 163, 171, 175, 188
Warren, S. F., 432, 445, 482, 505, 508
Waryas, C., 481, 508
Washburn, D. A., 150, 151, 157, 161, 163, 171, 174, 187
Watanabe, K., 171, 172, 188
Waters, R. S., 199, 207
Watkins, R., 418, 427, 435, 445, 457, 472, 480
Watson, R., 108, 115
Waxman, S. R., 95, 115
Weikart, D. P., 462, 477
Weinberg, A., 30, 60
Weiner, P., 451, 458, 468, 480
Weiskrantz, L., 150, 161, 233
Wellman, H., 119, 140
Wellman, H. M., 473, 479
Weninger, J. M., 279, 283
Werker, J. F., 17, 28
Werner, H., 41, 45, 65, 134, 140
Wertsch, J. V., 104, 115
Wetherby, A., 483, 500, 508
Wetstone, H., 309, 320
Wetzel, W. F., 200, 201, 207

Wexler, K., 8, 11, 25, 29, 30, 45, 49, 60, 65, 93, 115, 325, 337, 403, 405, 428
Whitesell, K., 39, 60
Wieman, L. A., 21, 27
Wilcox, K., 459, 460, 462, 474, 479
Wilkinson, K., 434, 445
Williams, E., 27, 30, 64, 311, 320
Williams, M., 171, 187
Williamson, C., 39, 60
Willis, M. P., 356, 362
Wilson, A., 33, 62
Wilson, M., 199, 207
Wilson, W., 191, 206
Wilson, W. A., Jr., 199, 207
Witelson, S. F., 147, 149, 164
Wittgenstein, L., 269, 285
Wolf, D., 44, 65
Wolff, P. H., 344, 362
Wolz, J. P., 211, 232
Woodsmall, L., 452, 453, 454, 455, 479
Wootten, J., 472, 480
Wroblewski, R., 418, 419, 427
Wulfeck, B., 56, 60

Y

Yeni-Komshian, G. H., 149, 164, 205, 207
Yoder, D. E., 481, 482, 507
Young, G., 149, 164
Younger, B., 41, 61

Z

Zetterstrom, R., 19, 26
Zigler, E., 432, 445
Zihlman, A. L., 235, 255
Zipser, D., 58, 61
Zivin, G., 277, 285
Zoloth, S., 150, 162, 179, 188
Zurif, E., 196, 207

Subject Index

A

AAMD classification system, use of and severe mental retardation, 484, 488, 494

Actions and objects relationship between, 243–244, 250

Adaptation, 11, 31, 33, 35, 46, 152, 158, 168, 343
for predation, 168

Adults, 14, 15, 192, 193, 194
acquisition of grammar, 322, 324–325
speech in, 355

Alphabetic script, 374–376

American Sign Language (ASL), 146, 239, 262, 366, 367, 369–373, 374, 376, 378, 379, 381, 382, 388–389, 430
and Chinese Sign Language (CSL), differences between, 367–368
spatially organized syntax, 365–367
structure of, 363–368
universals of signed languages, 367–368

Analytic-holistic distinction, 43–45
Analytic/holistic learning strategies, 42–45
Analytic-holistic mechanisms, 45
Analytic vs. holistic children, 43–45
Apes, 153, 154, 155–157, 159, 170–173
and humans, differences between, 110
imitation and grammatical development, 235–251
learning language in, 155–157, 210–212

and protogrammar, 235–252
Articulation, 354, 358, 364, 407, 451
Assessment of Children's Language Comprehension (ACLC), 438
Associative learning, 125
great apes vs. rhesus monkeys, 151
Asymmetrical posture, 168
Asymmetries, *see also Handedness* 149–152, 171, 205
Attractors, 342–343, 348, 349
Auditory association cortex, 148
Auditory discrimination tasks, 175
Autistic children, 38, 46, 500

B

Babbling, *see also Canonical Babbling* 18, 19, 20, 21, 22, 43
Baboons, 172
Behavior
contingency-shaped vs. rule-governed, 275–277
and discriminations, 282–283
in humans, 275–276, 277, 278, 280
intraspecific vs. interspecific social behavior, 266–267
and learning, 265–266
rule-governed, 275–279, 281
Bilateral effects, 195, 196
Birds, 152
Brain, 190

damage of, 38, 56
learning and transfer, 147–149
lesions in, 179, 262, 380–383
maturational levels of, in various
    primates, 152
prefrontal lobe elaboration, 151
size and development in primates,
    147–149
stimulus and brain activity, 189
Brain hemispheres, 149, 191, 192, 193,
    196–197, 198, 200, 201, 202, 203,
    204, 262, 389
coordination, 356
left-damaged vs. right-damaged patients,
    178, 196–197
Brain hemisphere specialization, 175, 177,
    178, 181, 182, 183, 184, 352, 356,
    357
and auditory function in monkeys,
    178–179
handedness, preference for, 173
Brain lateralization
nonhuman primate patterns, changes in,
    189–206
Bush babies (Galago senegalensis), 150, 151,
    168, 169

C

Canalization, 13
Canonical babble, 18, 19, 20, 21,22
phonetic transcription, 19
stage of, 346, 349, 357
Categorical discrimination, 193
Categorical perception, 191, 194, 197
Central nervous system, 340
Cerebral hemispheric specialization, see
    Brain Hemispheres
Cerebral lateralization, 147, 150
Children, 9, 10, 11, 12, 13, 14, 37, 40, 67,
    86, 136, 192, 193, 194
analytic vs. holistic, 43–45
and articulation, 357
autistic, 38, 46, 500
and events, 105–107
and form-class errors, 71
and imitation, 47
language acquisition in, 259–262
and language comprehension, 301–319
lexical terms, acquisition of, 89–97
mentally retarded, 395, 396, 397, 429–430
mentally retarded (severe), 481–505

and nonactional verbs, avoidance of, 79
and organizational principles, 302
and perception of objects, 127, 295–297
problems with word meaning, 92
with specific language impairment,
    447–476
and taxonomic relations, 106
and verb-defining properties, 82
Children and perception of the world
whole vs. parts relations, 297–298, 299
Children vs. chimpanzees
in learning grammar, 238
Chimpanzees, 48, 141, 142, 143, 145,
    146–147, 148, 149, 151, 152, 153,
    154, 155–157, 158, 159, 209–231
bonobo or pygmy chimpanzees (Pan pa-
    niscus), 141, 142, 143, 146, 149, 155,
    156, 209–231, 230, 439
common chimpanzees (Pan troglodytes),
    47, 141, 149, 230, 235, 247, 248, 249,
    439
and computer game tasks, 157, 175
and gesture-after-lexigram rule, 245–247
and use of gestures, 239, 245, 246, 248,
    251
and imitation, 47
language learning in, 209–231
and learning routines, 214–231
lexigram symbols, acquisition of, 146,
    155–157, 211, 212, 215, 217, 218,
    219–231
and markers in learning routines, 216,
    217–231
pygmy or bonobo chimpanzees (Pan pa-
    niscus), 47, 235, 236–252
sounds and symbols, understanding of,
    212
Chinese Sign Language (CSL), 367–368,
    369, 374, 375, 377, 378
Classification, 87
Climbing, 154
Cognitive development, 8, 36, 38, 118, 146,
    158
Cognitive grammar, 37
Cognitivist perspective, 118
in child language, 118
on representation and expression, 117
Communication, 264, 265
development stages of, 299
skills and maturational factors, 152–155
Communication coding schemes (CCS),
    433, 434, 435

Communicative assessment protocols, 488
Competence-performance distinction, 6, 7
Comprehension, 372, 380, 409, 432, 452,
    453, 455
  in children, 40–42
  of early language, 260
  and language production, 40–42
  skills in, 396, 434–436, 437, 438, 439–440,
    441
Comprehension of language, see Language
    comprehension
Computer-based symbol system, 396
Computers
  and learning, 432, 433
  of early language, 260
  and language production, 40–42
  skills in, 396, 434–436, 437, 438, 439–440,
    441
Comprehension of language, see Language
    comprehension
Computer-based symbol system, 396
Computers
  and learning, 432, 433
  studies with chimpanzees, 157, 175
  and teaching, 409, 410, 422, 430
Concrete object references, 84, 85
Conduit metaphors, 263, 264
Consciousness, 117, 118, 121, 122, 124,
    125, 135
  representations in, 119
Consonant-vowel-consonant (CVC), 20
Consonant-vowel (CV), 20
Contingency-shaped behavior, 275–277
Continuity, 35–59
  continuous mechanisms, 36–45
  continuous motives, 45–48
  continuous representations, 48–59
  three parts of, 35–59
Continuity vs. discontinuity, 59
Continuous mechanisms, 36–45, 47, 48
Continuous motives, 36, 45–48, 48
Continuous representations, 36, 48–59
  competition, substitution, and blends,
    55–57
  connectivism, 36
  discontinuity, 48, 49
  learnability vs. nonlearnability of gram-
    mar, 49–50
  modularization, 57–59
  neural modeling, 36
  overgeneralization vs. underspecification,
    54

parallel distributed processing, 36
four solutions to discontinuity problem,
    51
submappings, 54–55
Undergeneralization vs. overspecification,
    52–54
Conversational circumstances and language
    advances, 414–421
Coordinated action
  dynamical systems interpretation, 341–344
Coordination, 340–341
Corpus callosum, 183, 184, 356
Cross-linguistic patterns, 69–70, 81
Cues, 121, 122, 123, 124, 125, 126, 134,
    135, 142, 189, 196, 197, 198, 212,
    260, 309, 311, 317, 357, 439, 454,
    455
  specific language-related, 191

D

Darwin and language development, 29–59
  continuous mechanisms, 36–45
  continuous motives in, 45–48
  continuous representations, 48–59
Deaf individuals, 20–21, 262, 356, 367–383
  children and grammar, 371, 372
  children and verb agreement, 371
  dissociation between language and spatial
    cognition in, 379–383
Development
  category formation, 353
  environment, effects of, 153
  mechanisms, 11
  sensorimotor stages, 152
Dialects, 274
Dichotic identification task, 196
Differentiation, 399, 417, 418, 419–421
Discontinuity problem
  four solutions for, 51
Discourse, 372–373
Discrimination, 193, 198, 352, 358
  auditory discrimination tasks, 175
  of behavior, 266
  and categorical perception, 191, 194, 197
  and learning, 158
  in nonhuman primates, 187–204
  of speech
Dolphins, 211
Domain-speciicity, 35, 45
Domain-specific mechanisms and content
  distinction between, 39

Dual function, definition of, 32
Dynamic process development, 344–345
Dynamic systems, 261, 342

E

Electroencephalogram, 189–190
Electrophysiological procedures, 189–191, 197
  and electroencephalogram (EEG), 189–190
  and event-related potential (ERP), 189–191
Elicited production and language acquisition, 321–336
  experimental research in children, 326–336
  long-distance Wh-movement, 330–334, 336
  structure dependence, 326–328
  wanna contraction, 328–330
  without experience, 322–326
Emotions, see also Expression of Emotion 268, 269
English as a second language (ESL) children, 463–464, 474–475
Enriched environments and learning, 154, 158, 159
Environment, 7, 8, 11, 12, 24, 141, 159, 178, 190, 345, 349, 351, 355, 400, 432, 440
  and development, 153
  effects of, 11, 24
  and learning grammar, 239–240
  neurological development, effects on, 147
  selective stimulation vs. sensory deprivation, 147
Equivalence classes, 279–282
Event category, 106
Event-related potential (ERP), 189–191, 192, 193, 197, 200, 203, 204, 206
  and brain hemisphere differences, 191
  rhesus monkeys, studies with, 200–204
  strengths, 190–191
Event representations in lexical development, 105–108
Events, 268, 316
Evolution, 110, 146, 177, 179, 184, 205, 213, 235, 259, 270, 274, 279
  and hemisphere specialization, 173
  of language, 277
  and language acquisition, 5–25, 31

  of speech, 179–180
Evolutionary theory, concepts of, 31–36
  dual function, 32
  functional branch points, 34–36
  heterochrony, 33–34
  limited recapitulation, 32
  preadaption, 31–32
Expansion stage, 346, 348, 349
Expression of emotion, 128, 129, 130, 132, 134
  and interpretation, 119
Expression and representation, see Representation and Expression

F

Fine-motor control factor, 45
Food, acquisition of, 167, 168, 169, 170, 174
Footedness, studies of, 166, 181–185
  and handedness, effects of, 181–184
Foraging, 170, 178
Form-class acquisition, 82
Frogs and tadpoles, 32–33
Fruit fly (Drosophila melanogaster), 11, 12
Functional branch points
  and domain-specificity, 35
  and genetic factors, 34
Functional grammar, 37

G

General analytic mechanisms, 84
Genetics, 34, 146
  effects of, 11, 12, 24
  and language acquisition, 6, 8, 13, 33
  mechanisms, 34
Gesture-after-lexigram rule, 245–247, 251
Gestures, 23, 42, 45, 46, 132, 178, 180, 239, 245, 246, 248, 251, 271, 292, 299, 340, 352, 358, 370, 371, 397, 437, 483, 486–487, 489, 495, 500, 501, 502, 503, 504
  auditory-vocal or visual manual, 125
  and chimpanzees, 216, 217, 218, 220, 230, 231, 245, 247
  in reptiles and lizards, 180
Gibbons, 173, 177
Gorillas, 148, 149, 151, 154, 173, 176, 177
Grammar, 1, 6, 29, 31, 32, 38, 39, 46, 47, 50, 57, 71, 72, 133, 143, 261, 324, 326

acquisition of, 50, 317, 318, 321–336
action-object relationships, 243–244
categories of, 108, 109
and deaf children, 371, 372
functional vs. cognitive grammar, 37
markers in, 365
rules of, 238, 322
Grammatical development and imitation
in apes, 235–251
Grasping, 154
Great apes, (Pongidae), 145, 148, 149, 173
handedness, preference for, 176–177
Growth recasts, 414–421
and normal vs. language-impaired children, 414–416

H

Handedness, 356
age, effects of, 170
and language lateralization, 183, 184
left-hand and right ear advantage, 183
left-hand preferences, 173
reaching for food, 169
right-handed preferences, 174, 174–178, 181
Handedness, preference for, 165, 166, 169–185
and footedness, 166, 181–185
in great apes, 176–177
in monkeys, 174–176
in primates, 150
right-handedness, evolution of, 177–178
right vs. left, studies of, 169–178
and visuospatial conditions, 172
Hedgehogs, 150, 151
Heterochrony, 33–34
definition of, 33
genetics and evolution, 33–34
Hominids, 271
Homo sapiens, 141, 146, 205, 209, 357
Humans, 177, 178, 191, 194, 197

I

Imitation, 46–48, 406, 415, 417
Imitation and grammatical development
chimpanzees, studies with, 235–252, 241–252
environment, effects of, 239–240
Individual selection, principle of, 6
Infants, 128, 192, 194, 345

and achieving independence, 290
and articulation, 354, 355, 356
early vocalizing, 17–21
and events and objects, 119
grammatical system, emergence of, 287
and imitation, 47
and language comprehension, 301–318
language development in, 14–25, 292–298
memory skills in, 135, 288–290
perception of constituent structure, 306–308
and perception of the world, 260, 298
phonation and articulation in, 348, 349
recognizing phonetic vs. acoustic invariants, 16
recognizing vowels, 16
sensitivity to linguistic environment, 349–352
sensitivity to vocal environment, 353
and social constructivism, 290–292
speech development stages, 350
speech perception, 16, 17
and visual components of speech, 353
and vocal behavior, 348
Innatism, 11, 12, 15, 30, 90, 149, 212, 213, 235, 261, 325, 335, 336, 351, 383
innate knowledge theories, 97–104
Instructed language learning
extant skills, 436–439
extant vs. instructed skills, 436
instructed skills, 439–441
patterns of, 436–441
Instruction, 431
Intentional communicative acts (ICAs), 489, 490–491, 492, 493, 496–497, 500, 501, 502
proto-imperatives and proto-declaratives, 490–493, 496, 500
Intermodal equivalencies, 352, 354
Intermodal perception, 302
Internal psychological circumstances
and language advances, 413–414
Interpretation and expression, 121, 127, 132

L

Language
and behavior, relationship between, 271
definition of, 5, 263
evolution of, 32
functions of, 263–283
structural theories of, 212–213

structure and function, 267–268
teachability of, 448–449
Language, acquisition of
in apes, 155–157, 210–212
in bonobo chimpanzees, 209–231
in children, 259–262
and children with specific language impairment, 447–476
comprehension vs. production, 40–42
and computer-based symbol system, 396
consonant and vowel class formation,
23–24, 25
and deaf infants, 20–21, 367–383
and early motor development, 339–359
first language, 93, 400, 406, 409, 429
form and function, zoologists vs. Darwin's views, 7
genetics vs. environment, 7, 8, 11, 12, 13,
24
and language-specific determinants, 369
man vs. chimpanzees, 212, 212–213
in mentally retarded individuals, 38, 395,
306, 397, 429–442, 481–505
modern study of, 6
nouns vs. verbs, 67–87, 302, 311–315,
318
problem of, 323, 325
second language, 56, 339, 400
and sign language, 409–410
variation in, 6, 11–14, 44–45
without experience, 322–336
Language acquisition and elicited production, see Elicited Production
Language acquisition device (LAD), 321,
322, 325
Language acquisition impairments, 429
Language Acquisition Preschool (LAP),
397, 460, 462, 463, 464, 465, 467,
473, 474, 475
Language and spatial cognitive dissociation
and Williams Syndrome, 383–388, 389
Language comprehension, 301–319
and word order, 308–311
in children and infants, 301–319, 326–336
preferential looking paradigm, 302–306
subcategorization frames and children,
311–315
Language development
concepts and event knowledge, acquisition of, 118
concepts of, 89–111
lexical development, 90–97, 104–111

meaning acquisition theories,
97–104
cultures, effect of, 287
Darwin's approach to, 29–59
dissociative patterns in, 43–44
and evolution, 5–25
Modern Evolutionary Theory, 1
predators and alarm calls, 152–153
social construction of, 292–298
and social interaction, 287–299
speech motor skills, development of,
339–359
theory of, 119
Language-impaired children, see also
Specific-Language Impaired Children
418, 421
and growth recasts, 414–415
Language learning difficulty
and auditory/vocal modality, 430–431
Language-learning models, 395, 399–424
conversational circumstances, 414–421
input and processing deficits, 408–411
and internal psychological circumstances,
413–414
rare-event learning mechanism (RELM),
400–408
Language learning task, 442
Language metaphors, 263–265
Language origins, 270–275, 357
and leaders, 272, 273, 274
and predation, 271
and verbal behavior, 272
vocal vs. verbal behavior, 273–275
vocal vs. verbal control, 272
Language Research Center, 431, 433
Language-specific determinants, 369
Language-specific patterns, 357
Language-specific vs. more general mechanisms, 84
Lateralization, 191, 193, 204, 205
Lateral specialization, 182
Learnability-theoretic research, 133
Lemurs, 170
black lemurs (Lemur macaco), 170
ring-tailed lemurs (Lemur catta), 169
Lesions, 162, 179
and language acquisition, effects on,
380–383
Lexical categories, 108, 109
Lexical contrast, theory of, 101
Lexical development
cognitive constructive view, 97

constraints on,93, 98, 99, 100, 101, 102, 103–104
definition of, 90
event schemas and infants, 105–107
event and slot-filler categories, 106, 107, 108
and nativism, 98–99
three distinct periods of, 2, 91–97
problems with, 97
revision, reorganization, and consolidation of terms, 96–97
social-cognitive perspective, 104–110
social determinism, 104
and specific language impairment (SLI) children, 451–456
Lexical items, 10, 24, 307, 315, 316, 318, 325, 372, 454, 464
Lexical terms, acquisition of
in children, 89–97
conceptual and semantic development, 91, 98
Lexicon, 22, 23, 24, 89–97, 110, 111, 239, 454, 464, 465, 472, 476
development of, 2, 9
rule for combining of, 248
Lexigram plus gesture combinations, 255–258
Lexigrams, 143, 146, 211, 212, 408, 409, 432
learning of in chimpanzees, 155–157, 215, 216, 217–231, 235–252
Limited Recapitulation
frogs and tadpoles, 32–33
ontogeny and phylogeny, 32–33
Linguistic and spatial development, see Spatial and Linguistic Development
Lizards, 180
Local homology model, 39
Long-distnace Wh-movement, 330–334

M

Marmosets (Callithrix jacchus), 172
Maturational factors
and communicative skills, 152–155
environmental enrichment, 154
and environment factors, 153–154
sensitive phase, 152–153
Mean length of utterance (MLU), 450, 451, 453, 455, 472

Memory, 45, 118, 119, 120, 125, 126, 127, 288–290, 400, 403, 404, 411, 412, 414, 421, 431, 454
object vs. action concepts, 68
and perception, 125
retention of objects and events in, 123
retrieval of information from, 120–121
storing information in, 127
Memory skills
adult-infant relationships, 288–289
social interaction, effects on, 288–290
subcultural variations, 288–289
Mentally retarded individuals
instructed language learning, patterns of, 436–441
insrruction via other modalities, 430–436
language acquisition in, 429–442
and technology-augmented progress in communication, 408–409
Mental retardation, 384–385
Mental retardation (severe), 481–505
AAMD classification system, use of, 484, 488, 494
and intentional communicative acts (ICAs), 489, 490–491, 492, 493, 496–497, 500, 501, 502
prelinguistic development period, stages of, 482–483, 485–487, 488, 489, 491, 494–495, 497–499
studies in communication of, 487–501
treatment programs for, 482–483
Mental spaces, 121, 122–126, 128, 132, 133, 135
Mind and language, contents of, 120–122
Modularization, 57–59
Monkeys, 170–173, 178, 179
and computer game tasks, 175
handedness, preference for, 174–176
macaques, 154, 175, 180, 280
Japanese macaques (Macaca fuscata), 170, 172, 179
stumptail macaques (Macaca speciosa), 172
Old World monkeys, 148
rhesus monkeys (Macaca mulatta), 142, 149, 150, 151, 152, 153, 157, 172, 174–175, 180, 199, 200–204, 205
squirrel monkeys (Saimiri sciureus), 172
vervet monkeys, 153
Motor behavior, development of, 261
Mutation, 33

N

Nativism, 51, 98
  dependency and adjacency, 37
  general vs. specific, 36–37
Natural selection, 7, 29, 31, 32, 37
Negative evidence, 325, 467–468
Neocortex, 148
Notation system
  for representations, 124–125
Nouns, acquisition of, 2, 67–87
  in children, 68, 77
  semantic vs. structural factors, 69
Nouns and small-scale structural properties
  problems with pronouns and proper
    names, 73–74

O

Object-action relationships, 243–244
Object classes, 92
Object-oriented communication, 45–46
Object permanence, 118
Object references, 82
Ontogeny, 7, 9, 10, 30, 31, 50, 104, 147,
    259, 344, 345
  and Postural Origins Theory, 185
Ontogeny and phylogeny of language func-
    tion, see Phylogeny and Ontogeny
Orangutans, 151, 153, 154, 157
Overgeneralizations, 67, 72, 73, 467
Overgeneralization vs. underspecification,
    54
Overspecification, 52–54, 54
Overspecification vs. undergeneralization,
    52–54

P

Partially dissociable memory devices, 45–46,
    47
Peabody Picture Vocabulary Test (PPVT),
    438, 453, 455, 465
Perception, 14–17, 47, 135
Perception-production match in infants, 353
Perceptuomotor development, 8
Perceptuomotor systems, 343
Phase shifts, 343, 344, 346–352, 355
Phenotypic variations, 12, 14
Phonation stage, 9, 346
Phoneme identification task, 192–193
Phonetic segments, 9, 14–25

Phylogenic problems
  and expression of emotion, 268–270
  learnability problem, 50
  private events, 269–270
  vocal language, 270
Phylogeny, 7, 9, 10, 30, 31, 50
Phylogeny and ontogeny of language func-
    tion, 263–283
  contingency-shaped vs. rule-governed be-
    havior, 275–277
  and discrimination of behavior, 282–283
  equivalence classes, 279–282
  language metaphor, 263–265
  language origins, 270–275
  phylogenic problems, 268–270
  primary function of language, 265–267
  rule-governed behavior, ontogeny of,
    277–279
  structure and function, 267–268
Pigeons, 275
Pitch, 351, 353, 355
Positive evidence, 467–468, 473
Postural differences, 172
Postural Origins Theory, 165–185
Posture, 169
  definition of, 166
  human asymmetry patterns, 181–184
  and primate origins, 166–167
  and sitting, 180
Preadaption, 31–32
Predation, 152, 167, 168, 173, 177, 185,
    269, 270, 271
  adaptation for, 168
  and alarm calls, 153
  and prey, relationship between, 266
Predicate-argument analysis, 74–76, 80–81,
    82
Preferential looking paradigm, 260, 309,
    315, 317
  studies in intermodal perception, 302–306
  visual fixation and latency, 303–305
Primary linguistic data (PLD), 321, 322,
    323
Primates, 165–185
  apes and learning language, 155–158
  asymmetries, 149–152
  behavioral and cognitive differences in,
    149
  biological relationship of man and ape,
    209–210
  brain comparisons, 147–149
  cerebral hemispheric specialization, 142

development, rearing, and adult competencies, 158–160
evolution and postural adaptation, 167
and footedness, 181–185
human vs. nonhuman, 189, 209–210
language, acquisition of, 141–160
man vs. chimpanzees, 212
maturational factors in, 152–155
neurobiological asymmetries in, 165–185
nonhuman speech discrimination, 187–204
perception of speech cues, 189–206
Primates, comparative perspectives of brain, cognition, and language, 145–160
Process-oriented theories of language behavior, 214
reinforcement, 214
Production constraints and supports, 407
Pronominal reference in spatial language, 370–371
Prosimians, 173, 181
and handedness, 169–170
Protogrammar and apes, 235–252
Psychophysical studies, 16

Q

Quick incidental learning (QUIL), 452, 453, 454, 470

R

Rare-event learning mechanism (RELM), 395, 399, 400–410, 412, 414, 417, 419, 423
selective domain organizing supports, 407–408
selective elicitation, 407
selective engagement, 401–402
selective imitation strategies, 406–407
Selective Linking and Integrating Networks of Knowledge (LINK), 408
selective retrieval, 403–404
selective storage, 402–403
Reaching, 175
Reentry multimodal mapping, 352–353
Reflexive crying, 18
Reflexivity tests, 280
Reinforcement, 214, 281
Relational learning
great apes vs. rhesus monkeys, 151
Repetition, 352

and chimpanzees, 240, 241
Representation and expression, 117–136
cognitive development and child language, 118–120
contents of mind and language, 120–122
in development, 126–128
developments for constructing mental spaces, 122–126
and language development, 128–132
overextensions in word learning, 133–134
Representations, 50, 51, 52, 53, 54, 55, 59, 146, 262, 315, 377, 378, 401, 405, 410, 412
schemes, concepts, and events, 118
Reptiles, 180
and gestures, 180
Retardation, *see Mentally Retarded Individuals*
Routines
definition of, 215
experiments with chimpanzees, 214–231
and rules, 56
Rule-governed behavior, 275–279
and contingency-shaped behavior, 275–277
and ontogeny, 277–279

S

Second language acquisition, 56
Segmental phonology, 9
Segmentation, 18, 23, 53, 454
Selective domain organizing supports, 407–408
Selective elicitation, 407
Selective engagement, 401–402
Selective imitation and strategies, 406
Selective Linking and Integrating Networks of Knowledge (LINK), 408
Selective retrieval, 403–404
Selective storage, 395, 402–403
Semantic-based models, 83–84
Semantic Bootstrapping Hypothesis, 83
Semantic-structural analysis, 75
Semantic system, 96
Sensitive phase, 152–153
Sensorimotor stages, 38, 152
Signals, 145
Skill theory, 39
Slender lorises (Loris tardigradus), 170
Slot-filler categories, 106, 107, 108
Small-scale analysis, failures of,, 74

Snails, fresh water (Limnaea stagnalis, L. lacustris, L. bodamica), 12
Social interaction, 294, 298–299
Social skills, 152
Spatial and linguistic development, 363–389
American Sign Language (ASL), structure of, 363–368
language and spatial cognition
in deaf individuals, 379–383
in Williams Syndrome, 383–389
Spatially organized language
acquisition of, 368–373
pronominal reference in, 370–371
referential framework for syntax and discourse, 372–373
and spatialized verb agreement, 371
and spatial cognition, 377–379
and spatial script, 373–377
and syntax, 365–366
Spatial perception, 262
Spatial representations, 377, 378
Special education services, 409, 448, 484
Specialization, 149, 173, 181
Species, 13, 29, 30, 31, 95, 145, 148, 205, 210, 271
cross-species rearing project, 210
and evolution of language, 30
fixed vs. not fixed, 7
variations in, 11
Species-characteristic vocalizations, 152
Species-specific patterns, 152
Specificity hypothesis, 39
Specific language impairment (SLI), 396, 448
academic consequences, 458–459
causal factors, 456–458
definition of, 449–450
environment, effects of, 458
genetic basis for, 457–458
problems with morphology, 451
Specific language impairment (SLI) children, 447–476
and computer-assisted presentations, 410
and corrective feedback, use of, 463, 467
language development and cognitive/social skills, 462–464
language limitations of, 457, 475
language of, 450–451
and learning verbs, 465–473
and lexical development, 451–456
morphology and word learning problems, 464–465

nonverbal testing of, 456–457
positive vs. negative evidence teaching techniques, 467–468, 473
problems in language acquisition and morphology, 453–456, 460, 461, 464
problems with reading, 458–469
social adjustments and academic failures, 473–475
and social consequences, 459–460
Speech
and attractors, 342–343
early stages in, 17–25
evolution of, 179–180
and errors in, 56, 57
and nonspeech signals and sounds, 194, 196
perception of, 189–206
phase shifts in, 346–352
prespeech sounds, 261, 339–340
production of, 17–25, 341
Speech development
canonical stage, 346, 349, 357
expansion stage, 346, 348, 349
maturation and vocal motor system, 17
phonation stage, 346
Speech discrimination in nonhuman primates, 187–204
behavior indices, 199
and categorical perception for voicing, 199–204
Speech motor skills
and coordination, 340–341, 342
development of, 339–359
dynamical systems interpretation of coordination, 341–344
motor aspects of speech, 353–357
and reentry multimodal mapping, 352–353
speech to language, 357–359
transition from prespeech to speech, 346–352
Stimulus, 145, 189, 190
Structural descriptions, 402, 403, 404, 405, 411, 412, 414
Structural properties, 87
Structural theories of language, 212–213
chimpanzees vs. man, 212
innatism and language, 212–213
universal grammar (UG), 212–213
Structures, definition of, 267
Subcategorization frames
studies in children, 311–315

Subdomain-specific physiological supports, 407–408
Subjacency, 330, 333
Subject/Auxiliary inversion, 327
Submapping, 54–55
Superposition, 53, 54
Syllable discrimination, 15
Symbolic interactionalism, 292
Symbol learning task, 440
Symbols, 44, 49, 53, 56, 58, 143, 155, 210, 212, 267, 296, 396, 408, 409, 431, 432, 433, 434, 435, 436, 439, 440, 441, 442, 481, 502, 503, 504
 and chimpanzees, 155–157, 235, 236–252
 comprehension of, 440
 symbol manipulation tasks, 44
 and syntax, development of, 29–59
 use of in communication, 145
Symmetry, tests in, 279–280, 282
Syntactic and semantic development
 lexical vs. grammatical categories, 108, 109
 paradigmatic and syntagmatic relations, 108, 109
 parallels between, 108–110
Syntax, 372–373

T

Tagalog, acquisition of, 71–73, 82
Tarsiers, 168
Teaching techniques
 positive vs. negative evidence, 467–468, 473
Temporal patterns, 275
Test of Auditory Comprehension of Language (TACL), 438
Thermodynamic nonequilibrium, 341
Tone onset time (TOT), 194, 195,196
Transcription, 129
Transformational/Generative Grammar Theory, 322
Transformations, 265
Transitivity tests, 280, 282
Tree shrews, 150

U

Undergeneralization, 52–54
Undergeneralization vs. overspecification, 52–54
Underspecification, 54

Underspecification vs. overgeneralization, 54
Universal attractors, 343
Universal grammar (UG), 7, 11, 30, 33, 212–213, 261, 322–323, 324, 325, 328, 329, 330, 335, 336
 chimpanzees and man, 213
 domain specificity, 30
 poverty of stimulus, 30
 universality, 30

V

Variegated babbl, 18, 21
Vegetative sounds, 18
Verbal behavior, 275–279, 280, 282, 283
 verbal vs. vocal, 264–265
Verbal control, 275, 280, 282, 283
Verb-defining properties, 82
Verbs
 actional vs. nonactional, 86
 and small-scale structural properties, 70–71
 and specific language impairment (SLI) children, 465–473
 and tenses, 71
Verbs vs. nouns, acquisition of, 67–87
 concrete object reference, 76–77
 cross-linguistics patterns, 69–70
 development of nouns, 77–78
 form-class development theories, 82–83
 Predicate-augument analysis, 74–76, 80–81
 semantic-based models, 83–94
 small-scale structural properties and nouns, 73–74
 Within-language patterns, 70–73
Visual association cortex, 148
Visual cortex, development of, 154
Visual fixation
 studies in children, 308, 310–311, 313, 314
Visuospatial language, 379
Visuospatial modality, 368, 373
Visuospatial script, 376–377
Vocal behavior, development of, 358
Vocalization, early stages of, 353
Vocal motor apparatus, 347–349
Voice onset time (VOT), 15, 142, 189, 201, 203, 204, 205

W

Wanna contraction, 328–330, 331
Weismann barrier, 6
Williams Syndrome, 262, 383–388, 389
  cognitive deficits in, 384–385
  definition of, 383
  grammatical abilities, selective preservation of, 386–388
  and language testing, 386–388
  and spatial cognition in, 385
  visuoperceptual testing in, 385
visuospatial tests in, 384–385
Within-language patterns
  verbs vs. nouns, 70–73
Word meaning, acquisition of, 97–104
  and overextensions, 133, 134
  species-specific linguistic constraints on, 98, 100
Word order, comprehension of, 308–311
  children and sensitivity to, 309, 311
  strategies in, 309
Word order tests, 307